~ VOLUME 3 ~

CITIZENS
OF
MISSOURI TERRITORY

TO – 1835

GRANTS IN
PRESENT DAY MISSOURI,
ARKANSAS AND OKLAHOMA

Frances T. Ingmire

Heritage Books
2024

HERITAGE BOOKS
AN IMPRINT OF HERITAGE BOOKS, INC.

Books, CDs, and more—Worldwide

For our listing of thousands of titles see our website
at
www.HeritageBooks.com

Published 2024 by
HERITAGE BOOKS, INC.
Publishing Division
5810 Ruatan Street
Berwyn Heights, MD 20740

Heritage Books by the author:

Citizens of Missouri Territory: 1787-1810, Grants in Present Day Missouri, Arkansas and Oklahoma, Vol. 1
Citizens of Missouri Territory: 1810-1812, Grants in Present Day Missouri, Arkansas and Oklahoma, Vol. 2
Citizens of Missouri Territory to-1835, Grants in Present Day Missouri, Arkansas and Oklahoma, Vol. 3
North Carolina Marriage Bonds and Certificates Series: Craven County, North Carolina, Marriage Records, 1780–1867
North Carolina Marriage Bonds and Certificates Series: Cumberland County, North Carolina, Marriage Records, 1803–1878
North Carolina Marriage Bonds and Certificates Series: Guilford County, North Carolina, Marriage Records, 1771–1868
North Carolina Marriage Bonds and Certificates Series: Lincoln County, North Carolina, Marriage Records, 1783–1866
North Carolina Marriage Bonds and Certificates Series: Orange County, North Carolina, Marriage Records, 1782–1868
North Carolina Marriage Bonds and Certificates Series: Rowan County, North Carolina, Marriage Records, 1754–1866
North Carolina Marriage Bonds and Certificates Series: Stokes County, North Carolina, Marriage Records, 1783–1868
North Carolina Marriage Bonds and Certificates Series: Surry County, North Carolina, Marriage Records, 1783–1868
North Carolina Marriage Bonds and Certificates Series: Wake County, North Carolina, Marriage Records, 1781–1867
North Carolina Marriage Bonds and Certificates Series: Wilkes County, North Carolina, Marriage Records, 1779–1868

International Standard Book Number
Paperbound: 978-0-7884-2753-4

PREFACE

The first American settlement in what is now Missouri was
in 1787. In 1795 American settlements were established in what
is now St. Charles County, north of St. Louis. It was then
called Upper Louisiana or New Spain. Until 1803 France and
Spain passed control of the Louisiana Territory back and forth.
In the Louisiana Purchase ownership passed into the hands of
the United States.

In 1805 Missouri became part of the Territory of Louisiana
and remained so until 1812 when it became a Territory in its
own name. At that time the population was 20,000 inhabitants.
This area of Missouri Territory included the present states of
Arkansas and Oklahoma until 1819 when Missouri applied for
statehood. Congress then created the Arkansas Territory and
included the area that is now the state of Oklahoma,

The grants included in this volume are those which were
presented and confirmed until 1835. Many of the citizens had
lived on their land for many years. The applicant gave the
information regarding how he acquired the land, how long he had
lived on it, and frequently gives information as to his occupation
and the size of his family.

Much genealogical and historical data is included in these land
records and it is hoped that the publication of these records with
an index will benefit researchers in the future.

Office of the Recorder of Land Titles
                                    St. Louis Missouri Oct. 1st, 1832
        Pursuant to an act of Congress entitled "An Act for the Final Ad-
justment of private land claims in the State of Missouri" approved the
9th day of July, 1832, the commissioners appointed by and under said act,
did on the 11th day of last month (Sept.) give public notice, through
Sundry Newspapers printed in this State, that on this day, the office
of the Recorder of Land Titles would be open and the board of commissioners organised and ready to receive testimony. In pursuance to said
notice, L.F. LINN and Fred R. CONWAY appeared and having been duly qualified, preceeded to take into consideration the appointment of translator interpreter and clerk. Resolved by the Board that the said officer
or officers shall hold his or their appointment at the pleasure of said
Board or a majority thereof.
        On motion, adjourned untill tomorrow 10 o'clock A.M.

            Tuesday October 2nd, 1832 Board Met
            Commissioners Present-Lewis F. LINN & F.R. CONWAY
(Unless otherwise stated, the above mentioned commissioners will one
or both be present when the Board is in session.)

The Board proceeded to the appointment of a translator of the French
& Spanish languages who should also act as Clerk to the Board. Whereupon Julius (cannot read name) being agreed upon as a suitable person
to fill that office, was accordingly appointed. Whereupon the said
(Cannot read name) after being duly qualified, entered upon duties of
his office.
It appearing that there was no further business before the Board adjourned to tomorrow 10 o'clock A.M.
            Wednesday October 3rd, 1832-Board Met-Both Commr's. present
        After keeping the office open several hours and no business
appearing before them, they adjourned until tomorrow at 10 o'clock A.M.
            Thursday October 4th, 1832-Board Met-Both Comm'rs. Present
    (Same as Above)
            Friday October 5th, 1832-Board Met-Both Commr's. Present
Pascal CERRE claiming as devisee of Gabriel CERRE 800 arpents of land
situate on the Marameck, District of St. Louis. See Book No. 1, pg.
514 and Book No. 5, pg. 544. The two original concessions being produced (See Livre Terrien No. 4, pg. 6) one being dated the 12th of October, 1782, signed by Francisco CRUSAT, the other on the 10th of January, 1798, signed by Zenon TRUDEAU, was also produced a paper purporting
to be the survey of the same, signed by James RANKIN, deputy Surveyor
and by Antoine SOULARD, Surveyor General, see Book A, pgs. 532 & 533.
M.P. LEDUC having been duly sworn, saith that the signature to the first
petition is the handwriting of Gabriel CERRE and the signature to the
concession is the handwriting of Francisco CRUSAT, that the signature
to the second petition is the handwriting of the said Gabriel CERRE and
the signature to the decree of concession is the handwriting of
Zenon TRUDEAU, that the signatures to the aforesaid survey are the hand
writing of the said James RANKIN and A. SOULARD. (Decision No. 1, pg. 286)

Pascal L. CERRE claiming a tract of land of a league square to be surveyed, etc. See Book No. 2, pg. 30 & Book No. 4, pg. 511.
M.P. LEDUC, being duly sworn, saith that the signature to the petition
is the handwriting of the claimant and that the signature to the concession is the handwriting of Carlos Dehault DELASSUS, see Record Book
B, pgs. 512 & 13. The Claimant also produces a paper purporting to be
an original letter from Gallore de LEMOS, late governor of Louisiana,
bearing date the 25th day of April, 1798. M.P. LEDUC, saith taht the
signature to the said letter is the handwriting of said Gallore de
LEMOS. (Decision No. 2, pg. 287)

James MACKEY's heirs claiming 30,000 arpents of land, see Book No. 1,
pg. 415, Book No. 3, pg. 21 & Book No. 4, pg. 186, produces a paper
purporting to be a concession of the same and certificates of survey,
one for 13,835 arpents dated 8th March, 1802, the survey executed 25th
March, 1801. Another for 10,340 arpents dated 28th February, 1806,
survey executed the 7th of February, 1803 and signed by Antoine SOULARD.
And a third for 5,280 arpents executed the 20th of December, 1804 and
certified by Ant. SOULARD as received for record on the 28th of February

1

1806. See Record Book B, pgs. 435, 436, & 473. Also, a paper purporting to be an original letter from Manuel Galloso de LEMOS, Governor of Louisiana to James MACKEY, dated 20th March, 1799. Also, a paper purporting to be an affidavit of Antonio SOULARD taken before F.M. GUYOT, a Justice of the Peace for the county of St. Louis, dated 5th December, 1817' authenticated on the 15th December, 1817, under the great Seal of the Territory of Missouri by Fred. BATES, exercising the government of said Territory. Also, a paper purporting to be an original letter from Zenon TRUDEAU, to said MACKEY. M.P. LEDUC, being duly sworn, saith that the signature to the decree of concession aforesaid as the handwriting of Lt. Governor Carlos Dehault DELASSUS, that the signature to the first survey is the handwriting of Ant. SOULARD, that the signature to the Survey of 10,340 arpents is the handwriting of Ant. SOULARD, that the signature to the Survey of 5,280 arpents is the handwriting of Ant. SOULARD, that the signature to the said letter of M. Galloso de LEMOS, that the signature to the affidavit are the handwriting of Ant. SOULARD, of F.M. GUYOT & Fred. BATES, that Antoine SOULARD died about six or seven years ago; that the signature to the letter of Zenon TRUDEAU, above mentioned is the handwriting of Zenon TRUDEAU. (Decision #3, pg. 287)

D.DELAUNAY claiming 800 arpents of land (See Book No. 1, pg. 269 & Book No. 4, pg. 464) produces a paper purporting to be a concession from Carlos Dehault DELASSUS, dated 18th January, 1800 and a survey of the same taken the 3rd January, 1804, certified the 15th April, 1804, signed by A. SOULARD, Surveyor General, see Book C, pg. 247 & 248. M.P. LEDUC, duly sworn, saith that the signature to the said concession is the handwriting of C.D. DELASSUS, that the signature to the certificate of Survey is the handwriting of A. SOULARD.(Decision 5, pg. 288)

John SMITH T & C, assignees of Alexander DUCLOS claiming 420 acres of land, see Book No. 3, pg. 313, Bk. No. 5, pg. 530. produces a paper purporting to be the original Survey for 12,400 arpents taken the 3rd February and certified the 15th of March, 1804, signed Ant. SOULARD, Surveyor General. (Said Survey not heretofore recorded). For the record of the claim see Book D, pg. 73. M.P. LEDUC, duly sworn, saith that the signature to the aforesaid Survey is the handwriting of said Antoine SOULARD. The said claimant, also, files a paper purporting to be original depositions taken in behalf of said claimant, before the District Court of the United States.

Jacob BOISSE claiming 400 arpents, see Book No. 5, pg. 525, produces the same paper as in the claim of John SMITH T & Co., assignees of A. DUCLOS. M.P. LEDUC, duly sworn, saith same as above in the case of John SMITH T & Co. Said claimant, also, files a paper purporting to be a Deed from Jacob WISE to E. LAMARQUE, also, depositions taken in the case of E. LAMARQUE, agst. the United States before the District Court in support of said claim. (Decision No. 9, Old Mine Concession pg. 289)

John SMITH T, assignee of Jacques ST. VRAIN claiming 14,000 arpents of land, see Book C (Record) pgs. 336 & 337 and Book D, pg. 57 for Deed. For testimony, see minute Book No. 1, pg. 514 and No. 5, pg. 540. The claimant files a paper purporting to be original depositions taken in the case of J.M. WHITE in the District Court of the United States in support of said claim. Also, depositions taken in the case of Thomas A. SMITH, guardian, against the United States. (Decision No. 4, pg. 287)

Richard CAULK claiming 4,000 arpents of land, see Book C, pgs. 120 & 121. For Testimony, the claimant refers to Minute Book No. 1, pg. 418, Book No. 3, pg. 259 & Book No. 4, pg. 376, produces affidavit of James MACKY, sworn to before Jeremiah CONNOR on the 25th of October, 1819. Also, an affidavit of Antoine SOULARD, sworn to before F.M. GAZOL, a Justice of the Peace, on the 26th October, 1819. Also, the affidavit of Thomas CAULK sworn to & subscribed before Wm. LONG, a Justice of the Peace on the 21st October, 1819. Also, an affidavit of Martin WOOD taken before Benjamin COTTLE, a Justice of the Peace, on the 28th September, 1819. Also, a paper purporting to be a concession dated 5th December, 1799, granted by Charles Dehault DELASSUS, and a

Survey made on the 17th of December, 1804 and certified 30th October, 1805 by Antoine SOULARD, Surveyor General. M.P. LEDUC, duly sworn, saith that the signature to the decree of concession is the handwriting of C.D. DELASSUS, Lt. Governor, that the signature to the Survey is the handwriting of Ant. SOULARD, Surveyor General of Louisiana; that the signature to the affidavits of MACKY & SOULARD are in their proper hand-writing.   (Decision No. 6, pg. 288)

Thomas CAULK claiming 400 arpents, see Record Book D, pg. 368. (said claim has not been acted upon by the former Board), produces a paper purporting to be a concession granted by Carlos Dehault DELASSUS, da-ted 10th March, 1800, and a paper purporting to be a Survey taken on the 19th February and certified the 28th March, 1804 by Ant. SOULARD, Surveyor General. M.P. LEDUC, duly sworn, saith that the signature to said concession is the handwriting of Carlos Dehault DELASSUS and that the signature to the Survey is the handwriting of A. SOULARD, Surveyor General. The Claimant refers to the affidavits of James MACKY and Ant. SOULARD taken on the above claim of Richard CAULK. Also, the affi-davit of Martin WOODS taken before Benjamin COTTLE, Justice of the Peace dated 28th September, 1819. (Decision No. 132, pg. 332)

Nota. The Witness M.P. LEDUC, after having given the testimonies above, states that in the case of MACKEY's heirs claiming 30,000 arpents of land he is interested.
     The Board adjourned untill tomorrow 10 o'clock A.M.
          Saturday 6th October, 1832-Board Met-Both Comm'rs. Present

M.P. LEDUC claiming 7,944 arpents of land, being the balance of 15,000 arpents granted for Services, see Record Book C, pgs. 443 & 444. The quantity of 7056 arpents of said claim having already been confirmed. In support of said claim, the claimant refers to the evidences produced before the late Board of Commissioners. See Minute Books No. 1, pg. 274, No. 3, pgs. 11 & 284 and Book No. 4, pg. 182. And for the con-firmation aforesaid, see the report of the late recorder of land titles and the laws of Congress, second Section of land Laws No. 290, pgs. 699 & 700. (Decision No. 7, pg. 288)

William DUNN, by his assignee Arend RUTGERS claiming 7056 arpents of land, see Record Book D, pgs. 117 & 118 and Minute Book No. 5,.pg. 490, produces a paper purporting to be a concession from C.D. DELASSUS to Wm. DUNN, dated 18th June, 1802. Also, two plats and certificates of Survey, the one for 800 arpents executed the 17th of November, 1803 and certified by Antoine SOULARD, Surveyor General on the 22nd December, 1803. The other for 6,256 arpents executed on the 13th of December, 1803 and certified by said SOULARD on the 15th January, 1804. M.P. LEDUC, duly sworn, saith that the signature to said concession is the handwriting of C.D. DELASSUS, Lt. Governor. That the signatures to the said certificates of Surveys are the handwriting of A. SOULARD, Surveyor General. (No. 251, Book No. 7, pg. 75)

James MCDANIEL by his assignee, James MACKAY claiming 1,800 arpents of land on River Des Peres, see Record Book F, pg. 358, Recorder's Minutes pages 80 and 163 & 164, produces a paper purporting to be a concession from Zenon TRUDEAU, Lt. Governor, dated 1st February, 1798. Also, a plat and certificate of Survey of same, executed the 29th (month not mentioned), 1802, and certified by A. SOULARD 15th March, 1803. Also, a report made by Frederick BATES, late Recorder of Land Titles to Jonah MEIGS, Comm'r. of the General Land Office, together with the accom-panying documents marked A,B,C,D & E. Also, a paper purporting to be an original letter from Gabriel LONG dated October 29th, 1818. M.P. LEDUC, duly sworn, saith that the signature to the concession above mentioned is the handwriting of Z. TRUDEAU, that the signature to the Surveys a-bove mentioned is the handwriting of A. SOULARD and that the signature to the letter above mentioned is the handwriting of Gabriel LONG. (Decision No. 8, pg. 289)

David COLE by his assignee, Jesse RICHARDSON, assignee of James MACKAY, see Book B, pg. 15 and Minute Book No. 3, pg. 268 and Book No. 4, pg. 380 claiming 400 arpents of land, produces a paper purporting to be a concession from Z. TRUDEAU, dated 23rd January, 1798. Also, a Plat and certificate of Survey certified by Antoine SOULARD and dated 10th December, 1805. Also, an affidavit of James MACKAY taken before Jeremiah CONNOR, a Justice of the Peace for the County of St. Louis, dated 21st October, 1818, authenticated by F. BATES, Secretary exercising the government of the Territory of Missouri, dated 10th November, 1818. M.P. LEDUC, duly sworn, saith that the signature to said concession is the handwriting of Zenon TRUDEAU, that the signature to the above Survey is the handwriting of Antoine SOULARD. (Decision No. 10, pg. 290)

John BASYE by his assignee, Jacques ST. VRAIN claiming 1,600 arpents of land, see Record Book C, pg. 327, Minutes No. 1, pg. 303 and No. 5, pg. 318, produces a paper purporting to be a concession from C.D. DELASSUS, Lt. Governor, dated 8th of January, 1801. Also, a Plat and certificate of Survey signed by Antoine SOULARD, Surveyor General, executed the 16th of February and certified the 20th of March, 1804. M.P. LEDUC, duly sworn, saith that the signature to the concession is the handwriting of Carlos Dehault DELASSUS and that the signature to the certificate of Survey is the handwriting of Antoine SOULARD. (Decision No. 11, pg. 290)

Toussaint CERRE by the heirs of Auguste CHOUTEAU claiming an Island in the Mississippi, the Payla Island, see Record Book B, pg. 55, Minutes Book No. 3, pg. 239 and Book No.4, pg. 369, produces a paper purporting to be a concession from C.D. DELASSUS, Lt. Governor, dated 15th January, 1800. Also, a plat and certificate of Survey signed by William MILBURG, without date. M.P. LEDUC, duly sworn, saith that the signature to the said concession is the handwriting of C.D. DELASSUS, Lt. Gov., and that the signature to the said Plat is the handwriting of said MILBURG. (Decision No. 12, pg. 291)

Wilkins UPDIKE, Esq., Comm'r., appeared, having been qualified, took his seat.
On motion the Board adjourned until Monday at 10 o'clock A.M.
Monday 8th October, 1832 Board Met-Both Comm'rs. Present &
also Wm. UPDIKE

Auguste CHOUTEAU by his heirs claiming 1,281 arpens of land, see Record Book B, pgs. 58 & 59 and Minutes Book No. 1, pg. 427, Book No. 3, pg. 245 and Book No. 4, pg. 370, produces a paper purporting to be a concession from C.D. DELASSUS, dated 5th January, 1800 to Auguste CHOUTEAU. Also, a plat of Survey executed 5th March, 1801 and certified 10th April 1801. Also, a paper purporting to be a petition dated 5th November, 1799, signed by A. CHOUTEAU and addressed to C.D. DELASSUS, Lt. Gov., together with the answer of said DELASSUS to said petition. Also, a letter from Mauel Galloso de LEMOS dated 20th March, 1799 to A. CHOUTEAU. Pascal CERRE, duly sworn, saith that the signature to the petition is the handwriting of A. CHOUTEAU and the signature to the concession is the handwriting of C.D. DELASSUS, that the signature to the above mentioned letter is the handwriting of said Galloso, that the signature to the plat of Survey and certificate is the handwriting of A. SOULARD, Surveyor General, that the signature to the petition dated 5th of November, 1799, is the hand writing of A. CHOUTEAU and that the signature to the decree is the handwriting of C.D. DELASSUS, knows that A. CHOUTEAU had a Distillery in operation several years before 1800. Believes said Distillery was in operation 12 or 15 years that to his knowledge, CHOUTED cut the wood for his distillery on said tract of land; that the Cote Brillante tract was generally known by the inhabitants of St. Louis to be the property of said CHOUTEAU. (Decision No. 141, pg. 343)

Auguste CHOUTEAU by his heirs claiming 7,056 arpens of land, see Record Book D, pgs. 121 & 122 and Minute Book 5 pg. 395, produces a paper purporting to be a concession dated 8th January, 1798 from Zenon TRUDEAU, Lt. Governor, also, a plat of Survey executed the 20th of December, 1803 and certified 29th of December, 1803. Pascal CERRE, duly sworn, saith that the signature to the concession is the handwriting of Z. TRUDEAU, that the signature to the plat of survey and certificate is the handwriting of Antoine SOULARD, that in the year 1798 and long before that time, Auguste CHOUTEAU was considered a man of large property possessed of large herds of cattle of all descriptions, owned 50 or 60 slaves, in fact was the richest man in upper Louisiana.

Pierre Delassus de LUZIERE claiming 100 arpens of land, see Record Book B, pg. 515 and Minutes Book No. 2, pg. 25 & Book No. 4, pg. 515, produces a paper purporting to be a concession from Zenon TRUDEAU dated 20th January, 1798. Pascal CERRE, duly sworn, saith that the signature to said concession is the handwriting of said Z. TRUDEAU. States that he knew LUZIERE as commandant of New Bourbon and believes he was yet commandant of said place at his death. The claimant refers for evidence to Minutes Book No. 2, pg. 25. (Decision No. 14, pg. 291)

Louis COWETOIS, Junr., claiming 7,056 arpens of land, see Record Book E, pgs. 217 & 218, it being special location, produces a paper purporting to be a concession from C.D. DELASSUS, dated 15th December, 1799. Pascal CERRE, duly sworn, saith that the signature to the concession is the handwriting of C.D. DELASSUS and that the signature to the certificate of Record of said concession is the handwriting of Ant. SOULARD. (This claim has not been acted upon by the former Board). (Decision No. 123, pg. 325)

Francois CAILLON claiming 1,600 arpens of land, see Minutes Book No. 5, pg. 394, Record Book C, pg. 443, claimed under a concession from Carlos Dehault DELASSUS, said to be dated 3rd January, 1800 (this conconcession is not produced), produces a Deed Certified by C.D. DELASSUS dated 12th of August, 1800. Pascal CERRE, duly sworn, saith that the signature to the certificate of the above deed is the handwriting of said DELASSUS. (Decision No. 18, pg. 293)
                On Motion the Board Adjourned untill tomorrow 10 o'clock A.M.
                Tuesday 9th October, 1832-Board Met-All Comm'rs. Present

Pierre Delassus de LUZIERE claiming 7,056 arpens of land, see Minutes Book No. 1, pgs. 347 & 388, Book No. 5, pgs. 521, 541, and 571, Record Book C, pgs. 450 & 451, produces a paper purporting to be an original concession from Z. TRUDEAU, dated 1st April, 1795 to P.D. de LUZIERE. Also, a certificate of delivery of property by Francois VALLE dated 17th of April, 1795. Also, an order of Survey dated 29th November, 1799 by Carlos Dehault DELASSUS. Also, a plat of Survey executed on the 14th December, 1799 and certified 5th March, 1800 by Antoine SOULARD. Also, an original letter signed the Baron de CARONDELET and addressed to Don Zenon TRUDEAU, dated 7th May, 1793; alos, an original letter purporting to be signed by the Baron de CARONDELET addressed to Dehault DELASSUS dated 8th May, 1793, also a certificate of Wm. MILBURN of the position of the tract upon the general map. Pascal CERRE, duly sworn, saith that the signature to the certificate of delivery is the handwriting of Francois VALLE, that the signature to the concession is the handwriting of Zenon TRUDEAU; that the signature to the certificate of survey is the handwriting of Antoine SOULARD; that the signatures to the two above mentioned letters are the handwriting of the Baron de CARONDELET. (Decision No. 64, pg. 309)

Pierre MENARD claiming 20 arpens front by 20 arpens in depth on River a la fromme (apple creek), see Record Book E, pg. 25, Minutes Book No. 4, pgs. 74 & 298, produces a paper purporting to be a concession from Zenon TRUDEAU to P. MENARD dated 5th November, 1798. Pascal CERRE, duly sworn, saith that the whole concession and the signature to it is the handwriting of Zenon TRUDEAU. (Decision No. 15, pg. 291)

Francois SAUCIER claiming 8,800 arpens of land of which 1,000 arpens is confirmed, see Minutes Book No. 1, pg. 271, Book No. 4, pg. 464, Record Book C, pg. 248. For confirmation, see Recorders report on the 15th of November, 1815, produces a paper purporting to be a concession from C.D. DELASSUS to Francois SAUCIER dated 18th September, 1799; also, a Survey of 6,800 arpens (part of said concession) executed 26th December, 1805 and certified by Antoine SOULARD on the 20th December, 1817. Also, an original letter of Zenon TRUDEAU to F. SAUCIER dated 15th March, 1799. Pascal CERRE, duly sworn, saith that the signature to the petitions is the handwriting of Francois SAUCIER. That the signature to the concession is the handwriting of C.D. DELASSUS. That the signature to the Survey is the handwriting of Fremon DETAURIERA, Deputy Surveyor and that the signature to the Certificate of Survey is the handwriting of Antoine SOULARD, Surveyor General. That the signature to the above mentioned letter is the handwriting of Z. TRUDEAU. (Dec. No. 16, pg. 292)

Charles Dehault DELASSUS claiming 30,000 arpens of land, see Record Book B, pgs. 515 & 516, Minutes Book No. 3, pg. 286, No. 4, pg. 387, produces a paper purporting to be an original concession from Z. TRUDEAU to C.D. DELASSUS, dated 10th February, 1798. Also, a Survey executed 2nd of January, 1806 signed by Fremon DELAURIERE. Pascal CERRE, duly sworn, saith that the signature to the petition is the handwriting of C.D. DELASSUS. That the signature to the concession is the handwriting of Z. TRUDEAU. That the signature to the certificate of record of concession is the handwriting of Antoine SOULARD. That the signature to the Survey is the handwriting of Fremon DELAURIERE. Claimant refers to a letter which was offered in evidence under the claim of Piere Delassus de LUSIERE, dated 8th of May, 1793, signed El Baron de CARONDELET and addressed to said DELASSUS. (Dec. #17, pg. 292)

Louis BISSONET by the heirs of Auguste CHOUTEAU claiming 40 arpens, see Record Book D, pg. 199, Book B, pg. 75, see Minutes Book 3, pg. 485, produces a paper purporting to be an original concession from Francois CRUSAT to Louis BISSONET dated 28th August, 1777. Also, a document purporting to be an adjudicated sale certified by Amos STODARD, Commandat of Upper Louisian, of said tract of land amongst others, to Augste. CHOUTEAU, dated 28th September, 1804. Also, a certificate with a plat of Survey dated 28th February, 1806 signed by James MACKAY. Pascal CERRE, duly sworn, saith that the signature to the concession is the handwriting of Francisco CRUSAT. He believes the signature to said document is the handwriting of STODARD, but is not very sure. That the signature to the Survey is the handwriting of James MACKAY. (Dec. #127, pg. 326)

Silvestre LABBADIE claiming 7,056 arpens of land, see Record Book A, pg. 526, Minutes Books No. 1, pg. 283, No. 3, pg. 373 and No. 4, pg. 425, produces a paper purporting to be an original concession from Carlos Dehault DELASSUS, dated 18th November, 1799. Also, a plat of survey executed the 15th of February, 1804 and certified the 8th of March, 1804 signed by Antoine SOULARD. Pascal CERRE, duly sworn, saith that the signature to the concession is the handwriting of C.D. DELASSUS and the signature to the Survey and Certifiecate is the handwriting of A. SOULARD.

The Sons of VASQUEZ, Benito, Antoine, Hipolite, Joseph and Pierre VASQUEZ claiming 800 arpens each under a concession dated 17th February, 1800, see Record Book C, pgs. 474 & 475, Minutes Books No. 1, pg. 491, No. 4, pgs. 67 & 502, produces a paper purporting to be an original concession dated 17th of February, 1800 from C.D. DELASSUS, Also, a plat of Survey dated 7th of February, 1806 of 800 arpens. Pascal CERRE, duly sworn, saith that the signature to the concession is the handwriting of DELASSUS, that the signatures to the survey are in the handwriting of MACKAY and Ant. SOULARD. (Dec. # 19, pg. 293)

Aaron QUICK claiming 800 arpens of land under a concession from C.D. DELASSUS, see Record Book D, pg. 312, Minutes Book 5, pg. 484, produces a paper purporting to be an original concession from DELASSUS dated the 20th of March, 1801 with a certificate at the foot thereof dated 17th December, 1803 signed A. SOULARD and an order at the foot of last mentioned certificate dated 20th December, 1803 and signed C.D. DELASSUS. Also, produces a survey of 800 arpens dated January 8th, 1804, certified by Antoine SOULARD the 15th March, 1808. Pascal CERRE, duly sworn, saith that the signature to the above mentioned papers are the respective handwriting of DELASSUS, SOULARD, DELASSUS & SOULARD. (Dec. No. 20, pg. 293)

Peter CHOUTEAU, Senr. claiming a tract of land about 20 arpens above the town of St. Charles, see Books No. 3, pg. 442, No. 4, pg. 434, Record Book B, pg. 510, produces a paper purporting to be an original concession DELASSUS dated 26th of November, 1800. Pascal CERRE, duly sworn, saith that the signature to the above mentioned concession are the signature of the respective persons they proffer to be. (Dec. No. 21, pg. 294)

    On motion, the Board Adjourned until tomorrow 10 o'clock A.M.

Wednesday 10th October, 1832 Board Met-All Commr's. Present

Louis LOREMIER claiming 8,000 arpens of which 7,056 arpens have been confirmed. Confirmation is prayed for the balance, see Book No. 4, pg. 73 & 299, Record Book E, pgs. 22 & 23. For confirmation see BATES decision pg. 67, produces a paper purporting to be an original order of Survey by the Baron de CARONDELET dated 26th October, 1795; also, a plat of survey executed 26th October, 1797 and certified 11th December, 1797 by A. SOULARD. (Dec. No. 22, p.g 294)

It is the opinion of this Board that it would be expensive and oppressive to the claimants & witnesses (who may reside at a distance) to attend at this place.
Resolved unanimously that a deputation of one of the members of the Board of Commissioners proceed to the Town of St. Genevieve for the purpose of taking testimony and that he shall attend at said place on Wednesday the 17th Inst: for such object. That the power to take such testimony be continued till the 1st day of November next.
Resolved that said depution give public notice in writing or otherwise when and where he will be ready in said Town to receive testimony.
Lewis F. LINN proposing to go as such deputation. The other two Commissioners agreed thereto.
On motion, the Board Adjourned until tomorrow at 10 o'clock A.M.
Thursday 11th October, 1832-The Board Met-All Comm'rs. Present

Bartholome COUSIN claiming 7,935 arpens of land of which 7,056 arpens have been confirmed. For confirmation see BATES report (Decision) pg. 67. For record of claim, see Book B, pg. 314, Minutes Book No. 1, pg. 512, Book No. 4, pgs. 70 & 294. (Dec. No. 61, pg. 308)

Carlos D. DELASSUS by his assignee Madame Delore SARPY claiming 20,000 arpens of land of which 7,056 arpens have been confirmed. For confirmation, see BATES decision pg. 40, for record of claim, see Book C, pg. 499, Minutes No. 3, pgs. 92 & 368, Book No. 4, pg. 423, produces a paper purporting to be an original concession from Z. TRUDEAU dated 18th June, 1796, also, a plat of survey executed the 15th of April, 1801 & certified 20th May, 1801 for 12,100 arpens. Refers to a letter dated 8th May, 1793 purporting to be addressed by the Baron de CARONDELET to Zenon TRUDEAU already offered in evidence under the claim of P. Delassus de LUZIERE for 7,056 arpens. (Dec. #23, pg. 294)

The Board Met & Adjourned on Friday 12th October, Saturday 13th October, 1832.
Monday 15th October, 1832 Board Met-Two Comm'rs. Present

James JOURNEY claiming 400 arpens of land, see Book F, pg. 104, BATES report pg. 103, produces a paper purporting to be a concession from Carlos D. DELASSUS, dated 21st September, 1799. Also, a translation of said concession signed by said DELASSUS. M.P. LEDUC, duly sworn, saith that the signature to the concession is the handwriting of Carlos D. DELASSUS and that the signature to the recommendation attached to said concession is that of James MACKAY. (Dec. No. 126, pg. 326)
No other business appearing before the Board, they Adjourned until tomorrow at 10 o'clock A.M.
The Board Met & Adjourned on October 16th, 17th, 18th, 19th, 20th, 22nd, 23rd, 24th,25th, 26th, 27th, 29th, 30th, 31st, Nov. 1st, 2nd, 3rd, 5th, 6th, 7th, 8th, 9th, 10th, 12th, 13th, 14th, 15th, 16th, 17th, & 19th, 1832.
Tuesday November 20th, 1832 Board Met-Two Comm'rs. Present
Old Mine Concession for 12,400 arpens of land, see Book D, pgs. 67 & following record of Survey Book D, pg. 73, for Testimony see Book No. 5, pgs. 524 & following. The following additional testimony was taken in the foregoing case in compliance with a resolution of this Board of the 10th of October last.
State of Missouri, County of St. Genevieve
The inhabitants of the old mine, thirty one in number, and their heirs and legal representatives each claiming four hundred arpens of land situated at a place called the Old Mine in the former District of St.

Genevieve, now the County of Washington, when Joseph PRATTE on his own right and Joseph PRATTE under Antoine SOVEREAU and Walter WILKINSON under Basil VALLE and Charles E. VALLE in his own right and Francois B. VALLE in his own right and St. Gemme BEAUVAIS under Thomas ROSS and the heirs and legal representatives of Jacques GUILBURG and Bartholomew St. GEMME under Bste. PLACET, produces the original concession dated the 4th day of June in the year one thousand eight hundred and three, granted on the petition of the said inhabitants, dated the 25th May, 1803 and granted & signed by Charles Dehault DELASSUS, Lt. Governor of Louisiana. The claimants also produce general & particular plats of survey made according to law, made by the proper authorities under the Spanish and American Governments. When Pascal DETCHMENDY, who is aged seventy one years, being produced and duly sworn as the law directs deposeth and saith that he came to this country in the year one thousand seven hundred and ninety six and that he has remained in the country ever since; that he is well acquanited with the handwriting and signature of Charles Dehault DELASSUS, who was at the date of this grant or concession, the Lt. Governor of upper Louisiana, that he has frequently seen him write his name and signature to the said concession dated the 4th day of June, 1803 is the proper handwriting of the said Charles Dehault DELASSUS, and the body of the said concession is in the handwriting of Antoine SOULARD, then Surveyor General of Upper Louisiana. This deponent further states that he knows personally (for he was frequently on the land granted, as he traded to said place) that the lands conceeded to each of the claimants here above stated was taken possession of by them in person or by some person for them and for their use and for their use and in their behalf. And this deponent further says that he knows that the lands aforesaid conceeded to each individual was not only taken possession of as aforesaid, but that many of the tracts were actually inhabited and cultivated by the concessioners in person or by some person for them or under them from the date of the concession aforesaid till the present time. And this deponent further states that as early as the year 1797, he made application to Zenon TRUDEAU, who was then Lt. Governor of Upper Louisiana, for a grant of land at this very place and that said Zenon TRUDEAU refused him the grant stating as his reason for refusing that the land was already promised to the said inhabitants of the Old Mine and would be granted to them so soon as they should make the application in form. And this deponent further states that he knows that each of the original concessioners aforesaid were at the date of the concession aforesaid actual inhabitants and citizens of this country and that the others in general continued inhabitants during their lives and that the present claimants are all citizens and residents of this state. And this deponent further states that he has been informed from a source entitled to credit that Moses AUSTIN asked for and wanted a grant for the same land aforesaid and was refused by the Spanish authorities for the same reasons that this deponent was refused. Sworn to and subscribed before me the subscriber Lewis F. LINN, one of the Commissioners appointed to finally settle and adjust land claims in Missouri. This 29th day of October, 1832. (Dec. #9, pg. 289) Signed L.F. LINN - P. DETCHMENDY

TRANSLATION

In the year one thousand eight hundred on the fourth of January, I have supplied the ceremonies of Baptism to Charles Francois Pierre Auguste VALLE, legitimate son of Francois VALLE, Civil and Military Commandant of St. Genevieve and of Marie CARPENTIER, his wife, born on the fifth of March of the preceding year and sprinkled (Ondoye) the same day. The Godfather has been Dr. Carlos Auguste DELASSUS, Lt. Governor of Illinois, the Godmother, Miss Julia VALLE, who have signed with us.

Signed Maxwell, Curat

I, the undersigned priest officiating at the old Mine and being for the present in St. Genevieve, certify that the above certificate of Baptism of Charles Francois Pierre Auguste VALLE is a true copy, faithfully extracted from the registers of the church of St. Genevieve. Given and signed in St. Genevieve the 30th October, 1832. The curate of the said St. Genevieve, Rev'd. Mr. DAHMEN, having declared to be unable to do it on account of sickness.

Signed T. BOULLIER

Adjourned untill tomorrow at 10 o'clock A.M.

Antoine DUBREUIL claiming 10,000 arpens of land, see Book 5, pg. 403,
Record Book B, pg. 95, Record of Survey Book B, pg. 95, produces a
paper purporting to be a concession from Carlos Dehault DELASSUS dated
19th December, 1799, Registered by Antoine SOULARD. Albert TISON, duly
sworn, saith that the signature to concession is the handwriting of
C.D. DELASSUS; that the signature to the registering is that of
A. SOULARD; that the signature to petition is the handwriting of
Antoine DUBREUIL. Witness further saith that in December, 1803, he
accompanied James RANKIN, deputy Surveyor, to survey this and other
tracts of land, that three tracts were surveyed to the South of the
above mentioned tract, but were prevented of surveying the same being
driven away by a party of Indians. Witness, when he went on said land
saw some kettles which had been used in making salt and the remains of
salt furnaces and the places where they had been digging for salt water.
Witness understood that said tract was afterwards surveyed by
Fremon DELAURIERE, who resides in this county. David DELAUNAY, being
duly sworn, saith that the signature to the aforesaid paper are in the
respective handwriting of the three individuals who signed it; that to
the best of his recollection, the claimant went before the change of
government on said land to make an attempt in manufacturing salt, but
was driven off by the Indians and to the best of his belief, it was in
1802. (Decision No. 24, pg. 295)

Charles Fremon DELAURIERE for himself and as assignee of
Louis LABEAUME by his legal representatives claiming 10,000 arpens of
land, see Record Book D, pgs. 287, 88, 89 & 290. Book No. 5, pg. 545,
produces a paper purporting to be the petition of Louis LABEAUME and
Fremon DELAURIERE, dated 7th May, 1799 to Zenon TRUDEAU, Lt. Gov. and
the concession of said TRUDEAU dated 13th May, 1792. Also, a paper
purporting to be the petition of said LABEAUME and Fremon DELAURIERE
dated 25th March, 1801 to Carlos Dehault DELASSUS, Lt. Governor of
Louisiana. Also, the concession of said DELASSUS dated 26th March,
1801, Registered by SOULARD, Record Book D, pgs. 288 & 289. Also, a
plat and certificate of survey signed by Antoine SOULARD, see Book D,
pg. 285. Albert TISON, being duly sworn, saith that the signatures
to petition are in the respective handwriting of Louis LABEAUME and
Fremon DELAURIERE; that the signature to first concession is the handwriting of TRUDEAU; that the signatures to second petition are in the
respective handwriting of Louis LABEAUME and Fremon DELAURIERE and the
signature to second concession is in the handwriting of C.D. DELASSUS.
David DELAUNAY, being duly sworn, saith that the signatures to second
petition and concession are in the respective handwriting of the three
individuals who signed them; that the signature to plat and certificate
of survey is the handwriting of A. SOULARD and that the signature to
the affidavit by James RANKIN on the back of said plat of Survey is in
the handwriting of said RANKIN. Claimant produces, also, a paper purporting to be a deed of conveyance from Louis LABEAUME to
F.DELAURIERE recorded Book D, pgs. 289 & 290. David DELAUNAY saith that
the signatures to said deed are in the handwriting of L. LABEAUME and
F. DELAURIERE. Albert TISON saith that he was present when
James RANKIN surveyed the said 10,000 arpens of land at the time stated
in the affidavit, that he saw the salt furnaces in operation by
Fremon DELAURIERE, that the family of said DELAURIERE had been residing
on said (cannot read) since either 1801 or 1802. In fact, a long time
before the land was surveyed, at least two years before, that they made
a great quantity of salt at said works for the supply of the inhabitants;
that they sustained losses of salt by boats upsetting in the Mississippi
and more yet in Salt River itself. That at the beginning of their undertaking there was great danger on account of the Indians. They they
were obliged to fortify themselves, had a piece of canon and were
several times threatened of being attacked. That the place where they
made salt was the extreme frontier of the settlements. That by this
undertaking, Fremon DELAURIERE was reduced to poverty.
(Decision # 119, pg. 324_)

Maria Luisa Valle VILLARS by her legal representatives claiming 7,056
arpens of land, see Book of Record B, pg. 422, Commissioners Minutes
Book No. 1, pg. 325, No. 5, pg. 509. The following additional testi-

mony was taken in the foregoing case in compliance with a resolution
of this board of the 10th of October last:
   St. Genevièvé Missouri 23rd October, 1832
The heirs and legal representatives of Marie Louise VILLARS, dec'd.,
claiming seven thousand and fifty six arpens of land situate on the
waters of Saline in the former District of St. Genevieve in pursuance
of and by virtue of a plat of survey. When Colonel Baptiste VALLE,
Senior personally appeared before Lewis F. LINN, one of the commissioners appointed finally to settle and adjust the land claims in
Missouri and authorised by the Commissioners to receive testimony in
this behalf, said VALLE, being duly sworn, deposeth and saith that he
knew of a concession to Marie Louise VILLARS for seven thousand and
fifty six arpens of land on the waters of the Saline, that he knew of
the Intendant or Governor of Lower Louisiana sending up instructions
to the Lt. Governor of upper Louisiana, directing that the survey of
PEYROUX should be run in such a way as to respect the concessions of
Marie Louisa VILLARS and Francois VALLE; that said concessions were
given to the Rev. James MAXWELL, Vicar of Upper Louisiana, to take to
New Orleans for the purpose of being laid before the Intendant; that
he understood and believes that they were either lost by the said
MAXWELL or left in some of the offices for confirmation.
Question by the Commissioner: Do you know or believe that these con-
cessions were antidated? Answer, No.
Question by the Commissioner: Have you any knowledge or reason to be-
lieve that any Spanish or French concessions were antidated? Answer,
No. For when I was in New Orleans during the existence of the Spanish
Government, the Baron de CARONDELET told me that if I wanted any lands
in upper Louisiana to make out a list and he would grant them.
Question by the Commissioner: Whilst you were at New Orleans, in your
conversations with the Baron de CARONDELET, did you understand from him
that the power to grant lands by the subdelegates was denied? Answer,
No, on the contrary, when he pressed me to accept lands for myself and
family, I informed him that the subdelegates had given me and my family
grants of land to which he replied, if you have not enough ask for more.
Sworn to and subscribed the day and year first above written, before
L.F. LINN, land Commissioner. (Decision #25, pg. 295)
   Signed J.Bste. VALLE - L.F. LINN
In behalf of this claim the following papers were produced. A paper
purporting to be a copy (certified by D. MAXWELL, Curate of St. Gene-
vieve) of the claimant's petition to, and concession of Zenon TRUDEAU,
Lt. Governor. Also, a plat and certificate of Survey by
Ant. SOULARD. References as above.
   On motion, the Board Adjourned untill tomorrow at 10 o'clock A.M.
   Thursday November 22nd, 1832 Board Met-Two Comm'rs. Present

Francois VALLE by his legal representatives claiming 7,056 arpens of
land, for record of Survey see Record Book C, pg. 396, Minutes Book
No. 4, pg. 325, No. 6, 53, produces a paper purporting to be the original concession from Zenon TRUDEAU dated 9th September, 1796. The
following additional testimony was taken in the foregoing case in compliance with a resolution of this Board of the 10th of October last:
   St. Genevieve, Missouri October 19th, 1832.
The heirs and legal representatives of Francois VALLE, dec'd., claiming
seven thousand and fifty six arpens of land situated on the river Saline
in the former District of St. Genevieve in pursuance of and by virtue of
a concession and survey heretofore filed with the former Commissioners,
when Bartholomew ST. GEMMES personally appeared before Lewis F. LINN,
one of the Commissioners appointed to finally settle and adjust land
claims in Missouri and authorised by said Board of Commissioners to receive testimony in this behalf, who being duly sworn deposeth and saith
in the year seventeen hundred and ninety eight he, the said ST. GEMMES
knew of Francis VALLE and by his hands did cultivate the aforesaid
tract of land, that the said VALLE had a house and field and resided on
the premises; that the claim existed and was duly surveyed by
Thomas MADDEN about that time, as he saw the marks made by said MADDEN
when surveying and that the said VALLE did cultivate the land continually and held possession during his life time and further knows that
the heirs and representatives of said VALLE have continued to hold
possession and cultivate said land ever since; that he is well acquainted
with the handwriting and signatures of Francois VALLE and Z. TRUDEAU and

has seen them write it frequently and knows the signatures to the
original petitions and concession are the proper handwriting and signatures of the said Francois VALLE and Zenon TRUDEAU and knows that
the said Zenon TRUDEAU was acting as Lt. Governor at that time and
further this deponent saith not. (Dec. #26, pg. 295)
Sworn to and subscribed this day and year first above written.
Signed   Bste. ST. GEMME
Before L.F. LINN, Land Commissioner.
      The Board adjourned untill tomorrow at 10 o'clock A.M.
            Friday November 23rd, 1832 Board Met- Two Comm'rs. Present

St. Gemme BEAUVAIS claiming 1,600 arpens of land, Book No. 1, pg. 316,
No. 5, pg. 546, Record Book C; pgs. 455 & 466, produces a paper pur-
porting to be an original concession from Zenon TRUDEAU dated Septem-
ber 2nd, 1796. Also, a paper purporting to be a copy of a plat of
Survey by Thomas MADDEN. The following additional testimony was taken
in the foregoing case in compliance with a resolution of this Board of
the 10th of October last:
State of Missouri, County of St. Genevieve, October 25th, 1832
St. James BEAUVAIS, the heirs and legal representatives of
St. James BEAUVAIS claiming 1,600 arpens of land situated in the late
District of St. Genevieve, now County of Madison in the State of Missouri by virtue and in pursuance of a grant or concession made and
given by Zenon TRUDEAU, formerly Lt. Gov. of Upper Louisian, dated the
second day of September, 1796, produces the original petition of said
St. James BEAUVAIS dated the 2nd August, 1796, and the recommendation
of Francois VALLE, then commandant of the 15th August, 1796 for the
concession. Also, the concession itself dated as aforesaid. The
claimant produces, also, a platt of survey dated, made and recorded by
Antoine SOULARD, the former Surveyor General of Upper Louisiana, dated
the 26th April, 1805 and October the 1st, 1805 and then the said
claimants, also, produce Francois Cabot LACHANCE, aged sixty five years
who being duly sworn as the law directs deposeth and saith that he is
well acquainted with the said St. James BEAUVAIS and has been from the
time he was able to know or recognize any person in the world, and that
he has known him as a residenter in this county ever since, that he well
knows his children, all of them, the present claimants, that they were
all born and all natives of this county, where they and him have always
resided and still live, in number ten, that he knows that the land here
claimed was and has been in the possession of the said
St. James BEAUVAIS from the year 1799 and he further states that the
said tract of land has been in the actual possession of the said
St. James BEAUVAIS and his children ever since, and that the same was
from the date aforesaid ever since and now is in the possession as
aforesaid and was by the said St. James BEAUVAIS and his children and
others under him, actually inhabited and cultivated from the year 1799
up to the present date; that houses were built in 1803 or 1804, and
rails split and fields cleared and actually cultivated for more than 20
years, which houses and fields are still there, that this claim was one
of the first grants of the Spanish Government in that quarter of the
country and the other grants for mine a La Motte and the village claim
(respected and refered to the lines of this grant) Sworn to and subscribed before me, Lewis F. LINN, one of the Commissioners for settling
and adjusting land claims in Missouri the day and date above.
Signed L.F. LINN   F. Cabot LACHANCE
(Decision #26, pg. 296)

And, also, personally came John Bste. VALLE, Senr., aged seventy two
years, who being duly sworn as the law directs, deposeth and saith
that he was well acquainted with Zenon TRUDEAU, late Lt. Gov. of Upper
Louisian, that he has frequently seen him write and that he knows that
the signature of the said Zenon TRUDEAU to the Concession for 1,600
arpens of land given to St. Gemme BEAUVAIS, dated the second day of
September, 1796 is in proper handwriting of the said Zenon TRUDEAU, and
he also knows that the said Zenon TRUDEAU was, at the date of said grant,
the Lt. Gov. of Upper Louisiana, and he also personally knows that the
signature of F. VALLE, who recommended said grant, is in the proper handwriting of said Francois VALLE.
Sworn to and subscribed before me, Lewis F. LINN, one of the Comm'rs.
appointed to finally settle and adjust the titles and claims of lands

11

in Missouri. This 30th day of October, 1832 (Dec. #28, pg. 296)
signed   L.F. LINN   J. Bste. VALLE

Annexed to the above testimony is an affidavit, signed by J.B. JANIS
and Julien LABRIERE, proving the cultivation and habitation of said
land, before the change of government up to the date of said affidavit, which was sworn to and·subscribed on the 30th day of November,
1818 before M. AMOUREUX, a Justice of the Peace for the county of St.
Genevieve.
        The Board Adjourned untill tomorrow at 10 o'clock A.M.
            Saturday November 24th, 1832 Board Met-Two Comm'rs. Present

Raphael St. GEMME, BEQUET and others claiming 1,600 arpens of land,
see Book No. 3, pg. 164, Book No. 4, pg. 358, Record Book D, pgs. 49
& 50, produces a paper purporting to be an original concession from
Zenon TRUDEAU dated 1st February, 1798. Also, a paper purporting to
be a plat of Survey executed on the 16th February, 1806 by
Thomas MADDEN, Dept. Surveyor. The following additional testimony was
taken in the foregoing case in compliance with a resolution of this
Board of the 10th of October last.
State of Missouri County of St. Genevieve
Bartholomew ST. GEMME and Raphael ST. GEMME and Charles GREGOIRE under
Vital ST. GEMME, dec'd., and Thomas MADDIN, Richard MADDIN and
James MADDIN, under Baptiste BEQUETTE and Raphael ST. GEMME claiming
1,600 arpens of land situate in the late District, now County of St.
Genevieve in the State of Missouri by virtue of a concession, produces
the original concession from Zenon TRUDEAU, late Lt. Governor of upper
Louisiana, dated the first day of February, 1798, given to
Raphael ST. GEMME, Vital ST. GEMME, Baptiste BEQUETTE and
Bartholomew ST. GEMME for 1,600 arpens of land, and a plat of the same
surveyed by Thomas MADDIN, late deputy Surveyor, and there upon came
Paschal DETCHMENDY, aged seventy one years, who being duly sworn as
the law directs, deposeth and saith that he was well acquainted with
Zenon TRUDEAU, late Lt. Gov. of Louisiana, that he was Lt. Gov. of
upper Louisiana in the year 1798, and that he was well acquainted with
the handwriting and signature of said Z. TRUDEAU, having frequently seen
him write and that the name and signature of said Z. TRUDEAU to the con-
conession made by him to Raphael ST. GEMME, Vital ST. GEMME,
Baptiste BEQUETTE and Bartholomew ST. GEMME for 1,600 arpens of land,
dated the first day of February, 1798 is in the proper handwriting of
said Z. TRUDEAU, and is his signature, and the deponent further says
that he was well acquainted with the said Raphael ST. GEMME,
Vital ST. GEMME, Baptiste BEQUETTE and Bartholomew ST. GEMME, the concessionees in the said grant named, and that they and each of them were
at the date of the grant aforesaid, citizens and residents in this
country. Sworn to and subscribed before me Lewis F. LINN, one of the
commissioners appointed to settle and adjust the titles and claims to
land in Missouri, this 30th day of October, 1832. (Dec. #29, pg. 296)
Signed L.F. LINN   P. DETCHMENDY

And, also, at the same time and place came Sebastian BUTCHER, aged
fifty two years, who being duly sworn as the law directs, deposeth &
saith that he was well acquainted with the grantees in the above conconcession, that they were in the year 1798 citizens and residenters
in this country and he further says that he well knows the land in the
above concession named and claimed, having frequently travelled by and
through the same about the year 1804, and that he saw one or more men
working on the land and making rails, preparing to enclose a field.
That there was a considerable quantity of rails.
Sworn to and subscribed before me, Lewis F. LINN, one of the commissioners appointed to settle and adjust the titles and claims to land
in Missouri this 30th day of October, 1832. Signed L.F. LINN
Sebastian (X) BUTCHER
        his mark

And, also, at the same time and place came Basile MESPLAS, aged fifty
three years, who being duly sworn, deposeth and saith that he knows
all the grantees named in the aforesaid concession. That they were
residenters in the country at the date of the concession in 1798. And
he further says he is well acquainted with the land claimed and named

in the said concession and that in the year 1804, he went on the land claimed by the direction of the grantees; and aided in carrying the chain to Survey the same in 1806. That in 1804, when he went on the land, he saw a house and fields on the same; that the house was built by one man called BLACK and the fields cleared by him. That the said BLACK was put there by the claimants, who gave him horses, stock, hogs, cattle, etc. on the shares. · That said BLACK remained there for a considerable time and he believes died there. And that the said land has been cultivated to the best of his knowledge ever since, either by the claimants or others under them.

Sworn to and Subscribed before, Lewis F. LINN, one of the Commissioners appointed to finally settle and adjust land claims in Missouri, this 30th day of October, 1832.

Signed L.F. LINN   Basile MASPLAS

Thomas MADDIN by his legal representatives claiming 1,500 arpens of land, see Book No. 1, pg. 333, Book No. 4, pg. 470, Record Book A, pgs. 514 & 515 & 204 of this Book, produces a paper purporting to be an original concession from Zenon TRUDEAU, dated 29th January, 1799. The additional testimony here below, was taken in the foregoing case in compliance with a resolution of this Board of the 10th of October last.

State of Missouri, County of St. Genevieve

Thomas MADDIN, now Antoine JANIS, the legal representative by regular transfers claiming one thousand five hundred arpens of land situate in the former district, now county of St. Genevieve in the State of Missouri, in the county of St. Genevieve, filed with the former Board of Commissioners, produces the original concession for the same from Z. TRUDEAU, late Lt. Gov. of upper Louisiana, dated the 29th January, 1799 and refers to the plat of Survey heretofore filed and produced to the former Board of Commissioners. And thereupon, the claimant produces Bartholomew ST. GEMME of the age of fifty eight years, who being duly sworn as the law directs, deposeth and saith that he is well acquainted with the handwriting and signature of Z. TRUDEAU, late Lt. Gov. of Upper Louisiana, and that the name and signature of the said Z. TRUDEAU to the concession for fifteen hundred arpens of land to Thomas MADDIN, dated 29th day of January, 1799 is in the proper handwriting of the said Z. TRUDEAU and that the name of Pierre Delassus de LUZIERE to the recommendation for said concession is in the proper handwriting of the said Pierre Delassus de LUZIERE to the recommendation for said concession is in the proper handwriting of the said Pierre Delassus de LUZIERE; and this deponent further says that in the year 1803 he personally saw the said Thomas MADDIN and his hands working on the said land and preparing timber to build a mill and that about the same time said MADDIN built a house for the purpose of accomodating himself, his hands and workmen and that about the same time said MADDIN actually cleared and enclosed a small field. And this deponent further says that at the date of the grant aforesaid, the said MADDIN was a residenter in the province, and has continued a residenter ever since; and this deponent further says that the said tract has been actually enclosed, improved, and cultivated ever since either by the said MADDIN or those claiming under him. And this deponent further saith that about that time the settlements distant from the towns were very much retarded by the hostile and repeated depredations of the Indians who frequently made incursions into the settlements and drove off or frightened the inhabitants.

Sworn to and subscribed before me, Lewis F. LINN, one of the commissioners appointed to finally settle and adjust the titles and claims to land in Missouri this 29th day of October, 1832. (Dec. #30, pg. 296)

Signed L.F. LINN, land Commissioner   Bar. ST. GEMME

And, also, came Francois VALLE, aged fifty two years, who being duly sworn as the law directs, deposeth and saith that in the latter part of the winter or spring of 1800, he understood that Thomas MADDIN was about to commence building a mill on the land mentioned in the concession aforesaid and that himself or his hands, amongst whom was Job WESTOVER, had gone out to the land for that purpose, that shortly after the same men returned saying they had been fired on and driven off by the Indians (Osage); that this deponent, with several others, went immediately to the place and found the facts as represented for

they saw the (cannot read) in the trees where the firing had been and
saw the tracts and signs of the Indians that this deponent with the
others followed the Indians all day without success, and that said
MADDIN, afterwards, continued from time to time to progress in building
the mill, and in 1803, this deponent assisted in building and finishing
the mill. That said MADDIN built a small house and opened some land,
and that he well knows that the said mill has been in operation generally ever since and that the said land was actually inhabited and cultivated from the date aforesaid ever since and still is. That said
MADDIN continued to clear and improve the land till, he believes, there
was more than one hundred, perhaps one hundred and fifty acres improved,
and in cultivation. That said MADDIN, at the date of the grant and
ever since was and has been a residenter of the Country.
Sworn and subscribed before me, Lewis F. LINN, one of the Commissioners
appointed to finally settle and adjust the titles and claims to land in
Missouri, this 30th day of October, 1832.
Signed L.F. LINN, Commissioner   Francois VALLE

And, also, came Joseph VITAL about fifty years of age, who being duly
sworn, deposeth and saïth that he has been a citizen of this country
from since he was eight years old, that he is well acquainted with the
tract of land claimed in the concession aforesaid, as also with
Thomas MADDIN, who was at the date of the grant and still is a citizen
and residenter of this Country. That he knows that about the year 1800
or 1801, Thomas MADDIN went, or sent, or took hands, he does not remember, and began to prepare to build a mill on the same and that they
were fired on by the Indians and driven off. That this witness was one
of the party who went out in pursuit of the Indians, who were then very
troublesome at any distance from the villages, and this deponent further
says that in 1803, to the best of his recollection, he assisted in person to raise the mill, which was put into operation and a mill continued
on said land ever since. That about that time or shortly afterwards,
said MADDIN begun and built a house and opened some land and continued
to improve said land and open more land till he had from one hundred to
one hundred & fifty acres opened, and he further knows that from about
the date of the concessions to the present time, the said land has been
inhabited, improved and cultivated.
Sworn to and Subscribed before me, Lewis F. LINN, one of the commissioners appointed to finally settle and adjust the titles and claims
to land in Missouri, this 30th day of October, 1832.
Signed L.F. LINN   Jph. V. BEAUVAIS

Jean Baptiste LABRECHE claiming 500 arpens of land, Book No. 1, pg.
319, No. 4, pg. 350, No. 5, pg. 536, C, pg. 419, produces a paper purporting to be an original concession from Carlos Dehault DELASSUS,
dated September 5th, 1799. The following additional testimony was
taken in the foregoing case in compliance with a resolution of this
Board of the 10th October last.
State of Missouri, County of St. Genevieve
Bazil MESPLAIS and Therese RANGE and the heirs and legal representatives of Lambert RANGE claiming five hundred arpens of land under
Baptiste LABRECHE, situate in the late District of St. Genevieve, now
County of Washington in the State of Missouri by virtue of a concession, produces the original concessions from Charles Dehault DELASSUS
late Lt. Gov. of Upper Louisiana to the said Baptiste LABRECHE, dated
the third day of September, 1799, for five hundred arpens of land. No
plat of Survey is produced, but reference is made to the record for the
same. Whereupon, Paschal DETCHMENDY, aged seventy one years, being
duly sworn as the law directs, deposeth and saith that he was well acquainted with the handwriting and signature of the said
Charles Dehault DELASSUS, that he often saw him write and that the signature and name of said C.D. DELASSUS to the concession for five hundred arpens of land given by him to Baptiste LABRECHE, dated the fifth
day of September, 1799, is in the proper handwriting of the said
C.D. DELASSUS.
Sworn to and subscribed before me, Lewis F. LINN, one of the commissioners appointed to finally settle and adjust the titles and claims
to lands in Missouri, this 30th Day of October, 1832. (Dec. #27, pg. 295)
Signed   L.F. LINN   P. DETCHMENDY

And, also, personally came Francois OGE, aged eighty five years, who being also duly sworn, deposeth and saith that he was well acquainted with Baptiste LABRECHE, named in the aforesaid grant, that he was a residenter of this country at the date of the grant in 1799, and continued a citizen, that about the date of the said concession in 1799, the said Baptiste LABRECHE took possession of the land granted, that he settled on the land, built a house, opened a field and cultivated the same, and that the said tract of land from about the date of the said concession, has been, by the said LABRECHE (Baptiste) and those claiming under him actually inhabited and cultivated ever since and now is inhabited and cultivated.

Sworn to and subscribed before me, Lewis F. LINN, one of the Commissioners appointed to settle and adjust the titles and claims to lands in Missouri, this 30th of October, 1832.   his
Signed L.F. LINN   Francois (X) OGE
                                                    mark

        The Board Adjourned untill Monday next at 10 o'clock A.M.
        Monday November 26th, 1832 Board Met-Two Comm'rs. Present

William JAMES claiming 600 arpens of land, see Book No. 3, pg. 157, Record Book D, pgs. 40 & 41, produces a paper purporting to be an original concession from Zenon TRUDEAU dated 20th February, 1798. The following additional testimony was taken in the foregoing case, in compliance with a resolution of this board of the 10th of October, last.

State of Missouri, County of St. Genevieve.

William JAMES claiming six hundred arpens of land situate in the late District of St. Genevieve, now County of St. Genevieve, in the State of Missouri on the right bank of the river aux Vases, by virtue of a concession from Z. TRUDEAU, late Lt. Gov. of Louisiana, dated the 20th of February, 1798, made in conformity of a petition of the said JAMES dated the 7th February, 1798 and an order of Survey to A. SOULARD, late Surveyor General under the Spanish Government, of the date first aforesaid. Produces the original concession and order of Survey above referred to.

When James I. FENWICK of lawful age, being duly sworn as the law directs, deposeth and saith that he is well acquainted with the claimant in this case, William JAMES, that he came to this country in the year 1797 and settled in the country, that he has remained a residenter of this country from that time to the present moment, that he settled on a tract of land purchased of one Robert SMITH, on the river Aux Vases, a few miles from and below the tract claimed, that he has remained in the country and on the land aforesaid ever since.

Sworn to and subscribed before me, Lewis F. LINN, one of the commissioners for finally settling and adjusting the titles and claims to lands in the State of Missouri this 26th day of October, 1832.
Signed L.F. LINN   James I, FENWICK
(Dec. #31, pg. 297)

John Bste. VALLE aged seventy two years being duly sworn in the case as the law directs, deposeth and saith that he is well acquainted with the handwriting and signature of Zenon TRUDEAU, who was the Lt. Gov. of Louisiana under the late Spanish government, that the signature to the concession of William JAMES for 600 arpens of land, dated the 20th February, 1798 and order of Survey of the same date is in the handwriting of the said Zenon TRUDEAU and that the memorandum at the bottom of said concession (that the same was duly recorded) is in the proper hand of Charles Dehault Delassus de LUZIERE, then commandant, that he knows that the said William JAMES came to this country in the year 1797 or 98, to the best of his recollection and that he has remained a residenter of the country ever since. That said JAMES settled on the river Aux Vases, a few miles below the land claimed in the concession where he has remained ever since. That he knows it was considered very dangerous for many years after said JAMES came to the country to make settlements or make Surveys at any distance from the towns and settled parts of the country.

Sworn to and subscribed before me, Lewis F. LINN, one of the commissioners for finally settling and adjusting titles and claims to lands in Missouri, this 26th day of October, 1832.
Signed L.F. LINN   Bste. VALLE

Charles Fremon DELAURIERE by his legal representatives claiming 300
arpens of land, see Book No. 5, pg. 447, Record C, pgs. 401 & 402,
produces a paper purporting to be an original concession from
Carlos Dehault DELASSUS, dated 10th December, 1799. The following
additional testimony was taken in the foregoing case, in compliance
with a resolution of this Board of the 10th October last.
State of Missouri, County of St. Genevieve
The heirs and legal representatives of Marie Louise LECLERC, who
claimed under Augustin Charles Fremon DELAURIERE, claiming three hundred arpens of land situate in the late district of St. Genevieve, now
County of St. Genevieve in the State of Missouri, produces the original
concession dated the 10th day of December, 1799, made to the said
Augustin Charles Fremon DELAURIERE on his petition by
Charles Dehault DELASSUS, the Late Lt. Governor of Louisiana, together
with the original assignment of the said Augustin Charles Fremon DELAU
Augustin Charles Fremon DELAURIERE to the said Marie Louisa LECLERC.
When Henry MORRIS aged seventy three years being produced and sworn as
the law directs, deposeth and saith that under and by the orders and
directions of the said Marie Louisa LECLERC, now deceased, as early as
the year 1799, he actually worked on the said land claimed in the concession, that he cut logs and built a house on said land and made a
garden on the land. That the negroes of the said Madame LECLERC were
by her orders and directions with him and worked with him and that in
the year 1800, a field was made and corn planted, and that from the
year 1799 up to the present time, the said tract of land has been continually inhabited and cultivated and stock left thereon. That when
he worked there in 1799, he understood that the said Madame LECLERC
had purchased the said land of the said DELAURIERE. And further this
deponent saith that at the date of the grant aforesaid, the said
Augustin Charles Fremon DELAURIERE and the said Madame LECLERC were
both residenters of this country, that he was well acquainted with
them both, and that they continued residenters.
Sworn to and subscribed before me, Lewis F. LINN, one of the commissioners appointed to finally settle and adjust the titles and claims
to lands in Missouri, this 30th of October, 1832. (Dec. #32, pg. 297)
Signed L.F. LINN   H. (X) MORRIS
                                        his mark

And, also, came Francois VALLE, aged fifty two years, who being duly
sworn as the law directs, deposeth and saith that he was well acquainted with Charles Dehault DELASSUS, that he was in the year 1799 the
Lt. Gov. of Upper Louisian, that he was well acquainted with the hand
writing of said C.D. DELASSUS, having seen him write and that the name
and signature to the said concession dated the 10th day of December,
1799 given by said C.D. DELASSUS to said A.C.F. DELAURIERE for three
hundred arpens of land is in the proper handwriting of the said
C.D. DELASSUS.
Sworn to and subscribed before me, Lewis F. LINN, one of the commissioners appointed to finally settle and adjust the titles and claims
to lands in Missouri, this 30th of October, 1832.
Signed L.F. LINN   F. VALLE
     The Board Adjourned untill tomorrow at 10 o'clock A.M.
          Tuesday November 27th, 1832 Board Met-Two Commr's. Present

Manuel LISA, by her legal representatives claiming 6,000 arpens of
land, see Book B, pg. 91, Book No. 2, pg. 33, Book No. 3, pg. 365,
produces a paper purporting to be an original concession from
Z. TRUDEAU, dated 17th July, 1799. Charles Fremon DELAURIERE, being
duly sworn, saith that the signatures to said concession and registering are in the proper handwriting of said Zenon TRUDEAU and of
Antoine SOULARD. M.P. LEDUC, being duly sworn, saith that the signatures to petition is in the proper handwriting of said Manuel LISA.
(Dec. #33, pg. 298)

Om tje Case of Francois VALLE's legal representatives claiming 7,056
arpens of land (entered 22nd inst:) M.P. LEDUC, Charles F. DELAURIERE
and Albert TISON, being duly sworn, say that Francois VALLE, had at
the date of his petition, seven children and at least from forty to
fifty slaves and that he was then Commandant of St. Genevieve.
Albert TISON & C. Fremon DELAURIERE say that he was then possessed of

16

a great number of cattle. (Decision #26, pg. 295)

In the case of Francois CAILLON claiming 1,600 arpens of land (entered 8th October) the original concession is produced. M.P. LEDUC, being duly sworn, saith that the signature to the original concession is in the proper handwriting of Carlos Dehault DELASSUS. (Dec. #18, 293)

In the case of James MACKAY claiming 30,000 arpens for services (entered 5th October), Charles Premon DELAURIERE, being duly sworn, saith that the signature to the original concession is in the proper handwriting of C.D. DELASSUS and the signature to MACKAY's petition is in the proper handwriting of said MACKAY. That he was well acquainted with MACKAY, that he was an officer who stood very high in the estimation of the Spanish Government and was looked upon as a very usefull man to the country that he was commandant of St. Andre, and that the only salary he received as such, was hardly sufficient to pay for the stationary that he recollects his return from New Orleans, where, it was understood, he had been to make his report to the general government of his voyage of discovery in the Western part of Upper Louisiana towards the Pacific Ocean; that he continued commandant of St. Andre till the cession of this country to the United States, that he acted also as deputy surveyor to Antonio SOULARD. Albert TISON, being duly sworn, saith that said James MACKAY was also commandant of St. Charles. That said District of St. Charles comprehended then, all the country North of Missouri at the exception of the small district of Portage des Sioux. Charles F. DELAURIERE and Albert TISON prove the signature to the letter of Zenon TRUDEAU, heretofore presented in evidence in this case. Fremon DELAURIERE proves the handwriting of Manuel Galloso de LEMOS to a letter dated 20th May, 1799. That he, said DELAURIERE, being a public officer had occasion to see it often. He also proves the signature of Ant. SOULARD to an affidavit dated 5th December, 1817 and to three plats of Surveys. (Dec. #3, pg. 287)

In the case of Pierre Delassus de LUZIERE claiming 7,056 arpens of land (entered 9th October). Albert TISON and Fremon DELAURIERE, being duly sworn, prove the signature of said De LUZIERE to his petition dated 3rd March, 1795. They also prove the handwriting of Francois VALLE to a certificate dated 10th March, 1795. Also, the handwriting of said Delassus de LUZIERE to a petition dated November, 25th, 1799. Also, the handwriting of Carlos Dehault DELASSUS to an order of survey dated 29th November, 1799. Also, the handwriting of Antonio SOULARD to a plat of survey of a league square. (the above papers allready presented in evidence on the 9th October last). Said witness also proves the handwriting of Francois VALLE to a certified copy of a letter of Dn. Luis de las CASAS, Captain General of Havana, addressed to the Chevalier Delassus de LUZIERE, dated 20th May, 1794. Also, the handwriting of Zenon TRUDEAU to a decree of concession of a league square to Pierre Delassus de LUZIERE dated 1st April, 1795. Also, the handwriting of Francois VALLE, Commandant of St. Genevieve to a certificate of delivery of possession of a league square situated on a branch of the St. Francis called Gabory, also prove the signature of the Baron de CARONDELET to a letter dated 17th May, 1793, addressed to Mr. Dehault DELASSUS. Albert TISON saith taht Pierre de LUZIERE was known in France and by the Baron De CARONDELET by the name of Dehault DELASSUS and during the French Revolution, he took the name of de LUZIERE. The above named witnesses also prove the handwriting of the Baron de CARONDELET to an original letter dated 7th May, 1793, addressed to Dn. Zenon TRUDEAU, also, that said de LUZIERE had no (cannot read) as commandant of New Bourbon. That he enjoyed the confidence and esteem of the governor general and of the Lt. Gov. of Upper Louisiana. That he was a personal friend and allied by blood to the Baron de CARONDELET/ (Dec. #64, pg. 309)

In the case of Carlos Dehault DELASSUS claiming 30,000 arpens of land (entered 9th October) Albert TISON and Charles Fremon DELAURIERE, being duly sworn, prove the handwriting of Carlos Dehault DELASSUS to a petition dated 3rd February, 1798. Also, the handwriting of Zenon TRUDEAU to a decree of concession dated 10th February, 1798. The above named witnesses say that the claimant had no salary as Lt. Gov. and received but sixty dollars a month as his pay for his rank in the

Army. They also say that he acted as civil and military governor & judge. That his jurisdiction and command extended from Arkansas to the Northern extremity of the Spanish possession on the Western side of the Mississippi. That he was highly considered by the Spanish Government and that his administration of the Government of Upper Louisiana gave general satisfaction to the people under his command. Albert TISON states that Carlos Dehault DELASSUS was an officer in the European Spanish Army, that by his good military conduct and the great bravery he showed in the several engagements wherein he fought, he acquired great honour. That knowing the destitute circumstances of his father in this country, he was, at his own request, promoted from the Guard (cannot read) to the Stationary regiment of Louisiana. The above named Fremon DELAURIERE acknowledges his own handwriting to a plat and certificate of survey. The above papers have allready been offered in evidence in this case.

Toussaint GENDRON, by Albert TISON, claiming 800 arpens of land, see Book C, pg. 438 & 9, Book No. 4, pg. 193, produces a paper purporting to be the original survey for 800 arpens of land taken on the 13th of February and certified 20th March, 1804. Said plat of survey comprising 10 concessions of 800 arpens each. M.P. LEDUC, being duly sworn, saith that the signature to said plat of Survey is in the proper handwriting of Antonio SOULARD, Surveyor General. ((2d, 137, No. 7, 240)

Gabriel CONSTANT by Albert TISON claiming 800 arpens of land, see Book C, pgs. 436, 438 & 9, Book No. 1, pg. 286 and No. 4, pg. 474, produces a concession dated 24th March, 1800 from Carlos Dehault DELASSUS. Also, a deed of conveyance from said CONSTANT to said TISON. Also, plat & certificate of Survey as above. M.P. LEDUC, being duly sworn, saith that the signature to said concession is in the proper handwriting of Carlos Dehault DELASSUS. (2d,128, No. 7, 238)

Antoine DESNOYERS by Albert TISON claiming 800 arpens of land, see Book C, pgs. 437, 8 and 9, Books No. 1, pg. 286, No. 4, pg. 475, produces a paper purporting to be an original concession from Carlos Dehault DELASSUS, dated 7th February, 1800, and a deed of conveyance from said DESNOYERS to said TISON. Survey as above. M.P. LEDUC, being duly sworn, saith that the signature to the above concession is in the proper handwriting of Carlos Dehault DELASSUS. (2d,129, No.7, 239)

Gabriel HUNAULT by Albert TISON claiming 800 arpens of land, see Book C, pgs. 437, 8 and 9, No. 1, pg. 286, No. 4, pg. 475, produces a paper purporting to be an original concession Carlos Dehault DELASSUS dated 9th May, 1800. Also, deeds of conveyances of the same. Also, plat & certificate of Survey as above. M.P. LEDUC, duly sworn, saith that the signature to the above concession is in the proper handwriting of said Carlos Dehault DELASSUS. (2d 130, No. 7, 239)

Jean Baptiste THIBAULT by Albert Tison claiming 800 arpens of land, see Books C, pgs. 438 & 9, No. 1, pg. 287, No. 4, pg. 475, produces a paper purporting to be a concession from Carlos Dehault DELASSUS, dated 7th December, 1799. Also, a deed of conveyance for the same. Plat & certificate as above. M.P. LEDUC, duly sworn, saith that the signature to said concession is in the proper handwriting of the said Carlos Dehault DELASSUS. (2d, 131, No. 7, 239)

Joseph DESNOYERS by Albert TISON claiming 800 arpens of land, see Books C, pgs. 437, 8 & 9, No. 1, pg. 286, No. 4, pg. 474, produces a paper purporting to be an original concession from Carlos Dehault DELASSUS, dated 15th January, 1800. Also, deeds of conveyances for same. Plat & certificate as above. M.P. LEDUC, duly sworn, saith that the signature to said concession is in the proper handwriting of said Dehault DELASSUS. (2d, 132, No. 7, 239)

Augustin LANGLOIS claiming 800 arpens of land, see Books C, pgs. 438, & 9, No. 1, pg. 287, No. 4, pg. 475, produces a paper purporting to be an original concession from Carlos Dehault DELASSUS, dated 4th June, 1800, and deeds of conveyances for same. Plat as above. M.P. LEDUC-duly sworn, saith that the signature to said concession is in the proper handwriting of said Dehault DELASSUS. (2d, 133, No. 7, 239)

Louis DESNOYERS by Albert TISON claiming 800 arpens of land, see Books
C, pg. 437, 8 & 9, No. 1, pg. 286, No. 4, pg. 475, produces a paper
purporting to be an original concession from Carlos Dehault DELASSUS,
dated 15th January, 1800. Also, deeds of conveyances for same. Plat
& Certificate as above. M.P. LEDUC, duly sworn, saith that the signature to said concession is in the proper handwriting of said
Carlos DELASSUS. (2d, 134, No. 7, 240)

Amable CHARTRAN by Albert TISON claiming 600 arpens and said CHARTRAN
200 arpens of land, see Book C, pgs. 436, 8 and 9, No. 1, pg. 285, No.
4, pg. 474, produces a paper purporting to be an original concession
from Carlos Dehault DELASSUS dated 18th June, 1800. Also, Plat & certificate as above. M.P. LEDUC, duly sworn, saith that the signature
to said concessions in the proper handwriting of the said
Carlos Dehault DELASSUS. (2d, 135, No. 7, 240)

Francois DESNOYERS by Albert TISON claiming 800 arpens of land, see
Books C, pgs. 438, & (; No. 1, pg. 287, No. 4, pg. 475, produces a
paper purporting to be an original concession from
Carlos Dehault DELASSUS, dated 15th January, 1800. Also, deeds of
conveyances for same. Plat and certificate as above. M.P. LEDUC,
duly sworn, saith that the signature to said concession is in the
proper handwriting of said Carlos Dehault DELASSUS. (2d, 136, No. 7, 240)
    The Board Adjourned untill tomorrow at 10 o'clock A.M.
        Wednesday November 28th, 1832 Board Met-Two Comm'rs. Present

Nicolas BOILEVIN by his legal representatives claiming 400 arpens of
land, situated at the Old Min, see Books D, pgs. 173, 4 & 5, No. 4, pg.
528.

Francois LACOMBE By Manuel LISA's legal representatives claiming 400
arpens of land, see Books D, pg. 232, No. 3, pgs. 330 and 364, No. 4,
pg. 421, produces a paper purporting to be an original concession from
Carlos Dehault DELASSUS, dated 26th February, 1800. Also, a deed of
conveyance for same. M.P. LEDUC, duly sworn, saith that the signature
to said concession is in the proper handwriting of C.Dehault DELASSUS.
(Dec. No. 34, pg. 298)

Joachin LISA by Manuel LISA's legal representatives claiming 6,000 arpens of land, see Books B, pg. 91, No. 2, pg. 33, No. 3, pg. 365, &
No. 4, pg. 421, produces a paper purporting to be an original concession from Zenon TRUDEAU dated 17th July, 1799 and a deed of conveyance
for same. M.P. LEDUC, duly sworn, saith that the signature to said
concession is in the proper handwriting of the said Zenon TRUDEAU, Lt.
Governor. (Dec. 133, pg. 333)

François LACOMBE by Manuel LISA's representatives claiming 400 arpens
of land, see Books C, pgs. 442 & 3, No. 3, pg. 330 & 364, No. 4, pg.
421, produces a paper purporting to be an original concession from
Carlos Dehault DELASSUS, dated 1st August, 1799. M.P. LEDUC, duly
sworn, saith that the signature to the said concession is in the proper handwriting of the said C. Dehault DELASSUS. (Dec. 125, pg. 326)

Philipe BACANE by Manuel LISA's legal representatives claiming 480
arpens of land, see Books C, pg. 443, No. 1, pg. 285, No. 3, pg. 368
for survey see Book C,pg. 443, produces a paper purporting to be an
original concession from Zenon TRUDEAU, dated 15th December, 1796.
M.P. LEDUC, duly sworn, saith that the signature to the said concession is in the proper handwriting of Zenon TRUDEAU. (Dec. 35, pg. 298)

Baptiste RIVIERE by Manuel LISA's legal representatives claiming 400
arpens of land, see Books C, pgs. 442 & 3, No. 1, pg. 285, No. 3, pg.
368 and No. 4, pg. 386, produces a paper purporting to be an original
concession from Zenon TRUDEAU dated 17th October, 1796. Also, a concession from Carlos Dehault DELASSUS, dated 8th January, 1803.
M.P. LEDUC, being duly sworn, saith that the signatures to the above
concessions are in the proper and respective handwriting of said
Zenon TRUDEAU and said Carlos Dehault DELASSUS, and that the signatures

to report of SOULARD on first concession is in the proper handwriting
of said SOULARD. Claimant also, produces a paper purporting to be a
plat of Survey executed by James RANKIN, deputy Surveyor on the 25th
February, 1806. M.P. LEDUC, saith that the signature to said plat of
Survey for the above concessions is in the proper handwriting of said
RANKIN and that said RANKIN was acting as deputy Surveyor under SOULARD
before and after the change of government. (Dec. No. 36, pg. 299)

In the case of Antoine DUBREUIL claiming 10,000 arpens of land (entered 21st inst: pg. 31) Charles Fremon DELAURIERE, being-duly sworn
saith that in the year 1802 Antoine DUBREUIL came to the witness's
salt lick and there made an arrangement with him to assist said
DUBREUIL in settling his salt works on Buffaloe Creek. That he, (witness) furnished said DUBREUIL with 10 salt kettles, besides oven, carts
and three of his best men. Among them was Benjamin SPENCER, now deceased, they built a house for said DUBREUIL on his concession at said
Buffaloe Creek. Also, erected his furnaces and actually made salt and
lived on said place till about February of 1803, when they were driven
away by the Indians, who killed the oxen, burnt the house and broke
several kettles, and the men who were at work there made their escape
to said DELAURIERE's salt works. That several months afterwards said
witness went down in a pirogeu to save as much as he could of what the
Indians had left. He found but seven kettles, the others having been
broke. Saw the remains of the burnt buildings and the furnaces destroyed. Witness further states that on the 24th February, 1806, he was
applied to by Antoine DUBREUIL to have his land surveyed as said
DUBREUIL had no opportunity to have it surveyed before that time having
been several times driven off by the Indians. That he, said DELAURIERE
proceeded there and surveyed the plat of survey of said land on the
Record Book B, pg. 95. He fines it to correspond exactly with the plat
of his Survey returned to Antoine SOULARD, Surveyor General with the
exception of the figures 1,000 on the face of said survey and in the
certificate, which he is sure is a mistake. That at that time, there
was in the whole province of Upper Louisiana, but three salt works in
operation; that salt was then very scarce and worth six dollars a
bushell. That in consequence of his working his saline salt fell to
three dollars a bushell. That the province of Upper Louisiana was de-
pendent mainly on foreigners from the Ohio for their supply of salt.
Witness further states that in the year 1805, he was appointed deputy
Surveyor and officially acted as such in that year and in 1806.
(Dec. No. 24, pg. 295)
     The Board Adjourned untill tomorrow at 10 o'clock A.M.
          Thursday November 29th, 1832 Board Met-Two Commr's. Present

Francois COLEMAN by his legal representatives J.P. CABANE and
J.N. MACKLOT claiming 2,500 arpens of land, see Books C, pgs. 121 & 122,
No. 4, pg. 316, produces a paper purporting to be a decree from
Manuel PEREZ, Lt. Gov. dated 12th March, 1788 and also a concession
from H. PEYROUX, late Commandant of St. Genevieve, dated 15th March,
1788. Also, a paper purporting to be a plat of survey executed by
Thomas MADDIN, deputy Surveyor on the 21st February, 1806, received
for record by A. SOULARD, Surveyor General February 28th, 1806.
M.P. LEDUC, duly sworn, saith that the signatures to the foregoing
papers are in the proper handwriting of the above named persons, who
signed them. (Dec. No. 37, pg. 299)

Jean Rene Guiho de K. LEGAND by his assignee Mathew DUNCAN claiming
500 arpens of land, see Book B, pg. 500, No. 1, pg. 386, No. 3, pg.
346, produces a paper purporting to be an original concession from
Carlos Dehault DELASSUS, dated 15th January, 1800. Also, a deed of
conveyance. M.P. LEDUC, duly sworn, saith that the signature to said
concession is in the proper handwriting of said
Carlos Dehault DELASSUS. (Dec. No. 38, pg. 299)

Marie Nicolle LESBOIS by her legal representatives claiming 244-1/2
arpens of land, see Book C, pgs. 73, 4 & 75, No. 3, pg. 282, No. 5, pg.
328, produces a paper purporting to be an original concession for 213
arpens of land, more or less, from Carlos Dehault DELASSUS, dated 11th
May, 1803. Also, a paper purporting to be a plat and certificate of
Survey for 244 arpens and 50 perches, taken 27th May and certified the

20th August, 1803 by Antoine SOULARD. M.P. LEDUC, duly sworn, saith
that the signature to said concession is in the proper handwriting of
the said Carlos Dehault DELASSUS and the signature to said certificate
of Survey is in the proper handwriting of said SOULARD. (Dec. 39, pg.300)

Jean Francois PERREY by his legal representatives claiming 3,000 arpens
of land, see Books B, pg. 93, No. 1, pg. 488, No. 5, pg. 322, produces
a paper purporting to be an original concession from Zenon TRUDEAU, dated 18th July, 1798. M.P. LEDUC, duly sworn, saith that the signature
to said concession is in the proper handwriting of said Z. TRUDEAU.
(Dec. 40, pg. 300)

William LOUGHRY by his legal representatives claiming 450 arpens of
land, see Books D, pg. 282, No. 5, pg. 450, produces a paper purporting
to be an original concession from Carlos Dehault DELASSUS, dated 19th
March, 1802. M.P. LEDUC, duly sworn, saith that the signature to said
concession is in the proper handwriting of said Carlos Dehault DELASSUS.
(Dec. No. 41, pg. 300)

Francois MOREAU and Antoine MARECHAL by their legal representatives,
Edw. HEMPSTEAD's heirs and devisees claiming 15 by 20 arpens of land,
see Books D, pg. 228, No. 3, pg. 271 and No. 4, pg. 381, produces a
paper purporting to be an original concession from Z. TRUDEAU, Lt. Gov.
dated 20th November, 1796. Also, a deed of conveyance. M.P. LEDUC,
duly sworn, saith that the signature to said concession is the handwriting of said Zenon TRUDEAU. (Dec. 124, pg. 325)

Mathias VANDERHIDER by his legal representatives claiming 10 by 40 arpens of land, see Books E, pg. 17, No. 5, pg. 511, produces a paper
purporting to be an original concession from Zenon TRUDEAU, dated 16th
March, 1797. Also, a deed of conveyance. M.P. LEDUC, duly sworn, saith
that the signature to said concession is in the proper handwriting of
the said Zenon TRUDEAU. (Dec. No. 42, pg. 300)

Andre PELLETIER by his legal representatives claiming 800 arpens of
land, see Books D, pgs. 258 & 9, No. 5, pg. 480, produces a paper purporting to be an original concession from Carlos Dehault DELASSUS, dated 15th May, 1800, and deed of conveyance. M.P. LEDUC, duly sworn,
that the signature to said concession is in the proper handwriting of
said C.D. DELASSUS. (2d-143, No. 7, 241)

Baptiste MARION by his legal representatives Edward HEMPSTEAD's heirs
and devisees claiming 800 arpens of land, see Books C, pg. 423, No. 5,
pg. 455, produces a paper purporting to be an original concession from
Carlos Dehault DELASSUS, dated 21st February, 1800. Also, deeds of
conveyances. M.P. LEDUC, duly sworn, saith that the signature to the
aforesaid concession is in the proper handwriting of said
Carlos Dehault DELASSUS. (2d, 126, No. 7-238)

Toussaint TOURVILLE by his legal representatives claiming 800 arpens
of land, see Books C, pg. 423, No. 5, pg. 505, produces a paper purporting to be an original concession from Carlos Dehault DELASSUS, dated 18th January, 1800. Also, deeds of conveyances. M.P. LEDUC, duly
sworn, saith that the signature to said concession is in the proper
handwriting of the said C.D. DELASSUS. (23, 127, No. 7 - 238)

John COONTZ and Edward HEMPSTEAD claiming 450 arpens of land, see Books
D, pg. 259, No. 5, pg. 399, produces a paper purporting to be an origi-
nal concession from Carlos Dehault DELASSUS, dated 30th May, 1800.
M.P.LEDUC, duly sworn, saith that the signature to the said concession
is in the proper handwriting of the said Carlos Dehault DELASSUS.
(Dec. No. 44, pg. 302)

Pierre LORD by his legal representatives, Edward HEMPSTEAD's heirs and
devisees claiming 800 arpens of land, see Books C, pg. 424, No. 5, pg.
445, produces a paper purporting to be an original concession from
Carlos Dehault DELASSUS, dated 14th December, 1799. Also, deeds of
conveyances. M.P. LEDUC, duly sworn, saith that the signature to said
concession is in the proper handwriting of said
Carlos Dehault DELASSUS. (2d-144, No. 7-242)

Joseph LAFLEUR by same as above claiming 800 arpens of land, see Books
D, pgs. 225 & 6, No. 3, pg. 360, No. 4, pg. 420, produces a paper purporting to be a copy of a concession from Carlos Dehault DELASSUS, dated 18th September, 1800. Said copy certified by Antoine SOULARD on
the 10th January, 1805. Also, deed of conveyance. M.P. LEDUC, duly
sworn, saith that the signature to said copy of concession is in the
proper handwriting of said Antoine SOULARD. (2d-145 No.7 -242)
    The Board Adjourned untill tomorrow at 10 o'clock A.M.
        Fryday November 30th, 1832 Board Met-Two Comm'rs. Present

Etienne and Louis BOLDUC by their legal representatives claiming two
tracts of land, each of 12-1/2 arpens in front by 40 arpens in depth,
produce a paper purporting to be an original concession from
Zenon TRUDEAU, dated 15th February, 1798. The following additional
testimony was taken in the foregoing case in compliance with a resolution of this Board of the 10th of October last.
St. Genevieve, November 6th, 1832
Etienne and Louis BOLDUC by their legal representatives claiming one
thousand arpents of land on the South branch of the Saline in the former District of St. Genevieve. Said claimants present the original
petition and concession. When Henry DIEL personally appeared before
Lewis F. LINN, one of the Commissioners appointed for the purpose of
finally settling private land claims in Missouri, said DIEL after
being duly sworn, deposeth and saith that he is sixty three years of
age. That he is well acquainted with the handwriting of Etienne and
Louis BOLDUC and knows that the signatures to the above mentioned petition are in their proper handwriting and furthermore that the signature to the concession is in the hand writing of Zenon TRUDEAU. He
furthermore swears that the petitioners were farmers, hard working and
industrious men, and believes they never had any other concession for
land in upper Louisiana or elsewhere.   (Not Recorded)
Sworn to and subscribed before L.F. LINN, Land Commissioner.
Signed L.F. LINN   H. DIEL
    The Board adjourned untill tomorrow at 10 o'clock A.M.
        Saturday December 1st, 1832 Board Met-Two Comm'rs. Present

In as much as the Board of Commissioners have come to the conclusion
not to report to the Commissioner of the general land office at the
next session of Congress on any of the land claims on which the law
requires them to act, in consequence of the resignation of
Witkins UPDIKE, Esq., one of the Commissioners, and of the prevalence
of the Cholera which prevented the attendance of witnesses, etc.
Furthermore, the time being limited for the reception of evidence to
the 9th of July next, and it being the opinion of this Board that it
would be opressive and expensive to witnesses who reside at a distance
to attend at this place (being mostly aged persons). Resolved, that
a Deputation of one of the members of the Board of Commissioners, proceed to the Southern part of the State for the purpose of taking evidence at the following places, to wit: At St. Genevieve, County of
St. Genevieve, Potosi, County of Washington; St. Michael, County of
Madison, Jackson, County of Cape Girardeau, and New Madrid, County of
New Madrid. Resolved, also, that Lewis F. LINN, be and is hereby
appointed to proceed to the above mentioned places to take such testimony and that he gives public notice, in writing or otherwise, when
and where he will be ready to receive such testimony as may be presented to him. Resolved, also, that the powers hereby given to
Lewis F. LINN, Esq., be continued untill this Board shall be officially
notified of the appointment of a successor to W. UPDIKE, Esq., resigned.
It is further resolved, that F.R. CONWAY, Esq., Recorder of land titles,
ex officio Commissioner, be and is hereby appointed to take testimony
at the Recorders Office in St. Louis, County of St. Louis, which power
shall be continued to him untill it is resolved otherwise by this board.
Resolved, that the Board Adjourn untill Wednesday the 12th instant.
    The Board Met & Adjourned on December 12th, 1832.
        Thursday December 13th, 1832 Board Met-F.R. CONWAY Present

John B. PRATTE by his legal representatives claiming 1,000 arpens of
land, see Book No. 1, pg. 454, No. 5, pg. 537, Record Book C, pg. 221
& pg. 200 of this Book. The following additional testimony was taken
in the foregoing case in compliance with a resolution of this Board

of the 10th October last.
St. Genevieve October 25th, 1832
The heirs and legal representatives of John B. PRATTE claiming one
thousand arpents of land situated on Grand river waters in the former
district of St. Genevieve in pursuance of and by virtue of a concession
and order of survey heretofore filed with the former Commissioners.
When Louis LASOURCE personally appeared before Lewis F. LINN, one of
the Commissioners appointed to finally settle and adjust land claims
in Missouri and authorised by said Board of Commissioners to receive
testimony in this behalf. When said LASOURCE, after being duly sworn,
deposeth and saith that he knows of the cultivation and habitation of
said tract ofland by John B. PRATTE in eighteen hundred or in eighteen
hundred and one. That he has seen the said PRATTE when residing on
the place where and when he had all his work hands. That his number
of hands was very numerous and that the land under cultivation was
quite a large field. How many arpents he does not know. Sworn to and
subscribed this day and date before writen in presence of L.F. LINN.
                              Signed   Louis LASOURCE

Col. Bste. VALLE appeared in behalf of said claimant and after being
duly sworn, deposeth and saith that the signature to the concession is
in the handwriting of Carlos Dehault DELASSUS and the signature to the
petition is the handwriting of John B. PRATTE and that, to the best of
his knowledge, the land claimed under said concession and now before
the Board of Commissioners was in a state of cultivation in 1801. And
that it has always been cultivated and inhabited ever since by PRATTE,
his heirs or representatives. Subscribed in presence of L.F. LINN.
                              Signed   Bste. VALLE

Henry DIELLE claiming 400 arpens of land. Also, one arpent in front
by 40 in depth, Book No. 3, pg. 168, No. 4, pg. 360, Record Book D,
pg. 54, produces a paper purporting to be an original concession from
Zenon TRUDEAU, dated 15th February, 1798 for 400 arpents of land.
Also, a paper purporting to be an original concession from Z. TRUDEAU
dated 15th February for one arpent in front by forty in depth. The
following additional testimony was taken in the foregoing case in compliance with a resolution of this Board of the 10th of October last.
St. Genevieve, November 2nd, 1832
Henry DIELLE claiming 400 arpents of land lying on the waters of the
Saline in the former District of St. Genevieve. When
Catherine BOLDUC, after being duly sworn, deposeth and saith that she
is acquainted with the handwriting of Zenon TRUDEAU and knows that his
name, attached to the concession here presented, is the handwriting of
said TRUDEAU, and she knows that Henry DIELLE took possession of the
land in 1798. Sworn to and subscribed before L.F. LINN, one of the
Commissioners appointed for the final adjustment of land claims in
Missouri. (Dec. 45, pg. 303)
Signed L.F. LINN   V. BODEU

Julien RATTE by his heirs and legal representatives claiming 150 arpents of land, see Book F, pgs. 127 & 8, BATES' decision, pg. 104,
produces a paper purporting to be an original concession from
Carlos Dehault DELASSUS, dated 18th October, 1799. The following
additional testimony was taken in the foregoing case in compliance
with a resolution of this Board of the 10th of October last.
St. Genevieve, October 27th, 1832.
Julien RATTE by his heirs and legal representatives claiming one hundred and fifty arpents of land on the waters of the Saline in the former district of St. Genevieve, in pursuance, and by virtue of an original concession. When Pierre ROBERT and Joseph St. GEMME appeared before L.F. LINN, one of the Commissioners appointed for the purpose of
settling the private land claims in Missouri, when the said ROBERT and
St. GEMME, being duly sworn, deposeth and saith that they know that
said RATTE occupied and cultivated said land in 1804, had built cabins
on it then, that it has been in his possession and occupation and that
of his family and representatives ever since. (Dec. 46, pg. 303)
Signed L.F. LINN   J. Bste. ST. GEMME
       Land Comm'r.   Pierre ROBERT (X) His Mark

St. Gemme BEAUVAIS claiming 60 feet in circumference around each hole at mine a Breton, where he may find mineral, see Book No. 1, pg. 316, No. 5, pg. 532, Record Book C, pg. 456, produces a paper purporting to be an original concession from Manuel PEREZ dated 27th November, 1788. (2d, 61, No. 7, p. 191)

F.R. CONWAY, Esq., adjourned untill tomorrow at 10 o'clock A.M.
Friday December 14th, 1832 Board Met-F.R. CONWAY, Present

Pierre L. VASQUEZ, by his legal representatives Gabriel PAUL claiming 800 arpents of land under a concession from Carlos Dehault DELASSUS dated 17th February, 1800 (said concession already produced to this Board on the 9th October last). See Minutes Book No. 1, pg. 491, No. 4, pgs. 67 & 502, Book C, pgs. 474 & 5, produces a plat of survey dated 7th October, 1830 by Joseph C. BROWN. Also, deed of conveyance. (Included in Dec. No. 19, pg. 293)

ST. VRAIN by his legal representative Charles GREGOIRE claiming 1,500 arpents of land, see Book No. 5, pg. 498, Record Book D, pg. 360, produces a paper purporting to be an original concession from Z. TRUDEAU, dated 22nd November, 1797. The following additional testimony was taken in the foregoing case, in compliance with a resolution of this Board of the 10th of October last.
St. Genevieve, Missouri, November 1st, 1832
Jacques MARCELIN, Cerand Dehault DELASSUS de ST. VRAIN by his legal representative Charles GREGOIRE, Junr., claiming fifteen hundred arpens of land situate on the waters of the river Aux Vases in the former district of St. Genevieve, in pursuance of and by virtue of a concession heretofore filed with the former Commissioners when Bartholomew ST. GEMMES personally appeared before Lewis F. LINN, one of the Commissioners appointed to finally settle and adjust land claims to Missouri and authorised by the said Board of Commissioners to receive testimony in this behalf, who being duly sworn, deposeth and sayeth that in the year seventeen hundred & ninety seven, he, the said deponent, was making sugar at a subar orchard belonging to his father. That then, and there, the above named Jacques M.C.D. DELASSUS came and requested to know where the lines of his said father's claim were run as he wanted to examine the creek in and about that neighbourhood, to see if he could not find a suitable place for a mill seat, that he proceeded on that examination (after he had been shown the supposed lines of said deponent's father) and deponent understood that said DELASSUS obtained grant or concession of a tract adjoining that of deponents's father, from Zenon TRUDEAU, said TRUDEAU being then Gov. of Upper Louisiana and that it was well understood at that time and always has been that said tract was claimed under said grant, by the said Delassus de ST. VRAIN and his legal representatives. This deponent further saith that he is well acquainted with the handwriting of Zenon TRUDEAU, late Governor of Upper Louisiana, that he has often seen him write and that the concession here shown for fifteen hundred arpents of land, dated 22nd of November, one thousand seven hundred & ninety seven and the signature thereto is in the proper handwriting of said Zenon TRUDEAU. That he is also well acquainted with the handwriting of Antoine SOULARD, late Surveyor General of Upper Louisiana. That he has often seen him write, and that the signature to the certificate annexed to said concession is in the proper handwriting of said SOULARD. Signed B. ST. GEMME   L.F. LINN (Dec.122, pg. 325)

Sebastian BUTCHER and the heirs and legal representatives of Bartholomew BUTCHER, Michael BUTCHER and Peter BLOOM, claiming 1,600 arpents of land, see Book No. 5, pg. 352, Record Book D, pgs. 46 & 47, produces a paper purporting to be their petition to the Intendant General of Louisiana and a recommendation to the same of Pierre Delassus de LUZIERE, Commandant of New Bourbon, dated 15th June, 1802. Also, a paper purporting to be a plat and certificate of survey dated 25th February, 1806 by Nathl. COOK, Deputy Surveyor. The following additional testimony was taken in the foregoing case in compliance with a resolution of this Board of the 10th October last.
The Claimants state that by virtue of their said claim, they located four hundred arpents thereof about six miles from Mine a la Motte as in their petition prayed for. That finding no further vacant land at that place of value for cultivation, they located the remaining 12 hundred arpents at a place on the waters of Grand or Big river, agree-

ably to the tenor of their said petition and the plat of survey herewith shewn to the Board of Commissioners. The petitioners further
state that the plat of Survey for the said four hundred arpents so located near Mine a la Motte is now in the land office at Jackson, so
that they cannot now produce it, but believe the same is of record in
the office of the Recorder of land titles at St. Louis. Joseph PRATTE,
being duly sworn in this behalf, deposeth and sayeth that he has seen
the recommendation of the said LUZIERE, late Commander of the Post of
New Bourbon, annexed to the petition of the said claimants for a grant
or concession of sixteen hundred arpents of land; that he is well acquainted with the handwriting of said LUZIERE and that the said recommendation dated June 15th, 1802 and the signature thereunto affixed,
are in the handwriting of the said LUZIERE. This deponent further
saith that he is well acquainted with the handwriting of A. SOULARD,
late Surveyor General of Upper Louisiana and that his signature to the
plat of Survey here shewn is as this deponent verily believes, genuine
and written by himself. This deponent further sayth that he is fifty
seven years of age and has resided in St. Genevieve vicinity in what
was formerly Upper Louisiana, all his life. That he is well acquainted with the nature of 'Spanish Concessions and requests and Recommendations of Commandants of Posts, of which latter class the claim here
shewn appears to be one. That after the year 1799 or 1800 (as near
as he can recollect) the Commandants did not give concessions, but
recommendations to the Intendant General at New Orleans (as in this
case) and that said recommendations were uniformly considered of equal
validty with concessions and were passed and transferred from hand to
hand, as such and that it was the uniform custom of the Intendant
General at New Orleans to grant and confirm all such claims. This
affiant further sayth that he has no doubt that the claim here shewn
would have been confirmed by the said Intendant, under the usages and
custom of the Spanish Government. That he has known the said
Sebastian (or Bastian), Michael & Bartholomew BUTCHER and Peter BLOOM
to have come to the country in the year 1797, and that it was the custom of the government to give lands to persons of their description
when applied for, and he has never heard that they received any other
lands than those in the present claim mentioned. Signed J. PRATTE
L.F. LINN, Land Commissioner.(Dec. 142, pg. 346)

John Bste. VALLE, Senior, being duly sworn in this behalf, deposeth &
sayth that he has seen the recommendation of the said LUZIERE, late
Commandant of the Post of New Bourbon, annexed to the petition of the
said claimants for a grant or concession of sixteen hundred arpents of
land. That he is well acquainted with the handwriting of the said
LUZIERE and that the said recommendation to the Intendant General and
the signature thereunto affixed, are in the handwriting of the said
LUZIERE. This deponent further says that he was well acquainted with
Antoine SOULARD, late Surveyor General of Upper Louisiana, and that
his signature to the plat of Survey here shewn, this deponent believes
to be genuine and written by said SOULARD. This deponent further says
that he is now seventy two years of age and has resided in St. Genevieve, in the District, (now County) of St. Genevieve all his life, &
is well acquainted with the manner of granting concessions by the
Spanish Government in Louisiana and he always considered incipient
titles of the kind here shewn, as much entitled to a confirmation as
any other; and that, frequently, lands granted by the said Spanish
Government were not surveyed untill several years after they were
granted and confirmed. Signed J. Bste. VALLE   L.F. LINN

And as a witness in this behalf, Mary Ann LAPLANTE, personally appeared
before Lewis F. LINN, one of the Commissioners appointed to settle and
finally adjust the land claims in Missouri and authorised by the Board
of Commissioners to receive testimony in this behalf, who being duly
sworn, deposeth and saith that she is about fifty eight years of age,
that she came from France to Upper Louisiana in the family of
Mr. LUZIERE, late Commandant of the Post of New Bourbon and has resided
in St. Genevieve and New Bourbon ever since the said LUZIERE came to
the country. That some time before the change of government (she thinks
about the year 1802) she was in the office of the said LUZIERE (he being
then Commandant of the Post of New Bourbon) and saw Mr. LUZIERE writing
a paper which said LUZIERE then told her was a concession or grant of

land to Bartholomew BUTCHER, Michael BUTCHER, Sebastian, (or Bastian)
BUTCHER and Peter BLOOM, which grant or concession said LUZIERE informed the witness was for four hundred arpens for each of said persons, for that, as those persons were such good stone masons, it was
a great object to the people and the government of the country to have
such good workmen and peaceable subjects retained in the country. This
affiant being now blind, cannot, of course, say whether the grant or
concession or recommendation now shewn to the Commissioner, is the
same she saw Mr. LUZIERE write. Signed Mary Ann (X) LAPLANTE
L.F. LINN   her mark
    Adjourned untill tomorrow at 10 o'clock A.M.
        The Board Met & Adjourned December 15th, 17th & 18th, 1832.
        Wednesday 19th December, 1832 Board Met-F.R. CONWAY Present

Louis LAJOIE by his legal representative John MULLANPHY claiming 800
arpents of land, see Book No. 5, pg. 316, Book C, pgs. 326, No. 1, pg.
302, No. 5, pg. 316, produces a paper purporting to be an original concession from Carlos Dehault DELASSUS, dated 19th February, 1800. Also,
a plat and certificate of Survey dated 20th March, 1804 by A. SOULARD.
Also, deeds of conveyances. M.P. LEDUC, being duly sworn, sayth that
the signature to said concession is in the proper handwriting of
Carlos Dehault DELASSUS and the signature to plat & certificate of Survey is in the proper handwriting of Antoine SOULARD. (2d,120, pg. 237)

Jacob EASTWOOD by his legal representative John MULLANPHY claiming 800
arpents of land, see Book C, pgs. 330, 31 & 32, Book No. 5, pg. 419,
produces a paper purporting to be an original concession from
Carlos Dehault DELASSUS dated February 8th, 1801. Also, a plat and
certificate of Survey dated 5th March, 1804 by Antoine SOULARD. Also,
deed of conveyance. M.P. LEDUC, being duly sworn, saith that the signature to the said concession is in the proper handwriting of
Carlos Dehault DELASSUS and that the signature to plat & certificate
of survey is in the proper handwriting of Antoine SOULARD.
(2d, 115, No. 7, 236)

Daniel HUBBARD, by his legal representative John MULLANPHY claiming
800 arpents of land, see Book C, pgs. 330, 31 & 32, Book No. 5, pg.
419, produces a paper purporting to be an original concession from
Carlos Dehault DELASSUS dated 20th November, 1800. Also, a paper purporting to be a plat and certificate of Survey dated 5th March, 1804
by Antoine SOULARD. Also, deed of conveyance. M.P. LEDUC, duly sworn,
saith that the signature to the said concession is in the proper handwriting of Carlos Dehault DELASSUS and that the signature to plat and
certificate of Survey is in the proper handwriting of Antoine SOULARD.
(2d, 117, No. 7-236)

Felix HUBBARD, by his legal representative John MULLANPHY claiming 800
arpens of land, see Book C, pgs. 330, 31 & 32, Book No. 5, pg. 418,
produces a paper purporting to be an original concession from
Carlos Dehault DELASSUS dated November 20th, 1800. Also, a plat and
certificate of Survey dated 5th March, 1804. Also, a deed of conveyance. M.P. LEDUC, being duly sworn, saith that the signature to the
said concession is in the proper handwriting of said DELASSUS, and that
the signature to plat and certificate of Survey is in the proper handwriting of Antoine SOULARD. (2d, 118, No. 7-236)

Eusebuis HUBBARD, by his legal representative John MULLANPHY claiming
800 arpents of land, see Book C, pgs. 330 & 332, No. 5, pg. 418, produces a paper purporting to be an original concession from
Carlos Dehault DELASSUS dated 7th January, 1803. Also, a plat and
certificate of Survey dated 5th March, 1804. (also, deeds of conveyances)
(Said Survey by Ant. SOULARD). M.P. LEDUC, being duly sworn, saith that
the signatures to the above papers are in the respective handwriting of
Carlos Dehault DELASSUS and Antoine SOULARD. (2d, 119, No. 7-237)

Bste. Joseph BILLOT, by his legal representative John MULLANPHY claiming
800 arpents of land, see Book C, pgs. 329 & 330, No. 1, pg. 304, No. 5,
pg. 318, produces a paper purporting to be an original concession from
Carlos D. DELASSUS dated 29th February, 1800. Also, a plat and certificate of Survey dated 28th March, 1804 (also, deed of conveyance).

M.P. LEDUC, duly sworn, saith that the signatures to the above papers
are in the respective handwriting of Carlos D. DELASSUS and
Antoine SOULARD. (2d, 122, No. 7-237)

Baptiste DELILLE, Junr., by his legal representative John MULLANPHY
claiming 800 arpents of land, see Book C, pgs. 329 & 330, No. 1, pg.
304, No. 5, pg. 318, produces a paper purporting to be an original
concession from Carlos Dehault DELASSUS dated 25th April, 1800. Also, a plat and certificate of Survey dated 28th March, 1804 by
Antoine SOULARD (Also, deeds of conveyances). M.P. LEDUC, duly sworn,
saith that the signatures to the above papers are in the proper handwriting of Carlos Dehault DELASSUS and Antoine SOULARD.(2d, 123, No.7-
237)

Baptiste DELILLE, Senr., by his legal representative John MULLANPHY
claiming 800 arpents of land, see Book C, pgs. 328, 29 and 330, Books
No. 1, pg. 304, No. 5, pg. 318, produces a paper purporting to be an original concession from Carlos Dehault DELASSUS, dated 9th October,
1799. Also, a plat and certificate of Survey dated 28th March, 1804
by Antoine SOULARD. (Also, deeds of conveyances.) M.P. LEDUC, duly
sworn, saith that the signatures to the above papers are in the proper handwriting of the said Carlos Dehault DELASSUS and
Antoine SOULARD. (2d, 124, No. 7-238)

Paul DESJARLAIS by his legal representative John MULLANPHY claiming
800 arpents of land, see Book C, pgs. 328 & 330, Books No. 1, pg. 304,
No. 5, pg. 318, produces a paper purporting to be an original concession from C.D. DELASSUS, dated 11th July, 1800. Also, a plat and certificate of Survey dated 28th March, 1804, by Antonio SOULARD. (also,
deeds of conveyances) M.P. LEDUC, duly sworn, saith that the signatures to the aforesaid papers are in the proper handwriting of
Carlos D. DELASSUS and Antonio SOULARD. (2d, 125, No. 7-238)

Joseph DECARRY, by his legal representative John MULLANPHY claiming
800 arpents of land, see Book C, pg. 335, Book No. 5, pg. 371, produces a paper purporting to be an original concession from
C.D. DELASSUS dated 8th March, 1802. M.P.LEDUC, duly sworn, saith
that the signature to the aforesaid concession is in the proper handwriting of the said C.D. DELASSUS. (2d,101, No. 7-233)

Joseph RIVET, by his legal representative John MULLANPHY claiming 800
arpents of land, see Book C, pg. 333, Books No. 1, pg. 303, No. 5, pg.
317, produces a paper purporting to be an original concession from
C.D. DELASSUS, dated 28th February, 1800. (also, deeds of conveyances)
M.P. LEDUC, duly sworn, saith that the signature to the aforsaid concession is in the proper handwriting of said C.D. DELASSUS.
(2d, 87, No. 7, pg. 230)

Dominique HUGE, by his legal representative, John MULLANPHY, claiming
800 arpents of land, see Book C, pg. 335, Book No. 5, pg. 371, produces
a paper purporting to be an original concession from C.D. DELASSUS,
dated 14th October, 1799. M.P. LEDUC, duly sworn, saith that the signature to said concession is in the proper handwriting of said DELASSUS.
(2d, 100, No. 7, 232)

Regis VASSEUR, by his legal representative, John MULLANPHY, claiming
800 arpents of land, see Book C, pgs. 334 & 335, Book No. 5, pg. 370,
produces a paper purporting to be an original concession from
C.D. DELASSUS, dated 23rd December, 1799. (also, deeds of conveyances)
M.P. LEDUC, duly sworn, saith that the signature to the said concession is in the proper handwriting of the above named C.D. DELASSUS.
(2d, 104, No. 7, 233)

Francois PACQUET, by his legal representative, John MULLANPHY, claiming
800 arpents of land, see Book C, pg. 336, Books No. 1, pg. 301, No. 5,
pg. 317, produces a paper purporting to be an original concession from
C.D. DELASSUS, dated 5th April, 1800. (also, deeds of conveyances)
M.P. LEDUC, duly sworn, saith that the signature to the said concession
is in the proper handwriting of the said Carlos Dehault DELASSUS.
(2d, 86, No. 7, pg. 229)

27

Joseph HEBERT, by his legal representative, John MULLANPHY, claiming 800 arpents of land, see Book C, pg. 336, Books No. 1, pg. 303, No. 5, pg. 317, produces a paper purporting to be an original concession from Carlos Dehault DELASSUS, dated 15th April, 1800. (Also, deeds of conveyances) M. P. LEDUC, being duly sworn, saith that the signature to the above concession is in the proper handwriting of the said C.D. DELASSUS. (2d, 103, No. 7-233)

William CLARK, by his legal representative, John MULLANPHY, claiming 800 arpents of land, see Book C, pgs. 332 & 333, Book No. 5, pg. 369, produces a paper purporting to be an original concession from C.D. DELASSUS, dated 30th October, 1800. M.P. LEDUC, being duly sworn, saith that the signature to said concession is in the proper handwriting of the said C.D. DELASSUS._(2d, 99, No. 7-232)

J.Bste. DUMOULIN, by his legal representative, John MULLANPHY, claiming 800 arpents of land, see Book C, pg. 334, Book No. 5, pg. 370, produces a paper purporting to be an original concession from C.D. DELASSUS, dated 7th November, 1800. M.P. LEDUC, being duly sworn, saith that the signature to the above mentioned concession is in the proper handwriting of the said Carlos D. DELASSUS. (23, 62(?), No. 7, 233)

Francois BELLANGER, by his legal representative, John MULLANPHY, claiming 800 arpents of land, see Book C, pgs. 325 & 6, Books No. 1, pg. 301, No. 5, pg. 316 & 317, produces a paper purporting to be a plat and certificate of Survey dated 20th March, 1804, by Ant. SOULARD. M.P. LEDUC. duly sworn, saith that the signature to said certificate of Survey is the proper handwriting of the said Ant. SOULARD. (23, 121, No. 7-237)

Joseph JAMISON, by his legal representative, John MULLANPHY, claiming 800 arpents of land, see Book C, pgs. 327 & 328, Books No. 1, pg. 304, No. 5, pg. 318, produces a paper purporting to be an original concession from C. D. DELASSUS, dated 9th February, 1802. Also, a plat and certificate of certificate of Survey, dated 10th February, 1804 by Antonio SOULARD. (also, deeds of conveyances) M.P. LEDUC, being duly sworn, saith that the signatures to the above mentioned concession & certificate of Survey are in the proper handwriting of said DELASSUS and SOULARD. (2d, 139, No. 7, 241)

Hiacinthe EGLIS, by his legal representative, John MULLANPHY, claiming 800 arpents of land, see Book A, pgs. 30 & 33, Minutes No. 1, pgs. 311 & 530, No. 4, pg. 194, produces a paper purporting to be an original concession from Carlos Dehault DELASSUS, dated 16th December, 1799. Also, a plat and certificate of Survey for 300 arpents dated 20th of February, 1806 by James MACKAY and Recorded by Ant. SOULARD. M.P. LEDUC, being duly sworn, saith that the signature to the concession is in the proper handwriting of said C.D. DELASSUS and that the signature to the plat and certificate of Survey are in the proper handwriting of said MACKAY and SOULARD. (Dec. 47, pg. 304)

Etienne PEPIN, by his legal representative, John MULLANPHY, claiming 1,600 arpents of land, see Book B, pg. 509, Minutes No. 5, pg. 477, produces a paper purporting to be an original concession from Carlos D. DELASSUS, Dated 18th October, 1800. Also, deeds of conveyances. M.P. LEDUC, duly sworn, saith that the signature to said concession is in the proper handwriting of Carlos D. DELASSUS and that the signatures to the plat and certificate of Survey are in the handwriting of said MACKAY and SOULARD. (Dec. 48, pg. 304)

Andre & J. Bste. Blondeau DREZY, by their legal representative, John MULLANPHY, claiming 480 arpents of land, see Book A, pg. 44, Minutes No. 1, pg. 490, No. 4, pg. 194, produces a paper purporting to be an original concession from Zenon TRUDEAU, L.G., dated 18th March, 1799. Also, a plat of Survey certified by James MACKAY, deputy Surveyor and recorded by A. SOULARD, Surveyor General. M.P. LEDUC, being duly sworn, saith that the signature to the concession is in the proper handwriting of the said Zenon TRUDEAU and that the signature to the plat and certificate of Survey are in the proper handwriting of the said MACKAY and SOULARD. (Dec. 49, pg. 304)

Francois DUNEGAN, by his legal representative, John MULLANPHY, claiming 800 arpents of land, see Book of Record C, pgs. 151, 2 & 153, No. 5, pg. 405, produces a paper purporting to be an original concession from Carlos Dehault DELASSUS, dated 17th December, 1802 and 8th January, 1803. Also, deed of conveyance. M.P. LEDUC, being duly sworn, saith that the signature to the decrees are in the proper handwriting of the said Carlos D. DELASSUS.

Gabriel CERRE, by his legal representative, John MULLANPHY, claiming an Island at the mouth of Cuivre in the Mississippi, See Book No. 1, pg. 394, No. 4, pg. 194, A, pg. 49 & 50, produces a paper purporting to be an original concession from Carlos Dehault DELASSUS, dated 25th May, 1800. Also, deed of conveyance. M.P. LEDUC, being duly sworn, saith that the signature to the concession is in the proper handwriting of Carlos D. DELASSUS. (Dec. 51, pg. 305)

Jacques de ST. VRAIN, by his legal representative, John MULLANPHY, claiming 4,000 arpents of land, see Book of Record A, pgs. 18 & 19, Minutes No. 1, pg. 271 &2, No. 4, pg. 193, produces a paper purporting to be an original concession from Dehault DELASSUS, dated 18th November, 1799. Also, a plat and certificate of Survey dated 5th of March, 1804 by Ant. SOULARD. (Also, deeds of conveyances) M.P. LEDUC, being duly sworn, saith that the signature to the concession is in the proper handwriting of the said Carlos Dehault DELASSUS and that the signature to the plat and certificate of Survey is the handwriting of Antonio SOULARD. (Dec. 62, pg. 308)
        Adjourned untill tomorrow at 10 o'clock A.M.
        The Board Met & Adjourned on December 20th, 21st, 22nd, 24th, 25th, 26th, 27th, 28th, 29th, 31st, 1832, January 1st, 2nd, and 3rd, 1833.
            Friday January 4th, 1833 Board Met-F.R. CONWAY Present

St. Gemme BEAUVAIS, by his legal representative, Jno. MULLANPHY, claiming 800 arpents of land, see Record Bk. C, pg. 332, Minutes No. 5, pg. 369, produces a paper purporting to be an original concession from Carlos Dehault DELASSUS, dated 23rd September, 1800. Also, deeds of conveyances. M.P. LEDUC, being duly sworn, saith that the signature to the said concession is in the proper handwriting of the said Carlos Dehault DELASSUS. (2d, 97, No. 7-232)

Pierre ROUSSEL, by his legal representative, John MULLANPHY, claiming 800 arpents of land, see Books C, pgs. 334 & 4, No. 1, pg. 302, No. 5, pg. 317, produces a paper purporting to be an original concession from Carlos Dehault DELASSUS, dated 25th January, 1800. Also, deeds of conveyances. M. P. LEDUC, being duly sworn, saith that the signature to the said concession is in the proper handwriting of the said Carlos Dehault DELASSUS. (2d, 98, No. 7-232)
            The Board Met & Adjourned January 5th, 7th, 8th, 9th, 10th, and 11th, 1833.
            Saturday 12th January, 1833 Board Met-F.R. CONWAY Present

Silvestre LABBADIE, by his heirs and legal representatives claiming 8 arpents of land in front by 40 arpents in depth, see Record Book A, pg. 525, Minutes No. 1, pg. 294, No. 3, pg. 373, No. 5, pg. 309, produces a paper purporting to be an original concession from Manuel PEREZ, dated 9th August, 1788, and an order of Survey dated 27th May, 1791 signed by Estevan MIRO, Gov. Genl. of Louisiana. M. P. LEDUC, being duly sworn, saith that having had many opportunities of seeing the official signatures of the above named Manuel PEREZ and Estevan MIRO, he is of opinion that the signatures affixed to the said concession and order of Survey are in their proper handwriting. P. CHOUTEAU, Sr., being duly sworn, saith that at the date of said concession, Manuel PEREZ was Lt. Gov. of Upper Louisiana and Estevan MIRO, Gov. Genl. of the Province of Louisiana, and that their signatures affixed to the above mentioned concession and order of survey are in their proper handwriting. He further saith that as soon as the said land was surveyed, he often went, in company with the said Silvestre LABADDIE, on said piece of land to look at LABBADIE's slaves working at the clearing of said land. That said Silvestre LABBADIE was his brother-in-law and confided to him all his affairs, and he perfectly knew that

the said land was improved by virtue of the concession he obtained
at the time of its date. (Dec. 50, pg. 304)

Benito VASQUEZ, by his legal representative, Bernard PRATTE, claiming
9 arpents of land in front by the depth comprised between the Mississippi and the Public Road leading to the village of Carondelet, see
Book B, pg. 417, Book D, pg. 342, Minutes No. 1, pg. 412, No. 5, pg.
319 & 562, L.T. No. 4, pg. 15, produces a paper purporting to be an
original concession from Francisco CRUZAT dated 20th November, 1786.
M.P. LEDUC, being duly sworn, saith that the signature to the said
concession is in the proper handwriting of the late Francisco CRUZAT.
Peter CHOUTEAU, Senr., being duly sworn, saith that the signature to
the said concession is in the proper handwriting of the said CRUZAT.
He further saith that immediately after getting the said concession,
the said Benito VASQUEZ had a house built on said land and had some
of his hands employed in improving the same. (Dec. 52, pg. 305)

J. Baptiste PUJOT, by his legal representative, Bernard PRATTE,
claiming 6 arpents of land in front by forty in depth, see Book C,
pg. 462, Minutes No. 4, pg. 429, No. 5, pg. 561, produces a paper
purporting to be an original concession from Zenon TRUDEAU, dated
11th November, 1796. M.P. LEDUC, being duly sworn, saith that the
signature to the concession is in the proper handwriting of the said
Zenon TRUDEAU. Peter CHOUTEAU, Senr., being duly sworn, saith that
the signature to the concession is in the proper handwriting of said
Zenon TRUDEAU. He further saith that before and about 1800, he bought
of said PUJOT several years in succession, the crops of tobacco he
raised on said tract of land, whereon said PUJOT resided, that he had
a garden, cornfields and large tobacco plantations. That he lived many
years on said land. (Dec. 53, pg. 306)

F.R. CONWAY, Esqr., having been summoned to appear before the Legislature of the State of Missouri on the 21st Instant, to testify in the
case of the State against William C. CARR, Judge of the Third Judicial
Circuit, on behalf of the state, and as he cannot disobey the summons
without great hazard on his part, upon mature deliverance has deter-
mined to obey it, and as it is uncertain as to the time when he will
be discharged by said Legislature, he adjourns untill such time as he
may return or one or more of the Commissioners may appear.
            The Board Met & Adjourned January 29th, 30th, 31st,
            February 1st, 2nd, 4th, 5th, 6th, and 7th, 1833.
            Friday February 8th, 1833 Board Met-F.R. CONWAY Present

Gabriel CERRE, by his legal representative, Fred. DENT, claiming 10
arpents of land in front by 40 arpents in depth, see Livre Terrien
No. 4, pgs. 21 & 22. For general notice, see Record Book F, pg. 146,
also, pg. 175, produces a paper purporting to be a certified copy of
a concession granted by Manuel PEREZ, Lt. Gov., dated March 15th, 1789.
Pascal CERRE, being duly sworn, saith that he is acquainted with the
tract mentioned in the above concession. That it was granted to his
father by Manuel PEREZ in the year 1789. That in the beginning of
June, 1789 or 1790, but he rather thinks it was in 1789, his father
had two ploughs at work on said land and planted a corn field, which
was not fenced in. That he had a cabin built and an Orchard planted.
That he, the said deponent, planted said orchard with his own hands and
had it fenced in, and had grass mowed on said land and had two hay stacks
made in the inclosure of said orchard. That his father remained in possession untill the deponent's mother died, when a division of the property took place, and the said land fell into the deponent's hands.
That now, he has no kind of interest in said property, having sold the
same to Abraham GALLATIN. That said land was surveyed by A. SOULARD,
under the Spanish Authorities. (Dec. 60, pg. 308)
            Adjourned untill tomorrow at 10 o'clock A.M.
                The Board Met & Adjourned Feb. 9th, 11th, 12th, 13th, &
                14th, 1833.
                Friday February 15th, 1833-Board Met-F.R. CONWAY Present

Pierre Francois DEVOLSAY, by his legal representative, J.P. CABANNE,
claiming 6 arpents of land in front by 40 in depth, see Livre Terrien
No. 1, pg. 14, Record Book F, pg. 152, produces a paper purporting to

be a copy of a concession from St. ANGE, Lt. Gov., dated 15th Sept., 1767. Also, a deed of conveyance from Francoise DUPUIS to J.P. CABANNE, dated 2nd October, 1817. Also, a copy of DEVOLSEY's Last Will & Testament & A translation of the same. Also, a paper purporting to be the deposition of Paul PORTNEUF, alias LADEROUTE, before F.M. GUYOT, a Justice of the Peace for the County of St. Louis on the 10th March, 1819. Pierre CHOUTEAU, Senr., being duly sworn, saith that DEVOLSEY was a Captain in the French Service and had a concession granted to him for the above mentioned piece of land that DEVOLSEY did not settle himself on said land because at that time no one would have dared to live out of Town on account of the Indians, but he cut his wood and made his hay on the same. That any one who wanted to cut timber on the same, had to ask DEVOLSEY's permission. He says, also, that the signature affixed to the concession in Livre Terrien No.1, pgs. 14 & 15, which is exhibited to him, is in the true handwriting of ST. ANGE, then Lt. Gov. He further states that he knew Paul PORTNEUF, alsias LADEROUTE, that he was the natural son of a former Commandant and a man of good repute. That he, the deponent, having been thirty years among the Indians he never paid attention, during his short stays in St. Louis, whether there was any field on said land at least he does not remember of having seen any. That at the time when Theodore HUNT was Recorder of land titles and receiving evidences under the Act of Congress of 1824, he, the deponent, went before said HUNT and gave his testimony in behalf of this claim, and Mr. Rene PAUL went with him as his interpreter. That said land is situated immediately south and adjoining Madame CHOUTEAU's land in the Little Prairie, South of St. Louis, and is bounded East by the Road to Carondelet, south & west by lands which were then vacant. Rene PAUL, being duly sworn, saith that in 1825, he, being then commissioned Deputy Surveyor, was requested by Theodore HUNT to go and identify all the possessions in the little Prairie according to their respective concessions and conformably to the testimonies given by Baptiste RIVIERE, alias BACANNE and Rene DODIER, who had been previously sworn to that effect. That he identified the claim of CABANNE under DEVOLSEY to be in the little prairie south of St. Louis bounded north by lands granted to Madame CHOUTEAU, East by the Carondelet Road, south by lands granted to BACANNE and West by lands said to be the commons of St. Louis, containing 6 arpents of land in front by 40 in depth. The north east corner thereof being on the West side of the Road and 8 linear arpents south of the South boundary line of SOULARD's land. He further states that in 1825, he went with P. CHOUTEAU, Senr. before T. HUNT and served as interpreter to said CHOUTEAU when he gave his testimony in behalf of this claim. Laurent REED, being duly sworn, saith that he is 73 years of age and when a boy he knew DEVOLSEY, who then lived in St. Louis, and he continued to know him till his death. He believes said DEVOLSEY died about 40 years ago, more or less, that he knew that one of DEVOLSEY's negroes cultivated a small field in the little Prairie, but does not remember exactly the place it being so long since. That said negro cultivated tobacco, melons and other articles of produce. (Dec. 59, pg. 307)

Adjourned until tomorrow at 10 o'clock A.M.
Saturday February 16th, 1833 Board Met-F.R. CONWAY Present
Adjourned untill Monday next at 10 o'clock A.M.
Monday February 18th, 1833 Board Met-F.R. CONWAY Present

James MACKAY, by his legal representatives claiming 200 & more arpents it being a special location, see Book B, pgs. 433 & 4, Minutes No. 1, pg. 417, Minutes of Recorder, pg. 117. The claimant further refers to Book B, pg. 486, in order to show that the claim for the common of St. Louis does not interfere with this claim. Also, to Book No. 5, pg. 552, produces a paper purporting to be a concession from Carlos Dehault DELASSUS, dated October 9th, 1799, See BATES Decisions pg. 36). M.P. LEDUC, being duly sworn, sayth that the signature to concession is in the proper handwriting of the said C.D. DELASSUS, Book No. 3, pg. 21, No. 4, pg. 186. For further testimony of M.P. LEDUC in behalf of this claim, see next claim below. (Dec. 54, 306)

Antoine SOULARD, by his legal representatives claiming 204 arpents 48 perches, see Book F, pgs. 244, 5 & 6, Recorders Minutes pgs. 80 & 81, Claimant further refers to Book B, pgs. 486, 7 & 8 in order to show

that the claim for the common of St. Louis does not interfere with
this claim, produces a paper purporting to be a concession from
Zenon TRUDEUA, dated 7th August, 1798. Also, a plat of Survey by
Antoine SOULARD, dated 20th January, 1800 and certified same day.
M.P. LEDUC, being duly sworn, sayth that the signature to the concession is in the true handwriting of the said Zenon TRUDEAU and
that the signature to the plat and certificate of Survey is the proper handwriting of Antoine SOULARD. Deponent further says that he
informed Mr. SOULARD that, in case he would abandon the part of his
claim which was included in the common of St. Louis, Mr. BATES would
confirm the balance of said claim. Thereupon SOULARD called on Mr.
BATES and made the abandonment upon which BATES confirmed the part of
said claim which lies East of the common, and at the same time, SOULARD
as agent for MACKAY, made the same abandonment on MACKAY's claim and
that since that time SOULARD told the Deponent that MACKAY disapproved
of said abandonment, and that he, the said deponent, never acted as
agent for MACKAY in said claim. That he does not know that SOULARD
ever was authorised by MACKAY to make said abandonment. That since
the time of said abandonment, MACKAY remained as ostensible owner and
claimant of said land. That he built thereon a house and lived and
died in it. The Deponent further says that what he understands by
these claims interfering with the common of St. Louis, is the part of
said claims included in the survey of said common, made by MACKAY in
1806 as recorded. Deponent believes that taxes were paid by MACKAY
and SOULARD on said lands until 1820, and that the part of MACKAY's
claim which was not confirmed was sold under an execution as being
the property of said MACKAY. (Dec. 63, pg. 309)

Bernard PRATTE claiming 7,056 arpens of land, see Book C, pg. 256,
No. 1, pg. 276, produces a paper purporting to be a concession from
Carlos Dehault DELASSUS, dated 19th October, 1799. Also, a plat of
Survey taken 15th & certified 19th February, 1806 by A. SOULARD.
M.P. LEDUC, duly sworn, saith that the signature to the concession
is in the proper handwriting of Carlos Dehault DELASSUS, and the sig-
nature to the plat of Survey is in the proper handwriting of
A. SOULARD. (Dec. 55, pg. 306)

Henry DIELLE, by his assignee Bernard PRATTE, claiming 5,000 arpens
of land on the waters of the St. Francis, see Record Book C, pg. 257,
Minutes No. 1, pg. 276, produces a paper purporting to be a concession
from Carlos Dehault DELASSUS, dated 29th February, 1799. Also, a plat
of Survey taken 3rd & certified 19th February, 1806 by A. SOULARD.
M.P. LEDUC, duly sworn, sayth that the signature to concession is in
the proper handwriting of Carlos Dehault DELASSUS, and the signature to
the plat of Survey is in the proper handwriting of A. SOULARD.
(Dec. 56, pg. 306)

Mathew SAUCIER, by his legal representative, Pierre CHOUTEAU, Sr.,
claiming 1,200 arpens of land, see Book D, pgs. 163 & 4, Book No. 5,
pg. 498, produces a paper purporting to be a concession from
Carlos D. DELASSUS, dated November 28th, 1800. M.P. LEDUC, duly sworn,
sayth that the signature to the concession is in the proper handwriting
of Carlos Dehault DELASSUS. (Dec. 57, pg. 307)

Pierre CHOUTEAU, Junr., by Pierre CHOUTEAU, Senr., claiming an Island
called DELASSUS' Island in the Missouri 3 miles above its mouth, see
Book C, pg. 384, produces a paper purporting to be a concession from
Carlos Dehault DELASSUS, dated 18th January, 1800. M.P. LEDUC, duly
sworn, sayth that the signature to the concession is in the true handwriting of said Carlos D. DELASSUS. (Confirmed, see BATES Decisions,
pg. 41)

Purnel HOWARD by his legal representative claiming 400 arpens of land,
see Record Book C, pgs. 384 & 5, Book No. 5, pg. 430, produces a paper
purporting to be a concession from Carlos Dehault DELASSUS, dated 25th
November, 1799. Also, a plat of Survey dated 28th March, 1804, by
A. SOULARD. M.P. LEDUC, duly sworn, sayth that the signatures to the
concession is in the proper handwriting of Carlos D. DELASSUS and the
signature to the Plat of Survey is in the proper handwriting of
A. SOULARD. (Dec. 58, pg. 307)

Etienne ST. PIERRE, by his assignee, Pierre CHOUTEAU, Senr., claiming a special location of which a league square has been confirmed, see Record Book B, pg. 510, Minutes No. 5, pg. 495, BATES decision No. 3, pg. 59, produces a paper purporting to be a concession from Carlos Dehault DELASSUS, dated 8th October, 1799. M.P. LEDUC, being duly sworn, saith that the signature to the concession is in the true handwriting of Carlos D. DELASSUS. (Dec. 128, pg. 327)

Charles TAYON, by his legal representative, Pierre CHOUTEAU, Senr., claiming 500 arpents of land, see Book C, pg. 380, No. 4, pg. 464, produces a paper purporting to be a concession from Zenon TRUDEAU, dated 28th January, 1798. Also, a plat of Survey taken the 8th & certified the 15th of January, 1800 by A. SOULARD. M.P.LEDUC, being duly sworn, saith that the signature to the concession is in the proper handwriting of said Zenon TRUDEAU and that the signature to the plat of Survey is the true handwriting of A. SOULARD. (Confirmed, see BATES Decision, pg. 61)

Francis TAYON, by his legal representative, Pierre CHOUTEAU, Senr., claiming the balance of 10,000 arpents of land, of which a league square has been confirmed, see Book C, pgs. 379 & 380, Minutes No. 4, pg. 464, BATES Book No. 3, pg. 64, produces a paper purporting to be a concession from Carlos Dehault DELASSUS, dated 15th October, 1799. Also, a plat of Survey dated 6th & certified 25th February, 1804 by A. SOULARD. M.P. LEDUC, being duly sworn, saith that the signature to the concession is in the proper handwriting of C.D. DELASSUS and the signature to the plat and certificate of Survey, the true handwriting of SOULARD. (Dec. 65, pg. 309)

Chalres TAYON, by his legal representative, Pierre CHOUTEAU, Senr., claiming 1,600 arpents of land, see Book D, pgs. 160 & 1, Minutes Book No. 5, pg. 506, produces a paper purporting to be a concession from Carlos Dehault DELASSUS, dated 16th of January, 1800. M.P. LEDUC, duly sworn, saith that the signature to the concession is in the proper handwriting of C.D. DELASSUS. (Dec. 67, pg. 309)
Adjourned untill tomorrow at 10 o'clock A.M.
The Board Met & Adjourned February 19th, 20th, 21st, 22nd, 23rd, and 25th, 1833.
Tuesday February 26th, 1833 Board Met-F.R. CONWAY Present

F.R. CONWAY, Esq. appeared pursuant to adjournment. Albert G. HARRISON, Esqr., also appeared having been appointed Commissioner in place of Wilkins UPDYKE, Esqr., resigned, and having been duly qualified took his seat. No business appearing before the Board adjourned untill tomorrow at 10 o'clock A.M.
The Board Met & Adjourned February 27th, 28th, March 1st, March 2nd, and March 4th, 1833.
Tuesday March 5th, 1833 Board Met-Two Comm'rs. Present

Nicolas BARSALOUX, by his legal representatives claiming 4 arpents of land in front by 40 arpents in depth. See Livre Terrien No. 1, pg. 16, Book F, pg. 153. Rene DODIER, being duly sworn, saith that he well knew Nicolas BARSALOUX, that he died a long time ago, perhaps 47 or 48 years ago. That he, the deponent, will be 71 years of age in June next. That to his knowledge BARSALOUX cultivated a piece of land south of the mill creek. That said BARSALOUX had a small house built upon wheels and used to have it hauled on said piece of land when he wanted to work on the same. That he saw said BARSALOUX work on said land several years in succession. That he was known as the lawfull owner of said land. He further states that the first tract of land south of said mill creek belonged to ORTEZ, then came CAMBAS, JERVAIS, Madame CHOUTEAU, DEVOLSEY, BACANNE, BARSALOUX, BEAUSOLEIF, etc. etc. He further saith that when a young man he heard that said BARSALOUX was one among the first settlers that came to this place and that said BARSALOUX had a wife and children. The claimant states that by referring to Livre Terrien for the concession, it is to be observed that said claim was not reunited to the Domain. Further, that said BARSALOUX being one of the first settlers, had no other lands granted to him by writen concession, but a town lot in St. Louis and no confirmation, but for the said town lot. (Dec. 66, pg. 309)
Adjourned till tomorrow at 10 o'clock A.M.

Wednesday March 6th, 1833 Board Met-Two Comm'rs. Present

In the case of Nicolas BARSALOUX, the claimant produces two papers
purporting to be copies of certificates of Baptism of Louis and
Marie ARCHANGE BARSALOUX and of Jean Baptiste BARSALOUX. Also, a
certificate of the Burial of Marie ARCHANGE and of Nicolas BARSALOUX,
her father, certified by E. SAULNIER, curate of St. Louis, 19th July,
1831. See pg. 110.

Esther, free mulatto woman claiming 80 arpents of land, see Livre
Terrien No. 5, pg. 10 & 11, Book C, pg. 159 & 160, No. 3, pg., 475,
No. 4, pg. 483. Rene DODIER, being duly sworn, says that he knew
Esther, a free mulatto woman, who lived with CLAMORGAN, That she
had a grant of land near the mound commonly called LaGrange de Terre,
that she lived with CLAMORGAN as if she had been his wife. That
CLAMORGAN had several children by her. That Esther had cattle which
were sent to pasture along with CLAMORGAN's cattle on said piece of
land and that she was generally known as being the lawful owner of
said land. That said land was comprised in the common field of St.
Louis. The fence of said field running on this side of where now
lives Mr. J. MULLANPHY. Witness further says that he thinks Esther's
land extended to the Bank of the Mississippi as it did not run West
of the road going to Belle fountain. (Dec. 70, pg. 310)
        Adjourned untill tomorrow at 10 o'clock A.M.
            The Board Met & Adjourned March 7th, and 8th, 1833.
            Saturday March 9th, 1833 Board Met-All Comm'rs. Present

Resolved that during the absence of a majority of the Baord of Commissioners, that the remaining Commissioner shall take and receive all
evidence that may be presented to or laid before the said Board of
Commissioners. No business appearing before the Board they adjourned
untill Monday next at 10 o'clock A.M.
            The Board Met & Adjourned Monday March 11, 1833.
            Tuesday March 12th, 1833 Board Met-Two Comm'rs. Present

In the case of M.P. LEDUC, see Pg. 8 of this Book, claimant produces
a paper purporting to be an original concession from C.D. DELASSUS,
dated 7th January, 1800. Also, a plat of Survey taken 18th February,
and certified by A. SOULARD 5th March, 1804. Charles F. DELAURIER,
being duly sworn, says that the signatures to the concession and plat
of Survey are in the respective handwriting of C.D. DELASSUS and of
A. SOULARD. Albert TISON, duly sworn, says the same.

Aaron QUICK, by his legal representative, Albert TISON, claiming 800
arpents of land, situate in Rich Wood County of Washington, see Book
D, pg. 312, Minutes No. 5, pg. 484, produces a certified copy of a concession under the hand and seal of I.V. GARNIER, Notary Public dated
9th of January, 1818. See pages 18 & 293. (No. 20)

Antoine GAGNIER, by Albert TISON, claiming 1,800 arpents of land on
the Missouri, Howard County, see Book B, pgs. 463 & 4, Minutes No. 5,
428, produces a paper purporting to be a concession from
Carlos Dehault DELASSUS, dated June 12th, 1800. Also, a plat and
certificate of Survey received for record by Ant. SOULARD Feb. 28th,
1806. Also, a deed from said GAGNIER to A. TISON, dated 11th January,
1805. Fremon DELAURIER, duly sworn, says that the signatures to the
concession and to plat of Survey are in the respective handwriting of
said DELASSUS and SOULARD. (Dec. 68, pg. 310)

John WATKINS claiming 7,056 arpents of land sitaute on the Merrimack,
see Book C, pgs. 367 & 8, Minutes No. 2, pg. 10, No. 3, pg. 262, No.
4, pg. 376, produces a paper purporting to be an original concession
from Zenon TRUDEAU, dated July 24th, 1797. Also, a plat and certificate of Survey received for record by A. SOULARD 27th February, 1806.
Albert TISON, being duly sworn, saith that the signatures to the above
papers are in the respective handwriting of said Zenon TRUDEAU and
said SOULARD. He further says that, to his knowledge, the above land
was inhabited and cultivated in about 1802 or 1803. (Dec. 69, pg. 310)

John WATKINS for self and as assignee of John NEIGHBOUR, claiming 800

arpents of land situate on the Merimack, see Book C, pgs. 536 &
following Minutes No. 3, pgs. 278 and 430, Livre Terrien No. 5, pg.
29., produces a paper purporting to be a concession from Z. TRUDEAU,
dated 22nd October, 1795 to John NEIGHBOUR for 400 arpents, an order
of Survey to John WATKINS for 800 arpents. Said Survey taken 5th
November and certified by Antoine SOULARD 7th December, 1800. A deed
from John NEIGHBOUR to Jno. WATKINS, a notice of A. SOULARD to said
WATKINS, copy of a petition from said SOULARD, certified by
Fredk. BATES, Recorder of Land Titles; affidavit of A. SOULARD and
James MACKAY. Affidavit of Jacques CLAMORGAN and a plat and certifi-
cate of Survey for 613 arpents, taken 9th November, & certified by
SOULARD the 7th December, 1800. M.P. LEDUC, C.F. DELAURIER and
A. TISON, being duly sworn, certify to the signatures of all the above
papers. A. TISON further states that to his knowledge the said tract
of land was inhabited and cultivated in about 1802 or 1803.
(Dec. 71, pg. 311)

Joseph M. PAPIN's legal representatives claiming 8 by 17 arpents of
land situated south of Little river or Mill Creek on the West side of
the road leading from St. Louis to Carondelet, which separates the
same from the arsenal, about 2-1/2 miles from St. Louis. See Book C,
pgs. 434 & 5 for first & second concession and certificate of SOULARD,
Livre Terrien No. 4, pg. 16, Minutes No. 5, pg. 479, produces a paper
purporting to be a concession from Francisco CRUZAT dated March 3,
1787. Also, an additional concession from Carlos Dehault DELASSUS,
dated 29th December, 1802, a certificate of A. SOULARD, Surveyor
General dated February 2nd, 1806, a plat of survey signed M.P. LEDUC,
dated August 27th, 1823. Albert TISON, being duly sworn, says that
the signatures to the above papers are in the respective handwriting
of the above named persons who signed them, except the signature of
Francisco CRUZAT with which he is not acquainted. (Dec. 72, pg. 311)

Antoine SAUGRIN, by his heirs claiming 20,000 arpents of land of
which a league square has been confirmed, see Book C, pgs. 252 & 3,
Minutes No. 1, pg. 289, No. 4, pg. 465, produces a paper purporting
to be a concession from Zenon TRUDEAU, dated 9th November, 1797, three
plats of Surveys, one of which is for 7,000 arpents and the two others
for 3,000 arpents each. M.P. LEDUC, duly sworn, says that the Decree
of concession and the signature to it is in the handwriting of
Zenon TRUDEAU, and the signature to the petition is in the handwriting
of A. SAUGRIN. C. Fremon DELAURIER, duly sworn, says that the three
above plats of surveys were executed by him being at the time commissioned Deputy Surveyor. (Dec. 73, pg. 312)

Baptiste JEFFREY, by his legal representatives, Henry Von PHIEL,
claiming 800 arpents of land, see Book D, pg. 290, Minutes No. 5, pg.
438, produces a paper purporting to be a concession from
C.D. DELASSUS, dated 9th October, 1800. Alsj, an affidavit of
Antoine SOULARD. M.P.LEDUC, duly sworn, says that the signature to
the concession is in the proper handwriting of said C.D. DELASSUS.
(2d, 142, No. 7-241)

Joseph MARIE, by his legal representative, claiming 800 arpents of
land, Book D, pg. 291, Minutes No. 5, pg. 458, produces a paper purporting to be a concession from Carlos Dehault DELASSUS, dated 10th
January, 1801. Also, an affidavit by A. SOULARD. M.P. LEDUC, duly
sworn, says that the signature to the concession is in the proper hand
writing of said Carlos Dehault DELASSUS. (2d, 141, No. 7-241)

Joseph Philip LAMARCHE, by his legal representative, Henry Von PHIEL
claiming 800 arpents of land, see Book D, pg. 292, No. 5, pg. 449,
produces a paper purporting to be an original concession dated 10th
February, 1800 from Carlos Dehault DELASSUS. Albert TISON, duly sworn,
says that the signature to the concession are in the proper handwriting
of said DELASSUS & SOULARD. (2d, 146, No. 7, 261)

Francois Lami DUCHOUQUET, by his legal representative, Henry Von PHIEL
claiming 800 arpents of land, see Book D, pgs. 293 & 4, Minutes No. 5,
pgγ 412, produces a paper purporting to be an original concession from
Carlos Dehault DELASSUS, dated 14th October, 1799. M.P. LEDUC, being
duly sworn, says that the signature to concession is in the proper

handwriting of C.D. DELASSUS.

The Sons of Jos. M. PAPIN, to wit: Joseph, Didier, Alexander, Hipolite, Silvestre, Theodore and Pierre, claiming 800 arpents of land each, under the same concession, see Book C, pg. 435, Minutes No. 3, pg. 286, No. 4, pgs. 386 &387, Spanish Record of Concessions No.2, pg. 15 No. 11. (Dec. #74, pg. 312)

Bernard PRATTE by his assignee Pelagie SARPI claiming 800 arpents of land, see Book C, pgs. 263 & 264, Minutes No. 5, pg. 478, produces a paper purporting to be an original concession from Zenon TRUDEAU, dated May 24th, 1799. Also, a plat of survey taken 4th January & certified 15th April, 1804; a deed of conveyance dated October 11th, 1819 and a concession from C.D. DELASSUS dated 6th May, 1803. M.P. LEDUC, being duly sworn, says that the signature to the concessions are in the proper handwriting of the said Zenon TRUDEAU and C.D. DELASSUS. (Dec. 75 pg. 312)

Adjourned untill tomorrow at 10 o'clock A.M.

Wednesday March 13th, 1833 Board Met-Two Comm'rs. Present

In the case of Francois SAUCIER claiming balance of 8800 arpents of land, see pg. 15 of this Book, claimant produces a paper purporting to be a commission from SOULARD appointing Charles Fremon DELAURIER his Deputy Surveyor, also a paper purporting to be a letter from said DELAURIER to A. SOULARD, dated 25th February, 1806 and receipt of same by SOULARD & signed by B. COUSINS as witness. M.P. LEDUC and Albert TISON, being duly sworn, say that the signatures to the receipt are in the respective handwriting of A. SOULARD & B. COUSINS, Charles Fremon DELAURIER, being duly sworn, says that the survey already produced is one of those included among the surveys mentioned in the above letter. That the survey was executed at the time it bears date that there was great difficulty and danger in executing surveys. That he was twice repulsed by the Indians and that the third time, he went up he could not execute several of the surveys being prevented by Indians of the Jack and Fox nations, although he and his companions were well armed; that surveyors were very scarce and it was difficult to procure any one to take a survey. That there was not half the number of surveyors necessary to execute the surveys that were then to be made. (Dec. 16, pg. 292)

In the case of C.D. DELASSUS claiming 30,000 arpents of land, claimant refers the Board of Commissioners to the Testimony given by C.F. DELAURIER in the above claim of F. SAUCIER. (see pag. 16 of this Book) (Dec. 17, pg. 292)

Charles GRATIOT, Junr., claiming 2,500 arpents of land on the left bank of river Merrameck between the rivers commonly called Cave and little Marameck, so as to include the bottom and situated about 54 or 60 miles from the mouth of the river Marameck, see Book D, pgs. 119, Book No. 5, pg. 427, produces a paper purporting to be a concession from Carlos Dehault DELASSUS, dated 16th December, 1802. M.P. LEDUC, duly sworn, says that the signature to the concession is in the proper handwriting of said C.D. DELASSUS. (Dec. 76, pg. 313)

Levy THEEL by Charles GRATIOT, Senr's. representatives claiming 200 arpents of land, see Book D, pg. 120, No. 5, pg. 507, produces a paper purporting to be an original concession from Carlos Dehault DELASSUS, dated 15th December, 1799 and an agreement between C. GRATIOT and THEEL dated January, 13th, 1811. M.P. LEDUC, duly sworn, says that the signature to the concession is in the proper handwriting of said DELASSUS. (Dec. 77, pg. 313)

Mathurin BOUVET by Ch. GRATIOT's representatives claiming 7,056 arpents of land, see Book A, pg. 534, Minutes No. 2, pg. 27, No. 3, pg. 379, No. 4, pg. 428, No. 5, pg. 556, Livre Terrien No. 5, pg. 14, produces a paper purporting to be a concession from Zenon TRUDEAU, dated 1st June, 1795. Also, an additional concession from C.D. DELASSUS, dated January 5th, 1801. Also, a plat of survey for 400 arpents certified by Fremon DELAURIER, Deputy Surveyor, dated 19th February, 1806. Also, a plat and certificate of survey for 7,056 arpents including the above 400, made by C.F. DELAURIER, Dep. Surveyor, received for record by SOULARD 15th April, 1806. M.P. LEDUC, duly sworn, says that the signature to the concession is in the proper handwriting of Zenon TRUDEAU, that the signature to additional concession is in the handwriting of C.D. DELASSUS and the signatures to the plat of Survey are in the respective handwriting of C.F. DELAURIER and A. SOULARD. Charles F. DELAURIER, duly sworn, says that in 1800 or 1801, he was on said tract and saw a well and the remains of houses and furnace, and several broken kettles and by appearances it was evident salt had been manufactured there and had often heard that salt had been manufactured there. As to the Survey witness states as follows: (see his testimony given in SAUCIER's case) Claimant produces copy of a public sale to C. GRATIOT. (Dec. 78, pg. 313)

Mathurin BOUVET by Ch. GRATIOT's representatives claiming 7,056 arpents of land, situated Bay de Charles, see Book C, pg. 230 & 231, Minutes Book No. 2, pg. 27, No. 3, pg. 379, No. 4, pg. 427, No. 5, pg. 556, Liv. Ter. No. 5, pg. 16, produces a paper purporting to be a concession from Zenon TRUDEAU dated June 12th, 1795. Also, a concession from C.D. DELASSUS to C. GRATIOT dated January 8th, 1801, a plat & certificate of Survey taken by C.F. DELAURIER, Deputy Surveyor, dated 17th February, received for record by SOULARD 15th April, 1806. M.P. LEDUC, duly sworn, says that the signatures affixed to the aforesaid papers are in the respective handwriting of Zenon TRUDEAU, C.D. DELASSUS, Ch. F. DELAURIER and A. SOULARD. Ch. Fremon DELAURIER, being duly sworn, says that in the fall of 1805 and spring of 1806, he went on said land and saw an old field and garden and the remains of old houses which had been burnt by the Indians and in which old BOUVET was burnt to death. For Survey, witness states as follows: (See SAUCIER's case) (Dec. 79, pg. 313)

Benito VASQUEZ by Charles GRATIOT's representatives claiming 7,056 arpents of land on the Merimack, see Book C, pg. 229, Book F, pg. 192, Minutes No. 1, pg. 506, No. 3, pg. 322, No. 5, pg. 544, Livre Terrien No. 4, pg. 10, produces a paper purporting to be a copy of a concession certified by C.D. DELASSUS, said certificate dated 3rd March, 1803. Also, said Liv. Ter. on which said grant bears date 8th Sept. 1784. Albert TISON, duly sworn, says that, in 1800 or 1801, he saw ground fenced in and a large quantity of stock that they were then making salt and by appearances had been making salt for some years prior to that time. And that the works continued in operation long afterwards, as said witness went occasionally on said place to procure salt. Charles Fremon DELAURIER, Senr., being duly sworn, says that in 1799, for the first time, he passed through said place and saw fields, furnaces, people at work, in fact, it was a pretty large establishment. That he saw the same for several years in succession in operation and that the first time he saw said place it had all the appearances of having been settled several years prior to that time. (Dec. 80, pg. 314)

John HILDERBRANT by the heirs of Charles GRATIOT claiming 320 arpents of land on the Merimack, see Book C, pg. 146, Minutes No. 1, pg. 438 & 439, No. 3, pg. 377 &8 for concession by LEYBA, dated 24th November, 1779, see Livre Terrien No. 3, pg. 31, produces a survey of the same received for record by SOULARD the 29th February, 1806. Albert TISON, duly sworn, says that from (cannot read) 1795 and 1804 & 5, he saw said land inhabited and cultivated and that it has been inhabited and cultivated ever since. He further says that the signature to receipt of survey is in the handwriting of Antoine SOULARD. (Dec. 81, pg. 314)

John SAUNDERS by Charles GRATIOT claiming 320 arpents of land on the Merimack, see Book C, pg. 146, for concession granted by LEYBA, dated 24th November, 1779, see Liv. Ter. No. 3, pg. 30, produces said Liv. Ter. for concession, a plat of Survey dated 28th February, 1806, received for record 29th, 1806, see Minutes No. 1, pg. 437, No. 3, pg. 377 & 8. Albert TISON, duly sworn, says that in 1800 or 1801, he was on said place and it was then inhabited and cultivated and had all the appearances of an old settled place. Witness, also, says that the signature to plat of Survey is in the proper handwriting of A. SOULARD.

Jacques CLAMORGAN by Charles GRATIOT's legal representatives claiming 800 arpents of land on the Merimack, see Book C, pg. 146, Minutes No. 1, pg. 438 & 9, No. 4, pg. 496, Livre Terrien No. 4, pg. 30, for concession granted to CLAMORGAN by Zenon TRUDEAU dated 1st June, 1793, produces a survey dated 20th February and received for record by A. SOULARD 29th February, 1806. Albert TISON, duly sworn, gives same testimony as in the above case. (Confirmed, see Comm'rs. Cert. No. 1331, M. 5, pg. 518)

Jacques CLAMORGAN by Charles GRATIOT's heirs claiming 1,600 arpents of land, see Book C, pg. 140, Minutes No. 1, pg. 438 & 9, No. 3, pg. 377, for concession granted by Zenon TRUDEAU 18th Sept, 1793, see Livre Terrien No. 4, pg. 35, produces a survey dated 28th & certified 29th of February, 1806. Albert TISON, duly sworn, says that in 1803, he was on said place, which was then inhabited and cultivated and had all the appearances of an old settled place. (Confirmed Cert. No. 1330, Commr's. M. 5, pg. 518)

Charles GRATIOT by his heirs claiming 500 arpents of land on River des Peres, see Book A, pg. 541, Minutes No. 2, pg. 18, No. 3, pg. 327, No. 4, pg. 408. Being a concession granted by Ch. Dehault DELASSUS to said GRATIOT dated January 18th, 1800. Survey taken November 28th, 1802 certified by A. SOULARD 5th Jany., 1803. (Dec. 82, pg. 314)
    Adjourned untill tomorrow at 10 o'clock A.M.
        Thursday March 14th, 1833 Board Met-All Comm'rs. Present

Pierre CHOUTEAU, Senr., claiming 30,000 arpents of land on River a la Mine, see Book B, pg. 509, Minutes No. 5, pg. 545, produces a paper purporting to be an original concession from Carlos Dehault DELASSUS dated 20th November, 1799. Also, assent of the Osage Indians to CHOUTEAU's taking as much land as he pleased on said spot, registered by SOULARD. Pascal L. CERRE, duly sworn, says that the signature to the concession is in the proper handwriting of C.D. DELASSUS and the signature to the registering that of SOULARD. (Dec. 83, pg. 314)

Joseph BRAZEAU by his legal representatives claiming 12 arpents front on the Mississippi, running back 30 arpents, see Book B, pg. 416, Min. No. 1, pg. 413, No. 5, pg. 320, produces a paper purporting to be an original concession from Carlos Dehault DELASSUS dated 19th November, 1799. Also, a plat and certificate of Survey dated 28th August, 1803. Pascal L. CERRE, duly sworn, says that the signature to the concession is in the proper handwriting of Carlos D. DELASSUS and the signature to certificate of Survey is in the proper handwriting of A. SOULARD. He further states that Joseph BRAZEAU, to his knowledge, inhabited and cultivated the land embraced in the concession of 1799, which land so cultivated was the same as contained in the concession of 1786 and which inhabitation and cultivation has continued from 1799 to the present time by him or his legal representatives. He believes that the land so cultivated was the whole embraced in the concession of 1786. (Dec. 84, pg. 315)

Newton HOWELL claiming 350 arpents of land, see Book D, pg. 37, Min. No. 3, pg. 301, No. 4, pg. 393, produces a paper purporting to be an original concession from C.D. DEALSSUS, dated 25th May, 1801. Also, a plat of survey dated 23rd August, 1823 by Nathaniel BOON, Dep. Surveyor. Pascal L. CERRE, duly sworn, says that the signature to the concession is in the proper handwriting of C.D. DELASSUS and the signature at the margin is in the handwriting of James MACKAY. William MILBURN, duly sworn, says that the signature to the plat of Survey is in the proper handwriting of Nath. BOON, at the time Dep. Surveyor. (Dec. 85, pg. 315)

Mackey WHERRY by his legal representatives claiming 1,600 arpents of land, see Min. Book No. 3, pg. 355, No. 4, pg. 420, produces a paper purporting to be an original concession from Carlos Dehault DELASSUS dated 18th April, 1802. Also, a plat of Survey dated 15th May, 1826 by Nathaniel BOON. Pascal L. CERRE, duly sworn, says that the petition is in the handwriting of PROVENCHERE, the concession in the handwriting of Ant. SOULARD and the signature to said concession is in the handwriting of Carlos Dehault DELASSUS. William MILBURN, duly sworn, says that the signature to the plat of Survey is in the proper handwriting of Nathl. BOON, and the signature to the Certificate is in the deponent's own handwriting. (Dec. 86, pg. 316)
    Adjourned untill tomorrow at 10 o'clock A.M.

Friday March 15th, 1833 Board Met-All Comm'rs. Present

Diego MAXWELL as Vicar General of Louisiana by the Bishop of Missouri, his representative claiming 112,896 arpents of land or 4 leagues square, see Book B, pg. 497, Mins. No. 3, pg. 161, No. 4, pg. 354 & 5.

In the case of Carlos Dehault DELASSUS claiming 30,000 arpents of land, see page 16 of this Book.
John Baptiste VALLE, being duly sworn, says that he is 72 years of age, that he was born in St. Genevieve, that under the Spanish Government a concession, although not surveyed, was nevertheless considered as lawfull property, transferrable by sale or otherwise. That previous to 1800, the Spanish government had no other means of rewarding its officers or other persons for their services, but by granting them lands. That to his knowledge it never happened that a grant made by a Subdelegate was ever refused by a Governor General. The deponent has no doubt that Mr. DELASSUS, as being Lt. Governor could have obtained any quantity of land he would have applied for. He further states that a grant obtained from a Lt. Gov. was considered in this country as equivalent to a complete title. That when a concession for a stock farm (Vachera) was obtained, although it was not settled in due time, said concession was nevertheless considered as the property of the grantee, it being known there was imminent danger to settle such places on account of the Indians. That it was the policy of the government to encourage as much as possible those remote settlements. That to his knowledge the government never sold an arpent of land even in MORALES's time. That the regulations of OREILLY, MORALES & BUYOSO were never in force in this country. Witness, further says that under the Spanish Government the communication between this country and New Orleans was very difficult and very expensive and that prevented people from sending their papers to said place, in as much as the approbation of the Governor General was then considered as mere formality and did not add, as they thought, any value to their concessions. That it was the custom to publish the regulations in the towns at the sound of the drum or at the Church door, and that MORALES, GAYOSO and OREILLY's regulations were never to published in St. Genevieve where he, the deponent, was born and always lived. That he had several concessions and never applied for the Governor General's approbation, althought he conversed on the subject in 1795 with the Baron de CARONDELET, who told him that if he wanted more land to ask for it to the Lt. Governor. The deponent thinks it is provable that if the inhabitants had not thought their property secured by the treaty, a number of them would have left the country and followed the Spanish Government.
Adjourned untill tomorrow at 10 o'clock A.M.

Saturday March 16th, 1833 Board Met-All Comm'rs. Present

Louis LORIMIER, Senr., by his legal representatives claiming 30,000 arpents of land for services, see Book C, pgs. 23 & 24, Mins. No. 4, pg. 302, produces a paper purporting to be an original concession from Carlos Dehault DELASSUS dated January 15th, 1800. Pierre MENARD, duly sworn, says that the signature to Petition is the handwriting of L. LORIMIER, Senr., that the signature to the concession is the handwriting of Carlos Dehault DELASSUS and the signature to the Registering is in the handwriting of Ant. SOULARD. Lecture being made of the aforesaid petition. Deponent says that it is a true statement of the petitioners' services. That he was well acquainted with said LORIMIER, since the year 1788 untill his death, which happened, he believes in 1815. That, at the sollicitation of the Spanish Government said LORIMIER brought a number of Shawnees and Delaware Indians to settle in the vicinity of Cape Girardeau and they (Cannot read) the depredations committed by the Osages. That the Shawnees and Delawares had ten villages between Cape Girardeau and Cape St. Come. (Dec. 87, pg.316)

In the case of St. Gemme BEAUVAIS claiming 1,600 arpents, see pg. 37 of this Book. Peter MENARD, duly sworn, says that he knows St. Gemme BEAUVAIS to be the father of 10 children. That when he first knew him he owned more than 40 negroes and a large stock of cattle. That he, the deponent, used to make St. Gemme BEAUVAIS' house his home when at St. Genevieve.

Louis LORIMIER, Senr. by his legal representatives claiming 1,000

arpents of land by way of extension of a former concession, see Book
E, pgs. 22 & 23, Mins. No. 4, pgs. 74 & 302, produces a document
signed C.D. DELASSUS, dated 31st July, 1800. Pierre MENARD, duly
sworn, says that the signature to said document is in the handwriting
of Carlos Dehault DELASSUS and the signature to the petition is in
the handwriting of L. LORIMIER, Senr. (2d class No. 1, No. 7, pg. 67)

Francois BERTHIAUME by his legal representatives claiming 420 arpents
of land, see Book E, pgs. 24 & 5, No. 4, pgs. 74 & 302, produces a
paper purporting to be an original concession from Carlos D. DELASSUS,
dated 28th December, 1799. Pierre MENARD, duly sworn, says that the
signature to the concession is in the proper handwriting of
C.D. DELASSUS. (Dec. 88, pg. 316)

Bartholomew COUSIN by his legal representatives claiming 8,000 arpents
of land, see Book B, pgs. 219, 317, 318 & 319, No. 4, pg. 68, No. 5,
pg. 14, produces a paper purporting to be an original concession from
C.D. DELASSUS, dated 31st March, 1803. Also, three plat's of Surveys.
Pierre MENARD, duly sworn, says that the signature to the concession
is in the proper handwriting of C.D. DELASSUS to the surveys the handwriting of SOULARD and the signature to the petition in the handwriting
of B. COUSIN. (Dec. 90, pg. 316)
    Adjourned untill Monday next at 10 o'clock A.M.
        Monday March 18th, 1833 Board Met-All Comm'rs. Present

Louis REED by his legal representatives claiming 6 arpents of land in
front by 40 in depth, situate in White Ox Prairie, for concession by
LEYBA dated 12th May, 1779, see Livre Terrien No. 3, pg. 25, Record
Book F, pg. 187. Baptiste RIVIERE, alias BACCANE, being duly sworn,
says that he is 86 years of age. That he was the first who ever
ploughed the land above mentioned, having been hired by said
Louis REED for that purpose. He thinks it is about 44 or 46 years
ago, more or less, that he believes the said REED Cultivated the said
land all his lifetime, but to his certain knowledge he cultivated the
same for 8 or 10 years in succession. (Dec. (Dec. 91, pg. 316)

    In as much as it has come to the knowledge of this Board by let-
ter and otherwise that it would be expensive and inconvenient on
account of age and distance for witnesses to attend at this place to
give testimony touching such land claims as are or may come before
this Board of Commissioners, therefore it is resolved that
Lewis F. LINN, a member of said Board, be and is hereby appointed to
proceed to take evidence in the counties south of St. Louis, relative
to any claim that may properly come within the purview of the powers
given to the Board of Commissioners by the law establishing the same,
and that he be and is hereby vested with all necessary power for that
purpose, so far as the Board of Commissioners can confer it on him;
and he shall give public notice of the time and places that he may
appoint for the taking of the same. Resolved further that if between
this time and the 9th of July next, it should be deemed expedient and
necessary to depute another member of the Board for the purpose of
taking testimony to be offered before the Board of Commissioners, that
a majority of said Board being present shall have the power to appoint
one of their body for that purpose, vesting him with such powers as
are mentioned in the above resolution.
    Adjourned untill tomorrow at 10 o'clock A.M.
        The Board Met & Adjourned March 19th, 1833.
        Wednesday March 20th, 1833 Board Met-Two Comm'rs. Present

Gabriel NICOLLE by his legal representative G.A. BIRD claiming 608 arpents of land, see Book C, pg. 386, produces a paper purporting to be
an original concession from Zenon TRUDEAU dated 1st February, 1798.
Also, a plat of Survey dated January 7th, 1806. Also, a Deed of conveyance dated 22nd February, 1812. L.F. LINN, being duly sworn, says
that he knows that C.L. BIRD resided on a piece of land, which Deponent is confident was said BIRD's property, situated at about 37 miles
in a S.S.W. direction from St. Genevieve on the main branch of the
river St. Francis and near Mine A Lamotte & St. Michael, that he was
on said piece of land in the spring of 1813 and that C.L. BIRD had
then 50 or 60 acres in cultivation and was preparing to build a mill

and that he lived on said place untill his death. Antoine CHENIER, duly sworn, says that the signature to the concession is in the proper handwriting of Zenon TRUDEAU, L.G. (Dec. 92, pg. 316)

Michel LACHANCE by G.A. BIRD, his legal representative claiming 72 arpents of land, see Book C, pgs. 386 & 7, Mins. No. 1, pg. 349, No. 4, pg. 478, produces a paper purporting to be a concession from Carlos D. DELASSUS, dated 24th January, 1800. Also, a plat of Survey dated 30th April, 1805 recorded by Ant. SOULARD. (Dec. 93,pg. 316)
        The Board Adjourned untill tomorrow at 10 o'clock A.M.
            Thursday March 21st, 1833 Board Met-F.R. CONWAY, Present

Manuel Gonzales MORO by his legal representatives claiming 7,056 arpents of land, see Record Book D, pg. 127, Mins. No. 5, pg. 459, produces a paper purporting to be an original concession from Carlos D. DELASSUS, dated 16th September, 1799. M.P. LEDUC, duly sworn, says that the said M.G. MORO was an officer under the Spanish Government, employed in the treasury department and highly considered by said government, but had a very small salary. He further says that the signature to the petition is in the proper handwriting of said MORO and the signature to the concession is in the proper handwriting of Carlos D. DELASSUS. (Dec. 94, pg. 317)

Manuel Gonzales MORO by his legal representatives claiming 800 arpents of land, see Book D, pg. 127, Mins. No. 5, pg. 459, produces a paper purporting to be a concession from C.D. DELASSUS, dated 20th June, 1800. M.P. LEDUC, duly sworn, says the same as in the above case and that the signature to the concession is in the handwriting of said C.D. DELASSUS. (Dec. 95, pg. 317)

William LORIMIER by his legal representatives claiming 1,000 arpents of land, see Book E, pgs. 25 & 6, produces a paper purporting to be an original concession from Carlos Dehault DELASSUS, dated December 28th, 1799. M.P. LEDUC, duly sworn, says that the signature to the concession is in the proper handwriting of Carlos Dehault DELASSUS. (Dec. 96, pg. 318)

Francois NORMANDAU by Albert TISON claiming 2,500 arpents of land, see Book B, pg. 94, Mins. No. 5, pg. 465, claimant refers also to the testimony given by Charles Fremon DELAURIER in F. SAUCIER's case, see pg. 118 of this Book, Spanish Record of Concession No. 2, pg. 51. (Dec. 97, pg. 318)

Andrew KINNAIRD by his legal representatives claiming 600 arpents of land, see Book C, pg. 480, Mins. No. 5, pg. 440, produces a paper purporting to be an original concession from Carlos Dehault DELASSUS, dated 28th January, 1800. M.P. LEDUC, duly sworn, says that the signature to the concession is in the proper handwriting of C.D. DELASSUS. (Dec. 98, pg. 318)

William HARTLEY by his legal representatives claiming 650 arpents of land, see Book C,pg. 480, Mins. No. 5, pg. 434, BATES Decisions Book No. 2, pg. 34, produces a paper purporting to be an original concession dated 14th January, 1800 from Carlos Dehault DELASSUS. M.P. LEDUC, duly sworn, says that the signature to the concession is in the proper handwriting of said C.D. DELASSUS. (No. 301, No. 7, pg.185)

John HENRY by his legal representatives claiming 900 arpents of land, see Book C, pg. 479, Mins. No. 5, pg. 433, produces a paper purporting to be an original concession from Zenon TRUDEAU dated 7th February, 1798. M.P. LEDUC, duly sworn, says that the signature to the concession is in the proper handwriting of said Zenon TRUDEAU. (Dec. 99, pg. 318)

Edward BRADLEY by his legal representatives claiming 500 arpents of land, see Book D, pg. 199, Mins. No. 5, pg. 375, produces a paper purporting to be an original concession from Carlos Dehault DELASSUS, dated 25th June, 1800. Also, a plat of survey dated 8th November, 1803. M.P. LEDUC, duly sworn, says that the signature to the concession is in the proper handwriting of said Carlos D. DELASSUS, and the signature to plat of Survey is in the proper handwriting of James MACKAY. (Dec. 100, pg. 319)

Jean GODINEAU by his legal representative J.P. CABANNE claiming 800 arpents of land, see Book C, pg. 349, for survey, see Book F, pgs. 54 & 55, Mins. No. 5, pg. 369, produces a paper purporting to be an original concession from Carlos Dehault DELASSUS, dated May 7th, 1800. Also, 2 Deeds of Conveyances from GODINEAU to LABEAUME. Also, a deed of conveyance from BENOIT To CABANNE. M.P. LEDUC, duly sworn, says that the signature to the concession is in the proper handwriting of C.D. DELASSUS.

George CRUMP by his legal representatives claiming 450 arpents of land, see Book C, pg. 477, No. 4, pg. 517, produces a paper purporting to be an original concession from Carlos Dehault DELASSUS, dated 9th May, 1800. Also, a plat of Survey dated 14th February, 1804 by MACKAY. M.P. LEDUC, duly sworn, says that the signature to the concession is in the proper handwriting of said DELASSUS and the signature to the plat of survey the true signature of said MACKAY. (Dec. 101, pg. 319)

Charles ROY by his legal representative J.P. CABANNE claiming 2 arpents of land in front by 40 arpents in depth, see Book F, pg. 190, Livre Terrien No. 4, pg. 2, produces said Liv. Ter. on which there is a Decree of concession to Charles ROY by Fernando de LEYBA dated March 25th, 1780 & Deed of conveyance from Ch. ROY to C. GRATIOT and from Ch. GRATIOT & Wife to J.P. CABANNE for said land. (Dec. 103, pg. 320)

Seneca ROLLINS by his legal representatives claiming 400 arpents of land, see Book C, pg. 477, Minutes No. 5, pg. 486, produces a paper purporting to be an original concession from C.D. DELASSUS, dated 22nd December, 1802. M.P. LEDUC, duly sworn, says that the signature to the concession is in the proper handwriting of said C.D. DELASSUS. (Dec. 104, pg. 320)

John LONG by his legal representatives claiming 10,000 arpents of land, see Book B, pg. 442, No. 5, pg. 444, produces a paper purporting to be an original concession from Zenon TRUDEAU, dated 1st September, 1797. Also, 2 plats of Survey, one for 5,000 arpents dated 20th January, 1806, the other for 5,050 arpents dated 21st March, 1805 by James MACKAY. M.P. LEDUC, duly sworn, says that the signature to the concession is in the true handwriting of Zenon TRUDEAU and the signatures to the Surveys are in the proper handwriting of James MACKAY & Ant. SOULARD. (Dec. 102, pg. 319)

Joachin ROY's legal representatives claiming 400 arpents of land on the river Marameck, under a concession from Zenon TRUDEAU, dated February 3rd, 1797, it being a special location, see Book F, pg. 138, as claimed by Pierre TORNAT's representative. (Dec. 105, pg. 320)

William LONG by his legal representatives claiming 400 arpents of land, see Book C, pg. 510, Minutes No. 5, pg. 448, produces a paper purporting to be an original concession from Carlos Dehault DELASSUS, dated 10th October, 1799. M.P. LEDUC, duly sworn, says that the signature to the concession is in the proper handwriting of said DELASSUS. (Dec. 106, pg. 320)

Edward YOUNG by his legal representatives claiming 800 arpents of land at a place called Manitou Saline, see Book D, pg. 199, Minutes No. 5, pg. 514, produces a paper purporting to be an original concession from Carlos Dehault DELASSUS dated 15th January, 1800. M.P. LEDUC, duly sworn, says that the signature to the concession is in the proper handwriting of Carlos Dehault DELASSUS. Dec. 107, pg. 320)
         Adjourned untill tomorrow at 10 o;clock A.M.
             Friday March 22nd, 1833 Board Met-F.R. CONWAY-Present

James MACKAY by his legal representatives claiming 10 arpents of land in front by 40 in depth on the Saline of the river called River Bonne femme, see Book C, pg. 476, Mins. No. 3, pg. 21, No. 4, pg. 186, produces a paper purporting to be an original concession from Z. TRUDEAU, dated 31st May, 1799. Also, a plat of Survey dated 2nd December, 1804 by MACKAY and certified on oath by Ant. SOULARD. M.P. LEDUC, duly sworn, says that the signature to the concession is in the proper handwriting of Zenon TRUDEAU and the signatures to the plat of Survey and

certificate in the respective handwriting of James MACKAY and
Ant. SOULARD. (Dec. 108, pg. 321)

Antoine GAUTIER by his legal representatives claiming 4,000 arpents
of land, see Book C, pg. 478, Mins. No. 2, pg. 32, No. 4, pg. 17, produces a paper purporting to be an original concession from Z. TRUDEAU,
dated 29th November, 1796. .Also, a plat of survey by SOULARD, dated
December 3rd, 1804. M.P. LEDUC, duly sworn, says that the petition,
Decree and the signature affixed thereto are in the proper handwriting
of said Zenon TRUDEAU and the signature to the plat of Survey is in
the proper handwriting of Ant. SOULARD. (Dec. 109, pg. 321)

John MCMILLAN by his legal representatives claiming 650 arpents of
land, see Book C, pg. 476 & 7, Mins. No. 4, pg. 517, produces a paper
purporting to be a concession from Carlos Dehault DELASSUS, dated 21st
September, 1799. M.P.LEDUC, duly sworn, says that the signature to
the concession is in the proper handwriting of Carlos D. DELASSUS.
(Dec. 110, pg. 322)

John COLLIGAN by his legal representatives claiming 1,200 arpents of
land, see Book C, pg. 479, Mins. No. 5, pg. 395, produces a paper purporting to be an original concession from Zenon TRUDEAU dated 14th of
December, 1798. M.P. LEDUC, duly sworn, says that the Decree and
signature thereto affixed are in the proper handwriting of Z. TRUDEAU.
(Dec. 111, pg. 322)

John BISHOP by his legal representatives claiming 350 arpents of
land, see Book B. pg. 439, Mins. Book No. 4, pg. 489, produces a paper
purporting to be an original concession from Carlos Dehault DELASSUS,
dated 14th November, 1799. Also, a plat of Survey dated 23rd August,
1803, by Antoine SOULARD. M.P.LEDUC, duly sworn, says that the signature to the concession is in the proper handwriting of said
DELASSUS and the signature to the plat of survey in the handwriting
of Ant. SOULARD. (Dec. 112, pg. 322)
    Adjourned untill tomorrow at 10 o'clock A.M.
        The Board Met & Adjourned on March 23rd, 1833.
        Monday March 25th, 1833 Board Met-F.R. CONWAY, Present

Charles Fremon DELAURIERE by Louis LABEAUME's legal representatives,
claiming 10,000 arpents of land situate Prairie Rondeau, now Richwood,
see Record Book D, pgs. 300 & 301, Mins. No. 5, pg. 539, produces a
paper purporting to be an original concession from Z. TRUDEAU, dated
17th January, 1797. Also, a deed between said DELAURIERE & LABEAUME
dated July 15th, 1806. Albert TISON, duly sworn, says that the signature to said concession is in the proper handwriting of Z. TRUDEAU,
that said land was surveyed in 1803. That it was settled by LABEAUME
in 1806 and possessed, cultivated & inhabited ever since by, or
through him. Ch. F. DELAURIERE, being duly sworn, says that in the
spring of 1800, he engaged & hired two men to go on said land in order
to build a bouse and make what improvements they could. That in the
fall of the same year, he sent another man on said land, but circumstances turning out differently to his expectations, he discontinued
improving said land. The deponent further declares that he is in no
way whatsoever interested in the above mentioned tract of land.
(Dec. 113, pg. 323)

Jean Bste. TISON by Louis LABEAUME's legal representatives claiming
7,056 arpents of land, see Book D, pg. 302, No. 5, pg. 507, for survey
claimant refers to the testimony given by Ch. F. DELAURIER in the case
of F. SAUCIER, see pg. 118 of this book, produces a paper purporting
to be a concession from Carlos Dehault DELASSUS, dated November 19th,
1799. A certified copy of a Deed from said TISON to LABEAUME. Also,
a Deed of partition between said TISON & LABEAUME. M.P. LEDUC, duly
sworn, says that the signature to the concession is in the proper handwriting of said Carlos Dehault DELASSUS. (Dec. 114- pg. 323)

Francois M. BENOIT by L. LABEAUME's legal representatives claiming 800
arpents of land, see Book D, pg. 310, Mins. No. 5, pg. 381, produces
a paper purporting to be an original concession from C.D. DELASSUS,
dated 14th August, 1800. Also, a Deed from said BENOIT to a LABEAUME
dated March 5th. 1805. M.P. LEDUC, duly sworn, says that the signa-

ture to the said concession is in the proper handwriting of said
Carlos D. DELASSUS. (No. 337, No. 7-243)

Louis GIGUIERE by L. LABEAUME's representatives claiming 800 arpents
of land, see Book D, pg. 298, Mins. No. 5, pg. 438, Spanish Record of
concessions No. 2, pg. 67, produces a paper purporting to be a certified copy of a concession, granted to said GIGUIERE by Ch. D. DELASSUS,
dated 13th June, 1800, and certified by Anto. SOULARD. Also, Deed
from GIGUIERE to Peter LORD dated 12th January, 1805. Also, deed from
said LORD to LABEAUME dated July 18th, 1806. M.P. LEDUC, duly sworn,
says that the certificate and the signature affixed to it are in the
proper handwriting of said Ant. SOULARD as registered in Book No. 2,
pgs. 67 & 8, of record in the office of the Recorder of Land Titles.
Albert TISON, duly sworn, says that he had once in his possession three
concessions, among which was the original of the above mentioned copy.
That on his way from Coldwater to this place, his pocket book containing the three concessions aforesaid, was lost. Witness, further,
says that in 1806 he went on said land and it was then inhabited and
cultivated, and has been so ever since, having now between 40 and 50
acres under cultivation. (No. 336, No. 7, 243)

Louis DELILLE by L. LABEAUME's representatives claiming 2,500 arpents
of land, see Book C, pgs. 340 and 341, Mins. No. 5, pg. 407, produces
a paper purporting to be an original concession from C.D. DELASSUS,
dated November 6th, 1799. A plat of Survey taken 14th February and
certified 20th March, 1804 by SOULARD. Also, a certificate of transfer signed M.P. LEDUC, Recorder. M.P. LEDUC, duly sworn, says that
the signature to the concession is in the proper handwriting of
Carlos D. DELASSUS, and the signature to Plat & Certificate of Survey
is in the proper handwriting of said SOULARD. (Dec. 115, pg. 323)

Charles MIVILLE by L. LABEAUME's legal representatives claiming 800
arpents of land, see Book C, pgs. 341 & 2, Mins. No. 5, pg. 456, produces a paper purporting to be an original concession from
Carlos D. DELASSUS, dated November 18th, 1799. Also, a Plat and certificate of Survey taken January 4th and certified by SOULARD, March
5th, 1804. Also, a Deed dated December 20th, 1811. M.P. LEDUC, duly
sworn, says that the signatures to the concessions and to the Plat of
Survey are in the respective handwriting of Carlos Dehault DELASSUS
and Antoine SOULARD.

Louis LAMALICE alias LEMONDE by Louis LABEAUME's legal representatives
claiming 800 arpents of land, see Book C, pgs. 342 & 3. For Survey
pg. 349, Mins. Book No. 5, pg. 365, produces a paper purporting to be
an original concession from Carlos Dehault DELASSUS dated November 18th,
1799. Also, a paper purporting to be an original plat of survey (part
of said paper torn & missing) embracing 35 concessions of 800 arpents
each, numbered from 1 to 35 inclusive, on which said LAMALICE is No.
1. Also, a certificate of transfer signed M.P. LEDUC, Recorder.
M.P. LEDUC, duly sworn, says that the signature to the concession is
in the proper handwriting of Carlos Dehault DELASSUS and that the torn
original Survey is of the proper handwriting of Antoine SOULARD.
(2d, 80, No. 7, p. 228)

Jean DEROUIN by L. LABEAUME's legal representatives claiming 800 arpents of land, see Book C, pg. 343 & 349, Mins. No. 5, pg. 365, produces a paper purporting to be a concession from Carlos D. DELASSUS,
dated October 5th, 1799. Also, a Plat of Survey (part of said paper
torn and missing) embracing 35 concessions of 800 arpents each, numbered from 1 to 35 inclusive, on which claimant is No. 4. M.P.LEDUC,
duly sworn, says that the signature to the concession is in the proper
handwriting of Carlos D. DELASSUS and that the torn original Survey
is of the proper handwriting of Ant. SOULARD. (2d, 111, No. 7, 235)

Francois MARECHAL by L. LABEAUME's legal representatives claiming 800
arpents of land, see Book C, pgs. 344 & 349 Mins. No. 5, 365, produces
a concession from Carlos D. DELASSUS, dated 11th April, 1800. Also, a
Plat of Survey, part of which is torn & missing, embracing 35 concessions of 800 arpents each & numbered from 1 to 35 inclusive, on which
claimant is No. 5. Also, Deeds dated 5th December, 1803 and July 7th,

1804. M.P. LEDUC, duly sworn, says that the signature to the concession is in the proper handwriting of Carlos Dehault DELASSUS and that the torn original Survey is of the proper handwriting of A. SOULARD.

Joseph HUBERT by L. LABEAUME's legal representatives claiming 800 arpents of land, see Book C, pgs. 344 and 349, Mins. No. 5, pg. 366, produces a paper purporting to be an original concession from Carlos Dehault DELASSUS, dated March 16th, 1800. Also, a plat of survey, part of the same being torn and missing, embracing 35 concessions of 800 arpents each and numbered from 1 to 35 inclusive, on which claimant is No. 6. Also, Deed dated December 12th, 1803. M.P. LEDUC, being duly sworn, says that the signature to the concession is in the proper handwriting of Carlos D. DELASSUS and that the torn original Survey is of the proper handwriting of A. SOULARD.

Jean Louis MARC by L. LABEAUME's legal representatives claiming 800 arpents of land, see Book C, pgs.345 & 9, Mins. No. 5, pg. 366, produces a paper purporting to be an original concession from Carlos D. DELASSUS dated January 24th, 1800. Also, a plat of Survey part of the same being torn and missing, embracin g 35 concessions of 800 arpents each, and numbered from 1 to 35 inclusive, on which claimant is No. 9. Also, a deed dated January 9th, 1804. M.P. LEDUC, duly sworn, says that the signature to the concession is in the proper handwriting of Carlos D. DELASSUS and that the torn original Survey is of the proper handwriting of A. SOULARD. (2d, 105, No. 7-233)

Jean Bste. BRAVIER by L. LABEAUME's legal representatives claiming 800 arpents of land, see Book C, pgs. 345 & 9, Mins. No. 5, pg. 364, produces a paper purporting to be a concession from Carlos D. DELASSUS, dated April 11th, 1800. Also, a plat of Survey, part of the same being torn and missing, embracing 35 concessions of 800 arpents each and numbered from 1 to 35 inclusive, on which claimant is No. 10. Also, Deeds dated December 12th, 1803 & July 11th, 1804. M.P. LEDUC, duly sworn, says that the signature to the concession is in the proper handwriting of Carlos D. DELASSUS and that the torn original Survey is of the proper handwriting of A. SOULARD. (2d, 113, No. 7, 235)

Baptiste MARLI by L. LABEAUME's legal representatives claiming 800 arpents of land, see Book C, pgs. 245 & 9, Mins. No. 5, pg. 366, produces a paper purporting to be a concession from Carlos D. DELASSUS, dated December 17th, 1799. Also, a plat of survey, part of the same being torn and missing, embracing 35 concessions of 800 arpents each, and numbered from 1 to 35 inclusive, on which claimant is No. 11. M.P. LEDUC, duly sworn, says that the signature to the concession is in the proper handwriting of Carlos D. DELASSU and that the torn original survey is of the proper handwriting of A. SOULARD.(2d, 96, No.7-231)

Baptiste DOMINE by L. LABEUAME's legal representatives claiming 800 arpents of land, see Book C, pgs. 345 6 & 9, Mins. No. 5, pg. 367, produces a paper purporting to be a concession from Carlos D. DELASSUS, dated October 28th, 1799. Also, a plat of survey, part of the same being torn & missing, embracing 35 concessions of 800 arpents each and numbered from 1 to 35 inclusive on which claimant is No. 12. Also, a certificate. M.P. LEDUC, being duly sworn, says that the signature to the concession is in the proper handwriting of Carlos D. DELASSUS, and that the torn original survey is of the proper handwriting of A. SOULARD.

Louis CHARLEVILLE by L. LABEAUME's legal representatives claiming 800 arpents of land, see Book C. pgs. 347 & 9, Mins. No. 5, pg. 367, produces a paper purporting to be a concession from C.D. DELASSUS, dated November 14th, 1799. Also, a plat of survey, part of the same being torn & missing, embracing 35 concessions of 800 arpents each & numbered from 1 to 35 inclusive, on which claimant is No. 13. Also, certificate of transfer signed M.P. LEDUC, Recorder. M.P. LEDUC, duly sworn, says that the signature to the concession is in the proper handwriting of Carlos D. DELASSUS, and that the torn original survey is of the proper handwriting of SOULARD.

Francois BERNARD by L. LABEAUME's legal representatives claiming 800 arpents of land, see Book C, pgs. 346 & 9, Mins. No. 5, pg. 364, produces a paper purporting to be a concession from Carlos D. DELASSUS, dated January 16th, 1800. Also, a plat of survey, part of the same being torn and missing, embracing 35 concessions of 800 arpents each and numbered from 1 to 35 inclusive, on which claimant is No. 14. Also, Deeds dated January August & December, 1804. M.P. LEDUC, duly sworn, says that the signature to the concession is in the proper handwriting of Carlos D. DELASSUS, and that the torn original Survey is of the proper handwriting of A. SOULARD. (2d, 95-No. 7-231)

Louis BOISSI by L. LABEAUME's legal representative claiming 800 arpents of land, see Book C, pgs. 346 & 9, Mins. No. 5, pg. 364, produces a paper purporting to be an original concession from C.D. DELASSUS, dated January 18th, 1800. Also, a plat of survey, part of the same being torn & missing, embracing 35 concessions of 800 arpents each & numbered from 1 to 35 inclusive, on which claimant is No. 15. Also, certificate of transfer signed M.P. LEDUC, Recorder. M.P. LEDUC, duly sworn, says that the signature to the concession is in the proper handwriting of Carlos D. DELASSUS and that the torn original survey is of the proper handwriting of A. SOULARD. (2d,91-No.7-230)

Joseph CHARLEVILLE by L. LABEAUME's legal representatives claiming 800 arpents of land, see Book C, pgs. 347 & 9, Mins. No. 5, pg. 367, produces a concession purporting to be from Carlos D. DELASSUS, dated 16th November, 1799. Also, a plat of Survey, part of the same being torn & Missing, embracing 35 concessions of 800 arpents each and numbered from 1 to 35 inclusive, on which claimant is No. 16. Also, certificate of transfer signed M.P. LEDUC, Recorder. M.P. LEDUC, duly sworn, says that the signature to the concession is in the proper handwriting of said DELASSUS and that the torn original survey is of the proper handwriting of Ant. SOULARD. (2d, 92, No. 7-231)

Joseph PRESSE by L. LABEAUME's legal representatives claiming 800 arpents of land, see Book C, pgs. 347 & 9, Mins. No. 5, pg. 367, produces a paper purporting to be an original concession from Carlos D. DELASSUS, dated November 12th, 1799. Also, a plat of survey, part of the same being torn & missing, embracing 35 concessions of 800 arpents each & numbered from 1 to 35 inclusive, on which claimant is No. 17. Also, Deeds to LABEAUME. M.P. LEDUC, duly sworn, says that the signature to the concession is in the proper handwriting of said DELASSUS and that the torn original survey is of the proper handwriting of said SOULARD.

Michel VALLE by L. LABEAUME's legal representatives claiming 800 arpents of land, see Book C, pg. 347 & 9, No. 5, pg. 368, produces a paper purporting to be an original concession from C.D. DELASSUS, dated March 16th, 1800. Also, Deeds to LABEAUME. Also, a plat of Survey, part of the same being torn and missing, embracing 35 concessions of 800 arpents each and numbered from 1 to 35 inclusive, on which claimant is No. 18. M.P. LEDUC, duly sworn, says that the signature to the concession is in the proper handwriting of said DELASSUS and that the torn original survey is of the proper handwriting of said SOULARD.

Antoine BIZET by L. LABEAUME's legal representatives claiming 800 arpents of land, see Book C, pgs. 347 & 8 & 9, Mins. No. 5, pg. 364, produces a paper purporting to be an original concession from Carlos D. DELASSUS, dated 13th September, 1800. Also, Deeds to LABEAUME & certificate of transfer signed M.P. LEDUC, Recorder. Also, a Plat of Survey, part of the same being torn and missing, embracing 35 concessions of 800 arpents each, on which claimant is No. 19. M.P. LEDUC, duly sworn, says that the signature to the concession is in the proper handwriting of said DELASSUS and the torn original survey is of the proper handwriting of Ant. SOULARD. (2d, 90, No.7-230)

Auguste LEFEVRE by L. LABEAUME's legal representative claiming 800 arpents of land, see Book C, pgs. 348 & 9, Mins. No. 5, pg. 368, produces a paper purporting to be an original concession from Carlos D. DELASSUS, dated June 11th, 1800. Also, deeds to LABEAUME. Also, a Plat of Survey, part of which is torn and missing, embracing 35 concessions of 800 arpents, numbered from 1 to 35 inclusive, on which claimant is No. 21. M.P. LEDUC, duly sworn, says that the signature to the concession is in the proper handwriting of said DELASSUS, and the torn original Survey is of the proper handwriting of Ant. SOULARD. (2d, 84, No. 7-229)

Jean Bste. PROVENCHER by L. LABEAUME's legal representatives claiming 800 arpents of land, see Book C, pgs. 348 & 9, Mins. No. 5, pg. 368, produces a concession purporting to be from Carlos D. DELASSUS, dated January 15th, 1800. Also, certificate & transfer signed M.P. LEDUC, Recorder. Also, a plat of Survey, part of which is torn and missing embracing 35 concessions of 800 arpents each, numbered from 1 to 35 inclusive, on which claimant is No. 20. M.P. LEDUC, duly sworn, says that the signature to the concession is in the proper handwriting of said DELASSUS and the torn original Survey is of the proper handwriting of Ant. SOULARD. (2d, 85, No. 7-229)

Joseph MORIN, Junr., by L. LABEAUME's legal representatives claiming 160 arpents of land, see Book D, pgs. 303, 4 & 5, Mins. No. 5, pg. 458, produces a paper purporting to be a concession from Z. TRUDEAU, dated September 9th, 1797. A Plat and certificate of Survey signed A. SOULARD, said Survey taken November 16th, 1799 and certificate dated February 26th, 1806. Also, Deed from said MORIN to J.B. PAQUET dated March 13th, 1804 and Deed from PAQUET to LABEAUME dated May 8th 1804. M.P. LEDUC, duly sworn, says that the signature to the concession and the concession itself are in the proper handwriting of Zenon TRUDEAU, and the signature to the plat of Survey is in the proper handwriting of A. SOULARD. Albert TISON, duly sworn, says that about 28 years ago he went on said land, built a house, dug a well & fenced in a field, that he resided on the same near two years, and about 10 years after he left said place, the claimant went on said land, and by, or through him, it has been inhabited and cultivated ever since.

James WILLIAMS by L. LABEAUME's legal representatives claiming 400 arpents of land, see Book D, pgs. 310, 11 & 12, Mins. Book No. 5, pg. 513, produces a paper purporting to be an original concession from Carlos D. DELASSUS, dated 15th April, 1803. Also, a Deed from said WILLIAM to LABEAUME dated April 29th, 1806. Also, assignment by LABEAUME to A. TISON and release from said TISON to said LABEAUME. Also, a Survey in support of said claim, as an evidence of the same not claiming the land contained in the Survey, but only produces it in support of the grant made in lieu thereof. M.P. LEDUC, duly sworn, says that the signature to the concession is in the proper handwriting of said DELASSUS and the signature to the Survey is in the proper handwriting of Antoine SOULARD.

Jean Marie CARDINAL by L. LABEAUME's legal representatives, claiming 40 arpents of land in White Ox Prairie, see Book D, pgs. 296, Livre Terrien No. 3, pg. 12, Book F, pg. 184, Mins. No. 3, pg. 485, produces a copy of a duly registered concession granted by Francisco CRUZAT, bearing date 28th August, 1777 taken from said Livre Terrien. Also, a certificate of SOULARD dated 5th August, 1804. Also, copy of a Survey of said land certified by M.P. LEDUC. Also, copy of a Deed from the heirs of CARDINAL to LABEAUME dated July 26th, 1804 certified by James MACKAY, Commandant of St. Charles. M.P. LEDUC, duly sworn, says that the signature to the above mentioned papers are in the proper and respective handwriting of the above mentioned individuals who signed them.)No. 299, No. 7, 185)
    Adjourned until tomorrow at 10 o'clock A.M.
       The Board Met & Adjourned March 26th, 27th, & 28th, 1833.
       Friday March 29th, 1833 Board Met-F.R. CONWAY Present

Gabriel CERRE by Josiah MCCLANAHAN claiming 300 arpents of land, see Book B, pgs. 233 & 389, Mins. No. 1, pg. 393, No. 4, pg. 484, No. 6, 241. Pascal L. CERRE, duly sworn, says that Gabriel CERRE was his father. That ke knows the conditions of the said grant to have been on the part of his father to build a bridge over the Ruisseau de Pierre. That his said father having gone to Canada previous to DELASSUS signing the grant, he, the deponent, remained charged with his business in this country. When DELASSUS, who had not yet signed the grant, hurried him to go on with the Bridge, but the deponent

would not do it until the grant was signed, which DELASSUS having
done, he sent his hands immediately to work, having already all
the materials on the spot and soon completed the Bridge.(Dec.118, 324)
     Adjourned untill tomorrow at 10 o'clock A.M.
     The Board Met & Adjourned March 30th, April 1st, & 2nd.
          Wednesday April 3rd, 1833 Board Met-F.R. CONWAY, Present
                              .

In the case of Joseph MORIN, Junior, claiming 160 arpents of land, see
pg. 149 of this Book. Joseph HEBERT, duly sworn, says that to his
knowledge the said land was inhabited and cultivated 32 or 33 years
ago, by or through Joseph MORIN, Junior and has been so inhabited and
cultivated ever since.
     Adjourned untill tomorrow at 10 o'clock A.M.
          The Board Met & Adjourned April 4th, 5th, 6th, and 8th, 1833.
          Tuesday April 9th, 1833 Board Met-F.R. CONWAY, Present

James RICHARDSON by his legal representatives claiming 400 arpents of
land situate River Maline, see Record Book B, pgs. 304 & 404, Mins. No.
3, pg. 454, No. 4, pg. 435, produces a paper purporting to be an original concession from Carlos Dehault DELASSUS, dated 16th December, 1799.
Also, copy of the Survey. William CAMPBELL, duly sworn, says that he
knows the tract of land here above mentioned, that in 1799 or 1800, deponent helped RICHARDSON to raise a building intended for a Distillery
that to his knowledge the said RICHARDSON distilled liquors there for
three seasons in succession from the time he built the said house.
That in 1802 or 3 Deponent saw corn growing in a small lot; that the
said RICHARDSON kept his stock, hogs, etc. on said place; and that
from the time it was first settled, it has been inhabited or held by
or through said RICHARDSON ever since. M.P. LEDUC, duly sworn, says
that the signature to the concession is in the proper handwriting of
Carlos Dehault DELASSUS. (Dec. 120, pg. 324)
     Adjourned untill tomorrow at 10 o'clock A.M.
          The Board Met & Adjourned April 10th, and 11th, 1833.
          Friday April 12th, 1833 Board Met-Two Comm'rs. Present

Pierre DELOR claiming 10 arpents of land in front by 40 arpents in
depth on river au Gravois, a special location, see Record Book F, pg.
96, BATES Decision No. 5, pg. 102, produces a paper purporting to be
an original concession from Zenon TRUDEAU, dated 6th December, 1796.
Also, a plat of survey dated May 1821 by Jos. C. BROWN. John BOLI,
duly sworn, says that he was present when Jos. C. BROWN surveyed a
tract of land for Pierre DELOR cn River Au Gravois. That near the
main road, he was several times shown a (cannot read) said to be the
corner of said land as before Surveyed and that in running the lines
he saw trees marked with old blazes and he heard of said DELOR and
others that these old lines were run by BOUVET, who was Commissioned
Surveyor at the date of the concession. That said DELOR was a Spanish
Officer and acted as Commandant at his father's decease, and he, the
deponent served under him. (Dec. 121, pg. 325)
     Adjourned untill tomorrow at 10 o'clock A.M.
          Saturday April 13th, 1833 Board Met-Two Comm'rs. Present

Melchior Amand MICHAU claiming 600 arpents of land, see Book B, pg.
328, produces a plat of Survey received for record by A. SOULARD,
February 28th, 1806. And, as evidence in support of said claim, produces a concession purporting to be from Carlos Dehault DELASSUS, dated 16th May, 1800 at the foot of which there is a certificate of said
DELASSUS dated July 14th, 1818, by which it appears that the land was
granted to claimant and not to J. MICHAU as appears by Mins. Book 5,
pg. 454. M.P. LEDUC, duly sworn, says that the signature to the Plat
of Survey is in the proper handwriting of Antoine SOULARD and that the
signatures to the concession and to the certificate are in the proper
handwriting of said Carlos Dehault DELASSUS. (Dec. 134, pg. 333)
     Adjourned untill Monday next at 10 o'clock A.M.
          The Board Met & Adjourned April 15th, 1833.
          Tuesday April 16th, 1833 Board Met-Two Comm'rs. Present

The Inhabitants of St. Ferdinand claiming 7,056 arpents of land, of
which 5,206-3/4 arpents have been confirmed, see Book C, pg. 489,
Mins. No. 1, pg. 497, No. 5, pg. 322. (2d class No. 21, No. 7, pg.169)

Adjourned untill tomorrow at 10 o'clock A.M.
Wednesday April 17th, 1833 Board Met-Two Comm'rs. Present

In the case of Pierre DELORE claiming 10 by 40 arpents of land, see
pg. 154 of this Book. Jos. C. BROWN, duly sworn, says that he made
the survey of the land above mentioned. That John BOLY was along
with several other neighbours for the purpose, he thinks, of showing
the land, as claimed by the proprietor. (Dec. 121, pg. 325)

In the case of ST.VRAIN claiming 4,000 arpents of land, see pg. 89 of
this Book, Albert TISON, duly sworn, says that the time the conces-
sion for the said tract of 4,000 arpents of land was granted to said
ST.VRAIN, he had four children living to wit; Charles, Felix, Odille
& Ciran.
Adjourned untill tomorrow at 10 o'clock A.M.
Thursday April 18th, 1833 Board Met-A.G. HARRISON-Present

Jacques BON claiming 800 arpents of land in virtue of a settlement
right in the county of Washington, see Record Book F, pg. 53, BATES
decision Book No. 2, pg. 28, BATES Decision pg. 28, No. 2.
(Dec. cannot read)
Adjourned untill tomorrow at 10 o'clock A.M.
The Board Met & Adjourned April 19th, 1833.
Saturday April 20th, 1833 Board Met-A.G. HARRISON-Present

Nicolas & Louis GAMACHE, heirs of Jean Baptiste GAMACHE, Senr., deceased, claim under settlement right 1,050 arpents of land at the
mouth of the Merrimack, see Book B, pg. 24, Mins. No. 5, pgs. 423 & 4
and 555. John Baptiste VIEN, duly sworn, says that he was acquainted
with John Baptiste GAMACHE, Senr., the grandfather of Nicholas &
Louis GAMACHE. That said John Baptiste GAMACHE cultivated a tract of
land on the Right Bank of the Mississippi, at the mouth of the Merri-
mac about fifty years ago. That his children inhabited and cultivated
the land under the Spanish Government and that they left it on account
of the sickness of their families, and that his grandchildren, Nicolas
and Louis, with their families, still reside on it, and have for the
last seven or eight years resided on it. That he, the Deponent, found
them (the GAMACHES) in possession and cultivation of the said tract of
land, when he, the Deponent, first came to the country, which was about
1783-4. He further says that John Baptiste GAMACHE, Senr., had five
or six children. That Auguste GAMACHE and John Baptiste GAMACHE, Jr.,
sons of John Baptiste GAMACHE, Sr., lived on the land with their families. Auguste had a wife and four children and John Baptiste Jr., a
wife and six or seven children. John Baptiste Maurice CHATILLON, duly
sworn, says that he knew John Baptiste GAMACHE, Sr., in 1780. That he
lived on the tract above spoken of at that time. That in 1782, GAMACHE
brought his wife to St. Louis sick when she died and afterwards, that
GAMACHE returned to live on the land. That GAMACHE, Sr., died about
the year 1800 and after his death, that his sons Auguste and
John Baptiste GAMACHE, Jr., lived on and cultivated the same place and
that Nicolas and Louis have been living there ever since with their
families.   (Dec. 145, No. 7, pg. 12)

Daniel GRIFFITH claiming 600 arpents of land, see Book D, pgs. 111 &
12, Mins. No. 3, pg. 308, No. 4, pg. 387, produces a paper purporting
to be an original concession from Carlos Dehault DELASSUS, dated April
18th, 1801. Also, a plat and certificate of survey signed by
John FERRY, dated somewhat defaced, and the affidavit of said FERRY
before Thos. F. REDDICK, Justice of the Peace. M.P. LEDUC, duly sworn,
says that the signature of Carlos Dehault DELASSUS is in the proper
handwriting of the same, that the signatures to the Survey and affidavit are in the proper handwriting of the said John FERRY. That the
signature to the certificate is in the proper handwriting of
Thomas F. REDDICK.   (Dec. 168, No. 7, pg. 30)

Jean Baptiste DECHAMP by his legal representatives Jos. F. ROBIDOUX
claiming 4 by 40 arpents on the right bank of River Aux Cardes, see
Livre Terrien No. 4, pg. 7, Record Book F, pg. 191, Also Mins. of Recorder. John Baptiste Maurice CHATILLON, duly sworn, says that in
the year 1780, Jno. B. DECHAMP inhabited and cultivated said tract

of land and continued thereon for about three years, when he was compelled by Indian depredations to abandon it. That he had then a wife and two children. John Baptiste VIEN, duly sworn, says that one Toussaint DECHAMP, alias HUNOT, inhabited and cultivated said lands about forty years ago, for or under Baptiste DECHAMP, for about one year, when he was compelled to abandon it, on account of Indian depredations, and further, that said tract was inhabited and cultivated by or under said Baptiste DECHAMP about 20 years ago and ever since. (Dec. 164, No. 7, pg. 11)

Adjourned untill Monday next at 10 o'clock A.M.

The Board Met April 22nd, 23rd, 24th, 25th, and adjourned without attending to any business.

Friday April 26th, 1833 Board Met-Two Comm'rs. Present

In the case of Esther claiming 80 arpents of land, see page 111 of this book. J. Baptiste RIVIERE, dit BACANE, duly sworn, says he knew Esther, a free mulatto woman, who lived with CLAMORGAN, that to his knowledge, said Esther had to the North of St. Louis, a small piece of land which had been given to her by the Public at the end of their common fields, and that Esther made use of said piece of land as a pasture for her calves and cows that the said land was situated between the mound commonly called LaGrange de terre and the next mound south of the said grange de terre and running from the descent of the hill between the above said two mounds, to the Mississippi, that he does not know exactly how long she possessed the said land. He further says that when he said that the said land had been given to Esther by the Public, he meant the Government. Francois DUCHOUQUET, duly sworn, says he knows that Esther owned a piece of land situated at the foot of the Grange de terre and running thence to the Mississippi, byt does not know what quantity of land; that said Esther was the reputed owner of said land for more than ten years. Elisabeth HORTEZ, duly sworn, says that she heard her husband and others say that Esther had a piece of land situated about the Grange de terre and running towards the Mississippi, that she always understood that Esther was the reputed owner of said land. That the cows which were at CLAMORGAN's were always called Esthers cows. (Dec. 70, pg. 310)

Adjourned untill tomorrow at 9 o'clock A.M.

The Board met & Adjourned April 27th, 29th, 30th, May 1st, 2nd, 3rd, 4th, 6th, 7th, 8th, 1833.

Thursday May 9th, 1833 Board Met-A.G. HARRISON, Present

Jacob ODAM by Andy KINNEY & George FORGUER claiming 800 arpents of land, under settlement right, situated on the creek commonly called Odam's creek, on the Mississippi, opposite Wood Island, including the big (Cannot read) formerly presented to the Board in the name of John MCFERRAN, see Mins. No. 5, pg. 467, D, pg. 58.

Joseph GERARD, duly sworn, says that he has been in this country about fifty eight years; that he was, well acquainted with Jacob ODAM. That he went with said ODAM in the year 1777 or 1778 to the Commandant at St. Genevieve by the name of CARTEBONE, and that said ODAM asked the Commandant for a concession, but the Commandant told ODAM that he could not then give him a concession, but told him to go and settle and improve a place and that this would be the best concession. That ODAM did, after this, go immediately and settled and improved a place called Usually Wood Island, from being opposite or nearly opposite that island that he saw said ODAM working and improving said place, and that said ODAM raised a crop on said land, That after being there a while, Mrs. ODAM took sick and died, leaving one child, a daughter, by the name of Mindy, and that some months after the death of Mrs. ODAM, ODAM took sick and died. That both were buried on the place. that their daughter Mindy grew up and married. That the place, after the death of ODAM, has never been cultivated. That from where he settled to the Mississippi is about a half or three quarters of a mile, which space formed a part of his claim as witness thinks. That ODAM settled about a quarter of a mile above the big spring on the creek called ODAM's Creek.

Adjourned untill tomorrow at 9 o'clock A.M.

The Board Met & Adjourned May 10th and 11th, 1833.

Monday May 13th, 1833 Board Met-Two Comm'rs. Present

Resolved that A.G. HARRISON, Esq., one of the Board, attend at different points in the NorthWestern part of the State for the purpose
of receiving such testimony as may be offered under the late act of
Congress for the final adjustment of private land claims in Missouri
and the act supplementary thereto, and that he give notice where and
at what time he will attend at the different points for such purpose.
See Resolution taken on the 18th March, page 130 of this book.
     Adjourned until tomorrow at 9 o'clock A.M.
          The Board Met & Adjourned May 14th, & May 16th, 1833.
          Friday May 17th, 1833 Board Met-F.R.CONWAY, Present

In the case of P.F. DEVOLSAY by his legal representative J.P. CABANNE,
claiming 6 by 40 arpents of land, see pg. 100 of this book.
Francois CAYON, duly sworn, says that he saw DEVOLSAY's mulatto man
make a field on said land, where he planted tobacco, melons, etc.
That said land is situated nearly opposite the small prairie and on
the left side of the road leading to BARRIERE & DESNOYERS. That he
thinks said land was cultivated by DEVOLSAY nearly 50 years ago, may
be a little less. That DEVOLSAY went there every day to see his
hands work, that the hands went there every day early and came back
late in the evening. That he does not recollect how long the said
land was cultivated by DEVOLSAY, but he is certain that it was for
more than one or two years. He neither can remember what quantity
of land was inclosed in said field. That DEVOLSAY died in St. Louis,
maybe 45 or 46 years ago, he cannot state precisely the time.
     Adjourned until tomorrow at 9 o'clock A.M.
          Saturday May 18th, 1833 Board Met-F.R. CONWAY, Present

AMIOT by his legal representatives the heirs of Robert BUCHANAN
claiming under settlement right 600 arpents of land situated at Creve
Couer, No. 3, pg. 517, see Book D, pgs. 232 & 3, Mins. No. 4, pg. 440,
No. 5, pg. 561.
     Adjourned until Monday next at 9 o'clock A.M.
          Monday May 20th, 1833 Board Met- F.R. CONWAY, Present

Joseph GERARD & Patrick FLEMING by their legal representatives
Rufus EASTON & the heirs of James BRUFF, claiming 840 arpents of land
situate in the District of St. Genevieve, on the waters of a fork of
Marameck called Big river, see Record Book E, pgs. 331 & 2, Minutes
No. 5, pg. 537, No. 6, pg. 205, produces a paper purporting to be an
original concession from Carlos D. DELASSUS, dated 25th September,
1799. Also, a plat of Survey by Antoine SOULARD, dated January 10th,
1800. Also, a paper purporting to be a copy of a concession referred
to in the original concession here produced, and certified by
Francois VALLE, late Commandant of St. Genevieve. M.P. LEDUC, duly
sworn, says that the signature to the concession is in the proper handwriting of Carlos D. DELASSUS, that the signature to the plat of Survey is in the proper handwriting of A. SOULARD, and that the signature
to the certified copy of a concession is in the proper handwriting of
F. VALLE.

Victor LAGAUTERIE by his legal representatives claiming 800 arpents of
land, to wit; 690 arpents on Salt River and 110 arpents on the Mississippi, see Boof F, pgs. 107 & 8, Recorders Mins. P. 51, produces a
paper purporting to be an original concession from C.D. DELASSUS, dated 8th February, 1800. Also, two plats of surveys, one for 690 arpents and the other for 110 arpents, both taken on the 29th December,
1803 and certified by SOULARD on the 20th January, 1804. M.P. LEDUC,
duly sworn, says that the signature to the concession is in the proper
handwriting of C.D. DELASSUS and the signatures to the two plats of
surveys are in the proper handwriting of Ant. SOULARD.

Alexis LOISE by his legal representatives claiming 3 arpents of land
in front by 40 arpents in depth, see Livre Terrien No. 3, pg. 27,
Record Book F, pg. 188, No. 6, pg. 219.
     Adjourned until tomorrow at 9 o'clock A.M.
          The Board Met & Adjourned May 21st, 1833.

Wednesday May 22nd, 1833 Board Met-F.R. CONWAY, Present

Mathurin BOUVET by his legal representatives claiming 6 arpents square of land, see Livre Terrien No. 4, pg. 27, Record Book F, pg. 197. Gregoire KIERCEREAU, duly sworn, says he knows that Mathurin BOUVET owned and established a piece of land at the upper part of the town of St. Charles. That said BOUVET employed the Deponent's father and himself to cut and haul the timber for building a house and a large horse mill. That, as well as he can recollect, it is more than forty years ago that said buildings were erected. As, also, several other small buildings. That said BOUVET remained on said place. He cannot say exactly how long, but thinks 20 or 22 years. That said land is situated on the Western side of the continuation of Main Street and is bounded South by the Deponent's land, North by land formerly belonging to the Deponent's father, West by lands claimed as commons, and East by said Main Street. He further says that he can show the places where the buildings stood.

John VALET by his legal representatives claiming 400 arpents of land, see Record Book B, pg. 214, Mins. No. 1, pg. 510, No. 3, pgs. 69 & 215, No. 4, pg. 224.

In the case of Gabriel CERRE claiming 10 arpents of land in front by 40 in depth, see pg. 98 of this Book, the claimant produces a paper purporting to be a plat of survey signed by Jos. C. BROWN and dated 13th February, 1822. Joseph C. BROWN, duly sworn, says that the plat of Survey, presented by the claimant, was executed by him conformably to the Survey he made of said land and that what is in there stated is true.

George AYREY claiming 750 arpents of land, see Record Book B, pg. 216, for plat of Survey, Mins. No. 5, pg. 356. (2d, 60, No.7, pg. 190)

Edmund CHANDLER by Arthur BURNS, Junra, claiming 640 acres of land under settlement right, see Record Book D, pg. 340, Mins. No. 3, pg. 460 and No. 4, pg. 439, produces original Deed of Conveyance from CHANDLER To BURNS. (Dec. No. 137, pg. 334)

Abraham SMITH by his legal representatives claiming 600 arpents of land under settlement right, see BATES Mins. pgs. 75 & 92, BATES Decisions, pg. 33, Commissioners Mins. No. 5, pg. 499, Record Book D, pg. 341.
    Adjourned untill tomorrow at 9 o'clock A.M.
        Thursday May 23rd, 1833 Board Met-F.R. CONWAY, Present

James MCDANIEL by his legal representatives claiming 800 arpents of land under settlement right, situated 3 or 4 miles above Belle Fountain, see Book B, pg. 262, Mins. Book No. 5, pg. 552. Albert TISON, duly sworn, says that he saw the said MCDANIEL living and residing on said land in 1801 or 02; that he had a cabin and a field of about 5 or 6 acres. That in 1805 or 6, the said MCDANIEL resided yet on said place. That when he first saw it, he judged that it had been settled a few years before. (Dec. 136 pg. 333)

In the case of Edmund CHANDLER claiming 640 acres of land, (see the beginning of this page) Albert TISON, duly sworn, says that in the winter of 1803 & 4, he saw said CHANDLER with his family, residing on said land, that he had a house and field. (Dec. 137, pg. 334)

In the case of John VALET claiming 400 arpents of land, see pg. 169 of this Book, Albert TISON, duly sworn, says that in 1803, about the middle of December, he staid one night at Mr. COOK, who had purchased VALET's improvement, and said COOK had then a large field and a cabin that the place appeared to have been settled several years before the Deponent saw it. That said COOK had his family residing along with him and lived on said place untill his death, which happened five or 6 years afterwards.
    Adjourned untill tomorrow at 9 o'clock A.M.
        The Board Met & Adjourned May 24th, 25th, 27th, 28th, 29th, 30th, and 31st, 1833.

Saturday June 1st, 1833 Board Met-F.R. CONWAY, Present

Absalom LINK by his legal representatives William RAMEY claiming 510
arpents of land situated on White Oak run, District of St. Louis, see
Mins. No. 5, pg. 444, B.H.B. pg. 269, produces a plat of survey by
James MACKAY dated November 21st, 1805, recorded by SOULARD, January
26th, 1806. William CAMPBELL, duly sworn, says that in the spring
of 1804, he saw on said place a small piece of ground inclosed and
the foundation of a cabin, as also the name of said LINK carved on a
tree. That said place was then considered as Absalom LINK's land, under a settlement right, see pg. 175 of this Book. (2d, 62, No. 7-pg.191)
        The Board Met & Adjourned June 3rd, 4th & 5th, 1833.
        Thursday June 6th, 1833 Board Met-F.R. CONWAY,Present

Jacob WICKERHAH by his legal representative William DRENEN, claiming
800 arpents of land situated on Balero's Creek, see Record Book F,
pg. 142, BATES Decisions pg. 104. William MOSS, duly sworn, says that
he is settled in this country since the year 1795 and knows the tract
now claimed. That in 1803 he went to the farm of
Jacob WICKERHAM's father to buy corn, and having lost his way, he met
with the said Jacob WICKERHAM, who took him through a piece of land on
which he had about 500 peach trees he had planted the year before and
was then hoeing. The said trees were inclosed with a strong fence,
and that the said WICKERHAM proposed to sell his improvement to him,
the said deponent. (Dec. 140, pg. 338)
        Adjourned till tomorrow at 9 o'clock A.M.
        Friday June 7th, 1833 Board Met-F.R. CONWAY, Present

Widow DODIER by Louis LABEAUME's representative claiming 3 by 40 arpents of land, see Record Book D, pgs. 306, 7 & 8, Mins. No. 5, pg.
414, produces Livre Terrien No. 2, pg. 38 and a copy of the same.
Also, deed from the heirs of said DODIER to L. LABEAUME. (No. 300,
No. 7, pg. 185)
        Adjourned untill tomorrow at 9 o'clock A.M.
        The Board Met & Adjourned June 8th, 10th & 11th, 1833.
        Wednesday June 12th, 1833 Board Met-F.R. CONWAY, Present

Joseph FENWICK by his legal representative, Jno. SMITH T., claiming
20,000 arpents of land situated on the waters of St. Francis River,
see Mins. No. 5, pg. 421, Record Book C, pg. 504, produces a paper
purporting to be an original concession granted by Z. TRUDEAU, dated
18th August, 1796. (2d, 148, No.7, 243)

Camille DELASSUS by his representative John SMITH, T., claiming 2,400
arpents 34 perches of land, see Mins. No. 5, pg. 539, Record Book C,
pgs. 447 & 8, produces a paper purporting to be an original concession
from Carlos D. DELASSUS, dated 12th October, 1799. Also, a plat of
Survey taken 1st November, 1799 and certified 10th January, 1800, by
Ant. SOULARD.
        Adjourned untill tomorrow at 9 o'clock A.M.
        Thursday June 13th, 1833 Board Met-F.R. CONWAY, Present

In the case of Absalom LINK claiming 510 arpents of land, see Pg. 172
of this Book. Sally WILLIAMS, duly sworn, says that she is in her
70th Year, that she knows the claimant, Absolom LINK, that in the year
1801 or 2, he settled and improved a place adjoining that of her husband, Joseph WILLIAMS. That one Robert YOUNG, who had a grant prior
to LINK improving said land, had the said LINK's improvement included
in his survey.
        Adjourned untill tomorrow at 9 o'clock A.M.
        The Board Met & Adjourned June 14th, 1833.
        Saturday June 15th, 1833 Board Met-F.R. CONWAY, Present

In the case of James MACKAY claiming 30,000 arpents of land, see pg.
3 & 53 of this Book, Claimant produces a paper purporting to be an
original concession, dated 1st of May, 1798 from Manuel GAYOSO de
LEMOS, then Governor General of Louisian, appointing James MACKAY,
Captain of the first company of Militia in Missouri.
        Adjourned untill Monday next at 9 o'clock A.M.
        The Board Met & Adjourned June 17th, 1833.

Tuesday June 18th, 1833 Board Met-F.R. CONWAY, Present

Jacob COLLINS claiming 890 arpents of land situate on Big River, Merrimack, bounded on one side by the said Big River on the upper side
by Hugh MCCULLICK, on the lower side by Mark WIDEMAN and back by public land, by virtue of a settlement right, see Mins. No. 4, pg. 399.
James ROGERS, duly sworn, says that he is about 52 years of age. That
some time in May, 1802, he came on to this country in company with the
claimant. That they arrived time enough to raise a crop of corn. That
he, the deponent, worked a few days for the claimant. That in that
same year the claimant raised corn. That they made a camp at being
too late to build a house. That in 1803, claimant got one
Charles PRUIT to work said place for him and said PRUIT sowed flax and
planted some corn. That said place is under cultivation now and, deponent thinks it has ever been so since the first settling of it. That
there is now about 40 acres under cultivation and never heard that any
body claimed it but the aforesaid Jacob COLLINS. That he never knew
of Jacob COLLINS laying any claims to any other lands. That when
claimant first moved to this country, he had a wife and three children.
That at present there is on the place a hewn two story log house with
shingle roof, a barn, two stables, a well, etc. The deponent further
says that he was absent two years, at Natchez and the Walnut hills,
his absence embracing the time when said COLLINS presented his claim
before the former Board of Commissioners. (Dec. 135, pg. 333)

James ROGERS, Junr., claiming 750 arpents of land on Big River, see
Record Book E, pg. 356, BATES Decision, pg. 94. Jacob COLLINS, duly
sworn, says that he knows the land claimed it being the same tract
confirmed to Hugh MCCULLICK, adjoining the one claimed by deponent,
that he is well acquainted with claimant. That said claimant improved
and cultivated the above mentioned tract and raised corn there on in
1802, to the best of his recollection. That the said James ROGERS
staid with him, the deponent, and did not build a house, he being a
single man. That claimant had a clever little field and raised sound
corn. (2d, 53 No. 7, pg. 188)
    Adjourned untill tomorrow at 9 o'clock A.M.
        The Board Met June 19th, 20th, 1833, and Adjourned without
    doing any business.
        Friday June 21st, 1833 Board Met-Two Comm'rs. Present

Pierre GAMELIN by Charles LUCAS legal representatives claiming 800
arpents of land, see Record Book C, pg. 399, Mins. No. 2, pg. 7, produces a copy of a Deed from P. GAMELIN to Auguste CHOUTEAU. Also, one
from CHOUTEAU to DELASSUS.

Louis DUPRE by Charles LUCAS legal representatives claiming 800 arpents
of land, see Record Book C, pg. 399, Mins. No. 2, pg. 7, produces copy
of Deed from DUPRE to CHOUTEAU and the original Deed from CHOUTEAU to
DELASSUS.

Jean Baptiste CHALIFOUX by Charles LUCAS' representatives claiming 600
arpents of land, see Record Book C, pg. 399, Mins. No. 2, pg. 7, produces copy of a Deed from CHALIFOUX to CHOUTEAU. An original Deed
from CHOUTEAU to DELASSUS and an original Deed for the three tracts
above mentioned from DELASSUS to Charles LUCAS.

James CLAMORGAN by his legal representative Pierre CHOUTEAU claiming
536,904 arpents, being 458,963 acres of land, see Book C, pg. 181, &
Record of Concessions Book No. 3, pg. 7 & following No. 7, produces
a paper purporting to be an original concession dated 9th August, 1796
by Carlos Dehault DELASSUS, Commandant of New Madrid. Also, a plat
of survey made from the 30th January to the 12th of February, 1806,
certified by SOULARD. Also, original Deed of Conveyance from CLAMORGAN
to CHOUTEAU. M.P. LEDUC, duly sworn, says that the decree of concession and the signature affixed to it are in the proper handwriting of
Carlos D. DELASSUS. That the petition and signature to the same, are
in the proper handwriting of James CLAMORGAN, and that the signature
to the record of Survey is in the proper handwriting of SOULARD. See
Book No. 5, pg. 417. (2d, 149, No. 7, 244)

James CLAMORGAN by his legal representative claimin g a tract of land
on the Cuivre and Dardenne (quantity not ascertained), see Record Book
D, pg. 314, Mins. No. 5, pg. 417, Record of Concession No. 3, pg. 21,
No. 13, produces in evidence seven letters purporting to be original
letters from Baron de CARONDELET to James CLAMORGAN. Also, a certificate of James MACKAY and one of Charles SANGUINET, both sworn to before a magistrate. Also, a paper purporting to be a translation from
Spanish into French, of a letter from Baron de CARONDELET to
CLAMORGAN, translated by M.P. LEDUC and certified by him to have been
so translated from the original letter in the proper handwriting of
said CARONDELET. Also, a paper purporting to be a receipt from
Risdon H. PRICE for two original letters from Baron De CARONDELET to
James CLAMORGAN. M.P. LEDUC, duly sworn, says that the saignatures
to the seven above mentioned letters are in the proper handwriting of
Baron De CARONDELET, and that the translation, here above produced, is
a faithful translation made by him from the original letter written
in Spanish in the proper handwriting of said Baron de CARONDELET.
L.E. LAWLESS, agent of claimant, being duly sworn, says that the two
original letters described in the receipt were delivered by him to
said R.H. PRICE on the day of the date of said receipt signed by said
PRICE. To the best of Deponent's belief, the concession in this case,
as recorded, was at same date in possession of said PRICE and that
said PRICE is at present out of this state. Deponent further thinks
that said documents have remained in the possession of said PRICE and
are now out of the reach of the present claimants. Deponent further
states that said PRICE obtained said documents for the purpose of laying the same before Congress in order to obtain the confirmation of
said claim.   (2d, 149, No.7, 244)
     Adjourned untill tomorrow at 9 o'clock A.M.
          The Board Met & Adjourned June 22nd, June 24th, 1833.
          Tuesday June 25th, 1833 Board Met-All Comm'rs. Present

Antoine PRATTE, heirs & legal representatives of by their guardian
Dubreiul VILLARS claiming 500 arpents of land, see Book D, pgs. 71 &
72, No. 5, pg. 481, produces a paper purporting to be an original concession from Carlos Dehault DELASSUS, dated 5th, September, 1799.
The following testimony was taken before L.F. LINN, Esq., one of the
Comm'rs.
State of Missouri, County of St. Genevieve
     John Bste. VALLE, aged about 72 years, being duly sworn, saith
that he was well acquainted with Charles Dehault DELASSUS, late the
Lt. Gov. of Upper Louisian. That the said Charles D. DELASSUS was
the Lt. Gov. in the year 1799 and this deponent further says that he
is well acquainted with the name, signature and handwriting of the
said Charles D. DELASSUS, having frequently seen him write and that
the name and signature of said Charles D. DELASSUS to the concession
from him to the said Antoine PRATTE for five hundred arpents of land
dated the 5th day of September in the year 1799 is in the proper handwriting of the said Charles Dehault DELASSUS. And this deponent,
further says that he was well acquainted with Antoine PRATTE, the
grantee. That he was at the date of the grant aforesaid a citizen &
residenter of the then Province of Louisiana, and that he remained &
continued a citizen residenter of the county till the time of his
death. Sworn to & subscribed before Lewis F. LINN, one of the Commissioners appointed to investigate and report on land claims in Missouri.
This 4th day of May, 1833. L.F. LINN, Comm'r. J.Bste. VALLE

Henry PRATTE, the heirs and legal representatives of claiming six hundred arpents of land situate on the waters of Big River in the late
District of St. Genevieve, now county of St. Genevieve, see Record Bk.
D, pg. 71, produces a paper purporting to be an original concession
from Carlos D. DELASSUS, dated 5th September, 1799. The following
testimony was taken before L.F. LINN, Esq., one of the Comm'rs.
John Bste. VALLE, being duly sworn, says that he was well acquainted
with Charles Dehault DELASSUS. That he was Lt. Gov. in the province
of Upper Louisiana in the year 1799. The deponent further states that
he is well acquainted with the name, signature and handwriting of said
Charles D. DELASSUS. That he has frequently seen him write and that
the name, signature and handwriting to the concession from the said
C.D. DELASSUS to the said Henry PRATTE dated 5th Sept., 1799 for 600

arpents of land, is in the proper name and signature and in the proper handwriting of the said Charles Dehault DELASSUS. And this deponent with the said Henry PRATTE and that he was, at the date of the grant a citizen and residenter of the province of Louisiana. That some time after the date of the grant, the said Henry PRATTE went or was sent to Canada to complete his education he being destined for a Priest. That when his education was finished he again returned to this country and entered on the discharge of his clerical functions and that he continued a citizen and residenter of this country till the time of his death. That the said Henry PRATTE was a branch of a very large and numerous family which emigrated to this country long before the transfer of the country to the United States. Sworn to and subscribed before me Lewis F. LINN, one of the comm'rs., appointed to report and investigate land claims in Missouri. This 4th day of April, 1833.
L.F. LINN, Comm'r.   J. Bste. VALLE

Pierre Auguste PRATTE claiming 600 arpents of land situate on the waters of Big River, see Book D, pg. 70, produces a paper purporting to be an original concession from C. D. DELASSUS, L.G. dated 5th September, 1799.
State of Missouri, County of St. Genevieve.
    John Bste. VALLE, aged about 72 years, being duly sworn, says that he was well acquainted with Charles D. DELASSUS, that he was Lt. Gov. of the province of Upper Louisiana in the year 1799. This deponent further says that he is well acquainted with the name, signature and handwriting of the said Charles D. DELASSUS, having frequently seen him write and that the name, signature and writing to the concession from him to said P.A. PRATTE, dated the 5th September in the year 1799 for 600 arpents of land, is the proper name, signature and handwriting of the said Charles D. DELASSUS, and this deponent further says that he is well acquainted with the said Pierre A. PRATTE and that he was at the date of the concession aforesaid, a citizen and residenter in the then Province of Louisiana and that he has continued a citizen of the country and still is so.
Sworn to & subscribed before me, Lewis F. LINN, one of the Comm'rs. appointed to investigate and report on land claims in Missouri. This 4th day of May, 1833.
L.F. LINN, Comm'r.   J.Bste. VALLE

Joseph PRATTE for himself and others, assignees under him, to wit; Francis VALLE, Charles C. VALLE, Robert T. BROWN & Catherine BROWN, his wife, Walter WILKINSON and Emily WILKINSON, and George BULLETT, the legal representative of Celeste M. ALLEN claiming 20,000 arpents of land situate in the late District of St. Genevieve, now County of Washington, produces a paper purporting to be an original concession from Zenon TRUDEAU, dated 17th October, 1797, see Book D, pgs. 70 & 71, Mins. No. 5, pg. 481, produces also, a plat of survey dated September 4th, 1817 by John HAWKINS. Also, Deed of conveyance from Joseph PRATTE & wife.
State of Missouri, County of St. Genevieve.
    Charles MCLANE, aged 55 years, being duly sworn, deposeth and saith that he is well acquainted with the said Joseph PRATTE and has been to ever since he can remember any body for both this witness and said PRATTE were born in this country and have always and still do, reside in the same. And this witness further says that some 32 or 33 years ago, this deponent does not particularly remember the year, but it was five or six years before the American Government took the possession of this country. He, this deponent in company with one Lewis CANON and one Stephen DALINEL, (now deceased) at the request of Mr. Francis VALLE, then the commandant of this Post, did go to a piece of land situate on the waters of the river St. Francis about sixteen miles distant from the mine a Breton for which he understood a concession had been or would be applied for, and on which it was then understood there was a large quantity of iron ore. That this witness and the others were sent to dig pitts and holes to ascertain the probable quantity of ore and bring samples of the same. And this deponent further says that himself and the others aforesaid did go and dig and work on said land and procure the sameples of the ore as aforesaid and further this deponent says that by instructions to him given he did mark and blaze the trees round the said land to ascertain the boundaries,

56

ant that said Francis VALLE, son of the Commandant, with Walter F., son in law of said Francis VALLE, Senr., and an American whose name he does not recollect, went again the next following year to the same place, for the purpose of showing the iron ore to the American Gentleman. And this deponent further says that it was well known in the country at the time that a concession had been obtained for the said land on which the said iron ore had been found as aforesaid. And he further says that the marks and blazes spoken of before to designate the place, were a few years ago, and perhaps still are visible and conspicuous. That said tract of land is remarkable being almost included in the fork of a creek called by the French thus: La Fourche du Pore, being a part of the waters of the River St. Francis. And this deponent further says that he has several times been on the said tract of land since it was surveyed under the said concession and that the said tract so surveyed is the same which he had to examined and marked and blazed some 30 odd years ago, and that he further knows that the said land has been and is continually claimed under the said concession ever since and now is so and this deponent further says, that he for the claimant built a cabbin on the said land at the time he worked there, and this deponent further says that he, the said, Joseph PRATTE, Robert T. BROWN and Francois VALLE and Walter WILKINSON with hands went in the neighbourhood of said land many years since to make a furnace, forge or bloomery to wash said ore and that they built cabbins, shop and dug for a seat to build the works. Sworn and Subscribed before me, Lewis F. LINN, one of the Comm'rs. appointed to finally settle and adjust land claims in Missouri. This 30th day of October, 1832.

L.F. LINN

his
Charles (X) MCLANE
mark

And also came John Bste. VALLE, Senr., aged about 72 years, who also being duly sworn, as the law directs deposeth and says that he is and was well acquainted Zenon TRUDEAU, late Lt. Gov. of Upper Louisiana. That he was the Lt. Gov. in the year 1797. This deponent says he is well acquainted with the handwriting and the signature of the said Zenon TRUDEAU having seen him write and that the name and the signature of the said Zenon TRUDEAU to the concession to Joseph PRATTE for 20,000 arpents of land dated the 17th day of October in the year 1797, is the proper name, handwriting and signature of the said Z. TRUDEAU. And this deponent further says that he is well acquainted with Joseph PRATTE, the grantee on said concession. That he was at the date of said concession a citizen and resident in the then province of Louisiana and that he has continued a citizen and residenter ever since and still is. That the said PRATTE was a member of a very large and respectable family and had in himself considerable means and property, wereon with such assistance as his connections were able to give him, placed it in his power to render the grant to him available. That he always understood that the grant was in trust for the said Joseph PRATTE to them named and that the family for whose use the said grant was obtained, had collectively large means, a great number of negroes & large stock and that the said PRATTE was influential with the Indians and in connection with his father aided and gave much assistance in keeping peace and maintaining relations of friendship and amity between them and the whites. That in the early settlement of the country, the Indians were troublesome, killed people, drove off the cattle and prevented the spreading of the settlements and it was considered as rendering both the people and the government great and essential services to suppress that disposition of the Indians and maintain peace so as to enable the settlements to expend and spread through the country. Sworn to and subscribed before me Lewis F. LINN, one of the Comm'rs. appointed to investigate and report on land claims in Missouri this 4th May, 1833.

L.F. LINN, Comm'r.   J. Bste. VALLE

Adjourned untill tomorrow at 9 o'clock A.M.

Wednesday June 26th, 1833 Board Met-Two Comm'rs. Present

Pierre TORNAT dit LAJOIE by his legal representatives claiming 600 arpents of land on the Merrimack by settlement right, see Book F, pg. 137, BATES decision No. 5, pg. 104, produces in evidence a sworn certificate of James MACKAY, sworn to and subscribed before

Jer. CONNOR, a Justice of Peace. Also, a certificate of Francis ROY, dated 23rd August, 1819, sworn to before F.M. GUYOT, a Justice of the Peace.

Joachin ROY by his legal representatives claiming 400 arpents of land, see Book F, pg. 138, BATES Decision No. 5, pg. 104, produces a paper purporting to be a concession from Zenon TRUDEAU, dated 3rd February, 1797, see pg. 136.

Jean Bste. DUMOULIN by his legal representatives claiming 800 arpents of land, see Book C, pgs. 334 and 349, Mins. No. 5, pg. 370. It being the same claim presented by John MULLANPHY as assignee of ST. VRAIN (see pg. 87 of this Book) claiming refers to the paper produced by said MULLANPHY.

Parfait DUFOUR and Louis BOLDUC by their heirs and legal representatives claiming 800 arpents of land situate on the waters of Fourche a Duclos (Duclos Fork) County of St. Genevieve, see Record Book B, pg. 88, Minutes No. 5, pg. 403, produces a paper purporting to be an original concession from Carlos D. DELASSUS, dated 25th April, 1803. Joseph PRATTE, being duly sworn as the law directs, deposeth and saith that he was well acquainted with Charles D. DELASSUS, that he was the Lt. Governor of the Province of Upper Louisiana in the year 1803, and this deponent further says that he is well acquainted with the name, signature and handwriting of the said Charles D. DELASSUS having frequently seen him write and that the name, signature and handwriting to the concession from the said Charles D. DELASSUS to the said Parfait DUFOUR and Louis BOLDUC for 800 arpents of land dated the 25th day of April in the year 1803, is the proper name signature and in the proper handwriting of the said Charles D. DELASSUS. And this deponent further says that he was well acquainted personally with the said Parfait DUFOUR and Louis BOLDUC. That at the date of the grant, they were both citizens and residenters of the then province of Upper Louisiana and that they both continued as such citizens and residenters in the country untill the time of their death, which took place some few years since. That they were both industrious labouring men, and both had families, houses and stock to a considerable amount. And this deponent further says that he was well acquainted with Francis VALLE, that he has frequently seen him write. That he was the commandant of the Post of St. Geneviéve in the year 1803, and that the name and signature to the recommendation to the said grant dated the 17th day of April in the year 1803, is the proper name and signature and in the proper handwriting of the said Francis VALLE. Sworn to & subscribed May 3rd, 1803.
L.F. LINN   Jh. PRATTE

And also came Sebastian BUTCHER, aged about 52 years, who being duly sworn as the law directs, deposeth and saith that he was well acquainted with the said Parfait DUFOUR and Louis BOLDUC. That they were citizens and residenters in this country when he came to it in the year 1797, and have hiterto continued to till their deaths. That he knows the tract of land above described, has been on the same, and knows they had small houses usually called cabbins on the same about 28 years ago, and that the cabbins had then the appearance of being several years old, one having been renewed. And he also knows that they continued to occupy the cabbins aforesaid and retained the unmolested possession of the property during their lives. And that when he first saw the land it was called and known as the land of said Parfait DUFOUR and Louis BOLDUC. Sworn to and Subscribed before me, Lewis F. LINN, one of the Comm'rs. appointed to investigate and report on land claims in the state of Missouri, this 4th of May, 1833.
L.F. LINN, Comm'r.   Sebastian (X) BUTCHER
                                                        his mark

John Bste. VALLE, Sr., claiming 7,056 arpents of land being 86 arpents wide by 86 arpents deep making (cannot read) league square, situate on the waters of the River Establishment in the County of St. Genevieve, see Book C, pg. 475, Mins. No. 5, pg. 510, produces a paper purporting to be an original concession from Z. TRUDEAU, dated 4th July, 1796. Joseph PRATTE, aged about 59 years, being duly sworn as the law

directs, deposeth and saith that he is well acquainted with the said
John Bste. VALLE, Sr., the claimant, and also with his handwriting,
having frequently seen him write and that the name, signature and
handwriting to the petition to the Lt. Gov. Zenon TRUDEAU, dated the
15th of June, 1796 is the proper name, signature and handwriting of
said John Bste. VALLE, Sr. And this deponent further says that he
was well acquainted with Francis VALLE and has frequently seen him
write and that the said Francois VALLE was the Commandant of the Post
and district of St. Genevieve in the year 1796, and that the name and
signature and handwriting to the recommendation for said grant dated
the 18th day of June, 1796 is the proper name, signature and handwriting of the said Francois VALLE. And this deponent further says that
he was well acquainted with Zenon TRUDEAU and has frequently seen him
write and that the name, signature and handwriting from him to the
said John Bste. VALLE, dated 4th July, 1796 is the proper name, signature and handwriting of the said Zenon TRUDEAU, and that the said
Zenon TRUDEAU was the Lt. Gov. of the Province of Upper Louisiana in
the year 1796. And this deponent further says that he well knows the
said John Bste. VALLE, the claimant and that he was at the date of the
grant or concession aforesaid and long a citizen and residenter of the
province of Upper Louiaiana and that he has hitherto continued and still
is a citizen and residenter of this country and further, that the said
John Bste. VALLE at the time of the grant or concession aforesaid and
ever since had a large and numerous family, a great number of slaves,
a large stock and was an active enterprising and useful citizen of the
country. And further this deponent says that he knows said VALLE
opened a farm of about 50 arpents more or less, but could not be over
or under much, that VALLE continued to hold and cultivate said land
from the date of concession.
Sworn & subscribed May 3rd, 1833.
L.F. LINN, Comm'r.   Jh. PRATTE

Francois VALLE, Jr., son of Francois VALLE, Sr., deceased, claiming
one league square or 7,056 arpents of land situate in the pinery on
the waters of the River aux Vases or Muddy Creek in the County of St.
Genevieve, see Record Book C, pg. 394, Minutes No. 3, pg. 107, No. 4,
pg. 326, produces a paper purporting to be a petition to the Indendant of Louisiana, dated 10th March, 1802, following which, is a recommendation dated 13th March, 1802 signed by Pierre Delassus DELUZIERE,
Commandant of New Bourbon and an order signed by MORALES, the Intendant General to have the said documents translated and presented to
the fiscal. Also, a certificate signed by Thomas MADDIN, Dep. Surveyor
and others before the Commandant of New Bourbon, (cannot read) demanded
belongs to the Royal Domain. Also, a receipt of MAXWELL dated 13th
March, 1802 for the above papers.
State of Missouri, County of St. Genevieve
    John Bste. VALLE, Sr., aged about 72 years, being duly sworn as
the law directs, deposeth and saith that he has often seen
Francois VALLE, Junr. (the son) write, that he is well acquainted with
him and that the name and signature to the said petition dated 10th of
March, 1802 is the name and signature and in the proper handwriting of
the said Francois VALLE, Jr. And this deponent further says that he
was well acquainted with Pierre Delassus de LUZIERE, that he has often
seen him wirte. That he was the Commandant of the Post and District
of New Bourbon in the year 1802, and the name and signature and handwriting to the recommendation for said grant dated 13th day of March,
1802, is the proper name and signature and in the proper handwriting
of the said Pierre Delassus de LUZIERE. And this deponent further
says that he is well acquainted with the tract of land claimed by the
said Francis VALLE, Jr., and that the said Francis VALLE, Jr., the
claimant, did in the course of the year 1802, build and erect a water
saw mill on the head waters of the River Aux Vases on the said tract
of land, for a grant of which he had petitioned and that the said saw
mill was in complete operation in the spring of the following year,
and continued in such operation untill about the year 1812 or 13, when
it was swept away by an extraordinary high flood. And this deponent
further says that he knows that the said Francis VALLE, Jr., his ser-
vants and workmen resided at the said mill on the said tract during
the time the said mill was in operation. And further this deponent
says that at the date of the application and long before, the said

Francis VALLE, Jr., was a citizen and residenter of this province of Upper Louisiana and has continued and still is a citizen & residenter of the province and of this county. That he was born in the province. Sworn to and subscribed before me, Lewis F. LINN, one of the comm'rs. appointed to investigate and report on land claims in the State of Missouri, this 4th day of May, 1833.
L.F. LINN, Comm'r.   .   J.B. VALLE

And also came John Bste. VALLE, Jr., as a witness, aged about 49 years who being also sworn as the law directs, deposeth and sayth that he was in company with Mr. Thomas MADDIN, Deputy Surveyor to Mr. A. SOULARD, his Catholic Majesty's Surveyor General over the upper parts of the province of Louiaian, when he the said Thomas MADDIN, surveyed the said tract of land of one league square for the said Francois VALLE, Jr., the claimant, that he, this deponent was employed as one of the chain carriers in the making of the said survey. The exact time, he does not now recollect. Sworn to and subscribed before me, Lewis F. LINN, Comm'r., this 20th day of May, 1833.
L.F. LINN, Comm'r.   Bste. VALLE, Jr.
    Adjourned untill tomorrow at 9 o'clock A.M.
        Thursday June 27th, 1833 Board Met-Two Comm'rs. Present

John Bste. VALLE and Francois VALLE, the heirs and legal representatives of the latter, claiming one league square of land or 7,056 arpents, situate in the pinery on the waters of the river aux Vases, County of St. Genevieve, see Record Book C, pgs. 475 and 476, produces a paper purporting to be a petition from the said J.B. VALLE and F. VALLE to the Indendant of the province of Louisiana, dated 11th August, 1801, followed by a recommendation from Pierre D. de LUZIERE, Commandant of New Bourbon, dated 27th February, 1802, and an order of MORALES, the Intendant, to have the papers here mentioned translated into Spanish and afterwards presented to the Fiscal. Also, a certificate signed by Thomas MADDIN, Dep. Surveyor and others certifying that the land demanded belongs to the King's Domain.
State of Missouri, County of St. Genevieve
    Bartholomew St. GEMME, aged about 59 years, being duly sworn as the law directs, deposeth and saith that he was well acquainted with both the said J.B. VALLE and F. VALLE, that they were for many years before the year 1801, and in the years 1801 & 2 citizens and residenters of the province of Upper Louisiana, and that the said J.B. VALLE is still a citizen and residenter of the country, and that the said Francois VALLE continued a citizen and residenter thereof till his death and that his heirs and legal representatives have continued citizens and residenters of the country ever since, and such of them as are living are still so. This deponent further says that the said J.Bste. VALLE and F. VALLE, both had large families of children and many slaves with other property. That they were active, enterprising industrious and usefull citizens. And this deponent further says that he knows the claimants had a saw mill in operation as stated in the petition, in the year 1801 & 2 and that it was usefull to the public. And this deponent further says that he was well acquainted with Pierre Delassus de LUZIERE. That he has seen him write and that the said P.D. DELUZIERE was the Commandant of the Post and District of New Bourbon in the year 1802, and that the name & signature to the recommendation for said grant, dated the 27th of February, 1802 is the proper name and signature and in the proper handwriting of the said Pierre Delassus de LUZIERE. And this deponent further says that the names of Thomas MADDIN, Francois JANIS, Fremon DELAURIERE, L. SARGEAU & Pierre Delassus de LUZIERE to the certificate by them signed, dated the 27th of February, 1802 is the proper name and signatures and in the proper handwriting of the certifyers, that he has seen them write. Sworn to & subscribed before me, Lewis F. LINN, Comm'r., this 27th day of May, 1833.
L.F. LINN, Comm'r.   Bste. ST. GEMME

John Bste. VALLE and Louis BOLDUC, the heirs and legal representatives of the latter claiming 800 arpents of land situate on the Mississippi River in the county of Cape Girardeau, see Book D, pg. 180 & 181, same Book pg. 69 & 70, produces a paper purporting to be an original concession from Henry PEYROUX, Civil & Military Commandant of St. Genevieve,

dated 23rd August, 1788, and granted in pursuance of the Decree of
Manuel PEREZ, Lt. Gov. of Upper Louiaiana, dated 13th August, 1788.
Also, a paper purporting to be an order of Survey from Z. TRUDEAU,
then Lt. Gov. of Upper Louisiana, dated 6th March, 1798.
State of Missouri, County of St. Genevieve
     Bartholomew ST. GEMME, being duly sworn as the law directs, de-
poseth and saith that he was well acquainted with John Bste. VALLE
and Louis BOLDUC, the original claimants. That he knows they were
citizens and residenters of the province of Upper Louisiana in the
year 1788 and the said VALLE is still a citizen and residenter and
the said BOLDUC continued so till his death and his children are
still so. And this witness further says that he was well acquainted
with Henry PEYROUX de la COUDRENIERE, that he has seen him write,
and that the said PEYROUX was the Commandant, Civil & Military of the
Post and District of St. Genevieve in the year 1788 and that the signature and name of the said Henry PEYROUX de la COUDRENIERE to the
recommendation for said grant dated the 1st day of August, 1788 and
to the grant by him made of date the 23rd August, 1788, is the proper
name and signature and in the proper handwriting of the said PEYROUX.
And this deponent further says that he was well acquainted with
Manuel PEREZ, personally. That he knows he was the Lt. Gov. of the
province of Upper Louisiana in the year 1788. And this deponent
further says that he was well acquainted with Zenon TRUDEAU, that he
has seen him write. That he was the Lt. Gov. of the province of upper Louisiana in the year 1798, and that the name and signature to
the warrant or order of Survey for said land dated the 6th day of March
1798, is the proper name and signature and in the proper handwriting of
the said Zenon TRUDEAU. And this deponent further says that in the
year 1788, the said John Bste. VALLE and Louis BOLDUC were both men of
families with slaves and other property. Sworn to and subscribed before me, Lewis F. LINN, Comm'r., this 27th day of May, 1833.
L.F. LINN, Comm'r.   Bste. ST. GEMME

Charles ROBIN and Louis CARON claiming 1,500 arpents of land situate
on the waters of the river Saline, see Book F, pg. 128, produces a
paper purporting to be an original concession dated 4th of April, 1800
from Carlos Dehault DELASSUS.
          Perry County, May 3rd, 1833
     Personally appeared before L.F. LINN, one of the Comm'rs. appoin-
ted for the final adjustment of private land claims in Missouri,
Joseph PRATTE, aged about 59 years, who after being sworn, deposeth
and says that he was well acquainted with Charles ROBIN and
Louis CARON and knows they had possession and a cabin built on this
tract of land named in the concession, previous to their having a
grant for the same. That he knows well the (cannot read) the concession is in the handwriting of Charles D. DELASSUS, former Lt. Gov. of
Upper Louisiana, further that the signature to the recommendation is
in the proper handwriting of Pierre Dehault DELASSUS, former Commandant of the District of New Bourbon, and further that they continued
to hold and use for their benefit and use, said tract of land.
Sworn to and subscribed day & date above written.
L.F.LINN, Comm'r.   Jh. PRATTE

John Bste. PRATTE by his heirs and legal representatives claiming 1,000
arpents of land situate on the waters of Big River, County of St.
Francis, see Book C, pg. 221 & foll. also pg. 71 of this Book, produces
a paper purporting to be an original concession from C.D. DELASSUS, dated 5th September, 1799. Also, a plat of Survey by A. SOULARD, dated
5th, March, 1801.
State of Missouri, County of Washington
Jacob MOSTELLER, a witness aged fifty six years, being duly sworn, deposeth and saith that he was well acquainted with John Bste. PRATTE,
Sr., and with a tract of land of, he thinks, about 1,000 arpents
claimed by him by concession on the waters of Big River in the late
District of St. Genevieve, now county of St. Francis. That he knows
that in the year 1801, the said John Bste. PRATTE had negroes on the
land claimed, a man, woman and children. That some land was cleared
and some small houses put up and he believes some digging was done.
That he saw Mr. MONITEAU (?) who said he was there doing business for
said PRATTE, and that the said tract of land has been inhabited and

and cultivated by said John Bste. PRATTE or those claiming under him
ever since, he had a stock on the farm and was frequently there in
person. Sworn to before me, the Commissioner, this 9th day of May,
1833.
L.F. LINN, Comm'r.   Jacob MOSTELLER

And,also, came John T. MCNEAL, a witness aged about 70 years, who
being duly sworn as the law directs, deposeth and sayth that he was
well acquainted with John Bste. PRATTE, the original claimant. He
also knows the tract of land claimed. That he understood it was
claimed by virtue of a Spanish concession. That in 1802, he saw on
the land a white man, who was said to be the manager of said PRATTE,
and some negroes on the land, and some land cleared, say 7 or eight
acres at least, and the same was in cultivation. That the houses and
field had the appearance of having been of several years standing.
He had oxen at work there, and he saw cattle & hogs there, but does
not know whose they were. Sworn to & subscribed before me, the
Comm'r., this 10th day of May, 1833.
L.F. LINN, Comm'r.   John T. MCNAILL

Also, came John STEWART, a witness aged about 64 years, who being
duly sworn, deposeth and saith that he was well acquainted with the
said John Bste. PRATTE, the original claimant. He also knows the
land claimed. That he understood it was claimed under a Spanish
grant. That he was there in 1801, and frequently passed there afterwards. That he saw John Bste. PRATTE, Jr., acting as a manager for
the claimant. There was some negroes there and in 1803 there was two
fields both in cultivation. That he saw stock of cattle, horses,
hogs, etc. at different times as he passed. That he understood the
same was inhabited and cultivated ever since. Sworn to and subscribed
before me, the Comm'r., this 20th day of May, 1833.
L.F. LINN, Comm'r.   John STEWART
        Adjourned untill tomorrow at 9 o'clock A.M.
            Friday June 28th, 1833 Board Met-Two Comm'rs. Present

Henry PEYROUX, by Henry DODGE & the heirs and legal representatives of
Edward HEMPSTEAD and John SCOTT, claiming 7,760 acres of land situate
on the Mississippi river and on the waters of the Saline, County of
St. Genevieve, see record Book C, pg. 258, Mins. No. 5, pg. 545, Book
F, pg. 258, produces a paper purporting to be an original concession
from Manuel PEREZ, L.G., dated 24th December, 1787. Also, a Plat of
Survey by John HAWKINS, Dep. Surveyor, dated 22nd and recorded by
SOULARD, Surveyor General 26th of February, 1806.
State of Missouri, County of St. Genevieve.
John Bste. VALLE, a witness aged about 72 years, being duly sworn as
the law directs, deposeth and saith that he was well acquainted with
Henry PEYROUX, otherwise called Henry Peyroux de la COUDRENIERE, the
original petitioner for said that he has often seen him write. That
the said PEYROUX at the date of the petition and grant was a citizen
and resident of this country, now the State of Missouri, and was civil and military Commandant at the Post and District of St. Genevieve,
and remained a citizen of the country from thence till long after the
purchase of the country by the American Government. This deponent,
also, says that the signature and name to the petition for said grant
dated the 15th of December, 1787, is the proper name and signature and
in the proper handwriting of said PEYROUX. And this deponent, further,
says that Manuel PEREZ was the Lt. Gov. of the Western Part of Illinois at the date of the grant in the year 1787. And this deponent,
further, says that he is well acquainted with the tract of land claimed
and that the same was at the date of the grant actually inhabited and
cultivated and used as a Saline where much salt, for the use of the
country, was made, and that after the grant aforesaid, the said land
was more or less continually inhabited and cultivated. That there were
several farms on the same and many buildings and houses with furnaces
for the making of salt and that the said property from the date of the
grant till about the year 1824 or 1825 and perhaps longer, was actually
inhabited and cultivated and extensively used in the making of salt,
and that the same was of great and extensive use to the whole country
for many years, and that the said tract of land has always been and
still is inhabited and cultivated and further that the said PEYROUX
was a man of property and useful in the country. And this deponent

further says that at the time said PEYROUX claimed said grant, he
understood that a grant had been formerly made for a part of said
tract as it now stands, which had been purchased by the said
PEYROUX. This witness, further, says that he saw the orders from
the Baron de CARONDELET for the Survey of this land and that in the
order, special instructions were given to respect the lands and lines
of Madame VILLARS and Francis VALLE.
Sworn to & subscribed before me, L.F. LINN, Comm'r., this 17th June,
1833.
L.F. LINN, Comm'r.   J. Bste. VALLE

In the case of Thomas MADDIN, by his legal representatives, claiming
1,500 arpents of land, see pg. 43 of this Book, the following testimony was taken by L.F. LINN, one of the Comm'rs.
State of Missour, County of St. Genevieve
John Bste. VALLE, aged 72 years, being duly sworn as the law directs,
deposeth and sayth that he was and is well acquainted with
Thomas MADDIN, the original grantee. That he knows he was a citizen
and residenter of the country called then the Province of Upper
Louisiana in the year 1799 and for several years before, and that he
has hitherto continued and still is a citizen and residenter of this
country and this deponent, further, says that the said Thomas MADDIN
in the year 1799 was the head of a family. That he had a wife, several children, many slaves and a large stock. That he was an active
enterprising and industrious citizen. Sworn to and subscribed before
me, the subscriber, Lewis F. LINN, one of the commissioners appointed
to investigate and report on land claims in Missouri this 4th day of
May, 1833.
L.F. LINN, Comm'r.   J. Bste. VALLE

In the case of Joseph GERARD & Patrick FLEMING claiming 840 arpents
of land, see P. 167 of this Book. Personally appeared before
L.F. LINN (one of the Comm'rs. appointed for the final adjustment
of private land claims in Missouri) Bste. VALLE, Senr., aged about
72 years, who deposes & says that he was well acquainted with
Patrick FLEMING and Joseph GERRARD, Senr., and knows that they were
inhabitants, long before the change of government to the United States.
Deponent, further, states that he always heard that said FLEMING and
GERARD had a concession for land under the Spanish Government and they
had located the same on flat River, a branch of Big River in the former District of St. Genevieve, but does not recollect the precise
place of their Survey or location.
Sworn to and subscribed May 27th, 1833.
L.F. LINN, Comm'r.   -   J.Bste. VALLE
    Adjourned untill tomorrow 9 o'clock A.M.
        Saturday June 29th, 1833 Board Met-Two Comm'rs. Present

In the case of James CLAMORGAN claiming lands on the Cuivre and Dardenne (See pgs. 179 and following). The following testimony was taken (Pg. 206 & 207 of this book are missing and therefore this claim
cannot be completed)
        Monday July 1st, 1833 Board Met-Two Comm'rs. Present

In the case of the Old Mine concession (See page 28 of this Book),
the following testimony was taken before L.F. LINN, Comm'r.
St. Genevieve, April 29th, 1833
John BOULLIER, being duly sworn, deposes and says that as Curate of
Joachin Parish (Old Mines) he is well acquainted with some of the
original claimants named in this concession, particularly with widow
COLMAN and knows that she has one hundred & sixty five children and
grandchildren, most of whom reside on the concession and great many
on that part, which it is said according to the numbers belongs to
her. Also, that he is well acquainted with Charlot BOYERS wife and
knows they have ninety seven children & grandchildren, nearly all
residing on the concession and on that part which is said belongs to
her according to the number. And, also, they have thirty five children and grandchildren, many of whom reside on the concession, and
that he knows they are generally worthy industrious honest people,
and that they have exerted themselves much with their limited means
to build a church and preserve their religious priviliges. That he

verily believes if many of these old respectable and venerable people
relying on the justice and liberality of the government, were at their
advanced age to be deprived of their lands, they would inevitably sink
under so heavy a calamity.
Sworn to and subscribed, day and date above written.
L.F. LINN, Land Comm'r.   J. BOULLIER
          Board Adjourned untill, tomorrow at 9 o'clock A.M.
               Tuesday July 2nd, 1833 Board Met-Two Comm'rs. Present

John MURPHY by his assignee, Jonah PARK claiming 550 arpents of land
on the waters of Fifi's creek, county of St. Louis, see Record Book C,
pg. 80 & following, Mins. No. 3, pg. 305, No. 4, pg. 396, Records of
Grants in St. Charles & St. Andrew No. 15. Hartley LANHAM, being duly sworn, says that he has known the said Jonah PARK, the present
claimant for upwards of thirty years and that in 1806 on the return
of the witness to this country from a journey to Kentucky, the said
Jonah PARK was inhabiting and improving the above mentioned tract of
land. That he has a stock of horses, cattle, hogs, etc. That the
said tract has been cultivated by through & for him ever since.

Resolved that F.R. CONWAY, Recorder of land titles be, and he is hereby authorised to proceed to Jefferson & Washington Counties in this
state for the purpose of receiving such testimony as may be offered
under the late Act of Congress for the final adjustment of private
land claims in Missouri & the act supplementary thereto. See Resolution passed by this Board on the 18th March last, pg. 130 of this
Book.
          Adjourned untill tomorrow at 9 o'clock A.M.
               Wednesday July 3rd, 1833 Board Met-L.F. LINN, Present

Joseph JARRETT by his legal representatives claiming 640 acres of land
situated at the grand Glaize, Jefferson County. Paschal CERRE, being
duly sworn, deposes and says that he knows that Joseph JARRETT occu
pied and cultivated land on the Grand Glaize Creek in Jefferson County
as early as 1789. The said JARRETT had a dwelling house on the same
and 15 or 20 acres of land in cultivation. Deponent says he saw said
Jarrett on this place for several years.
          Adjourned untill Friday 5th Inst. at 9 o'clock A.M.
               Friday July 5th, 1833 Board Met-L.F. LINN, Present

Louis COYTEUX, Jr., by his legal representatives, claiming 400 arpents
of land, produces a paper purporting to be an original concession from
Carlos D. DELASSUS, dated 18th October, 1799, with a recommendation
from Pierre Delassus DELUZIERE, Commandant of New Bourbon, dated 8th
of October, 1799, the whole headed by a petition from said COYTEUX.
By the recommendation it appears that the commandant of New Bourbon
recommends the said COYTEUX as worthy to obtain the grant which he
asks for as well on account of the signal services of his father in
the quality of Commissioner of Police of the Canton of Bois Brute, as
because the suppliant has no other means of subsistence, but that of
cultivator. Also, the following endorsement is found on the back of
the title papers. No. 17 Depot des titres de concessions d une Terre
accordes au Louis COYTEUX fils, enregistree sons le No. 17. Also:
Rejected for want of a plat of Survey.
                              Signed J.L. DONALDSON
                              Rec. St. Louis

M.P.LEDUC, duly sworn says that the signature to the concession is in
the proper handwriting of Carlos Dehault DELASSUS, that the signature
to the recommendation is in the proper handwriting of P. D. DELUZIERE,
Commandant of New Bourbon, that the signature to the endorsement by
J.L. DONALDSON is in the proper handwriting of said DONALDSON, then
Recorder of land Titles in St. Louis. Deponent, further, says that it
appears by said endorsement that the said DONALDSON rejected the recording of said claim for want of a plat of Survey.

In the case of LAMALICE and others, each claiming 800 arpents of land,
(See pg. 142 & following of this Book) claimants produce part of a
certificate of Survey, which was torn and missing. Said Survey being
a connected plat of 35 tracts of 800 arpents each. M.P.LEDUC, (cannot
read) to said plat and certificate of survey is in the proper hand-

writing of Antoine SOULARD.
Adjourned untill tomorrow at 9 o'clock A.M.
Saturday July 6th, 1833 Board Met-L.F. LINN, Present

Thomas REED, by his assignee W. SLOANE claiming 747 arpents of land,
see Book B, pgs. 246 & 7, Mins. No. 1, pgs. 373 & 375, No. 3, pg.
119 & 127, No. 4, pgs. 335 & 6, No. 6, 460.
State of Missouri, Washington County
Be it remembered that on this 11th January, 1832 before me,
Henry SHURLDS, a Justice of the peace in and for said county, the
following person appeared: Daniel PHELPS aged seventy seven years
and upwards, being duly sworn, deposeth and saith, that some time in
the fall of 1806, he was on the tract of land claimed as above set
forth, and there was at that time a crop of about six or eight acres
of corn grown on said place and a cabin there & occupied and from the
appearance of the place at that time, he believes it must have been
occupied and cultivated two or three years at least before that time
that the place, he understood from both REED and William SLOANE, that
he believes to have been occupied & cultivated ever since the period
above.
Sworn to & subscribed before me, Henry SHURLDS, Justice of the Peace
Daniel PHELPS

State of Missouri, Washington County
I, John C. BRICKER, Clerk of the County (cannot read) and for
said County do hereby certify that Henry SHURLDS, whose name is subscribed to the within affidavit as having taken the same, was at the
time of taking the said affidavit of Daniel PHELPS, an acting Justice
of the Peace within and for said County, duly commissioned and qualified as such and that full faith and credit is due to all his official
acts.
In testimony whereof I have hereunto set my hand and seal of
office at Potosi this 6th day of May, 1833.
(Seal)   J.C. BRICKER, Clerk

Potosi Washington County, May 6th, 1833
Personally appeared before L.F. LINN, one of the Comm'rs. appointed for the final adjustment of private land claims in Missouri,
Mr. Timothy PHELPS, who after being duly sworn, says that he is well
acquainted with the handwriting of Daniel PHELPS (who was deponent's
father). That the signature to the above deposition dated 11th January, 1832, taken before Henry SHURLDS, is in the handwriting of his
father, Daniel PHELPS. Sworn to and subscribed day above written.
L.F. LINN, Comm'r.   Timothy PHELPS

At the same time appeared Dr. Israel MCGREDDY, who after being
duly sworn, deposes and says that he was well acquainted with
Daniel PHELPS and from long personal acquaintance has no hesitation
in saying said PHELPS was a man of respectability, integrity and
truth.   Sworn to and subscribed day above written.
L.F. LINN, Comm'r.   Israel MCGREADY

Andre CHEVALIER by his legal representatives claiming 400 arpents of
land, see Record Book B, pg. 511 & 12, No. 2, pg. 25, No. 4, pg. 515,
produces a paper purporting to be an original concession from
Carlos Dehault DELASSUS, dated 18th October, 1799, preceded by a recommendation from Pierre Delassus de LUZIERE, Commandant of New Bourbon. M.P. LEDUC, being duly sworn, says that the signature to the
concession is in the proper handwriting of Carlos Dehault DELASSUS,
and that the recommendation and the signature affixed to it, are in
the proper handwriting of Pierre Delassus de LUZIERE, then Commandant
of New Bourbon.

Notice of Joseph EVANS to L.F. LINN, Comm'r.
I do hereby request that Lewis F. LINN, Comm'r., do attend at
the Old mines on the 13th of this month to take testimony about the
Old Mine Concession.
11th May, 1833   Jos. EVANS
And on the back of it, the following:
I wave the within request.
12th May, 1833   Jos. EVANS

William RAMSAY, Sr., by his legal representatives claiming 1,100 arpents of land situated on Ramsay's lick, see Book No. 7, pg. 105, B,
pg. 239.   Ira COTTLE, being duly sworn, says that he knows
William RAMSAY in 1802, that he then was cultivating land on Bryan's
Creek at the Saline since called after him, Ramsay's lick. That said
RAMSAY cultivated on a grand scale. Had a considerable stock. Had
quite a large farm and was strong handed. That he understood and believes that about the year, he thinks, 1804, but he is not now certain,
there were several families killed in Ramsay's neighbourhood. That
MCHUGH's family was killed and this was the cause of RAMSAY leaving
said place.

William MCHUGH, alias MCQUE claiming 640 acres joining the tract of
William RAMSAY, Sr., on RAMSAY's lick, (see pg. 499 of this Book).
Ira COTTLE, being duly sworn, says that he well knew MCHUGH. That he
had a considerably large family. That he had a house and a truck patch
on said piece of land adjoining RAMSAY's lick. That MCHUGH was on said
piece of land in 1803, and that his children were killed on said place
by the Indians in 1804.

John Bste. BELLAND, by his legal representatives claiming 480 arpents
of land on the waters of Perruque. Ira COTTLE, being duly sworn, says
that when he first came to this country in 1800, said BELLAND was living on said piece of land. That said BELLAND had a family and several
children. That he had a house and several acres under cultivation.
That this tract is situated on Belland's Creek, so named after the sd
BELLAND.

John DRAPER, by his legal representatives claiming 747 arpents of land
situated on Bob's Creek, see Book B, pg. 257, No. 1, pg. 400, No. 5,
pg. 319. Ira COTTLE, duly sworn, says that some time in 1802, he knew
John DRAPER having a house on Bob's creek. That DRAPER dug a well on
said place.

David MIRACLE claiming 640 arpents of land on the waters of the Dardenne, County of St. Charles, see Book C, pg. 511,No. 5, pg. 457.
Ira COTTLE, duly sworn, says that David MIRACLE's wife came to this
country before her husband, and had a house on said tract of land, as
soon at least as 1803. That it was certainly before the change of
Government.

John RAMSAY by his legal representatives claiming 848 arpents of land
situated on Sandy Creek, Book B, pg. 345, No. 5, pg. 485.
Ira COTTLE, duly sworn, says that he knew John RAMSAY and that said
RAMSAY was married before the change of Government. (2d, No.43, No. 7,
p. 182)

George GURTY by his legal representatives claiming 640 acres of land
near the village of St. Charles, see BATES Mins. p.134, Decisions p.37.
Ira COTTLE, duly sworn, says that he knew said GURTY he thinks it was
about the year 1800. That said GURTY then lived about half a mile
from the village of St. Charles. That he had a house and lived there
with his family and several children. That said GURTY resided there
some time. Deponent does not recollect how long, and then went on
the Dardenne where he died.
                Adjourned untill Monday next at 9 o'clock A.M.
                Monday July 8th, 1833 Board Met-L.F. LINN, Present

Calvin ADAMS' legal representatives in the name of said ADAMS & as
assignee of Patrick LEE, assignee of Joseph MOTTARD claiming 1,340 arpents of land on Mill Creek near the city of St. Louis, see Book B,
pg. 480 & following, Mins. No. 1, pg. 524, No. 3, pg. 323, No. 4, pg.
404 & 5, produces a paper purporting to be a translation of a concession sworn to & subscribed by Peter PROVENCHERE. Also, a translation
of a plat and certificate of Survey. Louis DUBREUIL, being duly
sworn, says that 40 years ago there was, to his knowledge, people
working under MOTTARD, on said piece of land. That he several times
wrote accounts for his father, for produce which his said father had
bought from said plantation. That MOTTARD had there some cattle.
That said place was occupied for a long time by one COTTARD, under
MOTTARD, and Deponent went often on said place to see said COTTARD,

and that said place continued to be occupied by or under MOTTARD,
till his death, which happened a short tine prior to the change of
government. Peter CHOUTEAU, Sr., duly sworn, says that 42 or 43
years ago, Jos. MOTTARD was cultivating said land and had one
COTTARD on said place, as his agent. That said land was cultivated
till MOTTARD's death. That after his death a mullato man lived on
said place. That at MOTTARD's death, said tract was sold and deponent thinks was bought by Patrick LEE. That MOTTARD cultivated said
land for 10 or 12 consecutive years by himself or through him. Deponent further says that the said tract did not interfere with the
commons. Alexander BELLASSIME, being duly sworn, says that he has
been in this country these forty five years. That when he arrived
to this country, the said MOTTARD was inhabiting and cultivating sd
tract of land. That deponent often went on said place to see said
MOTTARD, who had there an orchard bearing fine apples, and the place
continued to be cultivated by or under MOTTARD, till very near the
time of the taking of possession of the country by the American Government.

Charles ROY by John P. CABANNE claiming 2 by 40 arpents of land, see
Livre Terrien No. 4, pg. 2, Book F, pg. 190. Peter CHOUTEAU, Sr.,
being duly sworn, says that he has perfect knowledge of this tract.
That about the year 1780 or there about, it was cultivated by said
ROY, and was so cultivated for 4 or 5 consecutive years till the time
of his death.

Francois HEBERT by John P. CABANNE claiming 2 by 40 arpents of land,
see Livre Terrien No. 4, pg. 2, Book F, pg. 190. Peter CHOUTEAU, Sr.,
duly sworn, says that he is 75 years of age and saw the building of
the first house in St. Louis. That HEBERT cultivated said place for
5 or 6 consecutive years till his death.

Widow DODIER's legal representatives claiming 3 by 40 arpents of land
in the prairie near St. Louis, see Record Book F, pg. 169, Livre
Terrien No. 2, pg. 38, Recorder's Mins. pg. 128, where the same
appears to be confirmed. Peter CHOUTEAU, Sr., duly sworn, says that
he knows the said land was cultivated by said Widow DODIER 12 or 15
years prior to (cannot read) (1780) that the land adjoining St. Louis
were since the said year 1780 partly abandonned through fear of the
Indians.

Joseph ROY by Louis LABEAUME's representatives claiming 600 arpents of
land on the left saide of Bay de Roy, see Book D, pg. 302 & following,
Mins. No. 5, pg. 488, Record of Concessions under the Spanish Government, No. 2, pg. 54, to which claimant refers. Jean TAYON, being duly
sworn, says that during the Spanish Government he saw said ROY living
on said tract of land. That it might be 5 or 6 years prior to the
change of government that said ROY was inhabiting & cultivating said
piece of land.

In the case of Jean Marie CARDINAL claiming 40 arpents of land, see pg.
150 of this Book, claimant produces a paper purporting to be a plat
and certificate of Survey dated 28th February, 1806 by A. SOULARD.
M.P. LEDUC, duly sworn, says that the signature to said plat & certificate is in the proper handwriting of said Antoine SOULARD.

Alexis LOISE's legal representatives claiming 3 by 40 arpents of land,
see Livre Terrien No. 3, pg. 27, to which claimant refers, entered pg.
168 No. 6. Peter CHOUTEAU, Sr., being duly sworn, says that
Alexis LOISE, some time after the year 1780, cultivated said piece of
land during 5 ot 6 years, and that signs of cultivation are yet visible.

Jean Bste. MARTIGNY by his legal representatives claiming 12 arpents
in front (a special location) the ordinary depth, see Book F, pg. 191,
Recorders Minutes pg. 151, Livre Terrien pg. 7, No. 4.
Peter CHOUTEAU, Sr., duly sworn, says that said MARTIGNY had a house
on said land and lived there 4 or 5 years. That he had a corn field
and garden and had the place under cultivation till he sold it.

Baptiste DUCHOUQUET by his legal representatives claiming under a special location, a tract of land situated between the lands granted to Etienne ST. PIERRE and Silvestre LABADIE, on the waters of River Berger, right bank of the Missouri, see Book B, pg. 511, Mins. No. 5, pg. 404, produces a paper purporting to be an original concession from Carlos Dehault DELASSUS, dated December 30th, 1800. M.P. LEDUC, duly sworn, says that the signature to said concession is in the proper handwriting of said Carlos D. DELASSUS, see Book No. 7, pgs. 72 & 78.

Antoine V. BOUIS by his legal representatives F.V. BOUIS claiming 25 by 40 arpents of land situated near YOSTY's plantation, on the Missouri bottom on the road leading from St. Louis to St. Charles (a special location), see Book C, pg. 204, Mins. No. 4, pg. 175 and 184, produces a paper purporting to be an original concession from Zenon TRUDEAU dated November 11, 1796. M.P. LEDUC, duly sworn, says that the decree and signature to the same are in the proper handwriting of said Zenon TRUDEAU.

Hyacinthe ST. CIR's legal representatives claiming sections 9 & 16, Township 46 N. of Range 7 E. of the 5th principal meridian, containing 137 acres & 91/100 of an acre. The same being within the lines of the original survey made by Antoine SOULARD, late Surveyor General of Upper Louisiana under the Authority of the Spanish Government by virtue of a concession granted to H. ST. CIR, see Book A, pg. 267, Mins. No. 1, pg. 23, No. 3, pg. 11 & 391.

Antoine FLANDRIN by his legal representatives claiming 6,000 arpents of land, see Book B, pg. 94 & 5, Mins. No. 5, pg. 420. Claimant refers to Spanish Record of Concessions No. 2, pg. 52.

J.P. CABANNE claiming 2,000 arpents of land, see Book D, pg. 180, Mins. No. 3, pg. 283, No. 4, pg. 386, Spanish Record of Concessions, No. 2, pg. 44.

Jacques CLAMORGAN by his legal representatives William CLARK and W.C. CARR claiming 40 by 80 arpents of land situated on the waters of the Merrimack, see Record Book C, pg. 188 & 189, Livre Terrien, No. 5, pg. 6, Mins. No. 1, pg. 411, No. 5, pg. 519, produce a paper purporting to be an original concession from Zenon TRUDEAU dated 5th of October, 1793. Also, deed of conveyance. M.P. LEDUC, duly sworn, says that the signature to the concession is in the proper handwriting of the said Zenon TRUDEAU.

Regis LOISEL by Jacques CLAMORGAN's representatives claiming 44,800 arpents of land situated Cedar Island on the Missouri, see Book C, pg. 172 & following, Mins. No. 1, pg. 484, No. 4, pg. 500, produces a paper purporting to be an original concession from C.D. DELASSUS, dated March 25th, 1800. Also, a plat certified by Antoine SOULARD and dated November 20th, 1805. Also, a copy of an adjudication of the said land to Jacques CLAMORGAN, certified by M.P. LEDUC the 7th of October, 1805. Also, the affidavit of Antoine TABOT and Pierre DORION, taken before Charles GRATIOT, Judge Court of Common Pleas. M.P. LEDUC, being duly sworn, says that the signature to the decree of concession is in the proper handwriting of Carlos Dehault DELASSUS. That the signature to said plat & certificate is in the proper handwriting of A. SOULARD, and that the signature to the adjudication is in the deponents own handwriting.

Thomas WILKINSON by Alexander MCNAIR's legal representatives claiming 400 arpents on the waters of Fifi's creek, County of St. Louis, see Book D, pgs. 345, 6 & 7, Mins. No. 3, pg. 327 & 8, No. 4, pg. 408, produces a paper purporting to be an original concession from Zenon TRUDEAU, dated December 17th, 1796. Also, Deed from J. WILLIAM to (cannot read first name) SARPY dated March 2nd, 1797. Sheriff's Deed to Alexander MCNAIR dated June 29th, 1808. M.P.LEDUC, duly sworn, says that the decree of concession and signature to it are in the proper handwriting of Zenon TRUDEAU.

Jean Bste. LAMARCHE by Alexander MCNAIR's legal representatives claiming 800 arpents of land originally granted by Zenon TRUDEAU to said LAMARCHE on the 18th of November, 1798, see Book D, pg. 345 & following, Mins. No. 2, pg. 15, No. 4, pg. 512, Book C, pg. 263, produces Sheriff's Deed.

Alexander MCNAIR's legal representatives claiming 1 by 40 arpents of land, Barriere a Desnoyers, see Book D, pg. 345 & following.

David KINCAID claiming 500 arpents of land, see Book B, pg. 189, Mins. No. 1, pg. 219, No. 3, pg. 31, No. 4, pg. 200, produces a paper purporting to be an original concession from Carlos Dehault DELASSUS, dated 14th June, 1803. Also, a plat and certificate of Survey certified by Ant. SOULARD 27th, February, 1806. M.P. LEDUC, duly sworn, says that the signature to the concession is in the proper handwriting of Carlos D. DELASSUS, and the signature to the certificate of Survey is in the proper handwriting of Antoine SOULARD.

David MCKINNEY's legal representatives claiming 500 arpents of land, see Book C, pg. 36, Mins. No. 1, pg. 232, No. 4, pg. 206.

Silvestre LABADIE claims a special location, see Record Book A, pg. 524, Book D, pg. 100, Mins. No. 5, pg. 449.

Isidore LACROIX's representatives claiming 6,000 arpents of land situated Marais tenis Clair, county of St. Charles, see Book C, pg. 281 and Book D, pg. 178, two Surveys, Mins. No. 1, pg. 464, No. 3, pg. 73, No. 4, pg. 225.

William DAVIS's representatives claiming 800 arpents of land in St. Charles County, see Book D, pg. 203, Mins. No. 5, pg. 378 Under BARADA.
        Adjourned until tomorrow at 9 o'clock A.M.
        Tuesday July 9th, 1833 Board Met-L.F. LINN, Present

Old Mine concession, see pgs. 28 & 208 of this Book. The following notice was filed before L.F. LINN, Comm'r., May 6th, 1833.
NOTICE to the Commissioners appointed for the final adjustment of land claims in Missouri.
Land Office at St. Louis, Mo. Register's Office 4th October, 1832
        I hereby certify that applications for the purchase by and proof of, the right of preemption under the Act of Congress of 5th April, 1832, have been filed in this office by Samuel LATIMER, Obediah FERGUSON, N.P. HUBBARD, Jotham CLARK, (cannot read) Andrew CASEY, Charles ROBERT, John SETTLE, Morgan CASEY, Simon RODERICK, Adison DEARING, Wm. CONWAY, Simon RODERICK & John SETTLE, John RICE, Samuel ST. MARIA, John CASEY, Jr., Joseph EVANS, Peter BOYER, Richard MITCHELL, Jas. WILLIAMS, Anthony DUCLOS, Sr. & Anthony DUCLOS, Jr., Patrick LAWLER and Louis BOYER, and have been suspended by reason of their being covered by the unconfirmed land claim called the Old Mine concession or grant to 31 inhabitants.
        Given under my hand this 4th October, 1832
                        Wm. CHRISTY, Register
                By   Edm. T. CHRISTY, Clerk

Personally appeared before L.F. LINN, one of the Comm'rs. appointed for the final adjustment of private land claims in Missouri, Thomas MADDIN, aged ninety three years, who after being sworn, deposes and says that he was Deputy Surveyor under the Spanish and American Governments. Deponent says that he surveyed the tract of land called the Old Mine concession granted to thirty one heads of families. He surveyed the general survey in the year 1804, 3rd of February. Deponent further states that on the 22nd of December, 1805, he run the division lines by running across the original survey and marking a point on each division line, so that each individual might know his claim. Deponent further states that he run the Special lines between claims marked in the plat at the request of the individuals interested, who paid him for the same. Deponent, further, states that at the time, he heard of no complaints or dissatisfaction (cannot read bottom line on this page) made nor untill lately. Deponent, further, states that it appeared to him understood between the claimants, that in the event of

an individual who had made an improvement, being thrown on a tract
where there was no improvement, he was to be paid for his labour.
Sworn to and subscribed May 11th, 1833.
L.F. LINN, Comm'r.   Thos. MADDIN

Personally appeared before L.F.LINN, one of the Comm'rs. appointed
for the final adjustment of private land claims in Missouri,
Charlot BOYER, who after being sworn, deposes and says he came to the
place now called Old Mine in the year 1801, and has continued to reside at the place ever since. Deponent says that he is eighty three
years of age. Deponent, further, states that Bste. VALLE and
C.H.F. Auguste VALLE never resided or cultivated land on the Old Mine
concession. Deponent, further, states that he was well acquainted
with Manuel BLANCO, that he knew of said BLANCO having settled on and
improved a peice of land, which was claimed by Elias BATES and not embraced in the Old Mine concession. Deponent, further, states that sd
BLANCO never resided or cultivated land in the Old Mine Concession.
Deponent, further, states that he was well acquainted with John POTEL,
who came to and resided on the Old Mine concession in the year 1801.
That he commenced that year to build a house barn, after which began
to open lands for cultivation. Deponent, further, states that
John POTEL, Jr., resided in a house built on the same land, which
house joins the one built by his father. Deponent, further, states
that he was well acquainted with Pierre MARTIN and knows that said
MARTIN never resided or cultivated land in the Old Mine Concession.
Deponent further states that he was well acquainted with Jacob WISE,
that said WISE never resided on or cultivated in the Old Mine Concession. Deponent, further, states that he was well acquainted with
Alexander DUCLOS, who inhabited and cultivated land in the Old Mine
Concession. Deponent says he cannot recollect the time, but it was
many years since, perhaps in 1803 or 1804. Deponent, further, says
said tract of land so inhabited and cultivated lies near a place formerly inhabited by N. HEBERT in the Old Mine concession. Deponent,
further, states that he was well acquainted with his nephew,
Charles ROBERT, who inhabited and cultivated land on the Old Mine Concession, which was a tract of land adjoining one inhabited and cultivated by Alexander DUCLOS, their house being the width of one arpent
apart. Deponent, further, states that he was well acquainted with
Joseph PRATTE. That said PRATTE never resided on or cultivated land
in the Old Mine Concession. Deponent, further, states that he was
well acquainted with Francis MANICHE. That said MANICHE built a
house and cultivated a garden in the Old Mine Concession. He does
not recollect distinctly at what time, but it was many years since.
Same place is now inhabited by Francois PORTEL.
L.F. LINN, Comm'r.   Charles BOSEY
        Caledonia, Washington County.
Personally appeared before L.F. LINN, one of the Comm'rs. appointed
for the final adjustment of private land claims in Missouri.
John STEWART, formerly, Deputy Surveyor in Upper Louisiana, who after
being sworn, deposes and says that he came to this state and to this
now Washington County in the month of November, 1800 and transacted
business at and near the Old Mines in part of the years 1803 and 1804.
That he was well acquainted with the persons residing at that time in
the Old Mine Concession and knows that Joseph PRATTE resided in St.
Genevieve and never was to his knowledge an inhabitant of the Old Mine
Concession. Deponent, further, states C.F. Augt. VALLE, alias
Charles C. VALLE, was at that time very young and did not reside on
the old Mine Concession. Deponent, further, states that
Pierre MARTIN was a resident of Mine a Breton and never resident of
the Old Mines nor did he cultivate land on the same to the best of
his knowledge. Deponent, further, says he never heard of knew of
Bste. VALLE's being an inhabitant of the Old Mine Concession. He always heard or his residence being at St. Genevieve. Deponent, further states that Manuel BLANCO resided on a piece of land belonging to
Elias BATES adjoining Old Mine Concession. He never knew or heard of
said BLANCO residing on or cultivating land on the Old Mine Concession.
Deponent, states that Jacob WISE was a resident of Mine Breton and
never an inhabitant of the Old Mine Concession to the best of his
knowledge. Sworn to and subscribed May 14th, 1833.
L.F. LINN, Comm'r.   John STEWART

Old Mine May 11th, 1833
Personally appeared before L.F. LINN, one of the Comm'rs. appointed
for the final adjustment of private land claims in Missouri,
Mr. John TRIMBLE, who after being duly sworn, deposes and says that
he came to reside in Upper Louisiana in the year 1811 (now State of
Missouri); that he is acquainted with the general Survey of the Old
Mine Concession and knows that lots marked one & two on the plat of
Survey and said to belong to the VALLE's had no appearance of habi-
tation or cultivation up to the year 1817, when George BRECKENRIDGE
built a cabbin on the same and made no other improvement.
Sworn to and subscribed May 11th, 1833.
L.F. LINN, Comm'r.   J.F. TRIMBLE
        Adjourned untill tomorrow at 9 o'clock A.M.
            Wednesday July 10th, 1833 Board Met-L.F. LINN, Present

Auguste P. CHOUTEAU, son of Peter CHOUTEAU, Sr., claiming 800 arpents
situated in Washington County, see Book C, pg. 379, Mins. No. 1, pg.
282, No. 5, pg. 536, produces a paper purporting to be an original
concession from Carlos Dehault DELASSUS, dated January 5th, 1800.
M.P. LEDUC, duly sworn, says that the signature to the concession is
in the proper handwriting of the said Carlos Dehault DELASSUS.
The following testimony was taken before L.F. LINN, Comm'r.
Thomas MADDIN of lawful age, being first duly sworn, deposeth and
saith that he was deputy surveyor under the Spanish and American Governments in Upper Louisiana. That while he was Deputy Surveyor under the Spanish Government, he surveyed for Auguste CHOUTEAU, son of
Dr. Pedro CHOUTEAU, eight hundred arpents of land in virtue of a concession from the Lt. Gov. of Louisiana, situated in Washington County
at this time, formerly St. Genevieve. This Survey was made on December 6th, 1803, and it is bounded as follows: beginning at a post and
making corner at Elias BATES land, thence S. 20 E, 285 French Perches
to a stone near a post oak, S. 70 W. 280 perches to a Stone near a
post oak, 28 to N. near a white oak, N. 20 W. 285-1/2 perches to a
stone near a post oak, thence N. 70 E. 280 perches to the beginning.
Deponent, further, states that at the time this tract of land was surveyed by him, there was a house on the same occupied by the agent of
the said CHOUTEAU, who had negroes working on the land at the time.
Deponent further says he filed a regular plat of survey of this tract
which was recorded at St. Louis and to which deponent refers.
Sworn to and subscribed May 11th, 1833
L.F. LINN, Comm'r.   Thos. MADDIN

Joseph BECQUET, Sr., being duly sworn, deposes and says that
Auguste CHOUTEAU, son of Pierre CHOUTEAU, occupied and cultivated by
their agent Nicholas BOILEVIN a concession of land, quantity not recollected, joining the old mine tract or concession. Deponent, further, states that they had in cultivation in the year 1804, four or
five acres of land. He says said CHOUTEAU had said land in possession some years before. How many, he does not remember. Deponent,
says that before and during the year 1804, he had negroes working on
this property owned by said CHOUTEAU, as well as hired white men in
the employment of Mr. CHOUTEAU or his agent. Deponent, further,
states, said tract of land has been occupied and cultivated ever since
by CHOUTEAU or persons under him.
Sworn to and subscribed May 11th, 1833.
L.F. LINN, Comm'r.   Jh. BEQUET
        Adjourned untill tomorrow at 9 o'clock A.M.
            Thursday July 11th, 1833 Board Met-L.F. LINN, Present

In the case of Joseph ROY, by Louis LABEAUME's representatives
claiming 600 arpents of land on Bay de Roy, see pg. 219 of this book.
Francois CAILLON, being duly sworn, says that during the government
of Zenon TRUDEAU and about two years after Carlos D. DELASSUS was
Lt. Gov., the said Joseph ROY inhabited and cultivated said tract of
land, that he lived on the same with his wife and two children and
that he, the deponent, passed a winter with the claimant on said
place. Deponent, further, says that the claimant was driven off the
said place by the Indians.
        Adjourned untill tomorrow at 9 o'clock A.M.

Friday July 12th, 1833 Board Met-Two Comm'rs. Present

In the case of Absalom LINK claiming 510 arpents of land, see pg. 172 of this Book. Lewis MUSICK, duly sworn, says that at the latter end of 1803 or beginning of 1804, he was requested by the claimant to go with him on a piece of land, which claimant wanted to improve. They went together and said claimant laid the foundation of a cabbin, deadened some trees and cut his name on the bark of a tree.. Deponent further says, he heard that claimant had made an improvement, which had been taken away from him by a survey subsequently made, which induced claimant to make this new improvement.

   Adjourned until tomorrow at 9 o'clock A.M.
         Saturday July 13th, 1833 Board Met-Two Comm'rs. Present

David HORINE claiming 640 acres of land situate in the Richwood settlements Washington County on the waters of Big River, see Mins. No. 5, pg. 432, produces a plat of survey dated 12th Febr., 1806.
John STEWART, being of lawfull age and duly sworn upon his oath, doth depose and say that on the 12th day of February, 1806, he surveyed for David HORINE a settlement or head right of 639 acres 19 and 10 poles including David HORINE's improvement. That as to the settlement of the above claim, this deponent does not positively know, but there were large white oak stumps that from appearances had been made into rails within the survey. Deponent says he neither saw a house nor inclosure at the time above mentioned, though, there might have been without his seeing them, as his duties only required of him to make the survey.
Sworn to and subscribed May 9th, 1833
L.F. LINN, Comm'r.   John STEWART

Benjamin HORINE, being duly sworn, deposes and says that he was in the country before the change of government. That he is now fifty six years of age. That David HORINE came to the country in 1801. That at the time he came to the country, which was later than David HORINE had come, there were corn stalks in David HORINE's filed. At the time he came David HORINE was living on the place, which was afterwards surveyed by John STEWART for him, in the surveying of which he assisted in carrying the chain. That the land surveyed for David HORINE was on the waters of Big River.
L.F. LINN, Comm'r.   Benjamin HORINE
         Adjourned untill Monday next at 9 o'clock A.M.
            The Board Met & Adjourned July 15th, 1833; no business.
            Tuesday July 16th, 1833 Board Met-Two Comm'rs. Present

Therese CRELY, wife of Tesson HONORE, by his legal representatives claiming 3,528 arpents of land on the North side of the River Scoffrion, see Book D, pg. 129, Spanish Record of Concessions Book No. 2, pgs. 58, 59 & 60, Mins. No. 5, pg. 396. Col. Tho. H. BENTON, being duly sworn, says that about 14 or 15 years ago, the original concession, on which this claim is founded, was put in his hands by Therese CRELY Tesson HONORE and her son Louis HONORE to draw a petition upon it to Congress for its confirmation. The Petition was drawn and sent on and he believes the original was sent on with it; that he has since, at the request of those interested, searched among his papers for the original, but could not find them and does not know where they are. Deponent, further, says that the papers had all the appearances of genuine papers.

In the case of James CLAMORGAN claiming land on Cuivre and Dardenne, see pg. 179 of this Book. Jean Elie THOLOZAN, being duly sworn, says that he believes it was about the year 1816 that he gave to Risdon H. PRICE the concession and all the papers he had in his possession at the time of this claim, in order to have said claim presented to Congress for confirmation. That he has heard that said PRICE is now out of this state and does not know where those papers are and neither to whom to apply for them.
   Adjourned untill tomorrow at 9 o'clock A.M.
      (Cont. p. 249, Book 7
         The Board Met & Adjourned July 17th, 18th, 19th, 20th, 22nd,
         23rd, 1833 without attending to any business.

Wednesday July 24th, 1833 Board Met-All Comm'rs. Present

Gabriel LORD by his assignee Vincent CARICO claiming 400 arpents of
land, see Book C, pg. 323, Book No. 5, pg. 448, produces a paper purporting to be an original concession from Carlos Dehault DELASSUS, dated July 12th, 1800. Also, a plat of survey executed by MACKAY and
certified by SOULARD August·3rd, 1803 for 360 arpents. M.P. LEDUC,
duly sworn, says that the signature to the concession is in the proper
handwriting of Carlos D. DELASSUS, and the signature to the plat & certificate of Survey is in the proper handwriting of Antoine SOULARD.
Daniel QUICK, being duly sworn, says that about the year 1811 or 1812,
the said Gabriel LORD hired hands to work on said land and that it has
been cultivated ever since·by said LORD, or under him.

In the case of David COLE claiming 400 arpents of land, see pg. 9 of
this book, the following testimony was taken before A.G. HARRISON, Esq.,
one of the Comm'rs. Isaac VANBIBBER, Sr., being duly sworn, says that
in the year 1800, he (witness) rented of David COLE a field in Darst
bottom on the Missouri river, consisting of some three or four acres,
which field witness put in corn that year and raised a crop on it that
said field had been cultivated the year preceding by said COLE, that
said COLE had a cabbin on said tract of land and lived there. That
said place has been in cultivation ever since, and is the place where
one Zachariah MOORE now lives. That said place or tract of land was
bounded by Joshua DODSON claim, Joseph HAINE's, David DARST, by my
own, William HAYS & Col. Daniel BOONE's & by the Missouri river. That
Darst bottom is sometimes called Femme Osage Bottom.
Loutre Lick, June 26th, 1833
A.G. HARRISON, one of the Comm'rs.
      Adjourned untill tomorrow at 9 o 'clock A.M.
            The Board Met & Adjourned July 25th, 1833; no business.
            Friday July 26th, 1833 Board Met-All Comm'rs. Present

Auguste GAMACHE by his legal representatives claiming 300 arpents of
land under a concession from Carlos Dehault DELASSUS, dated December
20th, 1799. See Record Book C, pg. 319.
      Adjourned untill tomorrow at 9 o'clock A.M.
            The Board Met & Adjourned July 27th, 29th, 30th, 31st,
      Aug. 1st, 2nd, 3rd, 4th, 5th, 6th, 1833.
            Wednesday August 7th, 1833 Board Met-All Comm'rs. Present

In the case of Gabriel CERRE by Josiah MCCLANAHAN claiming 300 arpents
of land, see pg. 151 of this book. Andre LANDREVILLE, being duly
sworn, says that under the Spanish Government, he knows that
Gabriel CERRE at his own expence made and built a bridge over the
Rivisseau de pierre. That said bridge was of great public utility,
and that he, the deponent, passed many a time on said bridge.
      Adjourned untill tomorrow at 9 o'clock A.M.
            The Board Met & Adjourned August 8th, 9th, & 10th, 1833.
            Monday August 12th, 1833 Board Met-All Comm'rs. Present

Louis DESNOYERS by his legal representatives claiming 800 arpents of
land, see Book F, pg. 96, Recorder's Mins. pg. 40. Laurent REED,
duly sworn, says that Louis Desnoyers cultivated said land about 40
years ago and continued to inhabit and cultivate the said tract of
land for about 5 or 6 years consecutively, when he was plundered and
driven away by the Indians.

Bazile DESNOYERS by his legal representatives claiming 800 arpents of
land on the right bank of the Marameck, see Book F, pg. 96.
Laurent REED, duly sworn, says that Bazile DESNOYERS cultivated said
tract of land about 40 years ago and continued to inhabit and cultivate the same for about 5 or 6 years consecutively untill he was
plundered and driven away by the Indians.
      Adjourned untill tomorrow at 9 o'clock A.M.
            The Board Met & Adjourned Aug. 13th, 1833; no business.
            Wednesday August 14th, 1833 Board Met-All Comm'rs. Present

Charles TAYON, Jr., by his legal representatives claiming 800 arpents
of land, see Book C, pg. 366, Mins. No. 5, pg. 506, produces a paper

purporting to be an original concession from Carlos D. DELASSUS, dated 18th October, 1802. Also, depositions taken November 14th, 1817 before Andrew WILSON, J.P. Also, Deeds of conveyances. M.P.LEDUC, duly sworn, says that the signature to the concession is in the proper handwriting of Carlos Dehault DELASSUS.

Adjourned untill tomorrow at 9 o'clock A.M.

The Board Met & Adjourned Aug. 15th, 16th, 1833; No Business.

Saturday August 17th, 1833 Board Met-All Comm'rs. Present

In the case of Auguste GAMACHE claiming 300 arpents of land, see pg. 238 of this Book. Paul ROBERT, being duly sworn, says that in the year of the earthquakes in this country, to wit; in 1811, he was employed by Jeremiah CONNOR, then the Sheriff of St. Louis County, to aid in surveying the above mentioned tract. That said survey embraced also, as witness understood, a tract of 1,050 arpents belonging to the claimant and John Baptiste GAMACHE jointly, and that the claimant, Auguste GAMACHE, was present when the tract was surveyed. That he was informed CONNOR had a judgement against Jno. Bste. GAMACHE, and his object was to ascertain the situation of the land to enable him to give a description of the tract for the purpose of exposing it to public sale. That in, or about, the year 1816, Mr. Philip FINE, rented the said 300 arpents tract of Auguste GAMACHE, and he, the deponent, owing FINE, paid part of the rent for him to GAMACHE and that he always understood the tract to belong to said GAMACHE. That about 31 or 32 years ago, he saw corn growing on this tract and, as well as he can recollect, the field contained some 8 or 10 acres.

Adjourned untill Monday next at 9 o'clock A.M.

The Board Met & Adjourned Aug. 19th, 1833; No Business.

Tuesday Aug. 20th, 1833 Board Met-All Comm'rs. Present

Charles ROGER by his legal representatives claiming one lot of 150 ft. square and a tract of land of 1-1/2 arpents in front by 40 in depth, situated in prairie a Catalan, see Book F, pg. 182, Livre Terrien No. 3, pg. 9, produces a paper purporting to be an original concession from Francisco CRUZAT, dated 25th June, 1775. M.P. LEDUC, duly sworn, says that although he never saw said CRUZAT write, he really believes the signature to the said concession to be in his proper handwriting, as he, the deponent, had many opportunities when he was employed by the Spanish Government, to see said CRUZAT's signature to official papers.

Adjourned untill tomorrow at 9 o'clock A.M.

The Board Met & Adjourned Aug. 21st, 1833; No Business.

Thursday Aug. 22nd, 1833 Board Met-All Comm'rs. Present

In the case of Auguste GAMACHE claiming 300 arpents of land, see pg. 238 & 244 of this Book. Joseph GAMACHE, duly sworn, says he knows that 26 years ago, Auguste GAMACHE went with his, the deponent's, father, to J. BRINDLEY, who was then working on said land and told him it was his Auguste GAMACHE's land by virtue of a concession granted to him by the Spanish Government, but said BRINDLEY did not mind him and continued to work on said land.

Adjourned untill tomorrow at 9 o'clock A.M.

Friday Aug. 23rd, 1833 Board Met-All Comm'rs. Present

Samuel NEALE by his legal representatives claiming 800 arpents of land situated on the waters of the creek of mine a Breton, see Book C, pg. 498, produces a paper purporting to be an original concession from Carlos D. DELASSUS, dated November 29th, 1799. The following testimony was taken before L.F. LINN, one of the Comm'rs. John Bste. VALLE, aged about 72 years, being duly sworn as the law directs, deposeth and saith that he was well acquainted with Francois VALLE. That he has often seen him write. That he was the Commandant of the Post and District of St. Genevieve in the year 1799, and that the name and signature and handwriting to the recommendation to the Lt. Gov., dated the 22nd day of November, in the year 1799, is the proper handwriting of the said Francois VALLE. And this deponent, further, says that he was acquainted with Charles D. DELASSUS, that he has frequently seen him write. That the said C.D. DELASSUS was the Lt. Gov. of the Province of Upper Louisiana in the year 1799, and that the name, signature and handwriting to the concession from him to the said Samuel NEAL, dated the

29th day of November in the year 1799, is the proper name and signa-
ture and in the proper handwriting of the said Charles D. DELASSUS.
Sworn to and subscribed before me, Lewis F. LINN, one of the Comm'rs.
appointed to investigate and report on land claims in the State of
Missouri, this 4th day of May, 1833.
L.F. LINN, Comm'r.   J. Bste. VALLE

And, also, came John T. MCNEAL, a witness aged about 70 years, who
being duly sworn as the law directs, deposeth and saith that he was
well acquainted with Samuel NEAL, the original Grantee. That he was
a citizen and residenter in the Province of Upper Louisiana in the
year 1799. That he understood he had obtained a grant for land from
the Spanish Government and that he had prepared and started to make
an improvement thereon. That he was informed the land granted was on
the waters of Mine a Breton Creek or river. That he laboured with the
said Samuel NEAL in the furnace of Moses AUSTIN.
Sworn to & subscribed before me, Lewis F. LINN, Comm'r., this 8th day
of May, 1833.
L.F. LINN, Comm'r.   John T. MCNEAL

Jacob NEAL by his legal representatives claiming 800 arpents of land
situated on the waters of the river or creek of Mine a Breton, see
Book C, pg. 497, produces a paper purporting to be an original concession from Charles D. DELASSUS, dated the 29th day of November, 1799.
The following testimony was taken before Lewis F. LINN, Esqr., one of
the Comm'rs.
State of Missouri, County of St. Genevieve
     John Bste. VALLE, aged about 72 years being duly sworn as the law
directs, deposeth and saith that he was well acquainted with
Francois VALLE. That he has often seen him write. That the said
Francois VALLE was Commandant of the Post and District of St. Genevieve
in the year 1799, and that the name, signature and writing to the recommendation for said grant dated as aforesaid is the proper name and
signature and in the proper handwriting of the said Francois VALLE,
the Commandant as aforesaid. And this deponent, further, says that he
was well acquainted with Charles D. DELASSUS, that he has often seen
him write. That he was the Lt. Gov. of the said province of Upper
Louisiana in the year 1799, and that the name, signature and handwriting to the said concession from him to the said Jacob NEAL, dated the
29th day of November in the year 1799, is the proper name and signature
and in the proper handwriting of the said Charles Dehault DELASSUS.
Sworn to and subscribed before me, L.F. LINN, one of the Comm'rs. appointed to investigate and report on land claims in Missouri, this
4th day of May, 1833.
L.F. LINN, Comm'r.   J. Bste. VALLE

And, also, came John T. MCNEAL, a witness aged about 70 years, who
being duly sworn as the law directs, deposeth and saith that he was
well acquainted with Jacob NEAL, the original claimant, that he saw
him in this country, then called the province of Upper Louisiana in
the year 1799. That he was then a citizen and residenter of the
country. Had a wife and nine children. That he understood he had
obtained a grant for land from the Spanish Authorities, situated on
the Creek of River of Mine A Breton. That he understood it to be the
intention of the said NEAL to erect a powder mill on the land granted,
but that before he could carry the same into effect, he died.
Sworn to and subscribed before me, Lewis F. LINN, Comm'r., this 8th
day of May, 1833.
L.F. LINN, Comm'r.   John T. MCNEAL
     Adjourned untill tomorrow at 9 o'clock A.M.
          Saturday Aug. 24th, 1833 Board Met-All Comm'rs. Present

Walter FENWICK by his legal representatives claiming 10,000 arpents
of land situate near Mine a la Motte, see Minutes No. 5, pg. 422, Book
D, pgs. 41 & 43, produces a paper purporting to be an original concession from Zenon TRUDEAU, dated Aug. 23rd, 1796. The following testimony was taken before L.F. LINN, Esq., one of the Comm'rs.
State Of Missouri, County of St. Genevieve
     John Bste. VALLE, Sr., being duly sworn as the law directs, de-
poseth and saith that he is about 72 years of age. That he was well

acquainted with Zenon TRUDEAU. That he was the Lt. Governor of the
Province of Upper Louisiana in the year 1796. And this deponent,
further, states that he is well acquainted with the name, signature
and handwriting of the said Zenon TRUDEAU. That he has often seen
him write and that the name, signature and handwriting to the said
concession from Zenon TRUDEAU to said Walter FENWICK for the quantity of 10,000 arpents of land, dated the 23rd day of August, in the
year 1796, is the proper handwriting, name and signature of the said
Zenon TRUDEAU. And the deponent, further, says that he was well acquainted, personally, with Walter FENWICK, the grantee that the said
(pgs. 252 & 253 are missing from this Minutes Book).
Monday August 26th, 1833 Board Met-All Comm'rs. Present

Leo FENWICK claiming 500 arpents of land situated between the waters
of Apple Creek and Cape St. Come, see Minutes Book No. 5, pg. 423,
produces a paper purporting to be an original concession from
Zenon TRUDEAU, dated June 10th, 1797. The following testimony was
taken before L.F. LINN, Comm'r.
John Bste. VALLE, Sr., aged about 72 years, who being first duly sworn as the law directs, deposeth and says that said Z. TRUDEAU
was the Lt. Gov. in the then Province of Upper Louisiana in the year
1797. That this deponent was well acquainted with his name, signature and handwriting having frequently seen him write and that the
name, signature and hand writing to the concession from him to
Leo FENWICK dated the 10th of June, 1797 for 500 arpents of land is
the proper handwriting, name and signature of the said Z. TRUDEAU.
And this deponent, further, saith that he was and is well acquainted
with the said Leo FENWICK, the grantee and that he was at the date of
the grant a citizen and residenter in the then Province of Upper
Louisiana, and that he has continued a citizen and residenter ever
since, and still is so (except where absent on a visit or for the purposes of education).
Sworn to and Subscribed before me L.F. LINN, one of the Comm'rs. for
the settlement of land claims in Missouri, this 4th day of May, 1833.
L.F. LINN, Comm'r.   J. Bste. VALLE

Tuesday Aug. 27th, 1833 Board Met-All Comm'rs. Present

Thomas MADDIN, Sr., claiming 2,000 arpents of land, the residue of a
concession originally for 6,000 arpents situated on the waters of
River Aux Vases, see Minutes Book No. 4, pg. 470, Book A, pg. 516,
BATES Dec. pg. 35, produces a paper purporting to be an original con-
cession from Charles Dehault DELASSUS, dated 15th January, 1800, with
an additional permit to take the said quantity of land in two different places, and also, a recommendation from Pre. Delassus DELUZIERE,
Commandant of New Bourbon. The following testimony was taken before
L.F. LINN, Esq., one of the Comm'rs.
State of Missouri, County of St. Genevieve
John Bste. VALLE, aged about 72 years, being duly sworn as the
law directs, deposeth and saith that he was well acquainted with
Pierre Delassus DELUZIERE. That he has frequently seen him write,
that he was the Commandant of the Post and District of New Bourbon in
the year 1800, and that the name and signature to the recommendation
for said grant dated the 10th of January in the year aforesaid is the
proper name and signature and in the proper handwriting of the said
Pierre Delassus DELUZIERE. And this deponent, further, says that he
was well acquainted with Charles Dehault DELASSUS. That he has frequently seen him write. That he was the Lt. Gov. of the Province of
Upper Louisiana in the year 1800, and the the name and signature and
handwriting to the said concessions from said Charles D. DELASSUS,
(cannot read) January in the year 1800, and of the 15th of March, in
the same year to said Thomas MADDIN for said 6,000 arpents of land, is
the proper name and signature and in the proper handwriting of the said
Charles Dehault DELASSUS. And this deponent, further, says that at the
date of the grants aforesaid, the said Thomas MADDIN was a citizen and
residenter of the then, province of Upper Louisiana, that he had a large
family, slaves, stock and other property and was enterprising and industrious and that the said MADDIN has from thence hitherto and still
is a citizen and residenter in the country. That he opened a large
farm and built a great mill and saw mill on some of the land conceded

to him. Sworn to and subscribed before me, L.F. LINN, one of the
Comm'rs. appointed to investigate and report on land claims in the
State of Missouri, this 4th day of May, 1833.
L.F. LINN, Comm'r.   J.Bste. VALLE

Charles VALLE by his legal representatives claiming 4 arpents of
land in front by 40 arpents. in depth, situated at Glaize a Bequette
and Mississippi, see Livre Terrien No. 4, pg. 4, Book F, pg. 190.
Jean Baptiste MAURICE, alias CHATILLON, being duly sworn, sayth that
he was born on the 4th of March, 1759 at the town of Kaskaskins, Ill.
That he came to St. Genevieve in or about the year 1766 or 7. That
he travelled several times from St. Genevieve up to St. Louis and
Carondelet and resided at Carondelet ever since 1787 or 1788. That
about the year 1783 or 1784, the said Charles VALLE inhabited & cultivated the said tract of land. That he, said deponent, did put up
at the house of said Charles VALLE on said tract of land several
times untill the year 1787 or thereabout, when said claimant moved
from said tract of land on account of Indian depredation.
        Adjourned untill tomorrow at 9 o'clock A.M.
              Wednesday Aug. 28th, 1833 Board Met-Two Comm'rs. Present

Adrien LANGLOIS by his heirs and legal representatives claiming 1,500
arpents of land, situate District of St. Genevieve. The original conconcession in this case is not produced, the same, as is stated, being
lost, destroyed or mislaid by time and accident, but claimant produces
a copy thereof dated October 24th, 1799 by Charles D. DELASSUS. Also,
copy of the recommendation of Pierre Delassus DELUZIERE. Also, a plat
of Survey from the registers office to shew that the same has been
reserved from sale, etc. Book E, pg. 236, No. 5, pg. 451. The following
testimony was taken before L.F. LINN, Comm'r.
State of Missouri, County of St. Genevieve
        Paschal DETCHMENDY aged 71 years, being duly sworn as the law di-
rects, deposeth and saith that he was well acquainted with
Adrien LANGLOIS, that he was a residenter in this country and that he
continued to reside in the country for many years before and after the
country was purchased by the United States. That he never saw the
original concession relied on, but that he always understood he had a
grant or concession for land within a few miles of the town of St.
Genevieve. And he, further, states that he saw the said LANGLOIS at
work on the said land which he understood had been granted to him.
That there was a house and field thereon, and that the same was always
claimed by him during his life time and by his representatives ever
since. Sworn to and subscribed before me, L.F. LINN, one of the Comm'rs.
appointed to finally settle and adjust the titles and claims to lands
in the State of Missouri, this 29th day of October, 1832.
L.F. LINN, Comm'r.   P. DETCHMENDY

And, also, came Bartholomew St. GEMME, aged 58 years, who being, also,
sworn as the law directs, deposeth and saith that he has examined the
above and foregoing deposition of Paschal DETCHMENDY and that he personally knows substantially the same facts. Sworn to and subscribed
before me, Lewis F. LINN, one of the Comm'rs. appointed to finally settle and adjust land claims in Missouri this 29th day of October, 1832.
L.F. LINN, Comm'r.   B. ST. GEMME
        Adjourned untill tomorrow at 9 o'clock A.M.
              Thursday Aug. 29th, 1833 Board Met-Two Comm'rs. Present

Hipolite BOLON by his legal representatives, Israel DODGE &
Rufus EASTON claiming 18 arpents of land in front by 40 arpents in
depth, situated at Bois Brule adjoining the land of Mr. PATTERSON, see
Book C, pg. 492 & 3, No. 3, pg. 320, No. 4, pg. 402, produces a notice
to the recorder dated July 17th, 1807. Also, a certificate of the late
Lt. Gov. Charles Dehault DELASSUS.

Michael LACHANCE claiming 72 arpents of land situated on the waters
of the St. Francis, for record of concession see Book C, pg. 387, produces a plat of survey by Thomas MADDIN and certified by SOULARD April
30th, 1805. The following testimony was taken before L.F. LINN, one
of the Comm'rs.
State of Missouri, County of St. Genevieve.
Nicholas Caillote LACHANCE aged about 49 years, being duly sowrn as

the law directs, deposeth and saith that he is well acquainted with
the claimant Michel LACHANCE. That he was a citizen and residenter
in the province of Upper Louisiana in the year 1800 and for some time
before. That he is still a citizen and residenter of this country.
That in the year 1805, he assisted in the surveying the land claimed.
That he carried the chain. That he knows the land claimed. Sworn to
before me Lewis F. LINN, Comm'r. this 31st May, 1833.
L.F. LINN, Comm'r.   Nicholas (X) Caillote LACHANCE
                                                 his mark
        Adjourned untill tomorrow at 9 o'clock A.M.
          Friday Aug. 30th, 1833 Board Met-Two Comm'rs. Present

State of Missouri, County of St. Genevieve
Whereas Col. John Bste. VALLE of the county of St. Genevieve in the
town of St. Genevieve in the State of Missouri has been frequently
called on as a witness to testify in relation to land claims in
Missouri and wheras from the number of depositions given by him, some
doubt might exist in the mind of some persons. The Government of the
truth or accuracy of his statements. Now, I, Lewis F. LINN, one of
the Comm'rs. appointed to investigate and report on land claims in
Missouri, and before whom the most of the depositions of Col. VALLE
have been taken, I take this occasion with pleasure to state and certify that I have personally known Col. VALLE for twenty three years.
That he is an aged, wealthy, meritorious and highly respectable citizen of the county, who has all his life maintained the highest reputation for integrity and truth, and that there is not one spot or
stain in his character known to me, or ever heard of by me. That he
has been called on thus frequently, exclusively from the motive of
the case that most of the old inhabitants of the county having depar-
ted this life, but himself and two others are able to prove the facts
required and I have no hesitation in stating that the most implicit
faith and reliance can, ought and may be placed in all the statements
and testimonies which he has given or may give in relation to the
subject matter. This statement is made and filed, out of Justice to
Col VALLE that it may serve him and the people in the event of my absence from the Board.
                        L.F. LINN, Comm'r.
        Adjourned untill tomorrow at 9 o'clock A.M.
          The Board Met & Adjourned Aug.31st, Sept. 2nd, 3rd, 4th,
          5th,6th, 7th, 9th, 10th, 11th, 12th, 13th, 14th, 16th, 17th,
          18th, 19th, 20th, 21st, 23rd, 24th, 25th, 26th, 27th, 28th,
          30th, Oct. 1st, 2nd, 3rd, 4th, 5th, 7th, 8th, 1833.
          Wednesday Oct. 9th, 1833 Board Met-All Comm'rs. Present

In the case of ST. VRAIN, by John SMITH T., claiming 10,000 arpents
of land (see pg. 6 of this Book). John SCOTT, aged about 51 years,
being duly sworn, says that in the year 1810, he was employed by
John SMITH T., as his agent and attorney to attend at St. Louis with
the concession to said ST. VRAIN named in the deposition of
Joseph PRATTE, and to file the same for record with the recorder, and
to attend to the claim before the Board of Commissioners and for that
purpose he had put and placed in his hands and possession, the original concession from the Baron de CARONDELET to said ST. VRAIN, for
10,000 arpents of land, together with the petition preceding the
grant, and that both, the petition and the grant, were written in a
fair, intelligible hand, entirely free and clear of all blots, erasures and interlinations, and that he verily believes if the record
of the said petition and grant, presents any other aspect than those
of a fair, clear, intelligible paper, it must be entirely owing to the
mistake, negligence or want of room or accuracy in the person, who may
have committed or placed the same of Record. The following testimony
was taken before L.F. LINN, Esq., on the 3rd of May last.
Joseph PRATTE, witness, aged about 59 years being duly sworn as the
law directs, deposeth and saith that he has had in his hands and possession and frequently seen & examined the original petition and grant
aforesaid from the Baron de CARONDELET to said ST. VRAIN, both before
and after the same was sold and transfered by said ST. VRAIN to
John SMITH T., and that both the petition and the grant were written
in a fair, intelligible hand, entirely clear of all blots, erasures
or interlinations, and that he verily believes if the record of the

said petition and grant, presents any other aspect than that of a
fair, clear, intelligible paper, it must be entirely owing to the
mistake, negligence or want of accuracy in the person who may have
committed or placed the same of Record. Sworn to and subscribed
May 3rd, 1833. Signed Joseph PRATTE, L.F. LINN, Comm'r.
         Adjourned untill tomorrow at 9 o'clock A.M.
              The Board Met & Adjourned Oct. 10th, 11th,& 12th, 14th,1833.
              Tuesday Oct. 15th, 1833 Board Met-Two Comm'rs. Present

The Inhabitants of the County of Chicot present to the Board a petition relating to the de VILLEMONT claim, which petition is filed, by
order of the Board among the papers of this office.
         Adjourned untill tomorrow at 9 o'clock A.M.
              The Board Met & Adjourned Oct. 16th, 1833.
              Thursday Oct. 17th, 1833 Board Met-Two Comm'rs. Present

Jacques de ST. VRAIN's children claiming 4,000 arpents of land, under
the same concession produced by John MULLANPHY, see pg. 89 of this
Book, it being the same tract of land claimed by said MULLANPHY as
assignee. Albert TISON, duly sworn, says that at the time the concession for the said tract of 4,000 arpents of land was granted to said
ST,VRAIN, he had then four children to wit; Charles, Felix, Odelle &
Ceran. That said ST.VRAIN had, altogether nine children of whom 8
are now alive to wit; Charles, Ceran, Odelle, Isabelle, Savigny,
Domitille, Emma & Marcellin, and Felix, who died last year, leaving
a widow and four children. That at his death said ST.VRAIN was insolvent. That said ST.VRAIN sold said tract of land to
Jno. MULLANPHY for 12+1/2 cents an arpent, and received in payment goods
at an enormous price. The witness verily believes that said
MULLANPHY did not give more in real value for said land than 2 cents an
arpent. That said ST.VRAIN was not obliged to sell the said tract of
land for the support of his children, but did it unfortunately to suit
his own purposes. That he was not authorised by any authorities to
sell said property. Claimmants, for the purpose of showing that the
Spanish Government had made concessions to the said Jacques ST. VRAIN
without any stipulations in favour of his children, refers to the
following concession: One for 2,350 arpents dated in 1799, Surveyed
in 1801, another for 900 arpents, being a complete grant made by
MORALES dated 22nd April, 1802 & 3rdly, one for 10,000 arpents dated
in 1796.
         Adjourned untill tomorrow at 9 o'clock A.M.
              Friday Oct. 18th, 1833 Board Met-Two Comm'rs. Present

In the case of the Old Mine claim, the following testimony was taken
by F.R. CONWAY, Esqr. This day personally appeared Jacques BON before me, F.R. CONWAY, Recorder of land titles acting as a Comm'r. for
the final adjustment of private land claims in Missouri, this 6th day
of July, 1833 and being sworn, says that he is nearly 58 years of age
and that he is not interested for or against the part of the grant
about which he deposes or gives testimony. He says he settled in the
Old Mines in Washington County in the year 1801, and has resided there
ever since. When he came there, Charles BOYER, Bernard COLEMAN,
John POTEL, Joseph BOYER, John POLITE, Robert POLITE, P. BOYER,
Louis BOYER & Alexander COLEMAN resided there on small improvements,
having been there but a short time on what was afterwards surveyed to
31 persons by Thomas MADDIN about two years after this. That
BOILEVIN came to this (cannot read) and informed him he was obtaining
signatures to a petition in order to procure a concession for the land
on which they were residing, agreeing as this offiant then understood
that each of the settlers should have the improvement he had made and
that a village should be laid off on the land, and in this way, obtained their consent to sign the petition. This officiant does not
know who did sign, or the number, but has been informed that 32 were
obtained, but when or how the grant was obtained, he does not recollect.
He heard about that time, the names of some who had signed the petition
were stricken off without their consent, and others added to the petition before the grant was obtained, or about that time. The grant No.
l was granted to Bazile VALLE, No. 2 was granted to Charles FRANCIS,
Auguste VALLE' neither of whom ever lived on or cultivated the land
either before or since the grant was obtained. No. 5 was granted to

Pierre MARTIN, No. 6 to Jacob BOISE, neither of whom ever lived on, or cultivated the land. No. 7 was granted to Alexander DUCLOS and No. 8 was granted to Charles ROBERT, neither of whom ever lived on or cultivated his own land. They resided on the land granted to Jacob BOISSE, near where N.G. HEBERT resided. No. 9 was granted to Joseph PRATTE, who never lived on or cultivated the land. No..10 was granted to Francis MANICHE, he never lived on, or cultivated the land where his grant was made, he resided on the concession No. 4, as this officiant thinks. No. 11 was made to Amable PARTENOY, No. 12 to Joseph BLAY, No. 13 to Francis ROBERT, No. 14, to L. BOYER, neither of whom lived on or cultivated the land granted to him, nor did any one of the persons to whom a grant was made at the Old Mines as numbered & surveyed by Thomas MADDIN. This affiant assisted in making the survey of the exterior boundary. It was made by running all the lines, but the closing line, this was not run as this affiant believes, neither were the subdivision lines ever run by Thomas MADDIN between each grant. He run across each and stuck posts about the center of the tracts in 1805 or 6, at the request of those interested, and should this grant be confirmed, the improvements of those who did not settle, will be on the grants of other who never settled or improved. Several of those to whom a grant was made claimed land by settlement on the same place where they cultivated within the bounds of this survey, and some to whom a grant was made here, got land in other places. Of those claiming now, Jacob BOISSE is one. This affiant knows that Alexander DUCLOS did not live on this tract more than two years at any time, nor did Robert live on this survey three years before he sold it. Both of these persons settled under BOYER (Jos.) who had the land enclosed and they built in his enclosure, one of whom was his son-in-law and the other his nephew. Jos. BOYER lived on lot No. 6, granted to Jacob BOISE, and DUCLOS & Robert lived to the south of him. Robert POLITE & Francis MANICHE both resided on grant No. 4, granted to John POTEL. MANISH did not reside here more than one year. And further saith not.
Signed   Jacques (X) BON   Sworn to and subscribed before me,
                his mark   this 6th day July, 1833.
                    Signed   F.R. CONWAY

John TRIMBLE, being sworn, says that John POTEL lives on Lot No. 5 granted to P. MARTIN, he does not reside on the grant made to John POTEL, and N.P. HIBBARD formerly resided on lot No. 6 granted to Jacob BOISE. And, further, saith not. signed, John TRIMBLE.
Sworn to & subscribed before me the 9th day of July, 1833.
Signed F.R. CONWAY

Amable PARTENAY, appeared this day before me, F.R. CONWAY Recorder of land titles acting as a Comm'r. for the final adjustment of private land claims in Missouri, who being sworn saith that while he resided in St. Genevieve, he saw in the possession of Francis VALLE, who was Commandant, a petition for land at the Old Mines in Washington County. He offered to add thereto this affiant's name & finally did do so, asking for 400 arpents of land French measure. This affiant says this was in the year 1796 or 97, as it was shortly before he moved to Potosi in Washington County, which was in 1799. This petition contained the names of 31 persons. Some time after he went to Potosi, he thinks in 1802 or 1803, he was informed that Moses AUSTIN had a number of grants and was going to survey them at the old Mines and when the surveyor went there to survey said AUSTIN's claims, those who were interested & had settled there prevented him from making the survey believing that they owned the land, or ought to have it, having petitioned for it. This affiant went immediately to St. Genevieve to look for the petition & grant if any had issued on the petition that he had signed, but found neither or grant either there or at St. Louis.. While at St. Louis the Commandant (cannot read) informed this affiant if he would prove that a petition had existed, he might obtain from Francis VALLE, the Commandant at St. Genevieve, a copy of the first petition & he would give a grant for the land. This affiant went back to St. Genevieve and obtained certificates from different citizens there proving the existence, or that a petition had existed for this land, to 31 petitioners or applicants. The said Francis VALLE directed his clerk to make out a petition intended to be a copy of the original according to the instructions of LASSUS. Instead of this, he

left off the name of five, at least, who had been on the first petition and put on five who were not on the first petition, and the said
VALLE as this affiant believes, presented this petition & obtained
the grant of 400 arpents to each of the 31 petitioners. The out
boundary lines of this survey was made by Thomas MADDIN. This affiant
had become bound to him for the payment of his fees, but he does not
recollect at what time it was made, but not long after the grant was
made, but he did not at that time run the division lines, but claimed
his fees & sued for them, but could not recover them. Afterwards in
1806 or 1807, as this affiant thinks, the said MADDIN came back to
finish the survey and numbered them by a lottery drawn by two individuals. They were numbered from 1 to 31 both inclusive, to this several of the claimants objected as they might lose their improvements
but it was done not withstanding, and the survey was made by running
across each grant about the middle from East to West. This affiant
has no interest at this time. He has owned grants, but sold them
without any recourse on him. This affiant is 67 years of age and one
amongst the first settlers in this part of the country.
Signed   Amable PARTENOY
Sworn to & subscribed before me the 6th day of July, 1833
signed F.R. CONWAY

This day personally appeared Amable PARTENAY before me, F.R. CONWAY,
as aforesaid, who being duly sworn, says that he has no interest in
this claim and that he is 67 years of age. He knows that
Jacques BON settled in the Old Mines in the year 1801 and has been
cultivating a farm there ever since. He has been married for a number of years, but he does not know at what time. He still lives on
siad land & has had possession ever since he first settled the land
on which he lives. This affiant was one amongst the first settlers
in this part of the country.   Signed Amable PARTENOY
Sworn to and subscribed before me, this 6th day of July, 1833,
signed F.R. CONWAY
        Adjourned untill tomorrow at 9 o'clock A.M.
            Saturday Oct. 19th, 1833 Board Met-Two Comm'rs. Present

In the case of Nicolas BOISLEVIN claiming 400 arpents of land, see
pg. 60 of this Book, the following testimony was taken before
F.R. CONWAY, Esqr. John STEWART of lawful age, being first duly
sworn, deposeth & saith in the above case that John SMITH T., who
claims under the above Nicolas BOISLEVIN, as this affiant has heard,
had possession of the land surveyed for said Nicolas, situated in
the then District of St. Genevieve, now county of Washington, in the
year 1804. Said BOISLEVIN had possession thereof in the year 1803.
This affiant hauled mineral from them that year. BOISLEVIN had been
living there for some time previous as appeared from the age of the
buildings and improvements upon said. This affiant would, further,
show that the aforesaid John SMITH T., who represents the said
Nicolas BOISLEVIN, has, from the said year 1804 down to the present
time, been in the occupancy of the aforesaid tract of land. This
affiant was personally well acquainted with said Nicholas and, further,
this deponent saith not.
Subscribed, John STEWART
Sworn to and subscribed before me this 5th day of July, A.D. 1833.
signed F.R. CONWAY
        Adjourned untill Monday next at 9 o'clock A.M.
            The Board Met & Adjourned Oct. 21st, 22nd, 23rd,24th, 25th.
            26th, 28th, 29th, 30th, 1833.
            Thursday Oct. 31st, 1833 Board Met-All Comm'rs. Present

In the case of Gabriel CERRE claiming 300 arpents of land, see pages
151 & 241 of this Book. Hyacinthe LECOMTE, duly sworn, says that he
is about 58 years of age. That he knows perfectly well that
Gabriel CERRE caused a bridge to be built at his own expence on the
Ruisseau de pierre. Witness says further that said bridge was of the
greatest utility to the public. That by the old road there was almost
an impossibility of passing with loaded carts. That himself has had
his cart loaded with hay, very often overturned on said old road. That
when said bridge was built the Spaniards had possession of the country
and that as soon as said bridge was erected all the inhabitants abandoned the old raod. That it was built some time before the Americans

took possession of the country, but cannot recollect how long before.

Gabriel CERRE claiming 800 arpents of land, see pg. 2 of this Book. The Board are unanimously of opinion that this claim ought to be confirmed to said Gabriel CERRE or his legal representatives according to the concession.   (No. 1)

Pascal CERRE claiming 7,056 arpents of land, see pg. 3 of this Book. The Board are unanimously of opinion that this claim ought to be confirmed to said Pascal L. CERRE or to his legal representatives according to the concession.   (No. 2)

James MACKAY by his heirs claiming 30,000 arpents of land, see pg. 3. The Board, after a minute examination of the original papers, see no cause to entertain the belief that they are fraudulent or antidated as urged against the confirmation by the U.S. agent, before the former Board.   They are unanimously of opinion that this claim ought to be confirmed to said James MACKAY or his legal representatives. (No. 3)

Jacques ST.VRAIN by his assignee, John SMITH, T. claiming 10,000 arpents of land, see pg. 6. The Board remark that they are satisfied that there existed such concession which was presented to the former Board, as appears from their minutes, and then no objections made to it. They are also satisfied that the interlineations mentioned in said minutes as existing in the record of said concession, are merely the completing of words, abreviated by the Recorder for want of room. The Board are unanimously of opinion that this claim ought to be confirmed to said Jacques ST.VRAIN or his legal representatives according to the concession. (No. 4)

David DELAUNAY claiming 800 arpents of land, see pg. 5 of this Book. The Board are unanimously of opinion that this claim ought to be confirmed to said David DELAUNAY or his legal representative according to the concession. (No. 5)

Richard CAULK claiming 4,000 arpents of land, see pg. 6 of this Book. The Board are unanimously of opinion that this claim ought to be confirmed to said Richard CAULK or his legal representatives according to the concession. (No. 6)
       The Board Adjourned untill tomorrow at 9 o'clock A.M.
         Friday Nov. 1st, 1833 Board Met- All Comm'rs. Present

M.P. LEDUC claiming 7,944 arpents of land, it being the balance of 15,000 arpents of which 7,056 arpents have been confirmed. The Board are unanimously of opinion that this claim of 7,944 arpents being the balance of the said 15,000, ought to be confirmed to the said M.P. LEDUC or his legal representatives according to the concession. The Board after examining minutely the original concession produced in this case, see no cause to support the suggestion made by the agent of the United States, before the former Board of there being an erasure in the same. (No. 7)

Louis TAYON by his legal representatives claiming 800 arpents of land, see pg. 367 of Book C, produces a paper purporting to be an original concession from Carlos Dehault DELASSUS, dated 18th October, 1802, Book 5, pg.513.

James MCDANIEL claiming 1,800 arpents of land, see pg. 9 of this Book. The Board are unanimously of opinion that this claim ought to be confirmed to the said James MCDANIEL or his legal representatives according to the concession. (No. 8)

Old Mine Concession for 12,400 arpents of land granted to 31 heads of families, see pgs. 28, 208, 225 & 276. The Board are unanimously of opinion that this tract of 12,400 arpents ought to be confirmed to the 31 heads of families, or to their legal representatives according to the concession. (No. 9)

In the case of Camille DELASSUS claiming 2,400 arpents of land, see pg. 175 of this Book. Genl. Bernard PRATTE, duly sworn, says that the signature to the concession is in the proper handwriting of

C.D. DELASSUS, and that he knows that the petitioner, Camille DELASSUS, was an inhabitant of this country at the date of the grant.

In the case of ST.VRAIN by Jno. SMITH, T. claiming 10,000 arpents of land, see pg. 6 & 271 of this Book, claimant withdraws the depositions taken before the District Court.

David COLE claiming 400 arpents of land, see pg. 9 of this Book. The Board are unanimously of opinion that this claim ought to be confirmed to said David COLE or his legal representatives according to the concession for 400 arpents and not to the extent of 430 arpents shown by the plat of survey. (No. 10)

John BASYE claiming 1,600 arpents of land, see pg. 10 of this Book. The Board are unanimously of opinion that this claim ought to be confirmed to said John BASYE or to his legal representatives according to the concession. (No. 11)

Toussaint CERRE claiming an Island, see pg. 10 of this Book. The Board are unanimously of opinion that this claim ought to be confirmed to said Toussaint CERRE or his legal representatives according to the tenor of the concession. (No. 12)

Auguste CHOUTEAU claiming 7,056 arpents of land, see pg. 12 of this Book. The Board are unanimously of opinion that this claim ought to be confirmed to said Auguste CHOUTEAU or his legal representatives according to the concession. (No. 13)

Pierre Delassus DELUZIERE claiming 100 arpents of land, see pg. 13 of this Book. The Board are unanimously of opinion that this claim ought to be confirmed to the said Pierre Delassus DELUZIERE, or his legal representatives, according to the concession. (No. 14)

Pierre MENARD claiming 400 arpents of land, see pg. 15 of this Book. In this case the following testimony was taken before L.F. LINN, Comm'r.
State of Missouri, County of Cape Girardeau
Jonathan BUIS, being duly sworn, according to law, deposeth & saith that some time in the month of June, 1799, he was at the mouth of Apple Creek and saw BERTHEAUME, who then resided there. He had two log houses or cabbins and some cleared land under fence, a garden, etc. And, further, this deponent states that he was at the same place in the year 1804 or 1805, and the same BERTHEAUME, (whose given name he does not recollect) still resided there. signed
Jonathan BUIS
Sworn to & subscribed Oct. 17th, 1833.
Signed L.F. LINN, Comm'r.
The Board are unanimously of opinion that this claim ought to be confirmed to said Pierre MENARD, or his legal representatives according to the concession. (No. 15)

Francois SAUCIER claiming 7,800 arpents of land, it being the balance of 8,800 arpents of which 1,000 have been confirmed. see pg. 15 of this Book, for confirmation see BATE's decision pg. 41. The Board are unanimously of opinion that 7,800 arpents of land, being the balance of the said 8,800 arpents, ought to be confirmed to the said Francois SAUCIER, or his legal representatives, according to the concession. (No. 16)
    The Board Adjourned untill tomorrow at 9 o'clock A.M.
        Saturday Nov. 2nd, 1833 Board Met-All Comm'rs. Present

Charles Dehault DELASSUS claiming 30,000 arpents of land. see pg. 16. The Board are unanimously of opinion that this claim ought to be confirmed to the said Charles Dehault DELASSUS or his legal representatives according to the concession. (No. 17)

Francois CAILLON claiming 1,600 arpents of land, see pg. 13 of this Book. The Board are unanimously of opinion that this claim ought to be confirmed to the said Francois CAILLON, or to his legal representatives according to the concession. (No. 18)

The Sons of VASQUEZ, each claiming 800 arpents of land under a concession from Charles Dehault DELASSUS, see pg. 17. The Board remark
that they can see no cause for entertaining the idea that the said
concession was not issued at the time it bears date, as intimated in
the minutes of the former Comm'rs. The Board are unanimously of
opinion that this claim ought to be confirmed to the said Benito,
Antoine, Hipolite, Joseph and Pierre VASQUEZ, or their legal representatives according to the concession. (No. 19)

Aaron QUICK claiming 800 arpents of land, see pgs. 18 & 113. The
Board are unanimously of opinion that this claim ought to be confirmed to the said Aaron QUICK, or his legal representatives according to the concession. (No. 20)

Peter CHOUTEAU, Sr., claiming a special location situated 20 arpents
above St. Charles, see pg. 18 of this Book. The Board are unanimously of opinion that this claim ought to be confirmed to the said
Peter CHOUTEAU, Sr., or to his legal representatives according to the
concession. (No. 21)
    The Board Adjourned untill Monday next at 9 o'clock A.M.
         Monday Nov. 4th, 1833 Board Met-All Comm'rs. Present

Louis LORIMIER claiming 944 arpents of land, it being the balance of
8,000 arpents of which 7,056 have been confirmed, see pg. 19 of this
Book. For Confirmation, see BATES decision, pg. 67. The Board are
unanimously of opinion that 944 arpents of land ought to be confirmed
to the said Louis LORIMIER, or his legal representatives according to
the concession. (No. 22)

Charles Dehault DELASSUS claiming 12,944 arpents of land, it being
the balance of 20,000 arpents, of which 7,056 have been confirmed,
see pg. 20 of this book. The Board are unanimously of opinion that
12,944 arpents of land ought to be confirmed to the said
Charles Dehault DELASSUS, or his legal representatives according to
the concession. (No. 23)

Antoine DUBREUIL claiming 10,000 arpents of land, see pg. 31 of this
Book. The Board are unanimously of opinion that this claim ought to
be confirmed to the said Antoine DUBREUIL, or his legal representatives according to the concession. (No. 24)

Marie Valle VILLARS claiming 7,056 arpents of land, see pg. 34. The
Board are unanimously of opinion that this claim ought to be confirmed
to the said Maria Louisa Valle VILLARS, or her legal representatives
according to the concession. (No. 25)

Francois VALLE claiming 7,056 arpents of land, see pg. 35 of this Book.
The Board are unanimously of opinion that this claim ought to be confirmed to the said Francois VALLE, or his legal representatives, according to the concession. (No. 26)

Baptiste LABRECHE claiming 500 arpents of land, see pg. 46 of this
Book. The Board are unanimously of opinion that this claim ought to
be confirmed to the said Baptiste LABRECHE, or his legal representatives according to the concession. (No. 27)

St. Gemme BEAUVAIS claiming 1,600 arpents of land, see pg. 37 of this
Book. The Board are unanimously of opinion that this claim ought to
be confirmed to said St. Gemme BEAUVAIS or his legal representatives
according to the concession. (No. 28)
    The Board Adjourned untill tomorrow at 9 o'clock A.M.
         Tuesday Nov. 5th, 1833 Board Met-All Comm'rs. Present

Raphael ST. GEMME, BEQUET & others claiming 1,600 arpents of land,
see pg. 40 of this Book. The Board are unanimously of opinion that
this claim ought to be confirmed to the said Raphael ST. GEMME,
Baptiste BEQUET, Vital ST. GEMME, and Barthemi ST. GEMME, or their
legal representatives according to the concession. (No. 29)

Thomas MADDIN claiming 1,500 arpents of land, see pg. 43 of this Book. The Board are unanimously of opinion that this claim ought to be confirmed to the said Thomas MADDIN, or his legal representatives according to the concession. (No. 30)

William JAMES claiming 600 arpents of land, see pg. 48 of this Book. The Board are unanimously of opinion that this claim ought to be confirmed to the said William JAMES, or his legal representatives according to the concession. (No. 31)

Charles Fremon DELAURIERE claiming 300 arpents of land, see pg. 50 of this Book. The Board are unanimously of opinion that this claim ought to be confirmed to the said Charles Fremon DELAURIERE, or his legal representatives, according to the extent of the survey of 402 arpents unless it conflicts with claims previously granted, and then to the extent that it does not conflict and in no event, under 300 arpents. (No. 32)

Mathew RAMEY claiming 1,056 arpents of land under a settlement right by his assignee George GORDON, see Book No. 4, pg. 438, B, pg. 348, Daniel B. MOORE, duly sworn, says that in 1803, he frequently saw Mathew RAMEY and Nathan RAMEY, his son, pass & repass before his, the witness, residence, and it was said they were improving a place in the neighbourhood. That early in the spring of 1804, witness went on the land claimed and saw said RAMEY and his son, chopping and split- ting rails and clearing lands, and had, to the best of his recollection, a nursery of fruit trees, a small enclosure, and a kind of cabbin or shed to shelter themselves. That he has good reasons to believe that the said RAMEY died on said place, as he knows that his family resided there for several years. Leannah GREAGER, duly sworn, says that Mathew RAMEY, in 1803, had apple trees planted, a well dug, and a garden. That in the same year, 1803, said RAMEY raised a crop of corn. She, further, says that she heard the said Mathew RAMEY say that he had a grant for the said tract of land. That said Mathew RAMEY died on said place.

Manuel LISA claiming 6,000 arpents of land, see pg. 52 of this Book. The Board are unanimously of opinion that this claim ought to be confirmed to the said Manuel LISA, or his legal representatives according to the concession. (No. 33)

Francois LACOMBE claiming 400 arpents of land, see pg. 60 of this Book. The Board are unanimously of opinion that this claim ought to be confirmed to the said Francois LACOMBE, or his legal representatives, according to the concession. (No. 34)

Philipe BACANNE claiming 480 arpents of land, see pg. 61 of this Book. It appears from the testimony that the land, at the spot indicated in the petition, was already occupied, and that a new order of survey, dated 18th November, 1803 was issued by Charles Dehault DELASSUS for the same quantity of land, to be located in any other vacant place. The Board are unanimous opinion that this claim ought to be confirmed to the said Philipe BACANNE, or his legal representatives according to the said order of survey dated 18th November, 1803. (No. 35)

Baptiste RIVIERE claiming 400 arpents of land, see pg. 61 of this Book. The Board remark that the survey produced in this case is probably the survey of the tract claimed, but it is not so stated in the said plat. The Board are unanimously of opinion that this claim ought to be confirmed to the said Baptiste RIVIERE, or his legal representatives according to the concession. (No. 36)

Francis COLEMAN claiming 2,500 arpents of land, see pg. 64 of this Book. The Board are unanimously of opinion that this claim ought to be confirmed to the said Francis COLEMAN, or his legal representatives according to the concession. (No. 37)

Rene Guiho de KERLEGAND claiming 500 arpents of land, see pg. 64 of this Book. The Board are unanimously of opinion that this claim ought to be confirmed to the said Rene Guiho de KERLEGAND, or his legal representatives, according to the concession. (No. 38)

Marie Nicolle LESBOIS claiming 244-1/2 arpents of land, see pg. 64 of this Book. The Board are unanimously of opinion that this claim ought to be confirmed to the said Marie Nicolle LESBOIS, or her legal representatives, according to the concession. (No. 39)

Jean Francois PERREY claiming 3,000 arpents of land, see pg. 65 of this Book. The Board are unanimously of opinion that this claim ought to be confirmed to the said Jean Francois PERREY, or his legal representatives according to the concession. (No. 40)

William LOUGHRY claiming 450 arpents of land, see pg. 65 of this Book. The Board are unanimously of opinion that this claim ought to be confirmed to the said William LOUGHRY, or his legal representatives according to the possession, as admitted by the Lt. Gov. (No. 41)

Mathias VANDERHIDER claiming 400 arpents of land, see pg. 66 of this Book. The Board are unanimously of opinion that this claim ought to be confirmed to the said VANDERHIDER, or his legal representatives according to the concession. (No. 42)
    The Board Adjourned untill tomorrow at 9 o'clock A.M.
        Wednesday Nov. 6th, 1833 Board Met-All Comm'rs. Present

Jean Bste. PRATTE claiming 1,000 arpents of land, see pg. 71 of this Book & 200. The Board are unanimously of opinion that this claim ought to be confirmed to the said Jean Bste. PRATTE, or his legal representatives, according to the concession. (No. 43)

In the case of Joachin LISA claiming 6,000 arpents of land, see pg. 6 of this Book. John P. CABANNE, duly sworn, says that to the best of his knowledge, Joachin LISA came to this country in the year 1800. That he resided in this town with his family, consisting of his wife and four or five children. That he thinks said LISA had several slaves, but cannot say how many. That said LISA resided in this place from 1800 to the fall of 1804, at which time said LISA went down to New Orleans with him, the deponent. He, further, says that in 1792, when deponent arrived in New Orleans, said LISA was then employed in the Custom House in said place. That at that time, all the family of said LISA was living in New Orleans. That he had a plantation near Bayou St. John, and that he sold said plantation before he came to this country with the intention of settling himself as a farmer. That he, the deponent, first came to this country in 1799 and was married in 1800, and has resided in this country ever since. The deponent, further, says that he knows that Manuel LISA, brother of claimant, was in St. Louis in the summer of 1799, and that the signature to the petition, asking 6,000 arpents of land for the said Joachin LISA, is in the proper handwriting of the said Manuel LISA. That the claimant, Joachin LISA was the elder brother of said Manuel LISA.

John COONTZ & Edw'd. HEMPSTEAD claiming 450 arpents of land, see pg. 67 of this book. The Board are unanimously of opinion that this claim ought to be confirmed to said John COONTZ, or his legal representatives according to the concession. (No. 44)

Henry DIELLE claiming 400 arpents of land and a 40 arpents lot, see pg. 72 of this Book. The Board are unanimously of opinion that this claim of 400 arpents ought to be confirmed to the said Henry DIELLE, or his legal representatives. The Board remark that the 40 arpents lot is, in their opinion, confirmed by the 1st section of the Act of Congress of 13th June, 1812, otherwise, it is recommended for confirmation. (No. 45)

In the case of ST.VRAIN claiming 1,500 arpents of land, see pg. 75 of this Book. Dr. Lewis F. LINN, Comm'r., as a witness in behalf of claimant, says that he has known of a mill on this tract for many years, perhaps 16 or 17 years, and that, at this present time, there exist on said tract, a saw and grist mill, a dwelling house & out houses and fields.

Julien RATTE claiming 150 arpents of land, see pg. 73 of this Book.

The Board are unanimously of opinion that this claim ought to be confirmed to the said Julien RATTE or to his legal representatives,
according to concession. (No. 46)
     The Board Adjourned untill tomorrow at 9 o'clock A.M.
          Thursday Nov. 7th, 1833 Board Met-All Comm'rs. Present

Hyacinthe EGLIZ claiming 800 arpents of land, see pg. 87 of this Book.
The Board remark that the survey produced in this case, is only for
300 arpents. The Board are unanimously of opinion that this claim
ought to be confirmed to the said Hyacinthe EGLIZ, or his legal representatives, according to the concession. (No. 47)

Etienne PEPIN claiming 1,600 arpents of land, see pg. 88 of this Book.
The Board are unanimously of opinion that this claim ought to be confirmed to the said Etienne PEPIN, or to, his legal representatives,
according to the concession. (No. 48)

Andre & Jean Bste. Blondeau DREZY claiming 480 arpents of land, see
pg. 88 of this book. The Board are unanimously of opinion that this
claim ought to be confirmed to the said Andre & J.Bste. Blondeau DREZY
or their legal representatives, according to the concession. (No. 49)

Silvestre LABBADIE claiming 8 by 40 arpents of land, (cannot read).
The Board remark that the concession of Manuel PEREZ, Lt. Gov., is for
8 arpents in front by 8 in depth, but the order of survey of
Estevan MIRO, Governor General, is for 8 arpents in front by 40 in
depth. The Board are unanimously of opinion that this claim ought to
be confirmed to said Silvestre LABBADIE or his legal representatives
according to the concession made by MIRO. (No. 50)

Gabriel CERRE claiming an Island at the mouth of Cuivre in the Mississippi, see pg. 89 of this Book. The Board are unanimously of opinion
that this claim ought to be confirmed to said Gabriel CERRE, or his
legal representatives according to the concession. (No. 51)

Benito VASQUEZ claiming 9 arpents of land in front by the depth from
the Mississippi to the main road leading to Carondelet, see pg. 95 of
this Book. The Board remark that in the petition, the words in front
were evidently omitted after the word nine. The Board are unanimously of opinion that this claim ought to be confirmed to the said
Benito VASQUEZ, or his legal representatives, according to the boundaries asked for in the petition and expressed in the concession.
(No. 52)

Jean Baptiste PUJOL claiming 240 arpents of land, see pg. 96 of this
Book. The Board are unanimously of opinion that this claim ought to
be confirmed to the said Jean Bste. PUJOL, or his legal representatives according to the concession. (No. 53)

James MACKAY claiming 200 & more arpents, see pg. 103 of this Book.
The Board, after minutely examining the original papers in this case,
see no cause for entertaining even the suspicion of the concession
being antidated, as expressed by the former Board, and they are unanimously of opinion that this claim ought to be confirmed to the said
James MACKAY or to his legal representatives according to the concession. (No. 54)

Bernard PRATTE claiming 7,056 arpents of land, see pg. 104 of this
Book. The Board are unanimously of opinion that this claim ought to
be confirmed to said Bernard PRATTE, or his legal representatives,
according to the concession. (No. 55)

Henry DIELLE claiming 5,000 arpents of land, see pg. 105 of this Book.
The Board are unanimously of opinion that this claim ought to be confirmed to said Henry DIELLE, or his legal representatives according
to the concession. (No. 56)

Mathew SAUCIER claiming 1,200 arpents of land, see pg. 105 of this
Book. The Board are unanimously of opinion that this claim ought to
be confirmed to the said Mathew SAUCIER, or his legal representatives
according to the concession. (No. 57)

Purnel HOWARD claiming 400 arpents of land, see pg. 106 of this Book.
The Board remark that there is evidently a mistake in the certificate
of survey for it is therein stated five hundred arpents when the survey shows 400. The Board are unanimously of opinion that this claim
ought to be confirmed to the said Purnel HOWARD, or to his legal representatives, according to the concession. (No. 58)
        The Board adjourned until tomorrow at 9 o'clock A.M.
              Friday Nov. 8th, 1833 Board Met-All Comm'rs. Present

Pierre Francois DEVOLSEY claiming 6 by 40 arpents of land, see pg. 100
of this Book. The Board are unanimously of opinion that this claim
ought to be confirmed to the said Pierre Francois DEVOLSEY, or his
legal representatives, according to the concession; and they remark
that their opinion was formed, independently of the deposition of
Portneuf, produced in this case. (No. 59)

Gabriel CERRE claiming 400 arpents of land, see pg. 98 of this Book.
The Board are unanimously of opinion that this claim ought to be
confirmed to said Gabriel CERRE or his legal representatives according to the concession. (No. 60)

Bartholomew COUSIN claiming 899 arpents of land, it being the balance
of 7,935 arpents, of which 7,056 have been confirmed, see pg. 20 of
this Book. The Board are unanimously of opinion that this claim ought
to be confirmed to the said Bartholomew COUSIN, or his legal representatives according to the concession. (No. 61)

Jacques ST. VRAIN claiming 4,000 arpents of land, see pg. 89 & 274.
The Board are unanimously of opinion that this claim ought to be confirmed to the said Jacques T.VRAIN or his legal representatives, according to the concession. (No. 62)

Antoine SOULARD claiming 204 arpents 48 perches of land, see pg. 103
of this Book. The Board are unanimously of opinion that this claim
ought to be confirmed to the said Antoine SOULARD, or his legal representatives according to the concession. (No. 63)

Pierre Delassus de LUZIERE claiming 7,056 arpents of land, see pg.
14 of this Book. The Board are unanimously of opinion that this
claim ought to be confirmed to the said Pierre Delassus De LUZIERE,
or his legal representatives according to the concession. (No. 64)

Francis TAYON, Jr., claiming 10,000 arpents of land, see pg. 107 of
this Book. The Board are unanimously of opinion that this claim
ought to be confirmed to the said Francis TAYON, or his legal representatives according to the concession. (No. 65)

Nicolas BARSALOUX claiming 160 arpents of land, see pg. 110 of this
Book. The Board are unanimously of opinion that this claim ought to
be confirmed to the said Nicolas BARSALOUX, or his legal representatives, according to the concession.   (No. 66)

Charles TAYON claiming 1,600 arpents of land, see pg. 102 of this Book.
The Board are unanimously of opinion that this claim ought to be confirmed to the said Charles TAYON or his legal representatives according to the concession. (No. 67)

Antoine GAGNIER claiming 1,800 arpents of land, see pg. 114. The
Board are unanimously of opinion that this claim ought to be confirmed.
to said Antoine GAGNIER, or his legal representatives, according to
the concession. (No. 68)

John WATKINS claiming 7,056 arpents of land, see pg. 114 of this Book.
The Board upon a careful examination of the original concession, find
that there is a date to the same, in Zenon TRUDEAU's own handwriting,
and they are unanimously of opinion that this claim ought to be confirmed to the said John WATKINS or to his legal representatives, according to the concession. (No. 69)

Esther, free mulato woman claiming 80 arpents of land, see pg. 111 &

160. The Board are unanimously of opinion that this claim ought to be confirmed to the said Esther, or her legal representatives according to the concession. (No. 70)

John WATKINS, in his own name and as assignee of John NEIGHBOUR, claiming 800 arpents of land, see pg. 114 of this Book. The Board observe that, after a minute examination of John NEIGHBOUR's concession they see no good reasons for believing with the former Board, that the alteration mentioned, was (cannot read) as the word four altered into Eight, was sanctioned by the Lt. Gov., in the following in his own handwriting to wit: "the word eight, erased, to stand good". Immediately under which follows his signature, making the quantity of arpents granted, 8 in front by 40 in depth. The Board are unanimously of opinion that 160 arpents, (being the balance claimed by John NEIGHBOUR) should be confirmed, the former Board having already confirmed the other 160. The Board, also, are of opinion that 6 or 7 arpents in front by 40 in depth, granted to John WATKINS, should also be confirmed. (No. 71)

Joseph Marie PAPIN claiming 200 arpents of land, see pg. 115 of this Book. The Board are unanimously of opinion that this claim ought to be confirmed to the said Joseph Marie PAPIN, or his legal representatives, according to Charles Dehault DELASSUS's concession. (No. 72)

Antoine SAUGRAIN claiming 20,000 arpents of land, see pg. 115 of this Book. The Board are unanimously of opinion that this claim ought to be confirmed to the said Antoine SAUGRAIN, or his legal representatives according to the concession. (No. 73)
    The Board Adjourned untill tomorrow at 9 o'clock A.M.
        Saturday Nov. 9th, 1833 Board Met-All Comm'rs. Present

The Sons of Jos. M. PAPIN claiming 5,600 arpents of land, see pg. 117. The Board are unanimously of opinion that this claim ought to be confirmed to the said sons of Jos. M. PAPIN, to wit; Joseph, Didier, Alexander, Hipolite, Silvestre, Theodore & Pierre PAPIN, or to their legal representatives according to the concession. (No. 74)

Bernard PRATTE claiming 800 arpents of land, see pg. 117. The Board are unanimously of opinion that this claim ought to be confirmed to the said Bernard PRATTE, or to his legal representatives, according to the concession. (No. 75)

Charles GRATIOT, Jr., claiming 2,500 arpents of land, see pg. 119 of this Book. The Board are unanimously of opinion that this claim ought to be confirmed to the said Charles GRATIOT, Jr., or to his legal representatives, according to the concession. (No. 76)

Levy THEEL claiming 200 arpents of land, see pg. 119 of this Book. The Board are unanimously of opinion that this claim ought to be confirmed to the said Levy THEEL, or his legal representatives, according to the concession. (No. 77)

Mathurin BOUVET & Charles GRATIOT, claiming 7,056 arpents of land, see pg. 119 of this Book. The Board are unanimously of opinion that this claim ought to be confirmed to the said Mathurin BOUVET & Charles GRATIOT, or their legal representatives, according to the concession. (No. 78)

Mathurin BOUVET claiming 84 by 40 arpents of land, see pg. 120 of this Book. The Board remark that the alteration of the date of the concession consists in altering the 2 into one 1, but they think that nothing is to be inferred against this claim by said alteration, and they are unanimously of opinion that this claim ought to be confirmed to the said Mathurin BOUVET, or his legal representatives, according to DELASSUS's concession. (No. 79)

Benito VASQUEZ claiming 7,056 arpents of land, see pg. 121 of this Book. The Board are unanimously of opinion that this claim ought to be confirmed to the said Benito VASQUEZ or his legal representatives according to the concession. (No. 80)

John HILDERBRANT claiming 320 arpents of land, see pg. 121 of this
Book. The Board are unanimously of opinion that this claim ought to
be confirmed to the said John HILDERBRANT or his legal representatives according to the concession. (No. 81)

Charles GRATIOT, Sr. claiming 500 arpents of land, see pg. 123 of
this book. The Board are unanimously of opinion that this claim
ought to be confirmed to the said Charles GRATIOT, or his legal representatives according to the concession. (No. 82)

Pierre CHOUTEAU claiming 30,000 arpents of land, see pg. 123 of this
Book. The Board are unanimously of opinion that this claim ought to
be confirmed to the said Pierre CHOUTEAU or his legal representatives
according to the concession. (No. 83) The Board have decided upon
this claim without any reference to the agent of the Osage Nations to
CHOUTEAU's taking any quantity of land he pleased on river A la Mine.
   The Board Adjourned untill Monday next at 9 o'clock A.M.
      Monday Nov. 11th, 1833 Board Met-All Comm'rs. Present

Joseph BRAZEAU claiming 360 arpents of land, see pg. 123 of this book.
The Board are unanimously of opinion that this claim ought to be confirmed to the said Joseph BRAZEAU, or to his legal representatives,
according to the concession. (No. 84)

Newton HOWELL claiming 350 arpents of land, see pg. 124 of this Book.
The Board are unanimously of opinion that this claim ought to be confirmed to the said Newton HOWELL, or to his legal representatives
according to the concession. (No. 85)

Mackey WHERRY claiming 1,600 arpents of land, see pg. 124 of this
Book. The Board are unanimously of opinion that this claim ought to
be confirmed to the said Mackey WHERRY, or to his legal representatives, according to the concession. (No. 86)

Louis LORIMIER claiming 30,000 arpents of land, see pg. 127 of this
Book. By order of the Board the letter produced to the former Board
& which is of record in the Recorder's office, is to be translated
and attached to the concession. The Board are unanimously of opinion
that this claim ought to be confirmed to the said Louis LORIMIER, or
to his legal representatives, according to the concession. (No. 87)

Francois BERTHIAUME claiming 420 arpents of land, see pg. 128 of this
Book. The Board are unanimously of opinion that this claim ought to
be confirmed to the said Francois BERTHIAUME, or to his legal representatives, according to the concession. (No. 88)

Bartholomew COUSIN claiming 10,000 arpents of land, see pg. 129 of
this Book. The Board are unanimously of opinion that this claim
ought to be confirmed to the said Bartholomew COUSIN, or to his legal
representatives, according to the concession. (No. 89)

Bartholomew COUSIN claiming 8,000 arpents of land, see pg. 129 of
this Book. The Board are unanimously of opinion that this claim ought
to be confirmed to the said Bartholomew COUSIN, or to his legal representatives, according to the concession. (No. 90)

Louis REED claiming 240 arpents of land, see pg. 129 of this Book.
The Board are unanimously of opinion that this claim ought to be confirmed to the said Louis REED, or to his legal representatives, according to the concession. (No. 91)

Gabrielle NICOLLE claiming 608 arpents of land, see pg. 131 of this
Book. The Board are unanimously of opinion that this claim ought to
be confirmed to the said Gabriel NICOLLE, or to his legal representatives, according to the concession. (No. 92)

Michel LACHANCE claiming 72 arpents of land, see pg. 132 of this Book.
The Board are unanimously of opinion that this claim ought to be confirmed to the said Michel LACHANCE, or to his legal representatives,
according to the concession. (No. 93)

In the case of Louis LORIMIER claiming 1,000 arpents of land, see pg. 128 of this Book. Pierre MENARD, duly sworn, says that he was well acquainted with the said Louis LORIMIER. That he dealt largely with him. That he believes that in 1803 or 1804, said LORIMIER begun to build a saw and grist mill. That if some one had possessed the land below his mill, he might easily have rendered said mill useless by backing the water that the whole tract claimed was subject to over-flowing.

Manuel Gouralez MORO claiming 7,056 arpents of land, see pg. 132 of this Book. The Board are unanimously of opinion that this claim ought to be confirmed to the said Manuel Gonzales MORO, or to his legal representatives according to the concession. (No. 94)

Manuel Gonzales MORO claiming 800 arpents of land, see pg. 133 of this Book. The Board are unanimously of opinion that this claim ought to be confirmed to the said Manuel Gonzales MORO, or his legal representatives, according to the concession. (No. 95)

William LORIMIER claiming 1,000 arpents of land, see pg. 133 of this Book. The Board are unanimously of opinion that this claim ought to be confirmed to the said William LORIMIER, or to his legal represen-tatives, according to the concession. (No. 96)

Francois NORMANDEAU claiming 2,500 arpents of land, see pg. 133. The Board are unanimously of opinion that this claim ought to be confirmed to the said Francois NORMANDEAU, or to his legal representatives, ac-cording to the concession. (No. 97)

Andrew KINAIRD claiming 600 arpents of land, see pg. 133 of this Book. The Board are unanimously of opinion that this claim ought to be con-firmed to the said Andrew KINAIRD, or his legal representatives, ac-cording to the concession. (No. 98)

John HENRY claiming 900 arpents of land, see pg. 134 of this Book. The Board are unanimously of opinion that this claim ought to be confirmed to the said John HENRY, or to his legal representatives, according to the concession. (No. 99)
        Board Adjourned untill tomorrow at 9 o'clock A.M.
            Tuesday Nov. 12th, 1833 Board Met-All Comm'rs. Present

Edward BRADLEY claiming 500 arpents of land, see pg. 134 of this Book. The Board are unanimously of opinion that this claim ought to be con-firmed to the said Edward BRADLEY, or to his legal representatives, according to the concession. (No. 100)

George CRUMP claiming 450 arpents of land, see pg. 135 of this Book. The Board remark that in the entry of this claim, in the minutes of the former Board, there is a mistake, probably made by their Clerk, stating this land to lie on river Gingras District of St. Louis. This land being evidently in the District of St. Charles. The Board are unanimously of opinion that this claim ought to be confirmed to the said George CRUMP, or to his legal representatives according to the concession. (No. 101)

John LONG claiming 10,000 arpens of land, see pg. 136 of this Book. The Board remark that the survey exceeds the quantity granted by 50 arpents. The Board are unanimously of opinion that this claim ought to be confirmed to the said John LONG, or to his legal representa-tives, according to the concession. (102)

Charles ROY claiming 80 arpents of land, see pg. 135 of this Book. The Board are unanimously of opinion that this claim ought to be con-firmed to the said Charles ROY or his legal representatives, accor-ding to the concession. (103)

Seneca ROLLINS claiming 400 arpents of land, see pg. 135 of this Book. The Board are unanimously of opinion that this claim ought to be con-firmed to the said Seneca ROLLINS, or his legal representatives, ac-cording to the concession. (104)

Joachin ROY claiming 400 arpents of land, see pg. 136 of this Book. The Board are unanimously of opinion that this claim ought to be confirmed to the said Joachin ROY, or to his legal representatives, according to the concession. (105)

William LONG claiming 400 arpents of land, see pg. 136 of this Book. The Board are unanimously of opinion that this claim ought to be confirmed to the said William LONG, or to his legal representatives, according to the concession. (106)

Edward YOUNG claiming 800 arpents of land, see pg. 137 of this Book. The Board are unanimously of opinion that this claim ought to be confirmed to the said Edward YOUNG, or his legal representatives, according to the concession. (No. 107)

James MACKAY claiming 400 arpents of land, see pg. 137 of this Book. The Board after a minute examination of the original concession, are of opinion that the paper on which it is written, is in places, defective, but they see nothing to indicate fraudulent erazures, as suggested by the agent of the United States, before the former Board. They are unanimously of opinion that this claim ought to be confirmed to the said James MACKAY, or to his legal representatives, according to the concession. (No. 108)

Antoine GAUTIER claiming 4,000 arpents of land, see pg. 137 of this Book. The Board remark that by the petition the Clearweather swamp is asked for, but the surveyor general, Antoine SOULARD says at the foot of the concession, that the granting of said Swamp would lead into difficulties with the inhabitants of St. Charles and Portage des Sioux, and therefore being vested with the proper authority he gives order that this claim is to (cannot read) the King's Domain. The Board are unanimously of opinion that this claim ought to be confirmed to the said Antoine GAUTIER or to his legal representatives, according to the concession. (109)

John MCMILLAN claiming 650 arpents of land, see pg. 138 of this Book. The Board are unanimously of opinion that this claim ought to be confirmed to the said John MCMILLAN, or to his legal representatives, according to the concession. (110)

John COLLIGAN claiming 1,200 arpents of land, see pg. 138 of this Book. The Board are unanimously of opinion that this claim ought to be confirmed to the said John COLLIGAN, or to his legal representatives, according to the concession. (111)

John BISHOP claiming 350 arpents of land, see pg. 138 of this Book. The Board are unanimously of opinion that this claim ought to be confirmed to the said John BISHOP, or to his legal representatives, according to the concession. (112)
     The Board adjourned untill tomorrow at 9 O'clock A.M.
          Wednesday Nov. 13th, 1833 Board Met-All Comm'rs. Present

Charles Fremon DELAURIERE claiming 10,000 arpents of land, see pg. 139 of this Book. The Board are unanimously of opinion that this claim ought to be confirmed to the said Charles Fremon DELAURIERE, or to his legal representatives, according to the concession. (113)

Jean Bste. TISON claiming 7,056 arpents of land, see pg. 140 of this Book. The Board are unanimously of opinion that this claim ought to be confirmed to the said Jean Bste. TISON, or to his legal representatives, according to the concession. (114)

Louis DELILLE claiming 2,500 arpents of land, see pg. 141 of this Book. The Board are unanimously of opinion that this claim ought to be confirmed to the said Louis DELILLE, or to his legal representatives, according to the concession. (115)

Joseph MORIN, Jr. claiming 160 arpents of land, see pg. 152 of this Book. The Board are (cannot read) this concession is for 160 arpents and the survey for 162-48 perches. The Board are unanimously of opinion that this claim ought to be confirmed to the said

Joseph MORIN, Jr., or to his legal representatives, according to the concession. (116)

James WILLIAMS claiming 400 arpents of land, see pg. 149 of this Book. The Board are unanimously of opinion that this claim ought to be confirmed to the said James WILLIAMS, or to his legal representatives, according to the concession. (117)

Gabriel CERRE claiming 300 arpents of land, see pg. 151 of this Book. The Board are unanimously of opinion that this claim ought to be confirmed to the said Gabriel CERRE, or to his legal representatives, according to the concession. (118)

Charles Fremon DELAURIERE for himself & as assignee of Louis LABEAUME claiming 10,000 arpents of land, see pg. 32 of this Book. The Board are unanimously of opinion that this claim ought to be confirmed to the said Charles Fremon DELAURIERE and L. LABEAUME, or to their legal representatives, according to the concession. (No.119)

James RICHARDSON claiming 400 arpents of land, see pg. 153 of this Book. The Board are unanimously of opinion that this claim ought to be confirmed to the said James RICHARDSON, or to his legal representatives, according to the concession. (No.120)

Pierre DELOR claiming 400 arpents of land, see pg. 154 of this Book. The Board are unanimously of opinion that this claim ought to be confirmed to the said Pierre DELOR, or to his legal representatives according to the concession. (No. 121)

Jacques ST.VRAIN claiming 1,500 arpents of land, see pg. 75 of this Book. The Board are unanimously of opinion that this claim ought to be confirmed to the said Jacques ST.VRAIN, or his legal representatives. (No. 122)

Thomas CAULK claiming 400 arpents of land, see pg. 332 of this This.

Louis COURTOIS, Jr. claiming 7,056 arpents of land, see pg. 13 of this Book. The Board are unanimously of opinion that this claim ought to be confirmed to the said Louis COURTOIS, or his legal representatives according to the concession. (No. 123)

Francois MOREAU & Antoine MARECHAL claiming 300 arpents of land, see pg. 66 of this Book. The Board are unanimously of opinion that this claim ought to be confirmed to the said Francois MOREAU & Antoine MARECHAL, or to their legal representatives, according to the concession. (No. 124)

Francois LACOMBE claiming 400 arpents of land, see pg. 61 of this Book. The Board are unanimously of opinion that this claim ought to be confirmed to the said Francois LACOMBE, or his legal representatives, according to the concession. (No. 125)

James JOURNEY claiming 400 arpents of land, see pg. 22 of this Book. The Board are unanimously of opinion that this claim ought to be confirmed to the said James JOURNEY, or his legal representatives, according to the concession. (No. 126)

Louis BISSONET claiming 40 arpents of land, see pg. 16 of this Book. The Board remark that in the minutes of the former Board, it is there stated that this claim interferes with the claim of Widow and representatives of Antoine MORIN. The Board are unanimously of opinion that this claim ought to be confirmed to the said Louis BISSONET, according to the concession. (No. 127)
    The Board Adjourned untill Friday next.
    Friday, November 15th, 1833 Board Met

In the case of Etienne ST. PIERRE claiming a special location on River A Berger, Francois BOUCHER, being duly sworn, says he is 56 years of age. That he has travelled up and down the Missouri since he was a young man. That he has ascended said River perhaps forty times. That he believes the distance from the hills below Berger River to the hills opposite Moline Island, to be 3 leagues, in following the turn of the Missouri, which makes a great bend at that place. Witness, further, says that he never crossed Berger bottom by land and cannot say what is the distance in a straight line. James GUNSONLIS, being also duly sworn, says that he has often ascended the Missouri in Keel boats and steam boats, and that he believes the distance to be, from the hills below Berger River to the hills opposite Moline Island, 9 miles, more or less. Peter CHOUTEAU, the present claimant, (cannot read) and states that the line beginning at the foot of the hills below Berger River has always been understood to be one league in length, although, the petition expresses one league, more or less, and the sd line is to run parallel with the general course of said Berger River, and from the end of the said line of one league in length, another straight line is to be run to strike the foot of the hills opposite Moline Island, which foot of said hills is washed by the Missouri, and the quantity comprised between the said two lines and the Missouri is the quantity claimed, of which the number of arpents contained in a league square has been confirmed, see BATES decisions, pg. 59. The Board are unanimously of opinion that the balance of this claim ought to be confirmed to the said Etienne ST. PIERRE, or his legal representatives, according to the concession. (No. 128)

John ST. CLAIRE, Jr. claiming 640 acres of land situate on the waters of the St. Francois, in the late District of St. Genevieve, now county of Madison, see Record Book F, pg. 13, BATES Decision, pg. 97. The following testimony was taken before L.F. LINN, Comm'r.
State of Missouri, County of Madison
Thompson CRAWFORD, a witness aged about (cannot read)being duly sworn, as the law directs, deposeth & saith that he is well acquainted with the original claimant. That he came to this country, then the Province of Upper Louisiana, in the fall of the year 1803. That he was then a young man grown and made his home at his father's whose name was also, John ST.CLAIRE. Witness, also, knows the land claimed and that in the early part of the year 1804, the claimant made some improvements on the land, and he knows cultivated land that year, but wether the cultivation was on the land claimed or not, witness does not recollect, and that the land claimed has been inhabited, improved and cultivated ever since. Sworn to & subscribed before me,
L.F. LINN, Comm'r., this 22nd October, 1833.
L.F. LINN, Comm'r.   Thompson CRAWFORD

And, also, came John REAVES, a witness aged about 73 years, who also being duly sworn, deposeth & saith that he well knew John ST. CLAIRE, the claimant. That he came with the claimant to the country in 1803. That they lived a while together. Witness, also, knows the land claimed and knows that the claimant settled and improved and cultivated the same in 1803 and 1804. That the (cannot read) Indians in (cannot read the year) drove the inhabitants together, where they made a common defence and common crop in that year. And witness, further, knows that the land has been actually inhabited, improved and cultivated ever since. Sworn to and subscribed before me, L.F. LINN, Comm'r., this 23rd October, 1833.
L.F. LINN, Comm'r.   John (O) REAVES
                                              his mark
The Board are unanimously of opinion that 640 acres of land ought to be granted to the said John ST.CLAIRE, or to his legal representatives. (No. 129)

Daniel KRYTZ claiming by settlement right, 234 arpents 36 perches of land, see Minutes No. 4, pgs. 36 & 280. The following testimony was taken before Lewis F. LINN, Comm'r.
State of Missouri, County of Madison
Daniel BOLLINGER, aged about 80 years, being duly sworn as the law directs, deposeth and saith that he is well acquainted with the original claimant, Daniel CRITZ or CRITS. That said claimant came to the country, then the Province of Upper Louisiana, in the fall of the year 1802. Witness, also, knows the land claimed, and knows that the claimant got permission of Louis LORIMIER, then Commandant of Cape Girardeau, to settle lands. And witness, also, knows that claimant

94

settled on said land claimed (cannot read) built a good house, a
good barn and stables with Kitchen and out houses, fenced in and
cleared in 1803 and 1804 some ten acres or more and cultivated the
same in corn and other things necessary for a family. Claimant,
also, at that time, planted an orchard. Claimant had a wife and 7
or 8 children. Claimant had a good stock of horses, cattle, hogs,
etc. and the claimant has actually continued to inhabit, improve &
cultivate the said land from the time of the original settlement to
the present day and still actually resides on and cultivates the same
being his only home from the time he came to the country to the present day of himself and such of his family as remained with him at
home. Sworn to and subscribed before me, L.F. LINN, Comm'r., this
23rd day of October, 1833.
L.F. LINN, Comm'r.   Daniel (X) BOLLINGER
                                                 his mark
The Board are unanimously of opinion that 234 arpents 36 perches of
land, being the quantity originally claimed, ought to be granted to
the said Daniel KRYTZ, or to his legal representatives. (No. 130)

Jacob WALKER claiming 982 arpents 65 perches of land (by his heirs
and legal representatives), see Book No. 4, pg. 12 and 264, Book B,
pg. 293. The following testimony was taken before Lewis F. LINN,
Comm'r.
State of Missouri, County of Cape Girardeau
George F. BOLLINGER, aged about 60 years, and Joseph NISWONGER, aged
nearly 54, being severally duly sworn as the law directs, deposeth
and saith that they were well acquainted with Jacob WALKER, the original claimant. That he came to this country, then the Province of
Upper Louisiana, now State of Missouri in the year 1799. That he obtained a grant or permission to settle from Louis LORIMIER, the then
Spanish Commandant of this Post. They also know that he built a
house on the land claimed in the year 1801, and cultivated the same
land, and that the said (land) has been both inhabited and cultivated
ever since.
George F. BOLLINGER   Joseph (X) NISWONGER
                                                 his mark
Sworn to & subscribed October 19th, 1833. The Board are unanimously
of opinion that 640 acres of land ought to be granted to the said
Jacob WALKER, or to his legal representatives. (No. 131)

Thomas CAULK claiming 400 arpents of land, see pg. 7 of this Book.
The Board are unanimously of opinion that this claim ought to be confirmed to the said Thomas CAULK, or his legal representatives, according to the concession. (No. 132)

Joachin LISA claiming 6,000 arpents of land, see pg. 61 & 3 of this
Book. The Board are unanimously of opinion that this claim ought to
be confirmed to the said Joachin LISA, or to his legal representatives, according to the concession. (No. 133)

Melchior Aman MICHAU claiming 600 arpents of land, see pg. 155 of this
Book. The Board are unanimously of opinion that this claim ought to
be confirmed to the said Melchior Aman MICHAU, or his legal representatives according to the concession. (No. 134)

Jacob COLLINS claiming under settlement right 890 arpents of land,
see pg. 176 of this Book. The Board are unanimously of opinion that
640 acres ought to be granted to the said Jacob COLLINS, or to his
legal representatives. (No. 135)

James MCDANIEL claiming under settlement,right, 800 arpents of land,
see pg. 170 of this Book. The Board are unanimously of opinion that
640 acres of land ought to be granted to the said James MCDANIEL, or
to his legal representatives. (No. 136)

Edmund CHANDLER claiming under settlement right, 640 acres of land, see
pg. 170 of this Book. The Board are unanimously of opinion that 640
acres of land ought to be granted to the said Edmund CHANDLER, or to
his legal representatives. (No. 137)

William DILLON claiming under sttlement right, 640 acres of land, see

Book No. 3, pg. 386, No. 4, pg. 431, Record Book E, pg. 225. The following testimony was taken before L.F. LINN, Comm'r.
State of Missouri, County of Madison
Samuel CAMPBELL, aged about 68 years, who being duly sworn, deposeth and saith that he was well acquainted with the original claimant. That the witness became acquainted with him in the spring of 1803, and understood the claimant·had been here for some years before. Witness, also, knows the land claimed, and knows that the claimant was settled on the same and living thereon in the spring of 1803, and the place had the appearance of having been settled for several years, for there was then two houses (a dwelling house & Kitchen and several acres of land under fence and cleared and appeared to have been in cultivation before that time (cannot read)actually inhabited and cultivated the same in 1803, and that the same tract of land has been continually inhabited and cultivated by either the claimant or some other person ever since, till within a few years back, and may have been for these few years, but the witness cannot positively say as he removed to another part of the State. Sworn to and subscribed before me, L.F. LINN, Comm'r., this 22nd day of October, 1833.
L.F. LINN, Comm'r.   Saml. CAMPBELL

Also. came John CLEMENTS, a witness aged about 53 years, who being duly sworn as the law directs, deposeth & saith that he was well acquainted with William DILLON, the original claimant. That he found him in this country, then the Province of Upper Louisiana, in the spring of the year 1802. That witness, also, knows the land claimed and knows that the claimant was then settled on and living on the land claimed. That claimant had then a dwelling house and in the same year built a kitchen. That claimant had in 1802, some 3 or 4 acres under fence and cleared, which land was actually cultivated in 1802 in corn and other things. Claimant, also, had a garden. Claimant continued to inhabit and cultivate (cannot read) and the witness understood that he had afterwards remained there for some time, but witness went away in the fall of 1802 and cannot say positively. Witness lived with claimant and helped him build the house and attend the farm at the time. Sworn to and subscribed before me, L.F. LINN, Comm'r., this 22nd day of October, 1833.
                                   John (X) CLEMENTS
                                        his mark
Also, came John REAVES, a witness aged about 73 years, who being duly sworn as the law directs, deposeth and saith that he knew the original claimant. That he found him a citizen and residenter of this country in 1803, when the witness came to the country. Witness, also, knows the land claimed. Clamant was settled on the same in 1803, had a house in which he lived, and had several acres in actual cultivation cleared and under fence, and the same tract of land has been actually inhabited continually improved and cultivated ever since. Sworn to and subscribed before me, L.F. LINN, Comm'r., this 23rd October, 1833.
                                   John (X) REAVES
                                        his mark
The Board are unanimously of opinion that 640 acres ought to be granted to the said William DILLON, or to his legal representatives. (No.138)

Robert GIBONEY claiming 348 arpents 42 perches of land, see Book No. 3, pg. 507, Book No. 4, pg. 255, Book B, pg. 334. The following testimony was taken before L.F. LINN, Comm'r.
State Of Missouri, County of Cape Girardeau
This day personally appeared before me, Lewis F. LINN, one of the Comm'rs. appointed under an act of Congress to Settle and Adjust the unconfirmed land claims in the State of Missour, Alexander SUMMERS of lawful age, who being sworn, deposeth and saith that he emigrated to the District of Cape Girardeau in the year 1798, the District then being under the Spanish Government. That in the year 1800, this affiant knows that Robert GIBONEY made a settlement and improvement on the waters of Giboney's Creek in said District. This affiant knows that the said improvement has always been claimed by said Robert GIBONEY. That the same has been ever since improved and cultivated. That this affiant has lived here and still resides here.
Sworn to & subscribed October 15th, 1833.
L.F. LINN, Comm'r.   Alexander SUMMERS

State of Missouri, County of Cape Girardeau
This day personally appeared before me, Lewis F. LINN, one of the
Comm'rs., etc., William WILLIAMS of lawful age, who being duly sworn
according to the law, deposeth and saith that he emigrated to the
District of Cape Girardeau under the Spanish Government A.D. 1799.
This affiant recollects that as early as the year A.D. 1802, he saw
an improvement made & claimed by Robert GIBONEY in the District of
Cape Girardeau, and this affiant recollects that from his frequently
having passed the said improvement since that time, the same appears
to have been improved & cultivated up to the present time.
                       signed William WILLIAMS
Sworn to and subscribed October 15th, 1833. L.F. LINN, Comm'r.
The Board are unanimously of opinion that 348 arpents 42 perches of
land, it being the quantity originally claimed, ought to be granted
to the said Robert GIBONEY, or to his legal representatives. (No. 139)

Jacob WICKERHAM claiming 800 arpents of land, see pg. 173 of this Book.
The Board are unanimously of opinion that 640 acres of land ought to
be granted to the said Jacob WICKERHAM, or to his legal representatives.
(No. 140)

Israel DODGE claiming 7,056 arpents of land, see Book E, pg. 219, No.
5, pg. 407, produces a paper purporting to be an original concession
from Carlos Dehault DELASSUS, dated 11th December, 1800. M.P.LEDUC,
duly sworn, says that the signature to the above concession is in the
true handwriting of Carlos Dehault DELASSUS.

Ezekiel FENWICK claiming 500 arpents of land, situated between Apple
Creek and River St. Come, see Book D, pg. 44, Book No. 5, pg. 422,
produces a paper purporting to be an original concession from
Zenon TRUDEAU, dated 10th June, 1797. M.P. LEDUC, duly sworn, says
that the signature to the said concession is in the proper handwriting
of the said Zenon TRUDEAU.
     The Board Adjourned untill Tuesday next at 9 o'clock A.M.
     Tuesday Nov. 19th, 1833 Board Met-All Comm'rs. Present

Elijah BENTON by his legal representatives claiming 640 acres of
land on Big River, about 6 or 7 miles from Michael HORINE's, see Book
No. 3, pgs. 185 & 369, No. 4, pg. 361. John STEWART of Jefferson
County, being duly sworn, says that he was well acquainted with the
said Elijah BENTON and knows the tract claimed. That in August or
September of the year 1803, he was on the tract claimed and then there
was a field of corn of some 3 or 4 acres, a garden, a comfortable cabbin and out house, and to his knowledge, said tract has been inhabited
& cultivated ever since, by whom he can not say. Mason FRISELL, the
present claimant, observes to the Board that the above witness,
John STEWART, is a different man than John STEWART of Washington
county, who gave testimony in the same case before L.F. LINN, Comm'r.

The following resolutions were passed by the Board of Commissioners
on the 30th of October last.
R. 1st ₦ Resolved that it was the custom of both France & Spain &
formed a part of the policy of those nations in the settling of new
countries, to appoint officers whose business it was by express regulations, to grant lands to all such of their subjects as might wish
to settle in those countries, for the avowed purposes of improving &
populating said countries.
R. 2nd - That all acts in relation to grants, concessions, warrants &
orders of Survey done & performed by the French & Spanish officers,
during the time those governments had possession & exercised the
sovereignty over the province of Upper Louisiana, ought to be considered as prima facia evidence of their right to do those acts & per-
form those duties & ought to be held & considered binding on the
government of the United States in as much as the acts of the officers in said province were not only tolerated, but approved by their
superiors in power.
R. 3rd - That all grants, concessions, warrants or orders of Survey
made & issued by the Franch Or Spanish officers in the late province
of Upper Louisiana, on or before the 10th day of March, 1804, where
the same are not proved to be fraudulent, ought to be confirmed, pro-

vided the conditions annexed to the grant have been complied with
or a satisfactory reason given for not fulfilling the same.
R. 4th - That O"REILY's instructions or regulations of 18th February, 1770, those of GAYOSO of 9th September, 1797 & those of
MORALES of 17th July, 1799, were not in force in upper Louisiana,
except perhaps the provisions contained in those of GAYOSO, which
related to new settlers.
R. 5th - That subdelegates in making grants, etc., were not limited .
by any known law or custom as to the quantity of arpents they should
grant, except, perhaps as to new settlers. And that such grants
passed titles and that a survey was merely an incidental matter after
the title had passed by the grant, so as to identify the land. That
the grantee might take possession of it.
R. 6th - That what are called imcomplete (cannot read) country were
recognized as property, capable of passing by devise, transferable,
from one to another, and were liable to be sold for debt.
R. 7th - That those grants which are general in their terms pass as
good a title as those which are more special, the difference being
in the description of the land and not in the title.
R. 8th - That those officers of the French & Spanish Governments,
whose names are signed to concessions, must be presumed to have acted
agreeably to powers vested in them by their sovereign and that their
acts are accordingly legal, untill the contrary is shewn.
R. 9th - That fraud is an affirmative charge and as relates to the
French and Spanish claims, as well as in all other cases, must be
proved and not presumed.
R. 10th - That in all cases where there are conditions to a grant,
etc., if the grantee show satisfactorily that he has been prevented
from a fulfilment of the conditions by the Act of God, by the act of
law, by the enemies of the country, or by the act of the party making
the grant, or any other sufficient cause, that the grantee will be
considered as absolved from the performance of the same, and the
grant be regarded as absolute.
                    F.R. CONWAY, L.F. LINN, A.G. HARRISON,

Auguste CHOUTEAU claiming 1,281 arpents of land, see pg. 11th of this
Book. The Board are unanimously of opinion that this claim ought to
be confirmed to the said Auguste CHOUTEAU, or to his legal representatives, according to the concession. (No. 141)
        The Board Adjourned untill tomorrow at 9 o'clock A.M.
            Wednesday Nov. 30th, 1833 Board Met-All Comm'rs. Present

Whereas the Board of Commissioners are of the opinion that the report
to be made out by them, upon the unconfirmed Franch and Spanish land
claims in Missouri, which is to be transmitted to the Comm'r. of the
General Land Office, and by him to be laid before Congress at their
next session for their final decision thereon, should be confided to
the care only of a member of the same. And whereas being also of the
opinion that the report makes too great a bulk to be forwarded by mail,
and involves a matter too much importance to the Government and the
land claimant to be (cannot read) and whereas L.F. LINN, one of the
members of the Board having received the appointment of Senator to the
Congress of the United States, and being about to resign his office as
Comm'r., which will cause a vacancy and interrupt the further action
of the Board in the examination of the land claims during said vacancy.
Be it therefore resolved that Albert G. HARRISON, a member of the Board
be and is hereby authorized and required to take the City of Washington the report above mentioned and deliver the same to the Comm'r. of
the General Land Office, in order that it may be submitted to Congress
according to the requsitions of act creating the Board approved 9th
July, 1832.
        The Board Adjourned untill tomorrow at 9 o'clock A.M.
            The Board Met & Adjourned Nov. 21st, 22nd, 24th, 25th &
            26th, 1833.
            Wednesday Nov. 27th, 1833 Board Met-All Comm'rs. Present

Resolved unanimously that the thanks of this Board be hereby given
to Mr. Julius de MUN, as a small testimonial of regard for the intel-
ligence, untiring industry and faithfulness he has shown whilst per-
ming the duties of Clerk and Translator to the Commission.

Sebastian BUTCHER, Bartholomew BUTCHER, Bastian BUTCHER &
Peter BLOOM claiming 1,600 arpents of land, see pg. 76 of this Book.
The Board, although not considering themselves authorized by the provisions of the act of Congress to take cognisance of this claim, regarding it to be a meritorious claim, respectfully recommend it to
the examination of Congress for confirmation. (No. 142)
    The Board Adjourned untill tomorrow at 9 o'clock A.M.
        Thursday Nov. 28th, 1833 Board Met-All Comm'rs. Present

                    Recorder's Office
St. Louis, Missouri, November 28th, 1833
Received of the Commissioners on private land claims in Missouri, four
tin boxes or cannisters, enveloped in paper & sealed and directed to
the Hon. Elijah HAYWARD, Comm'r. of the Genl. Land Office, which boxes
or cannisters contain the report of said Comm'rs. on 142 private land
claims, together with the transcript of each claim and the transla-
tions of the concessions, etc. All which I promise to deliver to the
Comm'r. of the Genl. Land Office at Washington City in a reasonable
time from the date above written.
Teste,   '   Albert G. HARRISON
F.R. CONWAY

Lewis F. LINN, Esqr., announced to the Board that having accepted the
appointment of Senator to the Congress of the United States, he this
day resigned his situation as Comm'r.
    The Board Adjourned untill tomorrow at 9 o'clock A.M.
        Friday Nov. 29th, 1833 Board Met

F.R. CONWAY, Esqr. appeared pursuant to adjournment, being authorized
to receive evidence, by resolution passed on the 9th day of last
March. (see pg. 112 of this Book).

Jacob WICKERHAM by his legal representatives Wm. DRENEN claiming 800
arpents, see pg. 173 of this Book & 338. Richard EVERETT, being
duly sworn, says that he is 56 years of age, and is well acquainted
with Jacob WICKERHAM, the original claimant and also knows the land
claimed. That WICKERHAM had possession of the same in the fall of
1803, deadened some timber and, he thinks, made a small inclosure &
sowed some seeds, but is not certain as to his cultivating anything
on the place that year. That he was on the place in the summer of
the year 1804 & saw an enclosure of an acre or two of land on said
place and saw corn growing and knows that WICKERHAM did actually cultivate the same, and at that time, he also had peach and apple trees
planted on the place, had a cabbin & resided there at that time, and
to his knowledge, continued to reside there for 3 or 4 years. That
the present claimant purchased the same from WICKERHAM about 18 or 19
years ago, and has continued to inhabit and cultivate the same ever
since. That there is now a good orchard, dwelling house and other
out houses and some 40 or 50 acres of land in cultivation. The present claimant states that he paid taxes for the same for 16 years,
but as the government had not confirmed it, he deemed it most prudent
to pay taxes on it no more, untill it should be confirmed.

James CRAIG by his legal representative Richard EVERITT claiming 800
arpents of land on the Negro Fork of the Marameck, see Record Book F,
pg. 98, BATES decisions pg. 103. William DRENEN, being duly sworn,
says that he is 74 years of age, that he was well acquainted with
James CRAIG, the original claimant. That in the year 1801 or 1802,
he is not positive which, said CRAIG, the original claimant, went on
the tract claimed, cut house logs & planted peach & apple seeds on
the place. He does not think that CRAIG ever lived on the place, but
was at that time, or shortly thereafter, a married man. That CRAIG
sold the place to the present claimant, who resided on the same untill about two years ago, when he was forced to move off, in consequence of the United States selling the same. He knows that
EVERITT resided on & cultivated the same for twenty (cannot read)
years. (2d, 76, No. 7, pg. 226)
    Adjourned untill tomorrow at 9 o'clock A.M.
        Saturday Nov. 30th, 1833 Board Met-F.R. CONWAY, Present

In the case of Elijah BENTON claiming 640 acres of land, see pg. 339

of this Book. The claimant produces to the Board a paper purporting
to be the original survey of the land claimed. Said survey made by
John STEWART & dated 12th February, 1806, received for Record by
SOULARD February 27th, 1806. The following testimony was taken before Lewis F. LINN, Comm'r.
John STEWART, being of lawful age and duly sworn upon his oath, deposes and says that on the 12th day of January, 1806, he surveyed
for Elijah BENTON, a head or settlement right of 640 acres including
his improvement on Big River. That at the time, this deponent was
on the said tract of land to survey the same (at the time above mentioned) there had been, from the appearance of the field, at least
two crops made on the place, and from the appearance of the houses,
there was reason to believe that they had been used for two or three
years. The deponent, further, states that he feels great confidence
in the belief that at least two crops had been raised on this tract
of land at the time he surveyed the same. Sworn to and subscribed
Nov. (cannot read the date) 1833. signed John STEWART

Benjamin HORINE, being duly sworn upon his oath, deposes and says
that he was in this country before it passed under the government of
the United States. That he was well acquainted with the place on
Big River, settled by Elijah BENTON. That before the change of
government took place, Elijah BENTON had been at work on the place
making improvements. That the year after the change of government
took place, there was corn raised on the said place by
Elijah BENTON. That at the surveying of the said tract by
John STEWART, he assisted in carrying the chain, and that at this
time, he is fifty six years of age. Signed   Benjamin HORINE
L.F. LINN, Comm'r.

William REED claiming 727 arpents of land, see No. 1, pg. 369, No.
3, pg. 185, No. 4, pg. 336, Book B, pg. 464. The following testimony
was taken before Lewis F. LINN, Comm'r.
State of Missouri, Washington County
Be it remembered that on this tenth day of January, 1832, before me,
Henry SHURLDS, a Justice of the Peace within and for said County,
the following persons appeared.
John MCNEILL, aged sixty eight years & Upwards, being duly sworn, deposeth and saith that some time in the fall of the year 1804, he called
at Jacob JOB's, who was then living with his family (cannot read)
William REED, Jrs. claim, in, now Washington County aforesaid. That
he was living in a cabbin, and had a crop of corn growing, and he understood from said REED, that JOB was living there by his, REED's consent. In 1805, JOB moved off, and REED moved into the same place and
continued there untill 1815 or 16, as well as he remembers, and the
place has been inhabited and cultivated ever since. Subscribed and
sworn to by John T. MCNEILL who is personally known to me,
Henry SHURLDS, J.P.   John T. MCNEILL
Sworn to and signature acknowledged May 6th, 1833. L.F. LINN, Comm'r.

Potosi Washington County, May 6th, 1833
Personally appeared before L.F. LINN, one of the Comm'rs. appointed
for the final adjustment of private land claims in Missouri,
Mr. John STEWART, Deputy Surveyor under General WILKINSON, who after
being duly sworn, deposes and says that he surveyed this tract of
land for Wm. REED, Jr. in the year 1806. That there was a good cabbin & corn crib on said place. There was corn in the crib, a field
cleared and there was reason from appearances to believe said place
was in cultivation for two crops.   John STEWART
Sworn to & subscribed day above written. L.F. LINN, Comm'r.
     Adjourned untill Monday next at 9 o'clock A.M.
          Monday Dec. 2nd, 1833 Board Met-F.R. CONWAY, Esqr. Present

John PAUL claiming 640 acres of land under a settlement right on Big
River Bellview Township, see No. 1, pg. 371, No. 4, pg. 482, Book C,
pg. 3. The following testimony was taken before L.F. LINN, Comm'r.
Personally appeared before L.F. LINN, one of the Comm'rs. appointed
for the final adjustment of private land claims in Missouri,
John MCNEAL, who after being duly sworn, deposes and says that he was
well acquainted with John PAUL, who emigrated, he thinks, to this
country in 1799. In 1803, said PAUL made a settlement on Big River

in Belleview Township, and had permission from Joseph DESELLE to make an improvement. In the spring of 1803, said PAUL lived in a camp and was clearing land and raised a crop of corn that year. Deponent, further, states said PAUL continued on said place for several years and gradually improved the land by enlarging his fields and improving his houses. Said deponent saw peach trees growing on said land in 1804. Sworn to and subscribed May 7th, 1833.
L.F. LINN, Comm'r.   John MCNEAL

At the same time appeared Martin RUGGLES, who after being duly sworn, deposes and says that in the summer of 1804, he saw Mr. John PAUL with his family in a log cabbin on a tract of land claimed by said PAUL on Big River, Belleview Settlement. Said PAUL had a small field of corn growing, say 2 or 3 acres. Deponent thinks PAUL was forty years of age.
L.F. LINN, Comm'r.   Martin RUGGLES

Personally appeared before L.F. LINN, one of the Comm'rs., etc. Uriah HULL, aged about 56 years who after being sworn, deposes and says that he came to this now county of Washington, formerly St. Genevieve County in the month of July, 1804. Deponent, further, says that he was at the house of John PAUL on Big River in the month of August following. Said PAUL had built then a house and stable, 3 or 4 acres of ground cleared, peach trees growing. Deponent, further, says he saw corn growing on the same land at that time. Next year, 1805, said PAUL had improved his place by openning five acres more, which Deponent cultivated for said PAUL. He further deposes and says he eat in 1805 peaches from the trees planted on this land by PAUL some years before. Sworn to and subscribed May 10th, 1833.
L.F. LINN, Comm'r.   Uriah HULL

Bede MOORE claiming 640 acres of land situate on the waters of the Saline, now in the County of Perry, see Book No. 1, pg. 345, No. 3, pg. 130, No. 4, pg. 338, Book B, pg. 242, produces a paper purporting to be an affidavit of Pre. Delassus DELUZIERE, former Commandant of New Bourbon, certifying that, prior to the 20th December, 1803, he gave permission to the said Bede MOORE (cannot read) District of the said New Bourbon.
State of Missouri, County of Perry
Nicholas TUCKER, aged 51 years, being duly sworn as the law directs, deposeth and saith that he is well acquainted with Bede MOORE, the original claimant. That he came to this country, then the province of Upper Louisiana, in June 1803 and the witness is also well acquainted with the land claimed and that the claimant was settled and living on the same in November, 1803. There was a house on the land into which the claimant went. That he saw claimant engaged in getting rails, that there was a small piece of land under fence. That claimant remained on the land, himself, till some time in 1804, and that the tract of land has been improved, inhabited and cultivated ever since. Sworn to and subscribed before me, L.F. LINN, Comm'r. this 8th day of May, 1833.
L.F. LINN, Comm'r.   Nicholas TUCKER
And, also, came Joseph MANNING, a witness aged 62 years, who being duly sworn as the law directs, deposeth and saith that he is well acquainted with Bede MOORE, the claimant. That he came to this country in the year 1803. That in the summer & fll of 1803, he was settled on the land claimed & lived on the land. Witness saw him there with his wife & children. That there was a small piece of land under fence. Witness saw turnips growing there. That the claimant remained there for some time, and that the said tract of land has been continually under habitation and cultivation ever since. Sworn to and subscribed before me, L.F. LINN, Comm'r., this 8th day of May, 1833.
L.F. LINN, Comm'r.   Joseph MANNING
       Adjourned untill tomorrow at 9 o'clock A.M.
          Tuesday Dec. 3rd, 1833 Board Met-F.R. CONWAY, Esqr. Present

Bazile VALLE by his legal representative John PERRY claiming 639 acres of land situated at Mine a Breton, see Book C, pg. 497, Minutes No. 3, pg. 158, No. 5, pg 542.
State of Missouri, County of Washington
John T. MCNEAL aged about 70 years, being duly sworn as the law

directs, deposeth and saith that he was well acquainted with
Bazile VALLE, the original claimant. That the witness came to this
country in the year 1797, and that he found VALLE, the claimant at
the Mine a Breton in the year 1798. That in the year 1798 said VALLE
was settled and living on the land claimed, had a cabbin on the same
and some land cleared, and that the said VALLE continued to inhabit
and cultivate the same till he sold to PERRY, and that the said tract
of land has been actually inhabited & cultivated ever since and still
is. Sworn to and subscribed before me, Lewis F. LINN, Comm'rs., this
8th day of May, 1833.
L.F. LINN, Comm'r.   John T. MCNEAL
And, also, came John STEWART, who being duly sworn, deposeth and says
that he is about sixty years old. That he came to this country in
the year 1800. That he knew the original claimant Bazil VALLE. That
he was settled at that time, 1800, on the land claimed, had several
good cabins on the same, had several acres of land cleared and in cultivation and that he continued to inhabit and cultivate the same till
he sold out to John PERRY, Sr., and that said PERRY took possession
of the land and continued to inhabit & cultivate the same and that the
tract of land has been actually inhabited and cultivated ever since,
and this witness, further, says that he surveyed the land for the
claimants. Sworn to and subscribed before me, the Comm'r., this 10th
day of May, 1833.
L.F. LINN, Comm'r.   John STEWART
And, also, came Uriah HULL, a witness aged about 56 years, who being
duly sworn, deposeth and saith that he came to the country in the
year 1804, and that he found Bazile VALLE, the original claimant.
That he was settled on the tract of land claimed, had several houses
had land cleared & cultivated. That he raised wheat on the place in
1804. That he saw it thrashed out and that the said tract of land
has been actually inhabited and cultivated, by the said Bazil VALLE,
or those claiming under him, ever since. And from the appearance of
the place, it had been inhabited & cultivated for some years before.
Sworn to & subscribed before me, the Comm'r. this 10th day of May,
1833.
L.F. LINN, Comm'r.   Uriah HULL

James HAWKINS claiming 640 acres of land situate near Mine a Breton,
see Minutes Book No. 4, pg. 315, Book B, pg. 246. The following
testimony was taken before Lewis F. LINN, Comm'r.
John STEWART of lawful age, being first duly sworn in the above case,
deposeth and saith in January or February, 1805 this deponent assisted in bringing a cartload of corn from off the improvement of
James HAWKINS, and took the corn out of corn crib, the cart was sent
for another load. There were, also, on James HAWKINS improvement at
the same time, corn stocks of the growth of the previous season, and
off of which he supposed the corn to have come, which deponent assisted in hauling. This claim lies about four miles from Potosi on the
Mineral fork, and is known by the name of HAWKINS improvement. This
deponent surveyed this claim for said HAWKINS, and the annexed dia-
gram is a just representation of the claim of HAWKINS, containing
640 acres. (cannot read) HAWKINS removed from his claim aforesaid
that a certain James SCOTT occupied the field of HAWKINS from whence
this deponent, assisted in hauling the corn aforesaid, but whether
obtained by purchase from HAWKINS, this deponent cannot say.
L.F. LINN, Comm'r.   John STEWART

John PAUL of lawful age, being first duly sworn, deposeth and saith
that he came to Mine a Breton with his family in the year 1802, and
became acquainted with James HAWKINS, the above claimant in the latter part of that year. In the fall of the year 1803, the said
James HAWKINS wished to sell this deponent his settlement and improvement made by him on the mine creek or Mineral fork, about four miles
from Mine a Breton, in Washington County in a North West direction.
This affiant, further, states that James SCOTT, now deceased, lived
for many years on said claim and untill he died, and his widow,
Constance SCOTT and a part of the children now live on said claim.
How James SCOTT obtained this claim from HAWKINS, this deponent does
not know. This deponent has, also, heard that Samuel PERRY, late of
Potosi and now deceased, by his last Will and Testament gratuitously
gave to said Constance SCOTT, widow, all his right to said claim.

This deponent, further, states that James SCOTT died insolvent.
L.F. LINN, Comm'r.   John PAUL
        Adjourned untill tomorrow at 9 o'clock A.M.
                Wednesday Dec. 4th, 1833 Board Met-F.R. CONWAY, Present

Thomas BAKER, by his legal representative, William SHANNON claiming
640 acres of land situate in Bellview Settlement County of Washington,
see No. 1, pg. 376, No. 3, pg. 214, No. 4, pg. 367. The following
testimony was taken before Lewis F. LINN, Esqr., one of the Comm'rs.
State of Missouri, County of Washington
Uriah HULL, a witness aged about 56 years, being duly sworn as the
law directs, deposeth and saith that he was acquainted with
Thomas BAKER, the original claimant. That, he, the witness, came to
the country in the year 1804. That he knows the tract of land
claimed. That in July 1804, Thomas BAKER offered to sell him his
place, and that the witness went with said BAKER to the land that
said BAKER then lived on the land, had a cabbin and some land cleared
some two acres or perhaps more. That the land was then in actual cultivation in such articles as corn & other things that a family would
want. There was some fruit trees planted on the place, they were
peach trees. Then some were two feet high. The witness was told the
trees were planted (cannot read) before this witness was then hunting
a place to settle was the reason he went to see the land. That BAKER
continued to inhabit and cultivate the land for several years, and
then sold to SHANNON. Sworn to & subscribed before me, the Comm'r.
this 10th day of May, 1833.
L.F. LINN, Comm'r.   Uriah HULL
John STEWART, aged about 54 years being duly sworn as the law directs,
deposeth and saith that in the month of February, 1806, he surveyed
for Thomas BAKER a tract of land of 480 acres 3/4 & 32 poles, in the
Bellview settlement for which he made out a plat of survey and the
same was returned to the proper officer. That he states these facts
from the original plat & field notes of the survey made by himself
and still in his possession. That the same was surveyed as the head
right of said Thomas BAKER, and that he had the recording fees for
the same.   John STEWART

And, also, came Uriah HULL, John STEWART, Joseph N. REYBURN &
Timothy PHELPS, who being severally sworn as the law directs, deposeth and saith that they were well acquainted with Benjamin CROW, who
has heretofore testified in this case that he was always esteemed a
man of good character, standing & reputation, and that he was generally esteemed a man of veracity and truth and entitled to full credit in
all his statements and testimonies, and these affiants believe such to
be the fact. Sworn to and subscribed before me, the Comm'r., this 10th
day of May, 1833.
                Uriah HULL   John STEWART
                J.N. REYBURN   Timothy PHELPS
L.F. LINN, Comm'r.

Potosi, Washington County, May 6th, 1833
Personally appeared before me, L.F. LINN, one of the Comm'rs. appointed for the final adjustment of land claims in Missouri,
Samuel HENDERSON, who after being duly sworn, deposes and says that
he and Thomas BAKER were school fellows and were nearly of the same
age. That deponent was born in the year 1785, he verily believes
there was but four months difference in their ages. Deponent, further, states that in the year 1811, he moved into the same settlement
in now Belleview Township, Washington County, at which time the afore-
mentioned BAKER did not reside on said tract of land, now claimed by
him or his legal representatives. Sworn to & subscribed day above
mentioned.
L.F. LINN, Comm'r.   Samuel HENDERSON

John JOHNSON, of lawful age being duly sworn, deposes & says that in
the fall of 1832 he asked Thomas BAKER his age, his reply was that he
the said BAKER would be 47 during the next winter.
L.F. LINN, Comm'r.   Jno. JOHNSON

At the same time appeared John T. MCNEAL, (cannot read) also duly
sworn, deposes and says that he never knew of Thomas BAKER having any

claim to a settlement claim on Big River or any other place. Said deponent, further, says that Thomas BAKER improved a place for his father in the year 1804, which improvement was taken by his father in the fall of 1804 and continued to be held by him as his property. Deponent, further, states that he heard the father of Thomas BAKER say in the spring of 1805, that said Thomas was not of age at that time. Deponent says he never heard of Thomas BAKER having made an improvement for himself, but a tomahawk improvement, which was known by girdling trees.
L.F. LINN, Comm'r.   John T. MCNEILL

At the same time appeared William DAVIS, Sr., of lawfull age, who being duly sworn, deposes and says that he emigrated to this country in the year 1809 to Bellevue Settlement. That Thomas BAKER took said deponent to a tract of land on Big River, which said BAKER claimed as his property. Deponent saw a pole pen, like a hog pen. That he saw a few rails split laying on the ground. That this was all the improvement he saw on said place or parcel of land, until the year 1811, when Benjamin HARDEN took possession of it as public land who becoming alarmed at the prospect of an Indian war, quit the country and left it in the care of his nephew Joseph HARDEN. Deponent says that in the year 1812, whilst the said Joseph HARDEN was on a campaign against the Indians, Thomas BAKER broke open the house of said HARDEN and took possession and kept it until he sold his claim. Deponent further says that Thomas BAKER told him that his father and Benjamin CROW notified all those who claimed places to be on them by a certain day and accordingly on the day thus appointed, the said Thomas BAKER and many others did go and remain on certain pieces of land, and that the father of the said Thomas BAKER & the said CROW did go round, and saw the said Thomas & others thus in possession or occupancy of certain lands, and report says that they afterwards went to St. Louis as witnesses to prove up their claims to land thus occupied as aforesaid. Question by Wm. SHANNON, as assignee of Thos. BAKER. Were you a resident in Upper Louisiana or were you even in said Territory previous to 1809? Answer by witness: No, I emigrated to the Territory of Upper Louisiana in 1809.
L.F. LINN, Comm'r.   Signed   William (X) DAVIS
                                                  . his mark

        Adjourned untill tomorrow at 9 o'clock A.M.
            Thursday Dec. 5th, 1833 Board Met-F.R. CONWAY, Esq., Present

Pierre (cannot read last name or first line of entry) claiming 1,000 arpents of land, situate at the place called the Old Cape Girardeau, see Book E, pg. 27, Book No. 5, pg. 416, produces a paper purporting to be an original concession from Charles Dehault DELASSUS, dated 23rd January, 1800. M.P. LEDUC, duly sworn, says that the signature to the recommendation is in the proper handwriting of Louis LORIMIER, Commandant of Cape Girardeau, and the signature to the concession is in the proper handwriting of Carlos Dehault DELASSUS.

Joseph SILVAIN claiming 250 arpents of land, see Record Book E, pg. 27, Minutes No. 5, pg. 499, produces a paper purporting to be an original concession from Charles Dehault DELASSUS, dated 15th December, 1799. M.P. LEDUC, duly sworn, says that the signature to the recommendation is in the true handwriting of Louis LORIMIER, Comm't. of Cape Girardeau, and the signature to the concessios is in the proper handwriting of Carlos Dehault DELASSUS.(No. 293, No. 7, pg. 183)

Barthelemi RICHARD claiming 1,200 arpents of land, situate in the District of Cape Girardeau, see Book E, pg. 26, Minutes No. 5, pg. 492, produces a paper purporting to be an original concession from Zenon TRUDEAU dated 29th December, 1798. M.P. LEDUC, duly sworn, says that the signature to the recommendation is in the proper handwriting of Louis LORIMIER, Commandant of Cape Girardeau, and the the signature to the concession is in the proper handwriting of Zenon TRUDEAU. The following testimony was taken before Lewis F. LINN, Comm'r.
St. Genevieve, April 29th, 1833.
Personally appeared before me, one of the Comm'rs. appointed for the final adjustment of land claims in Missouri, Mr. Antoine LACHAPELLE, who after being duly sworn, deposeth & saith that he knew that Mr. Barth. RICHARD inhabited & cultivated a tract of land in Cape

Girardeau County, then Upper Louisiana, which tract of land was known by the name of the Old Cape. That he knew the same, RICHARD to be an active, industrious and worthy man. That the same RICHARD inhabited and cultivated said place at the Old Cape in 1798 & 1799.

Antoine (X) LACHAPELLE

Sworn to & subscribed before the under-   his mark
signed L.F. LINN, Land Comm'r.

Adjourned until tomorrow at 9 o'clock A.M.

Friday Dec. 6th, 1833 Board Met-F.R. CONWAY, Esq., Present

Israel DODGE by his legal representative claiming 1000 arpents of land (cannot read) see Book E, pg. 220, Minutes No. 1, pg. 292, No. 4, pg. 465.

John ANDERSON by his heirs & legal representatives, claiming 640 acres situated in Bellevue Settlement, County of Washington, see Minutes Book No. 1, pg. 357, No. 3, pg. 124, No. 4, pg. 334, Book B, pg. 215.
State of Missouri, County of Washington
John T. MCNEAL aged about 70 years, being duly sworn as the law directs, deposeth and saith that he was well acquainted with the original claimant, John ANDERSON, usually called John Crow ANDERSON. That he settled on the land claimed in the year 1802 or 1803. That he built a small house on the same and made a small field of some two or three acres and sowed turnips thereon in the fall of 1803. That he understood that the claimant was there at times coninueing to clear and improve on the same. That the claimant as he understood then, sold the claim and that John BEAR or BAR, took possession of the same and lived on the same and continued to improve & cultivate the same till he died. And at his death, James BEAR, his son, took possession of the same and he continued in possession of the same till he left the country, when the same was left in possession of William BEAR, his uncle, who is still in the actual possession and inhabitation of the same. Sworn to & subscribed before me, the Comm'r., this 9th day of May, 1833.
L.F. LINN, Comm'r.   John T. MCNEAL
And also came John STEWART, a witness aged 64 years who being duly sworn as the law directs, deposeth and saith that he was well acquainted with John ANDERSON, the original claimant and that he knows the land claimed. That he believes said ANDERSON came to the country in the year 1803. That he was informed he had a claim to a tract of land and that in 1806, he was called on to survey the same, which he did. And that he made out a plat of survey, which was duly returned and recorded and the recording fees were paid. That when he surveyed the same there was an improvement on the land and a house or cabbin. ANDERSON sold the claim to one John BEAR and the same has been inhabited & cultivated ever since, he believes. Sworn to and subscribed before me, the Comm'r., this 10th day of May, 1833.   John STEWART
L.F. LINN, Comm'r.
And also came Uriah HULL, a witness aged about 56 years, who being duly sworn, deposeth and saith that he was well acquainted with
John ANDERSON, the original claimant, that this witness came to the country in 1804 and then found said ANDERSON on the tract of land claimed. That he had a cabbin on the land and some improvement. That he understood that he had raised some crop in 1804. That said ANDERSON (cannot read) (Pgs. 369 & 370 missing)

John STEWART, being further sworn, deposeth & saith that James BROWN and his wife resided at Squire BOHERS at the time he, James BROWN, was building and making his improvement before he moved, and this was in the year 1804 that he was building and improving on the land. Then BROWN moved on the land in 1804. John STEWART
L.F. LINN, Comm'r.

Adjourned untill Monday next at 9 o'clock A.M.

Monday Dec. 9th, 1833 Board Met-F.R. CONWAY, Esq. Present

David STRICKLAND, by his legal representative John PERRY claiming 1,247 arpents & 62 perches of land situate near Mine a Breton, County of Washington, see Book No. 1, pg. 506, No. 3, pg. 282, No. 4, pg. 384.
State of Missouri, County of Washington
Claimant produces a paper purporting to be a permission to settle by Joseph DECELLE, dated December 5th, 1803. Also, produces as a witness, John T. MCNEAL, aged about 70 years, who being duly sworn as the law

directs, deposeth and saith that he, this witness, came to this country in the year 1797, and that he was well acquainted with the original claimant, David STRICKLAND. That he settled on the land claimed
in the fall or winter of 1803. That in the year 1804, he cleared a
field of about eight acres and actually raised corn thereon that year.
And that the said tract of land has been actually inhabited and cultivated either by the said STRICKLAND or those claiming under him ever
since. And this witness, further, says that he was acquainted with
Joseph DECELLE, that he has seen him write. That said DECELLE was the
acting Commandant or police officer at Mine a Breton in the year 1803,
and that the name and signature to the permission from him to the said
STRICKLAND to settle, dated the 5th day of December, 1803, is the proper name and signature and in the proper handwriting of the said
DECELLE. That at the time of the settlement on the land aforesaid, the
said STRICKLAND had a wife and some six or seven children at least.
Sworn to & subscribed before me L.F. LINN, Comm'r., this 8th day of
May, 1833.
L.F. LINN, Comm'r.   John T. MCNEAL
And, also, came John STEWART a witness aged about 64 years, who being
duly sworn as the law directs, deposeth and saith that he surveyed the
land claimed in the year 1806 for the claimant, and that at the time
the place was inhabited and cultivated and had the appearance of having
been settled on for some years. That there was buildings and cleared
land on the same. That he knows said STRICKLAND was on the land in
1804, and raised a crop that year. That said STRICKLAND had a wife and
some six seven or eight children. That he made a return of the survey
to the proper officer, and the recording fees were paid.
Sworn before L.F. LINN, Comm'r.   John STEWART
     Adjourned untill tomorrow at 9 o'clock A.M.
               Tuesday Dec. 10th, 1833 Board Met-F.R. CONWAY, Esqr. Present

John EARS by his legal representatives and heirs claiming 960 arpents
of land situate on the waters of Big River, County of St. Francis, see
Minutes No. 1, pg. 370, No. 4,pg. 481.
State of Missouri, County of Washington
Alexander MCCOY, a witness aged about 52 years, being duly sworn as
the law directs, deposeth & saith that he was well acquainted with the
original claimant, John EARS. That he was on the tract of land claimed
in the year 1802. That he had a house on the land & some land cleared
and that he raised a crop on the land in 1802. That said claimant came
to the country in 1801. That in the year 1802, the claimant sold his
improvement to Jacob DOGET. That said Jacob took immediate possession
of the place and died shortly after the purchase. And that the widow
of said Jacob lived on the land & raised a crop in 1803, and the widow
continued to live on the said land and cultivated the same till the
year 1806 cr 1807, when she died. That James RIETH then lived on the
land for some time, and this witness then as the administrator of
Jacob DOGET rented the land to Neeley STUART, who remained in the possession thereof for one year, and that after STUART left the place,
Lewis SIMMS, in right of his wife, one of the heirs of Jacob DOGET, lived
on and cultivated the same for several years. That the said Lewis SIMMS
and Mary DOGETT, now Mary TRIPP, are the only two surviving heirs and
children of the said Jacob DOGET, that this witness was told by
Jacob DOGET of the sale and purchase of the improvement and that he paid
a part of the money to said EARS, say fifty dollars, for the Estate of
Jacob DOGET, which was paid in 1803. That said John EARS had a wife and
four children. Sworn to & subscribed before me, the Comm'r., this 9th
day of May, 1833.   Alexander MCCOY
L.F. LINN, Comm'r.
Also, came Jacob MOSTELLER, a witness aged about 56 years who being duly
sworn as the law directs, deposeth & Saith that he was well acquainted
with John EARS, the original claimant, and with the tract of land
claimed. That the said John EARS settled on the land in the year 1801,
& built a house on the same. That he cleared some land in 1802, and
cultivated the same. That in the year 1803. (cannot read) improvement
and head right to Jacob DOGETT, as he was told by both EARS & DOGETT,
and that DOGETT took immediate possession of the house and tract of land
& lived on the same till he died, and that then his wife and family still
lived on the same for some time and raised a crop in 1803 and the widow
remained on the land till she died in 1806 cr 1807. Then one,
James REIGH lived a while on the land then one Nuley STUART, and after

STUART left the same, one Lewis SIMMS, who had married Olive DOGETT, in her right took possession of the land and continued to inhabit & cultivate the same. That said Olive DOGETT was one of the daughters of Jacob DOGETT. That Mary DOGETT now intermarried with Henry TRIPP, and Olive DOGETT now intermarried with said Lewis SIMMS, are the only two surviving heirs of the said Jacob DOGETT, deceased, that said EARS came to the county in the spring of the year 1801, built a house on this land in the fall of 1801 and had a wife & four children. Sworn to & subscribed before me, the Comm'r., this 9th day of May, 1833. L.F. LINN, Comm'r.   Signed, Jacob MOSTELLER
And also came James MCCOY, aged about 53 years, who being duly sworn as the law directs, deposeth & saith that he was well acquainted with the original claimant, John EARS. That he came to this country in the year 1801 and settled on the tract of land claimed in the fall of the same year, and that in 1802, he cleared land and raised a crop. The said John EARS then sold his improvement and head right to Jacob DOGETT, who took immediate possession of the place and continued to inhabit the same till he died, and the witness then went away and returned in 1805 or 1806 and found the widow and family of said Jacob DOGETT still in the possession and cultivation of the place. That after the widow died in 1806 or 1807, one James REITH took possession of the place and continued on the same and for about one year, and then one Nuley STUART inhabited and cultivated the same for some time. And that after STUART had left the place, Lewis SIMMS, who had married Alice DOGETT, one of the daughters of the said Jacob DOGETT, took possession of the place & inhabited & cultivated the same for some time. That said John EARS had a wife & four children and that the said Alice DOGETT, now Alice SIMMS, and Mary DOGETT, now Mary TRIPP, wife of Henry D. TRIPP, are the only two surviving heirs of the said Jacob DOGETT, deceased. Sworn to & subscribed before me, the Comm'r., this 9th day of May, 1833.
L.F. LINN, Comm'r.   John (X) MCCOY
                                         his mark
        Adjourned untill tomorrow at 9 o'clock A.M.
          Wednesday Dec. 11th, 1833 Board Met-F.R. CONWAY, Esq. Present

Henry TUCKER, by his legal representatives claiming 800 arpents of land situate on Custards Fork of the Saline, see Record Book F, pg. 13, BATES decision pg. 98, No. 6, pg. 429, Bk B, pg. 242, No. 5, pg. 505. Beverly ALLEN, being duly sworn, says that in the year 1825, he had in his possession a plat of survey of a tract of land claimed by William HANCOCK & Britain WEST, as assignees of Henry TUCKER, who claimed the same as a settlement right, he believes that the document appeared to be the original survey of the claim, for what quantity he does not recollect. That on the back of the plat was endorsed the words, "Confirmed 250 acres", (or "arpens"). J.L. DONALDSON, which endorsement & signature believes from a comparison of the same with the handwriting & signature of said DONALDSON, on papers in the office of the Recorder of Land Titles, to be the handwriting and signature of J.L. DONALDSON, once a Commissioner of Land Titles under the Act of Congress, providing for their adjustment in the Territory of Missouri. By whom the survey was made, he does not recollect. He also sates that the said plat was lost or stollen out of his office at St. Genevieve in the year 1825 or 1826. That the land embraced in the survey lay as it purported on the North Branch of the Sourth fork of the Saline Creek in the old District of St. Genevieve, Missouri.
        Adjourned untill tomorrow at 9 o'clock A.M.
          Thursday Dec. 12th, 1833-Board Met-F.R. CONWAY, Present

Paschal DETCHMENDY, by his legal representatives claiming 7,056 arpents of land, see Book D, pg. 109, Minutes No. 5, pg. 414, produces an original petition to Congress, letter of Paschal DETCHMENDY to SOULARD, dated 14th February, 1804, also a letter from Thos. MADDIN, Deputy Surveyor to Antoine SOULARD. Also, testimony of SOULARD, taken before F.M. GUYOT, Justice of the Peace, on the 7th day of December, 1818. On the back of Thomas MADDIN's letter to SOULARD, dated 14th February, 1804 is the following testimony:
Thomas MADDIN, being duly sworn as the law directs, says that the signature to the within letter is in his handwriting and that the facts stated in said letter are just and true. Sworn to & subscribed before me, the Comm'r., this 11th May, 1833.   Thomas MADDIN
L.F. LINN, Comm'r.

On the 28th day of October, 1818 before me, Joseph BOGG, one of the Justices of the Peace of the County of St. Genevieve in the Missouri Territory, personally appeared Thomas MADDIN, Esqr. of the said county, who being duly sworn according to law, deposeth and saith that in the beginning of February, 1804, he, as deputy for A. SOULARD, the Spanish Surveyor General of the Upper Part of the Province of Louisiana, received instructions from the said Surveyor to make a survey for Mr. Paschal DETCHMENDY of the said, now County, then District of St. Genevieve, a tract of land granted to him by the Spanish Commandant of several thousand arpents, but the exact quantity, he does not now recollect. That in company with the said Paschal DETCHMENDY, he the deponent, in consequence of such orders, went to a place now called Bellevue in the now County of Washington, in the said Territory and in the then District of St. Genevieve, for the purpose of making the said survey. That when they were there and preferring to make the same, they were met by a number of armed men, at least ten, who by force and with threats of personal violence, prevented him from doing so, in consequence of which he was obliged to leave the ground and desist from his operations. The said armed persons even following them some distance for fear as he then thought and now thinks, that he & the said DETCHMENDY should return to survey the said tract of land. (cannot read) that the said Survey would then have been made, if he had not been opposed in the manner as above mentioned, and that the said survey was so attempted to be made on or about the middle of the said month of February in the said year; and before the possession of the country was had by the United States. And, lastly, the deponent saith that he does not think nor does he now believes the said survey could at any time thereafter have been made, and that any further attempts to have done so, would have been attended with the like danger of personal violence and opposition.   Thomas MADDIN
Sworn to & subscribed the day & year within, before me, Joseph BOGY, J.P. Sworn to & signatrue acknowledged before me May 11th, 1833.
L.F. LINN, Comm'r.
John B. VALLE, aged about 70 years being duly sworn as the law directs, deposeth and saith that he was well acquainted with the said
Charles Dehault DELASSUS, that he was the Lt. Governor of the province of Upper Louisiana in the year 1799, and this deponent, further, says that he was and still is well acquainted with the said
Paschal DETCHMENDY, the original claimant. That he was a citizen and residenter in the province of Upper Louisiana, before and in the year 1799, and that he has continued a citizen and residenter ever since and still is. And that the date of the grant aforesaid the said
Paschal DETCHMENDY was a man of considerable property. That he had a family & slaves, active and enterprising, having built a mill and improved other property in the country.
Sworn to & subscribed before me, L.F. LINN, Comm'r., this 27th May, 1833.
L.F. LINN, Comm'r.   J.Bste. VALLE
     Adjourned untill tomorrow at 9 o'clock A.M.
          Friday Dec. 13th, 1833-Board Met-F.R. CONWAY, Present

William DAVIS by his legal representatives claiming 640 acres of land, (originally filed for a less quantity) situate in Bellevue settlement, County of Washington, see Book No. 5, pg. 404.
State of Missouri, County of Washington
John STUART, being duly sworn, deposeth and saith that he was called on by John LITTLE, who claimed under the same William DAVIS, to survey the tract of land here claimed, which he said was granted to said DAVIS by the Spanish Government, and that this deponent surveyed the same in January or February, 1806, and returned the plat of survey to the proper officer and the recording fees were paid. That when he surveyed the same there was a good improvement on the same and some houses and that the (cannot read) improvements had the appearance of being some two or more years old. Sworn to & subscribed before me, L.F. LINN, Comm'r., this 9th day of May, 1833.
L.F. LINN, Comm'r.   John STEWART
And, also, came John T. MCNEAL a witness aged about 70 years, who being duly sworn, deposeth and saith that he is acquainted with the tract of land claimed. That in the year 1805, he saw one John LITTLE on the same in the spring of the year. That the house and improvement had the appearance of having been made the year before. Said LITTLE told this

witness that he had purchased the land of a man of the name of DAVIS, who he said had procured a Spanish right for the same, and that he knows said LITTLE continued on the same land for several years and raised several crops. Sworn to and subscribed before me, L.F. LINN, the Comm'r., this 9th day of May, 1833.

L.F. LINN, Comm'r.   John T. MCNEAL

And, also came Uriah HULL, a witness aged about 56 years who being duly sworn, deposeth and saith that he knew John LITTLE. That he, LITTLE, was on this tract of land in the summer of 1804. That he raised a crop on the land that year. That there was a cabbin on the land, in which he lived. That he had a wife and several children. Sworn to and subscribed before me, the Comm'r., this 10th day of May, 1833.

L.F. LINN, Comm'r.   Uriah HULL

   Adjourned till tomorrow at 9 o'clock A.M.
     Saturday Dec. 14th, 1833-Board Met-F.R. CONWAY, Present

Joseph REED, Jr., by his legal representatives claiming 640 acres of land situate in Bellevue County of Washington, see Book B, pg. 222, Minutes No. 3, pg. 126, No. 4, pg. 336.

State of Missouri, County of Washington

The claimant produces James JOHNSON, as a witness aged 44 years, who being duly sworn as the law directs deposeth and saith that he was well acquainted with the original claimant, Joseph REED, Jr., that he, witness, came to the province of Upper Louisiana in the year 1804, and that in the month of July or August in that year 1804, as well as he recollects, he assisted in clearing and improving some land on the tract claimed and that about one acre more or less, was so cleared on which some turnips were sown and perhaps some grass seed, which work went to and was for the use of the said Joseph REED, Junior, in some three or four days afterwards, he, the said REED, raising a house on the said improvement and land. This deponent, further, states that at the time he assisted in clearing as aforesaid, there had been some work done on the same place and (cannot read) on a tree on the said improvement, the work had the appearance of having been done the year before this witness assisted to clear as aforesaid. That said REED sold his claim to one David GALLAGHER for the consideration of 140 dollars, and that the said GALLAGHER took possession of and lived on the same place and continued to cultivate the same till he died, and his widow and heirs continued on the same some time afterwards, and then sold the same to Philip T. MCCABE, for one thousand dollars, and said MCCABE has been in the possession of the said land ever since. That the said Joseph REED, Jr., was, he believes at the time, above the age of twenty one years when the improvements aforesaid were made.

Sworn to & subscribed before me, L.F. LINN, one of the Comm'rs. appointed to investigate & report on land claims in Missouri, this 7th day of May, 1833.   James JOHNSON

L.F. LINN, Comm'r.

And, also, came John STEWART a witness aged about sixty four, who being duly sworn as the law directs, deposeth and saith that William REED, Sr., the father of Joseph REED, Jr., with the said Joseph REED, Jr., came to the country, he believes in 1802, and that they moved to Bellvue in the year 1803 and cultivated land in Bellevue in 1803, and continued as residenters and cultivators untill they left the country.

L.F. LINN, Comm'r.   John STEWART

And, also, came Martin RUGGLES a witness aged about 58 years and upwards, who being duly sworn as the law directs, deposeth and saith that in 1802, he was at an improvement in Bellevue, said to be William REED's, and that after an absence of some time, he returned & was at the same improvement and there saw Joseph REED, Jr., the claimant and this deponent, further, says that he is well acquainted with Mr. James JOHNSON, the witness who has deposed above. That he is generally esteemed a man of good character and of veracity and truth.

L.F. LINN, Comm'r.   Martin RUGGLES

   Adjourned untill Monday next at 9 o'clock A.M.
     Monday Dec. 16th, 1833 Board Met-F.R. CONWAY, Present

Curtis MORRIS, by his legal representatives claiming 746 arpents, 75 perches of land situated in Bellevue Settlement, see Record Book B, pg. 227, Minutes Book No. 1, pg. 376, No. 4, pg. 482.

State of Missouri   The State of Missouri to any two Justices of
the Peace within and for the County of Washington Greetings
Know ye that in confidence of your prudence and fidelity, I do require
and authorise and command you to cause to come before you, James BEAR,
John SWAN, J.T. MCNEAL and Mary MCNEAL, his wife, Joseph MCMAURTRY,
Samuel BRIDGE and Bernard ROGAN, and each of them examine upon their
respective corporal oaths to be by you, or one of you, administered
touching their knowledge of any thing that may relate to the cultivation, inhabitation and claiming of the South West quarter of Section
No. 18 Township No. 35 N in Range 3 East of the 5th principal meridian
and also a part of the South East quarter of Section No. 13, in Township No. 35 N in Range No. 2, East of the said 5th principal meridian
by Thomas MORROW and William (cannot read last name) and William (cannot read last name) prior to the twelfth day of April, 1814, and also
to the cultivation inhabitation and claiming of the said land by
Curtis MORRIS, in order to perpetuate the remembrance of the said facts
on behalf of William HUDSPETH under Airs HUDSPETH and having reduced to
writing in the English language or the language of the deponents, the
depositions so by you takne as aforesaid, you send the same certified
by you, sealed up and directed, together with this writ to the Clerk
of the Circuit Court of Washington County, wherein the said lands are
said to be situated, with all convenient speed.
Given under my hand and seal in Washington County this 25th day of
June, A.D. 1827.   Will. C. CARR (Seal)

County of Washington
Be it remembered that in pursuance of a commission from the honorable
William C. CARR, Judge of the Third District in the State of Missouri,
directed to two Justices of the Peace in the County and state aforesaid and agreeably to an advertisement in the Missouri Republican by
William HUDSPETH and Airs HUDSPETH, we the undersigned
William HINKSON & Andrew GOFORTH, two Justices of the Peace in the
County aforesaid, have met at the house of Andrew GOFORTH, Esqr., in
the township of Bellevue on the 9th day of October, A.D. 1827, and
proceeded to take the depositions of witnesses as named in the aforesaid commission, touching their knowledge of the facts as contained in
the aforesaid commission, and proceded to take the depositions of witnesses as follows; to wit:

James BEAR of lawful age, being produced and sworn according to law,
upon his corporal oath deposeth and saith:
Question by A.W. HUDSPETH, agent for William And Aires HUDSPETH - Did
you know of Thomas MORROW and William INGE, inhabiting and cultivating
on the S.W. 1/4 Sec. No. 18 in Township No. 35 N. R. 3, E of the 5th
principal meridian, and also at the same time, a part of the S.E. 1/4
Sec. No. 13, Township No. 35 N. R. 2 E. of the 5th principal meridian?
Answer by Deponent: I was knowing to Thomas MORROW settling on the S.E.
1/4 Sec. No. 13 (agreeable to the surveying) in T. 35 N. R. 2 E. of the
5th principal meridian.   There was a piece of ground cleared on the
same part of which improvement is included in the S.W. 1/4 of Sec. No.
18, T. 35, N. R. 3 E. of the 5th principal meridian.
Q. by A.W. HUDSPETH.   In what year did Thomas MORROW settle there?
A. by Deponent: As well as I recollect, it was in the fall of 1811 or
1812.
Q. by A.W. HUDSPETH: Did you ever hear Thomas MORROW say that
William INGE was his partner?
A. by Deponent: I did.
Q. by A.W. HUDSPETH: Did you know of any ground being cultivated in
1812 or 13 on one or both of the above named 1/4 sections?
A. by Deponent: Yes, there was corn raised on the improvement that
was included on both of the above named quarter sections.
Q. by A.W. HUDSPETH: Who done the labour that raised that corn?
A. by deponent: I do not know.
Q. by A.W. HUDSPETH: Do you know of Jacob MAHAN working for
Thomas MORROW & William INGE on said improvement in 1812 or 13?
A. by Deponent: I saw Jacob MAHAN working with Thomas MORROW at the
Distillery on that place.
Q. by A.W. HUDSPETH: Did you understand from Thomas MORROW or
William INGE that the aforesaid improvement belonged to them?
A. by Deponent: I do not recollect.
Q. by A.W. HUDSPETH: Do you know who claimed and occupied the improve-

ment in the spring of 1814?
A. by Deponent: I do not recollect.
                                    James BEAR
Sworn and subscribed before us on the tenth day of October, 1827 at
the place and within the hours first aforesaid.

A. GOFORTH-Wilm. HINKSON, Justices of the Peace
Joseph MCMARTREY of lawful age being produced & sworn according to
law upon his corporal oath, deposeth & saith:
Q. by A.W. HUDSPETH: In what year did Curtis MORRIS settle & improve
the place whereon Daniel PEHLPS now lives?
Ans. by Deponent: In 1805 Curtis MORRIS married, and the next morning
he started, as he said, to fix a house, where Daniel PHELPS now lives,
to live in. Further, I do not know whether Curtis MORRIS had any im-
provement on that place before that time or not.
Q. by A.W. HUDSPETH: Did you know of Walter CROW cultivating the land
now in question in 1803 or 1804?
A. by Deponent: I was there in 1803 and saw an improvement and
Walter CROW told me that he made an improvement there.
Q. By Timothy PHELPS: Do you know who claimed the place in 1804?
A. by Deponent: I do not recollect. And further this deponent saith
not.   Joseph MCMURTREY
Sworn to & subscribed before us on the 10th day of October, 1827 at
the place and between the hours first aforesaid.

A. GOFORTH - Wm. HINKSON Justices of the Peace sworn to & signature
acknowledged May 9th, 1833. L.F. LINN, Comm'r.
John T. MCNEAL of lawful age, being produced and after being duly
sworn according to law, upon his corporal oath, deposeth and saith:
Q. by A.W. HUDSPETH: Do you know when Curtis MORRIS first settled on
and inhabited and cultivated the place whereon Daniel PHELPS and
Timothy PHELPS now live?
A. by Deponent: I do not know.
Q. by A.W. HUDSPETH: Were you acquainted with Curtis MORRIS in the
year 1804?
A. by Deponent: Yes, I was.
Q. by A.W. HUDSPETH: Where did Curtis MORRIS make his home in the
summer of 1804?
A. by Deponent: In the fore part of the summer, he made his home at
William ASHBROOK.
Q. by A.W. HUDSPETH: Did you ever hear Curtis MORRIS say that he
raised a crop on A. MCCOY's plantation or in that neighbourhood in the
(left blank) of 1804?
A. by Deponent: I am not certain.
Q. by A.W. HUDSPETH: How far do you think that William ASHBROOK lived
in the summer of 1804, from the place in question?
A. by Deponent: I suppose it to be about six miles.
Q. by A.W. HUDSPETH: In what year and month did Curtis MORRIS marry?
A. by Deponent: Agreably to my recollection, about the last of Janu-
ary, 1805.
Q. by Timothy PHELPS: When did you assist Curtis MORRIS to build a
cabbin on the place in question?
A. by Deponent: In February or March, 1804.
Q. By.A.W. HUDSPETH: Was the cabbin made ready for the reception of
a family and in what situation was the cabbin prepared in 1804?
A. by Deponent: It was raised to the cave bearers the day I assisted
and I do not recollect that I was on the place any more in that year.
Q. by Timothy PHELPS? Where was the place in question situated, and
by whose claims was it bounded?
A. by Deponent: It was situated on the South side of Cedar Creek, and
bounded by Benjamin STROTHER's claim on the North, by Walter CROW's on
the West, by Benjamin CROW's on the SouthWest, and by Bernard RAGINS
on the South.
Q. by Timothy PHELPS: Did you understand by Curtis MORRIS that he
claimed that improvement at the time you helped him to build the cabbin?
A. by Deponent: Yes, I did.
Q. By A.W. HUDSPETH: Did you know of Curtis MORRIS making any other
improvement on the place in question in the year 1804, except the part
of the cabbin aforesaid?
A. by Deponent: I do not know.
And furthermore this deponent saith not.

Sworn and subscribed to before us on the 11th day of October at the place & between the hours first aforesaid.

A. GOFORTH, Wm. HINKSON, Justices of the Peace
Sworn to and signature of John T. MCNEAL acknowledged May 9th, 1833.
L. F. LINN, Comm.
Here follows the certificate of the two Justices, A. GOFORTH &
W. HINKSON, dated 12th October, 1827 and also, the certificate of
John JONES, Clerk of the Circuit Court & en officio Recorder dated
November 3rd, 1827.
The State of Missouri, County of Wayne
Depositions of a witness examined on the 4th day of October in the
year of our Lord, 1827, between the hours of 8 o'clock in the fore-
noon & 7 o'clock in the afternoon of that day, in the Township of
Kelly at the dwelling house of Joseph PAIN, in the County aforesaid
in pursuance to an order from the Hon. William C. CARR, Judge of the
Third Judicial District, to any two Justices of the Peace in Wayne
County, ordered that the deposition of Jacob MAHAN be taken to per-
petuate the remembrance of facts on the papers and in the behalf of
Wm. HUDSPETH and Avis HUDSPETH relating to the improving, cultivating
& inhabiting of an improvement lying & being on the waters of Cedar
Creek, in Bellevue Township in the County of Washington and State of
Missouri, now claimed by the aforesaid W. HUDSPETH and Avez HUDSPETH
as a preemption right. And now at this day, Jacob MAHAN of lawful
age, being produced, sworn and examined, deposeth & saith as follows:
Question by Avez HUDSPETH: Were you ever employed by Thomas MORROW
& William INGE to work and improve a tract of land in Bellevue Township in the County of Washington & State of Missour?
Answer by Jacob MAHAN: I was employed by Thomas MORROW and I considered Thomas MORROW and William INGE in partnership and I was employed
to work on and build a still house on the said improvement lying &
being near the forks of Saline & Cedar Creek.
2nd Question: In what year and how long were you employed by
Thomas MORROW?
Answer: I begun to work with him the last week in November, 1812,
and continued with him five months and assisted him in planting corn
in the month of May, following in the same place.
Question: Did you consider MORROW and INGE in copartnership at the
time you were employed by MORROW?
Answer: I di, for they both frequently told me they were in copartnership.
Question: Do you know who succeeded MORROW & INGE on the aforesaid
improvement?
Answer: Yes, In the year 1814, the third week in February, I was employed by INGE to go out and take possession of the improvement for
him and carry on the work for him, and I continued for him one month
to attend the still house, and raised a crop of corn for myself the
following season, but considered the land to belong to INGE.
Question: Did INGE pay you for your services done in years 1812 &
1813?
Answer: Yes, he agreed to pay me all, and some time afterwards, he
paid me part and denied the partnership and refused to pay me the
balance after MORROW left the country.
Question: Did you understand that MORROW intended to return to this
country when he went away?
Answer: When I parted with MORROW, he told me he would come back.
Question: Did you understand what became of MORROW?
Answer: I did not.
Question: Do you know if INGE & MORROW built a Mill on Cedar Creek?
Answer: Yes. In the time of my work for MORROW, a few days before
my time was out, MORROW commenced building a mill on Cedar Creek, and
from that time till I came out to take possession for INGE, the mill
was grinding.
Question: Do you know the section this improvement is on, or who joins
it, and who occupied the improvement last, and how far the improvement
was from the said mill?
Answer: I do not know the sectional lines, but it laid near South of
Benjamin STROTHER's confirmation claim, and East of Daniel PHELPS's
claim, and East of the great road leading from Mine a Breton through
Bellevue; and when I was at the place last, I saw an old man there who
was called HUDSPETH and told me he lived there. The improvement was
about twenty five rods from the mill on Cedar Creek.

Question by Timothy PHELPS: Since MORROW left the country did you
not frequently hear INGE deny the partnership between him and MORROW?
Answer: Yes, I did.
Question: Did you not make a demand of upwards of one hundred dol-
lars for services rendered & corn made use of on that place, in con-
sequence of Wm. INGE denying the partnership between him and MORROW?
Answer: Yes, I did.
Question: Did not MORROW leave this country with the express decla-
ration of going to the Spanish Country in February, 1814?
Answer: Yes, he did.
And further this deponent saith not.
Given under my hand this 4th day of October in the year of our Lord,
one thousand eight hundred & twenty seven.
                                    Jacob MOHAN (Seal)

Here follows the certificate of the two Justices, Isaac E. KELLY &
Joseph PAIN, same date as above and also, the certificate of
John JONES, Clerk of the Circuit Court & en officio Recorder, dated
November 5th, 1827.
The following testimonies were taken before L.F. LINN, Comm'r.
Bellevue, Washington County
Nancy GRAGG, of lawful age being first duly sworn, deposeth & saith
that she was acquainted with Curtis MORRIS, before his marriage.
Curtis MORRIS married the sister of this deponent, and during the
courtship, the acquaintance with him was formed. At that time, this
affiant does believe the house or place of residence of said
Curtis MORRIS was at William ASHBROOK's and this deponent never has
understood that Curtis MORRIS changed his place of residence untill
after he was married to the sister of affiant as aforesaid.
Curtis MORRIS, after he was married, removed to a place about two
miles distant from deponent's father's place of residence, which is
the same now claimed by heirs of Danl. PHELPS, as Curtis MORRIS's
Settlement right situated in Bellevue Township, Washington County,
May 9th, 1833, L.F. LINN, Comm'r. Nancy GREGG

John MCNEAL of lawful age, being first sworn according to law to give
evidence in this behalf, deposeth & saith that in the year 1811 or
12, Thomas MORROW was in possession of an improvement in Bellevue, on
the South Side of Cedar Creek, it was near a Mill broke and MORROW
built another dam and removed the mill upon land that was considered
as public. MORROW continued in the occupancy of the said improvement
untill, this deponent believes, in the year 1813, when Wm. INGE, purchased out Thomas MORROW, and continued in the occupancy thereof, untill Saml. MORRISON purchased said mill and improvement. There was,
also, a distillery on the improvement. This deponent knows positively that there was cultivation on said improvement, to wit: corn &
potatoes in the year 1813, and does believe that the same was inhabited as well as cultivated in the year 1812.
L.F. LINN, Comm'r.   John T. MCNEAL

John STEWART of lawful age, being produced and sworn, deposeth and
saith that he, this affiant, was a surveyor by lawful appointment and
that agreeably to his authority, he surveyed in 1806, in the month of
January or February, 638 acres of land and 56 poles for Curtis MORRIS,
who then lived on the place where Timothy PHELPS now lives, claimed
by the heirs of Daniel PHELPS under Curtis MORRIS, at that time there
was a small turnip patch or improvement like a turnip patch at that
place, and Walter CROW and Curtis MORRIS agreed to divide and did divide the said truck patch between them, and then Curtis MORRIS agreed
and made his beginning at or near the spring where the said Timothy
now makes use of for family use, running North 65 East 2 poles, thence
North 26 poles, thence North 65, East 120 poles, thence Sourth 70 East
60 poles, thence North 70 East 140 poles, thence East 100 poles, then
South 217 poles, thence around to the beginning, agreeable to a plat
here unto annexed, bounded by Robert REED, Bernard ROGAN,
Benjamin CROW & Walter CROW. This original survey left a piece of vacant land up and down Cedar Creek, situated in the South East quarter
of Sec. No. 13 in T. 35 N in R. 2 East, on which the mill now owned by
A.W. HUDSPETH, and the sect that is said to be where MORROW & INGE did
build a mill is situated, and the forge sect with a part of the imp-
provement of the said HUDSPETH as the representative of the said

MORROW and INGE and INGE individually, is situated on the then vacant
part of the South West Fractional part of Sec. No. 18 in T. 35 N. in
range 3 East of the 5th principal meridian in the County of Washington
in Bellevue Township. The strip of vacant land was about 48 poles
wide, the whole of which vacant land original survey will more fully
appear by reference to the plat hereunto annexed. This deponent, further, says that he does not intend to say that the turnip patch above
spoken of was the only improvement on the land, for there was undoubted-
ly other improvements on the land, and corn had been raised on the land.
Sworn to & subscribed May 14th, 1833.
L.F. LINN, Comm'r.   John STEWART
      Adjourned untill tomorrow at 9 o'clock A.M.
            Tuesday Dec, 17th, 1833 Board Met-F.R. CONWAY, Present

In the case of Louis LAJOIE claiming 800 arpents of land, see pg. 81
of this Book. Louis LAJOIE, being duly sworn, says that under the
Spanish Government, he asked for a concession of 800 arpents of land;
that on his demand the said concession was granted to him. That he
asked for said concession through Mr. LABEAUME, who drew up the petition. That at the time the grant was made he, the deponent, lived in
Florissant and had a wife & two children. That he, in company with
about fifteen others, came to St. Louis for the purpose of asking
lands of the govenment. That he does not recollect of having ever
given any testimony before the (cannot read) have been drunk at the
time. That, then, he was oftener drunk than sober. That previous to
obtain the grant he had not made any contract with any one for said
land. That he recollects of having sold his interest in the grant to
DEJARLAIS when in a frolick, for a pint of whiskey. That he does not
recollect of having signed any Deeds for said land. Being asked what
was his occupation at that time, he answered: Drinking drams. The
witness, further, says that he supported his family by working by the
day when sober. That since a few years he has left off drinking. That
at the time the grant was made, the Lt. Gov., Charles D. DELASSUS, lived
in a house on Main Street near the market place.
      Adjourned untill tomorrow at 9 o'clock A.M.
            Wednesday Dec. 18th, 1833 Board Met-F.R. CONWAY, Present

Nicholas LACHANCE, alias Nich. CAILLOTE LACHANCE, claiming 640 acres
of land situated on the waters of St. Francis, see BATES's Decision
pg. 31.
State of Missouri, County of Madison
Francois CAILLOTTE LACHANCE aged about 66 years, being duly sworn as
the law directs, deposeth & saith that he has resided in this country
about 46 years. That he is well acquainted with the claimant who came
to this country, then the province of Upper Louisiana, about 43 or 44
years ago. This witness, further, says that he knows the land claimed
that the claimant settled on the same some 31 years ago, and while the
country yet belonged to Spain, that he made a cabbin on the same and
made sugar on the land at that time. That in one or two years after
he built the cabbin, the claimant moved and settled and that he continued to claim the said land, till one Charles L. BIRD pretended he had
a concession for the land and compelled him to go off. That he has continued a citizen of the country and cultivator of the soil ever since.
Sworn to & subscribed before me, L.F. LINN, Comm'r., this 31st day of
May, 1833.   F. CALLIOTE LACHANCE
And, also, came Michel Caillote LACHANCE, a witness aged about 62 years
who after having heard the above and foregoing deposition of
Francois CAILLOTTE LACHANCE read and explained to him, deposeth and
saith that he knows the same facts and that the statements and facts
contained therein are just and true.
Sworn to and subscribed before me, Lewis F. LINN, Comm'r., this 31st
day of May, 1833.   Michel (X) Caillote LACHANCE
L.F. LINN, Comm'r.   his mark
      Adjourned until tomorrow at 9 o'clock A.M.
            Thursday Dec. 19th, 1833 Board Met=F.R. CONWAY, Present

Benjamin HELDERBRAND claiming 640 acres of land, situate on the waters
of White Water, Cape Girardeau, see Minutes Book No. 4, pg. 269.
State of Missouri, County of Madison
Peter GROUND, aged about 73 years being duly sworn as the law directs,
deposeth and saith that he has been in this country about 33 years.

That he is well acquainted with Benjamin HELDERBRAND, the original
claimant. That he came to this country, then the province of upper
Louisiana, in the fall of the year 1803. That the claimant had a
wife and settled on the land claimed in the spring of 1804. That he
built a house. This witness helped to hew the logs and put up the
house, and then claimant went on to clear land and make fences, say
some four or five acres, and put in and raised a crop or corn thereon. This witness says he was present and marked the trees when the
land was surveyed in 1806 by one BOYD, the Deputy Surveyor, and that
the said tract of land has been actually inhabited and cultivated ever
since. Sworn to and subscribed before me, L.F. LINN, Comm'r., this
31st May, 1833.
L.F. LINN, Comm'r.   Peter (X) GROUND
                                          his mark
        Adjourned untill tomorrow at 9 o'clock A.M.
            Friday Dec. 20th, 1833 Board Met-F.R. CONWAY, Present

David GREEN claiming 347 arpents & 53-1/2 perches of land situate on
Byrd's Creek, Cape Girardeau, see Book B, pg. 331 and Minutes No. 4,
pgs. 15 & 264, produces a paper purporting to be a plat of survey of
the said land, dated 28th November, 1805, signed B. COUSIN & counter-
signed Antoine SOULARD, Sur. General.
State of Missouri, Cape Girardeau County, April 18th, 1833
Personally appeared before L.F. LINN, one of the Comm'rs. appointed
under the law for the final adjustment of land claims in Missouri,
Robert GREEN, who being duly sworn according to law, deposeth and
saith that some time early in the year 1802, he was at
Louis LORIMIER's, former Commandant at the Post of Cape Girardeau
(Upper Louisiana), who introduced a conversation with this deponent
by stating that David GREEN, son of the deponent, had applied to him
some time previous for a grant of land or permission to settle on public land. That, he, LORIMIER, intended the said David should have a
certain tract or piece of land that joined this deponent on the North.
David GREEN was anxious to go and improve the same, but as deponent
had settled on a new place and stood in need of his son's assistance
to open a farm on his own land, he told his son David, if he would
first assist this deponent to open and improve his farm, he would then
assist his son, David, to improve his tract. David expressed some
fears that if he did not immediately improve his claim it might be taken
from him. Some time after this deponent saw LORIMIER, the above named
Commandant, and held a conversation with him on the subject, who
assured the deponent that as David GREEN was settled permanently in the
country, it was not necessary for him to improve the land immediately,
but at some subsequent time. That his grant should not be taken from
him on that account. Some time after this, Bartholomew COUSIN, the
surveyor, came to this deponent's house and informed his son, David,
that the Commandant had ordered him to survey his claim of land, which
he did and was paid by said David for the same. The tract of land now
claimed by said David has been inhabited and cultivated twenty three
or twenty four years ago, is now inhabited and cultivated as the property of said David. This deponent states that he will be 78 years of age
in September next to the best of his knowledge & belief. Sworn to and
subscribed day and date above written.
L.F. LINN, Comm'r.   Robert GREEN
        Adjourned untill tomorrow at 9 o'clock A.M.
            Saturday Dec. 21st, 1833 Board Met-F.R. CONWAY, Present

Camille DELASSUS claiming 6,000 arpents of land situate Terre Bleue,
District of St. Genevieve, see Book C, pg. 448 & 9, Minutes Book No. 5,
pg. 547, produces a paper purporting to be an original concession from
Carlos Dehault DELASSUS, dated 19th September, 1802. Also, a paper
purporting to be an original plat of survey of said land, dated December 18th, 1805 by Thomas MADDIN, and certified by SOULARD under date
of February 20th, 1806. M.P. LEDUC, being duly sworn, says that the
signature to the concession is in the proper handwriting of
Carlos Dehault DELASSUS, and the signature to the certificate of survey
is in the proper handwriting of Ant. SOULARD, Surveyor General.
Claimant produces, also, a paper purporting to be a copy of a letter,
dated May 8th, 1793, from the Baron de CARONDELET to Dehault DELASSUS,
Sr., & certified by Fran. VALLE, Commandant of St. Genevieve.

115

Thomas RING by his assignee Camille DELASSUS, claiming 500 arpents of land situate County of St. Genevieve, see Book F, pg. 97, Bate's Decision pg. 103, Comm'r. Cert. No. 847, BATE's Decision, pg. 82, produces a paper purporting to be a copy of a deed of sale from Thomas RING (cannot read) dated April, 1804 and certified by J.Bste. VALLE, Commandant of St. Genevieve.
    Adjourned untill Monday next at 9 o'clock A.M.
        Monday, Dec. 23rd, 1833 Board Met-F.R. CONWAY, Present

Etienne PARENT & Etienne GOVEROT claiming 800 arpents of land situate on the Saline Creek, District of St. Genevieve, see Book C, pg. 459, Book No. 4, pg. 414, produces a paper purporting to be a copy of a concession from Zenon TRUDEAU dated 1st February, 1798.
St. Genevieve, March 4th, 1833
Personally appeared before the undersigned one of the Comm'rs. appointed for the final Settlement of Private land claims in Missouri, Joseph PRATTE, who being duly sworn gives testimony as follows in support of the above claim.
Question by the agent for the claimants: How old are you and how long have you lived in this state?
Answer by Deponent: I am 59 years of age and I was born in St. Genevieve.
Question: Are you acquainted with a concession which Etienne PARENT & Etienne GOVEROT obtained from Zenon TRUDEAU in the year 1798, on a branch of the South fork of the Saline for 800 arpents?
Answer: I have never seen the concession.
Question: Have you ever seen or do you know that Etienne GOVEROT, deceased, made an improvement on this concession of 800 arpents on the South fork of the Saline?
Answer: I have seen the improvement which E. GOVEREAU made on the Saline and I was there when GOVEROT was making sugar, and it was a general rule here that every individual made sugar upon his own claim.
Question: About what time did you see this improvement of Etienne GOVEROT, deceased, on the South fork of the Saline?
Answer: It was between the years 1798 and 1800, but the precise time I do not recollect.
Question by Commissioner: Do you know of any other grant of land to Etienne GOVEROT & Etienne PARENT?
Answer: I know of none.
                        Joseph PRATTE
Sworn & subscribed before L.F. LINN.
    Adjourned untill tomorrow at 9 o'clock A.M.
        Tuesday Dec. 24th, 1833 Board Met-F.R. CONWAY, Present

Antoine VILLARS & Joseph VILLARS claiming 6,000 arpents of land situate on the waters of Big river, see Book B, (cannot read), No. 4, pg. 415, produces a paper purporting to be an original concession from Carlos Dehault DELASSUS, dated 11th October, 1799. Also, a paper purporting to be an original plat of survey by Thomas MADDIN, Deputy Surveyor & received for record by Antoine SOULARD, Surveyor General, February 26th, 1806. M.P. LEDUC, being duly sworn, says that the signature to the recommendation is in the proper handwriting of F. VALLE, Commandant of St. Genevieve & of Pre. Delassus de LUZIERE, Commandant of New Bourbon, and the signature to the concession in the proper handwriting of Carlos Dehault DELASSUS.

Morris YOUNG claiming 300 arpents under a special permission to settle see Minutes No. 4, pgs. 40 & 282.
State of Missouri, County of Cape Girardeau
Personally appeared before L.F. LINN, one of the Comm'rs. appointed under the law for the final adjustment of land claims in Missouri, George F. BOLLINGER and Moses BYRD, who being duly sworn, deposeth and saith that they are well acquainted with Morris YOUNG the above named claimant; that said YOUNG emigrated to this country in the year 1804, that he is a mechanic (a Black Smith by trade); that he has resided in this country ever since and followed his trade, and also cultivated or tilled the earth as a farmer. And Moses BYRD, one of the (cannot read) further states that he was present at the Commandant Louis LORIMIER in the year 1802 or 3, when Joseph YOUNG the brother of the claimant applied to said Commandant for a permission or grant for the above claimant Morris YOUNG. Sworn to & subscribed Oct. 18th, 1833.
George F. BOLLINGER-Moses BYRD

Adjourned to tomorrow at 9 o'clock A.M.
Wednesday Dec. 25th, 1833 Board Met-F.R. CONWAY, Present

James CRAWFORD claiming 640 acres of land situate on the waters of
the St. Francis, County of Madison, see Record Book F, pg. 91, Recorder's minutes pg. 117, BATE's Decisions, pg. 36.
State of Missouri, County of Madison
John MATHEWS, aged about 62 years being duly sworn as the law directs,
deposeth and saith that he is well acquainted with James CRAWFORD,
the original claimant. That he came to this country, then the province of Upper Louisiana, in the spring of the year 1803. This witness also knows the land claimed and believes that the claimant settled on the same in the year 1803 & improved the same.
Sworn to and subscribed before me Lewis F. LINN, Comm'r. this 31st
day of May, 1833.
L.F. LINN, Comm'r.   John MATTHEWS
(Cannot read) 47 years, who being duly sworn as the law directs, deposeth and saith that he was well acquainted with the original
claimant, who was his brother. That he came to this country in the
spring of the year 1803. Witness also knows the land claimed and
knows that the claimant actually improved and cultivated the same in
the years 1803 & 4. That there was some two or three acres fenced in
cleared & cultivated in corn and perhaps other things, and that the
said land has been actually inhabited, improved & cultivated ever
since. Sworn to & subscribed before me, L.F. LINN, Comm'r., this 22nd
day of October, 1833.
L.F. LINN, Comm'r.   Thompson CRAWFORD

Paul DEGUIRE by his legal representatives claiming 800 arpents or 640
acres of land situate on the waters of the St. Francis, County of Madison, see Recorder's minutes pg. 41, BATE's Decisions, pg. 30.
State of Missouri, County of Madison
Nicholas CAILLOTE LACHANCE, a witness aged about 49 years, being duly
sworn, deposeth and saith that he has resided in this County about 43
or 44 years. That he is well acquainted with Paul DEGUIRE, the original claimant. That he believes he was born in the country, then the
province of Upper Louisiana. This witness, also, says that he knows
the land claimed. That the claimant built a cabbin on the same in the
year 1803, and made sugar on the same. That he had a wife & 4 or 5
children at the time, and that the claimant continued to occupy the
said cabbin & land for several years, and untill one Charles L. BYRD,
pretended to have a concession therefor and compelled the claimant to
give up the same. That the said DEGUIRE continued a citizen till the
time of his death and was a cultivator of the soil. That he always
understood the claimant as claiming and owning this land and that he
only relinquished the possession from the threats of said BYRD.
                              Nicholas (X) Caillotte LACHANCE
                                       his mark
Sworn to before me, L.F. LINN, Comm'r., this 31st day of May, 1833.
L.F. LINN, Comm'r.
And, also, came Francois Caillotte LACHANCE aged about 66 years, and
Michel Caillotte LACHANCE aged about 62 years who having severally
heard the above deposition of Nicholas Caillotte LACHANCE read & ex-
plained to them, say that they know the same facts and that the state-
ments & facts in said deposition contained are just and true.
Sworn to & subsctibed before me, L.F. LINN, Comm'r., this 31st day of
May, 1833.
L.F. LINN, Comm'r.   F. Caillote LACHANCE
                              Michel (X) Caillote LACHANCE
                                       his mark
          Adjourned untill tomorrow at 9 o'clock A.M.
            Thursday Dec. 26th, 1833 Board Met-F.R. CONWAY, Present

Benjamin PETTIT, Jr., by his legal representatives claiming 640 acres
of land situate on the waters of St. Francis, County of Madison, see
Record Book F, pg. 13, Recorder's Minutes, pg. 17, BATE's Decisions,
pg. 28..
State of Missouri, County of Madison
John CLEMENTS aged about 53 years being duly sworn as the law directs,
deposeth and saith that he was well acquainted with the original

claimant, Benjamin PETTIT, Jr., who was the son of
Benjamin PETTIT, Sr., they both bearing the same name. That
Benjamin PETTIT, Jr. had a wife and family. That he came to this
country, then the province of Upper Louisiana, in the year 1803. Witness, also, knows the land claimed. He was with the claimant when he
drove his waggon with his family on the land in the fall of 1803, and
settled on the same. That claimant immediately built a cabbin or
house on the same and resided thereon with his family till he became
sick and afflicted, when he went near to his father's where he died.
Sworn to & subscribed before me, L.F. LINN, Comm'r., this 22nd October, 1833.
L.F. LINN, Comm'r.   John (X) CLEMENTS
                                                   his mark
And, also, came Samuel CAMPBELL, a witness aged about 68 years, who
after hearing the above and foregoing deposition read, deposeth and
saith that he knows the same facts and that the statements in the
same are substantially correct and true. Sworn to & subscribed before me, L.F. LINN, Comm'r., this 22nd October, 1833.
L.F. LINN, Comm'r.   Saml. CLEMENTS
Also, came John L. PETTIT, a witness aged about 51 years, who being
duly sworn as the law directs, deposeth & saith that he was well acquainted with the original claimant, who was his brother. That he
had a wife and five children. That he came to this country, then the
province of Upper Louisiana in the fall of 1803. That he immediately
moved on the land claimed (which he, witness, also knew) & settled on
the same, built a house and lived there untill he became sick, when he
made a temporary removal near to his father's, who was also called
Benjamin PETTIT, for the purpose of having better attendance during
his sickness, when he died. Sworn to & subscribed before me,
L.F. LINN, Comm'r., this 23rd day October, 1833. John L. PETTIT
And, also, came John REAVES, a witness aged about 73 years, who being
also duly sworn as the law directs, deposeth & saith that he was well
acquainted with Benjamin PETTIT, Jr., the original claimant. That he
came to this country, then the province of Upper Louisiana, in the year
1802 or 1803. Witness, also, knows the land (cannot read) that the
claimant actually settled on the same in the spring of 1803, built a
cabbin on the land in which he resided with his family. Claimant had
some land fenced in and cleared in 1803, and a garden in cultivation
on the same. The claimant continued to reside on the land till he
became sick, when he was brought up by his father near himself, that
he might be attended to during his sickness, as there was no person
lived near the place where he settled and that some time in the year
1804, claimant died. Witness knows the land was claimed for him by
his father, Benjamin PETTIT, Sr., as he was present and paid the recording fees, and the witness, also, knows that the land claimed has always been called Benjamin PETTIT, Jr.'r place, and still is so, and
witness, also, knows that the land claimed has been actually inhabited
& cultivated ever since. Sworn to & subscribed before me, L.F. LINN,
Comm'r., this 23rd October, 1833.
L.F. LINN, Comm'r.   John (X) REAVES
                                                   his mark

Samuel CAMPBELL claiming 640 acres of land situate on the waters of
St. Francis River, County of Madison, see Book F, pg. 89, Recorder's
minutes pgs. 19 & 110.
State of Missouri, County of Madison
John CLEMENTS aged about 53 years being duly sworn as the law directs,
deposeth and saith that he is well acquainted with (cannot read) that
he first saw him in this country, then the province of Upper Louisiana,
in the spring of the year 1803. Witness, also, knows the land claimed
and knows that the claimant settled on the land in the year 1803,
built a house on the same and had his family there residing. Witness
also knows that there was several acres of land fenced in and cleared,
which were actually cultivated in the years 1803 and 1804, in corn &
other things and witness, also, knows that the said tract of land has
been actually inhabited and cultivated ever since. Sworn to & subscribed before me, L.F. LINN, Comm'r., this 22nd November, 1833.
L.F. LINN, Comm'r.   John (X) CLEMENTS
                                                   his mark
And, also, came Thompson CRAWFORD a witness aged about 47 years, who

being duly sworn as the law directs, deposeth and saith that he is
well acquainted with Samuel CAMPBELL, the original claimant. That he
was a residenter of this country, the province of Upper Louisiana, in
the year 1803. Witness, also, knows the land claimed, and that the
claimant settled on the same in the latter part of the spring or early
in the summer of 1803. Claimant built a house on the same, and moved
into the same. Claimant built a Blacksmith shop, also, on the land
about the same time, and did work thereon for the people around him.
Claimant had a family consisting of a wife and one child. Claimant
fenced in and cleared some three or four acres of land, which was actually cultivated in the years 1803 and 1804 in corn and other things
necessary, and the said tract of land has been continually, from that
time, inhabited and cultivated ever since. Sworn to & subscribed before me, L.F. LINN, Comm'r., this 23rd October, 1833.
L.F. LINN, Comm'r.   Thompson CRAWFORD
And, also, came John REAVES, a witness aged 73 years, who being duly
sworn, deposeth & saith that he well knew the original claimant. That
he found him a settler and cultivator of the soil in 1803, when witness came to this country. The witness knows the land claimed.
Claimant was residing on the same in 1803; had a house and Blacksmith
shop in which the witness worked in 1803 and 1804. Claimant, also,
lived there in 1804. There was a good large field under fence, cleared
and in cultivation by the claimant and the said tract of land has been
continually inhabited & cultivated ever since. Sworn to & subscribed
before me, L.F. LINN, Comm'r., this 23rd October, 1833.
L.F. LINN, Comm'r.   John (X) REAVES
                                                  his mark
        Adjourned untill tomorrow at 9 o'clock A.M.
          Friday Dec. 27th, 1833 Board Met-F.R. CONWAY, Present

Peter BURNS, Sr., by his legal representatives claiming 640 acres of
land situate on the waters of the St. Francis, County of Madison, see
Record Book F, pg. 53, BATE's Decisions, pg. 102.
State of Missouri, County of Madison
John MATTHEWS, a witness aged about 62 years, being duly sworn as the
law directs, deposeth and saith that he was well acquainted with
Peter BURNS, Sr., that this witness came to this country in the year
1800. That Peter BURNS, Sr., came to this country, then the province
of Upper Louisiana, in the year 1804. That he settled on the tract of
land in the summer of 1804. That he had a house on the land and lived
in it with his family, which was a wife and some seven or eight children. That he saw some land open on the place, and that there was
something growing thereon, but whether corn, potatoes or turnips, he
does not recollect. That there was a small field of some two or three
acres opened at the time, and he is sure some cultivation was done in
the year 1804. That said Peter BURNS, Sr., remained on the place
several years, and then was scared or run off by the Osage Indians, who
drove them into the Settlement where the family remained. That the Indians did at that time frighten off the people and comitted several depredations on the waters of the St. Francis, and forced the people, for
safety, to come into the settlements. Sworn to & subscribed before,
L.F. LINN, Comm'rs. this 31st May, 1833.
L.F. LINN, Comm'r.   John MATTHEWS
Also, came John CLEMENTS, a witness aged 53 years, who being duly sworn
as the law directs, deposeth and saith that he was well acquainted with
the original claimant. That he came to this country in the year 1803,
to the best of his recollection, or early in the year 1804. Witness,
also, knows the land claimed, and that shortly afterwards, he settled
on the land, built a house, fenced in and cleared several acres of land
& cultivated the same in corn, tobacco, cotton, vegetables, and a common garden, and that the land has been generally inhabited and cultivated ever since the settlement was begun shortly after he came to the
country. Sworn to & subscribed before me, L.F. LINN, Comm'r., this
21st October, 1833.
L.F. LINN, Comm'r.   John (X) CLEMENTS
                                                  his mark
Also, came Thompson CRAWFORD, a witness aged about 47 years, who being
duly sworn as the law directs, deposeth and saith that he was well acquainted with the original claimant. That he came to this country in
the spring of 1804. Witness, also, knows the land claimed, and knows

that the claimant settled on, inhabited, inproved & cultivated the
same in the year 1804. That he built a house thereon and resided in
the same, and that the land has been actually inhabited & cultivated
ever since. Sworn to & subscribed before me, L.F. LINN, Comm'r. this
22nd October, 1833.
L.F. LINN, Comm'r.   Thompson CRAWFORD
And, also, came John REAVES, a witness aged about 73 years (cannot
read) deposeth and saith that he knew the original claimant, who came
to this country, he believes in 1802. That the claimant was here in
1803, and then witness became acquainted with him, from which time
witness and claimant lived neighbours. Witness, also, knows the land
claimed and that claimant settled on the same early in the spring of
1804, having built a house and moved into the same on the land in the
winter of 1803 & 1804, and that in 1804, he cleared, fenced in and
cultivated several acres in corn & other things necessary for a family. In the summer or spring of 1804, the Osage Indians made a break
on the settlement and drove off the settlers, particularly the women
and in the fall claimant returned & gathered his crop, and the said
tract of land has been, from time to time, inhabited and cultivated
ever since. Sworn to & subscribed before me, L.F. LINN, Comm'r., this
23rd October, 1833.   John (X) REAVES
L.F. LINN, Comm'r.   his mark

Robert BURNS by his legal representatives claiming 640 acres of land
on the waters of the St. Francis, County of Madison, see Book F, pg.
53, Recorder's Minutes, pg. 117, BATE's Decisions, pg. 36.
State of Missouri, County of Madison
John MATTHEWS, aged about 62 years, being duly sworn as the law directs, deposeth and saith that he was well acquainted with the
claimant, Robert BURNS. That he came to this country, then the province of Upper Louisiana, in the year 1803 and that he continued a
citizen and resident in the country till he died about two years
since. Sworn to & subscribed before me, the subscriber, the 31st day
of May, 1833.   John MATTHEWS
L.F. LINN, Comm'r.
And, also, came Thompson CRAWFORD, a witness aged about 47 years, who
being duly sworn, deposeth and saith that he is well acquainted with
Robert BURNS, the original claimant. That he came to this country,
then the province of Upper Louisiana, in the year 1803. Witness, also,
knows the land claimed, and knows that the claimant settled on, improved, & cultivated the same in the years 1803 & 1804. That in 1804,
claimant made a crop, on the same, of corn & other things, and that he
continued to inhabit & cultivate the same till the time of his death,
a few years since. Sworn to & subscribed before me, L.F. LINN, Comm'r,
this 21st October, 1833.   Thompson CRAWFORD
L.F. LINN, Comm'r.
    Adjourned untill tomorrow at 9 o'clock A.M.
         Saturday Dec. 28th, 1833 Board Met-F.R. CONWAY, Present

Joseph DOUBLEWYE, alias DEBLOIS by his legal representative claiming
640 acres of land situate on the waters of St. Francis, County of
Madison, see Record Book F, pg. 50, Recorder's Minutes, pgs. 47 & 78,
BATE's Decisions, pg. 31.
State of Missouri, County of Madison
Samuel CAMPBELL, aged about 68 years, being duly sworn as the law directs, deposeth and saith that he was well acquainted with
Joseph DEBLOIS, the original claimant. That he was one of the old
settlers of the country, then the province of Upper Louisiana. Witness, also, knows the land claimed, and knows that the claimant settled on the same in the summer of 1803 and actually built a house thereon, and cleared & fenced in several acres of land. Claimant hired one
Thomas RING to help him do the work, for which he paid RING forty dollars in a horse, which was valued between the parties by this witness.
Witness, also, knows that the claimant inhabited the house in the fall
and winter of 1803 & 1804, and that in the spring of 1804, the claimant
planted corn, made garden and cultivated the land. In the summer, the
Osage Indians made a break in the settlement & drove the claimant, with
many others from their farms, but witness knows that claimant returned
in the fall and gathered his corn and then returned to the place, and
again inhabited the house, and that the claimant and others under him

from thence forward, for several successive years (cannot read) the same place and extend his improvements, the claimant had a family, or a wife and two children, and the said tract of land has been continually inhabited and cultivated ever since. Sworn to & subscribed before me, L.F. LINN, Comm'r., this 23rd day of October, 1833.
L.F. LINN, Comm'r.   Saml. CAMPBELL
Also, came John CLEMENTS, a witness aged 53 years, who being duly sworn, deposeth and saith that he knows the land claimed. That it was always called DEBLOIS's land or improvement. Witness saw Thomas RING at work there, in the fall of 1803, in building a house or cabbin, and was told by RiNG that it was for the claimant. Witness also, saw the horse, which claimant paid RING for his labour done on the said place. Witness, also, saw corn standing on the place in the fall of 1804. The house was fenced in by the land cleared, and that was the land that was in corn. Witness, afterwards, saw one HILL-HOUSE, or HILLIS, on the place and understood that he was there by permission of DEBLOIS. Sworn to & subscribed before me, L.F. LINN, Comm'r., this 23rd day of October, 1833.
L.F. LINN, Comm'r.   John (X) CLEMENTS
                                                his mark
And, also, came John L. PETTIT, a witness aged about 51 years, who being duly sworn, deposeth and saith that he knew the original claimant in this country as a citizen and residenter since the year 1801. Witness had a conversation with the Commandant of the Post in 1801, in which conversation the Commandant told the witness that claimant had his permission to settle on land. That claimant was entitled to lands being a mechanic, a carpenter, and at work for the government. Witness saw him at work for the government at St. Genevieve. Claimant was one of the old settlers in the country. Sworn to & subscribed before me, L.F. LINN, Comm'r., this 23rd October, 1833.
L.F. LINN, Comm'r.   John L. PETTIT

In the Case of Louis LAJOIE claiming 800 arpents of land, see pg. 81 of this Book. Benito VASQUEZ, being duly sworn, and being shown the original deed of sale from Louis LAJOIE to DEJARLAIS (said Deed dated July 10th, 1804) and signed by him, the said Benito, as witness, says that it is his own handwriting & signature.

Thompson CRAWFORD claiming 640 acres of land situate on the waters of the St. Francis, County of Madison, see Record Book F, pg. 91, Recorder's Minutes pg. 117, BATE's Decisions, pg. 36.
State of Missouri, County of Madison
John MATTHEWS, aged about 62 years, being duly sworn as the law directs, deposeth and saith that he is well acquainted with the claimant Thompson CRAWFORD, that he has know him from the year 1803, early (cannot read) grown up, and this witness believes, was working for himself. That this witness about that time hired him to work for him. That he believes the claimant lived at his father's and this land claimed lies adjoining the lands, then occupied by his father. That shortly afterwards the claimant settled on this land claimed, built a house and commenced to improve and cultivate the same, and has continued to improve, inhabit and cultivate the same ever since.and still resides thereon. Sworn to & subscribed before me, L.F. LINN, Comm'r., this 31st day of May, 1833.   John MATTHEWS
L.F. LINN, Comm'r.
Also, came Samuel CAMPBELL, a wintess aged about 68 years, who being duly sworn, deposeth & saith that he was well acquainted with the original claimant. That he came to this country, then the province of Upper Louisiana, in the spring of the year 1803, witness also knows that the claimant settled on, inhabited, improved and cultivated the same, in the year 1804. That the land settled on, improved & cultivated was about one mile from his father's where his father then lived, and this witness believes it was the same land now claimed, and that he knows the land was inhabited, improved & cultivated by the claimant till within some eight years since when witness went off from this place, but the same may have been (cannot read) and cultivated during even those eight years, for all the witness knows, as he was absent. Sworn to & subscribed before me, L.F. LINN, Comm'r., this 21st October, 1833.
L.F. LINN, Comm'r.   Saml. CAMPBELL
      Adjourned until Monday next at 9 o'clock A.M.

John L. PETTIT claiming 640 acres of land situate on the waters of
St. Francis, County of Madison, see Book F, pg. 13, BATE's Decision,
pg. 97.
State of Missouri, County of Madison
John CLEMENTS aged about 53 years, being duly sworn as the law directs,
deposeth and saith that he was well acquainted with the original
claimant who, he believes first came to this country in the year of
1801, and was sent back by his father to Kentucky to transact some
business. That the witness also knows the land claimed, and knows
that the father of the said John L. PETTIT, together with a negro boy
of the said claimant, for the use & benefit of the said John, settled
on, improved and cultivated the said land in the years 1803 and 1804.
There was a house built on the land, and in the year 1804, there was
fenced in, cleared and actually cultivated (cannot read) about 8 or
10 acres. The father of said John informed this witness that this
building improvement and culitvation was for the said John, his son,
as he had sent his son back to the State of Kentucky to wind up his
business there, and that the negro boy, who was then at work, was the
property of the said John. Witness, also, knows that said John returned to this country and still resides here and that the land claimed
has been actually inhabited & cultivated ever since. Witness, also,
worked on the land and hewed house logs and understood from the father
who was, he understood, acting as agent of the claimant, that the logs
house and improvements were for the use and benefit of the claimant,
he being absent on business as aforesaid. Sworn to & subscribed before
me, L.F. LINN, Comm'r., this 22nd October, 1833.
L.F. LINN, Comm'r.   John (X) CLEMENTS
                                                his mark
Also, came John REAVES, a witness aged about 73 years, who being duly
sworn, deposeth and saith that he was well acquainted with the original claimant, that he came to this country, then the province of Upper Louisiana in the year 1801 or 1802. Witness does not precisely
remember. Witness, also, knows the land claimed and knows that the
same was actually settled on in the year 1803. There was then a house
and other buildings on the land at that time, and the house, he believes, is still standing being cedar timber that (cannot read) father
of claimant lived on the land in 1803 and raised a crop thereon. There
was some 8 or 10 acres under fence, cleared and an actual cultivation
and the same land was still inhabited & cultivated in 1804 and further
improvements made. Witness, also, knows from the information of
Mr. Benjamin PETTIT, the father, that this was the claim of
John L. PETTIT, and said he was labouring and fixing the place for,
and under John L. PETTIT, his son, whom he had sent back to Kentucky
to finish & wind up his business there, and that in this way they had
exchanged work. Witness knows the claim was filed for John L. PETTIT
in his name by his father, for witness was present and paid the fees
for recording. That some time afterwards, John L. PETTIT returned to
this country and has remained here in to the present time, and is still
a citizen, and that the said tract of land has been from time to time
inhabited & cultivated ever since and still is. Witness, also, knows
that while the father was at work on the place for John, that the negro man of John was also there at work on the place. Sworn to & subscribed to before me, Lewis F. LINN, Comm'r. this 23rd October, 1833.
L.F. LINN, Comm'r.   John (X) REAVES
                                                his mark

John BURK by his legal representatives claiming 1,000 arpents of land
situated on the waters of Big River, see Record Book B, pg. 426,
Minutes No. 5, pg. 362, produces a paper purporting to be the original
plat of survey of said land, dated January 1st, 1806, by Thomas MADDIN,
Deputy Surveyor & received for record by SOULARD, Surveyor General on
the 25th February, 1806.
State of Missouri, County of St. Genevieve
John Bste. VALLE, aged about 72 years, being duly sworn as the law directs, deposeth and saith that he was well acquainted with John BURK,
the original claimant. That in the year 1799, and before & afterwards,
he was a citizen & resident of the province of Upper Louisiana, and
that he continued a citizen & residenter till the time of his death.

That the said John BURK was a Blacksmith and resided in the town of
St. Genevieve, and followed his trade. That he had a wife and several
children. That said BURK had other property and means and was an industrious and usefull citizen. And the deponent further says that he
was well acquainted with Charles Dehault DELASSUS, that he was the Lt.
Governor in the province of Upper Louisiana in the year one thousand
seven hundred & ninety nine. Sworn to & subscribed before me,
Lewis F. LINN, Comm'r., this 27th May, 1833.
L.F. LINN, Comm'r.   J. Bste. VALLE

Henry TUCKER by his legal representatives claiming 640 acres of land
lying on Custards or Cedar Creek, waters of Saline Creek, see Record
Book F, pg. 13, BATE's Decision, pg. 98, Book B, pg. 242, Book 5, pg.
505.
Perry County, May 2nd, 1833
Personally appeared before L.F. LINN, one of the Commissioners appointed for the final adjustment of land claims in Missouri,
Mr. Roland BOYD, who after being duly sworn, deposes & says that he
has resided in this State of Missouri, formerly Upper Louisiana, upwards of 31 or 32 years near St. Genevieve, and knows that a settlement was made by Henry TUCKER, on the Cedar Fork of Saline Creek in
the year 1803, and was cultivated by him in 1804. Said TUCKER built
a cabbin on this land in 1803 and lived in the same & cultivated 6 or
7 acres in 1804. Deponent says he always heard and has every reason
to believe said TUCKER had permission to settle on this land from the
Spanish authorities. He, further, states that all the settlement
claims in the neighbourhood, all of which were of a similar nature and
resting on the same testimony for confirmation, were confirmed by the
former Board of Commissioners. The deponent had a claim confirmed by
said Board on the Back of the plat of TUCKER's survey was written by
J.L. DONALDSON, Secretary or Clerk to the Board "Confirmed". He, deponent, as well as all concerned, thought for many years said tract
was confirmed and never knew or heard untill a few years back that
this claim was not confirmed, for he, himself, heard the Commissioners
pronounce this claim "Granted". Sworn to & Subscribed day & date a-
bove written.   Roland (X) BOYD
L.F. LINN, Comm'r.   his mark

Henry TUCKER states that in the year 1802, he settled a place on Cedar
or Custards fork of the Saline Creek, now in the County of Perry &
state of Missouri, and in that year & the following, cleared about 3
acres as he thinks, and in the year 1803, raised corn on his improvement, built a cabbin or corn crib on it, and resided on it with his
family during that year (1803). The same is the place where
William HANCOCK now resides. The said Henry TUCKER states that on the
10th day of February, 1804, he sold & transferred his said improvement
and conveyed it by Deed of that date, which is herewith filed, as a
part of this statement, and that he has no claim on said improvement
nor does he claim any thing by virtue thereof.
October 25th, 1833. L.F. LINN, Comm'r.   Henry TUCKER

Joseph THOMPSON, Jr. by his legal representatives (cannot read), see
Record Book F, pg. 146, BATE's Decision pg. 105. The said land situated on Caney Creek, Cape Girardeau.
Hugh CRESWELL, being duly sworn says that he is 68 years of age. That
he came to the then District of Cape Girardeau, Upper Louisiana, now
County of Cape Girardeau, State of Missouri (in the year) 1801, in
which year he became acquainted with the said Joseph THOMPSON, some
time in said year 1801 by permission of the then Commandant at that
place, settled upon & inhabited a tract of land in said District, and
being so settled upon & an inhabitant of said tract of land, he, said
Joseph THOMPSON, continued thereon as aforesaid, and in the year 1802,
inhabited, remained, settled upon, improved & cultivated the same by
clearing, fencing said land and raising a crop of corn thereon, in said
year 1802. That the said Joseph THOMPSON, Jr., continued to reside in
said District untill the year 1820.
                                    Hugh CRISWELL
Sworn to & subscribed October 17th, 1833.
L.F. LINN, Comm'r.
The aforesaid, Hugh CRISWELL, being again sworn, saith that the said

tract of land mentioned in the aforesaid deposition of this deponent
as having been settled upon, inhabited, improved, cultivated, and
corn growed & raised thereon by the said Joseph THOMPSON, Jr., in the
year 1802 mentioned, was lying on a creek called Caney Creek, in said
District of Cape Girardeau, when & where the said Joseph THOMPSON, Jr.,
settled upon, inhabited and cultivated the said tract of land mentioned as aforesaid.

                              Hugh CRISWELL
Sworn to & subscribed October 19th, 1833.
L.F. LINN, Comm'r.
          Adjourned untill tomorrow at 9 o'clock A.M.
               Tuesday Dec. 31st, 1833 Board Met-F.R. CONWAY, Present

Joseph THOMPSON, Sr., by his legal representatives claiming 640 acres
of land situated on Ramsay's Creek, County of Cape Girardeau, see
Book F, pg. 146, BATE's Decisions, pg. 105.
John ABERNETHIE aged about 71 years, being duly sworn, deposeth and
saith that he came to the then District of Cape Girardeau, Upper
Louisiana, now County of Cape Girardeau, in the year 1800, where he
has ever since resided,. that in the year 1801, or 1802,
Joseph THOMPSON, Sr., came to said District and with his family, settled upon a tract of land in said District by the permission of the
then Commandant, Lewis LORIMIER, at that place, and being so settled
upon, and inhabiting the said tract of land continued thereon as such
inhabitant, during the year 1802 or 1803 and in said year improved
cleared & cultivated said land, made the necessary buildings & planted
ground and raised a crop of corn and the vegetables necessary for
family use during the season of the said year 1802. Further, that the
said Joseph THOMPSON, Sr. continued to reside with his family and to
be engaged in the cultivation of land untill the time of his death,
which took place on his farm on Ramsay's Creek in said District.
                              Jno. ABERNETHIE
Sworn to & subscribed October 18th, 1833.
L.F. LINN, Comm'r.
John RODNEY of lawful age, being duly sworn, deposeth & saith that the
tract of land of Joseph THOMPSON, Sr., on which he resided at the time
of his death, has been reserved from sale as a private unconfirmed land
claim, by the Register and Receiver of the land District of Cape Girardeau, which tract of land is on Ramsey's Creek in Cape Girardeau County.
Sworn to & subscribed Oct. 18th, 1833.   John RODNEY
L.F. LINN, Comm'r.
Ithamer HUBBLE, aged 71 years, being duly sworn, deposeth & saith that
he first came in 1797 to the then District of Cape Girardeau, Upper
Louisiana, now County of Cape Girardeau, State of Missouri, where he
has ever since resided. That the aforesaid Joseph THOMPSON, Sr., as
early as the year 1801, with his family came to said District, and in
the year 1801 aforesaid the said Joseph THOMPSON, with his family, settled (cannot read)said county, by the permission of the then Spanish
Commandant. Made the necessary buildings thereon, cleared & fenced a
part of said land and in the said year 1801, so being an inhabitant
of, and settled on, said tract of land, he, said Joseph THOMPSON in
said year 1801, cultivated planted & raised a field of corn thereon
of about 15 acres. That said Joseph THOMPSON, Sr. lived in said District untill the time of his death, with his family, which took place
on his way from the town of Cape Girardeau to the place of his residence, on his farm on Ramsay's Creek in said District. That said
Joseph THOMPSON left a number of heirs who have ever since continued
in the possession of said farm & tract of land, on said Ramsay's Creek
in the cultivation of the same.   Ithamer (X) HUBBLE
Sworn to & subscribed Oct. 18th, 1833.   His mark
L.F. LINN, Comm'r.
Elijah DOUGHERTY & Alexander SUMMERS, being duly sworn deposeth &
saith that they were well acquainted with the said Joseph THOMPSON,
Sr. in his life time. That they well recollect that in the year 1801,
the said Joseph THOMPSON, with his family, resided on a tract of land
on Ramsey's Creek, on the waters of Ramsey's creek in the said Dis-
trict of Cape Girardeau mentioned in the foregoing depositions.
Sworn to & subscribed Oct. 18th, 1833.   Alex. (X) SUMMERS
L.F. LINN, Comm'r.   his mark

LABUXIERE by his legal representatives claiming about 2 arpents of land in front or more if vacant, adjoining on one side the Ruisseau de pierre, and on the other side, to the land of Widow HEBERT; fronting on the Mississippi, by the ordinary depth of 40 arpents, see Livre Terrien No. 1, pg. 30 & Book F, pg. 146 & 159.
Baptiste Riviere dit BACANE, being duly sworn, says that he is between 86 and 87 years of age. That he knows that LABUXIERE had a tract of land situated North of St. Louis, but does not recollect exactly the quantity. That about 46 or 50 years ago, more or less, he knows that said tract of land was cultivated by or through said LABUXIERE, and was so cultivated by him for many years until he was expelled from the country by the Spanish Government. That LABUXIERE's tract was next, south, to the Ruisseau de pierre. Then came Widow HEBERT, Ortez and DUBRUISSEAU, etc.
         Adjourned until tomorrow at 9 o'clock A.M.
               Wednesday Jan. 1st, 1834 Board Met-F.R. CONWAY, Present

Danile BOLLINGER, Sr. by his legal representatives claiming 640 acres of land situate (cannot read) Cape Girardeau, see Minutes Book 4, pgs. 32 & 279.
Mathias BOLLINGER, being duly sworn, deposeth and saith that he, Mathias BOLLINGER is aged about 64 years, that he emigrated in the year 1799 & came to the then District of Cape Girardeau, Upper Louisiana, now County of Cape Girardeau, State of Missouri, where he has ever since resided. That at the same time Daniel BOLLINGER, Sr. came to said District with this affiant. That said Daniel BOLLINGER in the year 1800, by permission of the then Spanish Commandant at that place, with his family, settled upon and inhabited a tract of land on White Water, in said District, and being so an inhabitant and settled upon said land, he, the said Daniel BOLLINGER in said year 1800, cleared, improved, fenced & cultivated the ground on said tract of land, planted, growed & raised corn thereon with the vegetables necessary for family use. Erected dwelling houses and other buildings necessary for his family on said land. That the said Daniel BOLLINGER continued to inhabit & cultivate said tract of land, raising corn, grains, etc. thereon annually each year on said tract of land in the several years from said year 1800 and 1801, 2,3,4 & untill 1808. And that said Daniel BOLLINGER still resides in this state.
Sworn to & Subscribed Oct. 17th, 1833.   Mathias BOLLINGER
L.F. LINN, Comm'r.

Dawalt BOLLINGER by his legal representatives claiming 640 acres of land, situated on White Water, County of Cape Girardeau, see Minutes No. 4, pgs. 32 & 279, Bk. B, pg. 294.
Adam STATLER, 60 years of age, and Phillip BOLLINGER, about 51 years of age, being duly sworn, deposeth & saith that in the latter part of the year 1799 they emigrated to the then District of Cape Girardeau, Province of Upper Louisiana, now County of Cape Girardeau, State of Missouri, where they have ever since resided in said State as residents of the same. That at the same time in said year, the said Dawalt BOLLINGER emigrated to said District with these affiants that the said DAWALT BOLLINGER in the beginning of the year 1800, by the permission of the then Spanish Commandant, settled upon & actually inhabited a tract of land on White Water, in said District, and being so an inhabitant and settled upon said land, he, the said Dawalt BOLLINGER, in the said year 1800, cleared, improved and cultivated the ground on said tract of land, by fencing & raising corn thereon and vegetables necessary for family use, and so continued settled upon as an inhabitant of said tract of land (dwellings and other buildings being erected thereon) to improve & cultivate said land from said year 1800 inclusive annually in continuation growing the necessary grains and vegetables thereon untill the change of Government to the United States. That said Dawalt BOLLINGER has ever since he first emigrated to said District continued to reside in said state.
Phillip (X) BOLLINGER   Adam (X) STATLER
     his mark   his mark
Sworn to & subscribed Oct. 18th, 1833. L.F. LINN, Comm'r.
         Adjourned untill tomorrow at 9 o'clock A.M.
               Thursday Jan. 2nd, 1834 Board Met-F.R. CONWAY, Present

Philip BOLLINGER by his legal representatives claiming 640 acres of
land, situated on White Waters, County of Cape Girardeau, see Minutes
Book No. 4, pgs. 33 & 279, Book B, pg. 293.
Adam STATLER about 66 years of age and William BOLLINGER about 56
years of age, being duly sworn, deposeth & saith that in the latter
part of 1799, they emigrated to the then District of Cape Girardeau,
Upper Louisiana, now County of Cape Girardeau, State of Missouri,
where they have remained as inhabitants of the same ever since. That
at the same time with these affiants, the said Philip BOLLINGER emigrated to said District, that said Philip BOLLINGER, in the beginning
of the year 1800, by the permission of the then Spanish Commandant at
that place, settled upon & actually inhabited a tract of land on the
waters of White water in said District and being so inhabitant & settled upon said land, said Philip BOLLINGER, in the said year, 1800,
cleared, growed, improved and cultivated the ground on said tract of
land, by fencing & raising vegetables necessary for family use, and
so continued settled upon as an inhabitant of said tract of land
(dwelling houses & other buildings being erected thereon) during the
years 1801, 2 & 3, to raise corn & the necessary vegetables for family
use. That the said Philip BOLLINGER has, from the year first above
named, continued to reside in the said Louisiana & Missouri aforesaid.

Adam (X) STATLER   William (X) BOLLINGER
his mark   his mark

Sworn to & subscribed Oct. 16th, 1833. L.F. LINN, Comm'r.

John BOLLINGER, son of John, by his legal representatives claiming
640 acres of land situated on White Water, see Minutes No. 3, pg. 480,
No. 4, pg. 239, Book B, pg. 293.
Frederick SIMBAUGH, 68 years of age, and John CALNER, about 49 years
of age, being duly sworn, deposeth & saith that they have been inhabitants & residents since the year 1800 of the then District of Cape
Girardeau, Upper Louisiana, now County of Cape Girardeau, State of
Missouri, that some time in the latter part of the summer, or the
first of the fall of 1803, the said John BOLLINGER, son of John, by
permission of the then Spanish Commandant at that place, settled upon
and actually inhabited a tract of land and began the improvement of the
same in said year, by cutting down trees and clearing the ground on
said tract of land that in the spring of the year 1804, said
John BOLLINGER so inhabiting as aforesaid having cleared & fenced a
field of ground on said land on White Water in said District, planted
corn & the vegetables necessary for family use, which grew & were
raised in the usual time in the said spring & summer of 1804 on said
land. That the necessary building and dwellings on said land having
been made by said John BOLLINGER from the time of his said settlement
continued so to inhabit, reside on and cultivate said land, by raising
the different kinds of grains thereon, clearing & fencing ground from
the time he first settled upon & inhabited said tract of land as is
herein mentioned untill the time of the formation of the state government of Missouri.

Frederick (X) SIMBAUGH   John (X) CALNER
his mark   his mark
Sworn to & subscribed Oct. 16th, 1833. L.F. LINN, Comm'r.
    Adjourned untill tomorrow at 9 o'clock A.M.
        Friday Jan. 3rd, 1834 Board Met-F.R. CONWAY, Present

Martin THOMAS by his legal representatives claiming 640 acres of land
situated on little White water, County of Cape Girardeau, see Minutes
No. 3, pg. 481, No. 4, pg. 241, Book B, pg. 292.
State of Missouri, County of Cape Girardeau
John COTNER, being duly sworn, states that he is well acquainted with
Martin THOMAS, who (cannot read) Louisiana, in 1803, and had an improvement on Little White Water in said District in the fall of that
year, at which time Turnips were sowed. Early the next spring, this
affiant worked on the said improvement for the said THOMAS and assisted him in planting out apple trees. The said THOMAS claimed and has
owned the place ever since, he occupied it in 1804.

John (X) COTNER
his mark

Sworn to & subscribed Oct. 16th, 1833. L.F. LINN, Comm'r.
Joseph NISWANGER, states that he is well acquainted with the above

Martin THOMAS. That he has read the foregoing statement of
John COTNER, and knows the facts therein contained to be true.
Joseph (X) NISWANGER
his mark
Sworn before L.F. LINN, Comm'r.

Dawalt CRITZ by his legal representatives claiming 640 acres of land,
see Book B, pg. 292.
State of Missouri, County of Cape Girardeau
George F, BOLLINGER, aged about 60 years, being duly sworn-as the law
directs, deposeth & saith that he was well acquainted with the said
Dawalt CRITZ, the original claimant, that the claimant came to this
country, then the province of Upper Louisiana, now State of Missouri,
in the year 1802. That he was a cripple & unable to go about much.
That Daniel BOLLINGER applied to, and obtained permission or grant
from Louis LORIMIER, Spanish Commandant of the District, for him to
settle. That said CRITZ selected the land claimed, which the witness
also knows. That the land was actually cultivated in the year 1804,
and had the same surveyed and has been actually cultivated ever since.
That valuable improvements were made on the same, such as a good
dwelling house, out houses, barn stable and orchards.
Sworn to & subscribed Oct. 19th, 1833.   George F. BOLLINGER
L.F. LINN, Comm'r.
        Adjourned untill tomorrow at 9 o'clock A.M.
            Saturday Jan. 4th, 1834 Board Met-F.R. CONWAY, Present

David REESE by his legal representatives claiming 640 acres of land,
situated on the waters of the St. Francis, see Minutes Book No. 1, p.
278, No. 5, pg. 309, Book B, pg. 469.
State of Missouri, County of Cape Girardeau
Francis CLARK (being duly sworn) states that he is well acquainted
with David REESE. First, he came acquainted with the said REESE
early in the year 1804 in the District of Cape Girardeau, Upper Louisiana. The said REESE was then living on the St. Francis River in
said District, his improvement was small. There was fruit trees then
growing on the said place. The trees (cannot read) had been set out
some time before. The said place is still claimed by the said REESE,
and there is a good house on it and some ten or fifteen acres cleared.
The said place is situated on the St. Francis river, about 12 miles
West of North of Greenville, Wayne County, Mo. There is no other old
settler, except himself (the deponent) & Mr. PAVICH, who is too old
& infirm to come to Jackson, now living in the section of country
where the above land is situated.
                            Francis (X) CLARK
                                his mark
Sworn to & mark made in presence of L.F. LINN, Comm'r. Oct. 15th, 1833.

Alexander SUMMERS by his legal representatives claiming 640 acres of
land situate on the waters of Hubble's creek, County of Cape Girardeau, see Book No. 4, pgs. 57 & 288, Book E, pg. 28.
State of Missouri, County of Cape Girardeau
Ithamer HUBBLE, being duly sworn, states that he is aged 71 years,
that he came to and settled in the District of Cape Girardeau, Upper
Louisiana, in the year 1797. That in the year 1799 or 1800, which,
this affiant is not positive, he became acquainted with one
Alexander SUMMERs, who in one of those years moved to said District
and settled a place on Fartin's Creek, which is a branch of Hubble's
Creek, that empties into White Water. The said Alexander at the time
mentioned built a cabbin on said place where he then resided, and
raised a crop of corn and other grain on the same. The said improvement is situated about six or seven miles outh of the present town of
Jackson, Cape Girardeau County, Mo. and is owned at this time by one
William WILLIAMS or his children. There was something like three or
four acres of land cleared on said place by said SUMMERS at the time
mentioned above.   Ithamer (X) HUBBLE
Sworn & subscribed to this 18th Oct., 1833 his mark
L.F. LINN Comm'r.
        Adjourned untill Monday next at 9 o'clock A.M.
            Monday Jan. 6th, 1834 Board Met-F.R. CONWAY, Present

John GUETHING by his legal representatives claiming 585 acres of
land situated in the late District of Cape Girardeau, see Minutes
No. 3, pg. 512, No. 4, pg. 261, Recorder's minutes pg. 89, BATE's
decisions, pg. 34, Book B, pg. 284.
State of Missouri, County of Cape Girardeau
George HACKER, being sworn, says he came to the District of Cape Girardeau in April 1802, in the fall of that year he saw the said John
and knew him from that time up to his death, about the year 1820.
the said John was a carpenter by trade and worked on the King of Spain's
house at the town of Cape Girardeau. He also worked at his trace for
other persons in said District. He died without children leaving
Elisabeth as his wife & sòle heir.   George HACKER
Sworn & subscribed Oct. 16th, 1833. L.F. LINN, Comm'r.
Elijah DOUGHERTY, being sworn, states that he knew the said land in
1800. He was then working for LORIMIER at the town of Cape Girardeau
at his trade, which was that of a carpenter. He afterwards in 1802
& 1803 worked at William DOUGHERTY in said District of Cape Girardeau.
This affiant also understood that he had a grant or permission to set-
tle land from the Commandant LORIMIER.   Elijah (X) DOUGHERTY
Sworn to & subscribed June 10th, 1833.   his mark
L.F. LINN, Comm'r.

Nicholas REVEILLEE by the heirs of Andrew RANNEY claiming 200 arpents
of land situated in the late District of New Madrid, see Book B, pg.
410, Book No. 4, pgs. 82 & 304.
State of Missouri, County of Cape Girardeau
James RAMSEY, Jr. knew the said Nicholas in the District of New Madrid
in the year 1799 or 1800. He was a mechanic, a Whitesmith by trade,
worked at his trade, both in New Madrid and Cape Girardeau.
                                        James (X) RAMSEY, Jr.
Sworn to & subscribed June 10th, 1833.   his mark
L.F. LINN, Comm'r.
John RODNEY, sworn, says he knew said Nicholas. He was acquainted
with him first about two years before the change of government. He
lived at that time in Cape Girardeau District. He was a mechanic and
affiant has seen him work as such.
                              John RODNEY
Sworn to & subscribed to June 10th, 1833. L.F. LINN, Comm'r.
     Adjourned untill tomorrow at 9 o'clock A.M.
          Tuesday Jan. 7th, 1834 Board Met-F.R. CONWAY, Present

John DOUGHERTY by his legal representatives claiming 640 acres of land
on the waters of Birds Creek, County of Cape Girardeau, see Record Bk.
F, pg. 13, BATE's Decisions pg. 99.
State of Missouri, County of Cape Girardeau
Elijah DOUGHERTY states that he moved to and settled in the District
of Cape Girardeau, Upper Louisiana, now State of Missouri in 1800.
That he was well acquainted with John DOUGHERTY, who came to the country at the same time that is in 1800. The said
John DOUGHERTY was a mechanic, a carpenter by trade, and worked on and
assisted in building the Commandant's house at the town of Cape Girardeau in 1801 & 1802. This affiant well recollects hearing the said
John apply to the Commandant Dr. Louis LORIMIER for land, soon after
his arrival in the above district in June 1800. LORIMIER told him to
select his place and he would take care of it for him. That as he was
a mechanic there was no need for him to improve his land and that he,
LORIMIER, wanted him to work on his house in the Cape. In the month
of July 1800, this affiant went, with the said John (cannot read)
Byrds Creek about four miles from the present town of Jackson in said
District. This affiant assisted the said John in making what was
called a tomahawk improvement, that is clearing out a place to build a
house and making brush heaps, after which the said John went to work on
the Commandant's house as stated above.   Elijah (X) DOUGHERTY
Sworn & subscribed to before L.F. LINN, Comm'r. His mark
Oct. 17th, 1833. L.F. LINN, Comm'r.
Robert GREEN, aged 78 years, states that he removed to and settled in
the District of Cape Girardeau, Upper Louisian, now state of Missouri,
in the year 1800. He was well acquainted with John DOUGHERTY, who
moved to & settled in said District in said year 1800. The said John
was a mechanic, a carpenter by trade, in the year 1800 this affiant was

128

present when the said John applied to the Spanish Commandant,
Dr. Louis LORIMIER, for land. LORIMIER told him he should have land
and had his name put down on the Books, but that he wanted him to work
for him, said LORIMIER, on his house at the Cape. The said John hesi-
tated, when LORIMIER said, "your land no run away; mechanics are not
obliged to cultivate their land, and I will take care of yours for you".
This affiant knows that the said John selected his land on the waters
of Birds Creek in said District (cannot read) camp and made brush heaps
on said place at said time. This affiant also knows that the said John
worked for the said Commandant on his house in Cape Girardeau in the
years 1801 & 1802, under the faith, as this affiant understood and believes, that it was not necessary for him to improve his land. The said
John lived in said District up to the time of his death in 1829 or 1830.
                                   Robt. GREEN
Sworn and subscribed to this 19th of Oct. 1833. L.F. LINN, Comm'r.
      Adjourned untill tomorrow at 9 o'clock A.M.
                Wednesday Jan. 8th, 1834 Board Met-F.R. CONWAY, Present

James RAMSAY, Jr. claiming 750 arpents of land situated in the late
District of Cape Girardeau, see minutes No. 4, pgs. 18 & 269.
State of Missouri, County of Cape Girardeau
John RODNEY, being sworn, states that he has known James RAMSAY, Jr.
ever since the year 1798. That he lived in the District of Cape Gi-
rardeau in that year. Knows of his inhabiting & cultivating land in
said District from the year 1798 up to the year 1816. Has seen him
cultivating corn, potatoes, etc. previous to the change of government.
He was a farmer by occupation & had a negro.
                                   John RODNEY
Sworn & subscribed to this 11th of June, 1833.   L.F. LINN, Comm'r.
Ithamer HUBBLE, being sworn, states that he is about 70 years of age.
That he knows the said James RAMSEY, Jr. well; has been acquainted
with him ever since the year 1797, when he, the said James, first came
to the District of Cape Girardeau, he knows of the said James Inhabi-
ting & cultivating land in the said District in the year 1802 or 1803.
He built a cabbin, cleared some land and planted peach trees in one of
those years. The said James has lived in this country ever since. His
occupation was that of a farmer.
                             Ithamer (X) HUBBLE
Sworn & subscribed to June 11th, 1833.   his mark
L.F. LINN, Comm'r.
Ebenezer HUBBLE states that he is well acquainted with the said
James RAMSEY, Jr. He became acquainted with him in the year 1797, when
the said James first moved to the District of Cape Girardeau. He thinks
in the fall of 1804, he was on the improvement of the said James, and
from the appearance of the house logs and peach trees, he would suppose
the improvement had been made two or three years.
Sworn & subscribed to June 11th, 1833.   Ebenezer (X) HUBBLE
L.F. LINN, Comm'r.   his mark
George HACKER, being sworn, says he knew the said James RAMSEY, Jr. in
1802. He then lived in the District of Cape Girardeau. The said
RAMSAY was a farmer and this affiant has seen him cultivating and in
said district, during the existence of the Spanish government. This
affiant knows that the said James RAMSEY went to New Madrid on an In-
dian expedition under the Spanish Government in the year 1802.
Sworn and subscribed to this 11th June, 1833.   George HACKER
L.F. LINN, Comm'r.

Lemuel CHENEY by the legal representatives of Andrew RAMSEY claiming
640 acres of land, see Minutes No. 3, pg. 505, No. 4, pg. 255.
James RAMSEY, Jr. states that he knew the said CHENEY well. He came
to this District of Cape Girardeau about the year 1798 or 1799. Knows
of the said CHENEY inhabiting & cultivating land in said District of
Cape Girardeau in the year 1799 or 1800, the precise year not recollected. He also, built a house & planted an orchard on the said land under the Spanish Government, and continued to reside on the same up to
the time of his death, which happened in the year 1805 or 1806, which
year deponent does not positively recollect. He cultivated the said
land in corn, potatoes, etc., and was a farmer by occupation.
Sworn & subscribed to 11th of June, 1833.   James (X) RAMSAY
L.F. LINN, Comm'r.   his mark

James WILBOURN by his legal representatives claiming 640 acres of
land in the late District of Cape Girardeau, see Minutes Book No. 5,
pg. 391, Book B, pg. 324.
John BALDWIN, aged about 62 years, is well acquainted with the said
James WILBOURN. The said James came to the District of Cape Girardeau
in the fall of 1803 and settled in Tywappity bottom. He built a cabbin so soon as he arrived. That is in the winter of 1803, so soon as
he built, he commenced opening a farm, and in 1804 he raised corn and
other things on said improvement. This affiant has seen the permission of the said James to settle, on the Books of COUSIN at Cape Girardeau. The said James was at the time of his settling this country, a
married man with a wife and one child.   John BALDWIN
Sworn to & subscribed this 11th day of June, 1833.
L.F. LINN, Comm'r.
          Adjourned until tomorrow at 10 o'clock A.M.
                Thursday Jan. 9th, 1834 Board Met-F.R.CONWAY, Present

Andrew RAMSEY, Jr. by his legal representatives claiming 750 arpents
of land in the late District of Cape Girardeau, see Record Book F,
pg. 13, BATE's Decisions pg. 98.
State of Missouri, County of Cape Girardeau
James RAMSEY, who is aged about 53 years, states that he knew the said
Andrew RAMSEY, Jr. well. That he was acquainted with him since his
infancy up to the time of his death in the year 1830. Knows that the
said Andrew had a permission to settle from LORIMIER, the Commandant
of the said Cape Girardeau District, in the year 1797 when he first
came to this country. He knows of his inhabiting and cultivating land
on the Big Swamp, insaid District in 1798, in pursuance of said permission, and that he lived on the same 12 or 15 years. He, also, knows
that the said Andrew built a dwelling house, stable, Barn, etc. and
cleared 25 or 30 acres of land under the Spanish Government, and that
he, also, planted an orchard on said land. The said Andrew was a married man when he moved to this country. Had a wife & 3 or 4 children,
and was the owner of two negroes. The said Andrew went to New Madrid
in 1802 on an Inidan expedition, and was promised by the Spanish Commandant, LORIMIER, 250 acres of land for his services on said expedition. The said Andrew died in this country in February, 1830, leaving
as his heirs & legal representatives the persons mentioned in the caption of this deposition.   James (X) RAMSEY
Sworn & subscribed to this 11th June, 1833.   his mark
L.F. LINN, Comm'r.
John RODNEY, sworn, states that he is about 44 years of age. That he
knew the said Andrew RAMSAY in the year 1798, and knows of his improving land in that year, at or near the Big Swamp in the District of
Cape Girardeau. He built a dwelling house and cultivated the land under the Spanish Government. He, also, had an orchard and fruit trees
was a married man, had a wife and 3 or 4 children previous to the
change of government; also negroes.
Sworn & subscribed to this 11th day of   John RODNEY
June, 1833. L.F. LINN, Comm'r.
Ithamer HUBBLE; who is aged about 70 years, knew Andrew RAMSEY, Jr.
well. The said Andrew moved to the District of Cape Girardeau in 1797;
was a man with a family. Had a wife and children. He knows of said
Andrew inhabiting & cultivating land in the Big Swamp in said District
previous to the year 1800. The exact time, he made his improvement, he
does not recollect. He knows of his building a dwelling and other
houses in the Spanish times, and also, claiming lands in the place mentioned and that he cultivated corn, potatoes, etc.
Sworn & subscribed to June 11th, 1833   Ithamer (X) HUBBLE
L.F. LINN, Comm'r.   his mark
Ebenezer HUBBLE, states that he was well acquainted with Andrew RAMSEY,
Jr. first saw him at Cape Girardeau in 1797, and knows that he inhabited and cultivated land in the Big Swamp in Cape Girardeau, previous
to the year 1803. He built houses, cleared land and raised grain under
the Spanish Government. He, also, built stables, corn cribs & etc. was
a man with a family; had a wife and children, the number, this affiant
does not know. The said Andrew continued to cultivate the said land
as this affiant knows long after the American Government was established.
Sworn & subscribed to June 11th, 1833.   Ebenezer (X)HUBBLE
L.F. LINN, Comm'r.   his mark
          Adjourned until tomorrow at 9 o'clock A.M.

Fryday Jan. 10th, 1834 Board Met-F.R. CONWAY, Present

William THOMPSON by his legal representatives claiming 640 acres of
land situated on Hubbles Creek, County of Cape Girardeau, see Book No.
5, pg. 505.
State of Missouri, County of Cape Girardeau
William WILLIAMS states that he is aged about fifty eight or nine;
that he moved to and settled in the District of Cape Girardeau, Upper
Louisiana, in 1799; that he was well acquainted with one W.
William THOMPSON; he knows that the said THOMPSON had an improvement
on the waters of Kandles creek in said District, in the year 1800 or
1801. The said THOMPSON had corn growing on said place in the year
1801, and this affiant from the best of his recollection, states that
the said THOMPSON occupied said place up to the year 1802. There was
something like two or three acres of land cleared on said place at the
time mentioned above. William WILLIAMS
Sworn to & subscribed Oct. 16th, 1833.
L.F. LINN, Comm'r.

Elijah FORD by his legal representative, Wm. HACKER, claiming 640
acres of land situated in the late District of New Madrid, see Minutes
Book No. 5, pg. 425, Book B, pg. 409.
State of Missouri, County of Cape Girardeau
James RAMSAY, Jr. knew the said FORD in the District of New Madrid
some time about the year 1800, where he then lived. The said HACKER
purchased the improvement of the said FORD. Lived in it, and cultivated it in the year 1802. This affiant knows that the said HACKER
inhabited and cultivated the said land for a number of years from 1802
up to 1804 or 1805. This settlement was in the neighbourhood of
Matthew's farm in the District of New Madrid. There was a house built
a well dug, and stables raised in Spanish times. The said HACKER
raised corn, cotton, etc. on said land before the change of government.
Sworn & subscribed to June 11th, 1833.   James (X) RAMSEY, Jr.
L.F. LINN, Comm'r.   his mark

James BEVINS by his legal representatives claiming 640 acres of land
situate on White Water, County of Cape Girardeau, see Minutes No. 4,
pgs. 41 & 283.
State of Missouri, County of Cape Girardeau
Isaac MILLER states that he moved to & settled in the District of Cape
Girardeau, Upper Louisiana, now State of Missouri, in the year 1803.
That he was well acquainted with one James BEVINS, who also moved to
and settled in said District in said year 1803. This affiant and the
said BEVINS in the same year they arrived in the country, called on
LORIMIER, the Spanish Commandant at Cape Girardeau, for land and got
permission to settle. This affiant knows that the said James worked
& made an improvement on main White Water in said District in the winter of 1803, and raised corn thereon the next year, where he lived.
The said James died in the fall of the year 1804; the said place is
now owned by the heirs of one John MILLER.
Sworn to & subscribed Oct. 19th, 1833.   Isaac MILLER
L.F. LINN, Comm'r.
     Adjourned untill tomorrow at 9 o'clock A.M.
        Saturday Jan. 11th, 1834 Board Met-F.R. CONWAY, Present

Frederick LIMBAUGH by his legal representatives claiming 640 acres of
land on White Water, County of Cape Girardeau, see Minutes Book No. 1,
pg. 263, No. 3, pg. 481 and No. 4, pg. 241, Book B, pg. 275.
State of Missouri, County of Cape Girardeau
William BOLLINGER states that he moved to & settled in the District of
Cape Girardeau, Upper Louisiana in 1800, and that he is well acquainted
with Frederick LIMBAUGH, who moved & settled in the said District in
the year 1803. That said Frederick settled a place on south White Water
in said District in that year 1803. Built a house (cannot read) the
said Frederick raised corn, etc. on said place and still resides on the
land. The said Frederick had a family at the time he settled, consisting of his wife and six children. He cleared the first year something
like eight or ten acres and resided on the same.
Sworn to & subscribed Oct. 16th, 1833.   William (X) BOLLINGER
L.F. LINN, Comm'r.   his mark

131

Joseph NISWANGER states that he moved to and settled in the District
of Cape Girardeau, Upper Louisiana in 1800. That he is well acquainted
with Frederick LIMBAUGH, who moved to and settled in said District in
the year 1803. This affiant knows that the said Frederick settled a
place on South White Water in that year 1803. He built a house thereon in the same year, and cleared eight or ten acres of land. The next
year 1804, he cultivated the said land and raised corn on it. The
said Frederick lived on said place in the years mentioned above, that
is 1803 & 1804 and still lives there.   Joseph (X) NISWANGER
Sworn & subscribed to Oct. 16th, 1833.   his mark
L.F. LINN, Comm'r.

Joseph WORTHINGTON by his legal representatives claiming 640 acres of
land situated on the waters of Hubbles Creek, County of New Madrid,
see Minutes Book No. 4, pgs. 71 and 295.
State of Missouri, County of Cape Girardeau
John FRIEND, who is aged about 52 years, states that he moved to the
District of Lanse a la grasse, Upper Louisiana, in the year 1799. That
he was well acquainted with Joseph WORTHINGTON of the District of Cape
Girardeau. He first knew him in 1801. In 1803, this affiant worked
for the said Joseph on his improvement at what was called the Pond
Place, on the waters of Hubbles in said District, now County of Cape
Girardeau, Missouri; the said Joseph had a house on said place in 1803,
where he then lived, and had some ten or twelve acres cleared and in
cultivation in corn and other things. This affiant knows that the said
Joseph was living on said place in 1804, and for several years there-
after.   John (X) FRIEND
Sworn to & mark made in presence of   his mark
L.F. LINN, Comm'r. Jackson, Oct.15th, 1833.
          Adjourned untill Monday next at 9 o'clock A.M.
          Monday Jan. 13th, 1834 Board Met-F.R. CONWAY, Present

Ebenezer HUBBLE by his legal representatives claiming 640 acres of
land on White Water, County of Cape Girardeau, see Minutes No. 1, pg.
240, No. 3, pg. 510 & No. 4, pg. 260.
State of Missouri, County of Cape Girardeau
Ithamer HUBBLE, being duly sworn, says that he is about 70 years of
age. That he moved to Upper Louisiana in the year 1797, and settled
in the then District of Cape Girardeau, where he has resided ever
since. The said Ebenezer HUBBLE came to this country at the same time
and settled in said District of Cape Girardeau, where he has, also, resided ever since. In the year 1803, the said Ebenezer obtained a written permission from LORIMIER, the Spanish Commandant at Cape Girardeau,
to settle lands, and in the same year, that is 1803, improved land on
the West side of White water, in said District of Cape Girardeau, and
sowed the same in turnips the fall of that year. The said land has been
in cultivation, by the said Ebenezer, ever since with the exception of
two or three years at different times, and with the exception of a part
of said claim, which has been entered by one Morris YOUNG, the said
head right on settlement right was duly surveyed by the proper officer
in the fall of 1805. That part of said claim, which has been entered
by the said YOUNG includes nearly all the tilable land in said survey,
the ballance being hilly and broken.   Ithamer (X) HUBBLE
Sworn & subscribed to June 11th, 1833   his mark
L.F. LINN, Comm'r.
Ithamer HUBBLE, the above witness, further, states that the above place
of Ebenezer HUBBLE was not only put in cultivation as stated above, but
was also inhabited in the month of February, 1804, at which time he
built a house on said place.   Ithamer (X) HUBBLE
Sworn & subscribed to Oct. 18th, 1833.   his mark
L.F. LINN, Comm'r.

In the Case of Thomas REED claiming 747 arpents of land, see pg. 212
of this book, the following testimony was taken before L.F. LINN,
Comm'r.
State of Missouri, County of Cape Girardeau
John T. MCNEAL, aged about 70 years, says he knew the said Thomas REED
well, from the year 1802 up; in the month of February, 1804, he passed
the improvement of the said Thomas REED in the District of St. Genevieve,
there appeared to be two or three acres cleared and a cabbin built. The
land such as if it had been in cultivation the year before. He after-

wards understood that turnips had been raised on the improvement. The timber from the deadening seemed to have been cut in 1802. This improvement was made in Bellevue Settlement. This affiant in the next year, moved from that neighbourhood and did not return untill 1809, when the said improvement was in the possession of William SLOANE, who had purchased the same from the said REED, and has been on his possession and that of his children ever since. This affiant knows the children of the said William SLOANE, and believes their names are all mentioned in the caption of this deposition.   John T. MCNEAL
Sworn to & subscribed this 11th of June, 1833.
L.F. LINN, Comm'r.
        Adjourned untill tomorrow at 9 o'clock A.M.
                Tuesday Jan. 14th, 1834 Board Met-F.R. CONWAY, Present

John HAND by his legal representatives claiming 640 acres of land situated in the county of Cape Girardeau, see Minutes Book No. 3, pg. 489, No. 4, pg. 244.
State of Missouri, County of Cape Girardeau
John HAYS, aged about 55 years, being duly sworn, says that he was well acquainted with John HAND, the original claimant, that the claimant came to this country, then the province of Upper Louisiana, in the spring of the year 1799, and stopped at New Madrid and moved to the District of Cape Girardeau, the same fall, when he remained a citizen & cultivator of the soil till his death a few years since.
Sworn to & subscribed Oct. 18th, 1833.   John HAYS
L.F. LINN, Comm'r.
Also came Martha DOUGHERTY, a witness aged about forty eight, who being duly sworn as the law directs, deposeth & saith that she was well acquainted with John HAND, the original claimant. Witness knows the land claimed, and knows that in 1802, the said John settled on & improved the land, cleared in that year some land and sowed turnips and continued to clear more land in 1803 & 1804. He cultivated corn thereon in 1803 & 1804; that there was a house or cabbin built on said land, and that the said tract of land has been continually inhabited and cultivated ever since.   Martha (X) DOUGHERTY
Sworn to & subscribed Oct. 18th, 1833.   her mark
L.F. LINN, Comm'r.
Also came Mary Goza, a witness aged about 43 years, who being duly sworn, deposeth & saith that she was well acquainted with John HAND, the original claimant. Witness, also, knows the land claimed, and she knows that John HAND settled on and improved and cultivated the same as early as the year 1803. There was several acres of land fenced and cleared, and a garden in cultivation. This witness dropped the corn for said HAND in 1803 herself. She, also, knew that house logs were then cut & hawled and laying on the ground, and she, further, knows that the house was raised and fenced the same year, and she, further, knows that the said land has been constantly inhabited and cultivated ever since.   Mary (X) GOZA
Sworn to & subscribed Oct. 19th, 1833.   her mark
L.F. LINN, Comm'r.

James COX by his legal representatives claiming 640 acres of land situate on Randal's Creek, County of Cape Girardeau, see Minutes Book No. 4, pg. 60, No. 5, pg. 15.
State of Missouri, County of Cape Girardeau
Richard WALLER states that he was well acquainted with James COX. He first knew him in the District of Cape Girardeau in the year 1798. He knows of the said James inhabiting and cultivating land on the waters of Randal's Creek in said District Upper Louisiana in the years 1801,2, 3, and 1804 and since. The said James had a house on said place, and about six or seven acres cleared in the years mentioned above. There was, also, stables and corn cribs on said place.
Sworn and subscribed to this 18th of Oct., 1833.   Richard WALLER
L.F. LINN, Comm'r.
David GREEN, who is 50 years of age, states that he moved to & settled in the District of Cape Girardeau, Upper Louisiana, now State of Missouri, in the year 1800. That in the spring of 1802 or 1803, which he cannot positively state. he was passing from the Big Swamp to Byrd's Settlement, in said District, when he came in view of two or three improvements on Randal's Creek, where he met James COX, whom he had known in said District for several years. This affiant asked the said James,

who lived there, and was told by the said James that his father lived
at the left hand place, and that he, the said James, owned the other
and lived there. This affiant was well acquainted with the said James,
though he had never been at his house. The said James continued to
live in said District up to the time of his death, one or two years
ago. He was a farmer and followed that occupation.
Sworn and subscribed to Oct. 18th, 1833.   D. GREEN
L.F. LINN, Comm'r.

John PATTERSON by his legal representatives claiming 640 acres of land
situated on Hubble's Creek, County of Cape Girardeau, see Record Book
F, pg. 13, BATE's Decisions pg. 97.
State of Missouri, County of Cape Girardeau
Hugh CRISWELL states that he moved to and settled in the District of
Cape Girardeau, Upper Louisiana, in the year 1801, and that he is well
acquainted with John PATTERSON, then, and still a resident of said
District. This affiant knows of the said PATTERSON's obtaining permission to settle from LORIMIER, the Commandant at Cape Girardeau in
said year, and that he actually settled a place on Hubble's creek in
said District in the year 1801, and in 1802, he, said PATTERSON,
raised corn and other grain on said place. This affiant knows that
the said PATTERSON inhabited and cultivated said place in the years
1802, 3, 4 & 1805. The said PATTERSON was a mechanic, a Blacksmith by
trade, which trade he carried on at said place in the years mentioned
above. The said PATTERSON was a man with a family, previous to the
change of Government, consisting of his wife and three children. The
said PATTERSON had a large hewed log house on said place, an orchard
of both apples & peaches, previous to 1804. The quantity of cleared
land this affiant cannot state. There was perhaps seven or eight acres.
Sworn to & subscribed Oct. 14th, 1833.   Hugh CRISWELL
L.F. LINN, Comm'r.
        Adjourned till tomorrow at 9 o'clock A.M.
            Wednesday Jan. 15th, 1834 Board Met-F.R. CONWAY, Present

In the case of John BOLLINGER, son of John, (Cannot read) Book, the
following testimony was taken by L.F. LINN, Comm'r.
William BOLLINGER states that he is aged 56 years; that he moved to
and settled in the District of Cape Girardeau, Upper Louisiana, now
State of Missouri, in the year 1800. That he was well acquainted with
John BOLLINGER, son of John, who also settled in said District in the
year 1800. He knows of the said John making an improvement on South
White Water, in said District, in the spring of 1801, in which year it
was run off by B. COUSIN, the Surveyor, in said year a house was built
on said place and a garden made. The next year, 1802, more gound was
cleared and corn raised on it. The said place has been in cultivation
ever since by different persons. The said place has in part been entered as this affiant is informed and believes. The said place was
inhabited and cultivated in the years 1801 and 1802 by
John BOLLINGER.   William (X) BOLLINGER
Sworn to & subscribed Oct. 17th, 1833.   his mark
L.F. LINN, Comm'r.

Joseph CHEVALIER by his legal representative, John HAYS, claiming 400
arpents of land situated in the County of Cape Girardeau, see Record
Book B, pg. 307, Minutes No. 4, pgs. 64 & 521, produces a paper purporting to be the petition of said CHEVALIER, the recommendation of
Pre. De LUZIERE, Commandant of New Bourbon and the original concession
from Carlos Dehault DELASSUS, dated 18th October, 1799. Also, a plat
of survey by Edw. F. BOND, D.S., dated 5th February, 1806 & received
for record, by SOULARD, Surv. General, February 28th, 1806.
State of Missouri, County of Cape Girardeau
John Bste. VALLE, aged about 72 years, being duly sworn as the law directs, deposeth and saith that he was well acquainted with
Pierre Delassus de LUZIERE. The he has often seen him write. That he
was the Commandant of the Post and District of New Bourbon in the year
1799, and that the name and signature to the recommendation for said
grant, made by said Pierre Delassus de LUZIERE, dated the 6th day of
October in the year 1799, is the proper name & signature and the proper
handwritingof the said Pre. Delassus de LUZIERE. And this deponent,
further, says that he was well acquainted with Charels Dehault DELASSUS,
that he has often seen him write, and that the said C.D. DELASSUS, was

the Lt. Gov. of the province of Upper Louisiana in the year 1799 and
that the name and signature to the said original concession from him
to the said Joseph CHEVALIER for 400 arpents of land, dated the 18th
October in the year 1799 is the proper name and signature and in the
proper handwriting of the said Charles Dehault DELASSUS. And this
deponent, further, says that he was well acquainted with the original
concessionee, Joseph CHEVALIER, and that he was, at the date of the
concession, a citizen & resident of the province of Upper Louisiana.
Sworn to & subscribed before me, L.F. LINN, Comm'r., this 27th May,
1833.   J.Bste. VALLE
L.F. LINN, Comm'r.
        Adjourned untill tomorrow at 9 o'clock A.M.
            Thursday Jan. 16th, 1834 Board Met-F.R. CONWAY, Present

Samuel DORSEY by his legal representatives claiming 800 arpents of
land situated in the late District of Cape Girardeau, see Minutes No.
4, pgs. 38 & 131, B, pg. 395,   .
State of Missouri, County of Cape Girardeau
Joseph LEWIS, aged near 62 years, says he came to this country, then
the province of Upper Louisiana, in the year 1797, in the month of
March of that year. The witness was well acquainted with
Samuel DORSEY, the claimant. Witness found him a citizen and resident
in the province of Upper Louisiana in the year 1797, and knows that
said DORSEY continued a citizen and resident of the country for several years after the American Government purchased the country.
Sworn to & subscribed before me, L.F. LINN,   Joseph LEWIS
one of the Comm'rs., this 15th Oct., 1833.
Also came William WILLIAMS as a witness aged about 59 years, who being
duly sworn as the law directs, deposeth and saith that he came to this
country, then the Province of Upper Louisiana, in the spring of the
year 1799. That he became soon acquainted with the original claimant
Samuel DORSEY, who was then a citizen and resident of the country, and
that the said DORSEY continued a citizen and resident of the country
for many years after the American Government purchased the country.
                                          William WILLIAMS
Sworn to & subscribed in presence of L.F. LINN, Comm'r., Jackson,
Oct. 15th, 1833.

Jephta CORNELIUS by his legal representative Henry HOWARD, claiming
640 acres of land situated on Cane Creek, County of Cape Girardeau,
see Minutes Book No. 1, pg. 232, No. 4, pg. 35 & 280.
State of Missouri, County of Cape Girardeau
Moses BYRD states that he moved to & settled in the District of Cape
Girardeau, Upper Louisiana, in the year 1799. That he was well acquainted with Jephta CORNELIUS, who moved to and settled a place on
Cane Creek, a branch of Byrd's Creek in said District, either in the
latter part of the year 1801, or fore part of the year 1802, which,
this affiant is not sure. The said CORNELIUS built a house on said
land, previous to 1803, and raised two crops of corn on said land,
and in September, 1803, sold & transferred the said land and improvements to one Joseph YOUNG. The said YOUNG sold & transferred the said
land to Henry HOWARD,- who moved on the said place early in the year
1804, when the said CORNELIUS moved out of the house on said place.
The said HOWARD continued to inhabit & cultivate said place (cannot
read) some 8 or 10 years ago, his widow & family still inhabit said
plantation. This affiant recollects that said place was inhabited &
cultivated many years after its first settlement, either by CORNELIUS
or HOWARD, untill many years after 1804. The said CORNELIUS had a
family consisting of his wife, himself, and a good many children, the
precise number this affiant cannot state. Henry HOWARD also had a
large family consisting of his wife and children, but the precise number this affiant cannot state. He speaks of their families as they
were when they first moved to the country. This affiant lived at the
time in the neighbourhood of said place mentioned above.
Sworn to & subscribed Oct. 17th, 1833.   Moses BYRD
L.F. LINN, Comm'r.

William TALBERT by his legal representatives claiming 640 acres of
land. (Relinquished N.M. Certif. No. 175)

Enos RANDALL, Sr. claiming 640 acres of land situate County of Cape

Girardeau, see Minutes No. 3, pg. 468, No. 4, pg. 235
State of Missouri, County of Cape Girardeau
William WILLIAMS states that he came to the District of Cape Girardeau, Upper Louisiana, in the year 1799, and has continued to reside
in said District ever since. That he was well acquainted with
Enos RANDALL, Sr. The said Enos RANDALL lived at that time on Randall's Creek in said District and had an improvement, say from twenty
to forty acres of land cleared previous to the change of government.
He had built on said improvement a dwelling house, stables, cribs,
etc. and had a large family consisting of himself, his wife, and five
or six children, four sons & one or two daughters, prior to the 4th
of March, 1804, at which time the said RANDALL cultivated and inhabited said place.   William WILLIAMS
Sworn to & subscribed Oct. 16th, 1833.
L.F. LINN, Comm'r.
        Adjourned untill tomorrow at 9 o'clock A.M.
              Friday Jan. 17th, 1834 Board Met-F.R. CONWAY, Present

Polly BOYD by her legal representatives claiming 640 acres of land
situate on Cane Creek, see Book E, pg. 32, Minutes No. 4, pgs. 54, 64,
75 & 287, BATE's Decisions, pg. 99..
State of Missouri, County of Cape Girardeau
Alexander SUMMERS states that he is well acquainted with Polly BOYD,
and has know her for a long time. He recollects passing her improvement on Cane Creek, a branch of Byrd's Creek, in the year 1802. There
was at that time, a cabbin on said place, and about two or three acres
cleared and in cultivation. That is to say in 1802, at which time the
said Polly lived on said place. Said place was situated on the water
course mentioned above, in the District of Cape Girardeau, Upper Louisiana, now County of Cape Girardeau, State of Missouri. The said
Polly BOYD has lived in said District ever since, though this affiant
cannot state that she has always lived on said place.
Sworn to & subscribed Oct. 18th, 1833.   Alexander SUMMERS
L.F. LINN, Comm'r.

Joseph NISWANGER, Jr. by his legal representatives claiming 640 acres
of land situated on White Waters, County of Cape Girardeau, see Book
B, pg. 294, Minutes No. 3, pg. 482, No. 4, pg. 242.
State of Missouri, County of Cape Girardeau
Martin THOMAS states that he is well acquainted with Joseph NISWANGER,
Jr., who was living in the District of Cape Girardeau, Upper Louisiana,
when this affiant moved to said District in 1803. The said NISWANGER
was living at that time on Big White Water in said District and something like 12 or 15 acres in cultivation in corn and other grains. He
had a house, a stable, cribs, and other buildings. He was a married
man previous to the change of government. He had peach trees growing
on said land when this affiant settled in the country in 1803 on the
place mentioned above, where the said NISWANGER resided in 1803 and
1804 and still lives on said place.   Martin (X) THOMAS
Sworn to before L.F. LINN, Comm'r. Oct. 16th, 1833.   his mark
Frederick LIMBAUGH states that he is well acquainted with the said
Joseph NISWANGER, Jr. That he has read the above statement of
Martin THOMAS and knows the facts therein contained are true.
Sworn before L.F. LINN, Comm'r.   Frederick (X) LIMBAUGH
                                                      his mark

Samuel RANDALL, Jr. claiming 640 acres of land, situate on Randall's
Creek, County of Cape Girardeau, see No. 5, pg. 390.
State of Missouri, County of Cape Girardeau
Abraham RANDALL, who is 50 years of age, states that he moved to &
settled in the District of Cape Girardeau, Upper Louisiana, in the
year 1797. That he was well acquainted with Samuel RANDALL, Jr.,for-
merly of said District. This affiant knows of the said Samuel's improving a place on Randle's Creek, in said District, in said year 1797,
which place the said Samuel continued to cultivate and inhabit from
the year 1797 up to his death, which took place in 1801. The said
Samuel had something like 30 acres cleared and in cultivation at the
time of his death mentioned above. There was, also, a dwelling house,
stables, corn crib and orchard on said place at the time mentioned
above. The said Samuel had, at the time of his death, a wife and two
children, and also two negroes. The said land is situated about three

miles South East from the present town of Jackson and is owned by one
John RANDLE. This affiant has frequently heard the Commandant,
Dr. Louis LORIMIER remark and tell the settlers that he wanted them to
live near each other as it was a frontier country, and if they settled
they should have additional grants, elsewhere. Abraham (X) RANDLE
Sworn to & subscribed this 18th Oct. 1833.   his mark
L.F. LINN, Comm'r.
        Adjourned untill tomorrow at 9 o'clock A.M.
            Saturday Jan. 18th, 1834 Board Met-F.R. CONWAY, Present

Alexander ANDREWS by his legal representative, John HAYS, claiming 640
acres of land, situate in the County of Cape Girardeau, see Minutes
Book No. 3, pg. 506, No. 4, pg. 255, Book B, pg. 101.
State of Missouri, County of Cape Girardeau
Moses BYRD, aged about 52 years, being duly sworn, deposeth & saith
that he, the witness, came to this country, then the province of Upper
Louisiana, in the year 1799, where he has remained ever since. Witness was well acquainted with the original claimant, and witness, also,
knows the land claimed, and further, this witness says that the claimant settled on the land in the year 1802, built a cabbin thereon, and
cleared and fenced in some three or four acres of land and raised corn
thereon, and witness believes it was inhabited and cultivated for several years afterwards in succession, and the said tract of land has
been inhabited & cultivated ever since.   Moses BYRD
Sworn to & subscribed this 15th Oct. 1833, before me, L.F. LINN, Comm'r.
And also, came George HENDERSON, a witness aged nearly 49 years, who
being duly sworn as the law directs, deposeth & saith that in 1802, to
the best of his recollection, he saw an improvement of several acres on
the land claimed, which was said to be the improvement of
Alexander ANDREWS and witness believes there was, also, a cabbin on the
land, but whether then tenanted or not, he cannot say, but believes
there was.   George HENDERSON
Sworn to & subscribed Oct. 17th, 1833.
L.F. LINN, Comm'r.
Also came David GREEN, a witness aged about 50 years, who being duly
sworn as the law directs, deposeth & saith that he was personally acquainted with the original claimant Alexander ANDREWS, Witness, also,
knows the land claimed, and that the said ANDREWS was settled and living on the same in the year 1802; claimant had a cabbin or a house
thereon; lived on the same, had a garden in cultivation and also had
several acres under fence, and had a part, if not all, in cultivation.
Sworn to & subscribed Oct. 18th, 1833.   D. GREEN
L.F. LINN, Comm'r.
Moses BYRD being further sworn, deposeth and saith that he knew another
man in the same neighbourhood with this claimant, called
Alexander ANDREWS, who was also a citizen of the country at the same
time.   Moses BYRD
Sworn to & subscribed Oct. 18th, 1833
L.F. LINN, Comm'r.
Also came Alexander SUMMERS, a witness aged about 53 years, who depo-
seth and saith that he was well acquainted with the original claimant,
and he, also, knows that there was two men in the same neighbourhood,
at the same time, both of the name of Alexander ANDREWS.
Sworn to & subscribed Oct. 18th, 1833.   Alex. SUMMERS
L.F. LINN, Comm'r.
        Adjourned untill Monday next at 9 o'clock A.M.
            Monday, Jan. 20th, 1834 Board Met-F.R. CONWAY, Present

Alexander ANDREWS by his legal representative, Jonathan BUIS, claiming
640 acres of land situate on Byrd's creek, County of Cape Girardeau,
see Minutes No. 1, pg. 466, No. 4, pgs. 54 & 287, Book B, pg. 320.
State of Missouri, County of Cape Girardeau
Philip YOUNG states that he moved to and settled in the District of
County of Cape Girardeau, Upper Louisiana, in the year 1801. That in
the same year he became acquainted with one Alexander ANDREWS, who then
resided on an improvement, situated on the waters of Byrd's Creek in
the now County of Cape Girardeau, State of Missouri. The said improvement was small, the precise quantity he cannot state. The said
ANDREWS had it in cultivation in corn at the time mentioned above. He
also had a dwelling house. The said ANDREWS had a family consisting
of a wife.   Philip YOUNG
Sworn & subscribed to Oct. 17th, 1833. L.F. LINN, Comm'r.

Also came Moses BYRD, a witness aged about 53 years, who being duly sworn, deposeth and saith that he was personally acquainted with Alexander ANDREWS, the original claimant, and he, also, knows that there was another Alexander ANDREWS in the same neighbourhood, and a citizen of the country at the same time.   Moses BYRD
Sworn to & subscribed Oct. 18th, 1833.
L.F. LINN, Comm'r.
Also came Alexander SUMMERS, a witness aged about 53 years, who deposeth & saith that he was well acquainted with the original claimant and he, also, knows that there was two men in the same neighbourhood at the same time, both of the name of Alexander ANDREWS.
Sworn to & subscribed Oct. 18th, 1833.   Alex. SUMMERS
L.F. LINN, Comm'r.

Frederick BOLLINGER claiming 640 acres of land situate on White Water District of Cape Girardeau, see Minutes Book No. 5, pg. 389, Book B, pg. 320, List A.
Dawalt BOLLINGER, 51 years of age, being duly sworn, deposeth and saith that he came to the then district of Cape Girardeau, Upper Louisiana, a province of the King of Spain, now county of Cape Girardeau, State of Missouri, in the year 1799, where this deponent has ever since resided as an inhabitant and resident of the same.   That at said time, the said Frederick BOLLINGER in the said year 1799, settled upon and actually inhabited a tract of land by permission of the Spanish Commandant, on White Water in said District, and being so an inhabitant and settled upon said land, he, the said Frederick BOLLINGER, in the year 1800 began the improvement and cultivation of the same by clearing ground, fencing fields, planting and growing corn and vegetables thereon.   That the said Frederick BOLLINGER during the years 1800, 1801, 2 & 1803, in each of said years, actually inhabited, settled upon and cultivated said tract of land, raised corn and vegetables thereon and remained on said tract of land as aforesaid (having erected the necessary buildings thereon) until the transfer of said country to the United States, and until the Spanish Government has ceased to exercise any authority over the same.   That the said Frederick BOLLINGER has continued to reside in said District from the time when he first emigrated to it as mentioned, untill the present time.
Signed & sworn to Oct. 16th, 1833.   Dayvalt BOLLINGER
L.F. LINN, Comm'r.
     Adjourned until tomorrow at 9 o'clock A.M.
          Tuesday Jan. 21st, 1834 Board Met-F.R. CONWAY, Present

Agnew MASSEY by his legal representatives claiming 640 acres of land, situate in Prairie St. Charles alias Mathew's prairie, see Book E, pg. 194, Book No. 4, pg. 108, No. 5, pg. 26.
State of Missouri, County of Cape Girardeau
George HACKER, being sworn, says he was well acquainted with Agnew MASSEY, who resided in the District of New Madrid.   He first knew him in April, 1802 in Prairie St. Charles in said District, where he inhabited and cultivated land.   He had cleared land, which was in cultivation and built a dwelling house, etc.   He had a wife, one son and one daughter.   George HACKER
Sworn & subscribed to June 11th, 1833.
L.F. LINN, Comm'r.
I do hereby swear that I came to and settled in Prairie St. Charles in Scott County and State of Missouri, in the spring of 1802 and that some time within the said year, I saw and became acquainted with Agnew MASSEY, who built a small cabbin without any other improvements and left it in a few months.   Daniel STRINGER
Sworn & subscribed to before me, a Justice of the Peace for Byrd Township in Cape Girardeau County & State of Missouri, this the 15th day October, 1833.   A.H. BREWARD
Sworn to & signature acknowledged Oct. 15th, 1833.
L.F. LINN, Comm'r.
This day personally appeared before me, Lewis F. LINN, one of the Comm'rs. appointed under an act of Congress for settling & adjusting the unconfirmed land claims in Missouri, Robert GIBONEY of lawful age, being duly sworn, deposeth & saith that he emigrated to the District of Cape Girardeau, then under the Spanish Government, in the year 1797, that in the year 1804 or 5, as well as this affiant recollects, that in an arrangement made between Agnew MASSEY and this affiant's brother,

about going to Mathews prairie and bringing his, said MASSEY's horses
to the Saline on the Mississippi, then in the District of St. Genevieve, that this affiant went for his brother and drove MASSEY's horses to the salt works as above, the compensation for the above labour
was paid in salt, but how much this affiant does not recollect.
L.F. LINN, Comm'r.   Robert GIBONEY
     Adjourned untill tomorrow at 9 o'clock A.M.
          Wednesday Jan. 22nd, 1834 Board Met-F.R. CONWAY, Present

Edward MATHEWS by his legal representatives claiming 640 acres of land
situate in Prairie St. Charles, alias Mathew's prairie in Scott County
see No. 5, pg. 453, Book A, pg. 465
State of Missouri, County of Cape Girardeau
Daniel STRINGER states that he moved to and settled in the District of
L Ause a la graisse (New Madrid), Upper Louisiana, in the year 1802.
That he was well acquainted with Edward N. MASSEY, who then in 1802,
resided in Prairie St. Charles or LORIMIER's prairie in said District.
This affiant knows that the said Edward inhabited and cultivated land
in said Prairie in the years 1802, 3 & 4, and that he continued to live
in said Prairie up to the time of his death, something better than a
year ago. There was a double cabbin on the land where the said Edward
lived in 1802, and a considerable improvement. The said Edward died on
said place, having a family, which still lives on said place.
L.F. LINN, Comm'r.   Daniel STRINGER
John FRIEND states that he moved to and settled in the District of
l'Ause a la graisse (New Madrid) Upper Louisiana, in 1799. That he
was well acquainted with Edward N. MATHEWS. This affiant first became
acquainted with the said Edward in the fall of 1801, who then resided
in Prairie St. Charles, where he had settled in the spring of that
year. This affiant knows that the said Edward inhabited & cultivated
land in said Prairie, in the years 1802, 1803 and 1804, and that he continued to live in said Prairie up to the time of his death, which
occured some thing like twelve months ago. His children still live on
said place, in said Prairie.   John (X) FRIEND
                                            his mark
Sworn to & subscribed in presence of L.F. LINN, Comm'r. Oct. 15th, 1833.
     Adjourned untill tomorrow at 9 o'clock A.M.
          Thursday Jan. 23rd, 1834 Board Met-F.R. CONWAY, Present

David BOLLINGER claiming 640 acres of land situated on White Water,
District of Cape Girardeau, see Minutes Book No. 5, pg. 389.
State of Missouri, County of Cape Girardeau
This day personally appeared before me, L.F. LINN, one of the Comm'rs.
appointed under an act of Congress to settle & adjust the unconfirmed
land claims in the state of Missouri, Mathias BOLLINGER of lawful age,
who being duly sworn according to law, deposeth & saith that he is well
acquainted with David BOLLINGER. That he emigrated with
David BOLLINGER and others from North Carolina to Upper Louisiana (now
State of Missouri) in the year 1799. That in the year 1803, this affiant knows that the said David BOLLINGER obtained of Louis LORIMIER,
then Commandant of the Post and District of Cape Girardeau, a permission or grant to settle 300 arpents of land on White Water in said District. That the said David BOLLINGER is a farmer. That he has made
valuable improvements on his land. That he has lived in the same neighbourhood ever since he came to the country in 1799. This affiant states
that said David BOLLINGER commenced improving & cultivating in 1803, and
has cultivated the same ever since.
Sworn to & subscribed Oct. 16th, 1833.   Mathias BOLLINGER
L.F. LINN, Comm'r.
     Adjourned until tomorrow at 9 0'clock A.M.
          Friday Jan. 24th, 1834 Board Met-F.R. CONWAY, Present

Mathias BOLLINGER claiming 640 acres of land situate in Cape Girardeau
County, see Book No. 4, pgs. 33 & 280.
State of Missouri, County of Cape Girardeau
This day personally appeared before me, Lewis F. LINN, one of the
Commissioners appointed under an act of Congress to settle & adjust
the unconfirmed land claims in the State of Missouri, Adam STOTLER, a
resident of Cape Girardeau County, of lawful age, who being duly sworn,
deposeth & saith that he is well acquainted with Mathias BOLLINGER, Sr.,

this affiant emigrated in company with him from North Carolina to
Upper Louisiana (now State of Missouri) in the year 1799. That the
said BOLLINGER settled on the waters of White Water in the District
of Cape Girardeau, in said year. This affiant knows that in the year
1803, the said Mathias BOLLINGER obtained from Louis LORIMIER, Commandant of Cape Girardeau District or Post, an additional permission of
300 arpents of land so that his original permission to settle 500 arpents might be augmented to 800 arpents, his family consisting of himself, his wife and seven children. This affiant assisted to carry
the chain in surveying the additional 300 arpents in 1803. This affiant knows that the said BOLLINGER has lived on the place he just
settled when he came to the country in 1799, and now lives on the same
being a farmer he has made valuable improvements in buildings & orchards. This affiant, further, states that on the additional permission, which the said BOLLINGER received, he has gone on improving the
same, making a plantation building a fine house, barn and other necessary buildings and growing a fine orchard. This affiant says that he
knows the said BOLLINGER commenced improving and cultivating the same
in 1800 up to the present time.   Adam STOTLER
Sworn to and signed Oct. 16th, 1833.
L.F. LINN, Comm'r.
        Adjourned until tomorrow at 9 o'clock A.M.
            Saturday Jan. 25th, 1834 Board Met-F.R. CONWAY, Present

Reuben MIDDLETON claiming 640 acres of land situated in Bois Brule
bottom, District of St. Genevieve, see Minutes Book No. 3, pg. 293,
No. 4, pg. 391, Book E, pg. 212.
Personally appeared before me, L.F. LINN, one of the Comm'rs. appointed
for the final settlement and adjustment of private land claims in
Missouri, Mr. Thomas ALLEN, aged about 57 years, who after being sworn,
states that he was acquainted with Reuben MIDDLETON, that said
MIDDLETON emigrated to the then Province of Upper Louisiana and District of St. Genevieve in the year 1800 or 1801, and settled in Bois-
brule Bottom near a creek of the same name. Deponent states that
MIDDLETON built a house in which he lived. He opened some land and
cultiavted it in potatoes, etc. perhaps 2 or 3 acres.
L.F. LInn, Comm'r. Oct. 25th, 1833.   Thomas (X) ALLEN
                                                 his mark
Also John KENNISON appeared who after hearing the above deposition
read, deposes and says he believes and knows the statements above
made by Mr. ALLEN, to be true.
                        John KENNISON
L.F. LINN, Comm'r. Oct. 25th, 1833.
        Adjourned until Monday next at 9 o'clock A.M.
            Monday Jan. 27th, 1834 Board Met-F.R. CONWAY, Present

Conrad STOTLER claiming 640 acres of land situated on White Water,
County of Cape Girardeau, see No. 3, pg. 483, No. 4, pg. 242.
State of Missouri, County of Cape Girardeau
This day personally appeared before me, Lewis F. LINN, one of the
Commissioners appointed under an act of Congress to settle & adjust
the unconfirmed land claims in the State of Missouri,
Mathias BOLLINGER and Adam STOTLER of Cape Girardeau County, of law-
ful age, who after being duly sworn, according to law, deposeth and
saith that they were well acquainted with Conrad STOTLER, both in
North Carolina & in Upper Louisiana (now State of Missouri). That he
came in company with these affiants and a number of others to the District of Cape Girardeau in the year 1799, then under the Spanish
Government. That the said Conrad STOTLER got a permission from
Louis LORIMIER, then Commandant of the District of Cape Girardeau, to
settle on 500 arpents of land on White Water in said District. That
the said STOTLER went on to improve the same by building dwelling
houses, barns and other necessary buildings & planted an orchard, which
bears fine fruits, and continued to live on, and cultivate the said
land for 21 or 22 years. That after the said Conrad STOTLER had settled, improved & lived on said land some time, the said
Louis LORIMIER, Commandant, gave to the said Conrad an additional permission in 1803, so as to make his original permission 700 arpents,
which addition the said Conrad laid adjoining his 500 arpents tract,
and had the same surveyed. These affiants, further, states that said

Conrad STOTLER commenced cultivating the first five hundred arpents tract in 1800.
Mathias BOLLINGER   Adam STOTLER
Signed & sworn to Oct. 16th, 1833.
L.F. LINN, Comm'r.
        Adjourned until tomorrow at 9 o'clock A.M.
              Tuesday Jan. 28th, 1834 Board Met-F.R. CONWAY, Present

Valentine LORR claiming 640 acres of land situated in the District of Cape Girardeau, see Minutes No. 3, pg. 484, No. 4, pg. 242.
State of Missouri, County of Cape Girardeau
Personally appeared before L.F. LINN, one of the Comm'rs. appointed under the law for the final adjustment of land claims in the State of Missouri, Joseph NISWANGER of lawful age, who being sworn deposeth & saith that he was well acquainted with Valentine LORR. That said LORR emigrated to this country with this deponent in the year 1799, and from that time till 1803, he had been without interruption honestly employed in the cultivation of the earth. That in the year 1803, he received a grant for 300 arpents from Louis LORIMIER, then Spanish Commandant of the Post of Cape Girardeau. That said LORR made some improvements on said land and had the same surveyed and that the same has been cultivated and improved ever since. That said LORR was a single man and had (cannot read)   Joseph (X) NISWANGER
Signed & Sworn to Oct. 17th, 1833   his mark
L.F. LINN, Comm'r.
Joseph BAKER of lawful age, being duly sworn, deposeth and saith that he emigrated to this country in the year 1800. That he was acquainted with the above named Valentine LORR. That he knew he was a farmer, and generally raised a crop of grain every year. That he purchased corn from him in the year 1800, and was present when he obtained the permission to settle on 300 arpents, from the Commandant at Cape Girardeau in the year 1803.
Question by Comm'r. Did he raise corn or any other production on this tract?
Answer: Can't say, do not know.
                              Joseph BAKER
Sworn to & subscribed Oct. 15th, 1833.
L.F. LINN, Comm'r.
        Adjourned until tomorrow at 9 o'clock A.M.
              Wednesday Jan. 29th, 1834 Board Met-F.R. CONWAY, Present

Joseph DENNIS claiming 640 acres of land situated on the Mississippi, in the County of Cape Girardeau, see Minutes Book No. 5, pg. 415.
State of Missouri, Cape Girardeau County
Personally appeared before L.F. LINN, one of the Comm'rs. appointed under the law for the final adjustment of land claims in the State of Missouri, Richard WALLER of lawful age, who being sworn as the law directs, deposeth and saith that he was personally acquainted with Joseph DENNIS. That he resided on the West Bank of the Mississippi river, above the Old Cape, in what is called the Big Bend. That said DENNIS had resided there some years, but, how many this deponent cannot say, but in the year 1808, this deponent assisted to move said DENNIS from said place to Illinois. That he had a dwelling house erected and a small farm opened on said place. That his family consisted of a wife and two children.   Richard WALLER
Signed & sworn to in presence of L.F. LINN, Comm'r. Jackson, Oct. 15th, 1833.

John GRENWALT, Jr. by his legal representatives claiming 640 acres of land, situated on Bois brule creek, Perry County, see Minutes No. 2, pg. 23, No. 4, pg. 514, Book E, pg. 218.
The claimant produces in support of said claim, John GREENWALT, the father of said settler who states that his son, John, Improved a place on Bois brule creek in the bottom of the same named now in Perry County & State of Missouri, adjoining to a tract of land of Jones NEWSOM, on one side, and John MORGAN on the other side. That he settled on said place as early as the winter of 1803 & 1804. That he built a cabbin on it and cleared a piece of ground, and planted fruit trees (cannot read) in which summer he raised corn & all other vegetables usual to be raised. On the ground he had 30 (arpents) cleared. This deponent knows

the above facts, because he lived with his son at the same time, that his said son was then more than 25 years of age and doing for himself.   John (X) GREENWALT
L.F. LINN, Comm'r.   his mark
John KENNISON, being sworn, states that he knows as to the correct-
ness of the above statement of John GREENWALT, and of the house built
and improvement made as stated in the above deposition, frequently
passing the place in the summer of 1804, the said John GREENWALT, Jr.,
then residing there and improving and had the same in corn & other
things, as stated in the foregoing deposition, and the place is yet
known in the neighbourhood by the name of John GREENWALT's improvement.   John KENNISON
L.F. LINN, Comm'r. Oct. 25th, 1833.
        Adjourned until tomorrow at 9 o'clock.
            Thursday Jan. 30th, 1834 Board Met-F.R. CONWAY, Present

Jacob MILLER by his legal representatives claiming 300 acres of land
situated in the County of Cape Girardeau, see Minutes No. 3, pg. 467,
No. 4, pg. 235, Book B, pg. 292.
State of Missouri, Cape Girardeau County
Personally appeared before L.F. LINN, one of the Comm'rs. appointed
under the law for the final adjustment of land claims in the state
of Missouri, Isaac MILLER of lawful age, who being duly sworn, deposeth & saith that his father, John MILLER, emigrated to the Upper
Province of Louisiana, now State of Missouri, in the month of October in the year 1803. That this affiant and the above named
Jacob MILLER, an elder brother moved with him. That in the same year
application was made to the Spanish Commandant of the Post of Cape
Girardeau, Louis LORIMIER, for a grant of land for each of them, and
the said Commandant granted to John MILLER 800 arpents and to this
affiant and Jacob MILLER, 300 arpents each, and that the application
for these grants was made for the express purpose of permanently settling on and improving the same, they all being farmers and cultivators of the soil. That they all settled on and cultivated those said
grants of land. That the grants made to this affiant and John MILLER
were confirmed to them by a former board of Commissioners. The grant
to Jacob MILLER, the elder brother, was not confirmed for some cause
to this affiant unknown. The deponent, further, states that said
Jacob MILLER made valuable improvements on the same, dwelling house,
out houses, orchard, etc. The dwelling house was built in the year
1803, the other, the other buildings imeediately afterwards, either
late in the fall of 1803 or (cannot read). Witness does not positively recollect which. Witness, further, states claimant commenced preparing ground for cultivation in 1803, and in the year 1804 raised a
crop of corn, vegetables, etc.
Sworn To & subscribed Oct. 19th, 1833.   Isaac MILLER
L.F. LINN, Comm'r.
Joseph NISWANGER of lawful age, being sworn, deposeth & saith that he
was intimately acquainted with the before named Jacob MILLER. That he
knows he emigrated to this country in the year 1803; perhaps in the
month of September or October. That the said Jacob MILLER immediately
commenced clearing land and preparing for a crop, and raised a crop in
the year 1804, and continued to cultivate his farm till he moved away
many years after. The time he left his farm, not recollected, probably
the year 1820.   Joseph (X) NISWANGER
Sworn to & subscribed Oct. 19th, 1833.   his mark
L.F. LINN, Comm'r.
        Adjourned until tomorrow at 9 o'clock A.M.
            Friday Jan. 31st, 1834 Board Met-F.R. CONWAY, Present

Absolom KENNISON by his legal representatives claiming 640 acres, situated in Bois Brule Bottom, Perry County, see Minutes Book No. 5, pg.
442, Book E, pg. 241. Claimants produce, in support of said claim,
Thomas ALLEN as a witness, who being duly sworn, deposes & says that he
emigrated to this state, then known as the Territory of Upper Louisiana,
in the spring of 1797, and settled in the Bois brule Bottom, in Perry
County, where he has had his home & resided ever since. This deponent
was well acquainted with the said Absolom KENNISON, deceased, and that
he well recollects that said KENNISON moved to & settled in the said
Bois brule bottom in the year 1799, on a place at or near the hill

bounding said bottom, and that he continued to reside there for several years. That he well recollects that in the year 1803, he had on said place a considerable field, he thinks, not less than 10 or 12 acres cleared, fenced & cultivated, and had built a dwelling house thereon in which he resided with his family, and other out buildings, such as were usual in the country at that time. This deponent, further, states that the place so settled & improved by the said Absalom KENNISON, deceased, is now covered by other claims, and that the same are held, as he believes & as in generally understood in the neighbourhood, by those deriving title to the same from the government, and that the said Absalom KENNISON continued to reside in the country until the time of his death, which was, as he thinks, about the year 1816.   Thomas (X) ALLEN
L.F. LINN, Comm'r. Oct. 25th, 1833.   his mark
Elizabeth LOCHERD, also being sworn, testifies & says that she came to this country, then Upper Louisiana, in the spring of 1800 and settled in the edge of Bois brule bottom aforesaid, and that very shortly after her arrival, she was at the house of Absalom KENNISON, Sr., deceased, where he resided with his family, described in the foregoing deposition of Thomas ALLEN, and continued to visit there frequently, having been the neighbour of the said KENNISON in Kentucky, and being also a neighbour here; and that the said KENNISON had a considerable field enclosed and cultivated, previous to, and in the year 1803, and saw corn & other things growing in said field. Elizabeth (X)LOCHERD
L.F. LINN, Comm'r. Oct. 25th, 1833.   her mark
Hezekiah P. HARRIS, being sworn, testifies and says that in the summer of 1804, he well recollects of the said Abasalom KENNISON inviting him to assist him in reaping wheat, at the place described in the foregoing depositions of Thomas ALLEN & Elizabeth LOCHERD, and that he accordingly went & assisted in reaping and that the said KENNISON was then residing there with his family, and had a considerable improvement more, he should think than 12 acres.   H.P. HARRIS
L.F. LINN, Comm'r. Oct. 25th, 1833.
        Adjourned until tomorrow at 9 o'clock A.M.
        Saturday Feb. 1st, 1834 Board Met-F.R. CONWAY, Present

Solomon THORN by his legal representatives claiming 600 arpents of land situated in Cape Girardeau County, see Minutes Book No. 5, pg. 508.
State of Missouri, County of Cape Girardeau
This day personally appeared before me, Lewis F. LINN, one of the Comm'rs. appointed under an act of Congress to settle & adjust the unconfirmed land claims in the State of Missouri, Robert GIBONEY of lawful age, who being sworn, according to law, deposeth & saith that he emigrated to the District of Cape Girardeau, then under the Spanish Government in A.D. 1797. This affiant recollects, that in the year A.D. 1798 or 9, Solomon THORN emigrated and settled at Cape Girardeau. That the said THORN made a settlement and improvement, built a dwelling house raised a shop for a gun smith shop (as the said THORN was a gun smith by trade). This affiant knows that Louis LORIMIER, Commandant of the Post of Cape Girardeau, frequently gave orders to the Indians to go to THORN in order to get work done in & about their guns, etc. This affiant knows that said THORN resided from the time of his first settlement, until his death, about Cape Girardeau & that he died in A.D. 1820, 21 or 22, as near as this affiant can recollect.   Robert GIBONEY
Signed & sworn to Oct. 18th, 1833.
L.F. LINN, Comm'r.
Also appeared William WILLIAMS of lawful age, who being duly sworn according to law, deposeth & saith that he moved to Cape Girardeau in the year A.D. 1799, he thinks a little while before Christmas. That when he landed he found Solomon THORN living there. That he was a gun smith. That he frequently worked for the Indians which were then living on Apple Creek, in the District of Cape Girardeau. This affiant knows that the said THORN continued to live in the District of Cape Girardeau for a great many years, but when he died, this affiant does not recollect.   William WILLIAMS
Sworn to & subscribed Oct. 15th, 1833.
L.F. LINN, Comm'r.

George HENDERSON claiming 300 arpents situated in Cape Girardeau County,

see Minutes Book No. 4, pgs. 82 & 304, B, pg. 309, produces a copy
of an affidavit of Louis LORIMIER, certified by the Clerk of Cape
Girardeau Circuit Court, proving that said HENDERSON has served in
the military expedition to New Madrid in December, 1802.
Isaac WILLIAMS aged about 53 years, and Moses BYRD aged about 52
years, being duly sworn, deposeth & saith that they first became acquainted with the said George HENDERSON in the then District of Cape
Girardeau, Upper Louisiana, now County of Cape Girardeau, State of
Missouri, as early as the year 1800. That he, said HENDERSON, was
then an inhabitant of said District and a subject of the King of
Spain, and has continued to reside in said District ever since. That
in the year 1802, the Indians commenced hostilities on the inhabitants
of New Madrid in said Province, now Missouri, and killed some, and for
the purpose of repelling said Indians, the Commandant of said District
issued an order in December of the year 1802 calling upon the militia
of said District of Cape Girardeau to turn out and march to said District of New Madrid to repel the Indian attack aforesaid. That amongst
others, by the orders of said Commandant of the District of Cape Girardeau, the said HENDERSON, as one amongst the troops, was called out, &
about the middle of December, A.D. 1802 marched to the said District
of New Madrid on said expedition, and was by said Spanish authority
kept in said service until some time in the month of January, A.D. 1803,
having been absent on said expedition in continuation six weeks. That
the said Commandant Louis LORIMIER, said Spanish authority promised to
pay said troops in grants for land as a reward for said services, that
each of the said men employed in said service received grants of land
for the same which has never been confirmed.
        Isaac (X) WILLIAMS   Moses BYRD
            his mark
Signed & sworn to Oct. 17th, 1833. L.F. LINN, Comm'r.
    Adjourned until Monday next at 9 o'clock A.M.
        The Board Met Feb. 3rd, 4th, 5th, 6th, 7th, 8th, 10th, 11th,
    12th, 13th & 14th, 1834, and adjourned, No business.
        Saturday Feb. 15th, 1834 Board Met-F.R. CONWAY, Present

William MCHUGH, Sr., by his assignee, James MORRISON claiming 640 acres
of land situate about 45 miles N.W. of St. Charles- see Record Book B,
pg. 369, Book F, pg. 112, Recorder's Minutes, pg. 78, BATE's Decisions,
pg. 33, produces a survey of 1,320 arpents executed by
John HARVEY, D.S., dated 14th of February, 1806 & certified by
Antoine SOULARD on the 21st February, 1806.(see pg. 215 of this Book)
Nathaniel SIMONDS, being duly sworn, says that he is 58 years of age,
that he became acquainted with the original claimant, MCHUGH, in the
spring of the year 1802, and knows the tract claimed. That in May or
June of the year 1803, he was on said tract and saw corn, potatoes,
cabbage and such vegetables, as was usual at that time to plant, growing on the said place. He does not now recollect how much was then in
cultivation, but supposes there was some four, five or six acres, which
were enclosed by a fence. There was a cabbin & smoke house on the
place, at the time last above mentioned. He, further, says that MCHUGH
had at that time 8 or 10 children. That this settlement was about 15
miles from the main Settlement. That the neighbouring Indians were considered hostile. That there had been Indian signs seen near MCHUGH's.
A cow beast had been killed, as supposed by them, and this deponent had
gone then to aid MCHUGH to collect his stock and remove his family to
the main settlement, which they did immediately. That in September,
1804, the Indians killed three of the sons of said MCHUGH. That said
MCHUGH continued to reside in the country until his death, which took
place in about the year 1809 or 1810.
Ad   Adjourned until Monday next at 9 o'clock A.M.
        The Board Met Feb. 17th, 18th, 19th & 20th, 1834 and
    Adjourned without attending to any business.
        Friday Feb. 21st, 1834 Board Met-F.R. CONWAY, Present

Jonathan HELDERBRAND by his assignee claiming 200 arpents of land situate on the Negro fork of theMarameck, see Book D, pg. 340, Minutes
No. 3, pg. 296, No. 4, pg. 392. (John HELDERBRAND original owner)

John PAYETT by his legal representatives claiming 464 arpents of land,
situate on Big River, Marameck, see Book B, pg. 259, Minutes No. 1, pg.
482, No. 3, pg. 292, No. 4, pg. 389.

Abraham HELDERBRAND, being duly sworn, says that he is 51 years of age. That in 1802, he helped said PAYETT to raise a house on the land claimed. That in the fall of 1803, he passed by said place and eat some water melons, which grew on said land, and saw a small patch of corn growing, and, in the same fall, the Indians becoming trouble-some, he moved to the Marameck Settlement, about 12 miles below, and returned, as well as witness recollects, in the spring of 1805, and lived there till his death. Witness, further, says that his own farm lies about 6 miles from the land claimed, and that he has lived there for 32 years. That he recollects that said PAYETT lived on the land claimed since, he, witness, was about 10 years old, during which time the said PAYETT inhabited said place, except when compelled by the Indians, at different times, to leave the said place.

Jonathan HELDERBRAND, being duly sworn, says that is in his 50th year. That in 1801 or 1802, he cannot say which of those years, he passed by said PAYETT's house, but did not see any white person there. He found an Indian with whom he passed the (cannot read) in said PAYETT's house. The said Indian being a friendly one and not an Osage, and that in 1805, he saw the said PAYETT living on said place. That he knows said PAYETT lived on the land claimed till his death. That said PAYETT had a family consisting of his wife & several children, but does not re-collect how many.

Jacob PAYETT, being duly sworn, says that he is 42 years of age. That in 1801, John PAYETT went on said place and planted some corn, and in 1802, he raised a house, but witness does not recollect whether said PAYETT moved there that same year, or in 1803. That in the said year 1803, the said PAYETT was driven away by the Indians and staid away about two years, and then returned and lived on said place until he died. Witness, further, says that, at that time, the said PAYETT had a wife and 8 or 9 children, that said PAYETT died about 5 years ago.

   Adjourned untill tomorrow at 9 o'clock A.M.
      The Board Met & Adjourned Feb. 22nd, 24th, 25th, 26th, 27th, 28th, March 1st, 3rd, 4th, 1834.
      Wednesday March 5th, 1834 Board Met-F.R. CONWAY, Present

John MCCORMACK by his heir at law , Henry COOK, claiming 1,000 arpents of land situated (cannot read) District of St. Louis settlement claim, see Record Book D, pg. 219, Comm'rs. Minutes No. 5, pg. 457.

James MCROBERTS, being duly sworn, says that he is upwards of 70 years of age, and knows the tract claimed, that he came to this country in the year 1786 & resided on the E. said of the Mississippi. That in the year 1789, he crossed to this, the West side of the Mississippi for the first time & passed by and saw this improvement, it then had the appearance of an old improvement, the stumps then looked old & were much decayed. The undergrowth had sprung up, the fences and buildings had been destroyed by fire; the place had not been cultivated for se-veral years, as he was informed.

MCCORMACK having died some years before, his widow had married & moved off the place; he was informed that the place was cultivated for some years before the death of MCCORMACK. The witness passed frequently by this place in 1789, 90 & 91, and thinks it was the oldest improvement in that part of the country. He understood that there had been a mill built near this improvement by a man by the name of Thomas TYLER, who built it for the purpose of grinding for a few families. MCCORMACK had charge of the mill; it was however soon washed away & never rebuilt.

   Adjourned untill tomorrow at 9 o'clock A.M.
      The Board Met & Adjourned March 6th, 7th, 8th, 1834.
      Monday March 10th, 1834 Board Met-F.R. CONWAY, Present

John BOLI claiming 260 arpents of land situate on the waters of the Marameck, see Record Book C, pg. 190, Minutes No. 1, pg. 410, No. 4, pg. 487.

Pierre DELOR, being duly sworn, says that he is passed 64 years of age. That he well knows the land claimed. That since about 38 or 40 years, he knows said land to be owned, inhabited and cultivated by said or through said John BOLI. That about 38 years ago, he saw se-veral cabbins built & corn growing, and at that time, he, witness, very often went on said place to procure sugar. That since the time above mentioned, the said land has been so inhabited and cultivated by said BOLI, or through him, to the present day. That he cannot say

exactly how many arpents were then in cultivation. That BOLI had
several tenants on said land, one might have about 6 arpents, another
about 10, and a third may be 15 arpents, more or less.
Jean Bste. Maurice CHATILLON, being duly sworn, says that he is 92
years of age. That he well knows the land claimed. That 32 or 33
years ago, he went on said land to build a house for said John BOLI,
remained there one year, and made sugar. That when he went on said
land he saw cabbins built, lands improved, cornfields, etc. That to
his knowledge, the said land had been possessed, inhabited & cultivated by or through said BOLI for several years previous to his, witness,
going on said place.
      Adjourned until tomorrow at 9 o'clock A.M.
          The Board Met & Adjourned March 11th, 12th, 13th, 14th, 15th,
      17th, 1834.
          Tuesday March 18th, 1834 Board Met-F.R. CONWAY, Present

James ROGERS by his legal representatives claiming 766 arpents of land
situate on Negro fork of Merrimack, see Record Book B, pg. 345, Minutes
No. 5, pg. 485.
John STEWART, being duly sworn, says that he is in the 73rd year of
his age. That he first saw claimant in this country in the year 1801.
That in 1803, he saw James ROGERS settled on the land claimed, he had
then a comfortable house to live in, a kitchen and corncrib, a cornfield of at least 9 acres, and about an acre fenced in near the house,
in which was his garden and a cotton patch. That by the looks of the
place, it appeared to have been cultivated the year before. That said
ROGERS continued to inhabit and cultivate the same until his death,
which happened in 1805 or 1806, he cannot say exactly when. That said
ROGERS had a wife and 9 children. That said tract of land is situated
at about 2 or 3 miles above Wideman's mill on Big River. Witness says
that he never knew any body laying claim to said land. That
James ROGERS was the first who settled the same. Witness, further,
says that claimant had his house and garden on the rise of the hill &
his cornfield in the river bottom.

Priscilla ESTEP by her legal representatives claiming 800 arpents of
land situated S.E. side of Big River, see Record Book E, pg. 356,
BATE's Decisions pg. 30, BATE's Minutes, pg. 33.
John STEWART, being duly sworn, says that he is in the 73rd year of
his age. That in the year 1803, he saw claimant living on the land
claimed. She had then a cabbin and a cotton patch and some gardening
in vegetation. That she came to the country at the same time with
her father, James ROGERS. That he, witness, first saw them in this
country in the year 1801. Witness, further, says that he carried cotton to her to spin. That she was an industrious woman, and that she
lived and died in the neighbourhood of witness.
      Adjourned until tomorrow at 9 o'clock A.M.
          The Board Met & Adjourned March 19th, 20, 21st, 22nd, 23rd,
      24th, 25th, 26th, 27th, 28th, 29th, 31st, April 1st,2nd, 3rd,
      4th, 1834.
          Saturday April 5th, 1834 Board Met-F.R. CONWAY, Present

Charles DENNE by his legal representative, James MORRISON, claiming
750 arpents of land situate near Dardenne under settlement right, see
Record Book B, pg. 231, Minutes No. 1, pg. 449, No.4, pg. 494.
Gabriel LATREILLE, duly sworn, says that he is 64 years of age. That
he came to this country in the year 1793. That he resided in St.
Charles for the last 38 years. That in the beginning of the year 1803,
he went on the land claimed in company with said DENNE, who had then a
cabbin built and peach trees planted; which appeared, by their growth,
to have been planted two years before, and were in a piece of ground
fenced in of about half an arpent in (cannot read) outside of the fence,
that said DENNE was single man, who lived with his brother in law, and
went on his land to work, without living on the same. That said DENNE
sold his improvement to James MORRISON. Claimant produces a plat of
survey, dated 22nd February, 1806 by John HARVEY, received for record
by SOULARD the 26th February, 1806.
      Adjourned until Monday next at 9 o'clock A.M.
          The Board Met & Adjourned April 7th, 1834.
          Tuesday April 8th, 1834 Board Met-F.R. CONWAY, Present

Baptiste AUMURE, alias TAUMURE by his heirs & legal representatives
claiming 240 arpents of land situate on south fork of river Lafourche,
County of St. Genevieve, see Book No. 5, pg. 507, produces a paper
purporting to be an original concession from Zenon TRUDEAU, dated 13th
November, 1797.
Bernard PRATTE, aged about 60 years, being duly sworn, deposeth and
says that he was personally acquainted with the original grantee,
Baptiste AUMURE or TAUMURE. That he was a citizen of and resident of
the province of Upper Louisiana, at the date of the grant in the year
1797. Witness was, also, well acquainted with Zenon TRUDEAU and knows
that he was Lt. Gov. of the Province of Upper Louisiana in the year of
1797. And witness, further, knows the handwriting of said Z. TRUDEAU,
from having seen him write, and knows that the name & signature of the
said Zenon TRUDEAU, to the original concession, or order of Survey, is
the proper name & signature, and in the proper handwriting of the said
Zenon TRUDEAU.
        Adjourned until tomorrow at 9 o'clock A.M.
            The Board Met & Adjourned April 9th, 10th,11th, 12th, 14th,
        15th, 17th, 18th, 19th & 21st, 1834.
            Tuesday April 22nd, 1834 Board Met-F.R. CONWAY, Present

Jacob SWANEY by his legal representatives claiming 640 acres of land
situate on the Merrimack, see Record Book E, pg. 317, BATE's Decisions,
pg. 91 (Not found in either)
George SIP, duly sworn, says that he is about 62 years of age. That
in the year 1797 or 98, he helped said Jacob SWANEY to improve the
tract claimed. That witness assisted in building a house, splitting
rails, and clearing lands & fencing in about an acre of ground. That
he staid with said SWANEY till the spring following, and that to his
knowledge said SWANEY cultivated said land during 4 or 5 years till he
sold it to one John COLEMAN. That he heard it reported in the neighbourhood, that said COLEMAN sold the said tract of land to
John GODFREY. That the last time he saw said place, about 2 years
after he had first worked on it, SWANEY had about 5 acres under cultivation. That SWANEY had then a wife and, he thinks, two children.
John BOII, duly sworn, says that he is about 79 years of age. That he
cannot say exactly in what year, but it was when Jacob SWANEY lived on
the land claimed that he went on the same and saw grain raised there.
That he always understood, and he believes John COLEMAN himself told
him, that SWANEY had sold the said tract of land to him, COLEMAN, and
deponent saw said COLEMAN living on said place then under cultivation.
That he supposes there is, now, about 25 acres in cultivation.
        Adjourned until tomorrow at 9 o'clock A.M.
            The Board Met & Adjourned April 23rd, 24th,25th, 26th,&
        28th, 1834.
            Thursday April 29th, 1834 Board Met-F.R. CONWAY, Present

Jean CAMBAS by his legal representatives claiming 1 by 40 arpents of
land, it being the North half of a concession granted to Jean CAMBAS
& Jean ORTEZ for 2 by 40 arpents of land, situated in the little
prairie, South of St. Louis, see Livre Terrien No. 1, pg. 13, Recorder's Minutes Book No. 2, pg. 5, No. 3, pg. 104.
Pierre CHOUTEAU, duly sworn, says that Jean CAMBAS was a carpenter by
trade, who obtained said concession in partnership with Jean ORTEZ for
the purpose of cutting timber to build houses in St. Louis. That
CAMBAS & ORTEZ used to make their hay in said piece of land. That, to
his knowledge, they did make hay and cut timber thereon for upwards of
15 consecutive years, under the French & Spanish Government, and before
the Americans took possession of the country. That it was known,
generally by all the people in St. Louis, that said piece of land was
the property of the said CAMBAS & ORTEZ. Witness, further, says that
he has no kind of interest in the claim of CAMBAS, a division having
been made between CAMBAS & ORTEZ representatives, about 8 or 9 years
ago.
        Adjourned until tomorrow at 9 o'clock A.M.
            The Board Met & Adjourned April 30th, May 1st, 10th, 12th,
        13th, 14th, 15th, 16th, 17th, 19th, 20th, 21st, 22nd, 23rd, 24th,
        26th, 27th, 28th, 29th, 30th, 31st, June 2nd, 1834.
            Tuesday June 3rd, 1834 Board Met-F.R. CONWAY & J.S. MAYFIELD

James H. RELFE, Esqr. appeared having been appointed Comm'r. in place of A.G. HARRISON, Esqr., resigned, and having been duly qualified, took his seat. No evidence being offered, Adjourned until tomorrow at 9 o'clock A.M.

The Board Met & Adjourned June 4th, 5th, 6th, 1834.

Saturday June 7th, 1834 Board Met-F.R. CONWAY, J.H. RELFE & J.S. MAYFIELD, Present

In as much as, under the existing laws fixing the time for the taking of testimony of witness, in support of private land claims before the Board of Commissioners for final settlement, will expire the 9th day of July next, and the Board being induced to believe that the advanced age of, and distance at which many witnesses live from this place, that it would be inconvenient and expensive to procure such testimony here; and the Board, further, taking into view the time when under law, (without further extension by Congress) this Board will terminate, as well as the fact that the report of the former Board is now before Congress, for confirmation, and believing that whatever action Congress may take in regard to said report, that it will afford to the present Board a rule for their consideration in passing upon said claims. Therefore be it resolved that James H. RELFE, a member of this Board, be and is hereby appointed to proceed and take testimony in the counties South of St. Louis, relative to any claim or claims that may properly come within the purview of the powers given to this Board by the laws governing the same, and that he be and is hereby vested with as full and ample power, for said purpose, as this Board can in any wise or manner, confer on him, and he shall give notice of the time & places he may appoint for the taking of the same.
Unanimously adopted.

Adjourned until Monday next at 9 o'clock A.M.

The Board Met & Adjourned June 9th, 1834.

Tuesday June 10th, 1834 Board Met-J.S. MAYFIED & F.R. CONWAY, Present

In the case of Therese CRELY claiming 3,528 arpents of land, see No. 6, pg. 234.

Pierre CHOUTEAU Sr., duly sworn, says that in 1800, Tesson HONORE, the husband of said Theresa CRELY, came to ask of the deponent, if he could help him to make an establishment on river a Jeoffrion, now called Two rivers. That deponent lent him a sum of money, and the sd HONORE immediately hired several men, went on said tract, built houses, cleared lands, had a good stock of cattle, and lived there with his wife & father in law. That in 1803, deponent, on his way to Prairie du Chien, saw said improvement, he does not recollect of having seen a field, but saw a large garden, dwelling house, out houses and stables. That said Tesson remained on said tract until driven away by Indian depredations. Deponent, further, says that although said Tesson owed him at his death, the sum of $1,200, he has no kind of interest in the claim. Jacque METTE, duly sworn, says that 34 years ago, on the 15th of June, he passed on the tract claimed. That he saw a dwelling house and out houses, a garden of about 2-1/2 arpents. That, back of the buildings, there was an enclosure of 7 or 8 arpents where the cattle was then kept. That said HONORE was living on said place with his wife & children.

Adjourned until tomorrow at 9 o'clock A.M.

The Board Met & Adjourned June 11th, 12th, 13th,&14th, 1834.

Monday June 16th, 1834 Board Met-J.S. MAYFIELD & F.R. CONWAY, Present

Solomon BELLEW by his legal representatives claiming 350 arpents of land, situate River Gravois in the County of St. Louis, see Record Book E, pg. 327, produces a paper purporting to be an original concession from Carlos Dehault DELASSUS, dated 11th December, 1800. M.P. LEDUC, duly sworn, says that the signature to said concession is in the proper handwriting of said Carlos Dehault DELASSUS.

Adjourned until tomorrow at 9 o'clock A.M.

Tuesday June 17th, 1834 Board Met-J.S. MAYFIELD & F.R. CONWAY, Present

In the case of David HORINE claiming 640 acres of land, see pg. 232 of this book. Benjamin HORINE, being sworn, states on his oath, that he came to this country the 22nd day of May, 1803. That David HORINE was

at that time in possession of the land above named.on Big River, on which the said David HORINE had in cultivation between 4 or 5 acres in corn. And deponent, further, states the land was cultivated and possessed by the said David for 15 years or more, afterwards, that is to say, after the arrival of deponent in this country. Deponent, further, states that in giving evidence on a former occasion, in relation to the above claim, the points to which his testimony now relates, were not brought to his recollection by any questions or circumstances at the time of giving such testimony. Deponent, further, states that by the will of David HORINE, deceased, he has no interest or claim in, or to, the said estate of David, his deceased brother.
   Adjourned until tomorrow at 9 o'clock A.M.
     Wednesday June 18th, 1834 Board Met-J.S. MAYFIELD &
                F.R. CONWAY, Present

Benjamin F. JAMES by his legal representatives claiming 690 arpents of land situate on Cold Water, County of St. Louis, see Record Book B, pgs. 183 & 4, Minutes Book No. 1, pg. 102, No. 3, pg. 211, No. 4, pg. 365.
Catherine S. JAMES, duly sworn, says that she is in her 65th year. That she is well acquainted with the land claimed. That in the spring of 1804, the said Benjamin F. JAMES lived on the place with his family consisting of his wife & one child. That in the summer of said year, 1804, witness saw a small field of corn growing on said land. That to her knowledge the said James lived on said place until his death, which took place in 1815. That said James, from his first settling, continued to improve his land until he died. That at the time of his death, he had about 20 or more acres in cultivation, several cabbins and an orchard of apple & peach trees, and deponent understood that he occasionally taught a school in the neighbourhood.
   Adjourned until tomorrow at 9 o'clock A.M.
    The Board Met & Adjourned June 19th, 20th, 21st, 23rd, & 24th, 1834.
     Wednesday June 25th, 1834 Board Met-J.S. MAYFIELD &
                F.R. CONWAY, Present

John SCOTT by his legal representatives claiming 800 arpents of land situate on the waters of Dardenne, County of St. Charles, see Book F, pg. 12, BATE's Decisions, pg. 96.
James (cannot read the last name), being duly sworn, says that he is about 58 years old. That he thinks it was in 1800 that he helped said John SCOTT to make the first improvement on this tract. That in 1801, he, the deponent, lived part of his time with said SCOTT on the said place. That SCOTT had then a house and between 10 or 20 acres cleared & in cultivation. That said SCOTT lived on the place till his death. That SCOTT's family has continued to live on said place and are still living on the same.
John MCCONNELL, duly sworn, says that he is in his 52nd year. That late in the year 1799, he helped said John SCOTT to build a house on the land claimed, and early in the year 1800, he assisted him in moving on the same. That said SCOTT lived on said place and that in the spring of 1800, he cleared & improved a field & raised corn that same year. That said SCOTT remained on the place till his death. That his family continued to improve & enlarge the farm and are still living on the same. Witness, further, says that he understood that this tract of land lies adjoining a tract confirmed to said John SCOTT, under JOHNSON (Thomas) of 500 arpents.
John HOWELL, duly sworn, says that in 1801 he laid the worm of a fence round a good large field on the land claimed. That in that same year, John SCOTT raised a crop in the field, which deponent helped to fence in. That said John SCOTT had a house and his family was living there with him at the time that he had then 4 or 5 children. Deponent, further, says that during the late war with the British & Indians, two of said John SCOTT's sons, served as rangers during the whole war.
Michael PRICE, duly sworn, says that in 1801 he was at John SCOTT's place and he had then a good smart field wherein corn was growing. That John SCOTT was living there with his family, consisting of his wife & 4 or 5 children. That said SCOTT had a good stock of horses, cattle & hogs. That from the first settling of said place, SCOTT & after his death, his family, lived on, improved & cultivated said place up to this day.

Adjourned until tomorrow at 9 o'clock A.M.
Thursday June 26th, 1834 Board Met-MAYFIELD & CONWAY, Present

In the case of Antoine FLANDRIN claiming 6,000 arpents of land, see No.
6, pg. 221, claimant produces a paper purporting to be an original concession from Carlos Dehault DELASSUS, dated 15th January, 1800.
M.P. LEDUC, duly sworn, says that the signature to the said concession
is in the proper handwriting of said Carlos Dehault DELASSUS.

In the case of Joseph Philip LAMARCHE claiming 800 arpents of land,
see No. 6, pg. 116, claimant produces a paper purporting to be a certified plat of survey dated November 15th, 1807 by A. SOULARD.
M.P. LEDUC, duly sworn, says that the signature to the said Plat &
certificate of Survey, is in the proper handwriting of A. SOULARD,
Sur. General.

In the case of Jos. MARIE claiming 800 arpents of land, see No. 6, pg.
116, claimant produces a certified plat of survey by SOULARD, dated
15th November, 1807. M.P. LEDUC, duly sworn, says that the signature
to the said plat & certificate of survey is in the proper handwriting
of A. SOULARD, S.G.

In the case of Baptiste GEFFREY claiming 800 arpents of land, see No.
6, pg. 116, claimant produces a certified plat of survey by
A. SOULARD, dated 15th November, 1807. M.P. LEDUC, duly sworn, says
that the signature to the said plat & certificate of survey is in the
proper handwriting of A. SOULARD.

In the case of Francois Lami DUCHOUQUETTE claiming 800 arpents of
land (No. 6, pg. 117) claimant produces a plat & certificate of survey signed by Fremon DELAURIERE, Deputy Surveyor, dated 27th, December, 1805. M.P. LEDUC, duly sworn, says that the signature to the
said plat & certificate of survey is in the proper handwriting of said
Fremon DELAURIERE, Deputy Surveyor, who commission as such has already
been filed before this Board.

Frederick DIXON by his legal representatives claiming 800 arpents of
land, see Record Book D, pg. 291, Minutes No. 5, pg. 411, produces a
certified plat of survey, signed by SOULARD & dated November 15th,
1807. M.P. LEDUC, duly sworn, says that the signature to said Plat
& certificate of survey, is in the proper handwriting of A. SOULARD,
Surv. General.

Rene DODIER by his legal representatives claiming 800 arpents of land,
see Record Book D, pg. 294, Minutes No. 5, pg. 412, produces a plat
& certificate of survey by Fremon DELAURIERE, Dep. Surveyor, dated
December 27th, 1805. M.P. LEDUC, duly sworn, says that the signature
to the said plat & certificate of survey is in the proper handwriting
of the said Fremon DELAURIERE, Deputy Surveyor.

Antoine DEJARLAIS by his legal representatives claiming 800 arpents
of land, see Record Book C, pgs. 334 & 349, Minutes Book No. 1, pg.
303, No. 5, pg. 317.

Louis GRIMAR or GRIMAUD, alias CHARPENTIER by his legal representatives claiming 800 arpents of land, see Record Book C, pgs. 334 & 349,
Book No. 5, pg. 370.

James HAFF claiming 800 arpents of land, see Record Book C, pgs. 333 &
349, Minutes Book No. 5, pg. 370.

Benjamin QUICK by his legal representatives claiming 800 arpents of
land, see Record Book C, pgs. 335 & 349, Minutes Book No. 1, pg. 303,
No. 5, pg. 317.

Daniel QUICK by his legal representatives claiming 800 arpents of land,
see Record Book C, pgs. 324 & 5, Minutes Book No. 1, pg. 301, No. 5,
pg. 316.

In as much as it has come to the knowledge of the Board of Comm'rs. of private land claims that there are a number of claimants residing in the County of St. Charles, who are solicitous to prove up, or offer evidence in support of their respective claims, and in as much as the time for taking such testimony will expire the 8th of next month (July), and as the advanced age of some witnesses, and the unwillingness on the part of others to come to St. Louis at this time, in consequence of the prevalence of the Cholera, render it impracticable to procure their attendance at St. Louis. Therefore, be it resolved that J.S. MAYFIELD, a member of this Board be, and he is hereby appointed to proceed to the County aforesaid to take such testimony as may be offered relative to any claim or claims as may properly come within the purview of the powers given to this Board, by the law regulating the same, and that he be & is hereby vested with as full and ample power for said purpose as this Board can in any wise or manner confer upon him.

Adjourned until tomorrow at 9 o'clock A.M.
The Board Met & Adjourned June 27th, 28th, 30th, July 1st, 2nd, 3rd, 4th, 1834.
Saturday July 5th, 1834 Board Met-F.R. CONWAY, Present

In the case of James ROGERS, Jr., claiming 750 arpents of land, see No. 6, pg. 177.
Samuel HARRINGTON, duly sworn, says that he is about 48 years of age, that he knew said James ROGERS, Jr. in the month of May, in the year 1801, or 1802, witness is not positive. That said ROGERS came to this country at the time above mentioned, made company with five or six families, which after resting a few weeks, scattered about Big River & made settlements. That said ROGERS lived in the same house with Jacob COLLINS and worked his improvement at a distance. Witness did not see said improvement at the time, saw it only about one year after said improvement was made. That he then saw house logs, trees deadened & land ploughed, but does not recollect of having seen corn growing on the same, but he was told that claimant had raised corn there the year before. There was then 3/4 of an acre or may be an acre cleared. Witness does not believe that the said tract was ever cultivated since. Deponent, further, says that said improvement lies about half way between the improvement of said Jacob COLLINS and that of MC CULLICK, being at about 600 yards from each. That at the time witness saw said improvement, MCCULLICK had not yet come to this country. That said MCCULLICK arrived in the country in the year 1803. Further, says that said ROGERS was an active, industrious, hard working man, who has ever since lived in the country, but witness never knew of his living on the place that claimant had no family, being a single man.

In the case of James ROGERS, Sr., claiming 766 arpents of land, see No. 6, pg. 509.
Samuel HARRINGTON, duly sworn, says that he is about 48 years of age. That said James ROGERS, Sr. came to this country in the month of May, in the year 1801 or 1802, witness is not certain, in company with 5 or 6 families, which after they had come over to this side, rested a few weeks and went to settle on Big river. That said ROGERS, witness heard, had made an improvement on which he staid during the winter, and on account of Indian depredations, went over to Illinois where he passed the summer, but returned in the same year to his improvement. That witness saw said improvement in 1804 in the month of July. There was then a couple of cabbins, five or six acres fenced, and corn, pumkins, etc. growing on the same, and that the place, by all appearances, seemed to have been under cultivation two years & upwards. Witness, further, says that said ROGERS had then with him a wife & 8 children. That said ROGERS lived on said improvement until his death, which happened about the year 1806 & was burried on said place, which has never since been cultivated, the widow having married again & gone to her husband's plantation.

In the case of Priscilla ESTEP claiming 800 arpents of land, see No. 6, pg. 509.
Samuel HARRINGTON, duly sworn, says that the said Priscilla ESTEP did arrive in this country, with her husband, in the year 1801 or 1802, in company with five or six families. That witness, afterwards, saw the

said Priscilla ESTEP several times & knows she lived on Big River, but never saw her improvement. That said Priscilla had two children and that she was an industrious, hard working woman. That about 3 years after their arrival, her husband abandoned & left her & went down the Mississippi.

Adjourned until Monday next at 9 o'clock A.M.

Monday July 7th, 1834 Board Met-F.R. CONWAY, Present

Pierre ROY by his legal representatives claiming 1 by 40 arpents of land situated near St. Louis, see Record Book D, pg. 221, Minutes Book No. 5, pg. 489, produces a deed of conveyance from Pierre ROY to James MORRISON, dated June 15th, 1805.

Adjourned until tomorrow at 9 o'clock A.M.

Tuesday July 8th, 1834 Board Met-J.H. RELFE & F.R. CONWAY, Present

In the case of Augste. P. CHOUTEAU claiming 800 arpents of land, see Book No. 6, pg. 229. Claimant produces a paper purporting to be an original plat of survey of said land, dated 6th September, 1803, by Thomas MADDIN, D.S. and certified 15th January, 1804, by Antoine SOULARD, Surveyor General. M.P. LEDUC, duly sworn, says that the signature to the said plat & certificate of survey is in the proper handwriting of the said A. SOULARD.

Charles GILL by his legal representatives claiming 400 arpents of land situate on (cannot read), see Record Book D, pg. 280, Minutes Book No. 5, pg. 428. Claimant refers the Board to the plat in the Register's Office, on which plat the said land has been reserved from sale.

William MORRISON by his legal representatives claiming 750 arpents of land, see Record Book C, pg. 470, Book No. 5, pg. (?)?, produces a paper purporting to be an original concession from Carlos Dehault DELASSUS, dated 9th June, 1803. M.P. LEDUC, duly sworn, says that the signature to the said concession, is in the proper handwriting of the said Carlos Dehault DELASSUS.

Andrew HARRIS by his legal representatives claiming 600 arpents of land, see Record Book C, pg. 470, Book No. 5, pg. (cannot read), produces a paper purporting to be an original concession from Carlos Dehault DELASSUS, dated 7th of June, 1803. M.P. LEDUC, duly sworn, says that the signature to said concession is in the proper handwriting of the said Carlos D. DELASSUS.

John MCNEAL claiming 640 acres of land situate on Big River, see Record Book B, pg. 236, Minutes Book No. 1, pg. 504, No. 3, pg. 134, No. 4, pg. 341, produces the original survey by John STEWART, Deputy Surveyor, dated January, 11th, 1806.
John STEWART, duly sworn, says that he is about 65 years of age. That he knows that said MCNEAL took possession of the land claimed prior to the month of December, 180- (cannot read date). That in the fall of 1803, witness went on the place and saw there a cabbin.
John MCNEAL was then clearing the land, and in 1804, he raised a crop of corn thereon, had a garden & other improvements. Witness, further, says that soon after the American Government took possession of this country, he was appointed deputy surveyor to Antoine SOULARD, and in 1806, witness surveyed, for said MCNEAL, the tract of land claimed as appeared by the original plat filed in this case.

Lewis MARTIN claiming 300 arpents of land situate near St. Ferdinand, see Record Book B, pg. 267, No. 1, pg. 487, No. 3, pg. 233, No. (cannot read), produces a paper purporting to be an original concession from Carlos Dehault DELASSUS, dated February 1801. Also, a plat of survey by James MACKAY, dated 25th June, 1805, certified by SOULARD, 10th December, 1805. M.P. LEDUC, duly sworn, says that the signature to the said concession is in the proper handwriting of the said Carlos Dehault DELASSUS, and the signature to the certificate of survey is in the proper handwriting of Antoine SOULARD. David MARTIN, duly sworn, says that he is in his 52 year. That in 1801 or 1802, he saw house logs and a corn crib on the land claimed. That in 1803,

witness saw said Lewis MARTIN at work on said place, he was then
grubbing & ditching, and that since the year 1805, the said
Lewis MARTIN has continued to live on said place and is still living
thereon. Witness, further, says that there is now about 70 or 80 acres
under fence & in cultivation, a good double dwelling house, stables,
barn and all other necessary out buildings, also an apple orchard, and
further, that the said Lewis MARTIN has served three campaigns in the
last English & Indian war, under Captain MUSICK and that the said
claimant has raised on said place a family of 13 children.
Daniel B. MOORE, being duly sworn, says that having heard read the
foregoing testimony of David MARTIN, he finds it exact & true, and
that he does entirely agree with said David in all he said in the above
deposition in relation to said claim.

In the case of Charles GILL claiming 400 arpents of land (cannot read)
he knows that James MACKAY has resided there more than 15 years ago
on the said land which is bounded on one side by Joseph SAPPINGTON's
land, that he does not know of his own knowledge of Charles GILL living
on this place now claimed, but he is positively sure that said
Charles GILL was one of the first settlers on Gravois.

Peggy JONES, now Peggy CARTER, claiming 640 acres of land situate on
Grand Glaize. Pascal L. CERRE, duly sworn, says that when the former
Board of Commissioners was settling, the said Peggy JONES came to St.
Louis to file her claim before said Board. That, he, witness went with
said claimant to give testimony in her behalf. That after she had
filed her claim, the witness was sworn and gave testimony. That the
claimant being requested to give more testimony, went back to her settlement for witnesses, but having met with an accident (a fall from her
horse) she was prevented from coming back for a long while. That
Clement B. PENROSE, one of the Commissioners, seeing the witness sometime afterwards, asked him the reason why the said Peggy JONES did not
come back with her witnesses. Deponent, further, says that previous
to the change of government he was several times in the land claimed
& saw cabbins and a field under cultivation. Claimant had also horses
& cattle. That said Peggy JONES lived there with her husband & children. That said place lies south of Little rock creek, West of
Samuel WILSON's tract & bounded East by the Sulphur Spring, at the distance of about 20 miles from St. Louis. That said place was much ex-
posed to incusions of the Osage Indians.

Batpiste LAURINS by his legal representatives claiming 12 by 40 arpents
of land, see Record Book D, pg. 313, Minutes No. 5, pg. 456, produces
a paper purporting to be an original concession from Zenon TRUDEAU,
dated December 14th, 1796. M.P. LEDUC, duly sworn, says that the signature to said concession is in the proper handwriting of the said
Zenon TRUDEAU.

Francois COYTEUX, Jr. by his legal representatives claiming 400 arpents
of land, produces a paper purporting to be an original concession from
Carlos Dehault DELASSUS, dated 18th, October, 1799. M.P. LEDUC, duly
sworn, says that the signature to the said concession is in the proper
handwriting of the said Carlos Dehault DELASSUS.
    The Board Adjourned untill tomorrow at 9 o'clock.
            Wednesday July 9th, 1834 Board Met-J.S. MAYFIELD, J.H. RELFE,
                                        & F.R. CONWAY, Present

In the case of David HORINE claiming 640 acres of land, see Book No. 6,
pg. 232, (cannot read) about 65 years of age. That since 1802, he was
personally acquainted in the country with David HORINE, the claimant,
and witness believes that said David had arrived in the country in the
year 1801, and has ever since lived in the same.

Amable PATRIOTE claiming 640 acres of land situate in Bellevue Settle-
ment, see Record Book B, pg. 232, Book No. 5, pg. 477.
John STEWART, duly sworn, says that in 1802 claimant had a house and
garden on the tract claimed, and that said claimant has ever since re-
sided in this country. The following testimony was taken before
James H. RELFE, Esqr. on the 21st of last June.
State of Missouri, County of Washington
Personally appeared before James H. RELFE, one of the Comm'rs. for the

adjustment of private land claims in Missouri, John T. MCNEAL, who
deposeth & saith that Amable PATRIOTE, a labouring man, lived in a
cabbin in Mine a Breton & cultivated a garden and other improvements,
in the year 1800, and continued to reside there for some years after
and that he never knew him to claim any other lands. John T. MCNEAL
Sworn to & subscribed before me this 21st June, 1834. James H. RELFE
        The Board adjourned until tomorrow at 9 o'clock A.M.
            The Board Met & Adjourned July 10th, 21st, 22nd, 23rd, 24th,
        25th, 26th, 28th, 29th, & 30th, 1834.
            Thursday July 31st, 1834 Board Met-All Comm'rs. Present

Where as the period alloted for taking testimony before this Board has
expired, and the Clerk has not had time to transcribe a sufficient number of claims with the accompanying testimony, to occupy the attention
of the Board longer than a few days, therefore Resolved that the Clerk
finish the transcript of such claims as have been noted in Minutes
Books No. 6 and 7 of the proceedings, at as early a day as practicable
and as soon as completed, notify the Recorder and Commissioners thereof, and that the Board do now adjourn to such time as said transcript
shall be completed.
            Tuesday Oct. 7th, 1834 The Board Met-All Comm'rs. Present

The following resolution was unanimously concurred in by the Board.
        Be it resolved that the several resolutions of the former Board
of Commissioners, of the 30th of October, 1833, adopted as the basis
of their report of November the 7th, 1833, be observed by this Board
as fundamental rules for their action in passing upon such claim or
claims as may come within the purvieio of their jurisdiction, under
the act for the final adjustment of private land claims, and the act
supplementary thereto, of 2nd of March, 1833, and that the same be
observed as the basis of their report to the next Congress, to be made
in pursuance of the law referred to.

Jacques BON claiming 800 arpents of land, see No. 6, pg. 157.
The Board are unanimously of opinion that 640 acres ought to be confirmed to the said Jacques BON, or to his legal representatives, provided it does not interfere with the Old Mines claim. (Dec. No. 143)

Jean Baptiste DECHAMP claiming 160 arpents of land, see Book No. 6,
pg. 159. The Board are unanimously of opinion that this claim ought
to be confirmed to the said Jean Baptiste DECHAMP, or to his legal
representatives, according to the concession. (Dec. No. 144)

In the case of Daniel GRIFFITH claiming 600 arpents of land, see Book
No. 6, pg. 158, the following affidavit is transcribed by order of
the Board.
Territory of Missouri, County & Township of St. Louis
        This will attest & make known to whom it shall concern that the
annexed plat & certificate made for Daniel GRIFFTTH for 600 arpents
of land, marked in the margin this (J.H.B.) was made by me at the time
it bears date; that I was then a deputy Surveyor under
Major Antoine SOULARD, Surveyor General for the Territory of Missouri,
and that I returned the said plat & certificate to him, which he rejected & refused to receive, on the ground that it interfered with the
village common of the village of Portage Des Dioux, after which I delivered it to Mr. GRIFFITH, and do now recognize it to be the same I
made, as above stated.
                                        John FERRY
Sworn to & subscribed before me a Justice of the Peace for the County
& Township aforesaid, this 12th day of Oct., 1817.
                        Thos. F. RIDDICK, J.P.
        The Board Adjourned until tomorrow at 9 o'clock A.M.
            Wednesday October 8th, 1834 The Board Met-All Comm'rs. Present

Jean Baptiste GAMACHE, Sr., claiming by his legal representatives, 1,050
arpents of land, see Book No. 6, pg. 157. The Board are unanimously of
opinion that this claim ought to be granted to the legal representatives
of the said Jean Baptiste GAMACHE, Sr., according to the possession,
reference being had to the 2d Sections of the acts of 1805 & 7.
(Dec. No. 145)

Jacob ODAM by his legal representatives claiming 800 arpents of land, see Book No. 6, pg. 163. The Board are unanimously of opinion that 640 acres of land ought to be granted to the legal representatives of the said Jacob ODAM. (Dec. No. 146)

In the case of Curtis MORRIS claiming 746 arpents, 75 perches of land, see Book No. 6, pg. 385, the following additional testimony was taken by James H. RELFE, Comm'r. on the 5th of July, 1834.
State of Missouri, County of Washington
Personally appeared before James H. RELFE, one of the Comm'rs. for the adjustment of private land claims, John PAUL, who deposes & says he is 67 years of age, or about that, and came to Mine a Breton in the District of Ste. Genevieve, province of Upper Louisiana, in the year 1802, and continued to reside there until in the month of March in the year 1804, when he removed to Bellevue in the same District & province. Deponent says he became acquainted with Curtis MORRIS in the year 1803 or 4, in Mine a Breton, but at which period, deponent is unwilling to say, but it was in the fall of the year. Said MORRIS resided with William ASHBROOKS and continued to live with him until the end of the year 1804, and until he was married to Polly CROW, which he believes was in the latter end of the year 1804 or beginning of 1805. Witness continued to reside in Bellevue for two crop seasons & never knew of any other Curtis MORRIS than the one first named, and resided about half a mile from Mr. ASHBROOKS, with whom Curtis MORRIS resided, when he, deponent, moved to Bellevue.   John PAUL
Sworn to & subscribed before me this 5th July, 1834.
                                        James H. RELFE
State of Missouri, County of Washington
Personally appeared before James H. RELFE, one of the Comm'rs. for the adjustment of private land claims, Martha PAUL, who deposes & says she is 63 years of age, and answers to the following interrogations:
Question 1st: Where did you reside in the years 1802 and 1803?
Answer: In Mine a Breton, District of St. Genevieve, Province of Louisiana.
Q. 2nd: Where did you reside in 1804? Answer: In Bellevue, in the same district & Province, on Big river.
Q. 3rd: Did you know Curtis MORRIS in 1804? Answer: I did know him. He came to the country & resided with William ASHBROOK and, to the best of my knowledge, resided with him that summer & fall. Deponent saw said MORRIS working with William ASHBROOKS, ploughing corn in that year. Witness resided between half a mile & a mile from the residence of said ASHBROOKS, and said Curtis MORRIS continued to reside with ASHBROOKS until after his marriage, to the best of her recollection, to Polly CROW, daughter of Benjamin CROW. Q.4th: How long did you continue to reside in Bellevue, and did you know of any other man named Curtis MORRIS, in that neighbourhood during your residence? Answer: I resided three years in Bellevue, and never knew but the one man named Curtis MORRIS.   Martha (X) PAUL
                                                   Her mark
Sworn to & subscribed before me this 5th July, 1834.
                                        James H. RELFE

In the case of John VALET claiming 400 arpents of land, see Book No. 6, pg. 169. the following testimony was taken by James S. MAYFIELD, Comm'r.
Charles DENNY produced & sworn, states on his oath that in the year 1801, John VALLET was in possession of the above named tract of land; that said VALET was a man of family. That he erected & built on said tract of land a house, and had in cultivation about six acres of ground. The said tract was not enclosed, as at that time the St. Charles Commons were enclosed, & cattle could not get to it, and, further, that the same tract always went by the name of the Cave Spring tract, there being upon the same a large cave spring. Deponent, further, states that about twenty (or twelve) years afterwards, the said VALET sold the same tract & improvements to John COOK, whose son in law lived on the same about one year, under COOK & whose name was Antoine MARECHAL & deponent, further, states that the said VALLET lived in the house on said place, when there at work and that COOK, above named, continued to reside in this country, where he died. And that the tract mentioned above was surveyed after COOK became the purchaser, by John HARVEY & deponent

assisted in making said survey.
Sworn to this 3rd day of July, 1834 at St. Charles.
J.S. MAYFIELD, Comm'r.
Joseph VOISARD, sworn, on his oath states by his interpreter,
Charles DENNY, who was sworn a true interpretations to give, that
about 35 or 36 years ago, VALET made a small improvement on the above
tract of land, that he built a house on the same & enclosed a garden
spot near the cave spring, then called VALET Spring. That VALET lived
there while at work. Deponent, further, states he was not at the sale,
but understood, VALET sold the same tract of land to John COOK, who put
his son in law, MARECHAL mentioned above, to live on it, which he thinks
was after the change of government.
Gabriel LATREILLE, produced & sworn, states that, in the year 1802,he
knows of Mr. VALLET cultivating the land alluded to above. That he
had in cultivation two or three arpents of land & built a house upon
the same, and deponent, further, states, he, VALET, cultivated the same
for about two years & sold to John COOK, who occupied & possessed the
same until sold under execution by the Sheriff, and deponent, further,
states that the tract, as he understood, amounted to four hundred or
450 arpents, and embraced what was then called, VALET Spring, a large
cave spring.
Sworn to this 4th day of July, 1834.
                    James S. MAYFIELD, Comm'r.

In the case of Abraham SMITH claiming 600 arpents of land, see Book No.
6, pg. 170, the following testimony was taken by James S. MAYFIELD,
Comm'r. Claimant at the same time produced a paper purporting to be
an affidavit of Charles TAYON, late Commandant of St. Charles, certifying to have given to Abram SMITH, verbal permission to settle on 400
arpents of land.
Charles DENNY produced & sworn, on his oath states that in the year
1801 or 1802, deponent saw land broke up on the said tract, which was
called Abraham SMITH's improvement. He saw no house or enclosure &
SMITH had then returned to Kentucky. Deponent, further, states at that
time none of the inhabitants enclosed their lands or improvements, that
is, near the Common fields. Deponent, further, states that the paper
shewn him, marked A, is signed in the proper handwriting of
Charles TAYON, he having seen him write, who was Commandant of St.
Charles from about 1800, up to the change of government.
Sworn to this 3rd July, 1834 at St. Charles.
                    James S. MAYFIELD, Comm'r.
Gabriel LATREILLE, produced & sworn on his oath states, through his
interpreter, who was sworn a true interpretation to give, that in 1797
a Mr. SMITH was living on a tract of land lying near the town of St.
Charles, said land now being in the possession of James LINDSEY. That
SMITH lived there with his family, and had 7 or 8 arpents of land enclosed and in cultivation. That Mr. SMITH lived there for sometime afterwards and the place was left vacant, unoccupied, and unclaimed by
any one else, until about 15 years ago, when Mr. James LINDSEY took
possession of it, and deponent, further, states he does not recollect
the given name of Mr. SMITH, but does not, or did not know, of any other
man of that name, who settled & improved a tract of land near the town
of St. Charles, during the existence of the Spanish government.
Sworn to before me the 4th day of July, 1834.
                    James S. MAYFIELD, Comm'r.

In the case of Charles DENNE claiming 760 arpents of land, see Book No.
6, pg. 513, the following testimony was taken by James S. MAYFIELD,
Comm'r. Andrew ZUMALT, produced & sworn, on his oath states that he
saw an improvement on the land mentioned, but does not recollect that
he ever saw Mr. DENNE at work on the land aforesaid. That the improvement mentioned was always called DENNE's Improvement, and at that time
the said DENNE was a single man and, further, that the said improvement
consisted of the clearing of a small spot of ground, and enclosing the
same with the erection of a small building or hut on the same. Deponent, further, states that said DENNE was in possession of the land or
improvement, two years or more, as he thinks, before the change of
government.   Andrew (X) ZUMALT
                                        his mark
Sworn to this 3rd day of July, 1834 at St. Charles. J.S. MAYFIELD, Comm'r.

In the case of John MCNEAL claiming 640 acres of land, see No. 7, pg. 2, the following testimony was taken before F.R. CONWAY, Comm'r. John MCNEAL of lawful age (being as he says 70 years of age) deposeth & saith that in the spring of the year 1803, he the said MCNEAL, commenced & had an improvement made, trees chopped round and the foundation of a house made & a garden made in the spring of the year 1804 & fruit trees planted & moved on said land in the year 1804, and had his land surveyed by John STEWART in the month of January, 1806, which land he claimed as a donation right from the Spanish government, as one of Moses AUSTIN's followers, as will appear from or on the Spanish Recores, and claimed 640 acres, and sold his claim and interest to Augustus JONES, and is in no ways interested in said claim of land at this time, having given a gent claim for the same.   John T. MCNEAL Sworn to & subscribed before me at Potosi, Missouri this 8th day of May, 1834.   F.R. CONWAY

In the case of George AYREY claiming 750 arpents of land, see Book No. 6, pg. 169, the following testimony was taken by A.G. HARRISON, late Comm'r., under a resolution passed by the Board on the 13th of May, 1833.
Isaac VANBIBBER, Sr., being duly sworn, says that said AYREY lived with Wm. RAMSAY, Sr. before the change of government, and lived with him in 1800, and his claim adjoined as witness understood, the claim of said RAMSAY.
Joshua STOGSDILL, being duly sworn, says that he, witness, in February, 1804, made for said AYREY, on Lick Branch, an improvement on a tract of land on said Branch; the improvements consisted in clearing ground & building a cabbin; that said AYREY put in a crop on said place that year, as well as witness now recollects.

In the case of John VALET claiming 400 arpents of land, see Book No. 6, pg. 169, the following testimony was taken by A.G. HARRISON, late Comm'r. under a resolution passed on 13th May, 1833.
Jean RIEUR, being duly sworn, says that about 34 years ago, the said John VALET, alias BOURBONNE made an improvement near the cave spring in St. Charles County. That his claim included said spring. That he had a house on it and some ploughed ground. That he had a wife & five children at the time mentioned.
Pierre QUEBEC, alias VIOLET, being duly sworn, says that about 33 or 34 years ago, John VALET settled & improved a place including the cave spring in St. Charles County. That he had a house & field on said place, at the time mentioned.

In the case of William MCHUGH, alias MCQUE, claiming 640 acres of land, see Book No. 6, pg. 215, the following testimony was taken by A.G. HARRISON, late Comm'r., under a Resolution passed by the Board on the 13th of May, 1833.
Clarksville May 24th, 1833
James BURNS, being duly sworn, upon his oath says that at least two years before the change of the Spanish Government to the American Government, and at the same time that William RAMSAY came to that place, said MCHUGH cultivated a place on MCHUGH's creek. That after RAMSAY was driven off by the Indians, about 1804, said MCHUGH was put in possession of said RAMSAY's land, by RAMSAY, as he supposes; that said MCHUGH had, at that time, a wife & nine children.
Joseph MCCOY, being duly sworn, upon his oath says that, having heard the above testimony of James BURNS, the same is in atl things substantially true, as he believes & recollects.

In the case of Abraham SMITH claiming 600 arpents of land, see No. 6, pg. 170, the following testimony was taken by A.G. HARRISON, late Comm'r., under a resolution of the Board, passed on the 13th of May, 1833.
Robert SPENCER, being duly sworn, says that in the year 1799, he saw Abraham SMITH cultivating a place near the mamelles and immediately below Point D' Aulm, where the said SMITH had a house & a field of corn of about ten acres on it. That the appearance of the improvement was new, and that he cultivated the same two or three seasons afterwards, as witness now recollects.
Gabrielle LATREILLE, being duly sworn, says that in the year 1797, Abraham SMITH settled near the Mammelles & in 1798, raised a crop on

the place he settled. That he had a house on it, and continued there until 1800, when, being ordered by Charles TAYON, Commandant, to keep up his cattle, he left the said place.

In the case of Victor LAGAUTERIE claiming 800 arpents of land, see No. 6, pg. 167, the following testimony was taken by A.G. HARRISON, late Comm'r., under a Resolution of the Board passed the 13th of May, 1833. Etienne GUENELLE, duly sworn, says that he knew said LAGAUTERIE very well. That he lived on a tract of land on the banks of the Mississippi, above the mouth of Salt river, where he made salt. That at the time he, witness, knew him living there, was under the Spanish Government. That said LAGAUTERIE had a house & garden on said land. Also, a small field near the prairie, as witness was (cannot read). Pierre PARLADI, being duly sworn, says that having read the testimony of Etienne QUENELLE as above, and that being well acquainted personally with all the facts, makes the above testimony his own, relation to all that is above testified to.
Peter TEAGUE, being duly sworn, says that he was acquainted with a place called LAGAUTERIE's lick, on the banks of the Mississippi river, above the mouth of Salt river, at the lower end of a little prairie, which said lick was not far from Fort Mason. Witness always understood that Victor LAGAUTERIE's claim included said lick, and that said LAGAUTERIE had made Salt there.

In the case of David MIRACLE claiming 640 acres of land, see Book No. 6, pg. 216, the following testimony was taken by A.G. HARRISON, late Comm'r., under a Resolution above mentioned.
Daniel KEATHLY, being duly sworn, says he saw the wife of Mr. David MIRACLE, who lived at that time, as she said on a tract of land on a branch, then called Walker's branch, and now called Scott's branch. That witness never saw the place mentioned, while said MIRACLE lived there, but from general report of the neighbourhood is certain that said claimant did live on said place at the time mentioned.
John ZUMALT, being duly sworn, says that he knew the wife of David MIRACLE, who lived somewhere in the neighbourhood as above spoken of, that she was living there before her husband, David MIRACLE, came to the country.
Jeremiah GROSHON, being duly sworn, says that 1802, the wife of David MIRACLE improved & cultivated a place in Walker's branch, some times called Lewis branch. That there was a cabbin built on it, in which she lived. That it adjoined the claim of John LEWIS.
William CRAIG, being duly sworn, says that in 1802, he saw the wife of David MIRACLE living on & cultivating a place on Walkers, some times called Lewis branch. That said improvement consisted of a cabbin and a small field.

In the case of Curtis MORRIS claiming 746 arpents 75 perches of land, see Book No. 6, pg. 385, the following testimony was sworn to & signature acknowledged before Lewis F. LINN, Comm'r.
State of Missouri, Washington, Cty.
Be it remembered that on this 10th day of January, 1832, the following persons appeared before me, Henry SHURLDS, a Justice of the Peace in & for said County.
Martin RUGGLES aged fifty seven years & upwards, being duly sworn, deposeth & saith that he was at the place, in now Washington County, commonly called & known as he believes, as the claim of Curtis MORRIS, some time in the month of August or September, 1804, at which time he saw a cabbin, or log house about 14 or 14 feet square at said place & saw corn growing at the same time & place, supposed to be two or three acres. The corn then appeared to be full grown. There was no person at the cabbin at the time, and it had the appearance of being inhabited, and the same has been inhabited & cultivated ever since.
Subscribed & sworn to the day & year aforesaid. Martin RUGGLES
Henry SHURLDS, J.P.
Sworn to & signature acknowledged before me, Lewis F. LINN, Comm'r. this 7th day of May, 1833. L.F. LINN, Comm'r.
John T. MCNEILL, aged 68 years & upwards, being duly sworn, deposeth & saith that he assisted Curtis MORRIS in raising a cabbin or log house on the claim of said MORRIS, in the month of Febraury or first of March, 1804, which claim is situate in what is now called Washing-

ton County aforesaid. That he saw MORRIS living on the same, in the
summer of the same year, and dined with him, he MORRIS, having cooked
dinner for them. There was, at the time the cabbin was built, an enclosure at the same place of an acre perhaps or upwards, and a
Mr. REED went to the inclosúre & brought from thence, some turnips of
which witness partook. He saw corn stalks he thinks, standing in the
same enclosure, but from the length of time, he cannot be entirely certain, and the place has been inhabited & cultivated ever since.
                                        John T. MCNEAL
Subscribed & sworn to by John T. MCNEAL, who is personally known to me
the day & year first aforesaid.   Henry SHURLDS, J.P.
Sworn to & signature of J.T. MCNEAL acknowledged before me this 7th
day of May, 1833.   L.F. LINN, Comm'r.
James JOHNSON, aged 43 years & upwards, being duly sworn, deposeth &
saith that in July or August, 1804, he saw a small piece of ground
cleared on the claim commonly called the claim of Curtis MORRIS, on
which there was at the time corn growing, and he believes the same has
been inhabited & cultivated ever since.
                                        James JOHNSON
Subscribed & sworn to the day & year first aforesaid.
                                        Henry SHURLDS, J.P.
Sworn to & signature of James JOHNSON acknowledged before me this 7th
day of May, 1833.   L.F. LINN, Comm'r.

In the case of Pascal DETCHMENDY claiming 7,056 arpents of land, see
Book No. 6, pg. 378, the following testimony was taken by
J.H. RELFE, Comm'r.
State of Missouri, County of Washington
Personally appeared before James H. RELFE, one of the Comm'rs. for the
adjustment of private land claims in the State of Missouri,
John STEWART, who deposeth & saith that in the month of November, 1805,
he was appointed Deputy Surveyor under Antoine SOULARD, for all operations to be made in the settlement of Bellevue, which appointment &
instructions from James WILKINSON, is herewith exibited. In obedience
to instructions, he called on Mr. MADDIN for a report of such claims
as had been surveyed by him within the District now assigned to this
deponent, in reply to which a communication was received, dated December 9th, 1805, stating Mr. BATES & Mr. STODARDS (STROTHERS) were the
only claims surveyed by him, which lay within the bounds assigned to
this deponent. No application was ever made for the survey of the
claim of Pascal (now MORRISON) nor does deponent recollect to have
heard of the claim until after the expiration of the time allotted for
the survey of the private land claims. In executing the surveys of
private land claims in Bellevue, deponent made a survey for
William REED, Sr., adjoining the lands of Moses BATES, which has been
confirmed, also a tract for William REED, Jr., adjoining the land of
Edward JOHNSON, which is now before the Board of Comm'rs., also executed a survey for Joseph REED, Sr., adjoining the land of Robert REED,
which has been confirmed and a tract for Joseph REED, Jr., adjoining
to & south of the land of Joseph REED, Sr., which is now before the
Board of Comm'rs. for their action, and which will more particularly
appear by reference to the plats & field notes returned by deponent to
the proper office in the months of January & February, 1806. The deponent, further, says that the said William REED, Sr., William REED,
Jr., Joseph REED, Sr. & Joseph REED, Jr., were four different tracts
named, when the surveys were made. Deponent says he removed to Upper
Louisiana from the State of Kentucky in the year 1800 & established
himself in Mine a Breton & has continued to reside in the District of
County, now called Washington County ever since. It was his practice
to hunt for some distance round the mines, and he believes himself to
have been one of the first Americans who discovered the valley of land
now called Bellevue, and it was trhough his information & advice the
first settlements were made by the REEDS & others in the year 1803.
For a considerable time after the commencement of the settlements a-
round the mines, it was dangerous for families to live remote from each
other on account of the Indians, who, if they could find a small party
of whites, would beat them severely & rob them of their horses & other
property, as late as the year 1808. The Osage Indians made an incursion on Bellevue & drove off between 25 & 30 horses, or nearly all the
work horses in the settlement.   John STEWART
Sworn to & subscribed before me this 25th June, 1833. J.H. RELFE
                            159

State of Missouri, County of Washington
Personally appeared before James H. RELFE, one of the Comm'rs., etc.,
John T. MCNEALL, who deposeth & Saith that in the year 1797, he arrived in the province of Upper Louisiana, and the following year took
up his residence at Mine a Breton, that he was well acquainted with
the country now called Bellevue, at the time of its settlements by
the REEDS & others. At its first settlement it was called Big lick,
but late in the year 1803, deponent understood an old Frenchman of in-
fluence at the mines, gave it the name of Bellevue, which it has retained ever since. And deponent, further, states he never heard of
the claim of Pascal, now attempted to be established by MORRISON, until after the settlements & surveys of the lands of the REEDS, BATES,
STROTHERS, & others nor until the attempt of Mr. MADDIN to survey the
claim when the settlers drove them off and would not permit the survey to be made to include their settlements, as the deponent understood.   John MCNEAL - Sworn to & subscribed before me this 21st day
of June, 1834.   James H. RELFE

In the case of Thomas REED claiming 747 arpents of land, see Book No.
6, pg. 212, the following testimony was taken by F.R. CONWAY, Comm'r.
Bellevue, Washington County State of Missouri
Personally appeared before F.R. CONWAY, Recorder of land titles for
the state of Missouri & one of the Comm'rs. appointed, etc.
John T.MCNEAL, who being first duly sworn, states in reference to
the above claim as follows: having heretofore deposed in the above
cause byt having omitted to state a fact which deponent hereby supplies
and which fact is believed to be material he states he knows the above
claim and passed by it in the year 1804, in the month of February.
There was on the land an improvement which appeared to have been made
the year before. It was then under fence, and had been cultivated in
turnips. There was also a small cabbin near the improvement, and at
the date aforesaid it was known to be the above named Thomas REED's
improvement. And, further, this deponent saith that the small cabbin
at the time aforesaid was occupied, and appeared to have been lived in
for some time previous, by the marks of fire & smoke on & about the
chimney & further, deponent saith not.   John T. MCNEAL
Sworn to & subscribed before me at Potosi Missouri this 7th day of May,
1834.   F.R. CONWAY

In the case of Joseph REED, Jr. claiming 640 acres of land, see No. 6,
pg. 383, the following testimony was taken by F.R. CONWAY, Comm'r.
John MCNEAL, being duly sworn, deposes & says that in the month of
November, 1803, he passed by Joseph REED's spring and saw chopping
done, timber cut round & some fallen down, and the foundation of a cabbin laid. In the month of April, 1805, he met some children coming from
said REED's turnip patch with turnip sallad, or turnip greens, and when
he went to said turnip patch, he saw a woman in the inside of the patch
gathering turnip tops for greens and the fence was made of split rails
& poles, which he supposed included about one acre and said REED claimed
the same as his head right & sold the same to David GOLAR, who lived on
the said farm for several years, and after said GOLAHAN's decease, the
heirs sold their claim to Philip MCCABE, who lives on the same and has
a large farm on said land and this deponent says that he has never heard
that said REED ever claimed any other land as his head right before or
since and claims 640 acres as his head right.   John T. MCNEAL
Sworn to & subscribed before me this 8th day of May, 1834 at Potosi,
Missouri. F.R. CONWAY

In the case of Amable PANOTE claiming 640 acres, see Book No. 7, pg. 6,
the following testimony was taken by J.H. RELFE, Comm'r.
State of Missouri, County of Washington
Personally appeared before James H. RELFE, one of the Comm'rs. appointed
etc., Baptist PLAGET, who deposeth & saith he removed to Mine a Breton
in the year 1808, and in the spring of the year 1809, removed to the
old Mines in the then County of St. Genevieve Territory of Missouri, and
was employed by Amable PATNOTE, to work on a tract of land and extend an
improvement, deponent thinks it had been made five or six years previous
to that time. Baptiste (X) PLAGET
                    his mark
Sworn to & subscribed before me this 25th July, 1834. J.H. RELFE

Thursday Oct. 9th, 1834 Board Met-All Comm'rs. Present

Jos. GERARD & P. FLEMING claiming 840 (1600) arpents of land, see Book No. 6, pg. 167. The Board are unanimously of opinion that this claim ought to be confirmed to the said Joseph GERARD & Patrick FLEMING, or to their legal representatives, according to the concession. (Dec. No. 147)

Daniel GRIFFITH claiming 600 arpents of land, see No. 6, pg. 158. The Board are unanimously of opinion that this claim ought to be confirmed to the said Daniel GRIFFITH, or to his legal representatives, to be located on any unappropriated land of the United States, according to the usages of the Spanish Government. (Dec. No. 148)

Victor LAGAUTERIE claiming 800 arpents of land, see Book No. 6, pg. 167. The Board are unanimously of opinion that this claim ought to be confirmed to the said Victor LAGAUTERIE or to his legal representatives according to the surveys. (Dec. No. 149)

_____ AMIOT claiming 600 arpents of land, see Book No. 6, pg. 167. The Board are unanimously of opinion that this claim ought to be granted to the said AMIOT, or to his legal representatives, according to possession. (Dec. 150)

Mathurin BOUVET claiming 6 arpents square of land, see Book No. 6, pg. 169. The Board are unanimously of opinion that this claim ought to be confirmed to the said Mathurin BOUVET or to his legal representatives, according to the concession. (Dec. 151)

John VALLET claiming 400 arpents of land, see Book No. 6, pg. 169. The Board are unanimously of opinion that 400 arpents of land ought to be granted to the said John VALLET, or to his legal representatives. (Dec. No. 152)

Camille DELASSUS claiming 2,400 arpents 36 perches of land, see Book No. 6, pg. 175. The Board are unanimously of opinion that this claim ought to be confirmed to the said Camille DELASSUS, or to her legal representatives, according to the concession. (Dec. No. 153)

Antoine PRATTE claiming 500 arpents of land, see Book No. 6, pg. 181. The Board are unanimously of opinion that this claim ought to be confirmed to the said Antoine PRATTE, or to his legal representatives, according to the concession. (Dec. No. 154)

Henry PRATTE claiming 600 arpents of land, see Book No. 6, pg. 182. The Board are unanimously of opinion that this claim ought to be confirmed to the said Henry PRATTE, or to his legal representatives, according to the concession. (Dec. No. 155)
     Adjourned until tomorrow at 9 o'clock A.M.
          The Board Met & Adjourned Oct. 10th & 11th, 1834
          Monday Oct. 13th, 1834 Board Met-All Comm'rs. Present

Abraham SMITH claiming 600 arpents of land, see Book No. 6, pg. 170. The Board are unanimously of opinion that 600 arpents of land ought to be granted to the said Abraham SMITH or to his legal representatives. (Dec. No. 156)

Pierre Auguste PRATTE claiming 600 arpents of land, see No. 6, pg. 184. The Board are unanimously of opinion that this claim ought to be confirmed to the said Pierre Auguste PRATTE, or to his legal representatives, according to the concession. (Dec. No. 157)

Joseph PRATTE claiming 20,000 arpents of land, see Book No. 6, pg. 185. The Board are unanimously of opinion that this claim ought to be confirmed to the said Joseph PRATTE, or to his legal representatives, according to the concession. (Dec. No. 158)

Parfait DUFOUR & Louis BOLDUC claiming 800 arpents of land, see No. 6, pg. 189. The Board are unanimously of opinion that this claim ought to be confirmed to the said Parfait DUFOUR & Louis BOLDUC, or to their legal representatives, according to the concession. (Dec. No. 159)

Jean Baptiste VALLE claiming 7,056 arpents of land, see Book No. 6, pg. 191. The Board are unanimously of opinion that this claim ought to be confirmed to the said Jean Baptiste VALLE, or to his legal representatives, according to the concession. (Dec. No. 159)

Roger CAGLE, by his legal representatives claiming 650 arpents of land, situate on Sandy Creek, County of Jefferson, see Record Book E, pg. 323, BATE's Decisions, pg. 91.
William HARRINGTON, duly sworn, says that he is about 46 years of age. That he has lived in this country for 36 years. That he was well acquainted with the said Roger CAGLE and knows the tract claimed. That in the fall of 1803, he went on said CAGLE's place for the purpose to get him to help deponent's father to gather his corn. That, at that time, said CAGLE was working on his place making clap boards to cover, as witness supposes a small cabbin he had put up. That said CAGLE had then his family living at a neighbour close by till he could get a house for them to live in. Witness, further, says that in the spring of 1804, he went to said place to have some blacksmith work done by said CAGLE, who was a blacksmith by trade. That said CAGLE had then a double cabbin for a dwelling house and also a shop. That claimant had then a field of about 5 or 6 acres, and witness went to plough for CAGLE, while he did witness's blacksmith work at the shop. Deponent, further, says that he was frequently on said place through the summer and that claimant raised a crop of corn in the said year 1804. That claimant had a wife and, he thinks, 8 or 10 children. That said CAGLE witness believes, lived there two years, till he sold, as witness heard, to William JOHNSON & that the place has been under cultivation ever since.

Pierre GAMELIN claiming 800 arpents of land, see Book No. 6, pg. 178. The Board are unanimously of opinion that this claim ought to be confirmed to the said Pierre GAMELIN, or to his legal representatives, according to the concession. (Dec. No. 161)

Louis DUPRE claiming 800 arpents of land, see Book No. 6, pg. 178. The Board are unanimously of opinion that this claim ought to be confirmed to the said Louis DUPRE, or to his legal representatives, according to the concession. (Dec. No. 162)

Jean Baptiste CHALIFOUX claiming 600 arpents of land, see No. 6, pg. 179. The Board are unanimously of opinion that this claim ought to be confirmed to the said Jean Baptiste CHALIFOUX, or to his legal representatives, according to the concession. (Dec. No. 163)

Jean Baptiste VALLE & Louis BOLDUC claiming 800 arpents of land, see No. 6, pg. 197. The Board are unanimously of opinion that this claim ought to be confirmed to the said Jean Baptiste VALLE & Louis BOLDUC, or to their legal representatives, according to the concession. (Dec. No. 164)

Charles ROBIN & Louis CARRON claiming 1,500 arpents of land, see No. 6, pg. 199. The Board are unanimously of opinion that this claim ought to be confirmed to the said Charles ROBIN & Louis CARRON, or to their legal representatives, according to the concession. (Dec. No. 165)

Henry PEYROUX claiming 7,760 acres of land, see Book No. 6, pg. 202. The Board are unanimously of opinion that this claim ought to be confirmed to the said Henry PEYROUX, or to his legal representatives, according to the concession. (Dec. No. 166)
Adjourned until tomorrow at 9 o'clock A.M.
Tuesday Oct. 14th, 1834 Board Met-All Comm'rs. Present

Charles ROY claiming 80 arpents of land, see Book No. 6, pg. 218. The Board are unanimously of opinion that this claim ought to be confirmed to the said Charles ROY, or to his legal representatives, according to the concession. (Dec. No. 167)

David MIRACLE claiming 640 acres of land, see Book No. 6, pg. 216.
The Board are unanimously of opinion that 400 arpents of land ought
to be granted to the said David MIRACLE, or to his legal representatives, it being the quantity claimed on record. (Dec. No. 168)

Joseph ROY claiming 600 arpents of land, see Book No. 6, pg. 219. The
Board are unanimously of opinion that this claim ought to be confirmed
to the said Joseph ROY, or to his legal representatives. Survey to be
made to include his improvements. (Dec. No. 169)

Jean Baptiste MARTIGNY claiming 12 arpents in front, see Book No. 6,
pg. 219. The Board are unanimously of opinion that this claim ought
to be confirmed to the said Jean Baptiste MARTIGNY, or to his legal
representatives, according to the concession. (Dec. No. 170)

Antoine FLANDRIN claiming 6,000 arpents of land, see Book No. 6, pg.
221. The Board are unanimously of opinion that this claim ought to be
confirmed to the said Antoine FLANDRIN, or to his legal representatives,
according to the concession. (Dec. No. 171)
      Adjourned until tomorrow at 9 o'clock A.M.
         Wednesday Oct. 15th, 1834 Board Met-All Comm'rs. Present

James CLAMORGAN claiming 3,200 arpents of land, see Book No. 6, pg.
221. The Board are unanimously of opinion that this claim ought to be
confirmed to the said James CLAMORGAN, or to his legal representatives,
according to the concession. (Dec. No. 172)

Thomas WILKINSON claiming 400 arpents of land, see Book No. 6, pg. 222.
The Board are unanimously of opinion that this claim ought to be confirmed to the said Thomas WILKINSON, or to his legal representatives,
according to the concession. (Dec. No. 173)

David KINCAID claiming 500 arpents of land, see Book No. 6, pg. 223.
The Board are unanimously of opinion that this claim ought to be confirmed to the said David KINCAID, or to his legal representatives,
according to the concession. (Dec. No. 174)

David MCKINNEY claiming 590 arpents of land, see Book No. 6, pg. 223.
The Board are unanimously of opinion that this claim ought to be confirmed to the said David MCKINNEY, or to his legal representatives,
according to the concession. (Dec. No. 175)

Antoine BARRADA, by his legal representative, William DAVIS claiming
800 arpents of land, No. 6, pg. 224. The Board are unanimously of
opinion that this claim ought to be confirmed to the said
Antoine BARRADA, or to his legal representatives, according to the concession. (Dec. No. 176)

David HORINE claiming 640 acres of land, see Book No. 6, pg. 232 & 530.
The Board are unanimously of opinion that 640 acres of land ought to be
granted to the said David HORINE, or to his legal representatives.
(Dec. No. 177)

Auguste P. CHOUTEAU claiming 800 arpents of land, see Book No. 6, pg.
229. The Board are unanimously of opinion that this claim ought to be
confirmed to the said Auguste P. CHOUTEAU, or to his legal representatives, according to the concession. (Dec. No. 178)
      Adjourned until tomorrow at 9 o'clock A.M.
         Thursday Oct. 16th, 1834 Board Met-All Comm'rs. Present

Therese CRELY claiming 3,528 arpents of land, see Book No. 6, pg. 234.
The Board are unanimously of opinion that this claim ought to be confirmed to the said Therese CRELY, or to her legal representatives,
according to the concession. (Dec. No. 179)

Gabriel LORD claiming 400 arpents of land, see Book No. 6, pg. 237.
The Board are unanimously of opinion that 360 arpents of land ought to
be confirmed to the said Gabriel LORD, or to his legal representatives,

according to the Survey. (Dec. No. 180)

Auguste GAMACHE claiming 300 arpents of land, see Book No. 6, pg. 238.
The Board are unanimously of opinion that this claim ought to be confirmed to the said Auguste GAMACHE, or to his legal representatives,
according to the concession. (Dec. No. 181)

Bazile DESNOYERS claiming 800 arpents of land, see Book No. 6, pg. 242.
The Board are unanimously of opinion that 640 acres of land ought to be
granted to the said Bazile DESNOYERS, or to his legal representatives.
(Dec. No. 182)

Charles TAYON, Jr. claiming 800 arpents of land, see Book No. 6, pg.
243. The Board are unanimously of opinion that this claim ought to be
confirmed to the said Charles TAYON, Jr., or to his legal representatives, according to the concession. (Dec. 183)

Thomas MADDIN claiming 2,000 arpents of land, see Book No. 6, pg. 255.
The Board are unanimously of opinion that this claim ought to be confirmed to the said Thomas MADDIN, or to his legal representatives,
according to the concession. (Dec. No. 184)

Charles VALLE claiming 160 arpents of land, see Book No. 6, pg. 257.
The Board are unanimously of opinion that this claim ought to be confirmed to the said Charles VALLE, or to his legal representatives,
according to the concession. (Dec. No. 185)

Louis TAYON claiming (cannot read amount) arpents of land, see Book
No. 6, pg. (cannot read number). The Board are unanimously of opinion
that this claim ought to be confirmed to the said Louis TAYON, or to
his legal representatives, according to the concession. (Dec. No. 186)

Elijah BENTON claiming 640 acres of land, see Book No. 6, pg. 339.
The Board are unanimously of opinion that 640 acres of land ought to
be granted to the said Elijah BENTON, or to his legal representatives.
(Dec. No. 187)
     Adjourned until tomorrow at 9 o'clock A.M.
          Friday Oct. 17th, 1834 Board Met-All Comm'rs. Present

Thomas BAKER claiming 640 acres of land, see Book No. 6, pg. 360.
The Board are unanimously of opinion that 480 acres, 3 quarters & 32
poles ought to be granted to the said Thomas BAKER, or to his legal
representatives, it being the quantity claimed on record. (Dec. 188)

John PAUL claiming 640 acres of land, see Book No. 6, pg. 353. The
Board are unanimously of opinion that 640 acres of land ought to be
granted to the said John PAUL, or to his legal representatives.
(Dec. No. 189)

Bede MOORE claiming 640 acres of land, see Book No. 6, pg. 359. The
Board are unanimously of opinion that 640 acres of land ought to be
granted to the said Bede MOORE, or to his legal representatives.
(Dec. No. 190)

James HAWKINS claiming 640 acres of land, see No. 6, pg. 358. The
Board are unanimously of opinion that 640 acres of land ought to be
granted to the said James HAWKINS, or to his legal representatives.
(Dec. No. 191)

John ANDERSON claiming 640 acres of land, see Book No. 6, pg. 367.
The Board are unanimously of opinion that 638 acres, 3 qrts. & 5 poles
ought to be granted to the said John ANDERSON, or to his legal representatives, it being the quantity claimed on record. (Dec. No. 192)
     Adjourned until tomorrow at 9 o'clock A.M.
          Saturday Oct. 18th, 1834 Board Met-All Comm'rs. Present

John EARS claiming 960 arpents of land, see Book No. 6, pg. 373. The
Board are unanimously of opinion that 640 acres of land ought to be
granted to the said John EARS, or to his legal representatives.
(Dec. No. 193)

Henry TUCKER claiming 640 acres of land, see Book No. 6, pg. 429.
The Board are unanimously of opinion that 640 acres of land ought to
be granted to the said Henry TUCKER, or to his legal representatives.
(Dec. No. 194)

Camille DELASSUS claiming 6,000 arpents of land, see Book No. 6, pg.
405. The Board are unanimously of opinion that this claim ought to
be confirmed to the said Camille DELASSUS, or to his legal representatives, according to the concession. (Dec. No. 195)
      Adjourned until Monday next at 9 o'clock A.M.
            Monday Oct. 20th, 1834 Board Met-All Comm'rs. Present

In the case of Francois HEBERT claiming 2 by 40 arpents of land, see
No. 6, pg. 218. Pierre CHOUTEAU, Sr., duly sworn, says that
Francois HEBERT worked for 5 or 6 years consecutively on the tract
claimed prior to the year 1780, and the said HEBERT was killed in said
year 1780 by the Indians, while he was cultivating said land, and his
body could never be found.

In the case of Alexis LOISE claiming 3 by 40 arpents of land, see No.
6, pg. 219. Pierre CHOUTEAU, Sr., duly sworn, says that if in the
testimony given by him in this case on a former occasion, he has said
that the cultivation on this land had been done after the year 1780,
it must have been through inadvertancy, for said cultivation was prior
to the said year 1780. That for at least three or four years after
1780, no body ventured to cultivate land in the grand Prairie, there
being almost every day, alarms caused by Indians.

Etienne PARENT & Etienne GOVEROT claiming 800 arpents of land, see No.
6, pg. 406. The Board are unanimously of opinion that this claim
ought to be confirmed to the said Etienne PARENT & Etienne GOVEROT,
or to their legal representatives, according to the concession.
(Dec. No. 196)

Antoine VILLARS & Joseph VILLARS claiming 6,000 arpents of land, No. 6,
pg. 407. The Board are unanimously of opinion that this claim ought
to be confirmed to the said Antoine VILLARS & Joseph VILLARS, or to
their legal representatives, according to the concession. (Dec. No. 197)

James CRAWFORD claiming 640 acres of land, see Book No. 6, pg. 409.
The Board are unanimously of opinion that 600 arpents of land (it being
the quantity claimed on record) ought to be granted to the said
James CRAWFORD, or to his legal representatives. (Dec. No. 198)

John BURK claiming 1,000 arpents of land, see Book No. 6, pg. 428.
The Board remark that the date of the concession is anterior to that
of the petition & recommendation, but observe that being written, in
these three instances, in the old French & Spanish way of abreviating,
they are inclined to attribute this discrepance to a mistake of the
recording clerk. The Board are unanimously of opinion that this claim
ought to be confirmed to the said John BURK, or to his legal representatives, according to the concession. (Dec. No. 199)

Joseph DOUBLEWYE, alias DEBLOIS claiming 640 acres of land, see Book
No. 6, pg. 420. A majority of the Board are of the opinion that 640
acres of land ought to be granted to the said Joseph DOUBLEWYE, alias
DEBLOIS, or to his legal representatives.
      James A. MAYFIELD, Comm'r., dissenting.
      Adjourned until tomorrow at 9 o'clock A.M.
            Tuesday Oct. 21st, 1834 Board Met-All Comm'rs. Present

Joseph CHEVALIER claiming 400 arpents of land, see Book No. 6, pg. 465.
The Board are unanimously of opinion that this claim ought to be confirmed to the said Joseph CHEVALIER, or to his legal representatives,
according to the concession. (Dec. No.200)
      Adjourned until tomorrow at 9 o'clock A.M.
            The Board Met & Adjourned Oct. 22nd, 1834.
            Thursday Oct. 23rd, 1834 Board Met-All Comm'rs. Present

Thursday Oct. 23rd, 1834 Board Met-All Comm'rs. Present

In the case of Curtis MORRIS claiming 746 arpents 75 perches of land, see Book No. 6, pg. 385. The Board are of opinion that Justice to the claimants requires that an order should be made to take the deposition of Walter CROW & others residing in the Territory of Arkansas; and that the party, to whom the said order shall be made, shall give notice to the other of the time & place of taking the same, which said depositions shall be sealed, certified and returned to the Board, in pursuance of the law in such cases, on or before the 9th day of July, next.

Samuel DORSEY claiming 800 arpents of land, see Book No. 6, pg. 467. The Board are unanimously of opinion that this claim ought to be confirmed to the said Samuel DORSEY, or to his legal representatives, according to the concession. (Dec. No. 201)

In the case of Jacques BON claiming 800 arpent of land, see Book No. 6, pg. 157. Louis BOLLEDUC, duly sworn, says that since the year 1816, or 1817, he knows the said Jacques BON and that, to the best of his knowledge, the said BON has been settled upon & within the boundaries of the Old mine concession. Witness, further, says that he does not know of the said BON having any other claim to land in this state.

Joseph THOMPSON, Jr. claiming 250 arpents of land in Record Book B, pg. 320 & following see Book No. 6, pg. 430, where this claim is entered for 640 acres. The Board are unanimously of opinion that 250 arpents of land ought to be confirmed to the said Joseph THOMPSON, Jr., or to his legal representatives, according to the concession and List A, on which claimant is No. 95. (Dec. No. 202)

Dewalt BOLLINGER claiming 300 arpents of land, in Record Book B, pgs. 320 & following, see Book No. 6, pg. 436 where this claim is entered for 640 acres. The Board are unanimously of opinion that 300 arpents of land ought to be confirmed to the said Dewalt BOLLINGER, or to his legal representatives, according to the concession and List A, on which claimant is No. 48. For concession, see Joseph THOMPSON, Jr. claim, Decision No. 202. (Dec. No. 203)

John BOLLINGER, son of John, claiming 250 arpents of land, Record Book B, pgs. 320 & following, see No. 6, pg. 439 where this claim is entered for 640 acres. The Board are unanimously of opinion that 250 arpents of land ought to be confirmed to the said John BOLLINGER, son of John, or to his legal representatives, according to the concession, and List A, on which claimant is No. 105. For concession, see Joseph THOMPSON Jr., claim, Dec. No. 202. (Dec. No. 204)

Alexander SUMMERS claiming 250 arpents of land, Record Book B, pgs. 320 & following, see Book No. 6, pg. 443 where this claim is entered for 640 acres. The Board are unanimously of opinion that 250 arpents of land ought to be confirmed to the said Alexander SUMMERS, or to his legal representatives, according to the concession and List A, on which claimant is No. 49. For concession, see Joseph THOMPSON, Jr.'s claim, Dec. No. 202. (Dec. No.205)

John GUETHING claiming 500 arpents of land, Record Book B, pgs. 320 & following, see Book No. 6, pg. 444 where this claim is entered for 585 arpents. The Board are unanimously of opinion that 500 arpents of land ought to be confirmed to the said John GUETHING, or to his legal representatives, according to the concession & List A, on which claimant is No. 37. For concession, see Joseph THOMPSON, Jr.'s claim, decision No. 202. (Dec. No. 206)

Nicholas REVEILLE claiming 200 arpents of land, Record Book B, pgs. 320 & following, see Book No. 6, pg. 445. The Board are unanimously of opinion that 200 arpents of land ought to be confirmed to the said Nicholas REVEILLE, or to his legal representatives, according to the concession & List A, on which claimant is No. 115. For concession, see Joseph THOMPSON, Jr.'s claim, Dec. No. 202. (Dec. No. 207)

John DOUGHERTY claiming 300 arpents of land, Record Book B, pgs. 320 & following, see Book No. 6, pg. 446 where this claim is entered for 640 acres. The Board are unanimously of opinion that 300 arpents of land ought to be confirmed to the said John DOUGHERTY, or to his legal representatives, according to the concession and List A, on which claimant is No. 39. For concession, see Joseph THOMPSON, Jr.'s claim, decision No. 202. (Dec. No. 208)

James RAMSAY, Jr. claiming 400 arpents of land, Record Book B, pgs. 320 & following, see Book No. 6, pg. 448, where this claim is entered for 750 arpents. The Board are unanimously of opinion that 400 arpents of land ought to be granted to the said James RAMSAY, Jr., or to his legal representatives, according to the concession and List A, on which claimant is No. 36. For concession, see Joseph THOMPSON, Jr.'s claim, Decision No. 202. (Dec. No. 209)

Lemuel CHENEY claiming 100 arpents of land, Record Book B, pgs. 320 & following, see Book No. 6, pg. 450, where the same is entered for 640 acres. The Board are unanimously of opinion that 100 arpents of land ought to be confirmed to the said Lemuel CHENEY, or to his legal representatives, according to the concession and List A, on which claimant is No. 142. For concession, see Joseph THOMPSON, Jr.'s claim, decision No. 202. (Dec. No. 210)

Andrew RAMSAY, Jr. claiming 220 arpents of land, Record Book B, pgs. 320 & following, see Book No. 6, pg. 451, where this claim is entered for 750 arpents. The Board are unanimously of opinion that 220 arpents of land ought to be confirmed to the said Andrew RAMSAY, Jr., or to his legal representatives, according to the concession and List A, on which claimant is No. 123. For concession, see Joseph THOMPSON, Jr.'s claim, decision No. 202. (Dec. No. 211)

Joseph WORTHINGTON claiming 150 arpents of land, Record Book B, pgs. 320 & following, see Book No. 6, pg. 457, where this claim is entered for 640 acres. The Board are unanimously of opinion that 150 arpents of land ought to be confirmed to the said Joseph WORTHINGTON, or to his legal representatives, according to the concession and List A, on which claimant is No. 155. For concession, see Joseph THOMPSON, Jr.'s claim, Dec. No. 202. (Dec. No. 212)

Ebenezer HUBBLE claiming 250 arpents of land, Record Book B, pgs. 320 & following, see Book No. 6, pg. 458, where this claim is entered for 640 acres. The Board are unanimously of opinion that 250 arpents of land ought to be confirmed to the said Ebenezer HUBBLE, or to his legal representatives, according to the concession and List A, on which claimant is No. 51. For concession, see Joseph THOMPSON, Jr.'s claim, Dec. No. 202. (Dec. No. 213)

John HAND claiming 300 arpents of land, Record Book B, pgs. 320 & following, see Book No. 6, pg. 461, where this claim is entered for 640 acres. The Board are unanimously of opinion that 300 arpents of land ought to be confirmed to the said John HAND, or to his legal representatives, according to the concession, and List A, on which claimant is No. 70. For concession, see Joseph THOMPSON, Jr.'s claim dec. No. 202. (Dec. No. 214)

James COX claiming 300 arpents of land, Record Book B, pgs. 320 & following, see No. 6, pg. 462, where this claim is entered for 640 acres. The Board are unanimously of opinion that 300 arpents of land ought to be confirmed to the said James COX, or to his legal representatives, according to the concession and List A, on which claimant is No. 47. For concession, see Joseph THOMPSON, Jr.'s claim, Decision No. 202. (Dec. No. 215)

John PATTERSON claiming 400 arpents of land, Record Book B, pgs. 320 & following, see No. 6, pg. 463, where this claim is entered for 640 acres. The Board are unanimously of opinion that 400 arpents of land ought to be confirmed to the said John PATTERSON, or to his legal representatives, according to the concession and List A, on which claimant is No. 2. For concession, see Joseph THOMPSON, Jr.'s claim dec. No. 202. (Dec. No. 216)

Jephta CORNELIUS claiming 600 arpents of land, Record Book B, pgs. 320 & following, see Book No. 6, pg. 468, where this claim is entered for 640 acres. The Board are unanimously of opinion that 600 arpents of land ought to be confirmed to the said Jephta CORNELIUS, or to his legal representatives, according to the concession and List A, on which claimant is No. 11. For concession, see Joseph THOMPSON, Jr.'s claim, Dec. No. 202. (Dec. No. 217)

Enos RANDALL claiming 300 arpents of land, Record Book B, pgs. 320 & following, see Book No. 6, pg. 469, where this claim is entered for 640 acres. The Board are unanimously of opinion that 300 arpents of land ought to be confirmed to the said Enos RANDALL, or to his legal representatives, according to the concession & List A, on which claimant is No. 149. For concession, see Joseph THOMPSON, Jr.'s claim, decision No. 202. (Dec. No. 218)

Joseph NISWANGER, Jr. claiming 300 arpents of land, Record Book B, pgs. 320 & following, see Book No. 6, pg. 471, where this claim is entered for 640 acres. The Board are unanimously of opinion that 300 arpents of land ought to be confirmed to the said Joseph NISWANGER, Jr. or to his legal representatives, according to the concession and List A, on which claimant is No.103. For concession, see Joseph THOMPSON Jr.'s claim, dec. No. 202. (Dec. No. 219)

Samuel RANDALL, Jr. claiming 400 arpents of land, Record Book B, pgs. 320 & following, see Book No. 6, pg. 472, where this claim is entered for 640 acres. The Board are unanimously of opinion that 400 arpents of land ought to be confirmed to the said Samuel RANDALL, Jr., or to his legal representatives, according to the concession, and List A, on which claimant is No. 135. For concession, see Joseph THOMPSON, Jr.'s claim, Dec. No. 202. (Dec. No. 220)

Frederick BOLLINGER claiming 300 arpents of land, Record Book B, pgs. 320 & following, see Book No. 6, pg. 476, where this claim is entered for 640 acres. The Board are unanimously of opinion that 300 arpents of land ought to be confirmed to the said Frederick BOLLINGER, or to his legal representatives, according to the concession & list A, on which claimant is No. 101. For concession, see Joseph THOMPSON, Jr.'s claim, Dec. No. 202. (Dec. No. 221)

David BOLLINGER claiming 300 arpents of land, Record Book B, pgs. 320 & following, see Book No. 6, pg. 481, where this claim is entered for 640 acres. The Board are unanimously of opinion that 300 arpents of land ought to be confirmed to the said David BOLLINGER, or to his legal representatives, according to the concession & List A, on which claimant is No. 102. For concession, see Jos. THOMPSON, Jr.'s claim, Dec. No. 202. (Dec. No. 222)

Mathias BOLLINGER claiming 300 arpents of land, Record Book B, pgs. 320 & following, see Book No. 6, pg. 482, where this claim is entered for 640 acres. The Board are unanimously of opinion that 300 arpents of land ought to be confirmed to the said Mathias BOLLINGER, or to his legal representatives, according to the concession and List A, on which claimant is No. 160. For concession, see Joseph THOMPSON, Jr.'s claim, Dec. No. 202. (Dec. No. 223)

Conrad STOTLER claiming 200 arpents of land, Record Book B, pgs. 320 & following, see Book No. 6, pg. 484, where this claim is entered for 640 acres. The Board are unanimously of opinion that 200 arpents of land ought to be confirmed to the said Conrad STOTLER, or to his legal representatives, according to the concession, and List A, on which claimant is No. 164. For concession, see Jos. THOMPSON, Jr.'s claim, Dec. No. 202. (Dec. No. 224)

Valentine LORR claiming 300 arpents of land, Record Book B, pgs. 320 &

following, see Book No. 6, pg. 486, where this claim is entered for 640 acres. The Board are unanimously of opinion that 300 arpents of land ought to be confirmed to the said Valentine LORR, or to his legal representatives, according to the concession & List A, on which claimant is No. 110. For concession, see Jos. THOMPSON, Jr.'s claim, Dec. No. 202. (Dec. No. 225)

Benjamin HELDERBRAND claiming 300 arpents of land, Record Book B, pgs. 320 & following, see Book No. 6, pg. 402, where this claim ie entered for 640 acres. The Board are unanimously of opinion that 300 arpents of land ought to be confirmed to the said Benjamin HELDERBRAND, or to his legal representatives, according to the concession and List A, on which claimant is No. 111. For concession, see Joseph THOMPSON, Jr.'s claim, dec. No. 202. (Dec. No. 226)

David GREEN claiming 300 arpents of land, Record Book B, pgs. 320 & following, see Book No. 6, pg. 403, where this claim is entered for 347 acres, 53-1/2/100. The Board are unanimously of opinion that 300 arpents of land ought to be confirmed to the said David GREEN, or to his legal representatives, according to the concession, and List A, on which claimant is No. 81. For concession, see Jos. THOMPSON, Jr.'s claim, Dec. No. 202. (Dec. No. 227)

George HENDERSON claiming 300 arpents of land, Record Book B, pgs. 320 & following, see Book No. 6, pg. 495, where this claim is entered for same quantity. The Board are unanimously of opinion that 300 arpents of land ought to be confirmed to the said George HENDERSON, or to his legal representatives, according to the concession and List A, on which claimant is No. 82. For concession, see Jos. THOMPSON, Jr.'s claim, Dec. No. 202. (Dec. No. 228)

Alexander ANDREWS claiming 300 arpents of land, Record Book B, pgs. 320 & following, see Book No. 6, pg. 475, where this claim is entered for 640 acres. The Board are unanimously of opinion that 300 arpents of land ought to be confirmed to the said Alexander ANDREWS, or to his legal representatives, according to the concession & List A, on which claimant is No. 13. For concession, see above. (Dec. No. 229)

Solomon THORN claiming 600 arpents of land, Record Book B, pgs. 320 & following, see Minutes Book No. 6, pg. 494. The Board are unanimously of opinion that 600 arpents of land ought to be confirmed to the said Solomon THORN, or to his legal representatives, according to the concession and List A, on which claimant is No. 126. For concession, see above. (Dec. No. 230)
　　　Adjourned until tomorrow at 9 o'clock A.M.
　　　　The Board Met & Adjourned Oct. 24th, 1834
　　　　Saturday Oct. 25th, 1834 Board Met-All Comm'rs. Present

Elijah FORD claiming 200 arpents of land, Record Book B, pg. 409, see Book No. 6, pg. 454, where this claim is entered for 640 acres. The Board are unanimously of opinion that 200 arpents of land ought to be granted to the said Elijah FORD, or to his legal representatives. (Dec. No. 231)

Polly BOYD claiming 200 arpents of land, see Book No. 6, pg. 470, where this claim is entered for 640 acres. The Board are unanimously of opinion that 200 arpents of land ought to be granted to the said Polly BOYD, or to her legal representatives. (Dec. No. 232)
　　　Adjourned until Monday next at 9 o'clock A.M.
　　　　Monday Oct. 27th, 1834 Board Met - Two Comm'rs. Present
　　　Not being a full Board adjourned until 2 o'clock P.M.
　　　　　　2 O'Clock P.M.
　　　Not being a full Board Adjourned until tomorrow at 9 o'clock A.M.
　　　　Tuesday Oct. 28th, 1834 Board Met-All Comm'rs. Present

Alexander ANDREWS claiming 240 arpents of land, see Book No. 6, pg. 452, where this claim is entered for 640 acres. The Board are unanimously of opinion that 240 arpents of land ought to be confirmed to

the said Alexander ANDREWS, or to his legal representatives, according to the concession. (Dec. No. 233)
Adjourned until tomorrow at 9 o'clock A.M.
Wednesday Oct. 29th, 1834 Board Met-All Comm'rs. Present

In the case of Joseph FENWICK claiming 20,000 arpents of land, see Book No. 6,pg. 175. M.P. LEDUC, duly sworn, says that the concession and signature to the same, is in the proper handwriting of Z. TRUDEAU, who was, at the time, Lt. Governor of Upper Louisiana.

In the case of several claimants, who have produced List A, in support of their claims. M.P. LEDUC, duly sworn, says that the signature to the concession at the foot of said List A, is in the proper handwriting of Carlos Dehault DELASSUS.

James ROGERS, Sr. claiming 766 arpents of land, see Book No. 6, pg. 509. The Board are unanimously of opinion that 640 acres of land ought to be granted to the said James ROGERS, Sr., or to his legal representatives. (Dec. No. 234)

John BOLI claiming 260 arpents of land, see Book No. 6, pg. 506. The Board are unanimously of opinion that 260 arpents of land ought to be granted to the said John BOLI, or to his legal representatives. (Dec. No. 235)

Benjamin JAMES, claiming 690 arpents of land, see Book No. 6, pg. 531. The Board are unanimously of opinion that 690 arpents of land ought to be granted to the said Benjamin JAMES or to his legal representatives. (Dec. No. 236)

Rene DODIER claiming 800 arpents of land, see Book No. 6, pg. 527. The Board are unanimously of opinion that this claim ought to be confirmed to the said Rene DODIER, or to his legal representatives, according to the concession. (Dec. No. 237)

Frederick DIXON claiming 800 arpents of land, see Book No. 6, pg. 537. The Board are unanimously of opinion that this claim ought to be confirmed to the said Frederick DIXON, or to his legal representatives, according to the concession. (Dec. No. 238)
Adjourned until tomorrow at 9 o'clock A.M.
The Board Met & Adjourned Oct. 30th, at 9 A.M. & 2 P.M., and Oct. 31st at 9 A.M.
Friday Oct. 31st, 1834 Board Met (2 P.M.)-All Comm'rs. Present

Andrew HARRIS claiming 600 arpents of land, see Book No. 7, pg. 2. The Board are unanimously of opinion that this claim ought to be confirmed to the said Andrew HARRIS, or to his legal representatives, according to the concession. (Dec. No. 239)
Adjourned until tomorrow at 9 o'clock A.M.
Saturday Nov. 1st, 1834 Board Met-All Comm'rs. Present

Lewis MARTIN claiming 300 arpents of land, see Book No. 7, pg. 2. The Board are unanimously of opinion that this claim ought to be confirmed to the said Louis MARTIN, or to his legal representatives, according to the concession. (Dec. No. 240)

Baptiste LAURINS claiming 480 arpents of land, see Book No. 7, pg. 5. The Board are unanimously of opinion that this claim ought to be confirmed to the said Baptiste LAURINS, or to his legal representatives, according to the concession. (Dec. No. 241)

John MCNEAL claiming 640 acres of land, see Book No. 7, pg. 2. The Board are unanimously of opinion that 639 acres 3 quarters & 33 poles of land (it being the quantity claimed on record) ought to be granted to the said John MCNEAL, or to his legal representatives. (Dec. 242)

Carlos de VILEMONT claiming 2 leagues of land in front by 1 league in depth, situate Point Chicot, see Record Book F, pg. 1, BATE's Minutes, pg. 58, BATE's Decisions, pg. 24, produces a paper purporting to be an

original concession from the Baron de CARONDELET, Governor General of Louisiana dated 17th June, 1795. M.P. LEDUC, duly sworn, says that the signature to the concession is in the true handwriting of the said Baron de CARONDELET.
Adjourned until Monday next at 9 o'clock A.M.
The Board Met & Adjourned twice Nov. 3rd, 4th, 5th, 6th, 7th, 8th, 10th, 11th, 12th, 13th, 14th, 1834.
Saturday Nov. 15th, 1834 Board Met-All Comm'rs. Present

Joseph REED, Jr. claiming 640 acres of land, see Book No. 6, pg. 383. The Board are unanimously of opinion that 632 acres, 1 quarter & 20 poles of land (it being the quantity claimed on record) ought to be granted to the said Joseph REED, Jr., or to his legal representatives. (Dec. No. 243)

Thomas REED claiming 640 acres of land, see Book No. 6, pg. 212. The Board are unanimously of opinion that 638 acres 2 quarters & 7 poles of land (it being the quantity claimed on record) ought to be granted to the said Thomas REED, or to his legal representatives. (Dec. 244)

Francois HEBERT claiming 80 arpents of land, see Book No. 6, pg. 218. The Board are unanimously of opinion that this claim ought to be confirmed to the said Francois HEBERT, or to his legal representatives, according to the concession. (Dec. No. 245)

Alexis LOISE claiming 120 arpents of land, see Book No. 6, pg. 168. The Board are unanimously of opinion that this claim ought to be confirmed to the said Alexis LOISE, or to his legal representatives, according to the concession. (Dec. No. 246)

Charles GILL claiming 400 arpents of land, see Book No. 7, pg. 1. The Board are unanimously of opinion that this claim ought to be confirmed to the said Charles GILL, or to his legal representatives, according to the concession. (Dec. No. 247)
Adjourned until Monday next at 9 o'clock A.M.
Monday Nov. 17th, 1834 Board Met-All Comm'rs. Present

Jean CAMBAS claiming 40 arpents of land, see Book No. 6, pg. 519. The Board are unanimously of opinion that this claim is confirmed by the 1st Section of the Act of Congress of 1812. (Dec. No. 248)

Francois DUNEGAN claiming 800 arpents of land, see Book No. 6, pg. 89. The Board are unanimously of opinion that 750 arpents of land ought to be confirmed to the said Francois DUNEGAN, or to his legal representatives, according to the survey. (Dec. No. 249)

Louis LORIMIER claiming 1,000 arpents of land, see Book No. 6, pg. 128. The Board cannot take cognizance of this claim, there being no concession, warrant, or order of survey.

Louis COYTEUX claiming 400 arpents of land, see Book No. 6, pg. 210. The Board cannot take cognizance of this claim, there being no registery of the same.

_____ COYTEUX claiming 400 arpents of alnd, see Book No. 7, pg. 5. The Board cannot take cognizance of this claim, there being no registery of the same.

Hipolite BOLON claiming 720 arpents of land, see Book No. 6, pg. 260. The Board are unanimously of opinion that this claim ought not to be granted, the said Hipolite BOLON having had a concession of record in Book A, pg. 94, in the Recorder's Office. (2d) No. 4)

Louis DESNOYERS claiming 800 arpents of land, see Book No. 6, pg. 242. The Board are unanimously of opinion that this claim ought not to be granted, the said Louis DESNOYERS having had a concession, recorded in Book C, pg. 438 in the Recorder's Office. ((2d) No. 5)

Regis LOISEL claiming 64,800 arpents of land, see Book No. 6, pg. 222.

The Board do not take cognizance of this claim, it being out of their jurisdiction. ((2d) No. 6)

Walter FENWICK claiming 10,000 arpents of land, see Book No. 6, pg. 251. The Board are unanimously of opinion that the above claim is destitute of merit, an alteration being apparent in the original concession on file, as noted in the translation of said concession. The word Huit (eight) in the original having been altered into (cannot read) Rescinded, see pg. 244)

Leo FENWICK claiming 500 arpents of land, see Book No. 6, pg. 254. The Board are unanimously of opinion that this claim is destitute of merit, an alteration being apparent in the original concession on file, as noted in the translation of said concession; the name of river a Brazee having been altered into that of river a laviande, alias St. Come, thus increasing the distance, for location of grant several miles. ((2d) No. 7)

Ezekiel FENWICK claiming 500 arpents of land, see Book No. 6, pg. 339. The Board are unanimously of opinion that this claim is destitute of merit, an alteration being apparent in the original concession on file, as noted in the translation of said concession. The name of river a Brazeau having been altered into that of river a LaViande, alias St. Come, thus increasing the distance, for location of grant, several miles. ((2d) No. 8)

James FENWICK claiming 500 arpents of land, see Book No. 6, pg. 252. The Board are unanimously of opinion that this claim is destitute of merit, an alteration being apparent in the original concession on file, as noted in the translation of said concession. The name of river a Brazeau having been altered into that of river a La Viande, alias St. Come, thus increasing the distance, for location of grant, several miles. ((2d No. 9)
    Adjourned until tomorrow at 9 o'clock A.M.
    Tuesday Nov. 18th, 1834 Board Met-All Comm'rs. Present

Philip BOLLINGER claiming 640 acres of land, see Book No. 6, pg. 438. The Board are unanimously of opinion that this claim ought not to be granted, the said Philip BOLLINGER having had a confirmation under a concession, see Comm'rs. Certificate No. 227. ((2d No. 10)

Daniel BOLLINGER claiming 640 acres of land, see Book No. 6, pg. 435. The Board are unanimously of opinion that this claim ought not to be granted, the said Daniel BOLLINGER having had a confirmation under a concession, see Comm'rs. Certificate No. 316. ((2d No. 11)

Paul DEGUIRE claiming 640 acres of land, see Book No. 6, pg. 410. The Board are unanimously of opinion that this ought not to be granted, the said Paul DEGUIRE having had a confirmation under a concession, see Minutes Book No. 4, pg. 515. ((2d No. 12)

Thomas RING claiming 500 arpents of land, see Book No. 6, pg. 405. The Board are unanimously of opinion that this claim ought not to be granted, the said Thomas RING having had 640 acres granted to him. See BATE's Decisions, pg. 82. ((2d No. 13)

Joseph THOMPSON, Sr. claiming 640 acres of land, see Book No. 6, pg. 432. The Board are unanimously of opinion that this claim ought not to be granted, the said Joseph THOMPSON, Sr. having had a confirmation under a concession, see Comm'rs. Certificate No. 240. ((2d No.14)

Nicolas LACHANCE claiming 640 acres of land, see Book No. 6, pg. 400. The Board are unanimously of opinion that this claim ought not to be granted, the said Nicolas LACHANCE having had a confirmation under a concession, see Minutes Book No. 4, pg. 515. ((2d) No. 15)

John HELDERBRAND claiming 200 arpents of land, see Book No. 6, pg. 501. The Board are unanimously of opinion that this claim ought not to be granted. The Said John HELDERBRAND having had a grant of 400 arpents, see Comm'rs. Certificate No. 359. ((2d) No. 16)

John PAYETT claiming 464 arpents of land, see Book No. 6, pg. 501.
The Board are unanimously of opinion that this claim ought to be
granted, the said John PAYETT having had a confirmation by the former
Board, see Comm'rs. Certificate No. 168. ((2d) No. 17)

John SCOTT claiming 800 arpents of land, see Book No. 6, pg. 534.
The Board are unanimously of opinion that this claim ought not to be
granted, the said John SCOTT having had a confirmation under a concession, see Comm'rs. Certificate No. 120. ((2d) No. 18)

Edward MATHEWS claiming 640 acres of land, see Book No. 6, pg. 480.
The Board are unanimously of opinion that this claim ought not to be
granted, the said Edward MATHEWS having had a confirmation. See
Comm'rs. Certificate No. 1038, BATE's Decisions, pg. 18, for extension to 640 acres. ((2d) No. 19)

Pierre ROY claiming 40 arpents of land, see Book No. 6, pg. 543. This
claim is already confirmed, see HUNT's proceedings, Book No. 3, pg. 81.
((2d) No. 20)

David STRICKLAND claiming 1,247 arpents 62 perches of land, Book No.
6, pg. 371. The Board are unanimously of opinion that (there being
no concession found on record, for land granted to claimant, as al-
ledged by a witness) 640 acres of land ought to be granted to the said
David STRICKLAND, or to his legal representatives. (Dec. No. 250)
        Adjourned until tomorrow at 9 o'clock A.M.
            Wednesday Nov. 19th, 1834 Board Met- F.R. CONWAY, Present

In the case of Baptiste DUCHOUQUET claiming under a special location,
etc., see Book No. 6, pg. 220. M.P. LEDUC, duly sworn, says that
(cannot read) to the plat in the surveyor's office, the (cannot read)
of land claimed in this case, is 3,840 acres, the tract being 2 miles
in front on the right bank of the Missouri, by 3 miles in depth.
        Adjourned until tomorrow at 9 o'clock A.M.
            The Board Met & Adjourned Nov. 20th, 21st, 22nd, 24th, 25th,
        26th, 27th, 1834.
            Friday Nov. 28th, 1834 Board Met-F.R. CONWAY, Present

In the case of William DUNN claiming 7,056 arpents of land, see Book
No. 6, pg. 8, the following testimony was taken by A.G. HARRISON,
then Comm'r.
Jeremiah GROSHON, being duly sworn, says that a man by the name of
DUNN, worked a while for RUTGERS on a mill, some time in the year
1804. That said DUNN did not finish said mill, nor was there any mill
built on said land claimed by RUTGERS, as above stated. That said DUNN
had no family as far as witness knew. That where said DUNN worked, was
on the waters of Dardenne, for RUTGERS. That said mill as under taken
or commenced, was on RUTGERs' claim and not on DUNN's. That witness
did the hewing for said mill, before DUNN came. That witness knew
nothing about the contract between DUNN & RUTGERS in relation to said
mill.
William CRAIG, being duly sworn, says that on what is commonly called
DUNN's claim, there was no mill built, nor attempted to be built.
That on RUTGERS claim, on the Dardenne, one DUNN did commence building
a mill for RUTGERS, but did not finish it, but that it was afterwards
finished by some one else. That DUNN's claim was on Cuivre, on which
there was no improvement made by DUNN or by RUTGERS.
        Adjourned until tomorrow at 9 o'clock A.M.
            The Board Met & Adjourned Sat. Nov. 29th, 1834.
            Monday Dec. 1st, 1834 Board Met-All Comm'rs. Present

William DUNN claiming 7,056 arpents of land, see Book No. 6, pg. 8.
The Board are unanimously of opinion that this claim ought to be confirmed to the said William DUNN, or to his legal representatives,
according to the concession. (Dec. No. 251)

Roger CAGLE claiming 650 arpents of land, see Book No. 7, pg. 34. The
Board are unanimously of opinion that 650 arpents of land ought to be
granted to the said Roger CAGLE, or to his legal representatives. (252)
        The Board Adjourned until tomorrow 9 o'clock A.M.

Tuesday Dec. 2nd, 1834 Board Met-All Comm'rs. Present

In the case of Carlos de VILEMONT claiming 2 leagues in front by 1
league in depth, see Book No. 7, pg. 62.
Pierre CHOUTEAU, Sr., duly sworn, says that the signature to the concession is in the true handwriting of the Baron de CARONDELET. That
he, CHOUTEAU, first became acquainted with said de VILEMONT in the
year 1776 or 1777. That he knows that said de VILEMONT was Captain
in the Spanish service. That in 1802, witness going down to New Orleans in a boat, stopped at the mouth of Arkansas river, having some
business to transact with Joseph BOUGY, Sr., who lived at the Post of
Arkansas. That said BOUGY told witness that de VILEMONT (who was
BOUGY's on in law) had made a settlement at Point Chicot. That witness, on his return in the summer of 1803, stopped at Point Chicot
expecting to meet with de VILEMONT, but de VILEMONT had gone down to
New Orleans. That his agent, living at point Chicot, gave witness
vegetables of all kinds, poultry, etc. That the improvements as
witness saw consisted of log houses and gardens, he did not see any
fields that might have been further in the interview (cannot read)
the houses, as well as he can recollect had the appearance of having
been built 2 or 3 years before. Witness, further, says that he was
well acquainted with Joseph BOUGY, Sr., who testified in this case
before Recorder BATES. That said BOUGY, Sr., was a man of good
character, known by everybody for a man of veracity and who could be
relied upon. Witness, further, says that the de VILEMONT family resided on said place, but does not know how long.

In the case of Silvestre LABBADIE claiming a special location, see
Book No. 6, pg. 224. Peter CHOUTEAU, Sr., being duly sworn, says
that the distance from the hills which come to the water's edge, at
the foot of Isle aux Boeufs, to the hills (coming also to the water's
edge) at the head of said Island, is from 90 to 100 arpents.
    Adjourned until tomorrow at 9 o'clock A.M.
        Wednesday Dec. 3rd, 1834 Board Met-All Comm'rs. Present

Carlos de VILEMONT claiming 2 leagues in front by 1 league in depth,
s-e No. 7, pg. 62 & 70. The Board are unanimously of opinion that
this claim ought to be confirmed to the said Carlos de VILEMONT, or
to his legal representatives, according to the concession, reference
being had to the opinion of the Honorable Joseph S. SMITH, Judge of
the Superior Court, for the District of East Florida, as afterwards
sustained by the decision of the Supreme Court of the United States,
in the case of Arredondo & others against the United States. (No. 253)
    The Board Adjourned until tomorrow at 10 o'clock A.M.
        Dec. 4th, 1834 Board Met-All Comm'rs. Present

Silvestre LABBADIE claiming a special location, see Book No. 6, pg.
224. The Board are unanimously of opinion that this claim ought to
be confirmed to the said Silvestre LABBADIE, or to his legal representatives, according to the concession. (Dec. No. 254)

Baptiste DUCHOUQUETTE claiming a special location, see Book No. 6,
pg. 220. The Board remark that the 4,000 arpents on the left bank of
the Missouri, asked for in the petition, have been confirmed by Recorder BATES. See BATE's decisions, pg. 59. The Board are unanimously
of opinion that the remainder of this claim, lying on the right bank
of the Missouri ought to be confirmed to the said Baptiste DUCHOUQUETTE,
or to his legal representatives, according to the concession. (No. 255)

Whereas one of the members of the Board of Comm'rs. of private land
claims in the state of Missouri, having necessarily to be absent for
a few weeks, in conveying to Washington City the report of the Board
of Comm'rs. which they are required to make to the Commissioner of the
General land office at the commencement of each session of Congress,
and whereas by reason of the absence of such Commissioner and there
being many individuals who are competent to give testimony in support
of claims before the Board for final settlement, but who, in consequence of either their advanced age or the great distance at which they
live from St. Louis, their testimony cannot be procured. Therefore, be

it resolved, that during the absence of the Commissioner aforesaid, that Frederick R. CONWAY, and James H. RELFE, or either of the, be and they are hereby authorised & empowered to attend at such places as they, or either of them may think most convenient to claimants, as well as witnesses, and take and receive such testimony as may be produced to them or either of them in support of any claim or claims that may come before the Board for their adjudication in pursuance of the Acts of Congress regulating and defining their duties as Commissioners aforesaid.
          Adjourned until tomorrow at 9 o'clock A.M.
               Fryday Dec. 5th, 1834 Board Met-All Comm'rs. Present

                         RECORDER'S OFFICE
St. Louis, Missouri, December 5th, 1834
          Received of the Commissioners on private land claims in Missouri 2 tin boxes or cannisters and one package envelopped in paper and sealed & directed to the Honorable Elijah HAYWARD, Commissioner of the General Land Office, which boxes or cannisters contain the report of said Commissioners on 113 claims numbered from 143 to 255, both inclusive, with the transcript of each claim and the translations of the concessions, etc. All which I promise to deliver to the Commissioner of the General Land Office at Washington City in a reasonable time from the date above written.   James S. MAYFIELD
Note: The words "and one package" interlined.
Attest
          The Board adjourned until tomorrow at 9 o'clock A.M.
               The Board Met & Adjourned Dec. 6th, 8th & 9th, 1834.
               Wednesday Dec. 10th, 1834 Board Met-F.R. CONWAY, Present

Francois MOTIER by his legal representatives claiming 800 arpents of land, see Book C, pg. 343, Book No. 5, pg. 365, produces a paper purporting to be an original concession from Carlos Dehault DELASSUS, dated 19th April, 1800. M.P.LEDUC, duly sworn, says that the signature to the concession is in the proper handwriting of the said Carlos Dehault DELASSUS.

(Cannot read this entry because of an ink blot)
          Adjourned until tomorrow at 9 o'clock A.M.
               The Board Met & Adjourned Dec. 11th, 12th, 13th,15th, 16th, 17th, 18th, 19th, 20th, &22nd, 1834.
               Tuesday Dec. 23rd, 1834 Board Met-F.R. CONWAY, Present

Jerusha EDMONDSON by her legal representatives, claiming 250 arpents of land, see Book F, pg. 100, BATE's Minutes pg. 30, BATE's decisions, pg. 28. The following testimony was taken before L.F. LINN, Esqr., then one of the Commissioners. John STEWART, aged about 74 years being duly sworn as the law directs, deposeth and saith that he was well acquainted with the said Jerutha EDMONDSON. That her & one Michael RABER lived together on the tract of land claimed, in the year 1803, and raised a crop thereon in 1804. That there was a dwelling house, kitchen, smoke house & other small houses on the land. That there was several acres of land cleared, a good garden and some fruit trees planted. The houses had the appearance of being one or two years old. That he surveyed the land twice, once for said Michael RABER & afterwards for the said claimant, she claiming this land as hers. That said RABER & her had some difficulty or quarrels and both told this witness they were not married to each other. He heard Jerusha say that the said RABER should not stay on the place, and he knows they separated and continued apart.   John STEWART
Sworn to & subscribed before me this 9th day of May, 1833.
L.F. LINN, Comm'r.
Israel MCGREADY aged about 55, being duly sworn as the law directs, deposeth & saith that he was well acquainted with Jerusha EDMONDSON. That she lived with one Michael RABER on the tract of land claimed. That she remained on the tract claimed after said RABER left her, and claimed the same as hers. That he has heard both, the said Jerusha & Michael RABER say they were not married, and that the tract of land claimed has been inhabited and cultivated ever since.   Israel MCGREADY
Sworn to & subscribed before me this 9th day of May, 1833.
L.F. LINN, Comm'r.

Henry PINKLEY aged about 50 years, being duly sworn as the law directs, deposeth & saith that he was well acquainted with Jerusha EDMONDSON. That she lived on the tract of land claimed, and that one Michael RABER lived with her. That he was about to settle at or near the place claimed and the said Jerusha forbid him to do so, as she said the land was hers. That the land or place was always called the place of Jerusha EDMONDSON by the people at large who spoke of the same, and that Michael RABER claimed land on the other side of the creek about one half mile from this place claimed. That he had his buildings on the place he claimed, and not on the place claimed by Jerusha, on which this witness wanted to settle. Henry PINKLEY
Sworn to & subscribed before me this 9th day of May, 1833.
L.F. LINN, Comm'r.
John STEWART, being further sworn, deposeth and saith that he knows that after the said Jerusha EDMONDSON & Michael RABER parted that the said RABER went off and left the said Jerusha in possession of the place, where she continued claiming the same as her property for some time, and the only way she could be got from the place was by the purchase of her right & interest, which both Jerusha & THOMPSON told him, the said THOMPSON being the purchaser of her right. John STEWART
Sworn to & subscribed before me this 10th day of May, 1833.
L.F. LINN, Comm'r.
Uriah HULL aged about 56 years, being duly sworn as the law directs, deposeth and saith that he knows the tract of land claimed that the said Jerusha EDMONDSON & Michael RABER lived together on the same in the year 1804. That some time afterwards, say 5 or 6 years, they separated, and the said RABER went off leaving the said Jerusha in the possession of the place. That she remained on the place for some time after RABER left her, & this witness understood she had sold her right to one or both of the Messrs. THOMPSONS. This witness has since understood they were not married. Uriah HULL
Sworn to & subscribed before me this 10th day of May, 1833.
L.F. LINN, Comm'r.
Benjamin HORINE, being duly sworn, deposeth & saith that he knew Jerusha EDMONDSON. That her & one Michael RABER lived together on the tract of land claimed in the year 1804, and perhaps before that time. That the land was some times called RABER's, some times her's and that the said RABER went off & left her in the possession of the place, where she remained for some time afterwards.
Benjamin HORINE
Sworn to & subscribed before me this 11th day of May, 1833.
L.F. LINN, Comm'r.
The following testimony was taken before F.R. CONWAY, Esqr.
John STEWART, being duly sworn, deposeth & saith that he has once before deposed before L.F. LINN, one of the Comm'rs., and wishes to amend the said deposition by adding the following facts: That the last of July or the first of August, 1804, he, said STEWART, was on or at the place claimed by said EDMONDSON, and that there were several acres of land cleared and a good crop of corn growing, and that the said Jerusha EDMONDSON then told him that her & Michael RABER were not married, and that all the property belonged to her, and that the said RABER, some time afterwards, told him that he & the said Jerusha were not married & were not man & wife. And, further, states that there were more than one house, a very comfortable cabbin for a dwelling house, on the last of July or first of August, 1804, and that she always claimed the premises afterwards until she sold. John STEWART
Sworn to & subscribed the 5th July, 1833. F.R. CONWAY, Comm'r.
     Adjourned until tomorrow at 9 o'clock A.M.
          The Board Met & Adjourned Dec. 24th, 25th, 26th, 27th, 29th, 30th, 31st, 1834, Jan. 1st, 2nd, 3rd, 5th, 6th, 7th, 8th, 9th, 10th, 12th, 13th, 14th, 15th, 16th, 17th, 19th, 20th, 21st, 22nd, 23rd, 24th, 26th, 1835.
          Tuesday Jan. 27th, 1835 Board Met-F.R. CONWAY, Present

Benjamin GARDINER by his heirs claiming 750 arpents of land, settlement right. See Record Book B, pg. 255, Minutes No. 5, pg. 426.
Jonathan BRYAN, being duly sworn, says that (cannot read) that he came to this country in the year 1800 in company with Benjamin GARDINER in whose right the above tract is claimed. That he knows the tract

claimed. That GARDINER built a cabbin on the place, in the latter
part of the year 1801, and moved in it that year. That in the year
1802, he raised a crop of corn on the place, he thinks about 5 acres.
The said GARDINER had no wife, his sister lived with & kept house for
him. Witness thinks he continued to occupy the place about one year.
He was in the habit of hunting & trapping. That he made three trips
of from 4 to 6 months each. He started on a 4th trip & was taken
sick & returned to the settlement & died in the year 1805. That said
GARDINER raised a crop of corn at Samuel WATKINS in the year 1801
about 5 miles from the place claimed.
      Adjourned until tomorrow at 9 o'clock A.M.
            The Board Met & Adjourned Jan. 28th, 29th, 30th, 31st,
      Feb. 2nd, 3rd, 4th, 5th, 6th, 7th, 9th, 10th, 11th, 12th, 13th,
      14th, 16th, 17th, 18th, 19th, 20th, 21st, 23rd, 24th, 25th, 26th,
      27th, 28th, Mar. 2nd, 3rd, 4th, 5th, 6th, & 7th, 1835.
            Monday March 9th, 1835 Board Met-F.R. CONWAY, Present

Benjamin GARDINER claiming 750 arpents of land, see pg. 93 of this
Book. Isaac DARST, being duly sworn, says that he is in the 46th
year of his age. That he was well acquainted with Benjamin GARDINER,
and knows the tract of land claimed. That GARDINER was the neighbour
to witness's father. That he settled the place claimed in the year
1802, and in that year, or in 1803, he, the witness, saw corn growing
on the said place. That GARDINER had at that time some 8 or 10 acres
enclosed & about half of that quantity under cultivation in corn.
GARDINER went out frequently on hunting expeditions. The last trip
that he made, he was taken sick while out, was brought into the settlement and died in a short time thereafter. Witness was present at
his death. He was a single man & appeared to be above the age of 21
years at the time he settled the place. Was a man of good reputation
in the country & well thought of by his neighbours.
      Adjourned until tomorrow at 9 o'clock A.M.
            The Board Met & Adjourned Mar. 10th, 11th, 12th, 13th, 14th,
      16th, 17th, 18th, 19th, 20th, 21st, 23rd, 25th, 1835.
            Thursday Mar. 26th, 1835 Board Met-F.R. CONWAY, Present

William RAMSAY, Sr. claiming 748 arpents & 8 perches of land situate
on RAMSAY's Creek, see Record Book B, pg. 239, Minutes Book No. 5, pg.
485.
The following testimony was taken in Clarksville on the 24th May, 1833
by A.G. HARRISON, then Comm'r.
Ralph H. FLAUHERTY, duly sworn, says that before the change of government took place, William RAMSAY was living on a tract of land on a
creek called Ramsay's Creek, named after the claimant. That said
RAMSAY's family while living there having been taken sick, he left
there and came down to witness father's house, where he stayed some
time. Witness says he does not recollect certainly the precise time
that RAMSAY was in possession of said land, but is sure that it was before the change of government took place. At the time that RAMSAY was
in possession of said land, he, the said RAMSAY, had a wife & five
children.
James BURNS, being duly sworn upon his oath, says that at least two
years before the change of the Spanish to the American Government, he
knew the said William RAMSAY cultivated a farm on what is now called
Bryan's creek. That on said creek there is a spring called Ramsay's
lick, named after the said William RAMSAY, which is on the above mentioned tract of land. That said RAMSAY had house, stables, & a field
of at least 20 acres, was in the habit of selling corn to the neigh-
borhood. That one BRYAN also lived on said creek near the above from
whom said creek took its name. That said creek is frequently mistaken
for another creek higher up called Ramsay's creek, where said RAMSAY
made a hunting camp & split some rails. That at the time of the possession aforesaid, said RAMSAY had a wife & several. That said land
is about 10 or 11 miles below Clarksville & about 22 miles above where
said Bryan's Creek empties into King's lake. That witness has frequently been at RAMSAY's house and would be able now to identify the place.
Joseph MCCOY, being duly sworn upon his oath, says that before the
change of the Spanish Government he was quite a youth & lived near where
Troy now stands, about 16 or 17 miles from the land above described.

That does not recollect ever to have been at RAMSAY's before the change of government, but often heard it said that the said RAMSAY lived at a place on the creek, now called Bryan's Creek near a Mr. BRYAN, who gave name thereto, that he has since frequently seen the improvements of said RAMSAY. He, further, says that he has frequently heard many persons call said creek Ramsay's creek through mistake, as he, supposes from the circumstance of Ramsay's lick being thereon. That Ramsay's creek is higher up where he understands RAMSAY made a hunting camp & split some rails. That Bryan's Creek is even yet, frequently, mistaken for Ramsay's creek. That he has often been called on to know if he could show certain land on Ramsay's creek (so expressed by the inquirer) that in the course of conversation, he would ascertain it was on Bryan's creek (now so called) & that he knew the places well. That Bryan's creek was by them called Ramsay's creek, but he always called another creek higher up Ramsay's creek.

Jonathan BRYANT, being duly sworn, says that in 1801 at what is called Ramsay's lick on Bryant Creek, Wm. RAMSAY, Sr. settled & cultivated a tract of land made some improvements, as building a cabbin, clearing ground, etc. & left there in company with witness, on account of sickness in 1801, and left a man by the name of MCHUGH to take care of his place.

Joshua STOGSDILL, being duly sworn, says that William RAMSAY, Sr. lived on & cultivated a place on Bryant's creek in 1801 or 1802. That witness lived with said RAMSAY on said place about 8 weeks at the time sd RAMSAY's family was sick, and left there a few days before the death of his wife. That said RAMSAY had about 15 or 20 acres of corn, stables & other buildings on said place.

George GIRTY claiming 640 acres of land, see Book No. 6, pg. 216. The following testimony was taken by A.G. HARRISON, one of the Comm'rs., in May, 1833.

Ralph H. FLAUHERTY, duly sworn, says that in the winter of 1799 & 1800, he saw George GIRTY in a habitation about a mile W. of St. Charles, that at that time he had a house & a field of about five or six acres improved around the house. He had also fruit trees planted on the place, and that he knew the said GIRTY to live there two or three years after the time he first saw him. He had been living there some time before witness saw him, judging from the appearance of the improvements. That said GIRTY, at the time witness first saw him, had a wife & five children (cannot read).

Peter TEAGUE, being duly sworn, says that to the best of his knowledge in the month of June, 1798, George GIRTY was living on a place about a half mile or three quarters of a mile N.W. of St. Charles. That he had a small improvement on it with some fruit trees & that he lived there about 3, 4, or 5 years cultivating the same, and had a wife & 5 children.

Noel John PRIEUR, being duly sworn, says that George GIRTY lived and cultivated a piece of land near a mile West of St. Charles, That said GIRTY had a field of about four acres, a house & an orchard on said place. That the time spoken of was before the change of government, & that he remained there three or four years. That he left said place, as witness now recollects, before the change of government & moved on Dardenne where he made an improvement. That said GIRTY told witness he had concession for his place on Dardenne. That said place of GIRTY is in what are now the commons of St. Charles. (No. 259)

Adjourned until tomorrow at 9 o'clock A.M.

Friday Mar. 27th, 1835 Board Met-F.R. CONWAY, Present

John ROURKE by his legal representatives claiming 756 arpents of land on Dardenn, see Record Book D, pg. 256, Comm'rs. Minutes Book No. 5, pg. 490, BATE's minutes, pg. 131. The following testimony was taken in May, 1833 by A.G. HARRISON, Esqr. then one of the Comm'rs.

Ralph H. FLAUHERTY, being duly sworn, says that he knew John ROURKE. That said ROURKE lived on Dardenne on a tract of land, which he claimed just below Arend RUTGERS. That at the time witness saw him living there, he had a cabbin & a small field around it in cultivation. That to the best of witness's recollection, the time that ROURKE lived there was about the last of the reign of the Spanish Government, or shortly after. (No. 260)

Joseph CHARTRAN by his legal representatives claiming 998 arpents
of land on river Charette, see Record Book B, pg. 219, Minutes Book
No. 1, pg. 440, No. 3, pg. 54, No. 4, pg. 218.
John Mary CARDINAL, being duly sworn, says that he knew said CHARTRAN.
That he made a settlement & improvement on a tract of land on the upper part of Charette. That he had an orchard on the same tract. That
said improvement, settlement, etc. were made under the spanish government about five or six years before the change of government. That he
was married at the time mentioned and that he cultivated it about a
dozen of years.
Charles REILLE, being duly sworn, says that having heard read the testimony of Jean Mary CARDINAL as above, that he testifies to the same
facts in every particular as above, except that witness thinks said
CHARTRAN cultivated said land about fourteen years.

Benjamin GARDINER claiming 750 arpents of land, see pgs. 93 & 101 of
this book. The following testimony was taken in June, 1833 by
A.G. HARRISON, Esqr., then one of the Comm'rs.
Joshua STOGSDILL, duly sworn, says that in the year 1802 or 1803, he
passed by a place in Darst's bottom on the Missouri river, which
Benjamin GARDINER was then improving. That said GARDINER had on said
place a cabbin & several acres of cleared ground and was living there
at the time mentioned. That said GARDINER left there shortly afterwards, and David BRYANT succeeded him in 1803, and cultivated and improved the same place.
John MANLY, being duly sworn, says that witness came to the country
in the spring of 1804, and that Benjamin GARDINER had settled the fall
before in DART's bottom on the Missouri. That he had a small piece
of cleared ground on said place & a cabbin. That he resided there
about two years & that said GARDINER told witness that he had sold his
claim on that place to David BRYANT.
        Adjourned until tomorrow at 9 o'clock A.M.
            Saturday Mar. 28th, 1835 Board Met-F.R. CONWAY, Present
        No Evidence being offered, adjourned until Monday next, at 9
        o'clock A.M.
            Monday Mar. 30th, 1835 Board Met-F.R. CONWAY, Present

Mordicai BELL by the legal representatives of Amos STODDARD claiming
350 arpents of land situate in the grand Prairie near St. Louis, see
Record Book A, pg. 93 & D pg. 361, Minutes Book No. 5, pg. 359, produces a paper purporting to be an original concession from
Carlos Dehault DELASSUS, dated Jan. 29th, 1800. Also, deed of conveyance from Mordicai BELL to James MACKAY & deed from said MACKAY
to Amos STODDARD. M.P. LEDUC, being duly sworn, says that the signature to the concession is in the proper handwriting of
Charles Dehault DELASSUS. Witness, further, says that in the year
1804, he went in company with Major STODDARD & several other gentle-
men, to the place now claimed, and from that time the said place has
always been called STODDARD's mound. (No. 261)
        Adjourned until tomorrow at 9 o'clock A.M.
            Tuesday Mar. 31st, 1835 Board Met-F.R. CONWAY, Present

Antoine LARMARCHE by his legal representatives claiming 750 arpents
of land on Larmarche creek, in St. Charles County, see Minutes Book
No. 5, pg. 444, Book B, pg. 264. The following testimony was taken
in May, 1833 by A.G. HARRISON, then one of the Comm'rs.
Pierre PALARDI, being duly sworn, says that he knew Antoine LAMARCHE.
That said LAMARCHE lived on & cultivated a tract of land on LAMARCHE's
run, under the Spanish Government, 4 or 5 years. That at that time,
he had a wife & four children. The land spoken of is in St. Charles
county.
Etienne QUENELLE, being duly sworn, says that having heard read the
evidence of Pierre PALARDI as above, that he knows the same facts and
makes the same his own.
Ralph H. FLAUHERTY, being duly sworn, says that he knew the said
LAMARCHE. That he lived on a tract of land, on a creek now called
LAMARCHE's creek, under the Spanish Government as witness believes.
That he had a house & a field on said land. That he had a wife &
several children at that time. (No. 262)

Samuel HOLMES by his legal representatives claiming 840 arpents of land on Perruque, see Minutes Book No. 5, pg. 432, Book B, pg. 262. The following testimony was taken in the month of May, 1833 by A.G. HARRISON, Esqr., then one of the Comm'rs.
Etienne QUENELLE, being duly sworn, says that he knew Samuel HOLMES lived on Perruque from his first recollection, and that he, witness, is 47 or 48 years old. That HOLMES lived there a long time before the change of government. That he had a wife & children.
Joseph CHARTRAN, being duly sworn, says that he knew said HOLMES. That he lived on Perruque on the North side of it, under the Spanish Government, that he stayed there a long time after the change of government. That he had a wife & 3 children. He had an orchard on the place & was well fixed.
Daniel KEATHLY, being duly sworn, says that in the month of November, 1803, he met with Samuel HOLMES, who was then a stranger to witness. That said HOLMES requested witness to show him some land to settle on. That witness took him on Perruque, somewhere about half a mile from the mouth to the head of it. That Samuel HOLMES commenced immediately to make improvements on the land, which witness had showed to him, built a cabbin on the same & cultivated it. (No. 263)

Pierre PALARDIE claiming 1,000 arpents of land on the Dardenne, see Record Book D, pg. 340, Minutes Book No. 5, pg. 482. The following testimony was taken in May, 1833 by A.G. HARRISON, Esqr., then one of the Comm'rs.
Gabriel LATREILLE, being duly sworn, says that he is well acquainted with said tract of land. That it is situated at the mouth of the Dardenne. That Palardie cut hay on said land to feed his cattle with the intention of establishing himself on said place.
    Adjourned until tomorrow at 9 o'clock A.M.
        Wednesday April 1st, 1835 Board Met-F.R. CONWAY, Present

David MCKINNEY claiming 590 arpents of land, see Book No. 6, pg. 223. The following testimony was taken in May, 1833 by A.G. HARRISON, Esqr., then one of the Comm'rs.
Joshua STOGSDILL, being duly sworn, says that David MCKINNEY cultivated, improved & inhabited a tract of land on the North bank of the Missouri, adjoining to Alexander MCKINNEY's confirmed claim on the West. In the year 1802, he had some buildings & an orchard on the place spoken of. Witness thinks the first improvement was made in the year 1802. (No. 175 pg. 38)

William MEEK by his legal representatives claiming 500 arpents of land on the Missouri, see Record Book B, pg. 198. The following testimony was taken in June, 1833 by A.G. HARRISON, then one of the Comm'rs.
John MANLY, being duly sworn, says that he came with said MEEK to this country. That said MEEK settled on a place on the Missouri about four miles above the mouth of Charette. That witness in the spring of 1804, assisted said MEEK in clearing ground & putting in a crop on said place. That a short time after putting in the crop, said MEEK took sick & died.
    Adjourned until tomorrow at 9 o'clock A.M.
        Thursday April 2nd, 1835 Board Met-F.R. CONWAY, Present

In the case of John BURK claiming 1,000 arpents of land, see Book No. 6, pg. 428, claimant produces a paper purporting to be the original concession from Carlos Dehault DELASSUS, dated 20th November, 1799. M.P. LEDUC, duly sworn, says that the signature to the recommendation is in the proper handwriting of Francois VALLE, Commandant of St. Genevieve and the signature to the concession is in the proper handwriting of Carlos Dehault DELASSUS, Lt. Governor. (Dec. No. 199 pg.44)

In the case of Adrien LANGLOIS claiming 1,500 arpents of land, see Book No. 6, pg. 258, claimant produces a paper purporting to be the original concession from Carlos Dehault DELASSUS dated 24th October, 1799. M.P. LEDUC, duly sworn, says that the signature to the concession is in the proper handwriting of the said Carlos Dehault DELASSUS.
    Adjourned until tomorrow at 9 o'clock A.M.

Friday April 3rd, 1835 Board Met-F.R. CONWAY, Present

Vincent LAFOIX & Nicolas PLANTE by their legal representatives,
claiming 640 arpents of land situate on Fourche a Duclos, see Record
Book C, pg. 72, BATE's Decisions, pg. 65 (224 arpents confirmed)
produces a paper purporting to be an original concession from
Zenon TRUDEAU, dated 13th November, 1797. Also, a plat & certificate
of survey for 224 arpents said survey was made on the 15th December
1797 & certified on the 17th of May, 1798 by Antoine SOULARD.
M.P. LEDUC, du-y sworn, says that the signature to the concession
is in the proper handwriting of Zenon TRUDEAU, then Lt. Governor, and
that the signature to the plat & certificate of survey is in the proper handwriting of Antoine SOULARD, Sur. General. The following testimony was taken on the 4th of May, 1833 in St. Genevieve County, by
L.F. LINN, Esqr., then one of the Comm'rs.
John Bste. VALLE aged about 72 years, being first duly sworn as the
law directs, deposeth & saith that he was well acquainted with the
said Nicholas LAPLANTE, alias PLANTE, and Vincent LAFOIX, and that
they & each of them, at the date of the grant, were citizens & residents in, the then province of Upper Louisiana, and that they continued to be citizens and residents till the time of their death. That
he said that the grantees made sugar on the tract at an early day.
J. Bste. VALLE   (No. 264)
Sworn to & subscribed before me this 4th day of May, 1833.
L.F. LINN, Comm'r.
        Adjourned until tomorrow at 9 o'clock A.M.
        Saturday April 4th, 1835 Board Met-F.R. CONWAY, Present

John STEWART claiming 640 acres of land situate in the District of
St. Genevieve, see Record Book C, pg. 510. The following testimony
was taken by F.R. CONWAY, Esqr., at Potosi.
John MCNEAL, deposeth & saith that in the fall season of the year
1802, he staid all night with John STEWART and that said STEWART had
raised his cabbins some short time before, one was a very large cabbin of good logs much larger and higher than any built in those times,
and the other a small cabbin of the usual size, adjoining the large
one, witness eat supper & breakfast with said STEWART. In the summer
of 1803, witness passed a night & eat supper & breakfast with the sd
STEWART and then saw a field of good looking corn growing near claimant's
house & witness told claimant that he had a large field of good corn,
the said STEWART replied that it might not be as large as I thought and
asked me how much I supposed there was. I told him, I supposed there
was 8 or 10 acres. He said No, there is but 6 or 7 acres in corn.
Witness, further, says that Moses AUSTIN told him that the said
John STEWART (cannot read) to land from the Spanish Government (cannot
read) of said AUSTIN followers. Said STEWART (cannot read)was under
good fence and witness thinks from the part he saw, that it was generally made of split rails. The said STEWART claims 640 acres of land &
witness never heard that he claimed any other land for his head or improvement right. (No. 265)   John T. MCNEAL
Sworn to & subscribed before me at Potosi, Missouri, this 8th day of
May, 1834.   F.R. CONWAY
        Adjourned until Monday next at 9 o'clock A.M.
        Monday April 6th, 1835 Board Met-F.R. CONWAY, Present

William BATES claiming 640 acres of land situate in the District of
St. Genevieve, see Record Book B, pg. 350, Comm'rs. Minutes No. 3, pg.
127, No. 4, pg. 336. The following testimony was taken at Potosi by
F.R. CONWAY, Esqr.
John T. MCNEAL, being duly sworn, deposeth & saith that, in the month
of February, 1804, William BATES and he, witness, went in company to
where said BATES had made & laid the foundation of a house, there were
some trees cut round, some brush heaps made, and his name marked on a
tree near the spring & dated 1803. That said BATES claimed the same as
his head right as one of Moses AUSTIN's followers as will fully appear
on the original records of land titles under the Spanish Government.
That said William BATES claims 640 acres & witness never heard of his
tilling or claiming any other land as his head right. J.T. MCNEAL
Sworn to & subscribed before me at Potosi, Missouri, this 8th day of
May, 1834.   F.R. CONWAY

Francis THIBAUT by his legal representatives claiming 500 arpents of
land situate in the District of St. Genevieve, see Record Book D, pg.
339. The following testimony was taken at Potosi by F.R. CONWAY,
Esqr.
John MCNEAL, being duly sworn, deposeth & saith that, in the years
1803 & 1804, Francis THIBAUT was an inhabitant of the now county of
Washington, State of Missouri, That said THIBAUT had a family & Cultivated several acres of land and claimed the same as a donation from
the Spanish government for 640 acres, and witness never heard of his
claiming any other lands as his improvement or head right.
                                        John T. MCNEAL
Sworn to & subscribed before me at Potosi, Missouri, this 8th day of
May, 1834.   F.R. CONWAY
     Adjourned until tomorrow at 9 o'clock A.M.
            Tuesday April 7th, 1835 Board Met-F.R. CONWAY, Present

Charles MCDORMET claiming 640 acres of land situate in the District
of St. Genevieve, see Record Book B, pg. 245. The following testimony
was taken at Potosi by F.R. CONWAY, Esqr.
John MCNEAL, being duly sworn, deposeth & saith that, in the month of
February, 1804, he, in company with William BATES, passed by what
(Cannot read) Charles MCDORMET's improvement (cannot read) the foundation of a house, some trees (cannot read) brush heaps made, rails
split and a promising prospect for an improvement. That the said
MCDORMET has ever since claimed the same as his head right as one of
Moses AUSTIN's followers as will fully appear by having reference to
the Spanish records and claimant's name was marked on a sugar tree
near the spring dated 1803. Witness never heard of his claiming any
other land under his head or improvement right. John T. MCNEAL
Sworn to & subscribed before me this 8th day of May, 1834 at Potosi,
Missouri.   F.R. CONWAY

Jacob WISE claiming 37-1/2 acres of land situate at mine a Breton, see
Record Book B, pg. 242, Book No. 5, pg. 535. The following testimony
was taken at Potosi by F.R. CONWAY on the 8th day of May, 1834.
John MCNEAL, being duly sworn, deposeth & saith that, in the years
1803 & 1804, Jacob WISE, then a labouring man, was a resident in this
country and had some acres of land in cultivation, with a comfortable
cabbin thereon. The whole inclosed with a good fence, that said WISE
claimed the same as a donation from the Spanish Government and witness
never heard of his claiming any other headright than the one above mentioned, which will fully appear from the records of surveys recorded
in the year 1806 in St. Louis.   John MCNEAL   (No. 267)
Sworn to & subscribed before me at Potosi, Washington County, this
8th day of May, 1834.   F.R. CONWAY
     Adjourned until tomorrow at 9 o'clock A.M.
            Wednesday April 8th, 1835 Board Met-F.R. CONWAY, Present

Zachariah DOWTY claiming 450 arpents of land situate on Hubble's Creek,
see Record Book E, pg. 239, Minutes No. 3, pg. 281, Book No. 5, pg. 12.
The following testimony was taken in June, 1834 by J.H. RELFE,
Comm'r.
Alexander SUMMERS, being sworn, states that he was well acquainted
with the widow and family of Zachariah DOWTY, formerly of the District
of Cape Girardeau in the province of Upper Louisiana, now state of
Missouri. He first became acquainted with them in the forepart of the
year 1800 or 1801. They then resided on the waters of Hubbles Creek in
said District and cultivated & inhabited land on the same. They built
a cabbin in the same year, that is in 1800 or 1801, which year this
affiant is not positive. They continued to live on said place up to
the death of the said widow.   Alexander SUMMERS   (No. 268)
Sworn to & subscribed before me this 30th June, 1834. James H. RELFE

William EASOM claiming 800 arpents of land on the St. Francis river,
see Record Book F, pg. 98, BATEs Minutes, pg. 42, BATE's decisions,
pg. 31. The following testimony was taken in Madison County by
J.H. RELFE, Comm'r.
Samuel CAMPBELL, deposeth & saith that he saw William EASOM in possession of a tract of land on the waters of the St. Francis river in the
spring of the year 1803. He had a house in which he lived, a kitchen
and about four acres of corn in cultivation, which said CAMPBELL saw

gathered the following fall by said William EASOM. Saml. CAMPBELL (280)
Sworn to & subscribed before me this 28th of June, 1834. James H. RELFE
          Adjourned until tomorrow at 9 o'clock A.M.
               Thursday April 9th, 1835 Board Met-F.R. CONWAY, Present

Jane LOGAN claiming 800 arpents of land, see Record Book F, pg. 13,
BATE's Decisions, pg. 99. The following testimony was taken in Cape
Girardeau County, by J.H. RELFE, Comm'r.
John RODNEY, being sworn, states that he was well acquainted with
Jenny or Jane LOGAN, he first became acquainted with her in 1802, she
then lived in what was called the district of Cape Girardeau. She
lived on Hubbles creek in said District, where she cultivated & inhabited a place. This was in the years 1802, 3 & 4, and she continued
to live on the same for a number of years afterwards. She had then
children living with her at the time mentioned. There were also fruit
trees on said place, which is distant about nine miles south of the
present town of Jackson. (No. 269)   John RODNEY
Sworn to & subscribed before me this 30th June, 1834. J.H. RELFE

Benjamin TENNEL claiming 800 arpents of land on Castor Creek, Cape
Girardeau, see Record Book F, pg. 139, BATE's Decisions, pg. 104.
The following testimony was taken in the County of Washington by
J.H. RELFE, Comm'r.
Samuel CAMPBELL, deposeth & Saith that he was at the residence of
Benjamin TENNEL on the waters of the St. Francois river in the then
District of St. Genevieve, Province of Upper Louisiana, now County of
Madison, State of Missouri, in the fall of the year 1803, he found
him residing in a comfortable cabbin, in the course of the winter, he
cleared upwards of ten acres of ground & in the spring of the year,
1804, planted said ten acres of ground in corn. Deponent, further,
says from the time it was taken possession of in the year 1803, until
the present time, and it has been regularly possessed & occupied by
said Benjamin TENNEL and his legal representatives ever since. Deponent, further, says he was present at New Bourbon when Benjamin TENNEL
obtained permission from the Commandant to settle on the Domain and
never knew TENNEL to claim any other land in this country. (No. 270)
                                             Saml. CAMPBELL
Sworn to & subscribed before me this 3rd July, 1834. James H. RELFE

Julius WICKERS claiming 600 arpents of land on the St. Francis river,
see Record Book F, pg. 142, BATES decisions, pg. 105. The following
testimony was taken in Washington County by J.H. RELFE, Comm'r.
Personally appeared Samuel CAMPBELL, who deposeth & Saith that he was
well acquainted with Julius WICKERS in the year 1803. That early in
the summer of said year, he raised a cabbin and cultivated & cleared
a turnip patch and the following winter, he extended his clearing &
planted & cultivated a field of at least 8 acres of corn in the spring
of the year 1804, and said Julius WICKERS & his legal representatives
has continued to occupy said tract of land ever since. Deponent, further says he lived in the neighbourhood of WICKERS for twenty four
years, was present when the Commandant at New Bourbon gave said WICKERS
permission to settle on the public domain and never knew of said
claimant making claim to any other land. (271)   Saml. CAMPBELL
Sworn to & subscribed before me this 3rd July, 1834. James H. RELFE
          Adjourned until tomorrow at 9 o'clock A.M.
               Friday April 10th, 1835 Board Met-F.R. CONWAY, Present

Louis MILHOMME claiming 620 acres of land in mine a Breton, see Record
Book B, pg. 249. The following testimony was taken in Washington
County by J.H. RELFE, Comm'r.
Personally appeared John T. MCNEAL, who deposeth & saith that he was
well acquainted with Louis MILHOMME, a labouring man with a family,
who resided in Mine a Breton, who had a house and cultivated a garden
and other improvements in the year eighteen hundred & two, three and
four, and he never knew him to claim other lands.   John T. MCNEAL
Sworn to & subscribed before me this 21st June, 1834. James H. RELFE

Louis LACROIX claiming 701 arpents of land in Mine a Breton, see Minutes
Books No. 1, pg. 379 & No. 5, pg. 534, B, pg. 225. The following testimony was taken in Washington County by J.H. RELFE, Comm'r.

Personally appeared John T. MCNEAL, who deposeth & saith that he was
well acquainted with Louis LACROIX, who lived in a house and cultivated corn at some distance from the village, his field was on Big River.
At that early day it was necessary to the safety of the inhabitants
to live in the villages to secure them from the attacks of savages &
for this convenience of working the mines. This deponent never knew
LACROIX to claim any other lands.   John T. MCNEAL
Sworn to & subscribed before me this 21st of June, 1834. J.H. RELFE

Alexander COLMAN claiming 800 arpents of land at the Old Mine, see
Record Book F, pg. 91, BATE's Minutes, pg. 18. (No. 333, pg. 227)

Peter BOYER claiming 639-3/4 acres of land on Old Mine Creek, see
Record Book C, pg. 509, Minutes No. 5, pg. 567, BATES Decisions, pg.
75.
                Saturday April 11th, 1835 Board Met-F.R. CONWAY, Present

Jacques VINCENT by his legal representatives Jean Elie THOLOZAN,
claiming 10,000 arpents of land situate on Black water, Arkansas Territory, see Record Book.F, pg. 138, BATE's Minutes, pg. 26, BATE's
decisions, pg. 30.
                St. Louis - Commissioners Office
                     December 1st, 1812
Jean Elie THOLOZAN claiming ten thousand arpens of land on Black water river, North fork of White River.
Claimant being duly sworn, declares that he conceives the testimony
of Antoine JANIS to be very material to him in support of his claim,
and that the extreme old age of the said JANIS together with a severe
indisposition with which said witness is at this time afflicted under
it impossible to remove him from St. Genevieve, where he now is to
this place. Thereupon, the said claimant is permitted to cause the
deposition of said Antoine JANIS to be taken de Bene esse by some
justice of the peace within the district of St. Genevieve, and certified forwith to this office, together with this order.
Attest, Frederick BATES
     In pursuance of the within order, I, Michael AMOUREUX, a Justice
of the peace in and for the St. Genevieve Township, in the District
of St. Genevieve, have taken de Bene esse the deposition of
Antoine JANIS, as within the said order directed & have annexed to
this order the said deposition. At. St. Genevieve this 6th day of
December, 1812.   M. AMOUREUX
Translation: District of St. Genevieve, Territory of Missouri. In
the County of St. Genevieve on the sixth day of the month of December of the year one thousand eight hundred & twelve, before me,
Michael AMOUREUX, one of the Justices of the Peace for said County,
by virtue of the Honorable Frederick BATES, Comm'r..of the United
States for the land claims in the said Territory, the said order being
dated St. Louis the first of December, inst. and annexed to these presents personally appeared Mr. Antoine JANIS, residing on the Black Water River, District of New Madrid, who after having sworn on the Holy
Evangelist to say the truth, has been summoned at the request of
Jean Elie THOLOZAN to declare what he knew concerning the settlement
of a concession of land originally claimed by Jacques VINCENT, Surgeon
Major in the service of Spain, to which summon the said Antoine JANIS
answered that he well knew the lands claimed by the said
Jacques VINCENT on the Black Water river, having visited them several
times. That he has perfect knowledge that the said Jacques VINCENT
had caused to be made, in the year 1795 & 1796, sundry clearings on
the said lands, had built cabins and planted fruit trees, and that he
knew that one Charles LOGAN was inhabiting & cultivating one part of
the said lands. And, further, this deponent saith not. In testimony
whereof the said Antoine JANIS has signed this, his present deposition,
at St. Genevieve, this 6th(Day) of December, 1812.
                (Signed) Antoine JANIS
Sworn to and subscribed before me, Michael AMOUREUX, a Justice of the
Peace in and for the Township of St. Genevieve aforesaid, date above.
                M. AMOUREUX, J.P.
I certify the above translation of Antoine JANIS's deposition to be
truly translated from the original filed in this office.
                Julius de MUN, T.B.
     Adjourned until Monday next at 9 o'clock A.M.

The Board Met & Adjourned April 13th, 14th, 15th, 16th,
17th, 18th, 20th, 21st, & 22nd, & 23rd, 1835
Friday, April 23rd, 1835 Board Met-F.R. CONWAY, Present
James F. RELFE

John Bste. VALLE claiming twenty thousand arpents of land situated
in the District of St. Genevieve, by virtue of a concession from
Zenon TRUDEAU, herewith filed, produces the testimony of
Bartholomew ST. GEMME, aged about sixty years, who being duly sworn,
deposeth & saith that he was well acquainted with Zenon TRUDEAU. That
he was Lt. Gov. of Upper Louisiana in the year 1797 at the date of
the concession in this case. He, further, says that he is acquainted
with the handwriting of the said Zenon TRUDEAU. That he has often seen
him write, and that the signature to the said concession is in the proper handwriting of the said Zenon TRUDEAU. This witness, further, says
that he well knows the said John Bste. VALLE, the claimant. That he
was long before the date of the Grant, and at the date of the Grant, a
citizen and resident of the then province of Upper Louisiana, and that
he has continued a citizen and residenter ever since, and the said
VALLE at the date of the grant was the father of a family, large and
numerous. That he had a large quantity of slaves, and a verry large
stock of horses, cattle and other animals. That his family and connections were large and respectable that he acted as the Commandant of
the Post, and was held in high estimation and repute by the Spanish
government.   Bartholomew ST. GEMME
Sworn to & subscribed the 22nd April, 1835 before James H. RELFE, Co.
see Book E, pg. 199.

Martin FENWICK claiming five hundred arpents of land under concession
from Zenon TRUDEAU, herewith filed, dated 10th June, 1797. Record D,
pg. 44, Minutes Book 5, pg. 422, (cannot read) one of the Comm'rs.
at St. Genevieve on the 22nd April, 1835 Bartholomew ST. GEMME, aged
about sixty years, who being duly sworn, deposeth & saith that he was
well acquainted with Zenon TRUDEAU and he was Lt. Gov. in upper Louisiana in the year 1797, he further says that the signature to the said
concession is in the proper handwriting of the said Zenon TRUDEAU.
That he has often seen him write. Witness, further, says that he knew
the claimant and he was the son of Joseph FENWICK. That there was a
large and respectable family of them, and that the claimant at the
date of the grant was a citizen and residenter of the province of Upper
Louisiana and continued so untill long after the change of government.
                       Bartholomew ST. GEMME
Sworn to & subscribed this 22nd April, 1835. James H. RELFE, Comm'r.

Louis OUBOUCHON claiming 800 arpents of land on waters of Big River,
District of St. Genevieve under concession from C.D. DELASSUS, dated
10th January, 1800, see Record Book C, folio 195, Minutes No. 1, folio
360. The following testimony was taken before L.F. LINN, Comm'r..on
7th May, 1833. John T. MCNEAL of lawfull age, being first duly sworn
as the law directs, states that he well knows James HEWIT and that he
held his claim under some Frenchman, but the name he does not recollect.
The above claim lies on the waters of Big River, Belleview Washington
County, HEWITT occupied the above land in the year 1804 in April as
well as this deponent recollects and raised a crop of corn thereon that
year. HEWITT resided on said land until the year 1813 or 1814, when he
died, and his family have continued to reside on said land ever since.
HEWITT left a wife and several children.   John T. MCNEALL
(No. 272)
L.F. LINN, Comm'r.
John STEWART, being first duly sworn in the above case, states that
on the 18th February in the year 1806, at the instance of James HEWITT
he surveyed a spanish concession granted to Louis OUBUCHON for 800 arpents lying in the Belleview Settlement now in Washington County. He
states the above survey to be butted and bounded as follows, to wit,
beginning at a white oak on a line of William DAVIS's grant thence
south 63 W 40 acres crossing hazle creek to a branch of Big river to a
spanish oak, thence N 27 W 20 acres crossing hazel creek to a spanish
oak, then S 63 E 40 acres to a Hickory, thence S 27 E 20 to the beginning including his improvement, all which will fully appear by reference
to the plat in the Recorders Office St. Louis. This deponent, further,

states that he was legally appointed and authorised to make the survey aforesaid and when he made the same James HEWITT was living on the land. The family of said HEWITT still live upon said tract of land. James HEWITT handed him the original concession to make the survey from and this deponent returned the same with the plat of survey to the proper offices in accordance with his duty as surveyor, as to the concession being for 800 arpents, this deponent is not quite certain, but supposes so in as much as he surveyed out under the OUBUCHON concession 800 arpents. (272) John STEWART
Sworn to and subscribed May 7, 1833 L.F. LINN, Comm'r.

In the case of Curtis MORRIS, see pg. 23 of this book. The following testimony was taken before James H. RELFE, Comm'r.
State of Missouri
County of Washington Personally appeared before James H. RELFE, Comm'r. for the final adjustment of land claims in the state of Missouri, John T. MCNEAL, who testifyes and says in (cannot read) heretofore taken on the claim of Curtis MORRIS to land in the County aforesaid. He wishes to be understood when having said that Robert REED or Mr. REED went into the lot or field or turnip patch, and brought in some turnips of which he, deponent, partook that said REED brought the turnips from the hole where they had been put for preservation through the winter, that the turnips had been gathered from the piece of ground in which they were buried, and there still was to be seen at that time in February or March eighteen hundred and four turnips growing in said inclosure, which had all the appearances and I have no hesitation in saying had been raised from cultivation the fall previous on the said piece of ground, and which said land has continued in the possession and cultivation of the said Curtis MORRIS and his representatives to this day.   John T. MCNEAL
Sworn to & subscribed this 9th January, 1835. James H. RELFE, Comm'r.

In the case of James BROWN, see No. 6, pg. 369. The following testimony was taken before James H. RELFE, Comm'r.
State of Missouri, County of Washington
Personally appeared before James H. RELFE, one of the Comm'rs. for the adjustment of private land claims in Missouri, William DAVIS, Sr., who deposeth and says that in the fall of the year 1809, witness with James BROWN and others, were on Black river hunting land when James BROWN informed witness that, he, said BROWN had been employed by Joseph BEAR Or BARR, to build a cabbin on a tract of land in Belleview held by said BARR as assignee of CORDES, and after having built the cabbin, he moved into it, and kept possession of the land untill it was confirmed to BARR, believing he had as much right as BARR had to it and that while (cannot read) that he knows it to be the same land which has been confirmed to the legal representatives of CORDES, who are now in possession of the same, one King now living in the cabbin which BROWN informed witness he built.   William (X) DAVIS, Sr.
                                                                his mark
Sworn to this 18th December, 1835. James H. RELFE, Comm'r.

In the Case of Martin THOMAS, see No. 6, fol. 440. Joseph NISWANGER, Jr. states that he is the son of Joseph NISWANGER, Sr. That he and his father moved to the province of upper Louisiana, now state of Missouri in seventeen hundred and niety nine where he has resided ever since. He is the same person, who gave a deposition before Mr. Commissioner LINN in relation to Martin THOMAS's unconfirmed land claim. That he, this affiant, never gave testimony before any previous Board, but he has heard his father, Joseph NISWANGER, Sr. state that he was a witness in said claim before one of the previous Boards and this affiant has no doubt of the fact.   Joseph NISWANGER, JR.
Sworn to and subscribed before me, James H. RELFE, Comm'r. Apr. 6th, 1835.

In the case of James SUMMERS claiming 250 acres of land on White Water, District of Cape Girardeau, see Minutes 5, pg. 499 E, pg. 28. The following testimony was taken, Elijah DAUGHERTY being sworn, states that he has known the said James SUMMERS ever since the year 1800, the said James then resided in the District of Cape Girardeau, where he has continued to live ever since. This affiant has seen the said James cultivating land and improving the same under the Spanish Government about the years 1801-1802-1803 and 1804 in the said District of Cape Girardeau, and knows of his cultivating land up to this time June, 1833. Deponent does not know (cannot read)

Elijah (X) DAUGHERTY
his mark

The following testimony in relation to the claim of James SUMMERS, was taken before James H. RELFE, Comm'r.
State of Missouri, County of Cape Girardeau
James Summers claiming two hundred and fifty acres of land in the late District of Cape Girardeau by virtue of inhabitation and cultivation prior to and on the 10th day of March, 1804 and ever since, produces the permission to settle and refers to the records of the former Board of Commissioners for those facts, and for as much evidence as was then taken and filed and the said claimant, also, produces the following witnesses, First Ithamer HUBBLE, who being duly sworn as the law directs, deposeth and saith that he is aged about seventy three years, that he is well acquainted with the claimant, James SUMMERS, that he has known him ever since the year 1799. That in the year the said James SUMMERS moved to and settled in the District of Cape Girardeau, where he has resided ever since, that he was a Farmer and cultivator of the soil, but this affiant does not know from his own knowledge that the said James had a grant. The said James when he first came to this country was a young man, without a family.

Ithamer (X) HUBBLE
his mark

Sworn to and subscribed before me this 6th of April, 1835.
James H. RELFE, Comm'r.

In the case of Edward MATHEWS, (see attest Min. 6, pg. 479). The following testimony was taken before James H. RELFE, one of the Comm'rs.
Elizabeth SMITH, widow of Joseph SMITH, being sworn states that she moved to and settled in Mathews Prairie, province of Upper Louisiana in May, 1804. At that time she became acquainted with the MATHEWS, who lived in said prairie. There was two of them by the name of Edward, the son Edward MATHEWS, Jr. cultivated an (cannot read) adjoining his Father's (cannot read) to live untill the time (cannot read). This affiant acknowledges that Edward MATHEWS, Sr. had land confirmed him but never knew that Edward MATHEWS, Jr. ever had any. This affiant has always lived a near neighbour to the MATHEWS from the time she came to the country until their death.
Sworn to & subscribed this 10th April, 1835.   Elizabeth (X) SMITH
James H. RELFE, Comm'r.   her mark
Extended testimony in relation to the claim of Edward MATHEWS.
Daniel STRINGER, being sworn, states that he was well acquainted with the MATHEWS in Mathew Prairie, province of Upper Louisiana, now State of Missouri in Spanish times and afterwards. There was two of them by the name of Edward, one the Father, the other the son. Edward, Jr. had an improvement in cultivation seperate and distinct from his father in Spanish times. This affiant always understood that Edward MATHEWS, Sr. had land confirmed to him, and that he sold it to one GRAY. He never knew of Edward MATHEWS, Jr. ever having any land confirmed to him. This affiant has lived with both of said MATHEWS and was well acquainted with them up to the time of their deaths.

Daniel STRINGER

Sworn to and subscribed this 10th April, 1835.
James H. RELFE, Comm'r.

In the case of Silas FLETCHER (see Mins. 5, pg. 425 & E. pg. 271/
The following testimony was taken before James H. RELFE, one of the Comm'rs., Catharine GRIFFEY, formerly Catharine FINLEY, states that her husband Charles FINELY, was in the military expedition to New Madrid in the then province of upper Louisiana, now State of Missouri, under the Spanish Government, that some time previous to that year, she cannot state, she and her husband moved to and settled in the District of New Madrid in said province, there was a contest between PEROUX (cannot read) and LORIMIER, the (cannot read) who is given name she (cannot read) Silas lived on what was called the big (cannot read) near MATHEWS prairie in said Province. He and his family lived there

in a little cabbin, she cannot recollect as to the ballance of his
improvement.   Catherine (X) GRIFFEY
Sworn to and subscribed on this ··· her mark
9th April, 1835. James H. RELFE
        Adjourned until tomorrow morning 9 o'clock A.M.
            The Board Met & Adjourned Sat. Apr. 25th, 1835.
            Monday April 27th, 1835 Board Met- James H. RELFE, Present

In the claim of James WILBOURN, see Minutes Book 6, pg. 450. The
following testimony was taken before James H. RELFE, Comm'r. in Scott
County. Bridget LANE, widow, stated that she moved to and settled in
the District of New Madrid, then Province of Upper Louisiana, now
State of Missouri, about three years before the Americans took possession of said province (cannot read) . The same winter or next spring
the said James WILBOURN made a settlement and improvement in Tywappity
Bottom in said province. He built a verry good little cabin made a
garden and planted seed, which he brought from Georgia with him. This
affiant recollects he sowed some sower dock and she scolded him for it.
He had a smart little strip in cultivation. He had a wife and one
child, said WILBOURN has lived in the country ever since.
                                    Bridget (X) LANE
Sworn to and subscribed this 9th April, 1835.   her mark
James F. RELFE, Comm'r.

In the claim of Malachi JONES by his legal representative,
Nicholas SCHRAUM, see Book B, pg. 311, Minutes No. 5, pg. 437. The
following testimony taken before James H. RELFE, Comm'r. in Scott
County. Thomas FLETCHER, being sworn, states that he came to the province of upper Louisiana in the year eighteen hundred and three, in that
year, he passed up the Mississippi River and recollects passing Shrum or
SHUMS point on said river, about ten or twelve miles above the mouth of
the Ohio river in said province. There was an improvement on the point
which he was told belonged to Nicholas SHURM or SHRUM. There was a cabin on said place and some three or four acres cultivated in corn at the
time in 1803. The place is still called Shums Point. This affiant recollects seeing and conversing with the said SHUM at the time mentioned
and hearing him brag of what a fine place his was on the said point.
                                Thomas FLETCHER
Also, Bridget LANE states that she married and settled in the Province
of Upper Louisiana about three years before the Americans took possession of the country. She well recollects Nicholas SHUM or SCHRUM, a
resident of said province. She knew him early times in the country.
The year she cannot recollect, he used to pass his house in going to
his place on the Mississippi river (cannot read) called SHUMS or SHRUMS
Point, the place is still called SHUMS Point.   Bridget (X) LANE
                                                    her mark
Sworn to & subscribed this 9th April, 1835. James H. RELFE, Comm'r.

The following testimony was taken before Mr. Comm'r. LINN in relation
to the above claim, and now filed in this office.
                        June 11th, 1833
George HACKER, being sworn, says in the year 1802, he passed
Nicholas SHRUMS improvement on the Mississippi River, in the District
of New Madrid. He became acquainted with the said Nicholas in the year
1804. This affiant has understood that the said Nicholas purchased
his improvement from one Malachi JONES.   George HACKER
L.F. LINN, Comm'r.

In the claim of Agnew MASSEY, see Minutes No. 6, pg. 478. The following testimony was taken before James H. RELFE, Comm'r. in Scott County.
Elizabeth SMITH, states on his oath, that she moved to and settled in
Mathew Prairie, province of Upper Louisiana, now state of Missouri in
the year 1804. In the month of May that year, In the month of June that
year, she saw the improvement of Agnew MASSEY in said prairie, from the
appearance of the place she supposes it was in cultivation the year previous. The fence rails looked old as if they had been made several years
before. There appeared to be two or three acres under fence, which had
been in cultivation.   Elizabeth (X) SMITH
                                her mark

Also, Daniel STRINGER, being sworn, states that in eighteen hundred
and three he knew Agnew MASSEY in Mathews Prairie in the Province of
Upper Louisiana, in that year he was at the house of the said MASSEY
in said Prairie. He had a family. This affiant does not recollect
as to the size of his improvement. He lived in a log cabin, which
was the common kind of houses in the country at that time. He had in
that year ground inclosed. How much I cannot state.

                                              Daniel STRINGER
Sworn to and subscribed this 10th April, 1835.
                              James H. RELFE, Comm'r.
       Adjourned until tomorrow morning at 9 o'clock A.M.
          Tuesday April 28th, 1835 Board Met-Two Comm'rs. Present

William MCHUGH, Jr. by his legal representative, James MORRISON,
claiming 640 acres of land situate near Bryan's Creek, District of
St. Charles, see Record Book F, pg. 112- BATE's Minutes, pg. 78, BATE's
decisions, pg. 33.

John BALDWIN claiming 400 arpents of land situate in the District of
Cape Girardeau, see List B, in record Book B, pg. 324, Minutes Book
No. 5, pg. 391. The following testimony was taken before L.F. LINN,
Comm'r.
May 11th, 1833 State of Missouri, County of Cape Girardeau
James WILBORN, who is about 53 years old, has known the said
John BALDWIN between 35 & 40 years. The said John BALDWIN moved to
the District of Cape Girardeau in the fall of 1803 and settled in Tywappity bottom. He knows that the said John cleared land in the winter
of 1803 in said bottom and set out a nursery of fruit trees. He, also,
lived on the said land at the same time. The next season, 1804, he
planted (cannot read). The said John was a man with a family. He had
a wife and four children at the time he made the said improvement. The
said John BALDWIN has lived ever since, and now resides in the District
of Cape Girardeau.   James WILBORN
Sworn to & subscribed May 11th, 1833 before L.F. LINN, Comm'r.
       Adjourned until tomorrow at 9 o'clock A.M.
          Wednesday April 29th, 1835 Board Met-Two Comm'rs. Present

Charles SEXTON claiming 300 arpents of land situate District of Cape
Girardeau. For survey of 300 arpents, see Record Book B, pg. 303,
for list A, on which claimant is No. 48, see Book B, pg. 320, also,
Minutes Book No. 4, pgs. 61 & 293.
The following testimony was taken before L.F. LINN in October, 1833 by
L.F. LINN, Esqr. then one of the Comm'rs.
Daniel BRANT states that he was on the Indian Expedition to New Madrid
in the Province of Upper Louisiana in 1802, which was performed by order of the Spanish authorities at Cape Girardeau. Amongst others who
served a tour on said campaign, was Charles SEXTON, who acted as drum-
mer. He lived in Cape Girardeau District, and was absent from his
home something like six weeks. The men were promised land by the Spanish General and Commandant for serving on said expedition. (No. 276)
                                              Daniel (X) BRANT
Sworn to & subscribed 18th of October, 1833.
L.F. LINN, Comm'r.
       Adjourned until tomorrow at 9 o'clock A.M.
          The Board Met & Adjourned April 30th, 1835.
          Friday May 1st, 1835 Board Met-Two Comm'rs. Present

Nancy FERGUSON by her legal representatives claiming 300 arpents of
land situate in Tywappity, District of New Madrid, see Record Book E,
pg. 148, Book No. 4, pg. 97, No. 5, pg. 22. The following testimony
was taken before L.F. LINN, Comm'r. in June, 1833.
George HACKER, being sworn, says he is about 57 years old and that he
knew the said Nancy FERGUSON well. She came to the District of New
Madrid in the fall of 1802 and made an improvement in the winter of
that year. The next season, she planted corn and raised a crop on said
land, where she also resided. She had two children at that time. She
died in the year (cannot read) leaving her said two children,
Elizabeth (cannot read) & John JOHNSON, as her sole heirs & legal representatives. She inhabited and cultivated the said land in 1803 &
had a permission to settle from Don Henry PEYROUX, Commandant of New

Madrid.   George HACKER   Sworn to and subscribed this
11th day of June, 1833.
L.F. LINN, Comm'r.
        Adjourned until tomorrow at 9 o'clock A.M.
            The Board Met & Adjourned May 2nd, 4th, 5th, & 6th, 1835.
            Thursday May 7th, 1835 Board Met-Two Comm'rs. Present

In the case of Benjamin GARDINER claiming 700 arpents of land, see No.
7, pgs. 93, 101 & 109. William HAYS, being duly sworn, says he is
near 54 years of age. That he knows of Benjamin GARDINER, the claimant,
clearing several acres of land on the tract now claimed, in the year
1802, and in the same year said GARDINER had a potatoe patch, planted
& raised a crop of corn. Deponent thinks said GARDINER had in that
year about 7 acres under fence. This tract claimed is situated on the
North side of the Missouri river, between the said river and the land
of Daniel M. BOON & that of John LINSAY. Witness, further, says he
does not know of said GARDINER cultivating said land for more than one
year, he followed hunting, was a single man, and appeared at that time
to be upwards of 20 years of age. That in the year 1801, claimant lived
on the land of one Samuel WATKINS & there raised a crop of corn. His
sister, a widow, living at that time with him.

Urban ASHERBRAUNNER claiming 350 arpents & 95 perches of land, situate
on Castor creek, District of Cape Girardeau, see Book No. 3, pg. 479,
No. 4, pg. 238, Book B, pg. 294. The following testimony was taken
before James H. RELFE, Comm'r. in Cape Girardeau County.
William BOLLINGER, Sr. states that he moved to & settled in the District of Cape Girardeau in the year 1801. That he was well acquainted
with one Urban ASHERBRAUNNER then a resident of said District. This
affiant knows that the said ASHERBRAUNNER inhabited & cultivated a
piece of land on White Water in said District, in the year 1802. He
had a house built on said place in said year, some trees were deadened
on said place at the time mentioned, by said ASHERBRAUNNER. Said
ASHERBRAUNNER lived in said District upwards of 18 years. This improvement was made by the said Urban ASHERBRAUNNER, at the time mentioned, for his own use.   William (X) BOLLINGER
Sworn to & subscribed this 7th   his mark
of April, 1835. James H. RELFE, Comm'r.

            Friday May 8th, 1835 Board Met-Two Comm'rs. Present

Hugh CRISWELL by his heirs & legal representatives claiming 640 acres
of land situate on the waters of Randall's creek, Cape Girardeau
County, for list A, on which claimant is No. 139 for 100 arpents, see
Record Book B, pg. 323, Minutes Book No. 4, pgs. 60 & 293. The follow-
ing testimony was taken before L.F.LINN, Comm'r. in October, 1833.
State of Missouri, County of Cape Girardeau
Daniel BRANT, who is 59 years old, states that he moved to & settled
in the District of Cape Girardeau, Upper Louisiana in the year 1798.
That he was & still is well acquainted with Hugh CRISWELL of said District. That he knows of the said Hugh inhabiting & cultivating a place
on the waters of Randall's creek, adjoining one Anthony RANDALL in said
District in the year 1802. The said CRISWELL cultivated corn and other
grain on said place in said year 1802. The said CRISWELL had a cabin
& about seven acres of land cleared on said place at the time mentioned
above. He, also, had a family consisting of a wife and three children.
This affiant knows that the said CRISWELL continued to inhabit & cultivate said place for several years after the time mentioned above, but
the precise number of years he cannot recollect. This affiant has frequently heard the Spanish Commandant, Dr. Louis LORIMIER, say that he
wanted the people to settle close together, in order to protect them-
sleves from the Indians, and if they could not get land enough where
they lived, they should have it elsewhere.
Daniel (X) BRANT   Sworn to & subsctibed this 18th October, 1833.
    his mark   L.F. LINN, Comm'r.
        Adjourned until tomorrow at 9 o'clock A.M.
            The Board Met & Adjourned May 9th, 1835.

Monday May 11th, 1835 Board Met-Two Comm'rs. Present

Joseph FENWICK by his heirs & legal representatives claiming 800 ar-
pents of land, see Record Book E, pg. 335, BATE's decisions, pg. 93.
The following testimony was taken by L.F. LINN, Comm'r. on the 17th
day of June, 1833.
State of Missouri, County of St. Genevieve
John Bste. VALLE aged about 72 years, being sworn as the law directs,
deposeth & saith that he was well acquainted with the original claimant
Joseph FENWICK. That he came to this country, then the province of
Upper Louisiana in the year 1800 with a large & respectable family, &
had considerable property. That the said FENWICK settled on the land
claimed, made considerable buildings & improvements & cultivated the
same for some time, and that he then disposed of the same. That this
tract of land has passed through several hands and to several claimants,
but has always from the time of the original settlement up to the present day, been actually inhabited & cultivated and still is inhabited
& cultivated.
                         J. Bste. VALLE
Sworn to & subscribed before me, L.F. LINN, Comm'r. this 17th day of
June, 1833.   L.F. LINN, Comm'r.
       Adjourned until tomorrow at 9 o'clock A.M.
             Tuesday May 12th, 1835 Board Met-Two Comm'rs. Present

Mathew MULLINS claiming 726 arpents & 75 perches of land near Bellevue Settlement, see Record Book B, pg. 227, Book No. 5, pg. 545. The
following testimony was taken before F.R. CONWAY, Comm!r. in July,
1833.
John STEWART of lawful age, being first duly sworn, deposeth & saith
that in November, 1800, this affiant came to Mine a Breton in the District of St. Genevieve and was from that time for many years thereafter well acquainted with the above claimant, Mathew MULLINS. That
this affiant always understood from Moses AUSTIN & others that said
MATHEW was entitled to 400 arpents of land on account of his having
come to the Spanish country, under Moses AUSTIN & in virtue of an un-
derstanding between Moses AUSTIN & the Spanish authorities of the country, which will more at large appear by an examination of the records
of the courts in or about the year 1797. That being the year said
Mathew came to the country as this affiant has been informed. This
affiant would further show that Elias BATES was also a follower of
Moses AUSTIN, and obtained a gratuity of 400 arpents upon the identi-
cal principles upon which Mathew claims his. In January or February
1806, Mathew MULLINS called upon affiant, who was legally authorised
to make public surveys of land, to survey for him the above claim.
This affiant having been instructed to survey for each land claimant
640 acres, accordingly surveyed for Mathew MULLINS 640 acres of land
in Bellevue, then District of St. Genevieve, now County of Washington,
the plat whereof has been duly returned in order to its being recorded.
Mathew MULLINS shewed the land which was surveyed & pointed out to this
affiant the beginning corner of the same, which was accordingly fixed
and established as such by this affiant in virtue of his official duty
as surveyor. And, further, this deponent saith not.   John STEWART
Sworn to & subscribed before me this 5th day of July, A.D. 1833.
F.R. CONWAY, Comm'r.

Reuben BAKER claiming 640 acres of land, see Record Book B, pg. 230,
Book No. 3, pg. 314, No. 4, pg. 399. The following testimony was taken
before L.F. LINN, May, 1833.
John GREENWALT states that he was acquainted with Reuben BAKER very
shortly after witness came to the country in 1798. That previous to
the year 1804, as witness verily believes and according to the best of
his recollection, the said Reuben BAKER was settled on a piece of
ground fronting on the Mississippi in Bois brule bottom, had a cabin
built on it & had a nursery of peach & apple trees growing on it. That
previous to 1804, claimant had made his garden & had raised corn, pum-
pkins & other vegetables on the land claimed, and witness well recollects of said Reuben BAKER continuing to live on said land for several
years subsequent to 1804 and continued to occupy & cultivate it until
he sold his settlement right.   John (X) GREENWALT
Sworn to & subscribed May 5th, 1833. L.F. LINN, Comm'r.

In the case of Francis THIBAUT claiming 640 acres of land, see No. 7 pg. 118, the following testimony was taken before F.R. CONWAY, in July, 1833.
John STEWART, being duly sworn, says that in the year 1803, he, the deponent, resided in Mine A Breton & was well acquainted with the claimant THIBAUT, who also resided at Mine a Breton and in the year above mentioned, 1803, claimant had a house & lot & Cultivated a garden. That in the year 1804, he raised a crop of wheat on the tract claimed, it being public land, claimant having possessed & cleared the same in the year 1803, continued to cultivate the same for some years after, but how long this deponent does not know.
Sworn to & subscribed before me this 8th day of John STEWART
July, 1833.   F.R. CONWAY, Comm'r.
        Adjourned until tomorrow at 9 o'clock A.M.
            Wednesday May 13th, 1835 Board Met-Two Comm'rs. Present

William JANES by his legal representatives claiming 640 acres of land in Bellevue Settlement, see Record Book B, pg. 235, Book No. 3, pg. 214, No. 4, pg. 368. The following testimony was taken in May, 1833 before L.F. LINN, Comm'r.
State of Missouri, County of Washington
John T. MCNEAL, aged about 70 years, being duly sworn, as the law directs, deposeth & saith that he was acquainted with William JANES, the original claimant. That he improved the tract of land claimed in the year 1803 and continued on the same in 1804. Witness saw a cabin on said land in 1804, and in the winter of 1804 & 5, he was on the place & saw the corn stalks standing there, which must have been the corn stalks of the crop of 1804. There were several acres under fence and witness says he believes said JANES continued to live on said land till the year 1807, when he left the country.   John T. MCNEAL (332)
Sworn to & subscribed May 6th, 1833 - L.F. LINN, Comm'r.

William FLYNN, Jr. claiming 200 arpens of land, District of St. Genevieve, see Record Book E, pg. 256, Book No. 3, pg. 134, No. 5, pg. 327. The following testimony was taken in May, 1833 by L.F. LINN, Comm'r.
John GREENWALT testifies & says that he is about 68 years of age and emigrated to upper Louisiana in the spring of 1798, it being the spring after the high freshet of 1797, from which circumstance, he is eanbled to identify the time of his first coming to the country. Witness settled in Bois Brule bottom, now in the County of Perry & State of Missouri, where he has continued most of the time since. He further states that the father of the claimant, William FLYNN, Sr., emigrated to Louisiana & settled with his family in Bois Brule Bottom aforesaid as early as the year 1800 where he resided until the time of his death that William FLYNN, Jr., the claimant, came with his father to the country, and was, as witness believes, about 20 years of age, being a man grown & doing business for himself & on his own account. That witness knows of claimant cultivating a piece of ground in Bois Brule Bottom as early as the year 1804. That in the summer of 1804, claimant built a cabin, raised turnips & some vines on said land & also, as he thinks, grew some corn on it and then claimed & has ever since claimed the same as his settlement. Witness, further, states that claimant continued to occupy said ground until 1807, when the same lay idle for two or three years, but that afterwards for several years claimant rented it to men residing on it with their families for several years. Witness, further, states that he has been a neighbour to claimant since his first coming to the country in 1800, and that he has uniformly understood from him that the piece of ground above alluded to was the only land claimed by him as his settlement right, and that he has never had any lands confirmed to him.   John (X) GREENWALT
Sworn to & subscribed May 6th, 1833   his mark
L.F. LINN, Comm'r.
        Adjourned until tomorrow at 9 o'clock A.M.
            Thursday May 14th, 1835 Board Met-Two Comm'rs. Present

Sophia BOLAYE claiming 150 arpents of land situate on River aux Gravois, see Record Book E, pg. 327, BATE's decisions, pg. 91, produces a paper purporting to be an original concession from Zenon TRUDEAU,

dated 3rd June, 1796. Also, the deposition of Philip FINE taken
the 13th August, 1819 before Jos. CHARLESS, J.P. M.P. LEDUC, duly
sworn, says that the signature to the concession, or order of survey
is in the proper handwriting of the said TRUDEAU.
Territory of Missouri, County of St. Louis
Philip FINE of the Township of St. Louis in said County, being duly
sworn upon his oath, declares and says that he well knows the tract
described in the annexed petition of Sophia BOLAYE and has known it
for at least forty years past and that Sophia BOLAYE about thirty
years ago opened the ground, planted corn & potatoes and built a house
on said tract. (No. 279)   Philip (X) FINE
Sworn to & subscribed this 13th day of August, 1819 before me, A Justice of the Peace in & for the county of aforesaid.
                              Jos. CHARLESS, J.P.
        Adjourned until tomorrow at 9 o'clock A.M.
          Friday May 15th, 1835 Board Met-Two Comm'rs. Present

Charles MCLANE claiming 748 arpents 68 perches of land situated in
Bellevue, see Record Book B, pg. 227, Minutes Book No. 5, pg. 454,
produces a plat of survey executed by John STEWART, D.S. February 15th,
& received for record by A. SOULARD, S. Genl., February 29th, 1806.

Louis GRENIER claiming 701 arpents of land on Fourche a Courtois, District of St. Genevieve, see Record Book B, pg. 225. The following testimony was taken in July, 1833 by F.R. CONWAY in Washington County.
John STEWART, being duly sworn, deposeth & saith that he was well acquainted with Lewis GRENIER. That in the year 1803, the said GRENIER
was then a labouring man living in a cabin in Mine a Breton, he had a
garden & in 1804, he cultivated some acres of land on said place. That
in the year 1806, he called on witness to survey his land, but an old
Spanish right on the East, a conditional line on the West, a claim on
the South, and a Spanish concession on the North confined him to close,
witness could not get his complement of land and surveyed the balance
of his claim, in all 640 acres, about 18 miles, as witness supposes,
from the mine a Breton, in wood land not then claimed by any person,
which survey witness made, returned the plat for record & paid the recording fees.   John STEWART
Sworn to & subscribed before me this 9th day of July, A.D. 1833.
F.R. CONWAY
        Adjourned until tomorrow at 9 o'clock A.M.
          Saturday May 16th, 1835 Board Met-Two Comm'rs. Present

Charles BECQUETTE claiming 606 acres of land, situate in Bellevue,
District of St. Genevieve, see Record Book B, pg. 208. The following
deposition was taken in Washington County by F.R. CONWAY, Esqr.
This day personally appeared before me, John STEWART of lawful age,
who deposeth & saith that in the year 1803, Charles (otherwise called
Charlot) BECQUETTE was an inhabitant & resident of Mine a Breton and
cultivated some acres of land. In 1806, witness surveyed his improvement & the balance of the land including in all 640 acres, agreeably to
his instructions from the United States agent & Commissioners, which
survey I returned for record.   John STEWART
Sworn to & subscribed before me this 9th day of July, A.D. 1833.
                              F.R. CONWAY
        Adjourned until Monday next at 9 o'clock A.M.
          The Board Met & Adjourned Monday May 18th, 1835.
          Tuesday May 19th, 1835 Board Met-F.R. CONWAY, Present

Daniel RICHARDSON claiming 460 arpents of land situate on the Missouri
District of St. Louis, see Record Book B, pg. 346, Book No. 1, pg. 444,
No. 5, pg. 486. .T.ι
James COWEN, being duly sworn, says that in the month of November next
he will be 54 years of age. That in February 1803 he settled in the
neighbourhood of claimant and it was then reported that the said
Daniel RICHARDSON had begun to improve the land claimed in the spring
of said year 1803, but witness did not see it himself. The first time
witness saw the said improvement was in the fall of 1804 to the best of
his recollection, there were at that time some rails split, house logs
cut, a small piece of land, about a quarter of an acre, inclosed with

rails & ples, and a nursery of peach trees planted in said inclosure.
Witness, further, says that in the month of (cannot read), 1803, as
well as he can recollect, the Indians made an incursion on their
settlement, killed a man, burnt houses, and drove the settlers away.
Claimant was a single man and boarded with one STEVENS, whose land
was adjoining that of said claimant.
        Adjourned until tomorrow at 9 o'clock A.M.
            The Board Met & Adjourned May 20th & 21st, 1835.
            Friday May 22nd, 1835 Board Met-F.R. CONWAY, Esqr. Present

Jerome MATTIS by his legal representatives claiming 800 arpents of
land situate on the waters of river St. Francois, see Record Book F,
pg. 146, BATE's Decisions pg. 105. The following testimony was taken
in May, 1833 by L.F. LINN, then Comm'r.
State of Missouri, County of Madison
John BEEVE aged about 57 years, being duly sworn, as the law directs,
deposeth & saith that he was well acquainted with Jerome MATTIS. That
he knew him to be a citizen & resident of this country, then the province of Upper Louisiana, some years before the year 1800, and that he
continued to be a citizen of the country for many years afterwards &
until he died. This witness, further, says that he knows the land
claimed. That the claimant occupied the same in the year 1802 or 1803.
That he built a camp on the same & made sugar there. That the claimant
continued to occupy the same & made sugar there for several years.
That the claimant had a wife at the time.
                                    John (X) BEEVE
Sworn to & subscribed before me this 31st   his mark
day of May, 1833. L.F. LINN, Comm'r.
        Adjourned until tomorrow at 9 o'clock A.M.
            Saturday May 23rd, 1835 Board Met-F.R. CONWAY, Present

William EASOM claiming 800 arpents of land, see Book No. 7, pg. 120.
The following testimony was taken in October, 1833 by L.F. LINN,
Comm'r.
State of Missouri, County of Madison
Thompson CRAWFORD aged about 47 years, being duly sworn as the law directs, deposeth & saith that he well knew William EASOM, the original
claimant. That he came to this country, then the province of Upper
Louisiana, in the spring of 1803. Witness, also, knows the land
claimed & knows that claimant settled thereon & made a crop in 1803.
There were two cabins built on the place. Claimant fenced in, cleared
and cultivated 3 or 4 acres. Claimant remained on the place till some
time in the year 1804 when he removed, and that the said land has been
actually improved, inhabited and cultivated ever since. Claimant had
a wife and one child. (No. 280)   Thompson CRAWFORD
Sworn to & Subscribed before me this 23rd October, 1833. L.F. LINN,
Comm'r.
        Adjourned until Monday next at 9 o'clock A.M.
            Monday May 25th, 1835 Board Met-F.R. CONWAY, Present

Jonathan OWSLEY by his legal representatives claiming 1,200 arpents
of land on the waters of St. Francis river, see Record Book A, pg. 328,
Minutes Book No. 1, pg. 88, No. 3, pgs. 149 & 389, No. 4, pg. 345,
BATE's Dec. pg. 64, produces a paper purporting to be an original concession from Carlos Dehault DELASSUS, dated December 5th, 1799. The
following testimony was taken before L.F. LINN, Comm'r. in May, 1833.
Joseph PRATTE aged about 59 years, being duly sworn as the law directs,
deposeth & saith that he was well acquainted with Charles D. DELASSUS,
who was Lt. Gov. of Upper Louisiana in the year 1799. That he has frequently seen him write and that the name & signature to the said concession for 1,200 arpents of land to said Jonathan OWSLEY, is in the proper handwriting of said Charles Dehault DELASSUS. Deponent, further,
says that he was well acquainted with Pierre Delassus DELUZIERRE, who
was (cannot read) year 1799, Commandant of New Bourbon. That he has
frequently seen him write & that the signature to the recommendation
for said grant is in the proper handwriting of the said DELUZIERE.
And, further, this deponent says he was well acquainted with said
OWSLEY when he, said OWSLEY, resided on the waters of St. Francis. That
said OWSLEY emigrated to the best of his knowledge & belief, before the
year 1797. That said OWSLEY was honest, industrious & good farmer. That

he never knew of heard of said OWSLEY having more than one concession
for land.   Jh. PRATTE
Sworn to & subscribed May 3rd, 1833. L.F. LINN, Comm'r.
     Adjourned until tomorrow at 9 o'clock A.M.
          Tuesday May 26th, 1835 Board Met-F.R. CONWAY, Present

Gasper SCHELL claiming 640 acres of land in the district of Cape Girar-
deau, see Record Book F, pg. 146, BATE's decisions, pg. 105.   The
following testimony was taken in October, 1833 before L.F. LINN,
Comm'r.
State of Missouri, County of Cape Girardeau
Joseph NISWANGER of lawful age, being duly sworn, deposeth & saith
he is well acquainted with Gasper SCHELL, the above claimant. That
he emigrated to this country with his family in the District of Cape
Girardeau in the latter part of the month of June or beginning of
July in the year 1804. That in the same year he moved on & settled
the place where he now resides. That said SCHELL has continued to
inhabit & cultivate the same ever since. That he has made valuable
& lasting improvements on the same. That his family consisted of a
wife & seven or eight children.   Joseph (X) NISWANGER
Sworn to & subscribed Oct. 17th, 1833   his mark
L.F. LINN, Comm'r.
George F. BOLLINGER of lawful age, being sworn, deposeth & saith
that he is well acquainted with the claimant, Gasper SCHELL. That
he emigrated to this country in the spring of summer of 1804. That
some time after he settled on the place where he now lives & has resided there ever since. That he has made valuable improvements on
the same, to wit; a good dwelling house, out houses, barn, stables,
well, distillery, good orchard, etc.   George F. BOLLINGER
Sworn to & subscribed Oct. 18th, 1833.
L.F. LINN, Comm'r.
     Adjourned until tomorrow at 9 o'clock A.M.
          Wednesday May 27th, 1835 Board Met-F.R. CONWAY, Present

John TAYLOR by his legal representatives claiming 640 acres of land
situate on Hubble's creek in the County of Cape Girardeau, see Record
Book B, pg. 337, where this claim is entered for 481 acres 81 perches,
Book No. 4, pgs. 31 & 297. The following testimony was taken before
L.F. LINN, Comm'r. in June & October, 1833.
State of Missouri, County of Cape Girardeau
Richard WALLER, being sworn, says he knew John TAYLOR well. He first
became acquainted with him in 1802 in the District of Cape Girardeau
where the said TAYLOR then lived and continued to live up to the time
of his death 10 or 15 years ago. He saw him settled on a place in
said district in the year 1803, He had built a house to live in and
had cleared land. He had a wife & several children, the number not
recollected.   Richard WALLER
Sworn to & subscribed before me June 11th, 1833. L.F. LINN, Comm'r.
Hugh CRISWELL is about 67 years old, he was well acquainted with the
said John TAYLOR. He knew the said TAYLOR in this country, District
of Cape Girardeau in the year 1803. He was then a farmer & inhabited
& cultivated land in said District. He improved his head right or
settlement claim in the year 1803 in said district and lived on it until the time of his death, which happened some time about the year
1814. This affiant knows that he built a house in Spanish times & set
out peach and apple trees for an orchard. He had a wife, three boys
& two girls, that this affiant recollects.   Hugh (X) CRISWELL
Sworn to & subscribed this 11th June, 1833.   his mark
L.F. LINN, Comm'r.
William WILLIAMS states that he moved to & settled in the District of
Cape Girardeau, Upper Louisiana in the year 1794. That he was well
acquainted with John TAYLOR, deceased, formerly of said District. To
the best of his recollection, the said TAYLOR moved to & settled in
said District in the year 1802. In the next year (cannot read) he
moved to a place on the (cannot read) miles North east of the present
town of Jackson, opened land & raised a crop on the same in said year
1803. This affiant, also, assisted the said TAYLOR in building a
dwelling house on said place in said year. The said TAYLOR had a family at the time consisting of himself, his wife & four or five children.
The said TAYLOR had an apple orchard very early on said place, but the

the year when he set it out, this affiant cannot state. The said
TAYLOR lived on the said place up to the time of his death some six
or eight years after he settled. The said place is now owned by one
John CROSS.   William WILLIAMS
Sworn to & subscribed Oct. 16th, 1833, L.F. LINN, Comm'r.
Adjourned until tomorrow at 9 o'clock A.M.
            The Board Met & Adjourned May 28th, 1835.
            Friday May 29th, 1835 Board Met-Two Comm'rs. Present

Louis BUAT & twelve others claiming a tract of land situate between
the two forks of river (Cannot read) & adjoining the forty arpents
(cannot read), see Book No. 5, pg. 508, produces a paper purporting
to be an original concession from Zenon TRUDEAU, dated 1st September,
1797.   The following testimony was taken in June, 1833 by L.F. LINN,
Comm'r.
State of Missouri, County of St. Genevieve
John Bste. VALLE aged about 72 years, being duly sworn as the law directs, deposeth & saith that he was well acquainted with each & every
of them at the date of the said concession were citizens & residents
in the then province of Upper Louisiana, and that those who are dead
continued citizens & residents till their death, and that those who
are living are still citizens & residents of the country. This witness
further says that he was well acquainted with Zenon TRUDEAU, who was
Lt. Gov. of Upper Louisiana at the date of the concession. That he has
often seen him write, and that the name & signature to the concession
from said Zenon TRUDEAU to the said thirteen concessionees, is in the
proper handwriting of the said Zenon TRUDEAU. And this deponent, further, says that the claimants made a common field on the same & actually cultivated the same for several years.   (No. 282)
                                            J. Bste. VALLE
Sworn to & subscribed before me this 17th June, 1833. L.F. LINN,
                                                              Comm'r.

Dennis SULLIVAN by his legal representatives claiming 640 acres of
land situate in the District of Cape Girardeau, see Record Book B, pg.
320, for List A, on which claimant is No. 94, for 300 arpents of land,
Book No. 4, pgs. 59 & 288 & for survey (cannot read) pg. 337.   The
following testimony was taken in October, 1833 before L.F. LINN,
Comm'r.
Jonathan BUIS states that in the fall of 1802 after his return from
a visit to New Orleans, he saw & knew Dennis SULLIVAN O'SULLIVAN in
the District of Cape Girardeau, Upper Louisiana, now State of Missouri,
where the said O'SULLIVAN then resided and continued to reside up to
the time of his death, which took place some time after the change of
government. The said Dennis was a mechanic, a Blacksmith by trade,
which business he pursued & carried on in different places in the said
District. This affiant frequently heard the Commandant LORIMIER say
that mechanics were not required to settle & improve their lands.
                                            Jonathan BUIS
Sworn to & subscribed to Oct. 17t, 1833. L.F. LINN, Comm'r.
Moses BIRD, also, states that he was well acquainted with the said
Dennis SULLIVAN, who came to the District of Cape Girardeau, Upper
Louisiana, in 1801 or 1802. The said Dennis was blacksmith by trade,
which occupation he continued to follow in different parts of said
District up to the time of his death, which occured after the change
of government, the precise year he does not recollect. (No. 283)
                                            Moses BYRD
Sworn to & subscribed to before L.F. LINN, Comm'r. Cape Girardeau
County, October 17th, 1833.
        Adjourned until tomorrow at 9 o'clock A.M.
            The Board Met & Adjourned May 30th, 1835
            Monday June 1st, 1835 Board Met-Two Comm'rs. Present

Curtis WILBOURN by his legal representatives claiming 640 acres of
land situated in the former District of Cape Girardeau, see Record
Book B, pg. 324, for list B on which claimant is No. 10 for 600 arpents, Minutes Book No. 5, pg. 391. The following testimony was taken
before L.F. LINN, Comm'r. in June, 1833.
State of Missouri, County of Cape Girardeau
John BALDWIN knew said Curtis. He came to the District of Cape Girar-

deau in the year 1803 & settled in Tywappity in the fall of said
year. He built a house in the fall or winter of 1803 and immediately commenced clearing land, and in 1804, he raised corn & other things
on said place. This affiant saw his permission to settle on the Books
of LORIMIER. Claimant was a married man, had a wife & six children,
five sons and one daughter. The said Curtis was killed some six or
eight years ago. This affiant has understood & believes that all his
children are dead, except two who are the actual claimants. (No. 284)
                                    John BALDWIN
Sworn to & subscribed this 11th day of June, 1833. L.F. LINN, Comm'r.

Alexander BUTNER or BURTON claiming 300 arpents of land situated in
the district of Cape Girardeau, see Record Book B, pg. 324 for list
B, onwhich claimant is No. 38 for 300 arpents, Minutes Book No. 5, pg.
392. The following testimony was taken before L.F. LINN, Comm'r. in
June, 1833.
State of Missouri, County of Cape Girardeau
Philip YOUNG, being duly sworn, deposeth and saith that he was acquainted with the above named Alexander BUTNER or BURTON. That he
settled a place on the waters of Caney Creek in the year 1802, and
that he raised a crop of corn on said place in the year 1803, and
that he continued to reside & cultivate the same in 1804 & probably
1805. And, further, this deponent states that he resided within about
two miles from the said Alexander BURTON during the time above stated.
                                    Philip YOUNG
Sworn to & subscribed June 11th, 1833. L.F. LINN, Comm'r.
        Adjourned Until tomorrow at 9 o'clock A.M.
            Tuesday June 2nd, 1835 Board Met-Two Comm'rs. Present

Guillaume BIZET by his legal representative claiming 40 arpents of
land situated in the cul de sac of the grand Prairie, see Livre
Terrien Book No. 1, pg. 21, Book F, pg. 155.
Pierre GUERET, duly sworn, says that he is 57 years of age. That he
knows the tract claimed. That he owned land near the said tract, &
that, he has perfect recollection of having seen the late
Jean Baptiste PROVENCHER (who had married the widow of
Guillaume BIZET after said BIZET's decease) in possession of the
tract now claimed, and that said PROVENCHER cultivated the same for
many years, but how long, he cannot say. Witness, further, says that
said PROVENCHER did cultivate said land while under the government of
Francisco PEREZ or Zenon TRUDEAU or under both, he is not positive,
but he is certain that it was before Mr. DELASSUS was Lt. Governor.
        Adjourned until tomorrow at 9 o'clock A.M.
            Wednesday June 3rd, 1835 Board Met-Two Comm'rs. Present

The Clerk having completed a transcript of each unconfirmed land claim
entered upon the minutes of the present Board on the application of
the claimants or their agents, and whereas one of the members is unable from indisposition to attend its sittings. Therefore resolved
that a majority of the Board is competent to transact business, pass
upon the several claims & make reports thereof, reserving however to
the absent member the right of opening any decision made by said majority prior to the 1st day of September next, provided such absent
member shall apply in person for said purpose on or before the said
day.
        Adjourned until tomorrow at 9 o'clock A.M.
            The Board Met & Adjourned June 4th, 5th & 6th, 1835.
            Monday June 8th, 1835 Board Met-Two Comm'rs. Present

William MCHUGH, Sr. claiming 640 acres of land, see Book No. 6, pg.
215, No. 7, pg. 20. The Board are of opinion that 640 acres of land
ought to be granted to the said William MCHUGH, Sr. , or to his legal
representatives, according to possession. (Dec. No. 256)

The Inhabitants of St. Ferdinand claiming 1,849-1/4 arpents of land,
it being the balance of 7,056 arpents granted them for commons of which
5206-3/4 arpents have been confirmed, see Book No. 6, pg. 156. The
Board are of opinion that this claim ought not to be confirmed. The
said inhabitants having had the said commons surveyed conformably to
the boundaries asked for in their petition dated 1st April, 1797, and
the amount of said survey (5,206-3/4 arpents) having been confirmed

by the former Board of Commissioners.

Jerusha EDMONDSON claiming 250 arpents of land, see Book No. 7, pg. 84. The Board are of opinion that this claim ought not to be granted, the said 250 arpents being the same improvement claimed by and included in a survey made for, one Michael RABER by John STEWART, Deputy Surveyor on the 24th of February, 1806, the said Jerusha EDMONDSON living at that time with the said RABER as his wife or mistress.

William RAMSAY, Sr. claiming 748 arpents 8 perches of land, see Book No. 6, pg. 214, No. 7, pg. 105. The Board are of opinion that 748 arpents & 8 perches of land ought to be granted to the said William RAMSAY, Sr., or to his legal representatives, according to the survey. (No. 257)

Benjamin GARDINER claiming 750 arpents of land, see Book No. 7, pgs. 93 & 101, 109 & 143. The Board are of opinion that 750 arpents of land ought to be granted to the said Benjamin GARDINER, or to his legal representatives, according to possession. (No. 258)

George GIRTY claiming 640 arpents of land, see Book No. 6, pg. 216, No. 7, pg. 107. The Board are of opinion that 640 acres of land ought to be granted to the said George GIRTY, or to his legal representatives, according to possession, the same having been inhabited & cultivated before DELASSUS granted an increase to the common of St. Charles, which is now said to embrace this claim. (No. 259)

John ROURKE claiming 756 arpents of land, see Book No. 7, pg. 108. The Board are of opinion that 640 acres of land ought to be granted to the said John ROURKE, or to his legal representatives, the same to be taken within the original survey. (No. 260)

Joseph CHARTRAN, Sr. claiming 99-1/2 arpents of land, see No. 7, pg. 109. The Board are of opinion that this cannot be granted, the said Joseph CHARTRAN, Sr. having had two concessions confirmed, see Comm'rs. certificate No. 26 & 786.

Mordicay BELL claiming 350 arpents of land, see Book No. 7, pg. 110. The Board are of opinion that 350 arpents of land ought to be confirmed to the said Mordicai BELL, or to his legal representatives, according to the survey on Record in Book D, pg. 362. (No. 261)

Antoine LAMARCHE claiming 750 arpents of land, see Book No. 7, pg. 111. The Board are of opinion that 750 arpents of land ought to be granted to the said Antoine LAMARCHE, or to his legal representatives, according to the survey on record in Book B, pg. 264. (No. 262)

Samuel HOLMES claiming 840 acres of land, see Book No. 7, pg. 112. The Board are of opinion that 640 acres of land ought to be granted to the said Samuel HOLMES, or to his legal representatives, to be taken within the original survey. (No. 263)

Pierre PALARDIE claiming 1,000 arpents of land, see Book No. 7, pg. 113. The Board are of opinion that this claim ought not to be granted.

Vincent LAFOIX & Nicolas PLANTE claiming 640 arpents of land, see Book No. 7, pg. 115. The Board are of opinion that 416 arpents of land ought to be confirmed to said claimants, extending the survey already made to the above quantity of 640 arpents. (No. 264)

John STEWART claiming 640 acres of land, see Book No. 7, pg. 116. The Board are of opinion that 640 acres of land ought to be granted to the said John STEWART, or to his legal representatives, according to possession. (No. 265)

William BATES claiming 640 acres of land, see Book No. 7, pg. 117. The Board are of opinion that this claim ought not to be granted.

Francis THIBAULT claiming 500 arpents of land, see Book No. 7, pgs. 118 & 149. This claim is considered by the Commissioners of the

General Land Office, as confirmed, see his letter to the Recorder of Land titles under date of 28th January, 1833.

Charles MCDORMET claiming 640 acres of land, see Book No. 7, pg. 118. The Board are of opinion that this claim ought not to be granted.
     Adjourned until tomorrow at 9 o'clock A.M.
I have examined and concur in the foregoing decisions. (signed by the
                                          Comm'rs.)

        Tuesday June 9th, 1835 Board Met-Two Comm'rs. Present

William MEEK claiming 500 arpents of land, see Book No. 7, pg. 113. The Board are of opinion that this claim ought to be confirmed to the said William MEEK, or to his legal representatives, according to the survey recorded in Book B, pg. 198, in the Recorders Office. (No. 266)

Jacob WISE claiming 37-1/2 acres of land, see Book No. 7, pg. 119. The Board are of opinion that this claim ought to be granted to the said Jacob WISE, or to his legal representatives, according to the survey recorded in Book· B, pg. 242 in the Recorder's Office. (No. 267)

Zachariah DOWTY claiming 450 arpents of land, see Book No. 7, pg. 120. The Board are of opinion that this claim ought to be granted to the said Zachariah DOWTY, or to his legal representatives, according to possession. (No. 268)

Jane LOGAN claiming 800 arpents of land, see Book No. 7, pg. 121. The Board are of opinion that 640 acres of land ought to be granted to the said Jane LOGAN, or to her legal representatives, according to her possession.   (No. 269)

Benjamin TENNEL claiming 640 acres of land, see Book No. 7, pg. 121. The Board are of opinion that 640 acres of land ought to be granted to the said Benjamin TENNEL, or to his legal representatives, according to his possession. (No. 270)

Julius WICKERS having 600 arpents of land, see Book No. 7, pg. 122. The Board are of opinion that 600 arpents of land ought to be granted to the said Julius WICKERS, or to his legal representatives, according to possession. (No. 271)

Louis MILHOMME claiming 620 acres of land, see Book No. 7, pg. 125. The Board are of opinion that this claim ought not to be granted, there being no proof of possession or cultivation, the only testimony given having reference to a town lot.

Louis LACROIX claiming 701 arpents of land, see Book No. 7, pg. 124. The Board are of opinion that this claim ought not to be granted, the said Louis LACROIX, being one of the thirty one inhabitants claiming each 400 arpents of land under the old Mine concession.

Louis AUBUCHON claiming 800 arpents of land, see Book No. 7, pg. 130. The Board are of opinion that this claim ought to be confirmed to the said Louis AUBUCHON, or to his legal representatives, according to the survey of record in Book C, pg. 195 in the Recorders Office. (No. 272)

Silas FLETCHER claiming 300 arpents of land, see Book No. 6, pg. 135. The Board are of opinion that 300 arpents of land ought to be granted to the said Silas FLETCHER, or to his legal representatives, according to his possession. (No. 273)
     The Board Adjourned until tomorrow at 9 o'clock A.M.
      Wednesday June 10th, 1835 Board Met-Two Comm'rs. Present

Malachi JONES claiming 790 acres, see Book No. 7, pg. 137. The Board are of opinion that 640 acres of land ought to be granted to the said Malachi JONES, or to his legal representatives, to be taken within the original survey recorded in Book B, pg. 311 in the Recorders Office. (No. 274)

John BALDWIN claiming 400 arpents of land, see Book No. 7, pg. 139.

The Board are of opinion that 400 arpents of land ought to be granted to the said John BALDWIN, or to his legal representatives, according to his possession. (No. 275)

Charles SEXTON claiming 300 arpents of land, see Book No. 7, pg. 140. The Board are of opinion that this claim ought to be confirmed to the said Charles SEXTON, or to his legal representatives, according to the concession, and to be taken within the original survey recorded in Book B, pg. 303 in the Recorder's Office. (No. 276)

Nancy FERGUSON claiming 300 arpents of land, see Book No. 7, pg. 141. The Board are of opinion that this claim ought not to be granted.

Hugh CRISWELL claiming 640 acres of land, see Book No. 2, pg. 144. The Board are of opinion that 101 arpents 31 perches of land ought to be confirmed to the said Hugh CRISWELL, or to his legal represen- tatives, according to the original survey of record in Book B, pg. 287 in the Recorder's Office. (No. 277)

Urban ASHERBRAWNER claiming 350 arpents 95 perches of land, see Book No. 7, pg. 144. The Board are of opinion that this claim ought not to be granted.

Joseph FENWICK claiming 800 arpents of land, see Book No. 7, pg. 146. The Board are of opinion that this claim ought not to be granted, the said Joseph FENWICK had lands confirmed to him, see Commissioner's certificate No. 1243, BATE's decisions, pg. 57.

Mathew MULLINS claiming 726 arpents 95 perches of land, see Book No. 7, pg. 147. The Board are of opinion that this claim ought not to be granted.

Reuben BAKER claiming 640 acres of land, see Book No. 7, pg. 148. The Board are of opinion that 640 acres of land ought to be granted to the said Reuben BAKER, or to his legal representatives, according to the survey recorded in Book B, pg. 230 in the Recorder's office. (No. 278)

Sophia BOLAYE claiming 160 arpents of land, see Book No. 7, pg. 152. The Board are of opinion that this claim ought to be confirmed to the said Sophia BOLAYE, or to her legal representatives, provided the land belonged to the Domain at the date of the concession. (No. 279)

Charles MCLANE claiming 748 arpents 68 perches of land, see Book No. 7, pg. 153. The Board are of opinion that this claim ought not to be granted.

Louis GRENIER claiming 701 arpents of land, see Book No. 7, pg. 153. The Board are of opinion that this claim ought not to be granted.
     The Board adjourned until tomorrow at 9 o'clock A.M.
          Thursday June 11th, 1835 Board Met-Two Comm'rs. Present

William EASOM claiming 800 arpents of land, see Book No. 7, pg. 120 & 157. The Board are of opinion that 640 acres of land ought to be granted to the said William EASOM, or to his legal representatives, according to his possession. (No. 280)

Charles BECQUETTE claiming 606 acres of land, see Book No. 7, pg. 154. The Board are of opinion that this claim ought not to be granted.

Daniel RICHARDSON claiming 460 arpents of land, see Book No. 7, pg. 155. The Board are of opinion that this claim ought not to be granted.

Jerome MATTIS claiming 800 arpents of land, see Book No. 7, pg. 156. The Board are of opinion that this claim ought not to be granted, claimant had a confirmation for 400 arpents, see Comm'rs. Minutes Book No. 4, pg. 515.

Gasper SCHELL claiming 640 acres of land, see Book No. 7, pg. 159. The Board are of opinion that this claim ought not to be granted.

John TAYLOR by his legal representatives claiming 481-8 poles acres
of land, see Book No. 7, pg. 160, where this claim is entered for
640 acres. The Board are of opinion that 481 acres & 8 poles of land
ought to be granted to the legal representatives of the said
John TAYLOR, deceased, according to the survey recorded in Book B, pg.
337. (No. 281)
        The Board adjourned until tomorrow at 9 o'clock A.M.
            Friday June 12th, 1835 Board Met-Two Comm'rs. Present

Louis BUAT, Hippolite ROBERT, Joseph SALUMANDIERE, GIROUARD,
J. Bste. TAUMUR, Joseph BECQUETTE, Auguste AUBUCHON,
Jean SALUMANDIERE, Louis CARO, Vital BAUVAIS, DUFOUF, J.M. PEPIN,
claiming a special location between the 2 forks of Gaboury, see Book
No. 7, pg. 162. The Board are of opinion that this claim ought to
be confirmed to the said Louis BUAT & to the other above named twelve
individuals, or to their legal representatives, according to the petition and concession. (No. 282)

Dennis SULLIVAN claiming 300 arpents of land, see Book No. 7, pg. 163,
where it is entered for 640 acres, for concession see claim No. 202.
The Board are of opinion that 300 arpents of land ought to be confirmed
to the said Dennis SULLIVAN, or to his legal representatives, according
to the concession. (No. 283)

Curtis WILBOURN claiming 600 arpents of land, see Book No. 7, pg. 165,
where it is entered for 640 acres. The Board are of opinion that 600
arpents of land (it being the quantity claimed on record) ought to be
granted to the said Curtis WILBOURN, or to his legal representatives,
according to possession. (No. 284)

Alexander BUTNER OR BURTON (cannot Read) 165 where this claim is entered for 640 acres. The Board are of opinion that 300 arpents of
land ought to be granted to the said Alexander BUTNER or BURTON, or
to his legal representatives, according to possession. The said 300
arpents being the quantity claimed on record. (No.285)

Guillaume BIZET claiming 40 arpents of land, see Book No. 7, pg. 166.
The Board are of opinion that this claim ought to be confirmed to the
legal representatives of the said Guillaume BIZET, deceased, according to the concession. (No. 286)

Peter BOYER claiming 639-3/4 acres of land, see Book No. 7, pg. 124.
The Board are of opinion that this claim cannot be granted, the said
Peter BOYER claiming 400 arpents of land under the Old Mine Conces-
sion.

James WILBOURN claiming 300 arpents of land, see Book No. 6, pg. 450,
where this claim is entered for 640 acres. The Board are of opinion
that 300 arpents of land (it being the quantity claimed on record)
ought to be granted to the said James WILBOURN, or to his legal representatives, according to possession. (No. 287)

Charles DENNE claiming 750 arpents of land, see Book No. 6, pg. 513,
No. 7 pg. 17. The Board are of opinion that this claim ought not to
be granted.
        The Board adjourned until tomorrow at 9 o'clock A.M.
            Saturday June 13th, 1835 Board Met-Two Comm'rs. Present

Israel DODGE claiming 7,056 arpents of land, see Book No. 6, pg. 338.
The Board are of opinion that this claim ought to be confirmed to the
said Israel DODGE, or to his legal representatives, according to the
concession. (No. 288)

Agnew MASSEY claiming 248 arpents of land, see Book No. 6, pg. 478,
where this claim is entered for 640 acres. The Board are of opinion
that 248 arpents of land (it being the quantity claimed on record)
ought to be granted to the said Agnew MASSEY, or to his legal representatives, according to possession. (No. 289)

Joseph DOUBLEWYE alias DEBLOIS claiming 640 acres of land, see Book

No. 6, pg. 420. The Board are of opinion that this claim ought to
be granted to the said Joseph DOUBLEWYE, alias DEBLOIS, or to his
legal representatives, according to possession. (No. 290)

A.V. BOUIS claiming 1,000 arpents of land, see Book No. 6, pg. 220.
The Board are of opinion that this claim ought to be confirmed to the
said Antoine V. BOUIS, or to his legal representatives, according to
the concession. (No. 291)

Francois VALLE & J.B. VALLE claiming 7,056 arpents of land, see Book
No. 6, pg. 196. The Board have no jurisdiction on this claim there
being no concession, warrant or order of survey.

Francois VALLE, Jr. claiming 7,056 arpents of land, see Book No. 6,
pg. 193. The Board have no jurisdiction onthis claim, there being no
concession, warrant or order of survey.
        The Board Adjourned until Monday next at 9 o'clock A.M.
        Monday June 15th, 1835 Board Met-Two Comm'rs. Present

John RAMSAY claiming 848 arpents of land, see Book No. 6, pg. 216.
The Board are of opinion that this claim ought not to be granted.

John DRAPER claiming 747 arpents of land, see Book No. 6, pg. 215.
The Board are of opinion that this claim ought not to be granted.

Andre CHEVALIER claiming 400 arpents of land, see Book No. 6, pg. 213.
In this case the following certificate was sworn to & signature acknowledged before L.F. LINN, Comm'r.
I certify that it is not in my power to survey Andrew CHEVALIER's survey between now & the 1st of March. Given under my hand, February the
24th, 1806.   Thomas MADDIN
Sworn to & signature acknowledged May 11th, 1833. L.F. LINN, Comm'r.
The Board are of opinion that this claim ought to be confirmed to the
said Andre CHEVALIER, or to his legal representatives, according to the
concession. (No. 292)

Joseph SILVAIN claiming 250 arpents of land, see Book No. 6, pg. 365.
The Board are of opinion that this claim ought to be confirmed to the
said Joseph SILVAIN, or to his legal representatives, according to the
concession and to possession. (No. 293)

Jacob NEAL claiming 650 arpents of land, see Book No. 6, pg. 249 (entered for 800 arpents) The Board are of opinion that 650 arpents of
land ought to be confirmed to said Jacob NEAL, or to his legal representatives, according to the concession & number of persons in his
family. (No. 294)

Pierre DUMAIS claiming 1,000 arpents of land, see Book No. 6, pg. 364.
The Board are of opinion that this claim ought to be confirmed to the
said Pierre DUMAIS, or to his legal representatives, according to the
concession. (No. 295)

Barthelmi RICHARD claiming 1,200 arpents of land, see Book No. 6, pg.
365. The Board are of opinion that this claim ought not to be confirmed, the said RICHARD having abondoned said land, which was afterwards granted to Pierre DUMAIS under a concession, dated 23rd January,
1800.

Samuel NEAL claiming 200 arpents of land, see Book No. 6, pg. 248. The
Board are of opinion that 200 arpents of land ought to be confirmed to
the said Samuel NEAL, or to his legal representatives, according to the
concession. (No. 296)

Isidore LACROIX claiming 6,000 arpents of land, see Book No. 6, pg.
224. The Board are of opinion that this claim ought not to confirmed
claimant having had the lot in St. Charles confirmed, as also four
hundred arpents of land (See BATE's decisions pgs. 39 & 53) and nothing
more being granted by the concession.

Jean Bst. LAMARCHE claiming800 arpents of land, see Book No. 6, pg.
223. The Board are of opinion that 240 arpents of land, which is the

quantity asked for in the petition, ought to be confirmed to the said
Jean Bste. LAMARCHE, or to his legal representatives, to be taken
within the survey of record in Book C, pg. 263 in the Recorder's Office.
(No. 297)

John P. CABANNE claiming 2,000 arpents of land, see Book No. 6, pg.
221. The Board are of opinion that this claim ought to be confirmed
to the said John P. CABANNE, or to his legal representatives, according
to the concession. (No. 298)

Pierre TORNAT dit LAJOIE claiming 600 arpents of land, see Book No. 6,
pg. 189. The Board are of opinion that this claim ought not to be
confirmed. (Rescinded, see pg. 246)

Jean Marie CARDINAL claiming 40 arpents of land, see Book No. 6, pg.
150. The Board are of opinion that this claim ought to be confirmed
to the said Jean Marie CARDINAL, or to his legal representatives,
according to the concessions. (No. 299)

Widow DODIER claiming 120 arpents of land, see Book No. 6, pg. 174.
The Board are of opinion that this claim ought to be confirmed to
the said Widow DODIER, or to her legal representatives, according to
the survey in Livre Terrien No. 2, pg. 38. (No. 300)

William HARTLEY claiming 650 arpents of land, see Book No. 6, pg.
134. The Board are of opinion that this claim ought to be confirmed
to the said William HARTLEY, or to his legal representatives, according to the concession. (No. 301)

John MCCORMACK claiming 1,000 arpents of land, see Book No. 6, pg.
504. The Board are of opinion that this claim ought not to be granted.
    The Board adjourned unitl tomorrow at 9 o'clock A.M.
        Tuesday June 16th, 1835 Board Met-Two Comm'rs. Present

Absalom KENNYSON claiming 640 acres of land, see Book No. 6, pg. 481.
The Board are of opinion that 640 acres of land ought to be granted
to the said Absalom KENNYSON, or to his legal representatives, according to possession. (No. 302)

Jacob MILLER claiming 300 acres of land, see Book No. 6, pg. 489. The
Board are of opinion that this claim ought to be granted to the said
Jacob MILLER, or to his legal representatives, according to the sur-
vey. (no. 303)

John GREENWALT, Jr. claiming 640 acres of land, see Book No. 6, pg.
488. The Board remark that the testimony given by Thomas MADDIN before the former Board of Comm'rs. has no relation to this claim, but
refers to the claim of John GREENWALT, Sr. recorded in Book B, pg. 201,
& confirmed by BATES to Clement HAYDEN, assignee of said GREENWALT,
Sr. See BATES Decisions, pg. 64. The Board are of opinion that 640
acres of land ought to be granted to the said John GREENWALT, Jr., or
to his legal representatives, according to possession. (No. 304)

James BEVINS claiming 200 arpents of land, see Book No. 6, pg. 455,
where this claim is entered for 640 acres. The Board are of opinion
that this claim ought not to be granted.

William THOMPSON claiming 640 acres of land, see Book No. 6, pg. 454.
The Board are of opinion that 640 acres of land ought to be granted to
the said William THOMPSON, or to his legal representatives, to be taken
within the survey recorded in Book B, pg. 303. (No. 305)

Morris YOUNG claiming 300 arpents of land, see Book No. 6, pg. 408.
The Board are of opinion that this claim ought not to be granted.

David REESE claiming 640 acres of land, see Book No. 6, pg. 442. The
Board are of opinion that this claim (Cannot read)

Benjamin PETTIT, Jr. claiming 640 acres of land, see Book No. 6, pg.
(Cannot read). The Board are of opinion that this claim ought not to

be granted.

Robert RURNS claiming 640 acres of land, see Book No. 6, pg. 419.
The Board are of opinion that this claim ought not to be granted.
The Board Adjourned until tomorrow at 9 o'clock A.M.
Wednesday June 17th, 1835 Board Met-Two Comm'rs. Present

John MURPHY claiming 550 arpents of land, see Book No. 6, pg. 209.
The Board are of opinion that this claim ought to be confirmed to
the said John MURPHY, or to his legal representatives, according to
the survey recorded in Book C, pg. 81. (No. 306)

James ROGERS, Jr. claiming 750 arpents of land, see Book No. 6, pg.
177 & 540. The Board are of opinion that this claim ought .not to
be granted.

Reuben MIDDLETON claiming 640 acres of land, see Book No. 6, pg. (cannot read). The Board are of opinion that this claim ought not to be
granted.

Joseph DENNIS claiming 640 acres of land, see Book No. 6, pg. 487.
The Board are of opinion that this claim ought not to be granted.

Samuel CAMPBELL claiming 640 acres of land, see Book No. 6, pg. 414.
The Board are of opinion that this claim ought not to be granted,
claimant being a tenant in the years 1803 & 1804.

Amable PATNOTE claiming 640 acres of land, see Book No. 7, pg. 6.   The
Board are of opinion that this claim ought not to be granted.

William MORRISON claiming 750 arpents of land, see Book No. 7, pg. 1.
The Board are of opinion that this claim ought to be confirmed to the
said William MORRISON, or to his legal representatives, according to
the concession. (No. 307)

Solomon BELEW claiming 350 arpents of land, see Book No. 6, pg. 530.
The Board are of opinion that this claim ought to be confirmed to the
said Solomon BELEW, or to his legal representatives, according to the
concession. (No. 308)

Pascal DETCHMENDY claiming 7,056 arpents of land, see Book No. 6, pg.
378. The Board are of opinion that this claim ought to be confirmed
to the said Pascal DETCHMENDY, or to his legal representatives, according to the concession. (No. 309)

Baptiste AUMURE Or TAUMURE claiming 240 arpents of land, see Book No.
6, pg. 514. The Board are of opinion that this claim ought to be
confirmed to the said Baptiste AUMURE or TAUMURE, or to his legal representatives, according to the concession. (No. 310)

Priscilla EASTEPS claiming 800 arpents of land, see Book No. 6, pg.
509. The Board are of opinion that 640 acres of land ought to be
granted to the said Priscilla EASTEPS, or to her legal representatives,
according to possession. (No. 311)

William MCHUGH, Jr. claiming 640 acres of land, see Book No. 7, pg.
139.   The Board are of opinion that this claim ought not to be granted.

Adrien LANGLOIS claiming 1,500 arpents of land, see Book No. 6, pg. 258.
The Board are of opinion that this claim ought to be confirmed to the
said Adrien LANGLOIS, or to his legal representatives, according to
the concession. (No. 312)

Martin THOMAS claiming 640 acres of land, see Book No. 6, pg. 440, No.
7, pg. 133. The Board are of opinion that this claim ought not to be
granted.

George AYREY claiming 750 arpents of land, see Book No. 6, pg. 169.
The Board are of opinion that this claim ought not to be granted.

St. Gemme BAUVAIS claiming 60 feet in circumference around each hole in which he may find mineral, see Book No. 6, pg. 74. The Board are of opinion that this claim ought not to be confirmed.

Absalom LINK claiming 510 arpents of land, see Book No. 6, pgs. 172, 175 & 232. The Board are of opinion that this claim ought not to be granted.
The Board adjourned until tomorrow at 9 o'clock A.M.
Thursday June 18th, 1835 Board Met-Two Comm'rs. Present

Thomas POWERS by his legal representatives claiming 650 arpents of land, see Record Book B, pg. 266, Book No. 5, pg. 477, produces a paper purporting to be an original concession (the date of which has been omitted on record) from Charles Dehault DELASSUS, dated 9th of February, 1800, a plat of survey by James MACKAY, D.S. dated 22nd February, 1806, received for record by A. SOULARD. S.Genl. 27th of February, 1806. M.P. LEDUC, duly sworn, says that the signature to the concession is in the proper handwriting of the said Carlos Dehault DELASSUS, and that the signature to the plat of survey is in the proper handwriting of the said Antoine SOULARD. (No. 313)

Ludwell BACON by his legal representatives claiming 1,000 arpents of land, see Record Book E, pg. 315, Book No. 5, pg. 378 & BATE's Decisions, pg. 91, produces a paper purporting to be an original concession from Carlos Dehault DELASSUS, dated 14th December, 1802, a plat of survey signed William RUSSELL, dated August 18th, 1812. M.P. LEDUC, duly sworn, says that the signature to the concession is in the proper handwriting of the said Carlos Dehault DELASSUS. (No. 314)

(Peter) BUREL by his legal representatives claiming 2,000 arpents of land, see Record Book E, pg. 325, BATE's minutes, pg. 7, BATE's Decisions, pg. 27.

George PURSLEY by his legal representatives claiming 800 arpents of land, situate on Point LABBADIE Creek, see Record Book D, pg. 323 for notice of 1100 arpents, Record Book E, pgs. 331 for notice abandoning over 800 arpents, Minutes Book No. 3, pg. 336, No. 4, pg. 323, BATE's Minutes, pg. 24, where the same is "not granted". (No. 315)

Philip ROBERTS by his legal representatives claiming 1,050 arpents of land on waters of Grand Glaize, see Record Book F, pg. 39, Minutes No. 5, pg. 492, BATE's minutes, pg. 24, BATE's Decisions, pg. 29.
The Board adjourned until tomorrow at 9 o'clock A.M.
Friday June 19th, 1835 Board Met-Two Comm'rs. Present

Ephraim MUSICK claiming 800 arpents of land situate on Waters of Feefee's creek, see Record Book E, pg. 319, BATE's minutes, pgs. 1 &2, BATE's decisions, pg. 27. (No. 316)

Thomas P. BEDFORD claiming 800 arpents of land situate about 7 miles from St. Genevieve, see Record Book E, pg. 335, BATE's minutes, pg. 109, Decisions, pg. 35. (No. 317)

Joab LINE claiming 750 arpents of land on Wolf Creek, St. Genevieve, see Record Book E, pg. 341, for notice for 100 arpents, see Book B, pg. 95, Comm'rs. Minutes, Book No. 2, pg. 29, No. 4, pg. 344, BATE's Minutes, pg. 66, Decisions, pg. 32. (No. 318)

John DANIEL claiming 800 arpents of land situate on waters of Saline creek, St. Genevieve, see Record Book F, pg. 15 & 260, BATE's minutes, pg. 128, Decisions, pg. (Cannot read)

Walter SMOOT by his legal reprentatives claiming 800 arpents of land in St. Genevieve County, see Record Book F, pg. 260, BATE's Minutes, pg. 128, Decisions, pg. 21. (No. 319)

Michael RABER by his legal representatives claiming 748 arpents of land on waters of Big river, see Record Book B, pg. 245, Comm'rs. Minutes, Book No. 5, pg. 485, BATE's Minutes, pg. 114, BATE's decisions, pg. (not written in minutes)

Absalom RANDALL by his legal representatives claiming 778 arpents &
29 perches of land on Hubble's creek, for list A, on which claimant
is No. 52 for 300 arpents, see Record Book B, pg. 320, for survey of
778 arpents & 29 perches, see Book B, pg. 333, Minutes Book No. 3, pg.
477, No. 4, pg. 325. (No. 320)

John Bste. DARDENNE by his legal representatives claiming 1,600 arpents of land on Arkansas river, see Record Book F, pg. 235, BATE's
minutes, pg. 158, Decisions, pg. 26.   (Ark. No. 1, pg. 220)

John HYNAM by his legal representatives claiming 800 arpents of land
on Arkansas river, see Book F, pg. 226, BATE's minutes, pg. 158,
Decisions, pg. (?) (Ark. No. 2, pg. 220)

        COUISSAT by his legal representatives claiming 800 arpents of
land on Arkansas river, see Record Book F, pg. 226, BATE's Minutes,
pg. 158, Decisions, pg. (?) (Ark. No. 3, pg. 220)

John DORTILLIER by his legal representatives claiming 800 arpents of
land on waters of Arkansas river, see Record Book F, pg. 14, BATE's
minutes, pg. 160, Decisions, pg. (?) (Ark. No. 4, pg. 220)

Joseph DUCHASSIN by his legal representatives claiming 750 arpents
of land on the Arkansas river, see Record Book F, pg. 19, BATE's
minutes, pg. 159. (Ark. No. 5, pg. 221)

James MOORE by his legal representatives claiming 640 acres of land
situated on Stump creek, see Record Book F, pg. 227, BATE's minutes,
pg. 154, Decision, pg. (?) (Ark. No. 6, pg. 221)

Michael AQUETON by his legal representatives claiming 2,000 arpents
of land on White River, see Record Book F, pg. 227, BATE's minutes,
pg. 157. (Ark. No. 7, pg. 221)

James MCKIM by his legal representatives claiming 760 arpents of
land on Wappinock Bayou, see Record Book F, pg. 226, BATE's minutes
pg. 53. (Ark. No. 10, pg. 222)

GRAVER by his legal representatives namely John Bste. and
Francis GRAVER, alias GRABER claiming 1,600 arpents of land on Waters
of Black River, Arkansas Territory, see Record Book F, pg. 225, BATE's
minutes, pg. 157. (Ark. No. 8, pg. 221)

Baptiste SOCIER by his legal representatives claiming 760 arpents of
land at Pine Bluffs on the Southward side of White River, see Book F,
pg. 225, BATE's minutes, pg. 156, (Ark. No. 9, pg. 221)
        Adjourned until tomorrow at 9 o'clock A.M.
            The Board Met & Adjourned June 20th, 22nd, 23rd, 1835.
            Wednesday June 24th, 1835 Board Met-F.R. CONWAY, Present

John WELDON by his legal representatives claiming 500 arpents of land,
see Record Book D, pg. (cannot read), Book No. 4, pg. 309.

Robert MCCAY by his legal representatives claiming 320 arpents of land
in the District of Cape Girardeau, see Record Book E, pg. 125, Book
No. 5, pg. 17, BATE's Decisions, pg. 10, where the same is "Not confirmed", produces a paper purporting to be an original order of survey
signed by Jaun Ventura MORALES, acting Intendant & Manuel SERRANO,
Assessor General, dated May 7th, 1802. The following testimony was
taken on the 28th of May, & the 15th of October, 1833 before
L.F. LINN, Esqr. then one of the Comm'rs.
State of Missouri, County of Cape Girardeau
Joseph BOGY aged about 51 years, being duly sworn as the law directs,
deposeth & saith that he was well acquainted with Juan Venture MORALES
who was Intendant per interim in 1802 at New Orleans. That he has often seen him write and that the signature of the said MORALES to the
concession or grant appended to the original petition of the said
MCCAY is the proper name and signature and in the proper handwriting
of the said Juan Venture MORALES. Deponent was, also, well acquainted
with Manuel SERRANO, who was the Counsellor attorney, or legal adviser

under the Spanish government in 1802, and the signature to the grant aforesaid is the proper name & signature & in the proper handwriting of the said Manuel SERRANO. And this deponent, further, says that he knew Robert MCCAY, the original grantee. That he was an (cannot read) under the Spanish government, but the exact year he does not remember. Joseph BOGY   Sworn & Subscribed before me this 28th day of May, 1833. L.F. LINN, Comm'r.

John FRIEND, a witness aged 52 years being duly sworn as the law directs, deposeth & saith that he came to this country, then the province of Upper Louisiana in the year 1799 in the fall of that year. That he became acquainted in that year with Robert MCCAY, who was then a citizen & resident in New Madrid. That said Robert MCCAY has from the year 1799 to the present time remained & continued a citizen & resident of the country & still is.

John (X) FRIEND   Sworn to & Subscribed before me this 15th day of October, 1833. L.F. LINN, Comm'r.

Adjourned until tomorrow at 9 o'clock A.M.
Thursday June 25th, 1835 Board Met-F.R. CONWAY, Present

Francois LACOMBE by his legal representatives claiming 400 arpents of land situate on River Gravois, see Record Book F, pg. 143, BATE's minutes, pg. 61, BATE's Decisions, pg. 32, produces a paper purporting to be an original concession from Zenon TRUDEAU, dated November 26th, 1797. M.P. LEDUC, duly sworn, says that the signature to the concession is in the proper handwriting of the said Zenon TRUDEAU.

Adjourned until tomorrow at 9 o'clock A.M.
The Board Met & Adjourned June 26th, 1835.
Saturday June 27th, 1835 Board Met-J.M. MARTIN, Present

In the case of Jacques VINCENT claiming 10,000 arpents of land, see Book No. 7, pg. 128.
Jean Elie THOLOZAN, the legal representative of claimant, being duly sworn, says that in the year 1812, he started from New Orleans on horse back for the purpose of bringing to St. Louis the original papers relating to the case. That when he arrived at Natchez, he had the yellow fever & remained five weeks sick in said place. That when he started from Natchez he was very weak, and on his way from Washitaw to Arkansas, having had to cross a creek on a log, he carried his saddlebags, containing all his papers, on his arm and when about the middle of the stream, finding himself giddy, he was obliged to let go his saddlebags in order to prevent his falling into the water and in this manner lost the said papers.

Adjourned until Monday next at 9 o'clock A.M.
Monday June 29th, 1835 Board Met-J.M. MARTIN, Present

Jonathan VINEYARD claiming 500 arpents of land situate District of St. Louis, see Record Book B, pg. 251, Comm'rs. Minutes No. 1, pg. 475, No. 4, pg. 499.
John PRITCHETT, duly sworn, says that he is about 43 years of age. That in the beginning of the fall of 1804, he saw said
Jonathan VINEYARD inhabiting & cultivating the place claimed. That he had a temporary cabin werein he lived with his wife and, he believes, two children. Witness thinks there was about half an acre fenced in with a brush fence and may be some rails. He saw turnips growing in said inclosure. Witness, further, says that the land lies on Dubois Creek about 3 or 4 miles from Washington in Franklin County.

Adjourned until tomorrow at 9 o'clock A.M.
Tuesday June 30th, 1835 Board Met-F.H. MARTIN, Present

Jean HARVIN by his legal representatives claiming 600 arpents of land situate in Bois Brule bottom, District of St. Genevieve, see Record Book E, pg. 226, produces a paper purporting to be an original concession from Carlos Dehault DELASSUS, dated 22nd September, 1800.
M.P. LEDUC, duly sworn, says that the signature to the concession is in the proper handwriting of the said Carlos Dehault DELASSUS.
Francoise DANY, duly sworn, says that she is upwards of 59 years of age. That in the year 1803, she was on the tract claimed. That in the said year she saw on said place a dwelling house & several out buildings wherein said HARVIN lived with his family composed of himself, his wife & four children. That HARVIN had a field, but witness does not recollect how many arpents were then inclosed. There was a

good garden and said HARVIN had a good stock of horses & cattle.

Alexis MAURICE claiming 400 arpents of land situate Bois Brule, District of St. Genevieve, see Book No. 5, pg. 460, Record Book E, pg. 226, produces a paper purporting to be an original concession from Carlos Dehault DELASSUS, dated 24th May, 1800. M.P. LEDUC, duly sworn, says that the signature to the concession is in the proper handwriting of the said Carlos D. DELASSUS.

Joseph BELCOUR claiming 400 arpents of land situate Bois Brule, District of St. Genevieve, see Record Book E, pg. 226, Comm'rs. Minutes Book No. 3, pg. 383, No. 4, pg. 481, produces a paper purporting to be an original concession from Carlos D. DELASSUS, dated 18th March, 1800. M.P. LEDUC, duly sworn, says that the signature to the concession is in the proper handwriting of the said Carlos D. DELASSUS.
    Adjourned until tomorrow at 9 o'clock A.M.
        Wednesday July 1st, 1835 Board Met-F.H. MARTIN, Present

Jesse RAYNOR claiming 640 acres of land situate on Sandy Creek, District of St. Louis, see Record Book D, pg. 165, Minutes Book, No. 3, pg. 372, No. 5, pg. 337. (2d, 69, P. 223)

Philip ROBERT by his legal representatives claiming 1,097 arpents of land on waters of Grand Glaize, District of St. Louis, see Record Book E, pg. 234, Book No. 5, pg. 492. (2d,70, pg. 223)

Thomas JONES by his legal representatives claiming 1,000 arpents of land on Grand Glaize creek, District of St. Louis, see Record Book D, pg. 165, Minutes Book No. 5, pg. 439. (2d, 71 p. 223)

Thomas JONES by his legal representatives claiming 1,000 arpents of land on Big River, District of St. Louis, see Record Book E, pg. 326, BATE's minutes, pg. 6, BATE's Decisions, pg. 27. (2d, 72 p. 223)

John GERARD by his legal representatives claiming 320 arpents of land on Grand Glaize, District of St. Louis, see Record Book D, pg. 165, Minutes Book No. 5, pg. 430. (2d,73 p.223)

John GODFREY claiming 640 acres on the Maramec, see Record Book E, pg. 317, BATE's decisions, pg. 91, where the same is "Not Granted".
(2d, 150, pg. 246)
    Adjourned until tomorrow at 9 o'clock A.M.
        Thursday July 2nd, 1835 Board Met-F.R. CONWAY, Present

Gabriel CERRE by his legal representatives claiming 400 arpents of land situate on the Marameck, see Record Book A, pg. 246, Minutes Bk. No. 1, pg. 12, No. 5, pg. 523. (No. 326, pg. 222)

In the case of Curtis MORRIS, see Book No. 7, pg. 46. The following testimony was received by mail.
Territory of Arkansas, Hempstead County
Depositions of witness produced sworn & examined on the twelfth day of June, 1835, between the hours of 8 o'clock in the forenoon & 6 o'clock in the afternoon of that day in the Clerk's office in the town of Washington & County of Hempstead, Territory of Arkansas, before Birkett D. JETT & Henry DIXON, two Justices of the Peace within & for the County aforesaid, in pursuance of an order of the Honorable Board of Comm'rs. appointed for the final adjustment of private land claims in Missouri, passed on the 23rd day of October, 1834, authorising the claimants for the land claimed by Curtis MORRIS, or his legal representatives, to take the depositions of Walter CROW & others residing in the Territory of Arkansas, it appearing to us that the notice had been given to the adverse claimant agreeably to the order of the Board. Walter CROW of lawful age being first duly sworn, deposeth & saith: Question by James MCLAUGHLIN, agent for A.W. HUDSPETH: Do you know Curtis MORRIS's settlement right in Bellevue, Washington County, State of Missouri? Ans: I do. Quest. by same: When was it made? Ans: In the year 1804. Quest. by same: When was it inhabited & cultivated by MORRIS? Ans: In the year 1805 he moved on it & cultivated it. Quest. by same: Do you or do you not know from information obtained from

Curtis MORRIS whether he improved & settled said place for himself
or another? Ans: I heard Curtis MORRIS say, some time after he settled on the place aforesaid, that he settled it for himself, although
it had been said he settled it for James AUSTIN. Quest. by same: Have
you knowledge when he first claimed in his own name? Ans: I have not.
Quest. by same: When di he finish his cabin fit for the reception of
his family? Ans: He removed into his cabin early in the year 1805,
perhaps in the month of January or February. Quest. by same: Did
Walter CROW have an improvement in 1804 at the spring where
Curtis MORRIS settled and did he cultivate it in that year, hold his
land by it & take it within his lines, when confirmed, and did he sell
it to Daniel PHELPS? Ans: He had an improvement in 1804, but did not
cultivate it in that year and did hold his land by it. When his land
was confirmed & lines run they left out a part of his own improvement
and took in a part of said MORRIS's improvement. He sold a part of
said land to Daniel PHELPS and that part included his original improvement. Quest. by same: Did Curtis MORRIS cultivate or inhabit before
his marriage? Ans: I do not know. Quest. by same: Were you frequently at that place in the year 1804? Ans: I do not recollect being on
the place but once in that year, and then saw MORRIS there carrying on
work & building a house. Quest. by same: Did the original lines of
Curtis MORRIS take in the improvement & mill made by Thomas MORROW &
William INGE & Jacob MAHAN for INGE and now claimed by A.W. HUDSPETH
on Cedar creek in Bellevue aforesaid? Answ I do not know. Quest. by
same: Where did Curtis MORRIS make his home in 1804? Ans: I don't
certainly know, but am impressed with the belief that it was with
Wm. ASHBROOK about 5 miles from the improvement aforesaid. Quest. by
the Justices: Do you know of Curtis MORRIS, or any one for him having
performed any labour on the land mentioned, prior to the 20th of December, 1803? Ans: I do not. And, further, this deponent saith not.

                                              Walter CROW
Subscribed & sworn to before the undersigned two Justices of the peace
within & for the County of Hempstead, Arkansas Territory, at the place
& on the day & between the hours aforesaid. Given under our hands &
Seals this 12th day of June, A.D. 1835. Henry DIXON, J.P. (Seal)
Birkett D. JETT, J.P. (Seal)
James S.MCLAUGHLIN, being of lawfull age & first being sworn, deposeth
& saith. Quest: Do you know the land settled by Curtis MORRIS & now
claimed by the representatives of Daniel PHELPS in Bellevue, Washington County, State of Missouri? Ans: I do. Quest: When did MORRIS first
settle, inhabit & cultivate the same, and what do you know about it?
Ans: In the fore part of 1804, I saw said MORRIS working on the aforesaid land, building a cabin which he then raised about as high as a
man shoulders, which cabin he finished, I think, early in 1805. I frequently passed in 1804 & said unfinished cabin is all I recollect seeing until 1805. Mr. MORRIS married, I think, the 9th January, 1805, &
soon after removed to said cabin & cultivated it in that year. Quest:
Do you know of Curtis MORRIS or any person for him having performed
any labour upon the land mentioned prior to the 20th day of December,
1803? Ans: I do not. And further this deponent saith not, being no
further interrogated.
J.S. MCLAUGHLIN. Subscribed & sworn to before the undersigned two
Justices of the Peace within & for the County of Hempstead, Arkansas
Territory, at the place, and on the day and between the hours afore-
said. Given under our hands and seals this 12th day June, A.D. 1835.
Henry DIXON, J.P. (Seal)   Birkett D. JETT, J.P. (Seal)

The United States of America, Territory of Arkansas, County of Hempstead
I, James W. FINLEY, Deputy Clerk for Allen M. OAKLEY, Clerk of the
Hempstead County Court, do hereby certify that Henry DIXON and
Birkett D. JETT, whose names are affixed to the foregoing depositions,
are duly commissioned and acting Justices of the peace in & for the
Territory & County aforesaid and that as such due faith and credit is
and ought to be given to all their official acts. In Testimony where-
of I have hereunto set my hand & as Clerk & affixed the seal of said
County at Washington this 12th day of June, 1835, and of the Indepen-
dence of the United States the 59th.
James W. FINLEY, Dept. for Allen M. OAKLEY, Clk.
     Adjourned until tomorrow at 9 o'clock A.M.

The Board Met & Adjourned July 3rd, 1835.
Saturday July 4th, 1835 Board Met-F.R. CONWAY, Present

Louis OUVRAY by his legal representatives claiming 800 arpents of
land on River Au Cuivre. For concession, see Record Book F, pg. 54,
for Survey, Book C, pg. 349, Minutes Book No. 5, pg. 369.
Charles SANGUINET, duly sworn, says that he, witness, gave the original concession to his brother in law, H. COSIN, to have the same recorded in one of the upper counties. That said COSIN died a short
time afterwards, and since his death, witness has not been able to
discover what had become of said paper. (2d, 114, pg. 235)
      Adjourned until Monday next at 9 o'clock A.M.
      The Board Met & Adjourned July 6th, 1835.
      Tuesday July 7th, 1835 Board Met-F.R. CONWAY, Present

In the case of Pierre TORNAT claiming 600 arpents of land, see Book
No. 6, pg. 189. David FINE, duly sworn, says that he is about 71
years of age, that he came to this country in 1802 & settled a place
in 1803, about 3 miles from the land claimed. That in 1804, he went
on the tract claimed & there saw two men, GIGUIERE & BAUDOUIN working
on said land, they lived in a cabin, which appeared to be an old one.
Witness, further, says there was an inclosure of two or three arpents
and as well as he can recollect, there were some fruit trees planted
and some of them are yet standing. That said LAJOIE moved on said
place, he thinks, in 1806 and lived there till his death. That after
LAJOIE's death, his widow left the place for about one year, and
having married one ST.JOHN, came back to said place and lived till
the said ST.JOHN's death, which happened about 10 or 11 years ago.
Witness believes there must be now under cultivation about 40 or 45
acres.
Pascal S. CERRE, duly sworn, says that several years before the change
of government, under Mr. DELASSUS, he saw GIGUIERE and BAUDOUIN living
in a camp made with Clap Boards, and working on said piece of land for
& under Pierre TORNAT dit LAJOIE, who hired them by the year. That
said two men had, before the cession to the United States, a small
field of three or four arpents in which they raised corn & tobacco, &
had apple trees planted. That said LAJOIS moved to said place with
his family in 1806 or 1807, and continued to inhabit & cultivate the
same until his death. Witness, further, says that said LAJOIE was an
excellent & very industrious farmer. That this land is situated on the
North side of the Marameck, about two miles below John BOLI's ferry,
opposite the little Saline & bounded on one side by the Marrameck & on
the other side by (cannot read) line. LAJOIE's house was at about 25
arpents from the bank of the river.

Henry O'HARA by his legal representatives claiming 1,000 arpents of
land situate on Grand Glaize, District of St. Louis, see Record Book
D, pg. 166. Claimant refers to Comm'rs. Minutes Book No. 4, pg. 148,
for testimony of Antoine VACHARD, dit SARDOISE, in the case of
Charles VALLE claiming 320 arpents.
Baptiste DOMINE, duly sworn, says that he is 86 years of age. That
during the Spanish government, under either Manuel PEREZ or
Zenon TRUDEAU, witness saw the said O'HARA living on a tract of land
situate between the river Joachim and the little rock on the Mississippi. Claimant had on said piece of land a dwelling house, out houses
a field and a fine orchard.
Charles VACHARD, duly sworn, says that he is about 63 years of age.
That during the Spanish government he saw claimant on a piece of land
situated on the Mississippi about 1-1/2 miles below the Joachim. That
he had a large field in which he raised corn, wheat, etc. Also, had
a fine orchard. Witness's brother lived near O'HARA's improvement &
witness was often on said O'HARA's plantation. That said O'HARA had
a large family and that he was driven away from his place by the Indians. Witness, further, says that he cannot state exactly how long
said O'HARA remained on said land, but when witness went to reside with
his brother, O'HARA had settled his place several years before, and
witness remained 7 or 8 years with his said brother, during which time
said O'HARA continued to inhabit & cultivate said place.
Pierre CHOUTEAU, Sr., duly sworn, says that in the year 1778 or 79, as
he was coming from St. Genevieve in a boat, he was obliged on account

of the ice drifting in the Mississippi to unload his boat & put his goods in one Charles VALLE's house. That Henry O'HARA had a plantation adjoining that of said VALLE. Witness knew said O'HARA for many years having transacted business with him during the time O'HARA remained on said place, which was at least for ten consecutive years. Witness, further, says that after the attack of the Indians on the settlements in the year 1780, all the settlers were called in by the Lt. Gov., and said O'HARA, some time afterwards, sold his plantation, which was situated below the little rock near the Grand Glaize. Witness does not recollect whether it was ever cultivated afterwards. (No. 325, pg. 222)

Antoine VACHARD dit SARDOISE by his legal representatives claiming 640 acres of land in the District of St. Louis, see Record Book F, pg. 139, BATE's minutes, pg. 133, BATE's Decisions, pg. 37.
Baptiste DOMINE, duly sworn, says that he is 86 years of age. That under the Spanish Government, he saw said Antoine VACHARD inhabiting & cultivating a place between the Joachim creek and the little rock. That there was a house on said place and a field and witness as he went & came from Ste. Genevieve, saw the said VACHARD on said place for about 4 consecutive years.
Charles VACHARD, duly sworn, says that he is about 63 years of age. That under the Spanish Government, before Zenon TRUDEAU's time, witness's brother, Antoine VACHARD, settled a place between the Joachim and the little Rock. That there was on said place a dwelling house, a barn and a field in which said Antoine raised corn & wheat. Witness thinks his brother lived at least ten years on said place & was the last of the settlers, who left that settlement on account of the Indians. This was several years before the change of government. Witness says that Antoine VACHARD never returned on said place, but remained in the country about New Madrid. (2d, 79, pg. 227)

James SWIFT by his legal representatives claiming 640 acres of land in the District of St. Charles, see Record Book D, pg. 333.
Arthur BURNS, duly sworn, says that he is about 52 yeass of age. That he came to this country under the government of Zenon TRUDEAU. That before the change of government the said James SWIFT went on a piece of land, which had been improved by one BOON. That said SWIFT built thereon a cabin & cleared a small piece of land for the purpose of sowing turnips, but witness does not know whether the turnips were sowed. Witness, further, says that said SWIFT being out of provisions and the mosquitoes being very troublesome, he left said place about three weeks after he had first come there, and witness never knew that he returned to said place. (2d, 76, pg. 223)

In the case of Joseph MOTARD claiming 1,340 arpents of land, see Book No. 6, pg. 216. Pascal S. CERRE, duly sworn, says that he knew MOTARD's plantation from the year 1787 to 1791 & from 1794 till the change of government. That said plantation, as cultivated by, or under said MOTARD, was to his perfect knowledge, outside of the St. Louis common.
Michael MARLI, duly sworn, says that he is 56 years of age. That he knew MOTARD's plantation for forty years. That the fences of the commons went to MOTARD's field & thence run towards River des Peres, leaving said MOTARD's farm outside of the said common. Witness, further, says that he rented said plantation for two years from Calvin ADAMS. This was about 15 years ago. Witness does not know of any other improvement made in that neighbourhood.
Charles VACHARD, being duly sworn, says that he has known MOTARD's plantation for great many years. That he, witness, cultivated the same for two or three years. That it was outside of the common, and he can yet show where the fence of the common was laid, leaving said plantation entirely outside of said common. Witness never knew of any other improvement in that vicinity.
　　　Adjourned until tomorrow at 9 o'clock A.M.
　　　Wednesday July 8th, 1835 Board Met-F.R. CONWAY & J.H. RELFE

In the case of James BROWN claiming 640 acres of land, see No. 7, pg. 132, the following testimony was taken before James H. RELFE, Comm'r. in Washington County.

Zacaria GOFORTH deposeth & saith that he came to the settlement of Bellevue in the County of Washington in the Territory of Missouri, in the month of March, 1804. That in the month of July or August following a certain James BROWN came to the neighbourhood & established himself in a camp about 3 miles West of the present village of Caledonia, where deponent's father lived. That the said BROWN lived in his camp some short time & then erected a small cabin. Deponent has no recollection of any cultivation on said place as made by claimant BROWN that fall. As well as Deponent recollects, the next season, viz: in 1805, BROWN built a cabin for Joseph BARR, and when it was finished moved into it. This is the same improvement, which was confirmed to John CORDER's representatives. About the time BROWN moved into the cabin built on CORDER's place, he sold the cabin he first built to one Saul or Solomon HEWIT.   Z. GOFORTH Sworn to & subscribed this 30th June, 1835 before James H. RELFE, Comm'r.

In the case of Curtis MORRIS claiming, etc., see Book No. 6, pg. 385. The following testimony was taken before James H. RELFE, one of the Comm'rs. for the adjustment of private land claims. Elijah GRAGG, who on his oath deposeth & saith that in about the year 1816 or 1817, he was conversing with Curtis MORRIS on the subject of his land claim in Bellevue, and asked him why he sold his land so cheap, or told him he sold it too cheap. He replied he never thought it would be confirmed as it was not settled in time. As well as deponent recollects, PHELPS gave three hundred dollars for the claim.
Elijah GRAGG   Sworn to & subscribed this 6th July, 1835.
                                                    James H. RELFE, Comm'r.
    Adjourned until tomorrow at 9 o'clock A.M.
        Thursday July 9th, 1835 Board Met
    The Board Adjourned in order to give time to the Clerk to make up the transcripts and for the purpose of the examination of claims until the 15th of August.
        Monday August 17th, 1835 Board Met-F.R. CONWAY, J.H. RELFE,
                                            F.H. MARTIN, Present

Thomas POWERS claiming 650 arpents of land, see Book No. 7, pg. 191. The Board are unanimously of opinion that this claim ought to be confirmed to the said Thomas POWERS, or to his legal representatives, according to the concession and survey. (No. 313)

Sudwell BACON claiming 1,000 arpents of land, see Book No. 7, pg. 192. A majority of the Board are of opinion that this claim ought to be confirmed to the said Sudwell BACON, or to his legal representatives, according to the concession. James H. RELFE, Comm'r., dissenting. (No. 314)

Peter BURRELL claiming 2,000 arpents of land, see Book No. 7, pg. 192. The Board are unanimously of opinion that this claim ought not to be granted, the said Peter BURRELL having had a tract of 1,600 arpents confirmed. see BATE's decisions, pg. 25. (2d, No. 63)

Philip ROBERT claiming 1,050 arpents of land, see Book No. 7, pg. 193. The Board are unanimously of opinion that this claim ought not to be granted there being no proof of cultivation. (2d, No. 64)

George PURSLEY claiming 800 arpents of land, see Book No. 7, pg. 192. The Board are unanimously of opinion that 640 acres of land ought to be granted to the said George PURSLEY, or to his legal representatives, according to possession. (No. 315)

Ephraim MUSICK claiming 800 arpents of land, see Book No. 7, pg. 193. The Board are unanimously of opinion that 640 acres of land ought to be granted to the said Ephraim MUSICK, or to his legal representatives, according to possession. (No. 316)

Thomas P. BEDFORD claiming 800 arpents of land, see Book No. 7, pg. 193. The Board are unanimously of opinion that 640 acres of land ought to be granted to the said Thomas P. BEDFORD, or to his legal representatives, according to possession. (No. 317)

Adjourned until tomorrow at 9 o'clock A.M.
Tuesday August 18th, 1835 Board Met-All Comm'rs. Present

Joab LINE claiming 750 arpents of land, see Book No. 7, pg. 193.
The Board are unanimously of opinion that 750 arpents of land ought
to be granted to the said Joab LINE, or to his legal representatives,
(cannot read) (No. 318)

Walter SMOOT claiming 800 arpents of land, see Book No. 7, pg. 194.
The Board are unanimously of opinion that 640 acres of land ought to
be granted to the said Walter SMOOT, or to his legal representatives.
(No. 319)

Abraham RANDALL claiming 778 arpents of land, see Book No. 7, pg. 194.
The Board are unanimously of opinion that 300 arpents of land ought
to be confirmed to the said Abraham RANDALL, or to his legal represen-
tatives, according to the concession & list A, on which claimant is
No. 52 for 300 arpents. For concession & list A, see
Joseph THOMPSON, Jr.'s claim, decision No. 202. (No. 320)

Francois LACOMBE claiming 400 arpents of land, see Book No. 7, pg.
198. The Board are unanimously of opinion that this claim ought to
be confirmed to the said Francois LACOMBE, or to his legal representatives, according to the order of survey by C.D. DELASSUS. (No. 321)

Jean HARVIN claiming 600 arpents of land, see Book No. 7, pg. 200.
The Board are unanimously of opinion that this claim ought to be confirmed to the said Jean HARVIN, or to his legal representatives, according to the concession. (No. 322)

Alexis MAURICE claiming 400 arpents of land, see Book No. 7, pg. 201.
The Board are unanimously of opinion that this claim ought to be confirmed to the said Alexis MAURICE, or to his legal representatives,
according to the concession. (No. 323)

Joseph BELCOUR claiming 400 arpents of land, see Book No. 7, pg. 201.
The Board are unanimously of opinion that this claim ought to be confirmed to the said Joseph BELCOUR, or to his legal representatives,
according to the concession. (No. 324)

John DANIEL claiming 800 arpents of land, see Book No. 7, pg. 193.
The Board are unanimously of opinion that this claim ought not to be
granted.

Michael RABER claiming 748 arpents of land, see Book No. 7, pg. 194.
The Board are unanimously of opinion that this claim ought not to be
granted, the said Michael RABER having had a settlement right granted
to him. See BATE's decisions pg. 72.

John WELDON claiming 500 arpents of land, see Book No. 7, pg. 196.
The Board are unanimously of opinion that this claim ought not to be
confirmed, the said J. WELDON having relinquished the same. (2d, 67)

Jonathan VINEYARD claiming 500 arpents of land, see Book No. 7, pg.
200. The Board are unanimously of opinion that this claim ought not
to be granted.

The following ten claims situated in the Territory of Arkansas, were
presented by William RUSSELL and acted upon by the Board in pursuance
of an act of Congress entitled: An Act for the relief of
John Elie THOLOZAN & Willm. RUSSELL, approved June 28th, 1834.

John Bste. DARDENNE claiming 1,600 arpents of land, see Book No. 7, pg
194. The Board are unanimously of opinion that 640 acres of land
ought to be granted to the said John Bste. DARDENNE, or to his legal
representatives, according to possession. (Arkansas No. 1)

John HYNAM claiming 800 arpents of land, see Book No. 7, pg. 194. A
majority of the Board are of opinion that 640 acres of land ought to
be granted to the said John HYNAM, or to his legal representatives,

according to possession. James H. RELFE, Comm'r., dissenting. (Ark. #2)

COUISSAT claiming 800 arpents of land, see Book No. 7, pg. 194. The Board are unanimously of opinion that 640 acres of land ought to be granted to the said COUISSAT, or to his legal representatives, according to possession. (Arkansas No. 3)

John DORTILLIER claiming 800 arpents of land, see Book No. 7, pg. 195. The Board are unanimously of opinion that 800 arpents of land ought to be granted to said John DORTILLIER, or to his legal representatives, according to his possession. (Ark. No. 4)

Joseph DUCHASSIN claiming 750 arpents of land, see Book No. 7, pg. 195. The Board are unanimously of opinion that 750 arpents of land ought to be granted to the said Joseph DUCHASSIN, or to his legal representatives, according to possession. (Ark. No. 5)

James MOORE claiming 640 acres of land, see Book No. 7, pg. 195. A majority of the Board are of opinion that 640 acres of land ought to be granted to the said James MOORE, or to his legal representatives, according to possession. James H. RELFE, Comm'r., dissenting. (Ark. 6)

Michael AQUETON claiming 2,000 arpents of land, see Book No. 7, pg. 195. The Board are unanimously of opinion that 640 acres of land ought to be granted to the said Michael AQUETON, or to his legal representatives. The said 640 acres situated on Cash creek, adjoining Tessier, according to possession. (Ark. No. 7)

GRAVER claiming 1,600 arpents of land, see Book No. 7, pg. 195. The Board are unanimously of opinion that 640 acres of land ought to be granted to the said GRAVER, alias GRABER, or to his legal representatives, according to possession. (Ark. 8)

Baptiste SOCIER claiming 760 arpents of land, see Book No. 7, pg. 196. The Board are unanimously of opinion that 640 acres of land ought to be granted to the said Baptiste SOCIER, or to his legal representatives, according to the possession. (Ark. 9)

(cannot read the last entry)
        Adjourned until tomorrow at 9 o'clock A.M.
            Wednesday Aug. 14th, 1835 Board Met-All Comm'rs. Present

Henry O'HARA claiming 10,000 arpents of land, see Book No. 7, pg. 200. The Board are unanimously of opinion that 1,440 arpents of land ought to be granted to the said Henry O'HARA, or to his legal representatives, according to the possession.

Gabriel CERRE claiming 400 arpents of land, see Book No. 7, pg. 203. The Board are unanimously of opinion that this claim ought to be confirmed to the said Gabriel CERRE, or to his legal representatives, according to the concession.

Robert MCCAY claiming 320 arpents of land, see Book No. 7, pg. 197. The Board are unanimously of opinion that 320 arpents of land ought to be confirmed to the said Robert MCCAY, or to his legal representatives, according to the order of survey.

Jesse RAYNOR claiming 640 acres of land, see Book No. 7, pg. 202. The Board are unanimously of opinion that this claim ought not to be granted.

Philip ROBERT claiming 1,097 arpents of land, see Book No. 7, pg. 202. The Board are unanimously of opinion that this claim ought not to be granted.

Thomas JONES claiming 1,000 arpents of land, see Book No. 7, pg. 202. (Grand Glaize) The Board are unanimously of opinion that this claim ought not to be granted.

Thomas JONES claiming 1,000 arpents of land, see Book No. 7, pg. 202.

(Big River) The Board are unanimously of opinion that this claim
ought not to be granted.

John GERARD claiming 320 arpents of land, see Book No. 7, pg. 202.
The Board are unanimously of opinion that this claim ought not to be
granted.

James SWIFT claiming 640 acres of land, see Book No. 7, pg. 212.
The Board are unanimously of opinion that this claim ought not to be
granted.
        Adjourned until tomorrow at 9 o'clock A.M.
            Thursday Aug. 20th, 1835 Board Met-All Comm'rs. Present

Joseph MOTARD claiming 1,340 arpents of land, see Book No. 6, pg. 217,
No. 7, pg. 213. The Board are unanimously of opinion that 280 arpents
of land (it being the quantity ordered to be surveyed by the Lt. Gov.)
ought to be confirmed to the said Joseph MOTARD, or to his legal representatives, according to the said order of survey. (No. 328)

Diego MAXWELL claiming 112,896 arpents of land, see Book No. 6, pg.
125. The Board are unanimously of opinion that this claim ought not
to be confirmed, the conditions not having been complied with.
(2d, 75)

The following claim of Jacques VINCENT was presented by
Jean Elie THOLOZAN and acted upon by the Board conformably to an act
of Congress Entitled "An act for the relief of John Elie THOLOZAN &
William RUSSELL" approved June 28th, 1834.

Jacques VINCENT claiming 10,000 arpents of land, see Book No. 7, pg.
125 & 199. The Board are unanimously of opinion that this claim
ought to be confirmed to the said Jacques VINCENT, or to his legal
representatives, according to the order of survey. (Ark. 11)
        Adjourned until tomorrow at 9 o'clock A.M.
            Friday Aug. 21st, 1835 Board Met-All Comm'rs. Present

Curtis MORRIS claiming 746 arpents & 75 perches of land, see Book No.
6, pg. 385, Book No. 7, pgs. 12, 26, 46, 131 & 203. The Board are
unanimously of opinion that 746 arpents & 75 perches of land ought to
be granted to the said Curtis MORRIS, or to his legal representatives,
according to the survey executed by John STEWART on the 6th of Jan.,
1806, and recorded in Book B, pg. 227 in the Recorder's Office. (329)

John L. PETIT claiming 640 acres of land, see Book No. 6, pg. 425.
The Board are unanimously of opinion that 640 acres of land ought to
be granted to the said John L. PETIT, or to his legal representatives,
according to possession. (330)

Peggy JONES, now Peggy CARTER claiming 640 acres of land, see Book No.
7, pg. 4. The Board are unanimously of opinion that 640 acres of land
ought to be granted to said Peggy JONES, now Peggy CARTER, or to her
legal representatives, according to her possession. (331)

William JANES claiming 620 arpents & 27 perches of land, see Book No.
7, pg. 150. The Board are unanimously of opinion that 620 arpents &
27 perches of land ought to be granted to the said William JANES, or
to his legal representatives, according to possession & survey. (332)

James CRAIG claiming 800 arpents of land, see Book No. 6, pg. 349.
The Board are unanimously of opinion that this claim ought not to be
granted. (2d, 76)

James SUMMERS claiming 250 acres of land, see Book No. 7, pg. 133.
The Board are unanimously of opinion that this claim ought not to be
granted. (2d, 77)

William FLYNN, Jr. claiming 200 acres of land, see Book No. 7, pg. 150.
The Board are unanimously of opinion that this claim ought not to be
granted. (2d, 78)
        Adjourned until tomorrow at 9 o'clock A.M.

Saturday Aug. 22nd, 1835 Board Met-All Comm'rs. Present

Alexander COLEMAN claiming 800 arpents of land, see Book No. 7, pg.
124. The Board are unanimously of opinion that 640 acres of land
ought to be granted to the said Alexander COLEMAN, or to his legal
representatives, but not to interfere with the Old Mine Concession.
(No. 333)

John Bste. VALLE claiming 20,000 arpents of land, see Book No. 7, pg.
129. The Board are unanimously of opinion that this claim ought to
be confirmed to the said John Bste. VALLE, or to his legal reprsenta-
tives, according to the concession. (No. 334)

James BROWN claiming 640 acres of land, see Book No. 6, pg. 369, No.
7, pg. 214. The Board are unanimously of opinion that 640 acres of
land ought to be granted to the said James BROWN, or to his legal
representatives, according to the survey. (No. 335)

Antoine VACHARD claiming 640 acres of land, see Book No. 7, pg. 211.
A majority of the Board are of opinion that this claim ought not to
be granted, one John Bste. OLIVE having had a confirmation, under
said Antoine VACHARD, for a tract of 250 arpents in New Madrid, see
Comm'rs. Certificate No. 631. (cannot read) for granting 640 acres
on the gound that the tract confirmed to the above named
John Bste. OLIVE, was sold by said Antoine VACHARD prior to the act
of Congress of 1805, and consequently was not claimed by him at the
passage of that act. (2d, 79)
    Adjourned until Monday next at 9 o'clock A.M.
        Monday Aug. 24th, 1835 Board Met-All Comm'rs. Present

Louis LAMALICE claiming 800 arpents of land, see Book No. 6, pg. 142.
After a careful examination of the testimony and the various deeds
of transfer on the claims numbered from 80 to 147 inclusive. The
Board have decided to place them in the second class believing them
to have been founded in an extensive scheme of speculation by the
assignees, unknown to the Governor and that the ostensible object,
the population of the country, was not intended to be complied with
at the time of procuring the grant. The Board are unanimously of
opinion that this claim ought not to be confirmed. (2d, 80)

Francois MOTIER claiming 800 arpents of land, see Book No. 7, pg. 81.
The Board are unanimously of opinion that this claim ought not to be
confirmed. For reasons, see decision on the claim of Louis LAMALICE,
No. 80. (2d, 81)

Francois ARNAUD claiming 800 arpents of land, see Book No. 7, pg. 81.
The Board are unanimously of opinion that this claim ought not to be
confirmed. For reasons, see Decision on the claim of L. LAMALICE,
No. 80. (2d, 82)

Francois MARECHAL claiming 800 arpents of land, see Book No. 6, pg.
143. The Board are unanimously of opinion that this claim ought not
to be confirmed. For reasons, see decision on the claim of
Louis LAMALICE, No. 80. (2d, 83)

Auguste LEFEVRE claiming 800 arpents of land, see Book No. 6, pg. 148.
The Board are unanimously of opinion that this claim ought not to be
confirmed. For reasons, see as above. (2d, 84)

John Bste. PROVENCHER claiming 800 arpents of land, see No. 6, pg. 148.
The Board are unanimously of opinion that this claim ought not to be
confirmed. For reasons, see above. (2d, 85)

Francois PACQUET claiming 800 arpents of land, see Book No. 6, pg. 148.
The Board are unanimously of opinion that this claim ought not to be
confirmed. For reasons, see above. (2d, 86)

Joseph RIVET claiming 800 arpents of land, see Book No. 6, pg. 85.
The Board are unanimously of opinion that this claim ought not to be
confirmed. For reasons, see above. (2d, 87)

Joseph PRESSE claiming 800 arpents of land, see Book No. 6, pg. 147.
The Board are unanimously of opinion that this claim ought not to be
confirmed. For reasons, see decision on the claim of Louis LAMALICE,
No. 80. (2d, 88)

Michel VALLE claiming 800 arpents of land, see Book No. 6, pg. 147.
The Board are unanimously of opinion that this claim ought not to be
confirmed. For reasons, see above. (2d, 89)

Antoine BIZET claiming 800 arpents of land, see Book No. 6, pg. 148.
The Board are unanimously of opinion that this claim ought not to be
confirmed. For reasons, see above. (2d, 90)

Louis BOISSI claiming (cannot read amount) arpents of land, see Book
No. 6, pg. 146. The Board are unanimously of opinion that this
claim ought not to be confirmed. For reasons, see above. (2d, 91)

Joseph CHARLEVILLE claiming 800 arpents of land, see Book No. 6, pg.
146. The Board are unanimously of opinion that this claim ought not
to be confirmed. For reasons, see above. (2d, 92)

Baptiste DOMINE claiming 800 arpents of land, see Book No. 6, pg. 145.
The Board are unanimously of opinion that this claim ought not to be
confirmed. For reasons, see above. (2d, 93)

Louis CHARLEVILLE claiming 800 arpents of land, see Book No. 6, pg.
145. The Board are unanimously of opinion that this claim ought not
to be confirmed. For reasons, see above. (2d, 94)

Francois BERNARD claiming 800 arpents of land, see Book No. 6, pg. 146.
The Board are unanimously of opinion that this claim ought not to be
confirmed. For reasons, see above. (2d, 95)

Baptiste MARLY claiming 800 arpents of land, see Book No. 6, pg. 144.
The Board are unanimously of opinion that this claim ought not to be
confirmed. For reasons, see above. (2d, 96)

St. Gemme BAUVAIS claiming 800 arpents of land, see Book No. 6, pg.
92. The Board are unanimously of opinion that this claim ought not to
be confirmed. For reasons, see above. (2d, 97)

Pierre ROUSSEL claiming 800 arpents of land, see Book No. 6, pg. 93.
The Board are unanimously of opinion that this claim ought not to be
confirmed. For reasons, see above. (2d, 98)

William CLARK claiming 800 arpents of land, see Book No. 6, pg. 86.
The Board are unanimously of opinion that this claim ought not to be
confirmed. For reasons, see above. (2d, 99)

Dominique HUGE claiming 800 arpents of land, see Book No. 6, pg. 85.
The Board are unanimously of opinion that this claim ought not to be
confirmed. For reasons, see above. (2d, 100)

Joseph DECARRY claiming 800 arpents of land, see Book No. 6, pg. 85.
The Board are unanimously of opinion that this claim ought not to be
confirmed. For reasons, see above. (2d, 101)

Jean Bste. DUMOULIN claiming 800 arpents of land, see Book No. 6, pg.
87. The Board are unanimously of opinion that this claim ought not
to be confirmed. For Reasons, see above. (2d, 102)

Joseph HEBERT claiming 800 arpents of land, see Book No. 6, pg. 86.
The Board are unanimously of opinion that this claim ought not to be
confirmed. For reasons, see above. (2d, 103)

Regis VASSEUR claiming 800 arpents of land, see Book No. 6, pg. 85.
The Board are unanimously of opinion that this claim ought not to be
confirmed. For reasons, see above. (2d, 104)

Jean Louis MARC claiming 800 arpents of land, see Book No. 6, pg. 144.

The Board are unanimously of opinion that this claim ought not to be confirmed. For reasons, see decision in the claim of Louis LAMALICE, No. 80. (2d, 105)

James HAFF claiming 800 arpents of land, see Book No. 6, pg. 537. The Board are unanimously of opinion that this claim ought not to be confirmed. For reasons, see above. (2d, 106)

Louis GRIMARD claiming 800 arpents of land, see Book No. 6, pg. 537. The Board are unanimously of opinion that this claim ought not to be confirmed. For reasons, see above. (2d, 107)

Jean GODINEAU claiming 800 arpents of land, see Book No. 6, pg. 135. The Board are unanimously of opinion that this claim ought not to be confirmed. For reasons, see above. (2d, 108)

Antoine DEJARLAIS claiming 800 arpents of land, see Book No. 6, pg. 537. The Board are unanimously of opinion that this claim ought not to be confirmed. For reasons, see above. (2d, 109)

Benjamin QUICK claiming 800 arpents of land, see Book No. 6, pg. 538. The Board are unanimously of opinion that this claim ought not to be confirmed. For reasons, see above. (2d, 110)

DEROUIN claiming 800 arpents of land, see Book No. 6, pg. 142. The Board are unanimously of opinion that this claim ought not to be confirmed. For reasons, see above. (2d, 111)

Joseph HUBERT claiming 800 arpents of land, see Book No. 6, pg. 143. The Board are unanimously of opinion that this claim ought not to be confirmed. For reasons, see above. (2d, 112)

Jean Bste. BRAVIER claiming 800 arpents of land, see Book No. 6, pg. 144. The Board are unanimously of opinion that this claim ought not to be confirmed. For reasons, see above. (2d, 113)

Louis OUVRAY claiming 800 arpents of land, see Book No. 7, pg. 207. The Board are unanimously of opinion that this claim ought not to be confirmed. For reasons, see above. (2d, 114)
Adjourned until tomorrow at 9 o'clock A.M.
Tuesday Aug. 25th, 1835 Board Met-All Comm'rs. Present

Jacob EASTWOOD claiming 800 arpents of land, see Book No. 6, pg. 81. The Board are unanimously of opinion that this claim ought not to be confirmed. For reasons, see above. (2d, 115)

T. TODD claiming 800 arpents of land, see Book No. 6, pg. 82. The Board are unanimously of opinion that this claim ought not to be confirmed. For reasons, see above. (2d, 116)

Daniel HUBBARD claiming 800 arpents of land, see Book No. 6, pg. 82. The Board are unanimously of opinion that this claim ought not to be confirmed.. For reasons, see above. (2d, 117)

Felix HUBBARD claiming 800 arpents of land, see Book No. 6, pg. 83. The Board are unanimously of opinion that this claim ought not to be confirmed. For reasons, see above. (2d, 118)

Eusebius HUBBARD claiming 800 arpents of land, see Book No. 6, pg. 83. The Board are unanimously of opinion that this claim ought not to be confirmed. For reasons, see above. (2d, 119)

Louis LAJOIE claiming 800 arpents of land, see Book No. 6, pgs. 81 & 423 & 399. The Board are unanimously of opinion that this claim ought not to be confirmed. For reasons, see above. (2d, 120)

Francois BELLANGER claiming 800 arpents of land, see Book No. 6, pg. 87. The Board are unanimously of opinion that this claim ought not to be confirmed. For reasons, see above. (2d, 121)

Joseph BILLOT claiming 800 arpents of land, see Book No. 6, pg. 83.

The Board are unanimously of opinion that this claim ought not to be confirmed. For reasons, see decision in the claim of L. LAMALICE, No. 80. (2d, 123)

Baptiste DELISLE, Sr. claiming 800 arpents of land, see Book No. 6, pg. 84. The Board are unanimously of opinion that this claim ought not to be confirmed. For reasons, see above. (2d, 124)

Paul DEJARLAIS claiming 800 arpents of land, see Book No. 6, pg. 84. The Board are unanimously of opinion that this claim ought not to be confirmed. For reasons, see above. (2d, 125)

Baptiste MARION claiming 800 arpents of land, see Book No. 6, pg. 66. The Board are unanimously of opinion that this claim ought not to be confirmed. For reasons, see above. (2d, 126)

Toussaint TOURVILLE claiming 800 arpents of land, see Book No. 6, pg. 67. The Board are unanimously of opinion that this claim ought not to be confirmed. For reasons, see above. (2d, 127)

Gabriel CONSTANT claiming 800 arpents of land, see Book No. 6, pg. 57. The Board are unanimously of opinion that this claim ought not to be confirmed. For reasons, see above. (2d, 128)

Antoine DESNOYERS claiming 800 arpents of land, see Book No. 6, pg. 58. The Board are unanimously of opinion that this claim ought not to be confirmed. For reasons, see above. (2d, 129)

Gabriel HUNAULT claiming 800 arpents of land, see Book No. 6, pg. 58. The Board are unanimously of opinion that this claim ought not to be confirmed. For reasons, see above. (2d, 130)

Charles THIBAULT claiming 800 arpents of land, see Book No. 6, pg. 58. The Board are unanimously of opinion that this claim ought not to be confirmed. For reasons, see above. (2d, 131)

Joseph DESNOYERS claiming 800 arpents of land, see Book No. 6, pg. 58. The Board are unanimously of opinion that this claim ought not to be confirmed. For reasons, see above. (2d, 132)

Augustin LANGLOIS claiming 800 arpents of land, see Book No. 6, pg. 59. The Board are unanimously of opinion that this claim ought not to be confirmed. For reasons, see above. (2d, 133)

Louis DESNOYERS claiming 800 arpents of land, see Book No. 6, pg. 59. The Board are unanimously of opinion that this claim ought not to be confirmed. For reasons, see above. (2d, 134)

Amable CHARTRAN claiming 800 arpents of land, see Book No. 6, pg. 59. The Board are unanimously of opinion that this claim ought not to be confirmed. For reasons, see above. (2d, 135)

François DESNOYERS claiming 800 arpents of land, see Book No. 6, pg. 59. The Board are unanimously of opinion that this claim ought not to be confirmed. For reasons, see above. (2d, 136)

Toussaint GENDRON claiming 800 arpents of land, see Book No. 6, pg. 57. The Board are unanimously of opinion that this claim ought not to be confirmed. For reasons, see above. (2d, 137)

Daniel QUICK claiming 800 arpents of land, see Book No. 6, pg. 538. The Board are unanimously of opinion that this claim ought not to be confirmed. For reasons, see above. (2d, 138)

Joseph JAMISON claiming 800 arpents of land, see Book No. 6, pg. 87. The Board are unanimously of opinion that this claim ought not to be confirmed. For reasons, see above. (2d, 139)

Charles MIVILLE claiming 800 arpents of land, see Book No. 6, pg. 141. The Board are unanimously of opinion that this claim ought not to be confirmed. For reasons, see decision in the claim of L. LAMALICE, No. 80. (2d, 140)

Joseph MARIE claiming 800 arpents of land, see Book No. 6, pg. 537. The Board are unanimously of opinion that this claim ought not to be confirmed. For reasons, see above. (2d, 141)

Baptiste JEFFREY claiming 800 arpents of land, see Book No. 6, pg. 536. The Board are unanimously of opinion that this claim ought not to be confirmed. For reasons, see above. (2d, 142)

Andre PELETIER claiming 800 arpents of land, see Book No. 6, pg. 66. The Board are unanimously of opinion that this claim ought not to be confirmed. For reasons, see above. (2d, 143))

Pierre LORD claiming 800 arpents of land, see Book No.6, pg. 68. The Board are unanimously of opinion that this claim ought not to be confirmed. For reasons, see above. (2d, 144)

Joseph LAFLEUR claiming 800 arpents of land, see Book No. 6, pg. 68. The Board are unanimously of opinion that this claim ought not to be confirmed. For reasons, see above. (2d, 145)

Joseph Philip LAMARCHE claiming 800 arpents of land, see Book No. 6, pg. 535. The Board are unanimously of opinion that this claim ought not to be confirmed. For reasons, see above. (2d, 146)

Francois Lami DUCHOUQUETTE claiming 800 arpents of land, see Book No. 6, pg. 536. The Board are unanimously of opinion that this claim ought not to be confirmed. For reasons, see above. (2d, 147)

    Adjourned until tomorrow at 9 o'clock A.M.
        Wednesday Aug. 26th, 1835 Board Met-A-1 Comm'rs.Present

Louis GIGUIERE claiming 800 arpents of land, see Book No. 6, pg. 140. The Board are of opinion that this claim ought to be confirmed to the said Louis GIGUIERE, or to his legal representatives, according to the concession. (336)

F.M. BENOIT claiming 800 arpents of land, see Book No. 6, pg. 140. The Board are unanimously of opinion that this claim ought to be confirmed to the said F.M. BENOIT, or to his legal representatives, according to the concession. (337)

Israel DODGE claiming 1,000 arpents of land, see Book No. 6, pg. 366. The Board are unanimously of opinion that this claim ought to be confirmed to the said Israel DODGE, or to his legal representatives, according to the concession. (338)

Joseph FENWICK claiming 20,000 arpents of land, see Book No. 6, pg. 175, No. 7, pg. 58. A majority of the Board are of opinion that this claim ought not to be confirmed. F.R. CONWAY, Comm'r., voting for the confirmation. (2d, 148)

Jacques CLAMORGAN claiming 536,904 arpents of land, see Book No. 6, pg. 179. The Board are unanimously of opinion that this claim ought not to be confirmed, the conditions not having been complied with. (2d, 149)

Walter FENWICK claiming 10,000 arpents of land, see Book No. 6, pg. 251, No. 7, pg. 68. On motion the Board agree to reconsider the decision made on this claim on the 17th November, 1834, and on a re-examination of the original concession, find that the alteration above spoken of, is not made in the concession, but in the petition and the words "Diez mil arpanes" (ten thousand arpents) in the concession, are fairly written, it is believed in the proper handwriting of the Lt. Gov., Zenon TRUDEAU, and that the alteration in the petition must have been made anterior to the granting of the concession. The Board therefore, rescind their former decision in this case, and are unanimously of opinion that this claim of 10,000 arpents of land ought to be confirmed to the said Walter FENWICK, or to his legal representatives, according to the concession. (339)

The Board Adjourn until the 19th of Sept. to give time for the making out transcripts.

Saturday September 19th, 1835 Board Met-All Comm'rs. Present

Peter BURNS, Sr. claiming 640 acres of land, see Book No. 6, pg. 416. The Board are unanimously of opinion that 640 acres of land ought to be granted to the said Peter BURNS, Sr., or to his legal representatives, according to possession. (340)

William REED, Jr. claiming 727 arpents of land, see No. 6, pg. 351. The Board are unanimously of opinion that 727 arpents of land ought to be granted to the said William REED, Jr., or to his legal representatives, according to possession & survey. (341)

William DAVIS claiming 338 arpents & 7 perches of land. See Book No. 6, pg. 381 where this claim is entered for 640 acres. The Board are unanimously of opinion that 338 arpents & 7 perches of land ought to be granted to the said William DAVIS, or to his legal representatives, according to possession & survey. (342)

Thompson CRAWFORD claiming 600 arpents of land, see Book No. 6, pg. 423, where this claim is entered for 640 acres. The Board are unanimously of opinion that 600 arpents of land ought to be granted to the said Thompson CRAWFORD, or to his legal representatives, according to possession. (343)

Dawalt CRITZ claiming 200 acres of land, & 53 poles, see Book No. 6, pg. 441, where this claim is entered for 640 acres. The Board are unanimously of opinion that 200 acres & 53 poles of land ought to be granted to the said Dawalt CRITZ, or to his legal representatives, according to the survey recorded in Book B, pg. 292. (344)

Pierre TORNAT dit LAJOIE claiming 600 arpents of land, see Book No. 6, pg. 189, No. 7, pg. 208. The Board rescind their former decision on this claim (see Book No. 7, pg. 185) further testimony in behalf of this claim having been given since said decision. The Board are unanimously of opinion that 600 arpents of land ought to be granted to the said Pierre TORNAT or to his legal representatives, according to possession. (345)

John GODFREY claiming 640 acres of land, see Book No. 7, pg. 203. The Board are unanimously of opinion that this claim ought not to be granted. (2d, 150)

Martin FENWICK claiming 500 arpents of land, see Book No. 7, pg. 29. The Board are unanimously of opinion that this claim is destitute of merit, an alteration being apparent in the original petition on file, as noted in the translation. The name of river a Brazeau having been altered into that of river a la Viande, alias St. Come, thus increasing the distance for location of grant, several miles and the conditions not having been complied with. (2d, 151)

Leo FENWICK claiming 500 arpents of land, see Book No. 6, pg. 254. On request of the agent for claimant the Board agreed to reconsider this claim, and after a thorough reexamination are unanimously of opinion to adhere to the decision taken on this claim in Book No. 7, pg. 68, and add as a further reason that the conditions have not been complied with.

Ezekiel FENWICK claiming 500 arpents of land, see Book No. 6, pg. 339. On request of the agent for claimant the Board agreed to reconsider this claim, and after a thorough reexamination are unanimously of opinion to adhere to the decision taken on this claim in Book 7, pg. 69, and add as a further reason that the conditions have not been complied with.

James FENWICK claiming 500 arpents of land, see Book No. 6, pg. 252. On request of the agent for claimant, the Board agreed to reconsider this claim, and after a thorough reexamination are unanimously of opinion to adhere to the decision taken onthis claim in Book No..7, pg. 69, and add as a further reason that the conditions have not been complied with.

The majority of the Board, who rejected the claim of
Joseph FENWICK to 20,000 arpents of land on the St. Francois river,
& numbered 148 in the report (see Book No. 7, pg. 243) offer the
following reasons for the grounds of their opinion: The claimant was
an emigrant from the State of Kentucky and proposed to establish himself in Upper Louisiana and make certain improvements if a grant of
land should be given to him of 20,000 arpents on the river St. Francois,
his proposition, as set forth in his petition was acceded to. The
following year, viz; on 26th May, 1797, as a citizen of the United
States & an inhabitant of Kentucky, he makes a similar proposition,
asking for 3,000 arpents between the mouth of Apple Creek and the river St. Come, promising to remove to, settle, and cultivate the same
if it should be granted. Lt. Gov. TRUDEAU made the grant on the 10th
of June, 1797, and from the records of this office, it appears that
Joseph FENWICK complied with the conditions set forth in his petition,
and this government has confirmed to said FENWICK the claim of 3,000
arpents, but there is no evidence of his having made any improvement,
as promised in his petition for the 20,000 arpens on the river St.
Francois.
    The Board adjourned until Saturday 26th instant.
        Saturday Sept. 26th, 1835 Board Met-All Comm'rs. Present

In the case of James CLAMORGAN claiming land on Dardennes & Cuivre,
see Book No. 6, pgs. 179 & 235 & 205. The Board are unanimously of
opinion that this claim ought not to be confirmed, believing it to
have been disregarded by, both TRUDEAU, the Lt. Gov., who made the
grant and by his successor DELASSUS, for a full opinion and notice
of interferences, see the report of the Board to the Comm'r. of the
general Land Office. (152)
    The Board adjourned until 30th instant.
        Wednesday Sept. 30th, 1835 Board Met-All Comm'rs. Present

Received of the Commissioners on private lands claims in Missouri,
five tin boxes or cannisters, enveloped in paper, sealed and directed
to the Hon. Ethan Allen BROWN, Commissioner of the General Land Office, which boxes or cannisters contain the report of said Comm'rs.
on 242 private land claims, 94 of which are marked from 256 to 345
inclusive and 152 in the second class, marked from No. 1 to 152, inclusive, together with the transcript of each claim and the transla-
tions of the concessions, etc. all which I promise to deliver to the
Commissioner of the General Land Office at Washington City in a reasonable time from this day.
Note: The transcript marked No. 20 was withdrawn having been marked
inadvertently.
St. Louis, Recorder's Office, Sept. 30th, 1835.
signed duplicates

Office of the Recorder of Land Titles, St. Louis, Missouri
September 30th, 1835
Received of the Recorder & Comm'r. on private land claims in the
State of Missouri, one tim box or cannister containing their report
upon eleven private land claims in the Territory of Arkansas, and a
transcript of the evidence in each claim; directed to the Hon.
Martin VAN BUREN, President of the Senate of the United States,
Washington City, D.C., which I promise to deliver according to the
direction in a reasonable time from the date above written.
signed duplicates

Resolved unanimously by the Recorder & Comm'rs. for the final adjustment of private land claims in Missouri, that their thanks be
presented in the most cordial manner, to Julius DEMUN, Translator of
the French & Spanish languages & Clerk to the Board of Comm'rs. for
the able & faithful manner in which he has during the whole period
of the existence of the Board, performed the arduous duties assigned
to him.
Resolved that the above resolution be entered on the minutes of the
Board and that the Recorder be requested to furnish him with a copy
thereof.

Resolved that James H. RELFE, a member of the Board, be and is hereby authorised and required to take to the City of Washington the reports mentioned in his foregoing receipts and deliver the same as specified in the said receipts, in order that they may be submitted to Congress, according to the requisitions of the act creating the Board approved the 9th July, 1832.

On motion, the Board Adjourned. Sine die.

NAMES OF ORIGINAL CLAIMANTS & ASSIGNEES	ARPENTS	COMM.	MIN.
		Book #	pg.
AMIOT (Legal repr. of R. BUCHANAN	600	6	167
AYREY, George	750	6	169
ADAMS, Calvin (under MOTTARD	1340	6	216
ANDERSON, John (Leg. rep. of)	640	6	367
ANDREWS, Alexander (John HAYS	640	6	473
ANDREWS, Alexander (Jonathan BUIS	640	6	475
AUMURE OR TAUMURE, Baptiste	240	6	514
AYREY, George	756	7	19
AMIOT, (No. 150)	600	7	31
ANDERSON, John (192)	640	7	42
ANDREWS, Alexander (229)	640	7	56
ANDREWS, Alexander (233)	640	7	58
ARNAUD, François	800	7	81
AUBUCHON, Louis	800	7	130
ASHERBRAUNNER, Urban	350/95	7	166
AUBUCHON, Louis	800	7	174
ASHERBRAUNNER, Urban	350	7	176
AUMURE OR TAUMURE, Baptiste	240	7	140
AYREY, George	750	7	191
AQUETON, Michael	2000	7	196
AQUETON, Michael	2000	7	221
ARNAUD, Francois	800	7	229
BOISE, Jacob	400	6	5
BASYE, John	1600	6	10
BISSONET, Louis (Auguste CHOUTEAU's Heirs)	40	6	16
BEAUVAIS, ST. Gemme	1600	6	37
BOILEVIN, Nicholas (representatives of)	400	6	60
BACANNE, Philip (Manuel LISA's Representatives)	480	6	61
BOLDUC, Etienne & Louis (Not heretofore recorded)		6	68
BEAUVAIS, St. Gemme	60 ft.		
	in Circ.	6	74
BUTCHER, Sebastian and the heirs of B. & M. BUTCHER	1600	6	76
BILLOT, Bapt. Joseph (Jno. MULLANPHY)	800	6	83
BELLANGER, Francois (Same)	800	6	87
BLONDEAU, Andre & J. Bte. DRERY, (Jno. MULLANPHY)	480	6	88
BEAUVAIS, St. Gemme (Jno. MULLANPHY)	800	6	92
BARSALOUX, Nicolas (legal representatives of)	160	6	110,111
BOUVET, Mathurin (Chs. GRATIOT'r repre.)	7056	6	119
BOUVET, Mathurin (GRATIOT's Rep)	7056	6	120
BRASEAU, Joseph (Repres. of)	12 by 30	6	123
BEAUVAIS, St. Gemme	1600	6	128
BERTHEAUME, Francois (repres. of)	420	6	128
BRADLEY, Edward (repres. of)	500	6	136
BISHOP, John (represent. of)	350	6	138
BENOIT, Francois M. (LABEAUME's Repre.)	800	6	140
BRAVIER, Jean Bste. (LABEAUME's Repre.)	800	6	146
BERNARD, Francois (LABEAUME's Repre.)	800	6	146
BOISE, Louis (LABEAUME's Repre.)	800	6	148
BON, Jacques St. Right	800	6	157
BOUVET, Mathurin (Legal repres. of	6 arp. sq.	6	169
BELLAND, John Bste. (Legal repres. of	480	6	215
BOUIS, Antoine U. (F.V. BOUIS	1000	6	220
BOLON, Hipolite (HODGE & R. CASTON	720	6	---
BARLEVIN, Nicolas (repres. of (Old Mine)	400	6	260
BEAUVAIS, St. Gemme	1600	6	296
BACANNE, Philip	480	6	298
BLONDEAU, Andre & T.B. DRERY	480	6	304
BARSALOUX, Nicolas	160	6	309
BOUVET, Mathurin	7056	6	313
BOUVET, Mathurin	94 by 40	6	313
BRASEAU, Joseph (84)	360	6	315
BERTHEAUME, Francois	420	6	316
BRADLEY, Edward	500	6	319
BISHOP, John	350	6	322
BISSONET, Louis	40	6	326
BENTON, Elijah	640 acres	6	339
BUTCHER, Sebastian	1600	6	346
BENTON, Elijah	640 acres	6	350

NAMES OF ORIGINAL CLAIMANTS & ASSIGNEES	ARPENTS	COMM. MIN. Book #	Pg.
BAKER, Thomas	640 acres	6	360
BROWN, James (heirs & legal reps. of	640 acres	6	369
BURNS, Senr. Peter	640	6	416
BURNS, Robert	640	6	419
BURK, John	1000	6	428
BOLLINGER, Sen'r. Daniel	640	6	435
BOLLINGER, Dawalt	640	6	436
BOLLINGER, Philip	640	6	438
BOLLINGER, John, son of John	640	6	439
BEVINS, James	640	6	455
BOLLINGER, John, son of John	640	6	464
BOYD, Polly	640	6	470
BOLLINGER, Frederick	640	6	476
BOLLINGER, David	640	6	481
BOLLINGER, Mathias	640	6	482
BOLI, John	260	6	506
BARRADA, Antoine (Wm. DAVIS)	800	6	224
BELLEW, Solomon	350	6	530
BON, Jacaues (143)	800	7	10
BOUVET, M.	6	-	--
BARRADA, Antoine (William DAVIS) (176)	800	7	38
BENTON, Elijah (187)	640	7	41
BAKER, Thomas (188)	640	7	41
BURK, John (199)	1000	7	44
BON, Jacques (143)	800	7	47
BOLLINGER, Dewalt (203)	300	7	47
BOLLINGER, John (204)	640	7	48
BOLLINGER, Frederick (221)	640	7	53
BOLLINGER, David (222)	640	7	56
BOLLINGER, Mathias (223)	640	7	56
BOYD, Polly (282)	640	7	57
BOLI, John (235)	260	7	59
BOLON, Hipolite (2d)	720	7	68
BOLLINGER, Philip "	640	7	70
BOLLINGER, Daniel "	640	7	70
BELL, Mordicai (A. STODDARD's Reps.)	350	7	110
BURK, John	1000	7	114
BATES, William	640	7	117
BOYER, Peter	639-3/4	7	124
James BROWN	400	7	132
BALDWIN, John	400	7	139
BAKER, Reuben	640	7	148
BOLAYE, Sophia	150	7	152
BEQUETTE, Charles	606	7	154
BUAT, Louis & Twelve others	Special	7	162
BUTNER OR BURTON, Alexander	300	7	165
BISET, Guillaume	40	7	166
BELL, Mordicay	350	7	170
BATES, William	640	7	172
BALDWIN, John	400	7	175
BAKER, Reuben	640	7	176
BOLAYE, Sophia	150	7	176
BEQUETTE, Charles	606	7	177
BUAT, Louis & Twelve others	Special	7	179
BUTNER OR BURTON, Alexander	300	7	179
BISET, Guillaume	40	7	180
BOYER, Peter	639-3/4	7	180
BOUIS A. Vincent	1000	7	181
BEVINS, James	200	7	187
BURNS, Robert	640	7	188
BELIR, Solomon	350	7	189
BAUVAIS, St. Gemme	60 ft. (?)	7	191
BACON, Sudwell	1000	7	192
BEDFORD, Thomas P.	800	7	193
BURET, (Peter)	2000	7	192
BELIOUR, Joseph	400	7	201
BROWN, James	640	7	214
BACON, Sudwell	1000	7	216

NAMES OF ORIGINAL CLAIMANTS & ASSIGNEES		ARPENTS	COMM.	MIN.
			Book #	Pg.
BURRELL, Peter		2000	7	216
BELCOUR, Joseph		400	7	219
BEDFORD, Thomas P.		800	7	217
BROWN, James		640	7	227
BISET, Antoine		800	7	230
BOISSE, Louis		800	7	230
BERNARD, Francois		800	7	231
BAUVAIS, St. Gemme		800	7	232
BRAVIER, Jean Bste.		800	7	235
BELLANGER, Francois		800	7	237
BENOIT, F.M.		800	7	243
BURNS, Peter		640	7	---
Commissioners, Organisation of the Board of			6	1
Clerk, Appointment of and translator			6	1
CERRE, Gabriel	(Pascal CERRE devisee)	800	6	2
CERRE, Pascal L.		7056	6	3
CAULK, Richard		4000	6	6
CAULK, Thomas		400	6	7
COLE, David (	(Jesse RICHARDSON)	400	6	9
CERRE, Toussaint	(Auguste CHOUTEAU's heirs)	An Island	6	10
CHOUTEAU, Auguste	(heirs of)	1281	6	11
CHOUTEAU, Auguste	(heirs of)	7056	6	12
COURTOIS, Louis, Jun'r.		7056	6	13
CAILLON, Francois		1600	6	13
CHOUTEAU, Peter, Sen'r.			6	18
COUSIN, Bartholomew		7935	6	20
CAILLON, Francois		1600	6	53
CONSTANT, Gabriel	(Albert TISON)	800	6	57
CHARTRAN, Amable	(Albert TISON)	600	6	59
COLEMAN, Francois	(J.P. CABANNE & MACKLOT	2500	6	64
COONTZ, John and Edward HEMPSTEAD		450	6	67
CLARK, William	(John MULLANPHY)	800	6	86
CERRE, Gabriel	(Jno. MULLANPHY)	An Island	6	89
CERRE, Gabriel	(Frederick DENT)	400	6	98
CHOUTEAU, Jun'r.	(P. CHOUTEAU, Sen'r.)	An Island	6	105
CLAMORGAN, Jacques	(GRATIOT's Repres.)	800	6	122
CLAMORGAN, Jacques	(Same)	1600	6	122
CHOUTEAU, Pierre, Sen'r.		30,000	6	123
COUSIN, Bartholomew	(Repre. of)	10,000	6	129
COUSIN, Bartholomew	(Repre. of)	8000	6	129
CRUMP, George	(Repre. of)	450	6	135
COLLIGAN, John	(Repre. of)	1200	6	138
CHARLEVILLE, Louis	(LABEAUME's Rep.)	800	6	140
CHARLEVILLE, Joseph	(LABEAUME's Rep.)	800	6	140
CERRE, Gabriel	(Jonah MCCLANAHAN)	300	6	151
CERRE, Gabriel	(Frederick DENT)	400	6	169
CHANDLER, Edmund	(Arthur BURNS)	640 acres	6	170
CHANDLER, Edmund	(Same)	640 acres	6	170
COLLINS, Jacob		890	6	176
CHALIFOUX, Jean Bste.	(Chas. LUCAS's rep.)	600	6	179
CLAMORGAN, James	(Pierre CHOUTEAU)	536,904	6	179
CLAMORGAN, James	(Legal Repres. of)	Not Ascertained	6	179
CLAMORGAN, James	(Same)	Same Claim	6	205
CONTEAUX, Louis Jun'r. (Legal repr. of)		400	6	210
CHEVALIER, Andre	(Legal reprs. of)	400	6	213
CARDINAL, Jean Marie		40	6	219
CABANNE, John P.		2000	6	221
CLAMORGAN, Jacques	(Wm. CLARK & W.C. CARR (172))	3200	6	221
CHOUTEAU, Auguste P.		800	6	229
CRELY, Therin	(Legal repres. (No. 179))	3528	6	234
CLAMORGAN, James	(Claim on Dardenne & Cuivre)		6	234
COLE, David	(Jesse RICHARDSON)	400	6	237
CERRE, Gabriel	(Josiah MCCLANAHAN)	300	6	241
Certificate of Register on the Old Mine claim			6	224
Certificate of L.F. LINN, Comm'r. (Col. VALLE)			6	261
CERRE, Gabriel	(Josiah MCCLANAHAN)	300	6	286
CERRE, Gabriel		800	6	286
CERRE, Pascal L.		7056	6	287

NAMES OF ORIGINAL CLAIMANTS & ASSIGNEES	ARPENTS	COMM. Book #	MIN. Pg.
CAULK, Richard	4000	6	288
COLE, David	400	6	290
CERRE, TOUSSAINT	Island	6	291
CHOUTEAU, Auguste	7056	6	291
CAILLON, Francois	1600	6	293
CHOUTEAU, Peter, Sen'r.	Special	6	294
COLEMAN, Francis	2500	6	299
COONTZ, John & E. HEMPSTEAD	450	6	302
CERRE, Gabriel	400	6	308
COUSIN, Bartholomew	7935	6	308
CHOUTEAU, Pierre, Sen'r.	30,000	6	316
COUSIN, Bartholomew	10,000	6	316
COUSIN, Bartholomew	8000	6	317
CRUMP, George	450	6	319
COLLIGAN, John	1200	6	322
CERRE, Gabriel	300	6	324
COURTOIS, Jun'r. Louis	7056	6	325
CAULK, Thomas	400	6	332
COLLINS, Jacob	890	6	333
CHANDLER, Edmund	640 acres	6	334
CHOUTEAU, Auguste	1281	6	343
CRAIG, James	800	6	349
CRAWFORD, James (198)	640 acres	6	409
CAMPBELL, Samuel	640	6	414
CRAWFORD, Thompson	640	6	423
CUTZ, Dawalt	640	6	441
CHENEY, Lemuel	640	6	450
COX, James	640	6	462
CHEVALIER, Joseph (John HAYS)	400	5	465
CORNELIUS, Jeptha (Henry HOWARD)	640	6	468
CAMBAS, Jean	40	6	519
CRELY, Therese	3528	6	528
CHOUTEAU, Auguste P.	800	7	1
COYTEUX, Francois Jun'r.	400	7	5
CAYLE, Roger	650	7	31
CHALIFOUX, Jean Bste. (No. 163)	600	7	35
CLAMORGAN, James (172)	3200	7	37
CHOUTEAU, A.P. (178)	800	7	39
CRELY, Therese (179)	3528	7	39
CHEVALIER, Joseph (200)	400	7	40
CHENEY, Lemuel (210)	640	7	56
CORNELIUS, Jephta (217)	600	7	52
CAMBAS, Jean (248)	40	7	67
COYTEUX, Louis (2d)	400	7	67
COYTEUX, Francois "	400	7	67
CAYLE, Roger (252)	650	7	75
CHARTRAN, Joseph	998	7	109
COLMAN, Alexander	800	7	124
CRISWELL, Hugh	640	7	144
CHARTRAN, Joseph	998	7	170
CRISWELL, Hugh	640	7	175
CHEVALIER, Andre	400	7	183
CABANNE, John P.	2000	7	185
CARDINAL, Jean Marie	40	7	185
CAMPBELL, Samuel	640	7	189
COULISSAT	800	7	194
CERRE, Gabriel	400	7	203
COUISSAT	800	7	220
CERRE, Gabriel	400	7	222
CARTER, Peggy	640	7	225
CRAIG, James	800	7	226
COLEMAN, Alexander	800	7	227
CHARLEVILLE, Joseph	800	7	231
CHARLEVILLE, Louis	800	7	231
CLARK, William	800	7	232
CONSTANT, Gabriel	800	7	238
CHARTRAN, Amable	800	7	240
CLAMORGAN, Jacques	536,904	7	244
CRAWFORD, Thompson	600	7	245

NAMES OF ORIGINAL CLAIMANTS & ASSIGNEES	ARPENTS	COMM.	MIN.
		Book #	Pg.
CRETZ, Dawalt	200	7	246
CLAMORGAN, James	On Cuivre	7	249
DELAUNAY, David	800	6	5
DUELOS, Alexander (Jno. SMITH T) Old Mine Conc.)	400	6	5
DUNN, William (Arund RUTGERS)	7056	6	8
DELASSUS, Delusiere, Pierre	100	6	13
DELASSUS, Delusiere, Pierre	7056	6	14
DELASSUS, Charles Dehault	30,000	6	16
DELASSUS, Charles Dehault (Madame Delore SARPY)	20,000	6	20
DUBREUIL, Antoine	10,000	6	31
DELAURIERE, Charles Fremon	10,000	6	32
DELAURIERE, Charles Fremon (representatives ofO	300	6	50
DELASSUS, Delusiere, Pierre	7056	6	54
DELASSUS, Charles DEHAULT	30,000	6	56
DERNOYERS, Antoine (Albert TISON)	800	6	57
DERNOYERS, Joseph (Albert TISON)	800	6	58
DERNOYERS, Louis (Albert TISON)	800	6	59
DERNOYERS, Francois (Albert TISON)	800	6	59
DUBREUIL, Antoine	10,000	6	62
DIELLE, Henry	400	6	72
DELILLE, Baptiste Jun'r. (Jno. MULLANPHY)	800	6	84
DELILLE, Baptiste, Sen'r. (Jno. MULLANPHY)	800	6	84
DEJARLAIS, PAUL (Jno. MULLANPHY)	800	6	84
DECARRY, Joseph (Jno. MULLANPHY)	800	6	85
DUMOULIN, Jean Bste. (Jno. MULLANPHY)	800	6	87
DUNEGAN, Francois (J. MULLANPHY)	800	6	89
DEVOLSEY, Pierre Francois (J.P. CABANNE)	240	6	100
DIELLE, Henry (Bernard PRATTE)	5000	6	105
DUCHOUQUET, Francois (Same (Henry VON PHUL)	800	6	117
DELASSUS, Carlos DEHAULT	30,000	6	118
DELASSUS, Carlos Dehault	30,000	6	125
DELAURIERE, Chas. Fremon (LABEAUME's Rep.)	10,000	6	139
DEROUIN, Jean (LABEAUME's Rep.)	800	6	142
DELILLE, Louis (LABEAUME's Rep.)	2500	6	148
DELOR, Pierre	400	6	154
DELOR, Pierre	400	6	156
DECHAMP, Jean Bste. (Jos. F. ROBIDEUX (144))	160	6	159
DEVOLSAY, Pierre Francois (J.P. CABANNE)	240	6	166
DODIER, Widow (L. LABEAUME's Rep.)	120	6	174
DELASSUS, Camille (Jno. SMITH T)	2400/34	6	175
DUPRE, Louis (Charles LUCAS's repr)	800	6	178
DUMOULIN, Jean Bste. (Legal representatives)	800	6	189
DUFOUR, P. and Louis BOLDUC (Heirs & rep. of)	800	6	189
DRAPER, John (Legal rep. of)	747	6	215
DODIER, Widow (Legal repre. of)	120	6	218
DUCHOUQUET, Bste. (Legal repres. ofO	Special	6	220
DAVIS, William (representatives of A. BARRADA)	800	6	224
DERNOYERS, Louis (Legal reps. of)	800	6	242
DERNOYERS, Basile (Legal reps. of)	800	6	242
DELAUNAZ, David	800	6	288
DELASSUS, Camille	2400	6	290
DELASSUS de Lusiere	100	6	291
DELASSUS, Charles Dehault	30,000	6	292
DELASSUS, Charles Dehault	12,946	6	294
DUBREUIL, Antoine	10,000	6	295
DELAURIERE, Ch. Fremon	300	6	297
DIELLE, Henry	400	6	303
DIELLE, Henry	4000	6	306
DEVOLSEY, Pierre Francois	240	6	307
DELASSUS de Lusiere, Pierre	7056	6	309
DELAURIERE, Ch. Fremon	10,000	6	323
DELILLE, Louis	2500	6	323
DELAURIERE, Ch. Fremon	10,000	6	324
DELOR, Pierre	400	6	325
DILLON, William	640	6	334
DODGE, Israel	7056	6	338
(?), Pierre)	1000	6	364
DODGE, Israel (legal reps. of)	1000	6	366

NAMES OF ORIGINAL CLAIMANTS & ASSIGNEES		ARPENTS	COMM. MIN.	
			Book #	Pg.
DETCHEMENDY, Paschal	(Legal reps. of)	7056	6	378
DAVIS, William	(Legal reps. of)	640 acres	6	381
DELASSUS, Camille		6000	6	405
DEGUIRE, Paul		640 acres	6	410
DOUBLEWYE, Joseph Alias DEBLOIS		650	6	420
DOUGHERTY, John		640	6	446
DORSEY, Samuel		800	6	467
DENNIS, Joseph		640	6	487
DENNE, Charles	(James MORRISON)	750	6	513
DUCHOUQUETTE, Francois		800	6	536
DIXON, Frederick		800	6	537
DODIER, Rene		800	6	537
DEJARLAIS, Antoine		800	6	537
DECHAMP, Jean Baptiste (144)		160	7	11
DENNE, Charles		750	7	17
DECHMENDY, Pascal		7056	7	25
DELASSUS, Camille	(No. 153)	2400	7	31
DUFOUR, Parfait & Louis·BALDUC (no. 159)		800	7	33
DUPRE, Louis	(No. 162)	800	7	35
DERNOYERS, Basile	(No. 182)	800	7	40
DELASSUS, Camille	(No. 195)	6000	7	43
DORSEY, Samuel	(No. 201)	800	7	46
DOUGHERTY, John	(No. 208)	300	7	49
DODIER, Rene	(No. 237)	800	7	60
DUNEGAN, Francois	(No. 249)	800	7	67
DERNOYERS, Louis	(2d)	800	7	68
DEGUIRE, Paul	"	640	7	70
DUCHOUQUETTE, Baptiste		Special	7	72
DUNN, William		7056	7	74
DUNN, William	(No. 251)	7056	7	75
DUCHOUQUETTE, Baptiste (No. 255)		Special	7	78
DEVILEMONT		2 leagues	7	77
DOWTY, Zachariah		450	7	120
DOWTY, Zachariah		450	7	173
DENNE, Charles		750	7	180
DODGE, Israel		7056	7	181
DOUBLEWYE or DEBLOIS, Joseph		640	7	181
DRAPER, John		747	7	182
DUMAIS, Pierre		1000	7	183
DODIER, Widow		120	7	185
DENNIS, Joseph		640	7	189
DETCHMENDY, Pascal		7056	7	189
DANIEL, John		800	7	193
DARDENNE, John Pste.		1600	7	194
DORTILLIER, John		800	7	195
DUCHASSIN, Joseph		750	7	195
DANIEL, John		800	7	219
DARDENNE, John Bste.		1600	7	220
DORTILLIER, John		800	7	220
DUCHASSIN, Joseph		750	7	221
DOMINE, Baptiste		800	7	231
DECARRY, Joseph		800	7	233
DUMOULIN, Jean Bste.		800	7	233
DEJARLAIS, Antoine		800	7	234
DEROUIN, Jean		800	7	235
DELISLE, Jun'r. Baptiste		800	7	237
DELISLE, Senr., Baptiste		800	7	238
DEJARLAIS, Paul		800	7	238
DERNOYERS, Antoine		800	7	239
DERNOYERS, Joseph		800	7	239
DERNOYERS, Louis		800	7	240
DUCHOUQUETTE, Francois Same		800	7	242
DODGE, Israel		1000	7	243
DUNN, William		338/7	7	265
EASTWOOD, Jacob	(Jno. MULLANPHY)	800	6	81
EGLIS, Hyacinthe	(Jno. MULLANPHY)	800	6	87
ESTHER, Mulatress	(70)	80	6	111
ESTHER, Free Mulatto woman		80	6	160

NAMES OF ORIGINAL CLAIMANTS & ASSIGNEES		ARPENTS	COMM. MIN.	
			Book #	Pg.
EGLIS, Hyacinthe		800	6	306
ESTHER	(No. 70)	80	6	310
EARS, John		960	6	373
ESTEP, Priscilla	(legal reps. of)	800	6	509
ESTEP, Priscilla		800	6	562
EARS, John	(No. 193)	960	7	42
EDMONDSON, Jerusha	(THOMPSON)	250	7	84
EASOM, William		800	7	120
EASOM, William		Same	7	157
EDMONDSON, Jerusha		250	7	169
EASOM, William		800	7	177
EASTEPS, Priscilla		800	7	190
EASTWOOD, Jacob		800	7	236
FENWICK, Joseph	(John SMITH T)	20,000	6	175
FLANDRIN, Antoine	(Legal reps. of)	6000	6	221
FENWICK, Walter	(Legal reps. of)	10,000	6	251
FENWICK, James		500	6	252
FENWICK, Leo		500	6	254
FENWICK, Ezekiel		500	6	339
FORD, Elijah	(Wm. HACKER)	640 acres	6	454
FLANDRIN, Antoine		6000	6	535
FLANDRIN, Antoine	(171)	6000	7	37
FORD, Elijah	(231)	640	7	57
FENWICK, Joseph		20,000	7	58
FENWICK, Walter		10,000	7	68
FENWICK, Leo		500	7	68
FENWICK, Ezekiel		500	7	69
FENWICK, Martin		500	7	129
FLETCHER, Silas			7	135
FERGUSON, NANCY		300	7	141
FENWICK, Joseph		800	7	146
FLYNN, William		200	7	150
FLETCHER, Silas		300	7	174
FERGUSON, Nancy		300	7	175
FENWICK, Joseph		800	7	176
FLYNN, Jun'r., William		200	7	226
FENWICK, Joseph		20,000	7	243
FENWICK, Walter		10,000	7	244
FENWICK, Martin		500	7	246
FENWICK, Leo		500	7	247
FENWICK, Ezekiel		500	7	247
FENWICK, James		500	7	247
FENWICK, Joseph		20,000	7	248
GENDRON, Toussaint	(Albert TISON)	800	6	57
GAGNIER, Antoine	(Albert TISON)	1800	6	114
GRATIOT, Charles, Jun'r.		2500	6	119
GRATIOT, Charles Sen'r.	(Reps. of)	500	6	123
GODINAIR, Jean	(J.P. CABANNE)	800	6	135
GAUTIER, Antoine	(Reps. of)	4000	6	137
GEGUIERE, Louis	(LABEAUME'S reps.)	800	6	140
GAMACHE, Jean Bste. Sen'r. (by his heirs N. & L.				
	(GAMACHE)	1050	6	157
GRIFFITH, Daniel		600	6	158
GERARD, Joseph & Patrick FLEMING (R. EASTON &				
	J. BRUFF)	840	6	167
GAMELIN, Pierre (Charles LUCAS' reps.)		800	6	178
GERARD, Joseph and P. FLEMING		840	6	205
GURTZ, George	(Legal reps. of)	640 acres	6	216
GAMACHE, Auguste	(Legal reps. of)	300	6	238
GAMACHE, Augte.	(Same Claim)	300	6	244
GAMACHE, Augte.	(Same Claim)	300	6	247
GAGNIER, Antoine		1800	6	310
GRATIOT, Charles, Jun'r.		2500	6	313
GRATIOT, Charles, Sen'r.		500	6	314
GAUTIER, Antoine		4000	6	321
GIBONEY, Robert		348	6	336
GREEN, David		347/53-1/2		
		Per.	6	403

NAMES OF ORIGINAL CLAIMANTS & ASSIGNEES		ARPENTS	COMM. MIN.	
			Book #	Pg.
GUETHING, John		585 acres	6	444
GREENWALT, John		640	6	488
GEFFREY, Baptiste		800	6	536
GRIMAR Or GRIMAND, Louis Alias CHARPENTIER		800	6	537
GILL, Charles		400	7	1
GILL, Charles		400	7	3
GRIFFITH, Daniel		600	7	11
GAMACHE, Jean Bste. Sen'r.	(145)	1050	7	12
GERARD, Joseph & P. FLEMING	(No. 147)	1600	7	30
GRIFFITH, Daniel	(No. 148)	600	7	30
GAMACHE, Auguste	(No. 181)	300	7	39
GUETHING, John	(No. 206)	500	7	48
GREEN, David	(Mo. 227)	300	7	55
GILL, Charles	(No. 247)	400	7	66
GARDINER, Benjamin		750	7	93,101
GIRLY, George		640	7	107
GARDINER, Benjamin		750	7	109
GARDINER, Benjamin		Same	7	143
GRENIER, Louis		701	7	153
GARDINER, Benjamin		750	7	169
GIRLY, George		640	7	170
GRENIER, Louis		701	7	177
GREENWALT, Jun'r. John		640	7	186
GRAVER, alias, GRABER		1600	7	195
GERARD, John		320	7	202
GODFREY, John		640	7	203
GRAVER		1600	7	221
GERARD, John		320	7	223
GRIMARD or GRIMAND, Louis		800	7	234
GODINEAU, Jean		800	7	234
GENDRON, Toussaint		800	7	240
GIGUIERE, Louis		800	7	243
GODFREY, John		640	7	246
HUNAULT, Gabriele	(Albert TISON)	800	6	58
HUBBARD, Daniel	(John MULLANPHY)	800	6	82
HUBBARD, Felix	(same)	800	6	83
HUBBARD, Eusebius	(Same)	800	6	83
HUGE, Dominique	(Same)	800	6	85
HEBERT, Joseph	(Same)	800	6	86
HOWARD, Purnet	(Reps. of)	400	6	106
HILDERBRANT, John	(Ch. GRATIOT's Heirs)	320	6	121
HOWELL, Newton		350	6	124
HARTLEY, William	(Legal reps. of)	650	6	134
HENRY, John	(Legal reps. of)	800	6	134
HUBERT, Joseph	(LABEAUME's reps)	800	6	143
HEBERT, Francois	(J.P. CABANNE)	80	6	218
HORINE, David		640 acres	6	232
HOWARD; Purnel		400	6	307
HILDERBRANT, John		320	6	314
HOWELL, Newton		350	6	315
HENRY, John		900	6	318
HAWKINS, James		640 acres	6	358
HILDERBRAND, Benjamin		640 acres	6	402
HUBBLE, Ebenezer		640 acres	6	458
HAND, John		640 acres	6	461
HENDERSON, George			6	495
HELDERBRAND, Jonathan		200	6	501
HORINE, David		640	6	530
HAFF, James		800	6	537
HARRIS, Andrew		600	7	2
HORINE, David	(177)	640	7	38
HAWKINS, James	(191)	640	7	42
HEBERT, Francois		80	7	43
HUBBLE, Ebenezer	(213)	640	7	51
HAND, John	(214)	640	7	52
HENDERSON, George	(228)	300	7	56
HARRIS, Andrew	(239)	600	7	61
HEBERT, Francois	(245)	80	7	66

NAMES OF ORIGINAL CLAIMANTS & ASSIGNEES		ARPENTS	COMM. MIN.	
			Book #	Pg.
HELDERBRAND, John	(2d)	200	7	71
HOLMES, Samuel		840	7	112
HOLMES, Samuel		840	7	171
HARTLEY, William		650	7	185
HYNAM, John		800	7	194
HARVIN, Jean		600	7	200
HARVIN, Jean		600	7	218
HYNAM, John		800	7	220
HUGE, Dominique		800	7	232
HEBERT, Joseph		800	7	233
HAFF, James		800	7	234
HUBERT, Joseph		800	7	235
HUBBARD, Daniel		800	7	236
HUBBARD, Felix		800	7	236
HUBBARD, Eusebius		800	7	237
HUNAULT, Gabriel		800	7	239
JOURNEY, James		400	6	22
JAMES, William		600	6	48
JAMISON, Joseph	(John MULLANPHY)	800	6	87
JEFFREY, Baptiste	(reps. of)	800	6	116
JARRETT, Joseph	(legal reps. of)	640 acres	6	210
JAMES, William		600	6	297
JOURNEY, James		400	6	326
JAMES, Benjamin F.		690	6	531
JONES, Peggy		640	7	4
JAMES, Benjamin F.	(236)	690	7	59
JONES, Malachi	(Nicolas SHRUM)		7	137
JANES, William		640	7	150
JONES, Malachi		790	7	175
JONES, Thomas		1000	7	202
JONES, Thomas		1000	7	202
JONES, Thomas		1000	7	223
JONES, Thomas		1000	7	223
JANES, William		620	7	226
JONES, Peggy		640	7	225
JAMISON, Joseph		800	7	241
JEFFREY, Baptiste		800	7	241
KILEGAND, Jean Rene GUIHO De (Mathew DUNCAN)		500	6	64
KINNAIRD, Andrew	(Legal reps. of)	600	6	133
KINCAID, David		500	6	223
KERLEGAND, Jean Rene GUIHO de		500	6	299
KINAIRD, Andrew		600	6	318
KRYTZ, Daniel		234/36 per	6	330
KENNISON, Absalom		640	6	491
KINCAID, David	(174)	500	7	38
KENNYSON, Absalom		640	7	186
LEDUC, Mary Philip L.		7944	6	8
LABBADIE, Silvester	Record No. 2,	7056	6	17
LORIMIER, Louis	claiming the balance of	8000	6	19
LABRECHE, Jean Bste.		500	6	46
LISA, Manuel	(representatives of)	6000	6	52
LANGLOIS, Augustin		800	6	59
LACOMBE, Francois	(M. LISA's reps.)	400	6	60
LISA, Joachin	(M. LISA's reps.)	6000	6	61
LACOMBE, Francois	(M. LISA's reps.)	400	6	61
LESBOIS, Marie Nicolle		244-1/2	6	64
LOUGHRY, William	(Reps. of)	450	6	65
LORD, Pierre	(Reps. of)	800	6	67
LAFLEUR, Joseph	(Reps. of)	800	6	68
LAJOIE, Louis	(John MULLANPHY)	800	6	81
LABBADIE, Silvestre (Heirs of)		8 by 40	6	94
LADUC, Mary Philip		7944	6	113
LAMARCHE, Joseph Philip	(Henry Von PIEK	800	6	116
LORIMIER, Louis, Senr.	(Reps. of)	30,000	6	127
LORIMIER, Louis, Senr.	(Reps. of)	1000	6	128
LACHANCE, Michel	(G.A. BIRD)	72	6	132
LORIMIER, William (Legal reps. of)		1000	6	133
LONG, John	(Reps. of)	10,000	6	136

NAMES OF ORIGINAL CLAIMANTS & ASSIGNEES		ARPENTS	COMM.	MIN.
			Book #	Pg.
LONG, William	(Reps. of)	400	6	136
LAMALICE, Louis alias LEMONDE (LABEAUME's reps)		800	6	142
LEFEVRE, Auguste		800	6	148
LAGAUTERIE, Victor	(Legal Reps.)	800	6	167
LOISE, Alexis	(Legal reps.)	120	8	168
LINK, Absalom	(Wm. RAMEY)	510	6	172
LINK, Absalom	(William RAMEY)	510	6	175
LAMALICE and others each claiming 800 arpents			6	211
LOISE, Alexis	(Legal reps. of)	120	6	219
LOISIL, Regis	(J. CLAMORGAN's reps.)	44,800	6	222
LABADIE, Silvestre		Special	6	224
LACROIX, Isidore	(Reps. of)	6000	6	224
LINK, Absalom	(Wm. RAMEY)	510	6	232
LONG, Gabriel	(Legal Reps. of V. CASIED)	400	6	237
LANGLOIS, Adrian	(Heirs & Legs. & Reps.)	1500	6	258
LACHANCE, Michel		72	6	260
LEDUC, M.P.		7944	6	288
LORIMIER, Louis		944	6	294
LABRECHE, Baptiste		500	6	295
LISA, Manuel		6000	6	298
LES BOIS, Marie Nicolle	(No. 39)	244-1/2	6	300
LOUGHRY, William		450	6	300
LISA, Joachin		6000	6	301
LABBADIE, Silvestre		320	6	304
LORIMIER, Louis		30,000	6	316
LACHANCE, Michel		72	6	316
LORIMIER, Louis		1000	6	317
LORIMIER, William		1000	6	318
LONG, John		10,000	6	319
LONG, William		400	6	320
LACOMBE, Francois		400	6	326
LISA, Joachin		6000	6	333
LAJOIE, Louis		800	6	399
LACHANCE, Nicholas		640 acres	6	400
LAJOIE, Louis		800	6	423
LIMBAUGH, Frederick		640	6	456
LORR, Valentine		640	6	486
LABUXIERE			6	436
LAMARCHE, Joseph Philip		800	6	535
LAURINS, Baptiste	(241)	480	7	5
LAGOTERIE, Victor	(No. 149)	800	7	21
LAGOTERIE, Victor	(No. 149)	800	7	31
LORD, Gabriel	(180)	400	7	38
LOISE, Alexis		120	7	43
LORR, Valentine	(225)	300	7	55
LAURINS, Baptiste	(24L)	480	7	61
LOISE, Alexis	(246)	120	7	66
LORIMIER, Louis	(2nd)	1000	7	67
LOISEL, Regis	"	44,800	7	68
LACHANCE, Nicholas	"	640	7	71
LABBADIE, Silvestre		Special	7	77
LABBADIE, Silvestre	(256)	Special	7	78
LAMARCHE, Antoine		750	7	111
LANGLOIS, Adrien		1500	7	114
LAFOIX, Vincent & Nic. PLANTE alias LAPLANTE		640	7	115
LOGAN, Jane		800	7	121
LACROIX, Louis		40	7	124
LAMARCHE, Antoine		750	7	171
LAFOIX, Vincent & Nic. PLANTE		640	7	171
LOGAN, Jane		800	7	173
LACROIX, Louis		701	7	174
LACROIX, Isidore		6000	7	184
LAMARCHE, Jean Bste.		800	7	186
LANGLOIS, Adrien		1500	7	190
LINK, Abasalom		510	7	191
LINC, Joab		750	7	193
LACOMBE, Francois		400	7	198
LINC, Joab		750	7	217

NAMES OF ORIGINAL CLAIMANTS & ASSIGNEES		ARPENTS	COMM. MIN.	
			Book #	Pg.
LACOMBE, Francois		400	7	218
LAMALICE, Louis		800	7	228
LEFEVRE, Auguste		800	7	229
LAJOIE, Louis		800	7	237
LORD, Pierre		800	7	242
LAFLEUR, Joseph		800	7	242
LAMARCHE, Joseph Philip		800	7	242
MACKAY, James	(Heirs of)	30,000	6	3
MACDANIEL, James	(James MACKAY)	1800	6	9
MENARD, Pierre	(15)	400	6	15
MADDIN, Thomas		1500	6	43
MACKAY, James		30,000	6	53
MOREAU, Francois & Antoine MARECHAL (Reps. of)		15 by 20	6	66
MARION, Baptiste	(Reps. of)	800	6	67
MACKAY, James	(Reps. of)	Special	6	103
MARIE, Joseph	(Reps. of)	800	6	116
MAXWELL, Diego, Vicar General (By his reps. Bishop				
	of (?))	112,898	6	125
MORO, Manuel Gonzales	(Reps. of)	7056	6	132
MORO, Manuel Gonzales	(Reps. of)	800	6	133
MACKAY, James	(Reps. of)	400	6	137
MCMILLIAN, John	(Reps. of)	650	6	138
MEVILLE, Charles	(LABEAUME's reps.)	800	6	141
MARECHAL, Francois	(LABEAUME's reps.)	800	6	143
MARE, Jean Louis	(LABEAUME's reps.)	800	6	144
MARTY, Baptiste	(LABEAUME's reps.)	800	6	146
MORIN, Joseph Junr.	(LABEAUME's reps.)	160	6	149
MORIN, Joseph Junr.	(Same)	160	6	152
MICHAU, Melchior Amand		600	6	155
MCDANIEL, James	(Legal reps. of)	800	6	170
MACKAY, James	(Heirs of)	30,000	6	176
MADDIN, Thomas	(Legal reps.)	1500	6	204
MURPHY, John	(Jonah PARK)	550	6	209
MCHUGH, William alias MCGUE		640 acres	6	215
MIRACLE, David		640	6	216
MOTTARD, Joseph	(Calvin ADAMS)	1340	6	217
MARTIGNY, Jean Bste.	(Legal reps. of) (170)	12 in front	6	219
MCNAIR, Alexander	(Legal reps. of)	40	6	220
MCKINNEY, David	(Legal reps. of)	590	6	223
MADDIN, Thomas		2000	6	255
MACKAY, James		30,000	6	287
MACDANIEL, James		1800	6	289
MENARD, Pierre		400	6	291
MADDIN, Thomas		1500	6	296
MACKAY, James	(54)	200	6	306
MORO, Manuel Gonzales		7056	6	317
MORO, Manuel Gonzales		800	6	317
MACKAY, James		400	6	321
MCMILIAN, John		650	6	322
MORIN, Junr. Joseph		160	6	323
MOREAU, Francois & Ant. MARECHAL		300	6	325
MICHAU, Melchior Amand		600	6	333
MOORE, Bede		640 acres	6	354
MORRIS, Curtis	(legal reps. of)	746/75 per	6	385
MASSEY, Agnew		640	6	478
MATHEWS, Edward		640	6	479
MIDDLETON, Reuben		640	6	483
MILLER, Jacob			6	489
MCHUGH, William, Senr.	(James MORRISON)	640	6	499
MCCORMACK, John	(Henry COOK)	1000	6	504
MARIE, Joseph		800	6	536
MORRISON, William		750	7	1
MCNEAL, John		640	7	2
MARTIN, Lewis		300	7	2
MORRIS, Curtis		746/75 per	7	12
MCNEAL, John		640	7	18
MCHUGH, William		640	7	20
MIRACLE, David		640	7	22

NAMES OF ORIGINAL CLAIMANTS & ASSIGNEES	ARPENTS	COMM. Book #	MIN. Pg.
MORRIS, Curtis	746/75 per	7	23
MIRACLE, David (168)	640	7	36
MARTIGNY, Jean Baptiste (170)	12 in ft.	7	37
MCKINNEY, David (175)	590	7	38
MADDIN, Thomas (189)	2000	7	40
MOORE, Bede (190)	640	7	41
MORRIS, Curtis	746/75 per	7	46
MARTIN, Lewis (240)	300	7	61
MCNEAL, John (242)	640	7	62
MATHEWS, Edward (2d)	640	7	72
MOTIER, Francois	800	7	81
MCKINNEY, David	590	7	113
MEEK, William	500	7	113
MCDORMET, Charles	640	7	118
MILHOMME, Louis	20	7	123
MORRIS, Curtis	640	7	131
MATHEWS, Edward	540	7	134
MASSEY, Agnew	640	7	138
MCHUGH, Junr., William, Jas. MORRISON	640	7	139
MULLINS, Mathew	726	7	147
MCLANE, Charles	748/68 per	7	153
MATTIS, Jerome	800	7	156
MCHUGH, William, Senr.	640	7	168
MCDORMET, Charles	640	7	172
MEEK, William	500	7	172
MILHOMME, Louis	620	7	173
MULLINS, Mathew	726/95 per	7	176
MCLANE, Charles	748/68 per	7	177
MATTIS, Jerome	800	7	178
MASSEY, Agnew	248	7	181
MCCORMACK, John (2d-No. 47)	1000	7	186
MILLER, Jacob	300	7	186
MURPHY, John	550	7	188
MIDDLETON, Reuben	640	7	190
MUSICK, Ephraim	800	7	193
MOORE, James	640	7	195
MCKIM, James	760	7	189
MCCAY, Robert	320	7	197
MAURICE, Alexis	400	7	201
MORRIS, Curtis	746	7	203
MOTARD, Joseph	1340	7	213
MUSICK, Ephraim	800	7	217
MAURICE, Alexis	400	7	218
MOORE, James	640	7	221
MCKIM, James	760	7	222
MCCAY, Robert	320	7	223
MOTARD, Joseph	1340	7	224
MAXWELL, Diego	112,896	7	224
MORRIS, Curtis	746/75per	7	225
MOTIER, Francois	800	7	228
MARECHAL Francois	800	7	229
MARTY, Baptiste	800	7	231
MARC, Jean Louis	800	7	233
MARION, Baptiste	800	7	238
MIVILLE, Charles	800	7	241
MARIE, Joseph	800	7	241
NICOLLE, Gabriel (G.A. BIRD)	608	6	131
NORMANDAU, Francois (Albert TISON)	2500	6	133
Notice of Jos. EVANS to L.F. LINN, Comm'r.		6	214
Notice of Samuel LATIMER & others (Old Mine Conc.)		6	224
NEAL, Samuel (Reps. of)	800	6	247
NEAL, Jacob (Reps. of)	800	6	249
NICOLLE, Gabriel	608	6	316
NORMANDEAU, Francois	2500	6	318
NISWANGER, Junr., Joseph	640	6	471
NISWANGER, Joseph, Junr., (219)	650	7	53
NEAL, Jacob	650	7	183
NEAL, Samuel	200	-	---

NAMES OF ORIGINAL CLAIMANTS & ASSIGNEES		ARPENTS	COMM.	MIN.
			Book #	Pg.
Old Mine Concession		12,400	6	28
ODAM, Jacob (A. KINNEY & George FORGURS		800	6	163
Old Mine Concession		12,400	6	208
Old Mine Concession		12,400	6	225
Old Mine Concession		12,400	6	276
Old Mine Concession		12,400	6	289
ODAM, Jacob	(146)	800	7	12
OWSLEY, Jonathan		1200	7	158
OUVRAY, Louis		800	7	207
OHARA, Henry		1000	7	210
OHARA, Henry		1000	7	222
OUVRAY, Louis		800	7	235
PERRY, Jean Francois	(reps. of)	3000	6	65
PELLETIER, Andre	(reps. of)	800	6	66
PRATTE, J.B.	(reps. of)	1000	6	71
PACQUET, Francois	(Jno. MULLANPHY)	800	6	86
PEPIN, Etienne	(same)	1000	6	88
PAJCOL, Jean Bste.	(B. PRATTE)	240	6	96
PRATTE, Bernard		7056	6	104
PAPIN, Joseph	(reps. of)	8 by 17	6	115
PAPIN, Joseph M.	(Sons of each clmg.)	800	6	117
PRATTE, Bernard	(Pelagie SARPY)	800	6	117
PRESSE, Joseph	(LABEAUME's reps.)	800	6	147
PROVENCHER, Jean Bste.	(LABEAUME's reps.)	800	6	148
PRATTE, Antoine	(Heirs & legal reps. of)	500	6	181
PRATTE, Henry	(Heirs & legal reps. of)	600	6	182
PRATTE, Pierre Augste.		600	6	184
PRATTE, Joseph	(Heirs of & Others)	20,000	6	185
PRATTE, John Bste.	(Reps. of)	1000	6	200
PEYROUX, Henry	(Henry DODGE & Others)	7760 acres	6	202
PERREY, Jean Francois		3000	6	300
RATTE, Jean Bste.		1000	6	301
PEPIN, Etienne		1600	6	304
PAJCOL, Jean Bste.		240	6	306
PRATTE, Bernard		7056	6	306
PAPIN, Jos. M.		200	6	311
PAPIN, Sons of Joseph W.		5600	6	312
PRATTE, Bernard		800	6	312
PAUL, John		640 acres	6	353
PARENT, Etienne & Etienne GOVEROT		800	6	406
PETTIT, Benjamin, Junr.		640 acres	6	412
PETTIT, John L.		640 acres	6	425
PATTERSON, John		640 acres	6	463
PAYETT, John		464	6	502
PATRIOTTE, Amable		640	7	6
PRATTE, Antoine	(No. 154)	500	7	32
PRATTE, Henry	(No. 155)	600	7	32
PRATTE, Pierre Auguste	(No. 157)	600	7	33
PRATTE, Joseph	(No. 158)	20,000	7	33
PEYROUX, Henry	(No. 166)	7760 acres	7	36
PAUL, John	(No. 189)	640	7	41
PARENT, Etienne & Etienne GOVEROT (196)		800	7	44
PATTERSON, John	(216)	640	7	52
PATTENOTE, Amable		640	7	29
PAYETT, John	(2d)	464	7	71
PALARDIE, Pierre		1000	7	113
PLANTE, Nicolas alias LAPLANTE & V. LAFOIX		640	7	115
PALARDIE, Pierre		1000	7	171
PLANTE, Nicolas & V. LAFOIX		640	7	171
PETTIE, Junr., Benjamin		640	7	188
PATRIOTE, Amable		640	7	189
POWERS, Thomas		650	7	191
PURSLEY, George		800	7	192
POWERS, Thomas		650	7	216
PURSLEY, George		800	7	217
PETIT, John S.		640	7	225
PROVENCHER, John Bste.		800	7	229
PRESSE, Joseph		800	7	230

NAMES OF ORIGINAL CLAIMANTS & ASSIGNEES		ARPENTS	COMM. MIN.	
			Book #	Pg.
Pelletier, Andre		800	7	241
QUICK, Aaron		800	6	18
QUICK, Aaron		800	6	113
QUICK, Aaron	No. 20)	800	6	293
QUICK, Benjamin		800	6	538
QUICK, Daniel		800	6	538
QUICK, Benjamin		800	7	234
QUICK, Daniel		800	7	240
RIVIERE, Baptiste	(Manuel LISA's reps.)	400	6	61
RATTE, Julien	(Heirs of)	150	6	73
RIVET. Joseph	(Jno. MULLANPHY)	800	6	85
ROUSSEL, Pierre	(Jno. MULLANPHY)	800	6	93
REED, Louis	(Reps. of)	240	6	129
Resolution taken 10th October, 1832			6	19
Resolution taken 1st December, 1832			6	69
Resolution taken 9th March, 1833			6	112
Resolution taken 18th March, 1833			6	130
ROY, Charles	·(Reps. of)	80	6	135
ROLLINS, Seneca	(Reps. of)	400	6	135
ROY, Joachin	(Reps. of)	400	6	136
RICHARDSON, James	(Legal reps.)		6	165
ROGERS, James, Junr.		750	6	177
ROY, Joachin	(Legal reps.)	400	6	189
ROBIN, Charles & Louis CARON		1500	6	199
Resolution taken July 2nd, 1833			6	209
REED, Thomas	(Wm. SLOANE, assignees)	747	6	212
RAMSAY, William	(Legal reps. of)	1100	6	214
RAMSAY, John	(Legal reps. of)	748	6	216
ROY, Charles	(John P. CABANNE)	80	6	218
ROY, Joseph	(Louis LABEAUME's Rep.)	600	6	219
ROY, Joseph	(Same)	600	6	231
ROGR, Charles	(Legal Reps. of)	one lott 1-1/2 by 40	6	246
RAMEY, Mathew	(Settlement R.)	1056	6	297
RIVIERE, Baptiste		400	6	299
RATTE, Julien		150	6	303
REED, Louis		240	6	316
ROY, Charles		80	6	320
ROLLINS, Seneca		400	6	320
ROY, Joachin		400	6	320
RICHARDSON, J.		400	6	324
Resolutions passed 30th October, 1833			6	340
Resolution passed 20th November, 1833			6	343
Resolution passed 27th Nov., 1833			6	346
Receipt of A.G. HARRISON, Commr. for papers			6	347
Resignation of L.F. LINN			6	347
REED, William		727	6	351
RICHARD, B. h		1200	6	365
REED, Joseph (Legal reps. of)		640 acres	6	383
RING, Thomas (Camille DELASSUS)		500	6	405
REESE, David		640	6	442
REVEILLER, Nicolas		200	6	445
RAMSEY, James, Junr.		750	6	448
RAMSEY, Andrew		750	6	451
REED, Thomas	(Wm. SLOANE)	747	6	460
RANDALL, Enos		640	6	469
RANDALL, Samuel, Junr.		640	6	472
ROGERS, James, Senr.		766	6	509
Resolution passed June 7th, 1834			6	526
Resolution passed June 26th, 1834			6	538
ROGERS, James, Junr.		750	6	540
ROGERS, James Senr.		766	6	541
ROY, Pierre		40	6	543
Resolution (October 7th, 1834)			7	10
REED, Thomas		747	7	28
REED, Joseph, Junior		640	7	29
ROBIN, Charles & Louis CARRON	(No. 165)	1500	7	36
ROY, Charles	(167)	80	7	36

NAMES OF ORIGINAL CLAIMANTS & ASSIGNEES	ARPENTS	COMM.	MIN.
		Book #	Pg.
ROY, Joseph (169)	600	7	37
ROGERS, James Senior (234)	766	7	59
RAMSAY, James Junior (209)	750	7	49
RAMSAY, Andrew Junior (211)	750	7	50
RANDALL, Enos (218)	640	7	52
RANDALL, Samuel (220)	640	7	53
REED, Joseph Junior (243)	640	7	65
REED, Thomas (244)	640	7	66
RING, Thomas (2d)	500	7	70
ROY, Pierre "	40	7	72
Resolution 4th December, 1834		7	79
Receipt of James S. MAYFIELD		7	80
RAMSAY, William, Senr.	748/8 per	7	105
ROURKE, John	756	7	109
RICHARDSON, Daniel	460	7	165
RAMSAY, Senr., William	748/8 per	7	169
ROURKE, John	756	7	170
RICHARDSON, Daniel	460	7	178
RAMSAY, John	848	7	182
RICHARD, Barthelmi	1200	7	184
REESE, David	640	7	187
ROGERS, Junr., James	750	7	188
ROBERTS, Philip	1050	7	193
RABER, Michael	748	7	194
RANDALL, Abraham	778/29 per	7	194
RAYNOR, Jesse	640	7	202
ROBERT, Philip	1097	7	202
ROBERT, Philip	1050	7	216
RANDALL, Abraham	778/29 per	7	218
RAYNOR, Jesse	640	7	223
RABER, Michael	750	7	219
ROBERT, Philip	1097	7	223
RIVET, Joseph	800	7	230
ROUSSEL, Pierre	800	7	232
REED, Junr., William	727	7	245
Receipts of James H. RELFE, Esq. 30th Sept.		7	249,50
Resolutions 30th Sept., 1835		7	251
ST. VRAIN (Jno. SMITH, T.)	10,000	6	6
SAUCIER, Francois	8800	6	15
ST. GEMME, Raphael, BEQUETT & Others	1600	6	40
ST. VRAIN (Charles GREGOIRE)	1500	6	75
ST. VRAIN (Jno. MULLANPHY)	4000	6	89
SAUCIER, Mathew (Pierre CHOUTEAU, Senr.)	1200	6	105
ST. PIERRE, Etienne (P. CHOUTEAU, Senr.)	Spec location	6	106
SAUGRIN, Aantoine	20,000	6	115
SAUCIER, Francois	8800	6	118
SAUNDERS, John (Charles GRATIOT Heirs)	320	6	122
ST. GEMME, Beauvais	1600	6	137
ST. FERDINAND, Inhabitants of	1849-1/4	6	156
ST. VRAIN	4000	6	156
SMITH, Abraham (Legal reps. of)	600	6	170
ST. CIR, Hyacinthe (Legal reps. of)	137/91 per	6	221
ST. VRAIN (Jno. SMITH, T.)	10,000	6	271
ST. VRAIN (Children of (Same claimed by MULLANPHY)	4000	6	274
SOULARD, Antoine (63)	204/48per	6	103
ST. VRAIN, Jacques (Jno. SMITH, T.)	10,000	6	287
ST. VRAIN, Jacques (Same claim)	10,000	6	290
SAUCIER, Francois	7800	6	292
ST. GEMME, Raphael, BECQUET & Others	1600	6	296
ST. VRAIN, Jacques	1500	6	303
SAUCIER, Mathew	2100	6	307
ST. VRAIN, Jacques	4000	6	308
SOULARD, Antoine (No. 63)	204	6	309
SAUGRAIN, Antoine	20,000	6	312
ST. VRAIN, Jacques	1500	6	325
ST. PIERRE, Etienne	Special	6	327
ST. CLAIRE	640 acres	6	328

NAMES OF ORIGINAL CLAIMANTS & ASSIGNEES	ARPENTS	COMM. MIN. Book #	Pg.
SILVAIN, Joseph	240	6	365
STRICKLAND, David	1247/62 per	6	371
SUMMERS, Alexander	640	6	443
STOTTER, Conrad	640	6	484
SWANEY, Jacob	640	6	418
SCOTT, John	800	6	533
SMITH, Abraham	600	7	16,20
SMITH, Abraham (No. 156)	600	7	33
SUMMERS, Alexander (205)	640	7	48
STOTTER, Conrad (224)	640	7	56
SCOTT, John (2d)	800	7	71
STRICKLAND, David (250)	1247	7	72
STEWART, John	640	7	116
SUMMERS, James	250	7	133
SEXTON, Charles	300	7	140
SCHELL, G.	640	7	159
SULLIVAN, Dennis	640	7	163
ST. FERDINAND, Inhabitants of	1849-1/4	7	169
STEWART, John	640	7	171
SEXTON, Charles	300	7	175
SCHELL, Gasper	640	7	178
SULLIVAN, Dennis	300	7	179
SILVAIN, Joseph	250	7	183
SMOOT, Walter	800	7	196
SOCIER, Baptiste	760	7	196
SWIFT, James	640	7	212
SMOOT, Walter	800	7	218
SOCIER, Baptiste	760	7	221
SWIFT, James	640	7	223
SUMMERS, James	250	7	226
THIBAULT, Jean Bste.	800	6	58
TOURVILLE, Toussaint (reps. of)	800	6	67
TODD, T. (Jno.MULLANPHY)	800	6	82
TAYON, Charles (P. CHOUTEAU, Senr.)	500	6	106
TAYON, Francois (P. CHOUTEAU, Senr.)	10,000	6	107
TAYON, Charles (P. CHOUTEAU, Senr.)	1600	6	107
THEEL, Levy (Ch. GRATIOT's reps.)	200	6	119
TISON, Jean Bste. (LABEAUME's reps.)	7056	6	140
TORNAT, Pierre det LAJOIE (Legal reps. of)	600	6	189
TAYON, Charles, Junr. (SPICER)	800	6	243
TAYON, Louis	800	6	289
TAYON, Francis, Junr.	10,000	6	309
TAYON, Charles	1600	6	309
THEEL, Levy	200	6	313
TISON, Jean Bste.	7056	6	323
TUCKER, Henry	800	6	377
SAME	800	6	429
THOMPSON, Joseph, Junr.	640	6	430
THOMPSON, Senr., Joseph	640	6	432
THOMAS, Martin	640	6	440
THOMPSON, William	640	6	454
THOIN, Solomon		6	494
TAUMURE OR AUMURE	240	6	516
TAYON, Charles, Junior (183)	800	7	40
TAYON, Louis (186)	800	7	40
TUCKER, Henry (194)	640	7	43
THOMPSON, Joseph Junr. (202)	640	7	47
THORN, Solomon (230)	600	7	56
THOMPSON, Senr., Joseph (2d)	640	7	71
THIBAUT, Francis	500	7	118
TERMEL, Benjamin	800	7	121
THOMAS, Martin	640	7	133
THIBAULT, Francis	640	7	149
TAYLOR, John	540	7	160
THIBAULT, Francis	500	7	172
TENNEL, Benjamin	640	7	173
TAYLOR, John	640	7	178
TORNOT, dit LAJOIE, Pierre	600	7	185

NAMES OF ORIGINAL CLAIMANTS & ASSIGNEES		ARPENTS	COMM.	MIN.
			Book #	Pg.
THOMPSON, William		640	7	187
THOMAS, Martin		640	7	180
TORNAT, Pierre		600	7	208
TODD, T.		800	7	236
TOURVILLE, TOUSSAINT		800	7	238
THIBAULT, Charles		800	7	239
TORNAT, Pierre, dit LAJOIE		600	7	246
VASQUES, Sons of, each claiming		800	6	17
VILLARS, Marie Louise VALLE		7056	6	34
VALLE, Francois	(Reps. of)	7056	6	35
VALLE, Francois	(Reps. of)	7056	6	53
VANDERHYDER, Mathias	(Reps. of)	400	6	66
VASQUES, P.L.	(Gabriel PAUL)	800	6	74
VASSEUR, Regis	(Jno. MULLANPHY)	800	6	85
BASQUES, Benito	(Bernard PRATTE)	9 in front	6	95
VASQUES, Benito	(GRATIOT's reps.)	7056	6	121
VALLE, Michel	(LABEAUME's Reps.)	800	6	147
VALET, John	(Legal Reps. of)	400	6	169
VALET, Jno.	(Same)	400	6	171
VALLE, John Bste.		7056	6	191
VALLE, Francois Junr.		7056	6	193
VALLE, John Bste and Francois VALLE (Heirs of the latter)		7056	6	196
VALLE, John Bste. & Louis BOLDUC (Heirs & reps. of the latter)		800	6	197
VALLE, Charles	(legal reps. of)	160	6	257
VASQUES, the sons of each claimed 800			6	293
VILLARS, Marie Louise VALLE		7056	6	295
VALLE, Francois		7056	6	295
VANDERHYDER, Mathias		400	6	300
VASQUES, Benito		9 front	6	305
VASQUES, Benito		7056	6	314
VALLE, Basile		639 acres	6	356
VALLET, John		400	7	14
SAME		400	7	19
VALLET, John	(No. 152)	400	7	31
VALLE, Jean Bste.	(No. 160)	7056	7	33
VALLE, Jean Bste. & Louis BOLDUC (No. 164)		800	7	35
VALLE, Charles	(185)	160	7	40
VILLARS, Antoine & Joseph	(197)	6000	7	44
VILEMONT, Carlos de		2 leag. by 1	7	62
VILEMONT, Carlos de		Same	7	76
VILEMONT, Carlos de	(253)	2 leag. by 1	7	77
VINCENT, Jacques	J.E. THOLOZAN	10,000	7	125
VALLE, John Bste.		20,000	7	129
VALLE, Francois & J.B. VALLE		7056	7	182
VALLE, Francois, Junr.		7056	7	182
VINCENT, Jacques		10,000	7	199
VINEYARD, Jonathan		500	7	200
VACHARD, Antoine		640	7	211
VINEYARD, Jonathan		500	7	219
VINCENT, Jacques		10,000	7	225
VALLE, John B.		20,000	7	227
VACHARD, Antoine		640	7	227
VALLE, Michel		800	7	230
VASSEUR, Regis		800	7	233
WATKINS, John		7056	6	114
WATKINS, John		800	6	114
WHERRY, Mackay		1600	6	124
WILLIAMS, James	(LABFAUME's Reps.)	400	6	149
WICKERHAM, Jacob	(William DRENEN)	800	6	173
WILKINSON, Thomas	(MCNAIR's reps.)	400	6	222
WATKINS, John		7056	6	310
WATKINS, John		800	6	311
WHERRY, Mackey		1600	6	315
WILLIAMS, James		400	6	326
WALKER, Jacob		982	6	331
WICKERHAM, Jacob		800	6	338

NAMES OF ORIGINAL CLAIMANTS & ASSIGNEES	ARPENTS	COMM. MIN. Book #	Pg.
WICKERHAM, Jacob	800	6	348
WILBOURN, James	640	6	450
WORTHINGTON, Joseph	640	6	457
WILKINSON, Thomas (173)	400	7	38
WISE, Jacob	37-1/2	7	119
WICKERS, Julius	600	7	122
WILLBOURN, James	640	7	136
WILLBOURN, Curtis	640	7	165
WISE, Jacob	37-1/2	7	172
WICKERS, Julius	600	7	173
WILBOURN, Curtis	600	7	179
WILBOURN, James	300	7	180
WELDON, John	500	7	196
WELDON, John	500	7	219
YOUNG, Edward (Legal reps. of)	800	6	137
YOUNG, Edward	800	6	320
YOUNG, Morris	300	6	408
YOUNG, Morris	300	7	187

ABERNETHIE, Jogn 124
ADAMS, Calvin 66
ADAMS, Calvin 211
ADAMS, Calvins 224
ALAJOIE, Louis 114
ALLEN, ----- 140
ALLEN, Beverly 107
ALLEN, Celeste M. 56
ALLEN, Thomas 140
ALLEN, Thomas 143
ALLEN, Thomas 143
AMIOT, ----- 161
AMIOT, ----- 224
AMOUREUX, M. 12
AMOUREX, M. 184
ANDERSON, John 105
ANDERSON, John 105
ANDERSON, John 164
ANDERSON, John 224
ANDREWS, Alexander 137
ANDREWS, Alexander 138
ANDREWS, Alexander 169
ANDREWS, Alexander 170
ANDREWS, Alexander 224
AQUETON, Michael 206
AQUETON, Michael 214
AQUETON, Michael 224
ARNAUD, Francois 216
ARNAUD, Francois 224
ASHBROOK, William 111
ASHBROOK, William 113
ASHBROOKS, William 155
ASHERBRAUNNER, Urban 190
ASHERBRAUNNER, Urban 224
ASHERBRAWNER, Urban 200
AUBCHON, Louis 224
AUBUCHON, Auguste 201
AUBUCHON, Louis 199
AUBUCHON, Louis 224
AUMURE, Baptiste 147
AUMURE, Baptiste 204
AUMURE, Baptiste 224
AUSTIN, James 209
AUSTIN, Moses 8
AUSTIN, Moses 75
AUSTIN, Moses 80
AUSTIN, Moses 157
AUSTIN, Moses 181
AUSTIN, Moses 182
AUSTIN, Moses 191
AVERY, George 52
AWATKINS, Samuel 190
AYERY, George 204
AYREY, George 157
AYREY, George 224

BACANE, Baptiste Riviere dit 125
BACANE, Philipe 19
BACANNE, ----- 31
BACANNE, ----- 33
BACANNE, Philip 224
BACANNE, Philip 224
BACANNE, Philipe 85
BACON, Ludwell 205
BACON, Sudwell 212
BACON, Sudwell 225
BAKER, Joseph 141
BAKER, Joseph 141
BAKER, Reuben 191
BAKER, Reuben 191
BAKER, Reuben 225
BAKER, Rueben 200
BAKER, Thomas 103

BAKER, Thomas 104
BAKER, Thomas 164
BAKER, Thomas 225
BAKER, Thomas 225
BALDEIN, John 199
BALDWIN, John 130
BALDWIN, John 189
BALDWIN, John 189
BALDWIN, John 196
BALDWIN, John 197
BALDWIN, John 200
BALDWIN, John 225
BALDWIN, John 225
BAR, John 105
BARADA, ----- 69
BARLEVIN, Nicolas 224
BARR, Joseph 186
BARRADA, Antoine 163
BARRADA, Antoine 225
BARRADA, Antoine 225
BARSALOUX, Jean Baptiste 34
BARSALOUX, Marie Archange 34
BARSALOUX, Nicolas 33
BARSALOUX, Nicolas 34
BARSALOUX, Nicolas 88
BARSOLOUX, Nicolas 224
BASQUES, Benito 240
BASYE, John 224
BATES, ----- 7
BATES, ----- 31
BATES, ----- 32
BATES, ----- 33
BATES, ----- 41
BATES, ----- 57
BATES, ----- 66
BATES, ----- 84
BATES, ----- 94
BATES, ----- 99
BATES, ----- 116
BATES, ----- 117
BATES, ----- 120
BATES, ----- 121
BATES, ----- 122
BATES, ----- 123
BATES, ----- 124
BATES, ----- 128
BATES, ----- 134
BATES, ----- 136
BATES, ----- 144
BATES, ----- 147
BATES, ----- 149
BATES, ----- 160
BATES, ----- 162
BATES, ----- 170
BATES, ----- 174
BATES, ----- 181
BATES, ----- 183
BATES, ----- 184
BATES, ----- 189
BATES, ----- 195
BATES, ----- 205
BATES, ----- 206
BATES, ----- 207
BATES, ----- 212
BATES, Elias 71
BATES, Elias 191
BATES, F. 4
BATES, Frederick 3
BATES, Fredk. 35
BATES, Mr. 159
BATES, Willaim 225
BATES, William 198
BATES, William 225

BAUVAIS, St. Gemme 217
BAUVIAS, St. Gemme 204
BAYSE, John 4
BAYSE, John 83
BBURNS, Robert 120
BEAR, James 105
BEAR, James 110
BEAR, James 111
BEAR, John 105
BEAR, Joseph 186
BEAR, William 105
BEAUSOLEJF, ----- 33
BEAUVAIS, Jph. V. 14
BEAUVAIS, St. Gemme 11
BEAUVAIS, St. Gemme 29
BEAUVAIS, St. Gemme 84
BEAUVALS, St. Gemme 8
BEAUVIAS, St. James 11
BEAUVIAS, St. Gemme 39
BEAVAIS, St. Gemme 224
BECQUET, Joseph 71
BECQUETTE, Charles 193
BECQUETTE, Charles 200
BEDFORD, Thomas P. 205
BEDFORD, Thomas P. 212
BEDFORD, Thomas P. 225
BEDFORD, Thomas P. 226
BEEVE, John 194
BELCOUR, Joseph 208
BELCOUR, Joseph 213
BELCOUR, Joseph 226
BELEW, Solomon 204
BELIR, Solomon 225
BELL, Mordicai 179
BELL, Mordicay 198
BELL, Mordicay 225
BELLAND, John Bste. 66
BELLAND, John Bste. 224
BELLANGER, Francois 28
BELLANGER, Francois 218
BELLANGER, Francois 224
BELLANGER, Francois 226
BELLASSIME, Alexander 67
BELLEW, Solomon 148
BELLEW, Solomon 225
BENOIT, ----- 42
BENOIT, F. M. 220
BENOIT, F. M. 226
BENOIT, Francois M. 43
BENOIT, Francois M. 224
BENTON, Elijah 97
BENTON, Elijah 100
BENTON, Elijah 164
BENTON, Elijah 224
BENTON, Elijah 225
BENTON, Thos. H. 72
BEQUET, ----- 12
BEQUET, ----- 84
BEQUET, ----- 238
BEQUETTE, Baptiste 12
BEQUETTE, Charles 225
BERNARD, Francois 45
BERNARD, Francois 217
BERNARD, Francois 224
BERNARD, Francois 226
BERTHEAUME, ----- 83
BERTHIAUME, Francois 90
BEVINS, James 131
BEVINS, James 131
BEVINS, James 203
BEVINS, James 225
BEVINS, James 225
BILLOT, Bste. Joseph 26

BILLOT, Joseph Bapt. 224
BILLTO, Joseph 218
BIRD, Charles L. 114
BIRD, G. A. 40
BIRD, G. A. 41
BIRD, Moses 196
BISET, Antoine 226
BISHOP, John 43
BISHOP, John 92
BISHOP, John 224
BISSONET, Louis 6
BISSONET, Louis 6
BISSONET, Louis 93
BISSONET, Louis 224
BISSONETT, Louis 224
BIZET, Antoine 46
BIZET, Antoine 217
BIZET, Guillaume 197
BIZET, Guillaume 201
BLACK, ----- 13
BLANCO, Manuel 70
BLAY, Joseph 80
BLONDEAU, Andre 224
BLOOM, Peter 24
BLOOM, Peter 25
BLOOM, Peter 26
BLOOM, Peter 99
BOGG, Joseph 108
BOGY, Joseph 108
BOGY, Joseph 206
BOHERS, Squire 105
BOILEVIN, Nicholas 71
BOILEVIN, Nicholas 224
BOILEVIN, Nicolas 19
BOISE, Jacob 80
BOISE, Jacob 224
BOISE, Louise 224
BOISLEVIN, Nicolas 81
BOISSE, Jacob 2
BOISSE, Jacob 80
BOISSE, Louis 226
BOISSI, Louis 46
BOISSI, Louis 217
BOLAYE, Sophia 192
BOLAYE, Sophia 193
BOLAYE, Sophia 200
BOLAYE, Sophia 225
BOLDUC, Etienne 22
BOLDUC, Louis 22
BOLDUC, Louis 58
BOLDUC, Louis 61
BOLDUC, Louis 161
BOLDUC, Louis 162
BOLDUC, Louis 224
BOLDUC, Louis 228
BOLDUC, Louis 240
BOLI, ----- 146
BOLI, John 145
BOLI, John 147
BOLI, John 170
BOLI, John 225
BOLLEDUC, Louis 166
BOLLINGER, Daniel 94
BOLLINGER, Daniel 95
BOLLINGER, Daniel 127
BOLLINGER, Daniel 172
BOLLINGER, Daniel 225
BOLLINGER, Danile 125
BOLLINGER, David 139
BOLLINGER, David 168
BOLLINGER, David 225
BOLLINGER, Dawalt 125
BOLLINGER, Dawalt 138
BOLLINGER, Dawalt 225

BOLLINGER, Dayvalt 138
BOLLINGER, Dewalt 166
BOLLINGER, Frederick 138
BOLLINGER, Frederick 138
BOLLINGER, Frederick 168
BOLLINGER, Frederick 225
BOLLINGER, George F. 95
BOLLINGER, George F. 117
BOLLINGER, George F. 127
BOLLINGER, George F. 127
BOLLINGER, George F. 195
BOLLINGER, John 126
BOLLINGER, John 134
BOLLINGER, John 166
BOLLINGER, John 225
BOLLINGER, Marthia 168
BOLLINGER, Mathias 125
BOLLINGER, Mathias 139
BOLLINGER, Mathias 140
BOLLINGER, Mathias 141
BOLLINGER, Mathias 225
BOLLINGER, Philip 126
BOLLINGER, Phillip 125
BOLLINGER, Phillip 172
BOLLINGER, Phillip 225
BOLLINGER, William 126
BOLLINGER, William 131
BOLLINGER, William 134
BOLLINGER, William 190
BOLON, Hipolite 77
BOLON, Hipolite 171
BOLON, Hipolite 224
BOLY, John 49
BON, Jacaues 225
BON, Jacques 49
BON, Jacques 80
BON, Jacques 154
BON, Jacques 166
BON, Jacques 224
BOND, Edw. F. 134
BOON, Daniel M. 190
BOON, Nath. 38
BOONE, Daniel 73
BOSLEY, Charles 70
BOUCHER, Francois 93
BOUGY, Joseph 174
BOUIS, A. V. 202
BOUIS, A. Vincent 225
BOUIS, Antoine U. 224
BOUIS, Antoine V. 68
BOUIS, F. V. 68
BOULLIER, J. 64
BOULLIER, John 63
BOULLIER, T. 8
BOUVET, ----- 48
BOUVET, M. 225
BOUVET, Mathurin 36
BOUVET, Mathurin 52
BOUVET, Mathurin 52
BOUVET, Mathurin 89
BOUVET, Mathurin 161
BOUVET, Mathurin 224
BOYD, ----- 115
BOYD, Polly 136
BOYD, Polly 169
BOYD, Polly 225
BOYD, Polly 225
BOYD, Roland 123
BOYER, Charlot 70
BOYER, Jos. 80
BOYER, Joseph 79
BOYER, Louis 69
BOYER, Louis 79

BOYER, P. 79
BOYER, Peter 69
BOYER, Peter 184
BOYER, Peter 201
BOYER, Peter 225
BRADLEY, Edward 41
BRADLEY, Edward 91
BRADLEY, Edward 224
BRADLEY, Edward 224
BRANT, Daniel 189
BRANT, Daniel 190
BRASEAU, Joseph 224
BRAVIER, Jean Bste. 45
BRAVIER, Jean Bste. 218
BRAVIER, Jean Bste. 224
BRAVIER, Jean Bste. 226
BRAZEAU, Joseph 38
BRAZEAU, Joseph 90
BRECKENRIDGE, George 71
BREWARD, A. H. 138
BRICKER, John C. 65
BRIDGE, Samuel 110
BRINDLEY, J. 74
BROWN, ----- 212
BROWN, Catherine 56
BROWN, Ethan Allen 222
BROWN, James 105
BROWN, James 186
BROWN, James 216
BROWN, James 225
BROWN, James 225
BROWN, James 225
BROWN, James 226
BROWN, Jos. C. 48
BROWN, Jos. C. 49
BROWN, Jos. C. 52
BROWN, Joseph C. 24
BROWN, Robert T. 56
BROWN, Robert T. 57
BRUFF, James 51
BRYAN, Jonathon 176
BRYAN, Mr. 178
BRYANT, David 179
BRYANT, Jonathan 178
BUAT, Louis 196
BUAT, Louis 201
BUCHANAN, Robert 51
BUIS, Jonathan 83
BUIS, Jonathan 137
BUIS, Jonathan 196
BULLETT, George 56
BUREL, ----- 205
BURET, ----- 225
BURK, John 122
BURK, John 123
BURK, John 165
BURK, John 180
BURK, John 225
BURK, John 225
BURNS, Arthur 52
BURNS, Arthur 211
BURNS, James 157
BURNS, James 177
BURNS, Peter 119
BURNS, Peter 221
BURNS, Peter 221
BURNS, Peter 225
BURNS, Peter 226
BURNS, Robert 204
BURNS, Robert 225
BURNS, Robert 225
BURRELL, Peter 212
BURRELL, Peter 226

BURTON, Alexander 197
BURTON, Alexander 201
BUTCHER, Bartholomew 24
BUTCHER, Bartholomew 25
BUTCHER, Bartholomew 99
BUTCHER, Bastian 99
BUTCHER, Batholomew 26
BUTCHER, Michael 24
BUTCHER, Michael 25
BUTCHER, Michael 26
BUTCHER, Sebastian 24
BUTCHER, Sebastian 58
BUTCHER, Sebastian 99
BUTCHER, Sebastian 224
BUTCHER, Sebastian 224
BUTNER, Alexander 197
BUTNER, Alexander 201
BUYOSO, ----- 39
BYRD, Charles L. 117
BYRD, Moses 116
BYRD, Moses 135
BYRD, Moses 137
BYRD, Moses 138
BYRD, Moses 144

CABANNE, ----- 31
CABANNE, J. P. 30
CABANNE, J. P. 51
CABANNE, J. P. 68
CABANNE, John P. 67
CABANNE, John P. 86
CABANNE, John P. 203
CABANNE, John P. 226
CABANNE, John P. 227
CABBANE, J. P. 42
CAGLE, Roger 162
CAGLE, Roger 173
CAILLON, Francois 5
CAILLON, Francois 17
CAILLON, Francois 226
CAILLONN, Francois 83
CALLON, Francois 227
CALNER, John 126
CAMBAS, ----- 33
CAMBAS, Jean 147
CAMBAS, Jean 171
CAMBAS, Jean 227
CAMBAS, Jean 227
CAMPBELL, Saml. 121
CAMPBELL, Saml. 183
CAMPBELL, Samuel 96
CAMPBELL, Samuel 118
CAMPBELL, Samuel 119
CAMPBELL, Samuel 120
CAMPBELL, Samuel 204
CAMPBELL, Samuel 227
CAMPBELL, Samuel 227
CAMPBELL, William 48
CAMPBELL, William 53
CANON, Lewis 56
CARDINAL, Jean Marie 47
CARDINAL, Jean Marie 67
CARDINAL, Jean Marie 203
CARDINAL, Jean Marie 226
CARDINAL, Jean Marie 227
CARDINAL, John Mary 179
CARO, Louis 201
CARON, Louis 61
CARON, Louis 237
CARONDELET, Baron de 5
CARONDELET, Baron de 7
CARONDELET, Baron de 10
CARONDELET, Baron de 17
CARONDELET, Baron de 39

CARONDELET, Baron de 55
CARONDELET, Baron de 63
CARONDELET, Baron de 78
CARONDELET, Baron de 115
CARONDELET, Baron de 171
CARONDELET, Baron de 174
CARONDELET, El Baron de 6
CARR, W. C. 68
CARR, Will. C. 110
CARR, William C. 30
CARRON, Louis 162
CARTER, Peggey 215
CARTER, Peggy 227
CASAS, Luis de las 17
CASEY, Andrew 69
CASEY, John 69
CASEY, Morgan 69
CAULK, ARichard 2
CAULK, Richard 3
CAULK, Richard 82
CAULK, Richard 226
CAULK, Richard 227
CAULK, Thomas 2
CAULK, Thomas 3
CAULK, Thomas 93
CAULK, Thomas 95
CAULK, Thomas 226
CAULK, Thomas 227
CAYLE, Roger 227
CAYLE, Roger 227
CAYON, Francois 51
CERRE, Gabriel 1
CERRE, Gabriel 29
CERRE, Gabriel 30
CERRE, Gabriel 47
CERRE, Gabriel 52
CERRE, Gabriel 81
CERRE, Gabriel 82
CERRE, Gabriel 87
CERRE, Gabriel 87
CERRE, Gabriel 93
CERRE, Gabriel 208
CERRE, Gabriel 226
CERRE, Gabriel 227
CERRE, Gabriel 227
CERRE, Gabriell 214
CERRE, Pascal 4
CERRE, Pascal 5
CERRE, Pascal 6
CERRE, Pascal 30
CERRE, Pascal 82
CERRE, Pascal 226
CERRE, Pascal L. 1
CERRE, Pascal L. 38
CERRE, Pascal L. 38
CERRE, Pascal L. 47
CERRE, Pascal L. 153
CERRE, Pascal S. 210
CERRE, Pascal S. 211
CERRE, Paschal 64
CERRE, Toussaint 4
CERRE, Toussaint 83
CERRE, Toussaint 227
CERRE, Toussiant 226
CHALIFOUX, Jean Baptiste 54
CHALIFOUX, Jean Baptiste 162
CHALIFOUX, Jean Bste. 226
CHALIFOUX, Jean Bste. 227
CHANDLER, Edmund 52
CHANDLER, Edmund 52
CHANDLER, Edmund 95
CHANDLER, Edmund 226
CHANDLER, Edmund 227
CHARLESS, Jos. 193

CHARLEVELLE, Joseph 217
CHARLEVILLE, Joseph 46
CHARLEVILLE, Joseph 226
CHARLEVILLE, Joseph 227
CHARLEVILLE, Louis 45
CHARLEVILLE, Louis 217
CHARLEVILLE, Louis 226
CHARLEVILLE, Louis 227
CHARPENTIER, ----- 150
CHARPENTIER, Louis Alias 231
CHARTRAN, Amable 19
CHARTRAN, Amable 219
CHARTRAN, Amable 226
CHARTRAN, Amable 227
CHARTRAN, Joseph 179
CHARTRAN, Joseph 180
CHARTRAN, Joseph 198
CHARTRAN, Joseph 227
CHATILLON, Jean Baptiste 77
CHATILLON, Jean Bste. Maurice 146
CHATILLON, John Baptiste Maurice 49
CHENEY, Lemuel 129
CHENEY, Lemuel 167
CHENEY, Lemuel 227
CHENIER, Antoine 41
CHEVALIER, Andre 65
CHEVALIER, Andre 202
CHEVALIER, Andre 226
CHEVALIER, Andre 227
CHEVALIER, Joseph 134
CHEVALIER, Joseph 135
CHEVALIER, Joseph 135
CHEVALIER, Joseph 165
CHEVALIER, Joseph 227
CHEVALIER, Joseph 227
CHOUTEAU, A. P. 227
CHOUTEAU, Augste P. 152
CHOUTEAU, Auguste 4
CHOUTEAU, Auguste 6
CHOUTEAU, Auguste 54
CHOUTEAU, Auguste 83
CHOUTEAU, Auguste 98
CHOUTEAU, Auguste 226
CHOUTEAU, Auguste 227
CHOUTEAU, Auguste 227
CHOUTEAU, Auguste P. 71
CHOUTEAU, Auguste P. 163
CHOUTEAU, Auguste P. 226
CHOUTEAU, Auguste P. 227
CHOUTEAU, P. 29
CHOUTEAU, P. 226
CHOUTEAU, Peter 30
CHOUTEAU, Peter 67
CHOUTEAU, Peter 71
CHOUTEAU, Peter 84
CHOUTEAU, Peter 94
CHOUTEAU, Peter 226
CHOUTEAU, Peter 227
CHOUTEAU, Pierre 31
CHOUTEAU, Pierre 32
CHOUTEAU, Pierre 33
CHOUTEAU, Pierre 38
CHOUTEAU, Pierre 90
CHOUTEAU, Pierre 147
CHOUTEAU, Pierre 148
CHOUTEAU, Pierre 165
CHOUTEAU, Pierre 174
CHOUTEAU, Pierre 210
CHOUTEAU, Pierre 227
CHOUTEAU, Pierre 238
CHOUTED, ----- 4
CHRISTY, Edm. T. 69
CHRISTY, Wm. 69

CRELY, Therese 148
CRELY, Therese 163
CRELY, Therese 227
CRELY, Therese 227
CRELY, Therin 226
CRESWELL, Hugh 123
CRETZ, Dawalt 228
CRISWELL, Hugh 124
CRISWELL, Hugh 134
CRISWELL, Hugh 134
CRISWELL, Hugh 190
CRISWELL, Hugh 195
CRISWELL, Hugh 200
CRISWELL, Hugh 227
CRISWELL, Hugh 227
CRITS, Daniel 94
CRITZ, Daniel 94
CRITZ, Dawalt 127
CRITZ, Dawalt 221
CROSS, John 196
CROW, Benjamen 104
CROW, Benjamen 113
CROW, Benjamin 103
CROW, Polly 155
CROW, Walter 111
CROW, Walter 113
CROW, Walter 166
CROW, Walter 208
CROW, Walter 209
CRUMP, George 42
CRUMP, George 91
CRUMP, George 226
CRUMP, George 227
CRUSAT, Francisco 1
CRUSAT, Francois 6
CRUZAT, ----- 74
CRUZAT, Francisco 30
CRUZAT, Francisco 35
CRUZAT, Francisco 47
CURTY, George 66
CUTZ, Dawalt 227

DAHMEN, Mr. 8
DAJARLIAS, Antoine 229
DANIEL, John 205
DANIEL, John 213
DANIEL, John 229
DANIEL, Stephen 56
DANY, Francoise 207
DARDENNE, John Bste. 206
DARDENNE, John Bste. 213
DARST, David 73
DARST, Isaac 177
DAUGHTERY, Elijah 186
DAUGHTERY, Elijah 187
DAVIS, ----- 108
DAVIS, ----- 109
DAVIS, William 69
DAVIS, William 104
DAVIS, William 104
DAVIS, William 108
DAVIS, William 185
DAVIS, William 186
DAVIS, William 221
DAVIS, William 228
DAVIS, William 229
DEARING, Adison 69
DEBLOIS, ----- 120
DEBLOIS, ----- 121
DEBLOIS, Joseph Alias 229
DEBREUIL, Antoine 228

DECARRY, Joseph 27
DECARRY, Joseph 217
DECARRY, Joseph 228
DECARRY, Joseph 229
DECELLE, Joseph 105
DECELLE, Joseph 106
DECHAMP, Baptiste 50
DECHAMP, Jean Baptiste 49
DECHAMP, Jean Baptiste 154
DECHAMP, Jean Bste. 228
DECHAMP, Jean Bste. 229
DECHAMP, Jno. B. 49
DECHAMP, Toussaint 50
DECHMENDY, Pascal 229
DEGUIRE, Paul 117
DEGUIRE, Paul 172
DEGUIRE, Paul 229
DEJARLAIS, Paul 219
DEJARLIAS, Antoine 150
DEJARLIAS, Antoine 218
DEJARLIAS, Antoine 229
DEJARLIAS, Paul 228
DELASSU, Carlos D. 45
DELASSUS, ----- 48
DELASSUS, ----- 54
DELASSUS, ----- 198
DELASSUS, ----- 222
DELASSUS, C. D. 3
DELASSUS, C. D. 4
DELASSUS, C. D. 5
DELASSUS, C. D. 6
DELASSUS, C. D. 9
DELASSUS, C. D. 34
DELASSUS, C. D. 36
DELASSUS, C. D. 37
DELASSUS, C. D. 40
DELASSUS, C. D. 83
DELASSUS, C. D. 134
DELASSUS, C. D. 153
DELASSUS, C. D. 170
DELASSUS, C. D. 185
DELASSUS, C. D. 207
DELASSUS, Cahrles Dehault 108
DELASSUS, Camille 53
DELASSUS, Camille 82
DELASSUS, Camille 83
DELASSUS, Camille 115
DELASSUS, Camille 116
DELASSUS, Camille 161
DELASSUS, Camille 165
DELASSUS, Camille 228
DELASSUS, Camille 229
DELASSUS, Camille 229
DELASSUS, Carlo Dehault 152
DELASSUS, Carlo Dehault 179
DELASSUS, Carlos D. 7
DELASSUS, Carlos D. 27
DELASSUS, Carlos D. 41
DELASSUS, Carlos D. 44
DELASSUS, Carlos D. 46
DELASSUS, Carlos D. 46
DELASSUS, Carlos D. 47
DELASSUS, Carlos D. 51
DELASSUS, Carlos D. 58
DELASSUS, Carlos D. 64
DELASSUS, Carlos D. 69
DELASSUS, Carlos D. 74
DELASSUS, Carlos Dehault 1
DELASSUS, Carlos Dehault 9
DELASSUS, Carlos Dehault 14
DELASSUS, Carlos Dehault 16
DELASSUS, Carlos Dehault 17
DELASSUS, Carlos Dehault 18
DELASSUS, Carlos Dehault 21

DELASSUS, Carlos Dehault 22
DELASSUS, Carlos Dehault 23
DELASSUS, Carlos Dehault 24
DELASSUS, Carlos Dehault 26
DELASSUS, Carlos Dehault 28
DELASSUS, Carlos Dehault 29
DELASSUS, Carlos Dehault 32
DELASSUS, Carlos Dehault 33
DELASSUS, Carlos Dehault 38
DELASSUS, Carlos Dehault 39
DELASSUS, Carlos Dehault 42
DELASSUS, Carlos Dehault 43
DELASSUS, Carlos Dehault 45
DELASSUS, Carlos Dehault 65
DELASSUS, Carlos Dehault 68
DELASSUS, Carlos Dehault 71
DELASSUS, Carlos Dehault 73
DELASSUS, Carlos Dehault 82
DELASSUS, Carlos Dehault 97
DELASSUS, Carlos Dehault 115
DELASSUS, Carlos Dehault 116
DELASSUS, Carlos Dehault 148
DELASSUS, Carlos Dehault 150
DELASSUS, Carlos Dehault 175
DELASSUS, Carlos Dehault 180
DELASSUS, Carlos Dehault 205
DELASSUS, Carlos Dehault 208
DELASSUS, Carlos Dehault 228
DELASSUS, Charles D. 55
DELASSUS, Charles D. 75
DELASSUS, Charles Dehault 6
DELASSUS, Charles Dehault 8
DELASSUS, Charles Dehault 56
DELASSUS, Charles Dehault 61
DELASSUS, Charles Dehault 84
DELASSUS, Charles Dehault 85
DELASSUS, Charles Dehault 104
DELASSUS, Charles Dehault 123
DELASSUS, Charles Dehault 135
DELASSUS, Charles Dehault 194
DELASSUS, Charles Dehault 228
DELASSUS, Dehault 19
DELASSUS, Delusierre Pierre 228
DELASSUS, Lt. Gov. Carlos Dehault 2
DELASSUS, Mr. 197
DELASSUS, Mr. 210
DELASSUS, Pierre de Lusiere 228
DELAUNAY, D. 2
DELAUNAY, David 9
DELAUNAY, David 82
DELAUNAY, David 228
DELAUNAZ, David 228
DELAURIER, C. F. 36
DELAURIER, C. F. 37
DELAURIER, C. Fremon 35
DELAURIER, Charles F. 34
DELAURIER, Charles Fremon 36
DELAURIER, Fremon 34
DELAURIERE, Ch. Fremon 228
DELAURIERE, Charles Freemon 93
DELAURIERE, Charles Fremon 16
DELAURIERE, Charles Fremon 17
DELAURIERE, Charles Fremon 20
DELAURIERE, Charles Fremon 85
DELAURIERE, Charles Fremon 92
DELAURIERE, Charles Fremon 228
DELAURIERE, Fremon 6
DELAURIERE, Fremon 9
DELAURIERE, Fremon 18
DELAURIERE, Fremon 150
DELAURIERRE, Charles Fremon 43
DELAURIERRE, Chas. Fremon 228
DELILLE, Baptiste 27

EGLIS, Hyacinthe 230
EGLIZ, Hyacinthe 87
ESTEP, Priscilla 146
ESTEP, Priscilla 151
ESTEP, Priscilla 152
ESTEP, Priscilla 230
ESTHER, ----- 230
ESTHER, Mulatress 229
EVANS, Jos. 235
EVANS, Joseph 65
EVANS, Joseph 69
EVERETT, Richard 99
EVERITT, Richard 99

FENWICK, Ezekiel 97
FENWICK, Ezekiel 172
FENWICK, Ezekiel 221
FENWICK, Ezekiel 230
FENWICK, James 172
FENWICK, James 221
FENWICK, James 230
FENWICK, James I. 15
FENWICK, Joseph 53
FENWICK, Joseph 170
FENWICK, Joseph 185
FENWICK, Joseph 191
FENWICK, Joseph 200
FENWICK, Joseph 220
FENWICK, Joseph 222
FENWICK, Joseph 230
FENWICK, Leo 76
FENWICK, Leo 172
FENWICK, Leo 221
FENWICK, Leo 230
FENWICK, Martin 185
FENWICK, Martin 221
FENWICK, Walter 75
FENWICK, Walter 76
FENWICK, Walter 172
FENWICK, Walter 220
FENWICK, Walter 230
FERGUSON, Nancy 189
FERGUSON, Nancy 200
FERGUSON, Nancy 230
FERGUSON, Obediah 69
FERRY, John 154
FINE, David 210
FINE, Philip 74
FINE, Philip 193
FINE, Philip 193
FINELY, Charles 187
FINELY, James W. 209
FLANDRIN, Antoine 68
FLANDRIN, Antoine 150
FLANDRIN, Antoine 163
FLANDRIN, Antoine 230
FLANDRIN, Antoine 230
FLAUGHTERY, Ralph H. 177
FLAUGHTERY, Ralph H. 178
FLAUGHTERY, Ralph H. 179
FLEMING, P. 161
FLEMING, Patrick 51
FLEMING, Patrick 63
FLEMMING, P. 231
FLEMONG, Patrick 230
FLETCHER, Silas 187
FLETCHER, Silas 199
FLETCHER, Silas 230
FLETCHER, Thomas 188
FLYNN, William 192
FLYNN, William 215
FLYNN, William 230
FORD, Elijah 131
FORD, Elijah 169

FORD, Elijah 230
FORGUER, George 50
FRANCIS, Charles 79
FRIEND, John 132
FRIEND, John 139
FRIEND, John 207
FRISELL, Mason 97

GAGNIER, Antoine 34
GAGNIER, Antoine 88
GAGNIER, Antoine 230
GALLAGHER, David 109
GALLATIN, Abraham 30
GAMACHE, Auguste 73
GAMACHE, Auguste 74
GAMACHE, Auguste 164
GAMACHE, Auguste 230
GAMACHE, Auguste 231
GAMACHE, Jean Baptiste 154
GAMACHE, Jean Bste. 230
GAMACHE, John Baptiste 49
GAMACHE, John Baptiste 74
GAMACHE, Louis 49
GAMACHE, Nicholas 49
GAMELIN, Pierre 54
GAMELIN, Pierre 162
GAMELIN, Pierre 230
GAMMACHE, Jean Bste. 231
GARDINER, ----- 177
GARDINER, Benamen 176
GARDINER, Benjamen 177
GARDINER, Benjamen 179
GARDINER, Benjamen 190
GARDINER, Benjamen 198
GARDINER, Benjamen 231
GARDINER, Benjamen 231
GARNIER, I. V. 34
GAUTIER, Antoine 43
GAUTIER, Antoine 92
GAUTIER, Antoine 230
GAYOSO, ----- 39
GAYOSO, ----- 98
GAZOL, F. M. 2
GEFFREY, Baptiste 150
GEFREY, Baptiste 231
GEGUIERE, Louis 230
GEMME, Batholomew St. 12
GEMME, Batholomew St. 13
GEMME, Joseph St. 23
GEMME, Raphael St. 12
GEMMES, Batholomew St. 24
GENDRON, Toussaint 18
GENDRON, Toussaint 219
GENDRON, Toussaint 230
GENDRON, Toussant 231
GERARD, John 208
GERARD, John 215
GERARD, John 231
GERARD, Jos. 161
GERARD, Joseph 51
GERARD, Joseph 63
GERARD, Joseph 230
GERARD, Joseph 231
GERRARD, Joseph 50
GIBONEY, Robert 96
GIBONEY, Robert 97
GIBONEY, Robert 138
GIBONEY, Robert 139
GIBONEY, Robert 143
GIGIERRE, Louis 44
GIGUIERE, Louis 220
GIGUIERE, Louis 231
GILL, Charles 152
GILL, Charles 153

GILL, Charles 171
GILL, Charles 231
GILL, Charles 231
GIRLY, George 231
GIRTY, George 178
GIRTY, George 198
GODFREY, John 147
GODFREY, John 208
GODFREY, John 221
GODFREY, John 231
GODINAIR, Jean 230
GODINEAU, ----- 42
GODINEAU, Jean 42
GODINEAU, Jean 218
GODINEAU, Jean 231
GOFORTH, A. 111
GOFORTH, A. 112
GOFORTH, Zacaria 212
GOGORTH, Andrew 110
GORDON, George 85
GOVERET, Etienne 116
GOVEROT, Etienne 165
GOVEROT, Etienne 236
GOZA, Mary 133
GRABER, ----- 231
GRAGG, Nancy 113
GRATIOT, ----- 240
GRATIOT, C. 37
GRATIOT, Charles 36
GRATIOT, Charles 38
GRATIOT, Charles 68
GRATIOT, Charles 89
GRATIOT, Charles 90
GRATIOT, Charles 230
GRATIOT, Charles 238
GRAVER, ----- 206
GRAVER, ----- 214
GRAVER, ----- 231
GREEN, D. 134
GREEN, David 115
GREEN, David 133
GREEN, David 137
GREEN, David 169
GREEN, David 230
GREEN, David 231
GREEN, Robert 115
GREEN, Robert 128
GREEN, Robt. 129
GREENWALT, John 141
GREENWALT, John 142
GREENWALT, John 191
GREENWALT, John 192
GREENWALT, John 203
GREENWALT, John 231
GREGOIRE, Charles 12
GREGOIRE, Charles 24
GREGOIRE, Charles 238
GRENIER, Louis 193
GRENIER, Louis 200
GRENIER, Louis 231
GRENWALT, John 141
GRIFFEY, Catherine 188
GRIFFITH, Daniel 49
GRIFFITH, Daniel 154
GRIFFITH, Daniel 161
GRIFFITH, Daniel 230
GRIFFITH, Daniel 231
GRIFFITH, Daniel 231
GRIMAR, ----- 231
GRIMAR, Louis 150
GRIMARD, Louis 218
GRIMARND, ----- 231
GRIMAUD, Louis 150
GROHSON, Jeremiah 173

GROSON, Jeremiah 158
GROUND, Peter 114
GROUND, Peter 115
GUENELLE, Etienne 158
GUERET, Pierre 197
GUETHING, John 128
GUETHING, John 166
GUETHING, John 231
GUETHING, John 231
GUIHO, Jean Rene de 232
GUILBURG, Jacques 8
GUNSONLIS, James 94
GURTZ, George 230
GUYOT, F. M. 2
GUYOT, F. M. 58
GUYOT, F. M. 107
GUYOUT, F. M. 31

HACKER, George 128
HACKER, George 138
HACKER, George 188
HACKER, George 189
HACKER, George 190
HACKER, Goerge 129
HACKER, Wm. 131
HAFF, James 150
HAFF, James 218
HAFF, James 232
HAINE, Joseph 73
HANCOCK, William 107
HAND, John 133
HAND, John 167
HAND, John 231
HARDEN, Benjamen 104
HARRINGTON, Samuel 151
HARRINGTON, Samuel 151
HARRINGTON, William 162
HARRIS, Andrew 152
HARRIS, Andrew 170
HARRIS, Andrew 231
HARRIS, H. P. 143
HARRIS, Hezekiah P. 143
HARRISON, A. G. 49
HARRISON, A. G. 51
HARRISON, A. G. 73
HARRISON, A. G. 98
HARRISON, A. G. 148
HARRISON, A. G. 157
HARRISON, A. G. 158
HARRISON, A. G. 173
HARRISON, A. G. 177
HARRISON, A. G. 178
HARRISON, A. G. 179
HARRISON, A. G. 180
HARRISON, Albert G. 33
HARRISON, Albert G. 99
HARTLEY, William 41
HARTLEY, William 203
HARTLEY, William 231
HARTLEY, William 232
HARVEY, John 144
HARVEY, John 146
HARVEY, John 155
HARVIN, ----- 208
HARVIN, Jean 207
HARVIN, Jean 213
HARVIN, Jean 232
HAWKINS, James 102
HAWKINS, James 164
HAWKINS, James 231
HAWKINS, John 56

HAYS, John 133
HAYS, William 73
HAYS, William 190
HAYWARD, Elijah 99
HAYWARD, Elijah 175
HEBERT, Francois 67
HEBERT, Francois 165
HEBERT, Francois 171
HEBERT, Francois 231
HEBERT, Joseph 28
HEBERT, Joseph 48
HEBERT, Joseph 217
HEBERT, Joseph 231
HEBERT, Joseph 232
HEBERT, N. G. 80
HEBERT, Widow 125
HELDERBRAND, Abraham 145
HELDERBRAND, Benjamen 169
HELDERBRAND, John 144
HELDERBRAND, John 172
HELDERBRAND, John 232
HELDERBRAND, Jonathan 144
HELDERBRAND, Jonathan 145
HELDERBRAND, Jonathan 231
HEMPSTEAD, E. 227
HEMPSTEAD, Edw. 21
HEMPSTEAD, Edward 21
HEMPSTEAD, Edward 62
HEMPSTEAD, Edward 86
HEMPSTEAD, Edward 226
HENDERSON, ----- 144
HENDERSON, George 137
HENDERSON, George 137
HENDERSON, George 143
HENDERSON, George 169
HENDERSON, George 231
HENDERSON, Samuel 103
HENRY, John 41
HENRY, John 91
HENRY, John 231
HEWIT, Solomon 212
HEWITT, James 186
HILDERBRAND, Benjamen 114
HILDERBRAND, Benjamen 115
HILDERBRANT, John 37
HILDERBRANT, John 90
HILDERBRANT, John 231
HILLHOUSE, ----- 121
HILLIS, ----- 121
HINKINSON, William 110
HINKINSON, Wilm. 111
HINKINSON, Wm. 112
HOLMES, Samuel 180
HOLMES, Samuel 180
HOLMES, Samuel 198
HOLMES, Samule 232
HONORE, Tesson 72
HONORE, Tesson 148
HORINE, Benjamen 148
HORINE, Benjamen 176
HORINE, Benjamin 72
HORINE, Benjamin 100
HORINE, David 72
HORINE, David 148
HORINE, David 149
HORINE, David 153
HORINE, David 163
HORINE, David 231
HORINE, Michael 97
HORTEZ, Elisabeth 50
HOWARD, Henry 135
HOWARD, Purnel 32
HOWARD, Purnel 88
HOWARD, Purnel 231

HOWARD, Purnet 231
HOWELL, John 149
HOWELL, Newton 38
HOWELL, Newton 90
HOWELL, Newton 231
HUBBARD, Daniel 26
HUBBARD, Daniel 218
HUBBARD, Daniel 231
HUBBARD, Daniel 232
HUBBARD, Eusebius 231
HUBBARD, Eusebuis 26
HUBBARD, Eusebuis 232
HUBBARD, Felix 26
HUBBARD, Felix 218
HUBBARD, Felix 231
HUBBARD, Felix 232
HUBBARD, N. P. 69
HUBBLE, Ebenezer 129
HUBBLE, Ebenezer 130
HUBBLE, Ebenezer 132
HUBBLE, Ebenezer 167
HUBBLE, Ebenezer 231
HUBBLE, Ithamer 124
HUBBLE, Ithamer 127
HUBBLE, Ithamer 129
HUBBLE, Ithamer 130
HUBBLE, Ithamer 132
HUBBLE, Ithamer 187
HUBERT, Joseph 218
HUBERT, Joseph 231
HUBERT, Joseph 232
HUDSPETH, ----- 113
HUDSPETH, A. W. 111
HUDSPETH, A. W. 208
HUDSPETH, Airs 110
HUDSPETH, Avis 112
HUDSPETH, William 110
HUDSPETH, Wm. 112
HUGE, Dominique 27
HUGE, Dominique 217
HUGE, Dominque 231
HUGE, Dominque 232
HULL, Uriah 101
HULL, Uriah 103
HULL, Uriah 105
HULL, Uriah 109
HULL, Uriah 176
HUNAULT, Gabriel 18
HUNAULT, Gabriel 219
HUNAULT, Gabriel 231
HUNAULT, Gabriel 232
HUNOT, ----- 50
HUNT, ----- 173
HYMAN, John 206
HYNAM, John 213
HYNAM, John 232

INGE, ----- 114
INGE, William 110
INGE, William 112
INGE, William 209
INGE, Wm. 113

JAMES, Benjamen 170
JAMES, Benjamen F. 149
JAMES, Benjamen F. 232
JAMES, Catherine S. 149
JAMES, William 15
JAMES, William 85
JAMES, William 192
JAMES, William 232
JAMES, William 232

JAMISON, Joseph 28
JAMISON, Joseph 219
JAMISON, Joseph 232
JAMISON, Joseph 232
JANES, William 215
JANES, William 232
JANIS, Antoine 13
JANIS, Antoine 184
JANIS, J. B. 12
JARRETT, Joseph 64
JARRETT, Joseph 232
JEFFREY, Baptiste 35
JEFFREY, Baptiste 220
JEFFREY, Baptiste 232
JERVIAS, ----- 33
JETT, Birkett D. 208
JETT, Bricket D. 209
JOHNSON, James 109
JOHNSON, James 109
JOHNSON, James 159
JOHNSON, John 103
JOHNSON, John 189
JOHNSON, William 162
JONES, Augustus 157
JONES, John 112
JONES, John 113
JONES, Malachi 188
JONES, Malachi 188
JONES, Malachi 199
JONES, Malachi 232
JONES, Peggy 153
JONES, Peggy 215
JONES, Peggy 232
JONES, Thomas 208
JONES, Thomas 214
JONES, Thomas 232
JOURNEY, James 7
JOURNEY, James 93
JOURNEY, James 232

KEATHLY, Daniel 158
KEATHLY, Daniel 180
KELLY, Isaac E. 113
KENNISON, Abasol 143
KENNISON, Absalom 232
KENNISON, Absolom 142
KENNISON, John 140
KENNISON, John 142
KENNYSON, Absolam 203
KERLEGAND, ----- 232
KERLEGAND, Rene Guiho de 85
KIERDEREAU, Gregoire 52
KILEGAND, ----- 232
KINAIRD, Andrew 91
KINAIRD, Andrew 232
KINCAID, David 69
KINCAID, David 163
KINCAID, David 232
KINNAIRD, Andrew 41
KINNAIRD, Andrew 232
KINNEY, Andy 50
KRYTZ, Daniel 94
KRYTZ, Daniel 95
KRYTZ, Daniel 232

LABADDIE, Silvestre 233
LABADIE, Silvestre 68
LABADIE, Silvestre 69
LABBADIE, Silvestre 6
LABBADIE, Silvestre 29
LABBADIE, Silvestre 87
LABBADIE, Silvestre 174
LABBADIE, Silvestre 232

LABEAUME, ----- 42
LABEAUME, ----- 114
LABEAUME, L. 47
LABEAUME, Louis 9
LABEAUME, Louis 43
LABEAUME, Louis 53
LABEAUME, Louis 67
LABEAUME, Louis 71
LABEAUMES, Louis 93
LABEAUMES, L. 45
LABRECHE, Baptiste 15
LABRECHE, Baptiste 84
LABRECHE, Jean Baptiste 14
LABRIERE, Julien 12
LABUXIERE, ----- 125
LABUXIERE, ----- 233
LACHANCE, Caillote 114
LACHANCE, Francois Cabot 11
LACHANCE, Francois Caillotte 117
LACHANCE, Francois Cailotte 114
LACHANCE, Michael 77
LACHANCE, Michael 78
LACHANCE, Michel 41
LACHANCE, Michel 90
LACHANCE, Michel 233
LACHANCE, Michel C. 114
LACHANCE, Nicholas 114
LACHANCE, Nicholas 172
LACHANCE, Nicholas Caillote 77
LACHANCE, Nicholas Cailote 117
LACHANCE, Nicholas Cailotte 78
LACHAPELLE, Antoine 104
LACHAPELLE, Antoine 105
LACOMBE, Francois 19
LACOMBE, Francois 85
LACOMBE, Francois 93
LACOMBE, Francois 207
LACOMBE, Francois 213
LACOMBE, Francois 232
LACOMBE, Francois 234
LACROIX, Isadore 202
LACROIX, Isidore 69
LACROIX, Isidore 233
LACROIX, Isidore 233
LACROIX, Louis 184
LACROIX, Louis 199
LACROIX, Louis 233
LADEROUTE, ----- 31
LAFEVRE, Auguste 216
LAFLEUR, Joseph 22
LAFLEUR, Joseph 232
LAFLUER, Joseph 220
LAFLUER, Joseph 234
LAFOIX, Vincent 181
LAFOIX, Vincent 198
LAGAUTERIE, Victor 158
LAGAUTERIE, Victor 161
LAGOTERIE, Victor 233
LAGUATERIE, Victor 51
LAGUATERIE, Victor 233
LAJOHIE, ----- 210
LAJOIE, Louis 26
LAJOIE, Louis 121
LAJOIE, Louis 218
LAJOIE, Louis 234
LAMALICE, ----- 233
LAMALICE, L. 219
LAMALICE, Louis 44
LAMALICE, Louis 216
LAMALICE, Louis 217
LAMALICE, Louis 218
LAMALICE, Louis 234
LAMARCHE, ----- 69
LAMARCHE, Antoine 179

LAMARCHE, Antoine 198
LAMARCHE, Jean Bste. 68
LAMARCHE, Jean Bste. 202
LAMARCHE, Jean Bste. 203
LAMARCHE, Joseph Philip 35
LAMARCHE, Joseph Philip 150
LAMARCHE, Joseph Philip 220
LAMARCHE, Joseph Philip 233
LAMARCHE, Joseph Philip 234
LAMARQUE, E. 2
LANDREVILLE, Andre 73
LANE, Bridget 188
LANGLOIS, Adrian 233
LANGLOIS, Adrien 77
LANGLOIS, Andrien 180
LANGLOIS, Andrien 204
LANGLOIS, Andrien 233
LANGLOIS, Augistin 232
LANGLOIS, Augustin 18
LANGLOIS, Augustin 219
LANHAM, Hartley 64
LAPLANTE, Mary Ann 25
LAPLANTE, Mary Ann 26
LAPLANTE, Nicholas 181
LASOURCE, Louis 23
LASSUS, ----- 80
LATIMIER, Samuel 235
LATREILLE, Gabriel 146
LATREILLE, Gabriel 156
LATREILLE, Gabriel 156
LATREILLE, Gabriel 180
LAURINS, Baptiste 153
LAURINS, Baptiste 170
LAURINS, Baptiste 233
LAWLER, Patrick 69
LAWLESS, L. E. 55
LEBRECHE, Jean Bste. 232
LECLERC, Marie Louisa 16
LECLERC, Marie Louise 16
LECOMTE, ----- 81
LEDUC, M. P. 3
LEDUC, M. P. 4
LEDUC, M. P. 16
LEDUC, M. P. 17
LEDUC, M. P. 18
LEDUC, M. P. 19
LEDUC, M. P. 20
LEDUC, M. P. 21
LEDUC, M. P. 22
LEDUC, M. P. 26
LEDUC, M. P. 27
LEDUC, M. P. 28
LEDUC, M. P. 29
LEDUC, M. P. 30
LEDUC, M. P. 31
LEDUC, M. P. 32
LEDUC, M. P. 33
LEDUC, M. P. 34
LEDUC, M. P. 35
LEDUC, M. P. 36
LEDUC, M. P. 37
LEDUC, M. P. 41
LEDUC, M. P. 42
LEDUC, M. P. 43
LEDUC, M. P. 44
LEDUC, M. P. 45
LEDUC, M. P. 45
LEDUC, M. P. 46
LEDUC, M. P. 47
LEDUC, M. P. 54
LEDUC, M. P. 55
LEDUC, M. P. 64
LEDUC, M. P. 65
LEDUC, M. P. 67
LEDUC, M. P. 68

LEDUC, M. P. 69
LEDUC, M. P. 71
LEDUC, M. P. 73
LEDUC, M. P. 74
LEDUC, M. P. 82
LEDUC, M. P. 97
LEDUC, M. P. 104
LEDUC, M. P. 115
LEDUC, M. P. 116
LEDUC, M. P. 148
LEDUC, M. P. 150
LEDUC, M. P. 153
LEDUC, M. P. 170
LEDUC, M. P. 171
LEDUC, M. P. 173
LEDUC, M. P. 179
LEDUC, M. P. 180
LEDUC, M. P. 181
LEDUC, M. P. 193
LEDUC, M. P. 207
LEDUC, M. P. 233
LEDUC, Mary L. 232
LEE, Patrick 67
LEFEVRE, Auguste 46
LEFEVRE, Auguste 234
LEFVRE, Auguste 233
LEGAND, Jean Rene Guiho de K. 20
LEMONDE, Louis 233
LEMOS, Gallore de 1
LEMOS, Mauel Galloso de 4
LESBOIS, Marie Nicholle 232
LESBOIS, Marie Nicolle 20
LESBOIS, Marie Nicolle 86
LEWIS, John 158
LEWIS, Joseph 135
LEYBA, ----- 37
LIMBAUGH Frederick 132
LIMBAUGH, Frederick 131
LIMBAUGH, Frederick 136
LIMBAUGH, Frederick 233
LINC, Joab 233
LINE, Joab 205
LINE, Joad 213
LINK, Abasolam 233
LINK, Abasolom 233
LINK, Absalom 72
LINK, Absalam 53
LINK, Absolam 233
LINK, Absolom 205
LINN, ----- 188
LINN, Dr. Lewis F. 86
LINN, L. F. 1
LINN, L. F. 11
LINN, L. F. 12
LINN, L. F. 25
LINN, L. F. 55
LINN, L. F. 58
LINN, L. F. 59
LINN, L. F. 62
LINN, L. F. 63
LINN, L. F. 64
LINN, L. F. 65
LINN, L. F. 66
LINN, L. F. 70
LINN, L. F. 71
LINN, L. F. 72
LINN, L. F. 74
LINN, L. F. 76
LINN, L. F. 77
LINN, L. F. 79
LINN, L. F. 83
LINN, L. F. 94
LINN, L. F. 95
LINN, L. F. 96

LINN, L. F. 98
LINN, L. F. 101
LINN, L. F. 102
LINN, L. F. 103
LINN, L. F. 104
LINN, L. F. 105
LINN, L. F. 106
LINN, L. F. 107
LINN, L. F. 108
LINN, L. F. 109
LINN, L. F. 111
LINN, L. F. 112
LINN, L. F. 113
LINN, L. F. 114
LINN, L. F. 115
LINN, L. F. 116
LINN, L. F. 117
LINN, L. F. 118
LINN, L. F. 119
LINN, L. F. 120
LINN, L. F. 121
LINN, L. F. 123
LINN, L. F. 124
LINN, L. F. 125
LINN, L. F. 126
LINN, L. F. 127
LINN, L. F. 128
LINN, L. F. 129
LINN, L. F. 132
LINN, L. F. 133
LINN, L. F. 134
LINN, L. F. 135
LINN, L. F. 136
LINN, L. F. 137
LINN, L. F. 138
LINN, L. F. 139
LINN, L. F. 140
LINN, L. F. 141
LINN, L. F. 142
LINN, L. F. 143
LINN, L. F. 144
LINN, L. F. 159
LINN, L. F. 175
LINN, L. F. 176
LINN, L. F. 181
LINN, L. F. 189
LINN, L. F. 190
LINN, L. F. 191
LINN, L. F. 194
LINN, L. F. 195
LINN, L. F. 196
LINN, L. F. 197
LINN, L. F. 202
LINN, L. F. 206
LINN, L. F. 207
LINN, L. F. 226
LINN, L. F. 235
LINN, L. F. 237
LINN, Lewis F. 7
LINN, Lewis F. 10
LINN, Lewis F. 13
LINN, Lewis F. 14
LINN, Lewis F. 15
LINN, Lewis F. 22
LINN, Lewis F. 23
LINN, Lewis F. 40
LINN, Lewis F. 56
LINN, Lewis F. 57
LINN, Lewis F. 60
LINN, Lewis F. 75
LINN, Lewis F. 78
LINN, Lewis F. 97
LINN, Lewis F. 99
LINN, Lewis F. 100

LINN, Lewis F. 158
LINSAY, John 190
LINSAY, John 190
LISA, Joachin 19
LISA, Joachin 86
LISA, Joachin 95
LISA, Joachin 232
LISA, Joachin 233
LISA, Manuel 16
LISA, Manuel 19
LISA, Manuel 85
LISA, Manuel 86
LISA, Manuel 232
LISA, Manuel 233
LITTLE, ----- 109
LITTLE, John 108
LITTLE, John 109
LOCHERD, Elizabeth 143
LOCHERD, Elizabeth 143
LOGAN, Charles 184
LOGAN, Jane 183
LOGAN, Jane 199
LOGAN, Jane 233
LOGAN, Jenny 183
LOISE, Alexis 67
LOISE, Alexis 165
LOISE, Alexis 171
LOISE, Alexis 233
LOISE, Alexis 233
LOISE, Alexis 233
LOISEL, Regis 68
LOISEL, Regis 171
LOISIL, Regis 233
LONG, Gabriel 233
LONG, John 42
LONG, John 91
LONG, John 232
LONG, John 233
LONG, William 42
LONG, William 92
LONG, William 233
LONG, William 233
LONG, Wm. 2
LORD, ----- 44
LORD, Gabriel 73
LORD, Gabriel 73
LORD, Gabriel 163
LORD, Gabriel 233
LORD, Pierre 21
LORD, Pierre 220
LORD, Pierre 232
LORD, Pierre 234
LOREMIER, Louis 7
LORIMEIR, ----- 134
LORIMEIR, Lewis 124
LORIMEIR, Louis 39
LORIMEIR, Louis 115
LORIMEIR, Louis 127
LORIMEIR, Louis 144
LORIMEIR, Louis 171
LORIMEIRE, Louis 141
LORIMER, L. 39
LORIMIER, ----- 139
LORIMIER, ----- 187
LORIMIER, ----- 196
LORIMIER, L. 40
LORIMIER, Louis 84
LORIMIER, Louis 90
LORIMIER, Louis 91
LORIMIER, Louis 94
LORIMIER, Louis 95
LORIMIER, Louis 104
LORIMIER, Louis 128

LORIMIER, Louis 129
LORIMIER, Louis 137
LORIMIER, Louis 142
LORIMIER, Louis 232
LORIMIER, Louis 233
LORIMIER, William 41
LORIMIER, William 91
LORIMIIER, Louis 190
LORR, Valentine 141
LORR, Valentine 168
LORR, Valentine 169
LORR, Valentine 233
LOUGHRY, William 21
LOUGHRY, William 86
LOUGHRY, William 232
LOUGHRY, William 233
LOUISE, Alexis 51
LUDAC, M. P. 1
LUDAC, M. P. 2
LUSIERE, Piere Delassus de 6
LUZIERE, ----- 25
LUZIERE, ----- 26
LUZIERE, Delassus de 116
LUZIERE, P. Delassus de 7
LUZIERE, Pierre D. 60
LUZIERE, Pierre Delassus de 24
LUZIERE, Pierre Delassus de 65
LUZIERE, Pierre Delassus de 5
LUZIERE, Pierre Delassus de 13
LUZIERE, Pierre Delassus de 17
LUZIERE, Pierre Delassus de 88
LUZIERE, Pre. de 134

MACDANIEL, James 234
MACKAY, ----- 32
MACKAY, ----- 42
MACKAY, ----- 73
MACKAY, James 3
MACKAY, James 4
MACKAY, James 6
MACKAY, James 7
MACKAY, James 17
MACKAY, James 28
MACKAY, James 31
MACKAY, James 35
MACKAY, James 38
MACKAY, James 41
MACKAY, James 43
MACKAY, James 47
MACKAY, James 53
MACKAY, James 53
MACKAY, James 55
MACKAY, James 57
MACKAY, James 82
MACKAY, James 92
MACKAY, James 152
MACKAY, James 153
MACKAY, James 179
MACKAY, James 205
MACKAY, James 234
MACKAY, James 234
MACKAYY, James 87
MACKEY, James 1
MACKEY, James 2
MACKY, ----- 3
MADDEN, Thomas 11
MADDEN, Thomas 12
MADDIN, ----- 14
MADDIN, James 12
MADDIN, Mr. 159
MADDIN, Mr. 160
MADDIN, Richard 12

MADDIN, Thomas 13
MADDIN, Thomas 20
MADDIN, Thomas 59
MADDIN, Thomas 60
MADDIN, Thomas 63
MADDIN, Thomas 69
MADDIN, Thomas 71
MADDIN, Thomas 76
MADDIN, Thomas 79
MADDIN, Thomas 80
MADDIN, Thomas 81
MADDIN, Thomas 85
MADDIN, Thomas 107
MADDIN, Thomas 108
MADDIN, Thomas 115
MADDIN, Thomas 116
MADDIN, Thomas 152
MADDIN, Thomas 164
MADDIN, Thomas 202
MADDIN, Thomas 234
MADDIN, Thomas 235
MADDIN, Thos. 70
MAHAN, Jacob 112
MAHAN, Jacob 209
MANLY, John 179
MANLY, John 180
MANNING, Joseph 101
MARC, Jean Louis 45
MARC, Jean Louis 235
MARCELIN, Jacques 24
MARE, Jean Louis 234
MARECHAL, ----- 156
MARECHAL, Antoine 21
MARECHAL, Antoine 93
MARECHAL, Antoine 234
MARECHAL, Francois 216
MARIE, Jos. 150
MARIE, Joseph 35
MARIE, Joseph 220
MARIE, Joseph 234
MARIE, Joseph 234
MARIE, Joseph 235
MARION, Baptiste 21
MARION, Baptiste 219
MARION, Baptiste 234
MARION, Baptiste 235
MARLI, Baptiste 45
MARLI, Michael 211
MARLY, Baptiste 217
MARTIN, David 152
MARTIN, David 153
MARTIN, F. H. 208
MARTIN, F. H. 212
MARTIN, J. M. 207
MARTIN, Lewis 152
MARTIN, Lewis 153
MARTIN, Lewis 170
MARTIN, Lewis 234
MARTIN, Lewis 235
MARTIN, Pierre 70
MARTIN, Pierre 70
MARTIN, Pierre 80
MARTINGY, Jean Baptiste 163
MARTINGY, Jean Baptiste 235
MARTINGY, Jean Bste. 67
MARTINGY, Jean Bste. 234
MARTY, Baptiste 234
MARTY, Baptiste 235
MASPLAS, Basile 13
MASSEY, ----- 139
MASSEY, Agnew 138
MASSEY, Agnew 188
MASSEY, Agnew 189

MASSEY, Agnew 201
MASSEY, Agnew 234
MASSEY, Agnew 235
MASSEY, Edward N. 139
MATHEWS, Edward 139
MATHEWS, Edward 173
MATHEWS, Edward 187
MATHEWS, Edward 235
MATHEWS, Edwards 234
MATHEWS, John 117
MATHEWS, John 117
MATTHEWS, John 119
MATTHEWS, John 120
MATTIS Jerome 200
MATTIS, Jerome 194
MATTIS, Jerome 235
MATTIS, Jerome 235
MAURICE, Alexis 208
MAURICE, Alexis 213
MAURICE, Alexis 235
MAURICE, Jean Baptiste 77
MAXWELL, ----- 59
MAXWELL, Curat 8
MAXWELL, Diego 39
MAXWELL, Diego 215
MAXWELL, Diego 234
MAXWELL, Diego 235
MAXWELL, James 10
MAYFIELD, ----- 150
MAYFIELD, J. S. 148
MAYFIELD, J. S. 149
MAYFIELD, J. S. 151
MAYFIELD, J. S. 153
MAYFIELD, J. S. 156
MAYFIELD, James A. 165
MAYFIELD, James S. 155
MAYFIELD, James S. 175
MAYFIELD, James S. 238
MCCABE, Philip 160
MCCABE, Philip T. 109
MCCAY, Robert 206
MCCAY, Robert 207
MCCAY, Robert 214
MCCAY, Robert 235
MCCLANAH, Josiah 47
MCCLANE, Charles 56
MCCONNELL, John 149
MCCORMACK, John 145
MCCORMACK, John 203
MCCORMACK, John 234
MCCOY, Alexander 106
MCCOY, James 107
MCCOY, Joseph 157
MCCOY, Joseph 177
MCCULLICK, ----- 151
MCCULLICK, Hugh 54
MCDANIEL, James 3
MCDANIEL, James 52
MCDANIEL, James 82
MCDANIEL, James 95
MCDANIEL, James 234
MCDORMET, Charles 182
MCDORMET, Charles 199
MCDORMET, Charles 235
MCGREDDY, Israel 65
MCHUGH, ----- 66
MCHUGH, ----- 178
MCHUGH, William 144
MCHUGH, William 157
MCHUGH, William 189
MCHUGH, William 197
MCHUGH, William 204
MCHUGH, William 234

MCHUGH, William 234
MCHUGH, William 235
MCKIM, James 206
MCKIM, James 235
MCKINNEY, David 69
MCKINNEY, David 163
MCKINNEY, David 180
MCKINNEY, David 235
MCLANE, Charles 57
MCLANE, Charles 193
MCLANE, Charles 200
MCLANE, Charles 235
MCLAUGHLIN, James S. 209
MCMARTREY, Joseph 111
MCMAURTRY, Joseph 110
MCMILLAN, John 43
MCMILLAN, John 92
MCMILLIAN, John 234
MCNAILL, John T. 62
MCNAIR, Alexander 68
MCNAIR, Alexander 69
MCNAIR, Alexander 234
MCNEAL, J. T. 110
MCNEAL, John 101
MCNEAL, John 113
MCNEAL, John 152
MCNEAL, John 157
MCNEAL, John 170
MCNEAL, John 181
MCNEAL, John 182
MCNEAL, John 234
MCNEAL, John 234
MCNEAL, John 235
MCNEAL, John T. 62
MCNEAL, John T. 75
MCNEAL, John T. 75
MCNEAL, John T. 101
MCNEAL, John T. 102
MCNEAL, John T. 103
MCNEAL, John T. 105
MCNEAL, John T. 105
MCNEAL, John T. 106
MCNEAL, John T. 109
MCNEAL, John T. 111
MCNEAL, John T. 112
MCNEAL, John T. 132
MCNEAL, John T. 133
MCNEAL, John T. 154
MCNEAL, John T. 159
MCNEAL, John T. 160
MCNEAL, John T. 184
MCNEAL, John T. 186
MCNEAL, John T. 192
MCNEAL, Mary 110
MCNEIL, John 100
MCNEIL, John T. 100
MCNEIL, John T. 104
MCNEILL, John T. 158
MCQUE, William 66
MCREADY, Isreal 175
MCROBERTS, James 145
MEEK, William 180
MEEK, William 199
MEEK, William 235
MENARD, Peter 39
MENARD, Pierre 5
MENARD, Pierre 39
MENARD, Pierre 40
MENARD, Pierre 83
MENARD, Pierre 91
MENARD, Pierre 234
MERECHAL, Francois 235
MESPLAIS, Bazil 14

MESPLAS, Basile 12
METTE, Jacque 148
MEVILLE, Charles 234
MICHAU, J. 48
MICHAU, Melchior Aman 95
MICHAU, Melchior Amand 48
MIDDLETON, Reuben 140
MIDDLETON, Reuben 204
MIDDLETON, Reuben 234
MIDDLETON, Reuben 235
MILBURG, William 4
MILBURN, William 38
MILBURN, Wm. 5
MILHOMME, Louis 183
MILHOMME, Louis 199
MILHOMME, Louis 235
MILHOMME, Louis 235
MILLER, Isaac 131
MILLER, Isaac 131
MILLER, Isaac 142
MILLER, Jacob 142
MILLER, Jacob 203
MILLER, Jacob 234
MILLER, Jacob 235
MILLER, John 131
MINCHE, Francis 70
MINCHE, Francis 80
MIRACLE, David 66
MIRACLE, David 158
MIRACLE, David 163
MIRACLE, David 234
MIRACLE, David 234
MIRACLE, David 235
MIRO, Estevan 29
MIRO, Estevan 87
MITCHELL, Richard 69
MIVILLE, Charles 44
MIVILLE, Charles 219
MIVILLE, Charles 235
MOHAN Jacob 113
MONITEAU, ----- 61
MOORE, Bede 101
MOORE, Bede 164
MOORE, Bede 235
MOORE, Daniel B. 85
MOORE, James 206
MOORE, James 214
MOORE, James 235
MOORE, Zachariah 73
MORALE, ----- 39
MORALES, ----- 59
MORALES, Juan Ventura 206
MOREAU, Francois 21
MOREAU, Francois 93
MOREAU, Francois 234
MORIN, Antoine 93
MORIN, Joseph 47
MORIN, Joseph 48
MORIN, Joseph 48
MORIN, Joseph 92
MORIN, Joseph 93
MORIN, Joseph 234
MORO, Manuel Gonzales 41
MORO, Manuel Gonzales 234
MORO, Manuel Gouralez 91
MORRIS, ----- 159
MORRIS, Curtis 109
MORRIS, Curtis 110
MORRIS, Curtis 111
MORRIS, Curtis 155
MORRIS, Curtis 158
MORRIS, Curtis 166
MORRIS, Curtis 186

MORRIS, Curtis 208
MORRIS, Curtis 209
MORRIS, Curtis 212
MORRIS, Curtis 215
MORRIS, Curtis 234
MORRIS, Curtis 235
MORRIS, Curtis 235
MORRIS, H. 16
MORRIS, Henry 16
MORRISON, ----- 160
MORRISON, James 144
MORRISON, James 146
MORRISON, James 152
MORRISON, James 189
MORRISON, Saml. 113
MORRISON, William 152
MORRISON, William 204
MORROW, ----- 113
MORROW, ----- 114
MORROW, Thomas 110
MORROW, Thomas 110
MORROW, Thomas 112
MORRRISAON, William 234
MOSS, William 53
MOSTELLER, Jacob 61
MOSTELLER, Jacob 62
MOSTELLER, Jacob 106
MOSTELLER, Jacob 107
MOTARD, Joseph 211
MOTARD, Joseph 215
MOTARD, Joseph 235
MOTIER, Francois 175
MOTIER, Francois 216
MOTIER, Francois 235
MOTIER, Francois 235
MOTTARD, ----- 67
MOTTARD, Joseph 66
MOTTARD, Joseph 234
MULLANPHRY, Jno. 79
MULLANPHY, ----- 238
MULLANPHY, Jn. 238
MULLANPHY, Jno. 228
MULLANPHY, Jno. 240
MULLANPHY, John 26
MULLANPHY, John 26
MULLANPHY, John 27
MULLANPHY, John 28
MULLANPHY, John 29
MULLANPHY, John 58
MULLANPHY, John 79
MULLANPHY, John 226
MULLIN, Mathew 235
MULLINS, Mathew 191
MULLINS, Mathews 200
MULLINS, Mathews 235
MULPHANY, J. 34
MUN, Julius de 98
MURPHY, John 64
MURPHY, John 204
MURPHY, John 234
MURPHY, John 235
MUSICK, Ephraim 205
MUSICK, Ephraim 212
MUSICK, Ephraim 235
MUSICK, Ephraim 235
MUSICK, Lewis 72
Marc, Jean Louis 217

NEAL, Jacob 75
NEAL, Jacob 202
NEAL, Jacob 235
NEAL, Samuel 75
NEAL, Samuel 202
NEAL, Samuel 235

NEALE, Samuel 74
NEIGHBOUR, John 34
NEIGHBOUR, John 35
NEIGHBOUR, John 89
NEWSOM, Jones 141
NICOLLE, Gabriel 40
NICOLLE, Gabrielle 90
NICOLLE, Gabrielle 235
NISWANGER, Joseph 126
NISWANGER, Joseph 132
NISWANGER, Joseph 136
NISWANGER, Joseph 141
NISWANGER, Joseph 142
NISWANGER, Joseph 168
NISWANGER, Joseph 186
NISWANGER, Joseph 195
NISWANGER, Joseph 235
NISWINGER, Joseph 127
NISWONGER, Joseph 95
NORMANDAU, Francois 41
NORMANDEAU, Francois 91
NORMANDU, Francois 235

ODAM, Jacob 50
ODAM, Jacob 155
ODAM, Jacob 236
OGE, Francois 15
OHARA, Henry 210
OHARA, Henry 211
OHARA, Henry 214
OHARA, Henry 236
OREILLY, ----- 39
OREILLY, ----- 39
ORTEZ, ----- 33
ORTEZ, Jean 147
OUBOUCHON, Louis 185
OUVRAY, Louis 210
OUVRAY, Louis 218
OUVRAY, Louis 236
OWSLEY, ----- 194
OWSLEY, ----- 195
OWSLEY, Jonathan 236
OWSLEY, Jonathon 194

PACQUET, Francois 27
PACQUET, Francois 216
PACQUET, Francois 236
PAIN, Joseph 112
PAIN, Joseph 113
PAJCOL, Jean Bste. 236
PAJCOL, Jean Bste. 236
PALRDI, Pierre 179
PALRDIE, Pierre 180
PALRDIE, Pierre 198
PANOTE, Amable 160
PAPIN, ----- 236
PAPIN, Jos. M. 36
PAPIN, Joseph 236
PAPIN, Joseph Marie 89
PAPINS, Joseph M. 35
PAQUET, J. B. 47
PARENT, Etienne 116
PARENT, Etienne 165
PARENT, Etienne 236
PARK, Jonah 64
PARLADI, Pierre 158
PARTENAY, Amable 80
PARTENOY, Amable 80
PARTENOY, Amable 81
PATNOTE, Amable 204
PATRIOTE, Amable 153
PATRIOTE, Amable 154

PATRIOTTE, Amable 236
PATTENOTE, Amable 236
PATTERSON, ----- 77
PATTERSON, John 134
PATTERSON, John 167
PATTERSON, John 236
PAUL, Gabriel 24
PAUL, Gabriel 240
PAUL, John 100
PAUL, John 102
PAUL, John 103
PAUL, John 155
PAUL, John 164
PAUL, John 236
PAUL, Martha 155
PAUL, Mr. Rene 31
PAVICH, Mr. 127
PAYETT, ----- 145
PAYETT, Jacob 145
PAYETT, John 144
PAYETT, John 145
PAYETT, John 173
PAYETT, John 236
PAYETT, John 236
PELETIER, Andre 220
PELLETIER, Andre 21
PELLETIER, Andre 236
PELLETIER, Andre 237
PENROSE, Clement B. 153
PEPIN, Etiene 236
PEPIN, Etienne 28
PEPIN, Etienne 87
PEPIN, Etienne 236
PEPIN, J. M. 201
PEREZ, Francisco 197
PEREZ, Manuel 20
PEREZ, Manuel 29
PEREZ, Manuel 30
PEREZ, Manuel 61
PEREZ, Manuel 87
PEROUX, ----- 187
PERREY, Jean Francois 21
PERREY, Jean Francois 86
PERREY, Jean Francois 236
PERRY, ----- 102
PERRY, Jean Francois 236
PETTIT, Benjamen 117
PETTIT, Benjamen 118
PETTIT, Benjamen 122
PETTIT, Benjamen 203
PETTIT, Benjamen 236
PETTIT, John L. 118
PETTIT, John L. 121
PETTIT, John L. 122
PETTIT, John L. 215
PETTIT, John L. 236
PETTIT, Jr. Benjamen 118
PEYROUX, ----- 63
PEYROUX, Don Henry 189
PEYROUX, H. 20
PEYROUX, Henry 60
PEYROUX, Henry 61
PEYROUX, Henry 62
PEYROUX, Henry 162
PEYROUX, Henry 236
PHELPS, DDaniel 113
PHELPS, Daniel 65
PHELPS, Daniel 111
PHELPS, Daniel 209
PHELPS, Danl. 113
PHELPS, Timothy 65
PHELPS, Timothy 103
PHELPS, Timothy 111
PHELPS, Timothy 113
PHELPS, Timothy 113

PHIEL, Henry Von 35
PINKLEY, Henry 176
PLACET, ----- 8
PLAGET, Baptiste 160
PLANTE, Nicolas 181
PLANTE, Nicolas 198
POLITE, John 79
POLITE, Robert 80
PORTEL, Francois 70
PORTNEUF, Paul 31
POTEL, John 70
POTEL, John 79
POTEL, John 80
POWERS, Thomas 205
POWERS, Thomas 212
POWERS, Thomas 236
PRATTE, Antoine 55
PRATTE, Antoine 161
PRATTE, Antoine 236
PRATTE, Antoine 236
PRATTE, Bernard 30
PRATTE, Bernard 32
PRATTE, Bernard 36
PRATTE, Bernard 82
PRATTE, Bernard 87
PRATTE, Bernard 89
PRATTE, Bernard 147
PRATTE, Bernard 236
PRATTE, Bernard 236
PRATTE, Bernard 240
PRATTE, Henry 55
PRATTE, Henry 56
PRATTE, Henry 161
PRATTE, Henry 236
PRATTE, J. 25
PRATTE, J. B. 236
PRATTE, Jean Bste. 86
PRATTE, Jh. 58
PRATTE, Jh. 195
PRATTE, John B. 22
PRATTE, John B. 23
PRATTE, John Bste. 62
PRATTE, John Bste. 236
PRATTE, Jos. M. 236
PRATTE, Joseph 8
PRATTE, Joseph 25
PRATTE, Joseph 56
PRATTE, Joseph 57
PRATTE, Joseph 58
PRATTE, Joseph 61
PRATTE, Joseph 70
PRATTE, Joseph 78
PRATTE, Joseph 79
PRATTE, Joseph 80
PRATTE, Joseph 116
PRATTE, Joseph 161
PRATTE, Joseph 236
PRATTE, Pierre Auguste 56
PRATTE, Pierre Auguste 161
PRATTE, Pierre Auguste. 236
PRESSE, Joseph 46
PRESSE, Joseph 217
PRESSE, Joseph 236
PRESSE, Joseph 236
PRICE, Michael 149
PRICE, Ridson H. 55
PRICE, Ridson H. 72
PRIEUR, Noel John 178
PRITCHETT, John 207
PROVENCHER, Jean Baptiste 197
PROVENCHER, Jean Bste. 47
PROVENCHER, Jean Bste. 236
PROVENCHER, John Bste. 216

PROVENCHER, John Bste. 236
PROVENCHERE, Peter 66
PRUIT, ----- 54
PUJOL, Jean Baptiste 87
PUJOT, J. Baptiste 30
PURSLEY, George 205
PURSLEY, George 212
PURSLEY, George 236
PURSLEY, George 236

QUEBEC, Pierre 157
QUENELLE, Etienne 179
QUENELLE, Etienne 180
QUICK, Aaron 6
QUICK, Aaron 84
QUICK, Aaron 237
QUICK, Benjamen 150
QUICK, Benjamen 218
QUICK, Benjamen 237
QUICK, Daniel 73
QUICK, Daniel 150
QUICK, Daniel 219
QUICK, Daniel 237

RABER, Michael 175
RABER, Michael 176
RABER, Michael 198
RABER, Michael 205
RABER, Michael 213
RABER, Michael 238
RALFE, James H. 185
RAMEY, Mathew 85
RAMEY, Mathew 85
RAMEY, Mathew 237
RAMEY, Nathan 85
RAMEY, William 53
RAMSAY, Andrew 238
RAMSAY, James 131
RAMSAY, James 167
RAMSAY, James 238
RAMSAY, John 66
RAMSAY, John 202
RAMSAY, John 237
RAMSAY, William 66
RAMSAY, William 177
RAMSAY, William 198
RAMSAY, William 237
RAMSAY, Wm. 157
RAMSAY, Wm. 157
RAMSAY, Wm. 178
RAMSEY, Andrew 129
RAMSEY, Andrew 130
RAMSEY, Andrew 167
RAMSEY, James 128
RAMSEY, James 129
RAMSEY, James 130
RANDALL, Abosolam 206
RANDALL, Abraham 136
RANDALL, Abraham 213
RANDALL, Abraham 238
RANDALL, Enos 135
RANDALL, Enos 136
RANDALL, Enos 168
RANDALL, Enos 237
RANDALL, Enos 238
RANDALL, Samuel 136
RANDALL, Samuel 168
RANDALL, Samuel 237
RANDALL, Samuel 238
RANDLE, Abraham 137
RANDLE, John 137
RANGE, Lambert 14

RANGE, Therese 14
RANKIN, James 1
RANKIN, James 9
RANKIN, James 9
RANKIN, James 20
RANNEY, Andrew 128
RATTE, Julien 23
RATTE, Julien 86
RATTE, Julien 87
RATTE, Julien 237
RAY, Charles 237
RAYNOR, Jesse 208
RAYNOR, Jesse 214
RAYNOR, Jesse 238
RAYNOR, Jesse 238
REAVES, John 94
REAVES, John 96
REAVES, John 118
REAVES, John 119
REAVES, John 120
REAVES, John 122
REDDICK, Thos. F. 49
REED, ----- 65
REED, ----- 133
REED, Joseph 109
REED, Joseph 159
REED, Joseph 171
REED, Joseph 238
REED, Laurent 31
REED, Laurent 73
REED, Louis 40
REED, Louis 90
REED, Louis 237
REED, Mr. 159
REED, Robert 113
REED, Robert 186
REED, Thomas 65
REED, Thomas 132
REED, Thomas 171
REED, Thomas 237
REED, Thomas 238
REED, William 100
REED, William 159
REED, William 221
REESE, David 127
REESE, David 203
REESE, David 237
REESE, David 238
REILLE, Charles 179
REITH, James 106
RELFE, J. H. 152
RELFE, J. H. 159
RELFE, J. H. 182
RELFE, J. H. 183
RELFE, James H. 189
RELFE, James H. 147
RELFE, James H. 148
RELFE, James H. 153
RELFE, James H. 154
RELFE, James H. 155
RELFE, James H. 160
RELFE, James H. 175
RELFE, James H. 186
RELFE, James H. 188
RELFE, James H. 188
RELFE, James H. 211
RELFE, James H. 212
RELFE, James H. 214
RELFE, James H. 222
REVEILLE, Nocholas 166
REVEILLEE, Nicholas 128
REVEILLER, Nicolas 237
REYBURN, J. N. 103
RICE, John 69

RICHARD, ----- 105
RICHARD, B. 237
RICHARD, Barth. 104
RICHARD, Bathelemi 104
RICHARD, Bathelmi 202
RICHARDSON, Daniel 193
RICHARDSON, Daniel 200
RICHARDSON, Daniel 238
RICHARDSON, James 48
RICHARDSON, James 93
RICHARDSON, James 237
RICHARDSON, Jesse 3
RIDDICK, Thos. F. 154
RIEUR, Jean 157
RING, Thomas 116
RING, Thomas 120
RING, Thomas 121
RING, Thomas 172
RING, Thomas 237
RING, Thomas 238
RIVET, Joseph 27
RIVET, Joseph 216
RIVET, Joseph 237
RIVET, Joseph 238
RIVIERE, Baptiste 19
RIVIERE, Baptiste 31
RIVIERE, Baptiste 40
RIVIERE, Baptiste 85
RIVIERE, Baptiste 237
RIVIERE, J. Baptiste 50
ROBERT, Charles 69
ROBERT, Charles 70
ROBERT, Charles 80
ROBERT, Hippolite 201
ROBERT, Paul 74
ROBERT, Philip 208
ROBERT, Philip 212
ROBERT, Philip 214
ROBERT, Philip 238
ROBERT, Pierre 23
ROBERTS, Philip 205
ROBERTS, Philip 238
ROBIN, Charles 162
ROBIN, Charles 237
ROBINS, Charles 61
RODERICK, Simon 69
RODNEY, John 124
RODNEY, John 128
RODNEY, John 129
RODNEY, John 130
RODNEY, John 183
RODNEY, John 183
ROGAN, Bernard 110
ROGERS, Charles 74
ROGERS, James 54
ROGERS, James 146
ROGERS, James 146
ROGERS, James 151
ROGERS, James 151
ROGERS, James 151
ROGERS, James 170
ROGERS, James 204
ROGERS, James 237
ROGERS, James 237
ROGERS, James 238
ROGR, Charles 237
ROLLINS, Seneca 42
ROLLINS, Seneca 91
ROLLINS, Seneca 237
ROSS, Thomas 8
ROUKE, John 178
ROURKE, John 198
ROURKE, John 238
ROUSSEL, Pierre 217

256

ROUSSEL, Pierre 237
ROUSSELL, Pierre 29
ROUSSELL, Pierre 238
ROY, Charles 42
ROY, Charles 67
ROY, Charles 91
ROY, Charles 162
ROY, Francis 58
ROY, Joachin 58
ROY, Joachin 92
ROY, Joachin 237
ROY, Joachin 237
ROY, Joseph 163
ROY, Joseph 237
ROY, Joseph 238
ROY, Pierre 152
ROY, Pierre 173
ROY, Pierre 237
ROY, Pierre 238
RUGGLES, Martin 101
RUGGLES, Martin 109
RUGGLES, Martin 158
RUSSELL, William 205
RUSSELL, William 213
RUSSELL, William 213
RUSSELL, William 215
RUTGERS, ----- 173
RUTGERS, Arend 3
RUTGERS, Arend 178
RUTGERS, Arund 228

SALUMANDIERE, Jean 201
SALUMANDIERE, Joseph 201
SANGUINET, Charles 55
SANGUINET, Charles 210
SARPI, Pelagie 36
SARPY, Delore 228
SAUCIER, F. 36
SAUCIER, F. 41
SAUCIER, F. 43
SAUCIER, Francois 5
SAUCIER, Francois 36
SAUCIER, Francois 83
SAUCIER, Francois 238
SAUCIER, Mathew 32
SAUCIER, Mathew 87
SAUCIER, Mathew 238
SAUCIER, Mathew 238
SAUCIER, Raphael 238
SAUGRAIN, Antoine 89
SAUGRAIN, Antoine 238
SAUGRIN, Antoine 35
SAUGRIN, Antoine 238
SAUNDERS, John 37
SAUNDERS, John 238
SCHELL, G. 239
SCHELL, Gasper 195
SCHELL, Gasper 200
SCHRAUM, Nicholas 188
SCOTT, Constance 102
SCOTT, James 102
SCOTT, James 103
SCOTT, John 62
SCOTT, John 78
SCOTT, John 149
SCOTT, John 149
SCOTT, John 173
SCOTT, John 173
SCOTT, John 239
SERRANO, Manuel 206
SERRANO, Manuel 207
SETTLE, John 69
SEXTON, Charle 189

SEXTON, Charles 200
SEXTON, Charles 239
SEXTON, Charles 239
SHANNON, William 103
SHANNON, Wm. 104
SHURLDS, Henry 65
SHURLDS, Henry 100
SHURLDS, Henry 158
SHURLDS, Henry 159
SILIVAIN, Joseph 104
SILVAIN, Joseph 202
SILVAIN, Joseph 239
SILVAIN, Joseph 239
SIMBAUGH, Frederick 126
SIMMS, Alice 107
SIMONDS, Nathaniel 144
SLOANE, W. 65
SLOANE, William 65
SLOANE, William 133
SMITH, Abraham 52
SMITH, Abraham 156
SMITH, Abraham 161
SMITH, Abraham 238
SMITH, Abraham 239
SMITH, Elizabeth 187
SMITH, Elizabeth 188
SMITH, Jno. T. 83
SMITH, Jno. T. 228
SMITH, Jno. T. 238
SMITH, John 2
SMITH, John 2
SMITH, John 53
SMITH, John 78
SMITH, John 81
SMITH, John 82
SMITH, John T. 230
SMITH, Joseph 187
SMITH, Robert 15
SMITH, Thomas A. 2
SMOOT, Walter 205
SMOOT, Walter 213
SMOOT, Walter 239
SOCIER, Baptiste 206
SOCIER, Baptiste 214
SOCIER, Baptiste 239
SOULARD, ----- 20
SOULARD, ----- 36
SOULARD, ----- 37
SOULARD, ----- 53
SOULARD, ----- 54
SOULARD, ----- 73
SOULARD, ----- 100
SOULARD, ----- 107
SOULARD, ----- 122
SOULARD, ----- 134
SOULARD, ----- 146
SOULARD, A. 7
SOULARD, A. 25
SOULARD, A. 34
SOULARD, A. 38
SOULARD, A. 45
SOULARD, A. 61
SOULARD, A. 150
SOULARD, A. 193
SOULARD, A. 205
SOULARD, Ant. 41
SOULARD, Ant. 42
SOULARD, Ant. 43
SOULARD, Ant. 46
SOULARD, Ant. 47
SOULARD, Ant. 69
SOULARD, Antoine 1
SOULARD, Antoine 3
SOULARD, Antoine 4
SOULARD, Antoine 8

SOULARD, Antoine 9
SOULARD, Antoine 20
SOULARD, Antoine 21
SOULARD, Antoine 22
SOULARD, Antoine 26
SOULARD, Antoine 27
SOULARD, Antoine 31
SOULARD, Antoine 32
SOULARD, Antoine 35
SOULARD, Antoine 51
SOULARD, Antoine 65
SOULARD, Antoine 88
SOULARD, Antoine 92
SOULARD, Antoine 115
SOULARD, Antoine 144
SOULARD, Antoine 152
SOULARD, Antoine 154
SOULARD, Antoine 159
SOULARD, Antoine 181
SOULARD, Antoine 238
SOULARD, Antonio 2
SOULARD, Antonio 17
SOULARD, Antonio 18
SOULARD, Antonio 28
SOULARD, Antonio 29
SOULARD, Antonio 44
SOVEREAU, Antoine 8
SPENCER, Benjamin 20
SPENCER, Robert 157
ST VRAIN, Charles 49
ST. ANGE, ----- 31
ST. CIR, Hyacinthe 68
ST. CIR, Hyacinthe 238
ST. CLAIRE, ----- 238
ST. CLAIRE, John 94
ST. FERDINAND, ----- 238
ST. FERDINAND, ----- 239
ST. GEMME, Bartholomew 77
ST. GEMME, Bartholomew 185
ST. GEMME, Batholomew 60
ST. GEMME, Batholomew 61
ST. GEMME, Bauvais 226
ST. GEMME, Raphael 84
ST. JOHN, ----- 210
ST. MARIA, Samuel 69
ST. PIERRE, Etienne 33
ST. PIERRE, Etienne 68
ST. PIERRE, Etienne 93
ST. PIERRE, Etienne 94
ST. PIERRE, Etienne 238
ST. PIERRE, Etienne 238
ST. VAIN, Jacques de 29
ST. VRAIIN, ----- 83
ST. VRAIN, ----- 49
ST. VRAIN, ----- 78
ST. VRAIN, ----- 86
ST. VRAIN, ----- 238
ST. VRAIN, Ceran 79
ST. VRAIN, Charles 79
ST. VRAIN, Ciran 49
ST. VRAIN, Domitille 79
ST. VRAIN, Emma 79
ST. VRAIN, Felix 49
ST. VRAIN, Felix 79
ST. VRAIN, Jacques 2
ST. VRAIN, Jacques 4
ST. VRAIN, Jacques 82
ST. VRAIN, Jacques 88
ST. VRAIN, Jacques 93
ST. VRAIN, Jacques 238
ST. VRAIN, Jacques de 79
ST. VRAIN, Odelle 79
ST. VRAIN, Odille 49
ST. VRAIN, Savingy 79

STATLER, Adam 125
STATLER, Adam 126
STEVENS, ----- 194
STEWART, John 62
STEWART, John 70
STEWART, John 72
STEWART, John 81
STEWART, John 97
STEWART, John 100
STEWART, John 102
STEWART, John 103
STEWART, John 106
STEWART, John 109
STEWART, John 113
STEWART, John 114
STEWART, John 146
STEWART, John 146
STEWART, John 153
STEWART, John 157
STEWART, John 159
STEWART, John 175
STEWART, John 175
STEWART, John 176
STEWART, John 181
STEWART, John 186
STEWART, John 191
STEWART, John 192
STEWART, John 193
STEWART, John 198
STEWART, John 198
STEWART, John 215
STEWART, John 239
STODARD, Amos 6
STODDARD, Amos 179
STODDARDS, Mr. 159
STOGSDILL, Joshua 157
STOGSDILL, Joshua 178
STOGSDILL, Joshua 179
STOGSDILL, Joshua 180
STOTLER, Adam 140
STOTLER, Adam 141
STOTLER, Conrad 140
STOTLER, Conrad 141
STOTLER, Conrad 168
STOTTER, Conrad 239
STRICKLADN, David 239
STRICKLAND, David 105
STRICKLAND, David 106
STRICKLAND, David 173
STRINGER, Daniel 138
STRINGER, Daniel 139
STRINGER, Daniel 139
STRINGER, Daniel 187
STRINGER, Daniel 189
STROTHER, Benjamen 111
STROTHERS, ----- 159
STROTHERS, ----- 160
STRUTHERS, Benjamen 112
STUART, ----- 107
STUART, John 108
STUART, Neeley 106
STUART, Nuley 106
SULLIVAN, Dennis 196
SULLIVAN, Dennis 201
SULLIVAN, Dennis 239
SUMMERS, Alexander 96
SUMMERS, Alexander 124
SUMMERS, Alexander 127
SUMMERS, Alexander 136
SUMMERS, Alexander 137
SUMMERS, Alexander 138
SUMMERS, Alexander 166
SUMMERS, Alexander 182
SUMMERS, Alexander 239
SUMMERS, James 186

SUMMERS, James 187
SUMMERS, James 215
SUMMERS, James 239
SWAN, John 110
SWANEY, Jacob 147
SWANEY, Jacob 239
SWIFT, James 211
SWIFT, James 215
SWIFT, James 239

TABOT, Antoine 68
TALBERT, William 135
TAUMUR, J. Bste. 201
TAUMURE, Baptiste 204
TAUMURE, Baptiste 224
TAYLOR, John 195
TAYLOR, John 196
TAYLOR, John 201
TAYLOR, John 239
TAYLOR, John 239
TAYON, Charles 33
TAYON, Charles 73
TAYON, Charles 88
TAYON, Charles 156
TAYON, Charles 158
TAYON, Charles 164
TAYON, Charles 239
TAYON, Charles 239
TAYON, Charles 239
TAYON, Charles 239
TAYON, Francis 33
TAYON, Francis 88
TAYON, Francois 239
TAYON, Louis 82
TAYON, Louis 164
TAYON, Louis 239
TEAGUE, Peter 158
TEAGUE, Peter 178
TENNEL, Benjamen 183
TENNEL, Benjamen 183
TENNEL, Benjamen 199
THEEL, Levy 36
THEEL, Levy 89
THEEL, Levy 239
THERMEL, Benjamen 239
THIBAULT, Charles 219
THIBAULT, Charles 240
THIBAULT, Francis 198
THIBAULT, Jean Baptiste 18
THIBAULT, Jean Bste. 239
THIBAUT, Francis 182
THIBAUT, Francis 192
THIBAUT, Francis 239
THOIN, Solomon 239
THOLOZAN, J. E. 240
THOLOZAN, Jean Elie 72
THOLOZAN, Jean Elie 184
THOLOZAN, Jean Elie 207
THOLOZAN, John Eli 215
THOLOZAN, John Elie 213
THOMAS, Martin 126
THOMAS, Martin 127
THOMAS, Martin 136
THOMAS, Martin 186
THOMAS, Martin 204
THOMAS, Martin 239
THOMAS, Martin 240
THOMPSON, ----- 176
THOMPSON, Jos. 169
THOMPSON, Joseph 124
THOMPSON, Joseph 166
THOMPSON, Joseph 167
THOMPSON, Joseph 168
THOMPSON, Joseph 172

THOMPSON, Joseph 239
THOMPSON, William 131
THOMPSON, William 203
THOMPSON, William 240
THOPSON, Joseph 123
THORN, Solomn 169
THORN, Solomon 143
TISON, A. 35
TISON, Albert 9
TISON, Albert 9
TISON, Albert 16
TISON, Albert 17
TISON, Albert 18
TISON, Albert 19
TISON, Albert 34
TISON, Albert 36
TISON, Albert 37
TISON, Albert 38
TISON, Albert 41
TISON, Albert 44
TISON, Albert 49
TISON, Albert 52
TISON, Albert 79
TISON, Albert 228
TISON, Albert 230
TISON, Jean Bste. 43
TISON, Jean Bste. 92
TISON, Jean Bste. 239
TODD, T. 218
TODD, T. 239
TODD, T. 240
TORNANT, Pierre 42
TORNANT, Pierre 203
TORNAT, Pierre 57
TORNAT, Pierre 210
TORNAT, Pierre 210
TORNAT, Pierre 221
TORNAT, Pierre 239
TORNAT, Pierre 240
TORNANT, Pierre dit Lajoi
TORNOT, Pierre 239
TOURVILLE, ----- 21
TOURVILLE, Toussaint 239
TOURVILLE, Toussaint 240
TRIMBLE, J. F. 71
TRIMBLE, John 71
TRIMBLE, John 80
TRIPP, Henry 107
TRIPP, Mary 107
TRUDEAU, ----- 9
TRUDEAU, ----- 222
TRUDEAU, Z. 6
TRUDEAU, Z. 7
TRUDEAU, Z. 24
TRUDEAU, Z. 35
TRUDEAU, Z. 43
TRUDEAU, Z. 47
TRUDEAU, Z. 53
TRUDEAU, Z. 61
TRUDEAU, Z. 170
TRUDEAU, Zenon 2
TRUDEAU, Zenon 3
TRUDEAU, Zenon 4
TRUDEAU, Zenon 5
TRUDEAU, Zenon 10
TRUDEAU, Zenon 11
TRUDEAU, Zenon 12
TRUDEAU, Zenon 13
TRUDEAU, Zenon 15
TRUDEAU, Zenon 17
TRUDEAU, Zenon 19
TRUDEAU, Zenon 21
TRUDEAU, Zenon 23
TRUDEAU, Zenon 28

TRUDEAU, Zenon 30
TRUDEAU, Zenon 33
TRUDEAU, Zenon 34
TRUDEAU, Zenon 36
TRUDEAU, Zenon 37
TRUDEAU, Zenon 38
TRUDEAU, Zenon 41
TRUDEAU, Zenon 42
TRUDEAU, Zenon 48
TRUDEAU, Zenon 56
TRUDEAU, Zenon 57
TRUDEAU, Zenon 58
TRUDEAU, Zenon 59
TRUDEAU, Zenon 68
TRUDEAU, Zenon 75
TRUDEAU, Zenon 76
TRUDEAU, Zenon 88
TRUDEAU, Zenon 97
TRUDEAU, Zenon 116
TRUDEAU, Zenon 147
TRUDEAU, Zenon 153
TRUDEAU, Zenon 181
TRUDEAU, Zenon 185
TRUDEAU, Zenon 192
TRUDEAU, Zenon 196
TRUDEAU, Zenon 197
TRUDEAU, Zenon 207
TRUDEAU, Zenon 210
TRUDEAU, Zeon 1
TRUDEUA, Zenon 32
TSUART, Nuley 107
TUCKER, Henry 107
TUCKER, Henry 107
TUCKER, Henry 123
TUCKER, Henry 123
TUCKER, Henry 165
TUCKER, Henry 239
TUCKER, Nicholas 101

UPDIKE, Wilkins 4
UPDIKE, Witkins 22
UPDYKE, Wilkins 33

VACHARD, Antoine 210
VACHARD, Antoine 211
VACHARD, Antoine 216
VACHARD, Antoine 240
VALET, ----- 156
VALET, John 52
VALET, John 52
VALET, John 155
VALET, John 155
VALET, John 157
VALET, John 240
VALLE, ----- 71
VALLE, ----- 81
VALLE, Auguste 79
VALLE, Basile 240
VALLE, Bazile 101
VALLE, Bazile 102
VALLE, Bste. 70
VALLE, C.H. F. Auguste 70
VALLE, Charles 77
VALLE, Charles 77
VALLE, Charles 164
VALLE, Charles 210
VALLE, Charles 211
VALLE, Charles 240
VALLE, Charles C. 56
VALLE, Charles E. 8
VALLE, Col. Bste. 23

VALLE, Colonel Baptiste 10
VALLE, Fran. 115
VALLE, Francis 56
VALLE, Francis 57
VALLE, Francis 58
VALLE, Francis 59
VALLE, Francis 63
VALLE, Francis 80
VALLE, Francois 5
VALLE, Francois 10
VALLE, Francois 11
VALLE, Francois 14
VALLE, Francois 16
VALLE, Francois 17
VALLE, Francois 51
VALLE, Francois 59
VALLE, Francois 74
VALLE, Francois 75
VALLE, Francois 84
VALLE, Francois 180
VALLE, Francois 202
VALLE, Francois 240
VALLE, Francois B. 8
VALLE, J. B. 60
VALLE, J. Bste. 12
VALLE, J. Bste. 56
VALLE, J. Bste. 75
VALLE, J. Bste. 116
VALLE, J. Bste. 123
VALLE, J. Bste. 135
VALLE, Jean Baptiste 162
VALLE, Jean Bste. 240
VALLE, John B. 108
VALLE, John Baptiste 39
VALLE, John Bste. 15
VALLE, John Bste. 25
VALLE, John Bste. 55
VALLE, John Bste. 57
VALLE, John Bste. 58
VALLE, John Bste. 59
VALLE, John Bste. 61
VALLE, John Bste. 76
VALLE, John Bste. 78
VALLE, John Bste. 122
VALLE, John Bste. 134
VALLE, John Bste. 181
VALLE, John Bste. 185
VALLE, John Bste. 191
VALLE, John Bste. 196
VALLE, John Bste. 216
VALLE, John Bste. 240
VALLE, Marie Louise 240
VALLE, Michel 46
VALLE, Michel 217
VALLE, Michel 240
VALLE, Jr. Francis 60
VALLE, Jr. Francois 240
VALLET, John 161
VALLET, John 240
VAN BUREN, Martin 222
VANBIBBER, Isaac 73
VANBIBBER, Isaac 157
VANDERHIDER, Mathias 21
VANDERHIDER, Mathias 86
VANDERHYDER, Mathias 240
VASQUES, ----- 240
VASQUES, Benito 240
VASQUES, P. L. 240
VASQUEZ, ----- 84
VASQUEZ, Antoine 6
VASQUEZ, Benito 6
VASQUEZ, Benito 30
VASQUEZ, Benito 37

VASQUEZ, Benito 87
VASQUEZ, Benito 89
VASQUEZ, Benito 121
VASQUEZ, Hipolite 6
VASQUEZ, Joseph 6
VASQUEZ, Joseph 84
VASQUEZ, Pierre 6
VASQUEZ, Pierre 84
VASQUEZ, Pierre L. 24
VASSEUR, Regis 27
VASSEUR, Regis 217
VASSEUR, Regis 240
VASSEUR, Regis 240
VIEN, John Baptiste 49
VIEN, John Baptiste 50
VILEMONT, Carlos de 170
VILEMONT, Carlos de 174
VILEMONT, Carlos de 240
VILLARS, ----- 63
VILLARS, ----- 240
VILLARS, Antoine 116
VILLARS, Antoine 165
VILLARS, Antoine 240
VILLARS, Dudrieul 55
VILLARS, Joseph 116
VILLARS, Joseph 165
VILLARS, Joseph 240
VILLARS, Maria Louisa Valle 84
VILLARS, Maria Luisa Valle 9
VILLARS, Marie Louise 10
VILLARS, Marie Valle 84
VILLEMONT, ----- de 79
VINCENT, Jacques 184
VINCENT, Jacques 184
VINCENT, Jacques 207
VINCENT, Jacques 215
VINCENT, Jacques 215
VINCENT, Jacques 240
VINEYARD, Jonathan 207
VINEYARD, Jonathan 213
VINEYARD, Jonathan 240
VIOLET, ----- 157
VOISARD, Joseph 156
VRAIN, ----- St. 24

WALKER, Jacob 95
WALKER, Jacob 240
WALLER, Richard 133
WALLER, Richard 141
WALLER, Richard 195
WATKINS, John 34
WATKINS, John 35
WATKINS, John 88
WATKINS, John 89
WATKINS, John 240
WATKINS, Samuel 177
WELDON, John 206
WELDON, John 213
WELDON, John 241
WESTOVER, Job 13
WHERRY, Mackay 240
WHERRY, Mackey 38
WHERRY, Mackey 90
WHERRY, Mackey 240
WHITE, J. M. 2
WICKERAH, Jacob 53
WICKERHAM, Jacob 97
WICKERHAM, Jacob 99
WICKERHAM, Jacob 240
WICKERHAM, Jacob 241
WICKERS, Julius 183
WICKERS, Julius 199

WICKERS, Julius 241
WIDEMAN, Mark 54
WILBOURN Curtis 196
WILBOURN, Curtis 201
WILBOURN, James 130
WILBOURN, James 188
WILBOURN, James 189
WILBOURN, James 201
WILBOURN, James 241
WILKINSON, Emily 56
WILKINSON, James 159
WILKINSON, Thomas 68
WILKINSON, Thomas 163
WILKINSON, Thomas 240
WILKINSON, Thomas 241
WILKINSON, Walter 8
WILKINSON, Walter 56
WILKINSON, Walter 57
WILLBOURN, Curtis 241
WILLBOURN, James 241
WILLIAM, J. 68
WILLIAMS, Isaac 144
WILLIAMS, James 47
WILLIAMS, James 93
WILLIAMS, James 240
WILLIAMS, Jas. 69
WILLIAMS, Sally 53
WILLIAMS, William 97
WILLIAMS, William 127
WILLIAMS, William 131
WILLIAMS, William 135
WILLIAMS, William 136
WILLIAMS, William 143
WILLIAMS, William 195
WILLIAMS, William 196
WILSON, Andrew 74
WILSON, J. P. 74
WILSON, Samuel 153
WISE, Jacob 2
WISE, Jacob 70
WISE, Jacob 182
WISE, Jacob 199
WISE, Jacob 241
WOOD, Martin 2
WOODS, Martin 3
WORTHINGTON, Joseph 132
WORTHINGTON, Joseph 167
WORTHINGTON, Joseph 241

YOUNG, Edward 42
YOUNG, Edward 92
YOUNG, Edward 241
YOUNG, Joseph 135
YOUNG, Morris 116
YOUNG, Morris 132
YOUNG, Morris 203
YOUNG, Morris 241
YOUNG, Philip 137
YOUNG, Philip 197

ZUMALT, Andrew 156
ZUMALT, John 158

www.ingramcontent.com/pod-product-compliance
Lightning Source LLC
Chambersburg PA
CBHW080416270326

41929CB00018B/3046